CLASSICS OF TLINGIT ORAL LITERATURE

Edited by

Nora Marks Dauenhauer and Richard Dauenhauer

VOLUME 2

Haa Tuwunáagu Yís, for Healing Our Spirit:

Tlingit Oratory

Tlingit Oratory by:

Jessie Dalton
George Davis
Jimmie George
Austin Hammond
Johnny C. Jackson
Charlie Jim
George Jim
A. P. Johnson
William Johnson
Charlie Joseph
David Kadashan
Matthew Lawrence
Emma Marks
Jim Marks
Willie Marks
Tom Peters
Jennie Thlunaut
Thomas Young
Two unidentified speakers
from wax cylinders of 1899

Haa Tuwunáagu Yís, for Healing Our Spirit

TLINGIT ORATORY

Edited by Nora Marks Dauenhauer
and Richard Dauenhauer

UNIVERSITY OF WASHINGTON PRESS
Seattle and London
SEALASKA HERITAGE FOUNDATION
Juneau

The preparation of this volume was made possible in part by a grant from the National Endowment for the Humanities, an independent federal agency.

Sealaska Heritage Foundation gratefully acknowledges additional support for this book from: The Alaska State Legislature, Sealaska Corporation, Rainier Bank, Rasmuson Foundation, Kootznoowoo, Inc., and Huna Totem Corporation

This publication is funded in part by the Alaska Humanities Forum and the National Endowment for the Humanities.

Library of Congress Cataloging-in-Publication Data

Haa tuwunáagu yís, for healing our spirit : Tlingit oratory / edited by Nora Marks Dauenhauer and Richard Dauenhauer.
p. cm. -- (Classics of Tlingit oral literature ; v. 2)
English and Tlingit.
Includes bibliographical references.
ISBN 0-295-96849-4. -- ISBN 0-295-96850-8 (pbk.)
1. Tlingit Indians--Oratory. 2. Tlingit Indians--Religion and mythology. 3. Tlingit Indians --Rites and ceremonies. 4. Tlingit language--Texts. I. Dauenhauer, Nora. II. Dauenhauer, Richard. III. Title: Tlingit oratory. IV. Series.
E99. T6H23 1990
897' .2--dc20
90-43234
CIP

Cover art by Joanne George: "Your fathers' sisters would fly out over the person who is feeling grief." (Jessie Dalton, line 130)

for the Tlingit orators
living, departed, and to come—
peacemakers
between eternity and time

Ch'a a kayaa áyá yéi g̲ax̲tusanéi.
— Kaatyé

We will only imitate (our ancestors).
— David Kadashan

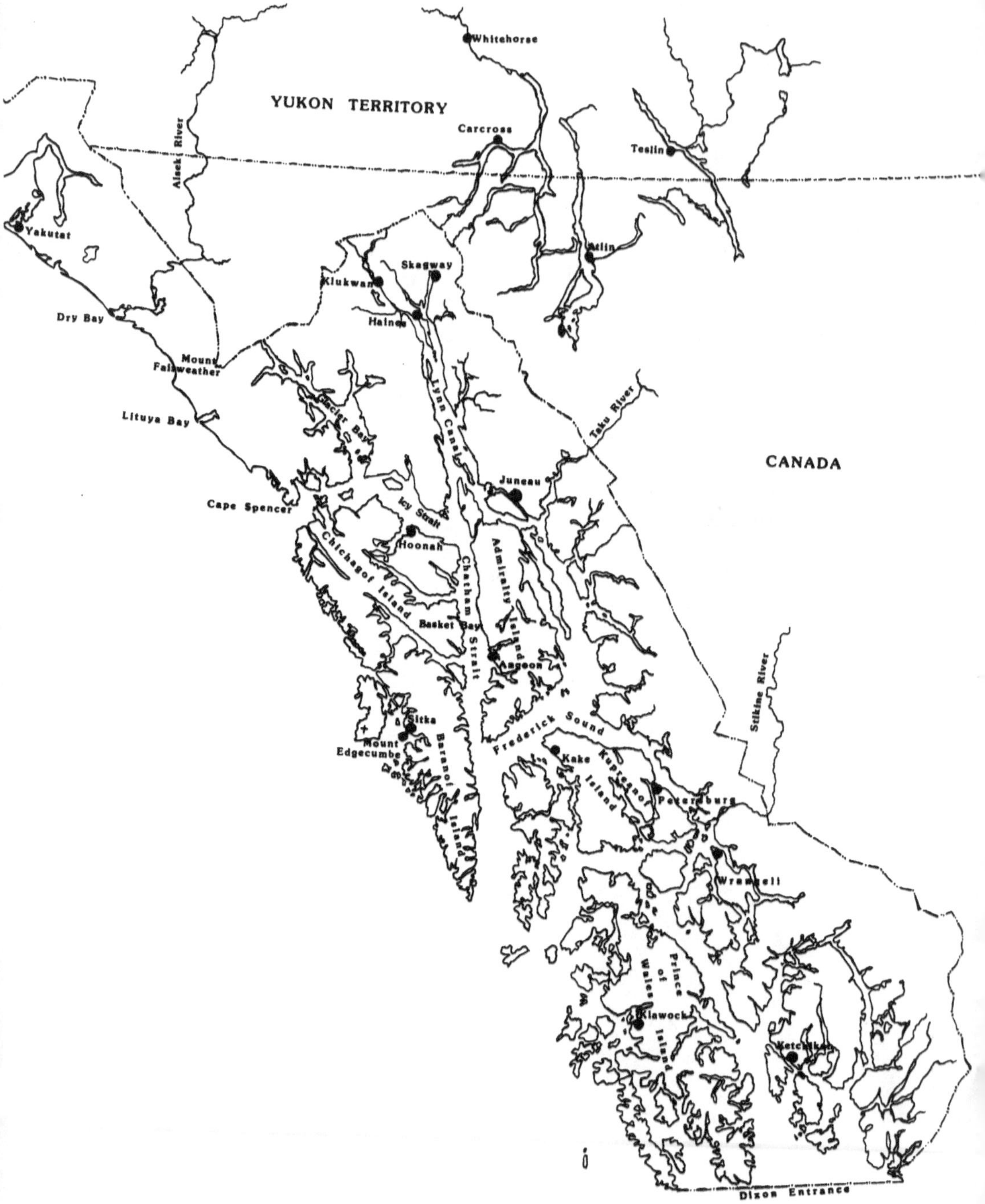
YUKON TERRITORY
Whitehorse
Carcross
Teslin
Alsek River
Yakutat
Atlin
Skagway
Klukwan
Haines
Dry Bay
Mount
Fairweather
Lituya Bay
Glacier Bay
Taku River
CANADA
Juneau
Lynn Canal
Cape Spencer
Icy Strait
Hoonah
Chichagof Island
Chatham Strait
Admiralty Island
Basket Bay
Angoon
Stikine River
Sitka
Mount
Edgecumbe
Baranof Island
Frederick Sound
Kake
Kupreanof Island
Petersburg
Wrangell
Prince of Wales Island
Klawock
Ketchikan
Dixon Entrance

Contents

Preface ix
Acknowledgments xxxi
Introduction 3
Speeches from Various Occasions

A. P. Johnson, Sitka 1971 156
Unidentified Speaker, Sitka 1899 156
Unidentified Speaker, Sitka 1899 158
Johnny C. Jackson, Kake 1971 162
Jimmie George, Kake 1971 166
Thomas Young, Klukwan 1972 168
Tom Peters, Teslin 1972 172
Charlie Joseph, Sitka 1972 176
Willie Marks, Mt. Edgecumbe 1976 182
David Kadashan, Hoonah 1976 186
Emma Marks, Juneau 1982 188
Jennie Thlunaut, Haines 1985 196
Jennie Thlunaut, Haines, 1985 206
Jennie Thlunaut, Klukwan 1985 208
Austin Hammond, Fairbanks 1988 214

Speeches for the Removal of Grief from the Memorial for Jim Marks, Hoonah 1968

Jim Marks (Posthumous) 230
Matthew Lawrence (1) 232
David Kadashan 234
William Johnson 240
Jessie Dalton 242
Austin Hammond 256
Matthew Lawrence (2) 260

"Because We Cherish You . . . :" Sealaska Elders Speak to the Future. (Selected Speeches from the First Sealaska Elders Conference, Sitka 1980)

Charlie Joseph (1)	264
George Davis (1)	276
William Johnson	282
Charlie Jim	284
George Davis (2)	296
George Jim	298
George Davis (3)	308
George Davis (4)	312
George Davis (5)	314
Charlie Joseph (2)	318

Notes	324
Glossary to the Speeches for the Removal of Grief	443
Biographies	521
References	559

Preface

More than by any other form of Tlingit literature, our personal and professional lives have been dramatically changed by oratory. Although these speeches are published as the second volume in the series, *Classics of Tlingit Oral Literature,* some of them actually got us started and have been foremost in our minds for many years. We have been living with some of the oratory, individually and as a professional collaborative team, as partners in marriage as well as in writing and scholarship, for over twenty years. We find the central images in the speeches by Jessie Dalton, David Kadashan, Austin Hammond and others included here to be among the most beautiful in world literature. Our lives have been changed by the dignity and power of their spoken words. We emphasize here, as always, that the words in these speeches are the words of the elders and are not our own. Where we do speak for ourselves, as in the introduction and notes, we have merely tried to explain and interpret the words of the elders, as we understand them.

The true success of public speaking is that it affects the listener. In education jargon, it is in the "affective domain," and, like many of the most important things in our lives, can't be measured on standardized tests. This impact is eloquently articulated by A. P. Johnson, whose speech about speech we have placed first in this book. He compares public speaking to a gaff hook: it reaches out over distance and becomes one with another person, who is "hooked." One set of speeches in this book was delivered to help remove the grief of a family and clan who had lost an honored member. The speakers in that Hoonah memorial in October 1968 had no way of knowing that their words would go far beyond the immediate audience to fall on ears of sympathetic listeners, both Tlingit and non-Tlingit, in other times and places, years later and around the world, allowing a new generation of listeners and readers to share in the beauty of the Tlingit spoken word and to appreciate the complexity of Tlingit oratory delivered in a traditional cultural setting. The reaching out in this case has included tape recording, transcription of the texts in Tlingit, translation into English, and publication as a book. In totally different cultural contexts, readers of previously published excerpts (including college students and participants in cultural retreats in Tlingit communities) and listeners from all walks of life who have heard the translations at poetry readings—in bookstores, libraries, and classrooms around the country, at readings in Austria, Germany, and Finland, around campfires on a rafting trip along the Alsek River, in elder-hostel courses on the Alaska State Ferry—have been visibly stunned by the power and beauty of the speeches for the removal of grief.

Our own personal experiences illustrate the unpredictable impact of oratory. We came to it from opposite directions. One of us came to Tlingit oral literature from long and detailed study of the languages and literatures, both oral and written, of Western tradition—Homeric and Slavic epic, Byzantine hymns, the poetry of Shakespeare, Donne, and T.S. Eliot. Richard was excited to find a Native American poetic tradition as intricate as anything in European tradition. From an immediate conceptual appreciation grew an emotional and personal attachment to Tlingit oral literature, and a professional commitment to working for academic and popular recognition of Tlingit literature as part of contemporary and traditional American literature, which, taken in its multi-ethnic fullness, embraces an entire continent rich in regional and ethnic traditions, both oral and written.

For the other of us, coming to the oratory from within the tradition, the perspective was different. It involved increasing conceptual appreciation of a tradition that was already emotionally there, immediate and personal—and at times so familiar as to be taken for granted. Nora's decision to study and write and present the material from a Tlingit point of view was taken at some risk. Because books are alien to Tlingit tradition, and because many negative and inaccurate things have been written about Tlingit culture, there was, and still is, great suspicion of and even hostility toward books and literacy among some members of the older generation of Tlingits. But she was encouraged by her professors and by many Tlingit elders of vision. Nora comments, "For years I heard the old folks say, 'If only someone could write this down!'"

A Description of the Book

Having addressed some of the personal basis and bias of this book, we turn to a more "nuts and bolts" description of how it is put together. *Haa Tuwunáagu Yís, for Healing Our Spirit: Tlingit Oratory,* the second volume of the series *Classics of Tlingit Oral Literature,* is the first publication ever of Tlingit oratory recorded in performance as well as the first of its kind edited by a Tlingit-speaking scholar. It features the original Tlingit texts with facing English translations and detailed annotations; many photographs of the orators and settings; discussion of the cultural contexts in which the speeches were delivered; biographies of the elders; a glossary for one of the most culturally important sets of speeches; and a bibliography. At the heart of the book are thirty-two speeches by twenty Tlingit elders, mostly tape recorded between 1968 and 1988. Two of the speeches, recorded on wax cylinders by the Harriman Expedition in Sitka in 1899, are the oldest known sound recordings of Tlingit. Leading into the speeches is a long introduction explaining the literary form of Tlingit oratory and its social and spiritual function. The introduction, while not entering into abstract or theoretical debate with existing scholarship, presents a new and different understanding of the "potlatch," the ceremonial setting at which much Tlingit oratory is delivered. The popular image of potlatch is often expressed in terms such as "feasting with enemies" or "fighting with property," but from the Tlingit point of view it is seen as the central ritual in traditional Tlingit ceremonial life for spiritual healing and removal of grief. The oratory itself, although intensely culture-specific, is also universal in its concern with grief and the ability of the human spirit to transcend death. Potlatch has often been described as more social than religious, its purpose being to validate social rights. We do not dispute this aspect of potlatch, but we feel that the spiritual dimensions—at least as they are explicit in the oratory—have been overlooked in favor of the social and economic functions. We submit that the textual evidence of the potlatch oratory itself and the group dynamics of its setting overwhelmingly support spiritual and psychological meaning as well. Accordingly, we have focused in the introduction on the spiritual dimensions as demonstrated by the style and content of the oratory. Readers interested in more rigorous conceptual analysis and dialogue with the secondary literature should examine the recent scholarly articles noted in the introduction and bibliography.

Our major scholarly goal in this book is to present primary data—the speeches themselves—as accurately and meaningfully as possible, and to present for the first time a substantial collection of new primary material not formerly available. From the primary data, additional analyses can follow later, whether by us or others. We feel that this new research has been made possible by two factors—the development of tape recorders that allowed for documentation of oratory in live performance, and, even more important, the commitment of a Native-speaking scholar with professional training in anthropology, linguistics, and literature, born and raised in the community and its traditions, who undertook to transcribe, translate, and annotate the oratory. Otherwise it is virtually impossible to understand the dynamics of live performance of oratory in the ceremonial setting.

The speeches are arranged in three sections. The first includes mostly unrelated speeches from various times, places, and occasions, generally arranged chronologically and in order of rhetorical complexity, so that readers can familiarize themselves gradually with the basic concepts and rhetorical forms of Tlingit oratory before moving to the more difficult sets. These speeches from various occasions illustrate a range of style and content and introduce the basic concepts of Tlingit oratory. The second section, a set of seven speeches, was delivered during a traditional memorial in Hoonah in 1968, in memory of Jim Marks. This set is a coherent example of traditional Tlingit spirituality in action. The third section, a set of ten speeches, is also traditional in form and content, but from a contemporary event. This set is excerpted from a modern elders conference sponsored by Sealaska Corporation in Sitka in 1980. Both sets of speeches are coherent examples of oratory as an expression of Tlingit spirituality. Both sets illustrate the host/guest relationship, but in different ways, and in each set the speeches and speakers interact with each other in very complicated ways.

The set from the elders conference is interesting because the elders publicly endorsed explicit instruction of the young, proceeding to explain aspects of Tlingit spirituality that were traditionally learned by observation and example. We still see the traditional belief system in operation, but the main theme of the speeches is that the elders are aware that only a few of those present understand them any more. This set of speeches is a kind of "benchmark" documenting a point in cultural history where Charlie Joseph, teacher of the G̱ajaa Héen Dancers of the Sitka Native Education Program, demonstrated the results of his teaching to his peers, who publicly responded with acceptance, emphasizing that no clan stands alone, that all are related and interconnected. The elders not only thanked and endorsed Charlie, they also seized the opportunity to join in the teaching, to explain the culture in their own words. Thus, this set of speeches is valuable for the content (in which the elders themselves interpret the culture) and as a social document in which they embrace the concept of teaching the young in community-based groups. Some of the speakers, such as George Davis and William Johnson, were founders of Sealaska Heritage Foundation, so that our work is based on such endorsements of the elders to document and teach.

When its parts are combined, the whole book becomes a striking illustration and documentation of social interaction in the Tlingit community. We see the hosts of one memorial as guests and orators at another, and after death, we see photographs from their memorials. Through their biographies we are given further insights into their personal history and world view, and relationship to others.

In our collaboration, we have tried to give careful attention to transcription, translation and annotation. We hope that the book will be of interest and importance to Native and non-Native readers alike. For those of Native American heritage the book articulates concepts understood and practiced by elders but difficult for them to explain, and often bewildering to younger generations. For people around the world interested in Northwest Coast culture, the book offers new insights into a traditional world view and the classics of Tlingit oral literature. Built of metaphor and simile and based on images of Tlingit visual art such as Chilkat robes, button blankets, hats, headdresses, and masks, the speeches should appeal to students of literature; they are poetic by nature and blend oral literature, visual art, and social structure through a living performance of the moment that binds eternity and time.

In addition to being of personal appeal to general readers, we hope that the book will also be of professional interest to students of literature, folklore, anthropology, and linguistics. The primary data feature Tlingit texts never before published, accompanied by detailed annotations and a glossary giving special attention to the analysis of verbs. Folklorists are offered a picture of contemporary Tlingit folklife presented in texts recorded in performance and accompanied by biographies, photographs, and background on the social context and group dynamics, especially memorials for the dead, as an interconnection of all aspects of Tlingit folklife—verbal and visual art; food, song, dance, and kinship; material culture and spirituality.

Structure and Format

The overall structure of this book is the same as the first volume, *Haa Shuká*: introduction, Tlingit texts and facing English translations, annotations, and biographies. The biographies illustrate the wide range of personalities and experiences that underlie the speeches. Many readers of *Haa Shuká* have mentioned their enjoyment of the biographies, commenting on their value and how much they add to the book. Accordingly, we increased the scope of the biographies for this book. But as publication neared, we realized that the biographies had outgrown the oratory book. The biographies alone were over 250 pages and included about seventy photographs. This would have increased the total size of the book to well over 800 pages, creating problems of binding and cost. We envisioned an affordable, quality paperback. When books get too thick, the glue won't hold, and they fall apart with repeated use. Clothbound is more expensive, as are thicker paperbacks.

Therefore, the decision was made by the editors of this book and the editors at the University of Washington Press to limit the biographies in the present volume to two pages each, including one photograph, but to publish the full biographies as soon as possible as a separate volume in this series. The volume dedicated exclusively to biographies allows for focus on themes of cultural importance articulated by each elder: land, subsistence, at.óow (crests), genealogy, and spirituality. We couldn't begin to do justice to these themes in the context of the present book, properly devoted to oratory.

A special addition to this volume is the glossary for the set of speeches for the removal of grief from the memorial for Jim Marks. The glossary is intended to link the study of language and the study of literature. To help readers who wish to use the speeches to learn Tlingit, the glossary lists every form of every word used in the speeches as it appears in the text, along with the underlying theoretical or dictionary form, grammatical analysis, and English translation. Linguistically, about 80% of the language used in the speeches is accessible with the help of a glossary to a learner who has worked his or her way through *Beginning Tlingit* (Dauenhauer and Dauenhauer 1976) and up to about lesson three or four of our *Intermediate Tlingit* (Dauenhauer and Dauenhauer, presently lecture notes, but projected as a book) or to more advanced students who have studied the grammatical appendix in the *Tlingit Verb Dictionary* (Story and Naish 1973). The main complexity of Tlingit is in the verb, and some verbal constructions will still require advanced linguistic skills or guidance from a teacher. Because of the detailed glossary, there are far fewer grammatical analyses in the notes than in *Haa Shuká,* and those are limited to the most interesting features of speeches not covered in the glossary. We hope that these grammatical notes and the glossary will be of use and benefit to students of the Tlingit language, and perhaps of casual interest to others who may have no need or desire to study Tlingit, but who might enjoy seeing how different it is from the totally unrelated languages more commonly taught and studied.

There is only minor duplication between the introductions to this book and *Haa Shuká.* Some basic concepts of Tlingit social structure first introduced in *Haa Shuká, Our Ancestors: Tlingit Oral Narratives* are reviewed here, and some discussion of at.óow (clan crests) is repeated here, but both topics are greatly expanded with new information and concepts important to oratory. Except for the review and expansion on social structure and at.óow, there is no duplication between the introductions to this book and *Haa Shuká*. Specifically, nothing is repeated here regarding format (the arrangement and numbering of lines, punctuation, etc.); the style of oral literature in general (repetition, etc.); translation theory and specific problems of translation; Tlingit language and grammar in general; and the alphabet used in this book. For help on any of this, we direct readers to the explanations in volume one in this series, *Haa Shuká, Our Ancestors: Tlingit Oral Narratives* (Dauenhauer and Dauenhauer 1987).

A few words are in order here on standardization of spelling. We should emphasize that there is no dispute regarding orthography: we use the popular and phonemically accurate writing system introduced by Constance Naish and Gillian Story about thirty years ago, in print since 1962, and in its present, revised form since 1972. As Tlingit literacy advances, certain conventions of word division are still being resolved. This is most evident in writing verb prefixes and compound nouns, especially names. As a general rule, where vowels are shortened in nouns appearing in verbal constructions, we have combined them into the verb as nominal prefixes rather than writing them as separate words; for example, in "a kát x̲'us.utsóowch" ("the sun would put its rays—literally, feet—on it") we treat x̲'us as a prefix and not as an independent word. In writing personal names, we combine as much as possible, but there is still no firm convention. Compare English, "Mary Ann," and "Marianne." Thus, we have combined in Yeilnaawú but not in Keet Yaanaayí; in both cases, the tone on the first part of the compound is "stolen" and we do not write it. In names of clan houses we have generally kept the component parts separate, but spelling without tone where it is stolen, and using short vowels where they are contracted. For example:

xóots	=	bear	*but*	Xuts Hít	=	Brown Bear House
Táax̲'	=	snail	*but*	Tax̲' Hít	=	Snail House.

The writing of suffixes involving labialized final consonants also presents problems. Léelk'w (grandparent) could be written léelk'wx̲ or léelk'ux̲ when suffixed as a predicate nominative. We have decided to write keeping the "w." Some vowels in Tlingit, especially in inflectional suffixes, may be written long or short. The earlier convention was to write them long, but, increasingly, over the last fifteen years the preference has changed to standardizing them short. For example, the irrealis morpheme was conventionally written -oo- but is now written -u-. We have tried to catch all of these in proofreading, but vestiges of the old conventions may remain. As a general rule, subject prefixes alternate long and short without contraction. For example, "too-" ("we") is pronounced and spelled long when it appears next to the stem, but is pronounced and written "tu-" when not next to the stem; likewise with i ~ ee, and yi ~ yee. The rest of the prefixes are short unless in contraction with the negative or a perfective prefix.

As users of the *Chicago Manual of Style* and similar tomes will attest, such conventions are often problematic in English, and we are slowly addressing them in Tlingit. We apologize for any inconsistencies. Also, we will not be surprised to find a few typographical errors in the Tlingit texts. We are blessed with many English proofreaders and many helpful friends and colleagues who took time to read the English parts of the book, but there are few proofreaders of Tlingit. Those upon whom we usually call (Michael Krauss, Jeff Leer, Constance Naish, Gillian Story, and Jürgen Pinnow) have read parts of the manuscript at various stages of its development, but all are deeply involved in work of their own, and it would have been beyond their time constraints to proofread all of the Tlingit, especially checking it against the audio tapes. So, we have imposed on them as little as possible, and we apologize for errors we have not caught. Alas, typos always hide in manuscript but leap out of the printed page.

Who Does What

We have received many requests from readers and reviewers to explain our work and how we do it, and which of the co-editors does what. The heart of the book, the Tlingit texts, are the work of Nora Dauenhauer. She is the principal researcher of the project. Tlingit is her first language, and it is she who conducts the interviews and does most of the fieldwork. It has been our experience that for most genres of Tlingit oral literature, the level of knowledge of the audience—in this case the fieldworker—contributes greatly to the style and content of the performance. Elders tend to shape their performance around what they feel the questioner needs to know, and will comprehend. Early in her fieldwork, one elder was surprised about a particular question, and asked, "How do you know that? You're too young to know about that. Nobody has asked me about that in years!"

In all of this, we work only with those elders who want to have their material recorded, written down in Tlingit, translated into English, and published. The ownership of the material remains their own and is the spiritual property of the clan. We view the books as the extension of their voices, not our own. To prevent commercial exploitation, copyright is held by Sealaska Heritage Foundation, a legally recognized Tlingit cultural organization founded by the elders themselves. We also respect the wishes of those elders who decline to be recorded. Many elders are reluctant to pass material on in written form, and many fear its leaving the community. Some have elected to die with their knowledge rather than to risk seeing it subject to ridicule or desecration. In this and in all aspects of our work we accept the values and standards of the Tlingit community regarding ownership of at.óow, including oral literature. This is not in conflict with scholarship, but reflects principles and ethics of folklore research. As in all communities, one cannot expect total consensus and agreement on issues as emotional and deeply rooted as the transmission of cultural material. Some elders will remain opposed on firm spiritual convictions (both traditional and fundamentalist Christian) to recording and publishing of oral material; others will be opposed for less noble reasons. While we respect the wishes of those who do not wish to be recorded, we believe that their feelings should not hinder those who do wish to see the traditions passed on. As noted, we work only with those who want to be recorded and published, and we have a long "waiting list" of elders yet to be interviewed and of tapes still to be transcribed.

Unless otherwise noted, all of the transcriptions in this book are the work of Nora Dauenhauer. Some of these date from the late 1960's and early 1970's. She writes down in Tlingit what the elders have said on the tape recordings. Careful attention is given to the line unit, as determined by breath, pauses, and sentence intonation. Only false starts are edited out, and these are usually noted in the annotations. At some point in the process we read the transcriptions back to the elders for their comments and approval. At the request of the elders, minor changes are sometimes made, and these are noted.

The Tlingit transcriptions are then translated into English. Nora Dauenhauer does the first draft. At this point, Richard Dauenhauer enters the process. He does most of the word processing. When the Tlingit text and English translation are prepared, both editors proofread the transcription and translation against each other and against the tape recordings, and discussion begins. The final text and final translation are the result of ongoing discussion and negotiation.

The annotations are written jointly. Most of those on cultural background are the work of Nora Dauenhauer, and most on grammar and style are by Richard Dauenhauer. Again, the final product is discussed and approved by both editors. Wherever possible, specific questions are clarified with the elders.

Unless otherwise noted, the biographies are written by both editors, but most of the research and fieldwork is done by Nora Dauenhauer. Then, either editor drafts the biography based on the fieldnotes and data. Most of the first drafts are done by Nora Dauenhauer, who often works directly from tape recordings of conversations in Tlingit, distilling the information, quoting, and paraphrasing. Unfortunately, we do not have time to transcribe the conversations in Tlingit, as we do with the oral literature texts. If possible, information is obtained from the living elders. In the case of departed elders, we work with family and friends. The final product is circulated to those who helped, to double check for accuracy, and to ask for additions and deletions. The two-page biographies in this book were condensed by Nora and Richard Dauenhauer and Barbara Cadiente Nelson from the longer versions that are forthcoming as a separate volume in this series.

The introduction is written jointly. Some sections were first composed by Nora Dauenhauer, others by Richard Dauenhauer. Some sections date from professional papers in the early and mid-1970's, others from the late 1980's. The final product is edited and approved by both. In addition, we have benefited from the suggestions of several readers, whose comments helped us make revisions.

The glossary is the work of Richard Dauenhauer, who has been living with it since 1972. It began with his needs and interests as a learner of Tlingit, and is published here in hopes that it will be of help and interest to other learners as well.

In all parts of this book, we have aimed the level of style toward the interested, intelligent reader. We have tried to keep technical words to a minimum, using them only where necessary and where not using them would increase confusion. As noted above, we try to focus on the speeches and orators themselves, rather than on literary or anthropological theory. This is old-fashioned "new criticism," a conservative, exegetical approach based on explication of text. We felt we had succeeded when one of our colleagues noted in a personal letter, "I like that you write as real advocates for the orators and the oratory, not that you own them, but that they kind of own you."

In translation, we have tried to achieve a balance of literal and emotional accuracy. If a line is translated too literally, it can easily lose the emotional impact of the original; if too freely translated it can be infinitely powerful, but perhaps not what the orator intended or said. Serious compromises are explained in the notes. In general, we have opted to use a looser translation in the text and explain the literal meaning in the notes, rather than to keep the literal translation in the text and bury the emotional meaning in the notes. In a similar vein, in writing the notes we have tried to convey our understanding and enthusiasm over certain passages, but without ruining the experience for the readers.

We should note here that the book was typeset in the Sealaska Heritage Foundation office. The primary typist for the earlier stages was Richard Dauenhauer. In the final stages we were assisted by Barbara Cadiente Nelson and Michael Travis. We have benefited greatly from the editorial advice of the staff of the University of Washington Press, but we wish to emphasize that any shortcomings at the level of typesetting, design, and style reflect on our own competence and not on the University of Washington Press.

Tradition

As in any literary tradition, Tlingit oratory operates on many levels and points in many directions, both in its content and its example. Ceremonial oratory is a gift and an invitation to respond appropriately, either verbally, if words are called for, or emotionally, through listening and becoming involved. The farther one goes, the more directions unfold, the more questions arise. So, the first step of transcription and translation of a single speech from a paternal uncle's memorial initiated a lifelong study and process of spiritual and intellectual growth and discovery.

Tlingit elders always caution one to be careful with words and speech, because they might have an impact of which we are unaware. In this case, the unforeseen impact of the oratory has been positive and beautiful. Careless words can bring pain and disaster, but words well thought out, well composed, and well delivered can heal and bring comfort. These speeches do bring comfort and healing. As they helped the original audience, they now help us to live with separation and loss, death and dying. They provide links with the personal and cultural past, with human and spiritual ancestors. The speeches show how knowledge of who we are helps us to bear the loss of loved ones, how reaffirmation of our relationships among the living helps us to understand our relationship to the dead.

The speeches included here may be considered a "vintage crop" of oratory by the last generation of traditionally raised elders. Many of these elders are now departed, and as this book goes to press, the living elders featured here are in their seventies, eighties, nineties. The oldest, Jimmie George, just turned one hundred. Their speeches are presented here as examples of the past and as models for the present and future.

By living example, the speeches are part of the transmission of culture from one generation to another and the communication of the human spirit from one state to another. Speaking of their ancestral models, Jessie Dalton and David Kadashan both make repeated reference to "only imitating." We understand this expression in two senses—that they are following cultural tradition, and also that they are spiritually engaged in ritual activity, because it is through ritual action that more abstract mythic patterns are expressed. Myth and ritual provide models for human behavior. Without them, we grope aimlessly in a spiritual void, like the spirits the elders describe. Jessie Dalton's and David Kadashan's statements are important, because they exemplify how, in the words of the American educator Chet Bowers, "traditions can only exist as individuals sustain them" (Bowers 1987:69).

Bowers also quotes Edward Shils (Shils 1981:14-15) on the subject of tradition. "Traditions are not independently self-reproductive or self-elaborating. Only living, knowing, desiring human beings can enact them and modify them. Traditions develop because the desire to create something truer and better or more convenient is alive in those who acquire and possess them. Traditions can deteriorate in the sense of losing their adherents because their possessors cease to present them or because those who once received and re-enacted them and extended them now prefer other lines of conduct or because new generations to which they were presented find other traditions of belief or some relatively new beliefs more acceptable" (1987:69).

All of what Shils describes has happened in Southeast Alaska. Some elders withheld from the younger generations, some elders changed, and some elders carried on the traditions, but the younger generations could no longer accept them. All of this has contributed to the sense of loss of traditional culture and cultural identity. This is a normal process and happens in all cultures all the time. But it often involves grief. Especially where tradition has been uprooted by force, there is often a residue of violence and hostility within the individual and the community. This has been particularly noted as a legacy of colonial situations, but the symptoms exist in so-called "mainstream" cultures as well.

This is an important psychological and cultural concern for all people. In a fragmented society such as twentieth-century America, where even deeply rooted and cohesive traditions such as Tlingit have been violently uprooted and shattered, and where the elements that divide the community are often stronger and longer lasting than the more fragile traditions that unite, the questions of personal and cultural identity almost always end up the same: Who am I? How am I related to others in the community? How am I related to my personal and cultural past?

In a society where ownership is so important, the negative aspects can easily take hold—fighting over who owns this song or that crest. Certainly the oratory emphasizes the pride of ownership and the importance of knowing what belongs to whom. But the speeches also emphasize the importance of knowing the history and significance and spiritual meaning of at.óow, including names. For this reason, some speeches in this book address only genealogy. Also, an important aspect of Tlingit tradition emphasized in the biographies and speeches is the practice of adoption. Concerned that some family names might die, elders often adopted people of other clans of the same moiety, giving them names and thereby uniting their families and clans. The most important factor in all the speeches is that everybody is related somehow, that no one is alone, and that in times of joy as well as sorrow, people need one another. The speeches stress the importance of community—of knowing who we are, so that we know how to relate to and be supportive of one other.

And indeed, the speeches are themselves models for all of us to emulate to the extent of our interest and needs. Having come now far beyond their original audience and intent, the speeches in this book remain alive and powerful with every reading. They are excellent models on many rhetorical levels, beginning with grammar and style, and opening like a flower offering insights into Tlingit spirituality and social structure. They offer not only culture-specific models for how to make a Tlingit speech, but more general and universal models for how to come to grips with death and grief. These are unique Tlingit expressions of a universal human condition—that to be human is to be aware of death. And our various cultural traditions offer ways in which the human spirit triumphs over death.

The Place of This Book in the Series

The narratives in *Haa Shuká* introduce the concept of at.óow (clan crests, names, land, etc.) and describe their acquisition by ancestors. The present volume expands the concept, with emphasis on spirits as at.óow. The oratory shows at.óow in action in their full spiritual context, especially the employment of at.óow in ceremonial use for healing, the removal of grief, and the prevention of harm. The narratives in *Haa Shuká* recall the fundamental covenants between humans and animals, the physical and the spiritual, and the symbolic representation of these covenents through at.óow. Oratory operates within this system of at.óow, kinship, and exchange. In the words of the orators, "imitating our ancestors."

Ritual is an enactment of myth. Thus, the speeches delivered in the context of a ceremony for the removal of grief are ritual enactments of myth as recalled in the narratives. For example, the "Glacier Bay History" by Amy Marvin in *Haa Shuká* explains the spiritual foundation for remembering the departed in memorials characterized by the giving of gifts of food and clothing. The memorial is the context in which the most significant Tlingit oratory is delivered. Just as the narratives explain the mythic covenants underlying the spirituality of the culture, oratory is the genre of memorial and ritual and operates against the spiritual background explained in the narratives.

Future volumes in the series will continue to address different genres of Tlingit oral literature and show how they fit into the total picture of traditional and contemporary Tlingit folklife. As noted above, the full-length biographies of the elders, too large for the present volume, will soon be published as a separate volume. An upcoming book explores Tlingit concepts of history and another will tackle humor—a genre often difficult to translate and to appreciate in translation—in the form of a collection of Raven stories. Raven is the well-known trickster and culture hero not only of the Northwest Coast and Interior Alaska, but of the Bering Sea coast and in adjacent Siberia. In addition to exploring different genres, we are also preparing another collection of narratives like *Haa Shuká*.

The Series in the Context of Oral Literature Research

For a background on the general scholarly context of our work, as well as for more theoretical detail, we direct interested readers to the substantial range of research of the last twenty years in ethnopoetics and ethnography of speaking, including Bauman and Sherzer (1974; reprinted 1989), Hymes (1981), Rothenberg (1968, 1972), Rothenberg and Rothenberg (1983), Sherzer and Woodbury (1987), Swann (1983), and Tedlock (1972, 1983), among others. For ethnopoetics, Sherzer and Woodbury (1987) is the best place to start because the introduction includes a definition of terms and a review of earlier work. For ethnography of speaking, the second edition of Bauman and Sherzer (1989) is valuable for the fifteen-year perspective presented in the introduction. All of these studies treat various aspects of Native American verbal art. Some of the texts in these studies are certainly related in spirit to Tlingit oratory, although not strictly oratorical in form and delivery. Tedlock (1983) discusses oratory at various places in his book, and Hymes (1981:200-208) discusses Chinookan oratory in relation to narrative and he points out (p. 90) that although oratory is important to Chinookan communities, it is rarely recorded. We note here also the important restorations by Nichols (1988) and Foster (1978) of oratory contained in historical documents. We have arbitrarily set our boundary at the Mexican border, but we note here work on Central American oratory by Léon-Portilla (1985) on Nahuatl, and Sherzer's (1983, 1987) on Kuna. Both of these contain interesting examples and valuable discussions of style and genre theory; likewise, many other essays in the above listed collections explore the linguistic and stylistic boundaries of various types of speaking, for example the boundary between narrative and other literary genres such as oratory. We also direct readers to the end notes to the introduction for further references to scholarly literature.

There is a strong folklore component in our work, and, as most of our generation, we have been influenced greatly by the writings of and/or discussions with Jan Harold Brunvand, Linda Dégh, Richard Dorson, Alan Dundes, Henry Glassie, Barre Toelken, and others. In an effort to keep our bibliography as short as possible, we have listed Brunvand (1978), Dorson (1972), and Toelken (1979) as good places to start. See also R. Dauenhauer (1975) for a bibliography.

For general anthropological background on Tlingit, we also direct readers to the standard (perhaps monumental) studies of Tlingit by Frederica de Laguna (1972), Catharine McClellan (1975; 1987), R. L. Olson, (1967) and others, as listed in the bibliographies of *Haa Shuká, Our Ancestors* and the present volume. Swanton (1970*a*, originally 1908) is sometimes tricky to use, but we are finding that it stands up to the test of time better than we at first thought.

We have also been influenced, at a more general level, as has an entire generation of scholars, by the work of Albert Lord and Milman Perry on Homeric and South Slavic oral literature. Though our own efforts in Tlingit are more modest in comparison, and our own work remains in its infancy, both in its volume and theoretical development, we aspire to similar goals, as expressed by Lord:

> We can learn not only how the singer puts together his words, and then his phrases, and then his verses, but also his passage and themes, and we can see how the whole poem lives from one man to another, from one age to another, and passes over plains and mountains and

> barriers of speech,—more, we can see how a whole oral poetry lives and dies (Lord 1954:5).

Lord continues:

> That particular form of thought which is sung or told—and in our own times written—and which we call literature, is only a more finished kind of thought, and is equally shaped by the character of the man and his times. Then to seize fully the style of a piece of literature would be to know everything about the author and the world in which he lived. The. . . poetry. . . can show us. . . how. . . points of style. . . can be grouped together in a pattern which can be followed back to that moment which criticism must seek to create—the instant when the thought of the poet expressed itself in song (Lord 1954:5).

Although we are dealing with on-the-spot composition of oratory, not epic songs, what Lord says about Serbian epic also applies to our editorial policy here:

> These volumes will present epic songs as they are sung, by both highly skilled and less highly skilled singers, with all the errors and inconsistencies which result from rapid performance. The texts do not represent what an editor feels that the singer should have said, but what he actually did say. It is necessary that the reader fully understand this principle (Lord 1954:18).

We want to emphasize here that we have tried to write down what the elders actually said, the way they actually said it. Readers should keep in mind that memorials are emotionally intense situations, and, especially in the widow's cry, orators may be choked up and under stress. Under such conditions, minor grammatical errors are sometimes made; some syllables seem to be "swallowed." We have noted such places but we have generally transcribed the speeches as performed. In other places we have restored text where the tape is obscure due to the overlap of responses or the sound of other activity in the hall. These places, too, we have noted. As a final comment on Lord, we point out that, although we are not dealing in Tlingit with heroic poetry and metrical composition in the European oral tradition and strictest definition, many important concepts do apply to Native American oral literature. Some of this is discussed in greater detail at the end of the introduction, in conjunction with Foster's work on Iroquois.

Themes and Community Use

We are concerned with practical application of our work in the community, and this book is designed to serve multiple purposes. As a social goal, in addition to our scholarly goals described above, we have made unceasing efforts over the last twenty years to introduce Tlingit and other Alaska Native language and literature into education at all levels, from preschool to college. Widespread acceptance of Tlingit literature in schools in Alaska is still a problem. But, with an 80% Native high school drop-out rate in some communities, and with rising rates of teen-age suicide and substance abuse, we think including Tlingit literature in the curriculum is worth a try. As this book goes to press, educators in Alaska are still debating the value and validity of teaching Alaska Native languages and culture in the schools. One school administrator in a Tlingit village in Southeast Alaska recently told us he could not possibly see how Tlingit literature fits into the curriculum in his school. Alaska Native literature is often stereotyped as simple and didactic, and as children's literature. Stories are frequently "retold" in English with a language and style associated with fairy tales and children's literature. In most school districts with which we have worked, Tlingit literature is most easily fitted into the curriculum as children's literature at the elementary level, and only with extreme political difficulty at the high school level, where we most often meet with considerable resistance, and where it is often trivialized or used as entertainment. Ultimately, in our opinion, these are forms of racism—either the effort to exclude or to diminish the value of things from another (non-white, non-European) tradition. The oratory in this book stands in sharp contrast to this stereotype of Native American oral literature—as a manifest of its beauty and complexity.

We have used some of the speeches for the removal of grief, with positive results, in our own college courses and seminars, and in community cultural retreats in Tlingit myth, ritual, and spiritual healing. The speeches are usually studied in conjunction with the narratives in *Haa Shuká, Our Ancestors.* Sergei Kan reports that he has used some of these speeches in his university course, "Anthropology of Death and Dying," and that many students were moved by them. We hope that the speeches in this book will be used not only in literature classes in schools and colleges and in cultural retreats, but that they will be used by individuals—privately and publicly, at home and with family and friends, and in community study groups sponsored by health and social organizations and churches. Helping ourselves and others to deal with grief is a most important part of our lives, one that affects us all.

We would suggest further that the missionary attack on the Tlingit memorial system had a two-fold, compound social impact: it removed the primary cultural institution for dealing with grief while at the same time it created a cause of additional grief in the form of cultural loss and the death of culture. Thus, an increase in grief was compounded by the suppression or elimination of the traditional way to resolve it. We feel that increased understanding of Tlingit oratory and its traditional ceremonial context will go a long way to help address personal and social disorders faced by Tlingit communities today.

To help with such practical applications, in the introduction to *Haa Shuká, Our Ancestors* we indicated several literary and cultural themes running through the stories, and we suggested that one might approach Tlingit literature using these topics thematically in comparative literature courses or community discussions. We feel that some of these themes, such as "conflict of loyalty," "alienation and self-concept," "pride and arrogance," and "revenge" might be of special interest and importance to high school and college students. These themes have been set forth in four thematic comparative literature curriculum modules designed for high school use and edited by Ron and Suzanne Scollon (1987) under contract from Sealaska Heritage Foundation.

This collection of Tlingit speeches also suggests several ideas for thematic, comparative study. Some of these ideas are: Death and Dying; Separation and Loss; Spirituality; Respect; Oratory and Rhetoric; and the Gift.

Death and Dying affects the physical, social, and spiritual lives of all of us. The work of Dr. Elizabeth Kübler-Ross has helped many people through this experience. Several of the speeches in this book reveal Tlingit attitudes toward certain aspects of death and dying; they could be used as departure points for discussion and study of death in different societies and literatures as well as in our own personal and immediate lives. Much Tlingit oratory is delivered for the removal of grief. More than any other aspect of Tlingit oratory, people who have heard or read earlier drafts of these speeches have commented on their beauty.

Separation and Loss can be experienced not only through death but also through divorce, exile, or imprisonment, resulting in loss of loved ones, homeland, or freedom.

Also closely related to the theme of Death and Dying is the theme of ***Spirituality and Afterlife***: how do various cultures and religions view their spirit world and life after death? This is a common theme in studies of anthropology and comparative religion, and may appeal to some students.

Most of the speeches in this book deal with spirituality, and parts of this introduction have treated topics relating to shaman spirits and other spirits. Another obvious study theme suggested by the speeches is ***Shamans and Shamanism,*** but the topic is extremely complicated and difficult, widely oversimplified, misunderstood, misrepresented, and often sensationalized. Therefore, we do not recommend it for casual involvement.

Respect is the single, major concept that most Tlingit elders place at the top of their list of imperatives to know, understand, and practice in the study of Tlingit culture. Respect is difficult to discuss in the abstract, but the speeches in this book offer excellent, concrete examples of respect in Tlingit literature and society; they can be used as a starting point for discussion of respect in Tlingit culture, including the study of protocol and ceremony. As a comparative theme, all cultures share the concept of respect, but respect is displayed differently from culture to culture, often in seemingly opposite ways. Ways of showing respect and politeness in one culture may be interpreted as disrespectful or rude in another. This is a fundamental fact in interethnic communication.

Another possible community or classroom use of the speeches in this book is the comparative study of ***Oratory and Rhetoric***—the study of "great speeches" from various times and places, for example Lincoln's Gettysburg Address, Marc Antony's speech in Shakespeare's *Julius Caesar*, the Easter Sermon of St. John Chrysostom, and others. One can study the form and function of great speeches, to learn how orators put their words together to create a desired effect on their audience. Other Native

American examples can be found in the anthologies listed in the bibliography. Examples from World War II range from Winston Churchill and Franklin D. Roosevelt to Adolph Hitler. Modern American examples are speeches by John F. Kennedy and the Reverend Martin Luther King, Jr.

Yet another theme is ***the gift***. This is the subject of two well-known books, Hyde (1983) and Mauss (1967). Hyde (1983:9, 26-36) discusses the Northwest Coast potlatch and the practice of gifts being used up, eaten, or otherwise consumed. Mauss includes oratory as a gift of speech, of the word. The themes of food and gift exchange also appears in religions around the world, Christianity among them, in human concern to transcend mortal life (bios, limited life, the life that dies) and gain eternal life (zoe, life that endures, eternal life, the gene pool). As is described in this book, exchange of food and other gifts not only defines the social world of host and guest, but also connects the human and spiritual worlds.

For the Tlingit community, we realize that the most important instruction of younger generations must come from the elders, but we hope that this book will support that effort by transmitting the words of elders now departed. We hope that this book will help people in learning how to make speeches, and will aid communities in how to conduct a memorial. As noted in the introduction, the ceremonial language will almost certainly be English in a few more years, much as the Catholic Mass or Orthodox Divine Liturgy are conducted in English, but the form and function can be the same.

Likewise, we call readers' attention to the many recurring themes within the speeches, spanning almost one hundred years, from 1899 to 1989: orators' concern with their ancestors and their grandchildren, with their relatives and reciprocity, with at.óow and the continuity of tradition. As our colleague Barbara Cadiente Nelson observed of these speeches: "The themes keep recurring, like waves caressing the beach."

Nora Marks Dauenhauer
Richard Dauenhauer
Juneau, April 1990

Acknowledgments

Our acknowledgments for this collection of Tlingit oratory, the second volume in the series *Classics of Tlingit Oral Literature,* are much the same as for the first volume, *Haa Shuká, Our Ancestors,* because the research on both projects was conducted simultaneously. We wish to thank the many people who have supported this work, even though the oratory and prose narratives found their way into print at different times.

The editors wish to acknowledge appreciation for the support of the Sealaska Heritage Foundation Board of Directors: Judson L. Brown (Chair, 1983-86) L. Embert Demmert, A. John Hope, Clarence Jackson, Toni Jones, Esther Littlefield, the late Robert Martin (Chair, 1986-87), Stella Martin, Conrad Mather, the late Roy Peratrovich, Sr., Robert Sanderson, Walter Soboleff (Chair, 1987-) Richard Stitt, Ed Thomas, the late Alfred Widmark, Sr., Ronald Williams, and Rosita Worl. We thank Carlton Smith, corporate secretary, and administrators David G. Katzeek, president; Tim Wilson, director of development; language and cultural studies production staff Fred White and Rhonda Mann, who were research assistants during the earlier stages of the manuscript; accountants Cindy Mar Mor and Rita Bowen; Celebration director Paul Marks, and all of our other colleagues at the Sealaska Heritage Foundation, who shared our vision of the possibility of using new technology to help document traditional ways. The map was drawn by Rhonda Mann. We thank also our colleagues in the Sealaska Corporation, especially

Edith McHenry, Ross Soboleff, and Ricardo Worl, for their timely assistance in helping us research the biographies and locate photographs. Also, we thank the staff at Tlingit and Haida Central Council for their help with photographs and biographies. Special words of appreciation go to Barbara Cadiente Nelson, editorial assistant for the final stages of this project. Her energy, skills, and enthusiasm greatly enhanced this book and helped propel it to completion.

We gratefully acknowledge the following institutions, agencies, organizations, and individuals, whose efforts and support helped make this work possible. Major funding for this project has come from the Alaska State Legislature, whose support has made it possible to document for posterity these treasures of the oral literature of Alaska that are the heritage of all Alaskans, regardless of ethnicity.

Major funding has also been provided through translation and research grants from the National Endowment for the Humanities (Grants RL-20533-86 and RO-21723-89). Some of the materials were collected, and earlier versions of some manuscripts were drafted with the support of the National Endowment for the Humanities Translation Grant RL-00160-80-1070 (1980-1981), and as projects of the Alaska Native Language Center, University of Alaska-Fairbanks, during its first year of operation 1972-73. Funds for publication of this volume were provided by a grant from the Alaska Humanities Forum. Any opinions, conclusions, or findings contained herein do not necessarily represent the views of the National Endowment for the Humanities or of the other supporting agencies.

Within Alaska and the greater Northwest, many private organizations have rallied to the cause, and we are happy to thank them here for their financial and moral support. Because the material with which we have been entrusted by the elders is the spiritual property of the Sealaska shareholders, we are especially gratified by the contributions we have received from Sealaska Corporation, Huna Totem Corporation of Hoonah, and Kootznoowoo, Inc., of Angoon. The Rasmuson Foundation of Anchorage provided grant support for the computer system on which this book was designed and typeset, and Rainier Bank of Seattle contributed substantially to the project.

We also gratefully acknowledge the personal and technical support of friends and colleagues who helped us pioneer in the development of software and firmware for fluent word processing, screen display, printing, and electronic transmission of Tlingit and other languages with character sets other than English; especially: Dr. James Levin of Interlearn and formerly of the University of California-San Diego, now of the University of Illinois, who helped us in earlier stages with software for the Apple II Plus and Apple IIe computers on which most of this material was first word-processed, and who has helped us most recently with upgrading to Macintosh; Dr. Moshe Cohen, of Interlearn and Hebrew University of Jerusalem; Mr. Allan Rogers of Hands-on Training Company, Bonita, California, who helped in the development of an inexpensive foreign language chip for the Apple IIe; and Drs. Ron and Suzanne Scollon, formerly of University of Alaska-Fairbanks, now of The Gutenberg Dump, Limited, Haines, Alaska. We thank the Scollons not only for their part in the computer work that helped make this possible, but for frequent and valuable discussions on the form, content, and philosophy of the work as well. Finally among the computer credits, special thanks and recognition go to our friend and colleague Tim Wilson of the Sealaska Heritage Foundation staff for his general expertise in Macintosh technology and specifically for his help in designing and installing the family of Tlingit Palatino fonts in which this book is typeset, and the accompanying software modifications that allowed us to wordprocess fluently in Tlingit as well as English on the Macintosh. In the final stages of this process we benefited immeasurably by the talents and attention to detail of Michael Travis, who designed or completed the family of Tlingit Palatino fonts, did the charts in the book, and typeset the entire manuscript.

The earliest transcriptions and translations in this book date back some eighteen years, so we are also happy for this opportunity to thank our many colleagues in linguistics, anthropology, and literature who have supported our work and who have encouraged us over the years. Among these are Michael Krauss, Irene Reed, Frederica de Laguna, Catharine McClellan, Fannie LeMoine, Robert Rehder, Peter Corey, William and Karen Workman, Kerry Feldman, O. W. Frost, Margritt Engel, Gary Holthaus, and H.-Jürgen Pinnow, Soterios Mousalimas, Lydia Black, Richard Pierce, Fr. Michael Oleksa, Sergei Kan, Karen Willmore, Walter Soboleff, Donald Bahr, and

Maxine Richert. We have benefited greatly from dialogue with these colleagues. Several read sections of the manuscript in progress and made careful notes and commentary.

Special thanks go to Jeff Leer, Constance Naish, and Gillian Story, not only for their insights and support over the years, but for their proofreading and discussion of the linguistic intricacies of the various Tlingit language texts. We are especially grateful to Jeff Leer for making time to help proofread the glossary; and to Emma Marks, John Marks and Katherine Mills for their help in clarifying many of the difficult Tlingit concepts involved in the speeches, especially the set from Hoonah. We thank all of these people for their time and effort, and for their share in improving the final product. Errors of omission or commission are entirely our own.

Some of the Tlingit texts included here were first transcribed in the early 1970's. We want to acknowledge those who helped with the typing in the early history of these manuscripts, especially Rosita Worl. For her administrative support in the early years we also thank Elaine Abraham.

We are grateful for the help of the families and friends of many of the elders, who assisted us with photographs and in the writing of the biographies. These people are noted in the biographies, notes, and photo credits. We thank the staff of the University of Washington Press not only for their boundless encouragement and technical assistance but equally for the singular joy they have brought to the project, for their advice, encouragement, and perennial optimism and good cheer.

We especially thank the Tlingit elders themselves for their faith, enthusiasm, courage, vision, and patience in supporting our work. It grieves us that so many have passed away since we first began working with them, but we are happy that their words will live on, as well as their names and memories. We hope that through this book their voices will continue to resonate over generations. It is to all of these elders and tradition bearers, known and unknown, living and departed, that this work is dedicated.

As we acknowledge the elders with whom it has been our privilege to work, we also acknowledge those with whom we have not yet been able to work, due to limitations of time and energy and to various circumstances beyond our control. This collection is but a tiny sample of Tlingit oratory. As with the narratives in *Haa Shuká*, this book is not the last word on Tlingit oratory, but only a first; it is by no means a complete collection of Tlingit oratory, but just a humble beginning, featuring the work of some of the elders with whom it has been our good fortune to study. We make no claim to being definitive. We hope this book is the first word on Tlingit oratory, not the last.

We see this book as a Tlingit book; it belongs ultimately to the Tlingit people and to the clans involved. The speeches in Tlingit are the words of the elders themselves, as they spoke them. We have tried to present their words in English through careful translation, and we have tried to bring additional meaning to them through commentary in the introduction, annotations, and biographies. The oratory presented here has been documented for our children and for all the younger generations in the Tlingit community that they may come to a greater understanding of and an appreciation for their heritage and traditions. But, as with all Tlingit oratory, the words are open to all who wish to listen. We hope that other persons reading the words of the elders will be as moved as we were upon first hearing them, and still are at hearing them over and over. The original speeches were directed primarily to a limited number of people, but the words have transcended time and space and have brought comfort, healing, and joy to many.

As editors, we are salaried to do this work, but we make no money from the sale of books. After publication expenses are met, all royalties normally accruing to the editors will go to Sealaska Heritage Foundation to be used for the publication of additional books "lifting up" the elders to whom the work is dedicated, honoring their achievement and their memories.

To all of these people who helped make this book a reality we are happy to say Gunalchéesh, hó hó!

Haa Tuwunáagu Yís, for Healing Our Spirit

George Davis at Chilkoot Lake, August 1980, during the filming of *Haa Shagóon*. He is wearing the Naatúxjayi tunic and holding the Sockeye Dance Staff. Naatúxjayi was woven by Jennie Thlunaut for her husband's (John Mark's) cousin (tribal brother) Jack David. It depicts a spirit helper that appeared to G̱éek'i, one of the Lukaax̱.ádi shamans, and is featured in oratory by Austin Hammond. According to oral history, G̱éek'i was beheaded by a sailor aboard a ship exploring the mouth of the Chilkat River. It is said that his body flew when he was decapitated. His head went in the water and sank. Later, his disembodied head crawled up the tide flats, its hair like tentacles. Photo by R. Dauenhauer.

Introduction:
The Form and Function of Tlingit Oratory

I. TLINGIT SOCIAL STRUCTURE

When dealing with any work of literature, the general reader who crosses the boundaries of time, place, or culture will require some introduction. Accordingly, in order to see the context in which these speeches were originally presented and are still understood by Tlingit people, we begin with an overview and some background on the Tlingit people and social structure. The Tlingit Indians[1] live in Southeast Alaska from Yakutat to Dixon Entrance, predominantly on the coast, but with inland communities along the Chilkat and Stikine Rivers in Alaska, and in Southwest Yukon and Northwest British Columbia. A variety of evidence as well as Tlingit tradition suggest that the Tlingits migrated to the coast at a very ancient date and spread along the coast from the southern range of their territory to the north where they were expanding toward the Copper River at the time of European contact.

The relationship of Tlingit to other Native American languages is uncertain. There is great cultural similarity between Tlingit and adjacent Northwest Coast groups but no obvious linguistic affinity. Tlingit is clearly not related to Tsimshian, and a possible ancient linguistic relationship to Haida is a subject of continuing scholarly debate, with most specialists maintaining that Haida and Tlingit are not related. On the other hand, many features of Tlingit phonology and grammar systematically parallel the Athabaskan languages (including Navajo, for example), but there are very few obvious similarities in vocabulary. Although there are some obvious Athabaskan loan words in Tlingit, there are very few undisputed lexical cognates, and it remains unproven whether the relationship is genetic or one of languages in contact. However, most linguists believe that Tlingit is genetically related to the Athabaskan family of languages and that the recently extinct Eyak language and nearly extinct Tongass dialect of Tlingit are the "missing links" in the language chain of Na-Dene. Still, the origin of much of the Tlingit vocabulary remains a puzzle.

Coastal Tlingits live in and on the edge of a rain forest, and this environment has shaped their lifestyle and material culture, along with those of other cultures of the Northwest Coast. Native American culture of this region has captured the imagination of explorers ever since first contact. These are the people of totem poles, elaborately carved wooden bowls and bentwood boxes, plank houses, ocean-going canoes, Chilkat robes, button blankets, and other well-known cultural objects and events, especially the ceremony known in Tlingit as k̲oo.éex', and most commonly in English as "potlatch." Many features of these cultures, especially totem poles and potlatch, have often been misunderstood by outsiders.

The speeches in this book are an integral part of this natural and social context. The orators derive their images from the physical and cultural environments, and the speeches are delivered according to patterns and protocol of social structure. Full understanding and enjoyment of the speeches (as well as of Tlingit visual and performing art) require familiarity with the basic concepts of Tlingit social structure.

Because of the length of the introduction, an outline may be helpful here. For easier reference, we have used the convention of ***boldface italic type*** to highlight topics.

The Form and Function of Tlingit Oratory

I. Tlingit Social Structure

  A. Moieties, Clans, and House Groups

B. Ownership and Reciprocity
II. At.óow (Clan Crests, etc.)
III. Social and Cultural Settings for Oratory
A. Informal Settings
B. Alaska Native Brotherhood
C. Forty Day Party
D. K̲oo.éex' (Memorial)
IV. The General Structure of a Tlingit Memorial
A. Preliminary Activities and Group Dynamics
B. Taking Up the Drum (Gaaw Wutaan)
i. The Cry (by the Hosts; K̲áa Eetí G̲aax̲í)
ii. The Widow's Cry (by the Guests; L S'aatí Sháa G̲aax̲í)
C. Food, Gifts, Songs, Dancing, and Dramatics
i. Fire Dishes
ii. Meals
iii. Songs, Dances, and Dramatics
a. "Regular" Dances and Love Songs
b. Yarn or Motion Dances
c. Spirit (Yéik utee; Shakee.át) Dances performed with an ermine headdress, behind a blanket
d. Haida Style (Deikeenaa) Dances
e. Dramatics (Yikteiyí)
iv. Distribution of Gifts
a. Dry Goods
b. Berries
c. Fruit
d. Soft Drinks
e. Canned Goods and Preserves
f. Miscellaneous Small Gifts
D. Distribution of Money
V. Simile and Metaphor in Tlingit and English Literature
VI. The General Structure of Tlingit Oratory
VII. At.óow in Action: Levels of Mediation in Tlingit Oratory
VIII. Treatment of Spirits in Tlingit Oratory
IX. Vocabulary of the Tlingit Spirit World
A. People
B. Spirits
C. Lands of the Dead

X. Conclusion: The Past, Present, and Future of Tlingit Oratory
  A. The Paper Trail: The Written Record of Tlingit Oratory
  B. Tlingit and Other Native American Oratory
  C. The Viability of Tlingit Oratory

Moieties, Clans, and House Groups

All of Tlingit society is organized in two reciprocating divisions called moieties (***moiety***: pronounced moy-uh-tee, meaning "half," or "one of two equal parts," and defined as "one of two basic complementary tribal subdivisions"). Tlingit society is also ***matrilineal***—organized through the mother's line. Although the words are often popularly confused, the term "matrilineal," meaning that a person's blood line is traced primarily through the mother, is not the same as "matriarchal," meaning "ruled by women." Tlingit society is matrilineal, but not matriarchal. A Tlingit individual is born into his or her mother's moiety, clan, and house group.

The two moieties are named Raven and Eagle. Raven is sometimes also known as Crow, and Eagle as Wolf. Crow and Wolf may in fact be older terms. For example, the word "wolf" always appears in songs as the term for that moiety, and women of the Raven moiety are usually referred to as Tsaxweil Sháa, meaning "Crow Women." Crow and Wolf are commonly used by the Inland Tlingit, and Raven and Eagle on the coast. In contrast to clans, moieties as such have no political organization or power, but exist for the purposes of ***exogamy*** (regulation of marriage) and exchange of other ritual services, especially mortuary ones. Traditionally, a person married into the opposite moiety, although this pattern is no longer strictly observed, and marriage within the same moiety and marriage to non-Tlingits are both common and accepted today. The moieties also group the clans for other kinds of reciprocal actions. For example, Ravens not only marry Eagles, but address songs and speeches to them as well, and vice versa. Because most formal speeches are delivered in the context of a host-guest relationship with one moiety hosting the other, oratory also crosses moiety lines. Most speakers begin by addressing relatives of the opposite moiety, such as fathers, paternal aunts, uncles, grandparents, and in-laws.

Each moiety consists of many ***clans***. Some of the Raven moiety clans mentioned in this book are Lukaax̲.ádi, L'uknax̲.ádi, T'ak̲deintaan, Kiks.ádi, Suk̲tineidí, Tuk̲.weidí, X'atka.aayí, K̲ak'weidí, and Deisheetaan. Among the Eagle (Wolf) moiety clans mentioned in this book are Kaagwaantaan, Wooshkeetaan, Chookaneidí, Shangukeidí, Yanyeidí, Teik̲weidí, Dak̲l'aweidí, and Tsaagweidí. Certain clans, such as the Kiks.ádi and Kaagwaantaan, are fairly well-known in English by these Tlingit names; others are less well-known. Also, some of the Tlingit clan names are more difficult for English speakers to pronounce than others. As a result, many of the clans now also have popular English names, usually derived from a major crest. Among these are:

Eagle Moiety

Shangukeidí - Thunderbird
Dak̲l'aweidí - Killer Whale
Teik̲weidí - Brown Bear

Raven Moiety

Deisheetaan - Beaver
L'uknax̲.ádi - Coho [Silver Salmon]
Lukaax̲.ádi - Sockeye [Red Salmon]
L'eineidí - Dog Salmon

Thus, when speaking Tlingit, a person might use the term Dak̲l'aweidí, but when speaking English he or she might say "Killer Whale," or "Killer Whale People." The English name is not a translation of the Tlingit name, but is based on the crest.

Most clans are dispersed though a number of communities, but in any given commmunity certain clans predominate for historical reasons. For example, the Kiks.ádi, Kaagwaantaan and L'uknax̲.ádi (Coho) are strong in Sitka; Deisheetaan and Teik̲weidí in Angoon; Chookaneidí and T'ak̲deintaan in Hoonah; Lukaax̲.ádi in the Chilkoot area, etc. Political organization rests at the clan level; clans own heraldic crests, personal names and other property. The Tlingit term for this property is at.óow, and it will be explained in detail below. Each clan has traditional leaders, but there is no single leader for all the Ravens or Eagles. The Tlingit terms for leaders include hít s'aatí (house master or house leader), naa shuháni (one who stands at the head of his clan), k̲áa sháadei háni (leader; one who stands at the head of men). Lingít tlein (big person) was also used for respected elders. A military leader or warrior was called x'eig̲aa k̲áa. The term "chief" is a European and American innovation. The Russians used the term "toion" for a Tlingit leader.

House Group, sometimes called "lineage" in anthropological literature, is a difficult concept because it applies both to kinship and residence, and these do not completely overlap. Most simply stated, the house was where people lived or once lived and this was part of their identity. Readers interested in more detail should consult works by de Laguna, Kan, McClellan, and others listed in the reference section of this book. For purposes of this introduction it is best to understand house groups as a kinship term, realizing that not all members of a house group physically reside in the ancestral house, that not all residents of a clan house are members of that house, and that most of the original houses are no longer standing. Various house groups are mentioned in the speeches, annotations, and biographies.

The easiest way to approach the term is to understand it as historically referring to both residence and kinship, but now used only as a term of kinship. Due to marriage and living patterns, not all residents of a house were members of the house group. Spouses, for example, were of the opposite moiety. In technical terms, Tlingit tradition was avuncilocal: a newly married couple would theoretically reside in the clan house of the husband's uncle, often because the nephew was already living there before his marriage. Also, not all members of a particular group were physical residents of the house, but might live in other houses or other villages. Women and their children, for example, would be genealogically of one house group but reside in another. As the population expanded, residents separated and new houses would be built. As houses grew in population and stature, they sometimes took on the status of independent clans, closely related to the parent clan. Thus, many contemporary clans began as house groups of an older clan and therefore share some of the original crests and personal names of their common ancestry. Many clan names (such as Kaagwaantaan and Deisheetaan) derive historically from house names.

Each clan traditionally included many house groups, although this genealogical awareness has been largely lost in recent generations due to changes in physical housing arrangements brought about by Protestant missionary and the Bureau of Indian Affairs (BIA) pressure. Other social changes in the twentieth century also contributed to the rise of single-family dwellings and led to the demise of traditional community houses. Changes in marriage practices were encouraged by the missionaries, and changes in the rules for inheritance were sanctioned by American law.

Finding English terms always presents a problem when discussing non-English concepts. For example, there is no single, generic term in Tlingit to cover what we call "clan" in this book, and what is sometimes referred to in anthropological literature as "sib." Likewise, there is no single Tlingit term for "moiety." The Tlingit word "naa" is used for both concepts and appears in Tlingit in various combinations: yéil naa, ch'áak' naa, naa káani, and naa yádi, meaning raven moiety, eagle moiety, an in-law of the moiety, and child of the moiety. Also, the word is used in such phrases as "Kaagwaantaan naa," which translates as Kaagwaantaan clan. The Tlingit term for "opposite moiety or clan" is g̲uneit kanaayí. Borrowed by linguists, this is also the origin of the "na" part of the linguistic term Na-Dene, referring to the greater Tlingit-Athapaskan-Eyak language family. Likewise, there is a Tlingit term for house group or lineage, "taan," a combining form that does not appear alone, but always in conjunction with the word for house, hít; for example, Xóots Hít Taan, People of the Brown Bear House, or Brown Bear House Group. The word also appears in many clan names, reflecting, as noted above, the origin of the clan as an earlier house group; for example, Deisheetaan, from Deishú Hít Taan, People of the House at the End of the Road, and Kaagwaantaan, from Kaawagaani Hít Taan, People of the Burned House. The English words "tribe" and "nation" are also heard in popular speech, and the meaning varies from speaker to speaker, ranging from a designation for all the Tlingit (Haida or Tsimshian) people, to moiety, or clan. In addition to the clan names as listed above, many appear in variant forms for women, such as Chookan sháa, L'uknax̲ sháa, and Shanguka sháa. The ending -sháa (meaning "women") is exclusively for women; -eidí and -ádi may be used for men or women or for a mixed group; it means "people of."

The father's clan of an individual is just as significant as that of the mother, but it functions and is recognized in a different way from that of the mother's clan. To be a socially recognized person in the traditional way requires actions by and references to both the mother's and the father's clans. Because the traditional social pattern called for marriage into the opposite moiety, a man's children were traditionally never of his own but of his wife's moiety and clan, because individuals follow not their father's but their mother's line. This is a very important concept in Tlingit social structure, visual art, and oral literature, especially songs and oratory. While a person is of his or her mother's clan, he or she is also known as a "child of" the father's clan. The Tlingit term for "child of" is yádi; the plural is yátx'i. For example, a man or woman may be Raven moiety, Kiks.ádi, and Kaagwaantaan yádi. The term Kaagwaantaan yádi or child of Kaagwaantaan does not mean that a person is of that clan, but that his or her father is of that clan.

This concept is basic to any serious understanding of the Tlingit culture in general, and of its oral literature in particular. Most songs, especially love songs, are addressed to members of the opposite moiety, who are identified according to their fathers' clan rather than their mothers' and their own. For example, if the Eagle Kaagwaantaan were singing to the Raven Kiks.ádi, the words of a song might be "Where are you, children of Kaagwaantaan." The song would never open with a phrase such as "Where are you, Kiks.ádis?" The father's clan is most often the clan of the composer as well; such a song would be owned by the clan directing it to their children (of the opposite moiety).

Not only the father's, but the paternal grandfather's clan is also very important in Tlingit oratory and social structure, especially where ceremonials for the departed are involved. The paternal grandfather and his grandchildren are ideally of the same clan, and always of the same moiety. The Tlingit term for this relationship is chushgadachx̱án, meaning "grandchildren of each other." The paternal grandparent relationship is especially important in ceremonial settings and will be discussed in detail in Sections IV and VII of this introduction.

Another concept of kinship basic to the oratory is reference to mothers and fathers in the plural. For example, all men of the father's clan, and, by extension, even all men of the entire opposite moiety may be considered tribal or clan fathers,

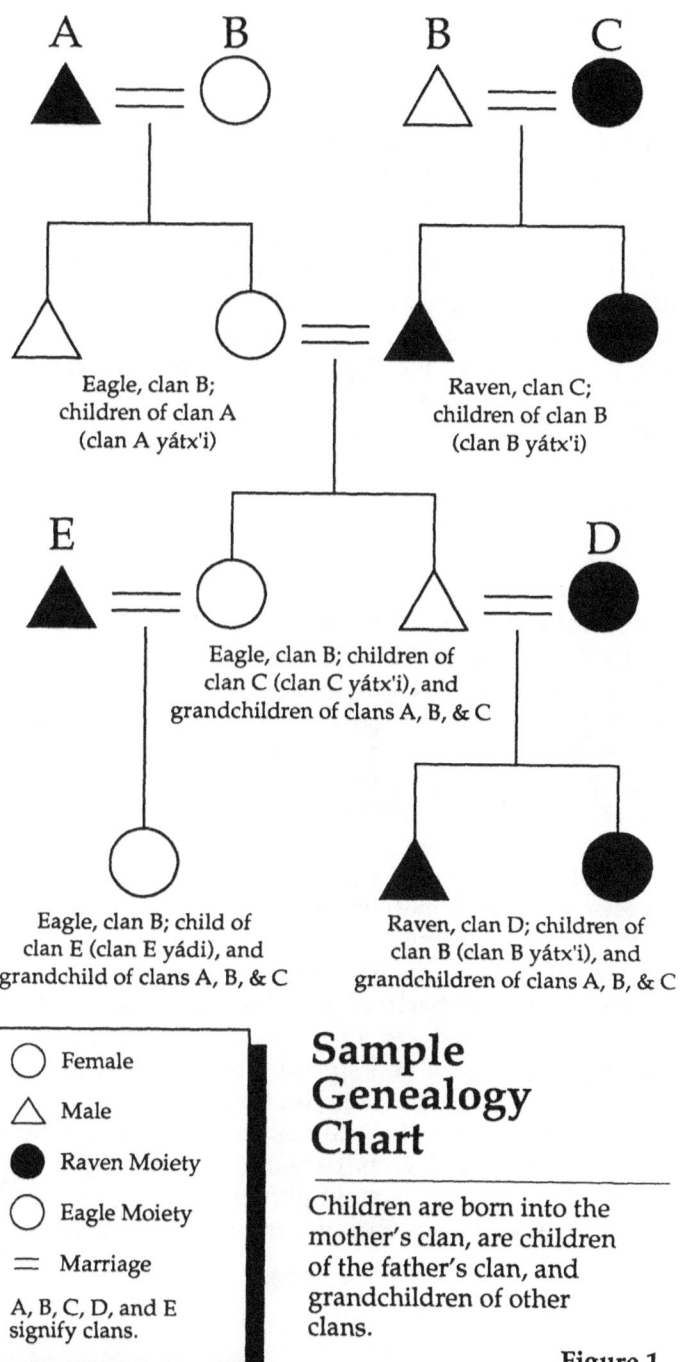

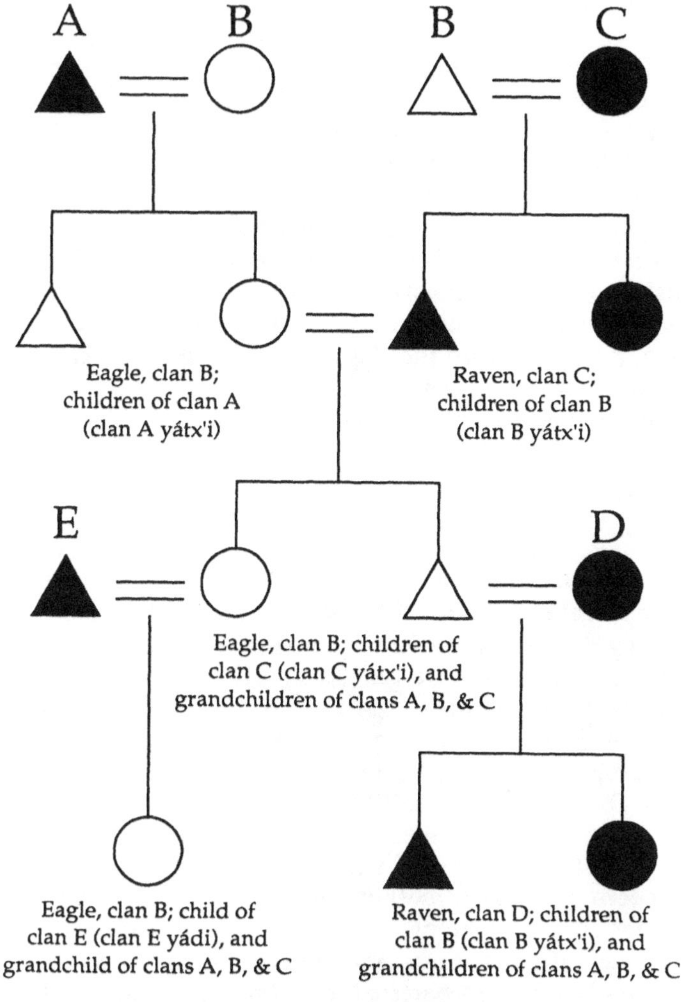

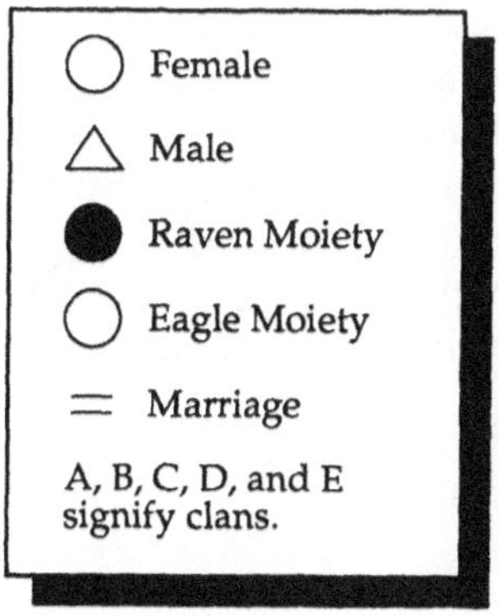

Sample Genealogy Chart

Children are born into the mother's clan, are children of the father's clan, and grandchildren of other clans.

Figure 1.

depending on the circumstances. The same kinship term is used for all of these relationships. This is likewise true for mothers: maternal aunts and by extension all women of the mother's clan may be referred to as clan mothers. Although a person has only one biological father and mother, according to the Tlingit kinship system an individual usually has more than one person who can be considered his or her father or mother. This can be confusing in English translation and transcription of oral records partly because the Tlingit use of terms is culturally different from English, partly because the English morpheme -s marks both plural and possession, and partly because of spelling conventions involving the apostrophe to mark possession. For example:

mother	—	singular
mothers	—	plural
mother's	—	singular, possessive
mothers'	—	plural, possessive.

At first glance, some of the plural possessives may seem to be typographical errors, but the speakers are in fact referring to something owned collectively by several women, all of whom are tribally considered to be a person's mother. This use of terms also extends to grandparents. A person need not be a biological ancestor to be considered a grandparent, if he or she is of the grandparent clan or house group.

The Tlingit term léelk'w, meaning grandparent, is used both biologically and ceremonially. Biologically it refers to a person of either sex and of either moiety. There are no separate Tlingit terms for grandmother and grandfather, or for maternal and paternal grandparents. Ceremonially, because of the pattern of exchange of gifts, songs, and speeches across moiety lines, the term usually refers to paternal grandparents, who use their at.óow to give help and support to their children and grandchildren in time of grief and spiritual need. The central example in this book is the memorial for Jim Marks, where speeches for the removal of grief are given to the mourning Eagles by the parent (Lukaax̱.ádi) and grandparent (T'ak̲deintaan) clans of the Raven moiety. Figure 1 is a simplified genealogy chart that summarizes the basic concepts of Tlingit social structure.

Ownership and Reciprocity

Two main features characterize Tlingit culture and oral tradition—ownership and reciprocity (popularly called "balance"). Songs, stories, artistic designs, personal names, land, and other elements of Tlingit life are considered either real or incorporated property of a particular clan. The Tlingit term for this concept of both tangible and intangible property is ***at.óow***, and the following section of this introduction is devoted entirely to this important concept. The use of at.óow, including the form, content, and immediate setting of oral tradition, operates in a larger context of reciprocity or "balance." The form and content of verbal and visual art or iconography are congruent with each other and with social structure. Stated simply, the patterns of the visual art and oral literature follow and reinforce the patterns of social structure.

The two moieties, Eagle and Raven, balance each other. Members of one moiety select marriage partners from the other, and they direct love songs and most formal oratory to each other. In host-guest relationships at ceremonials, they share in each others' joy and they work to remove each others' grief. This balancing is reflected in the oral literature itself. For example, the exchange of speeches follows the pattern of exchange of marriage, goods, and services, and the images in the songs and speeches are built around references of relationship to the opposite moiety. There are many examples of the principle of balance in this book. Raven guests address Eagle hosts in the "Speeches for the Removal of Grief" from the memorial for Jim Marks. The speeches for Charlie Joseph and the G̱ajaa Héen Dancers from the Sealaska Elders Conference demonstrate how a song or speech by a host must be answered by a guest—not in rivalry or competition, but so that the words of the speaker or singer may be received formally or somehow supported rather than "wandering aimlessly," or "lying unattended." Within the speeches themselves, information and images may be balanced artistically and emotionally: images of the physical and spiritual, the living and departed, humans and animals, living creatures and the land.

The art of public speaking is highly valued in traditional and contemporary Tlingit society. Tlingit oratory tends to be complex in style and content. As the examples in this collection show, a speaker must be the master of several areas of knowledge: genealogy—the family trees of everybody involved; kinship—the Tlingit clan and house group system; visual art or iconography—the Tlingit clan crests as portrayed in totems, masks, hats, dance headdresses, Chilkat robes, button blankets, tunics, and similar regalia; songs, histories, legends, and other narratives; traditional spirituality and concepts of the afterlife; and protocol—rules of order.

The speaker must know these in isolation and must also know how to connect them poetically, using simile, metaphor, and other rhetorical devices. The speaker must also be sensitive to human emotional needs. He or she must have a bearing of poise and dignity, and must know how to use his or her words to give comfort, encouragement, and strength to people in times of grief or at other rites of passage and times of crisis. A Tlingit public speaker must know how to build appropriate bridges between individuals, families, clans, and communities, and between the material and spiritual worlds. The speeches presented here provide an excellent introduction to Tlingit society because they illustrate how all aspects of Tlingit language and culture are interconnected.

II. AT.ÓOW

Most of the poetic images in Tlingit oratory are based on ***at.óow***. This concept is discussed at length in the introduction to *Haa Shuká*, the first book in this series (Dauenhauer and Dauenhauer 1987, hereafter referred to as *Haa Shuká*) but a review is useful here. At.óow is the single most important spiritual and cultural concept introduced through the narratives published in *Haa Shuká*. This fundamental concept underlies all dimensions of Tlingit social structure, oral literature, iconography, and ceremonial life. It is the spiritual, social, and rhetorical anchor for the oratory in this book.[2] The word at.óow means, literally, "an owned or purchased thing." The concepts of "thing" on the one hand, and "owned," or "purchased," on the other, are equally important.

The "thing" may be land (geographic features such as a mountain, a landmark, an historical site, a place such as Glacier Bay) a heavenly body (the sun, the dipper, the milky way) a spirit, a personal name, an artistic design, or a range of other "things." It can be an image from oral literature such as an episode from the Raven cycle on a tunic, hat, robe or blanket; it can be a story or song about an event in the life of an ancestor. Ancestors introduced in *Haa Shuká* can themselves be at.óow—Kaasteen, Kaats', Duktootl' and the others. These are the "léelk'w hás," the grandparents of a clan. At.óow can also be spirits of various kinds: shaman spirits and spirits of animals. These spiritual beings as at.óow are discussed at length at the end of this introduction.

The speeches in this book are rich in examples of at.óow. For example, Naatúxjayi mentioned by Austin Hammond is an at.óow, both the immediate physical woven Chilkat tunic, and the ancestral spirit it depicts. Jessie Dalton identifies the shirt named after the event in the Raven cycle, where Raven goes down to the bottom of the sea on bull kelp—Geesh Daa<u>x</u> Woogoodi Yéil K'oodás'. Matthew Lawrence uses images of Tsal<u>x</u>aan (Mt. Fairweather) and William Johnson mentions <u>G</u>aana<u>x</u>áa. These are at.óow of the Hoonah T'a<u>k</u>deintaan—not only the geographical places, but their representation on hats and other visual art, and the spiritual places and conditions the iconography represents. Jessie Dalton describes the Frog and Mountain Tribe Dog Hats; David Kadashan refers to the Sun Mask. These are all at.óow. The speeches by Charlie Joseph and those delivered in reply to him at the 1980 Sealaska Elders Conference are also based entirely on the concept of at.óow and their use.

Through ***purchase*** by an ancestor, a "thing" becomes ***owned*** by his or her descendants. The purchase and subsequent ownership may come through money, trade, or peacemaking, as collateral on an unpaid debt, or through personal action, usually involving loss of life. The at.óow central to the speeches in this collection recall the actions of ancestors whose deeds purchased them and the at.óow are therefore precious to the Tlingit people. Most often, and most seriously, the purchase is through human life—giving one's life for the image. In Tlingit tradition, the law is that a person pays for a life he or she has taken. Payment may be with one's own life, with someone else's life as a substitute, or with something of great value. Hence, if an animal (or natural object or force) takes the life of a person, its image may be taken by relatives in payment, and the descendants then own this image taken in payment. For example, in the "Glacier Bay History" by Amy Marvin in *Haa Shuká* all of the following are the "property" or at.óow of the Chookaneidí clan: the name Kaasteen, the land of Glacier Bay, the glacier itself, the story and the songs, the visual image of the Woman in the Ice, and the physical and now spiritual ancestor herself. All these at.óow were purchased with the life of a Chookaneidí ancestor. The clan histories and other stories recall how such an event happens in the life of an ancestor or progenitor and various aspects of the event become the clan's at.óow. The ancestor, the design, the spirit of the animal, the song, the story, and the land where it happened are all important in the spiritual, social, and ceremonial life of the people. The pattern is the same for most of the stories in *Haa Shuká*, for all of the at.óow mentioned in speeches in this book, and for all of Tlingit culture and oral literature.

An event, person, place or art object doesn't automatically receive instant status as at.óow. The design is usually executed initially as a mere piece of art. An individual or clan traditionally commissions an artist of the opposite moiety to create it, although it is becoming increasingly common for members of a clan to produce their own art work. The art object will always feature an at.óow of the clan, such as a frog or bear, a mountain, or a person such as Strong Man tearing the sea lion in half. These images don't "tell a story," but allude to or make reference to stories already known, in much the same way as a cross does not "tell" the Christmas or Easter "story," but alludes to the entire spiritual tradition. Once created, the art object is then brought out during a ceremonial and given a name. Speeches are made and the art is paid for by the person who commissioned it and his or her relatives. It was not the traditional practice to set or negotiate a fee in advance. Usually many members of the clan or house group joined to help pay for it and provide gifts to the artist, and in some cases contribute to the cost of materials.

When the individual owner dies, the at.óow is referred to by a special term: ***l s'aatí át***—a "masterless thing," an object with no owner. The object may then go to the stewardship of the next of kin in the same clan, or to a person who has contributed toward funeral expenses, or who in other ways gave moral, spiritual, or financial support to the owner. In most cases this support comes from a clan leader who then inherits the estate of the deceased. If there is no one to take it, then the l s'aatí át goes into communal ownership as part of the clan collection held by a steward. When there is no one to claim them individually as a steward, these at.óow are sometimes displayed on a table during ceremonials. They are worn or held in hand during the Widow's Cry. Under certain conditions, newly made at.óow may be added to the collection of l s'aatí át, as when Emma Marks included her new sets of beadwork and gave the beaded porpoises to the Chookaneidí women as part of the distribution of her deceased husband Willie's property.

William Johnson speaking on the T'a<u>k</u>deintaan at.óow during the Widow's Cry of the memorial for Willie Marks, Hoonah, October 1981. Hilda See holds the Mt. Tribe's Dog Hat (Shaatu<u>k</u>wáan Keidlí) and Elizabeth Govina holds the Mt. Fairweather Hat (Tsal<u>x</u>áantu Sháawu S'áaxw). Elizabeth Govina, T'a<u>k</u>deintaan, is the niece of Willie Marks. The Tsal<u>x</u>áantu Sháawu and Shaatu<u>k</u>wáan Keidlí spirits were visions of her Grandmother, Shkík, a shaman of the T'a<u>k</u>deintaan. This is the kind of setting in which William and his fellow orators delivered the speeches during the 1968 memorial for Jim Marks which are featured in this book. Photo by R. Dauenhauer.

In other situations, members of a clan may join in commissioning at.óow to be made for one of its leaders. In the event that the owner dies, this at.óow will become community-owned with a steward designated to care for it. For example, the Lukaax̱.ádi Raven House collection is a consolidation of at.óow from many house groups and deceased individuals now kept as a single collection with one steward.

In other words, while newly made art objects may depict already existing clan heraldic designs that are at.óow, the new objects themselves are not automatically at.óow, but may eventually become so through ceremonial use and dedication. For example, vests of felt or moosehide, hats and headbands and felt button blankets depicting at.óow are common in Tlingit communities. They are frequently worn for Indian dancing and at Forty Day Parties and memorials, both of which will be described in detail below. These are called ash koolyát kanaa.ádi—"play clothes." Once an owner of such a piece decides it is important enough, he or she will bring it out in memory of a deceased relative at a ceremonial and give it a name. It is then usually put on the owner by an appropriate member of the opposite moiety according to genealogy. Once this is done, the piece itself becomes an at.óow in its own right. It has been "purchased" or "paid for," as the at.óow it depicts was paid for in ancestral times. At.óow may also increase in value. Money brought out in a ceremonial in the name of an at.óow in memory of its owner increases the value of the at.óow, both monetarily and spiritually.

"Play clothes" may also be worn in formal settings that are not strictly Tlingit. For example, serving as eucharistic ministers at the January 1990 funeral mass at the Juneau Catholic Cathedral of the Nativity, Blessed Virgin Mary, for Kathy Isturis, a young woman of the L'uknax̱.ádi and Raven moiety, Barbara Nelson (Teik̲weidí of the Eagle moiety) wore her brown bear vest, and Carmela Ransom (Lukaax̱.ádi of the Raven moiety) wore her raven and sockeye vest. Both were beaded by Emma Marks. Carlos Cadiente (Teik̲weidí, Eagle moiety), who read the scriptures, wore the brown bear tunic passed to him by Eddie Jack, Teik̲weidí elder of Angoon. The use of the contemporary vests and the tunic gave strong Tlingit identity to the mass, and also increased the stature of the new regalia through the liturgical use in memory of a departed friend. In

Tlingit tradition, members of the opposite moiety joined in supporting the clan of the departed in their time of grief.

Two other terms are now ready for introduction: ***shagóon*** and ***shuká***, both of which mean "ancestor," but with slightly differing ranges of meaning. Shagóon can be an immediate parent and also human ancestors. Shuká, which is used in the title of the first book in this series, also means "ancestor," but in a more general way. The concept is pivotal because it is ambiguous and faces two directions. It means, most literally, "ahead," or "before." It refers to that which is before us or has gone before us in time—predecessors, "one before," "one who has gone before," those born ahead of us who are now behind us, as well as those unborn who wait ahead of us. Thus, the term refers to the past and also to the future—to that which lies ahead. There is a common expression in Tlingit, "we don't know our 'shuká'—our 'future.'" The term shuká includes both at.óow and shagóon. It includes all types of at.óow as well as all human ancestors who are not at.óow. Therefore, the term "shuká" embraces the narratives published in *Haa Shuká* themselves, the at.óow and ancestors within them, and the ancestors who told them.

These concepts are difficult to define, partly because the terms overlap but are not synonymous. In general, "shuká" is most often used for the images or heraldic designs, and at.óow for the material thing or object made with the design. L s'aatí át refers to at.óow left behind by a deceased ancestor or relative. The terms are sometimes used more loosely, sometimes even more precisely. For example, an at.óow owned by an ancestor (shagóon) may also be called shagóon, especially if it is the grandparents', the father's father's emblem.

A few examples may be helpful. The Raven design is a shuká of all Raven moiety clans. If a wooden Raven hat is made by a specific person or clan, brought out at a ceremonial and paid for, it becomes at.óow. In the "Glacier Bay History," the woman who remains behind and is killed by the advancing glacier is a shagóon of the Chookaneidí clan. She is also shuká and at.óow on specific art objects. Moreover, Glacier Bay, the glacier, and the icebergs are also at.óow because the woman paid for them with her life. In fact, icebergs are called Chookan sháa ("Chookaneidí women") for this reason. The songs and story are the property or at.óow of the Chookaneidí clan.

Likewise, Kaats' paid for the bear design with his life, and it is an emblem of the Teiḵweidí. Kaats' is also shuká, and he is shagóon to the grandchildren of Teiḵweidí. In the same way, Ḵaax̱'achgóok is a shuká of the Kiks.ádi; he is biological shagóon of the grandchildren of the clan. The song and story are at.óow of the Kiks.ádi, and the at.óow may be referred to as shagóon by the grandchildren of the clan.

It is probably not crucial for the general reader to worry too much about the terms; the main point is the general concept of at.óow, and how the concept underlies not only the stories in our first book, but also the oratory in the present volume.

Rules for the use of at.óow are very complex. Members of the owning clan use their own at.óow, although this is also regulated by custom according to the nature of the at.óow and the seriousness of the occasion. For example, beaded pendants or silver jewelry with clan crests are worn more casually in daily dress than Chilkat robes.

Under certain conditions, the at.óow of one clan may be used by members of other clans as well. While people may use the at.óow of another clan, this does not give them the right to claim them as their own, and the users must be careful not to do so. For example, relatives of the opposite moiety may hunt, fish, or pick berries with permission on another clan's land. The right extends to the use of songs and regalia. The most complicated examples of this usually happen in the context of ceremonials, and become important in the images of public speaking.

Such use shows love, courtesy, and mutual respect, especially where a grandparent-grandchild relationship is involved. For example, the songs from the "Glacier Bay History" are sung by the Hoonah Chookaneidí hosts during the cry portion of their memorials. They were sung at the memorial for Jim Marks included in this book, at the memorial for Willie Marks in October 1981, and most recently on October 8, 1988, at a Chookaneidí memorial for three recently departed members. But these Chookaneidí songs of Glacier Bay were also sung during the Cry section of the Kaagwaantaan memorial for Charlie Joseph in Sitka on October 10, 1987. Before he died, Charlie had requested that the songs be sung. Even though Charlie was not Chookaneidí, his people, the Kaagwaantaan, are part of the history of Glacier Bay. Moreover, Charlie lived part of his life in the Glacier Bay area, and had a personal connection with the land and history. In Sitka, members of the Hoonah Chookaneidí supported the Kaagwaantaan hosts in the ceremonial for Charlie Joseph, just as the Kaagwaantaan and Wooshkeetaan supported the Chookaneidí in the Hoonah memorials for Jim Marks and others. The main point is that the at.óow may be used by another clan with permission, under certain conditions, and according to protocol, but are not to be claimed by the other clan as their own.

One of the most common uses of at.óow by non-owners is use by grandchildren of the owner clan. The ***use of at.óow by grandchildren*** is explicit in the speech by Charlie Joseph and other speakers at the Sealaska Elders Conference. The custom is also followed in other settings. In Tlingit ceremonial life, a very important and prestigious relationship is that of a paternal grandfather—the father of one's father.

With proper permission, any descendant can use any at.óow, both of the maternal and paternal clans. However, a special relationship exists between grandchildren and the father's father's people, especially if they are of the same clan. Likewise, great-grandchildren may be related in special ways, according to the clan system. These special relationships show up in ceremonials most commonly during the Cry, at which time the hosts and guests generally select special people, always of the same moiety, but very often of different clans and usually grandchildren of the clan, to hold, wear, or otherwise use the l s'aatí át. The nearest of kin usually wear the deceased's at.óow. When this is done, the common practice is for persons of the opposite moiety (children of the hosts) to be honored by being asked to place or help place the at.óow on the person selected and honored to wear it. This is also done for newly made pieces being brought out and worn for the first time. For example, a man or woman of the Raven moiety would be asked by the Eagles to place an at.óow on an Eagle grandchild. This practice in general serves to remind all present that the at.óow are made for grandchildren—for those who will come after. It is also a way of strengthening family and community ties.

While such use by grandchildren is allowed, permission is traditionally difficult to obtain. A person must prove himself or herself by knowing the genealogy thoroughly—by knowing who the relatives are, and by assisting whenever help is needed. The most important help is usually in times of ceremonials, assisting with preparations and with the performing of the ceremony itself. In the memorial for Jim Marks, an example of such help is Naawéiyaa, a man of the Kaagwaantaan, but whose father was child of Chookaneidí, making Naawéiyaa a grandchild of Chookaneidí. Because of this special relationship, he came to the aid of his grandparent clan. It is very important to note that in Tlingit tradition this relationship applies not only to biological grandchildren in the narrowest sense, but to all who are members and grandchildren of the clan. In other words, Naawéiyaa may not have had any true biological grandparents involved, but in Tlingit tradition any member of the Chookaneidí clan, regardless of age, would be considered his grandparent, because his true biological grandparent was of the same clan. In this example he is not wearing or using at.óow, but is helping his grandparent clan. This is an extremely important concept to keep in mind. It underlies much of Tlingit social and ceremonial interaction, but is difficult for non-Tlingits and for many younger Tlingit people to grasp.

Many factors enter into a decision as to ***who inherits at.óow***. Obviously genealogy is very important in determining one's right to inherit, but there are other conditions as well, the most important of which is education. The inheritor would ideally have spent time with the present stewards and clan leaders, educating himself or herself on the responsibilities and obligations of handling at.óow. He or she would also have participated actively in ceremonies, and so through actual experience would understand the ceremonial use of the at.óow, including regalia and songs. An inheritor would have brought out money on the various at.óow during ceremonies. Finally, the inheritor would be chosen for leadership qualities and ability to work with people.

A person who inherits at.óow does not become the sole owner, but is the custodian or steward of property owned by the clan at large. A general responsibility is to ensure that the at.óow not be lost or sold for personal gain or to resolve personal or clan debt. The at.óow should not be sold, but should remain with the clan in the stewardship of its individuals and families for the life of the at.óow.

The ceremonial responsibility of a steward is to see that the at.óow are brought out at the appropriate time and worn by the appropriate people. In each case, clan elders will hold council to decide on procedures and protocol, and will select someone from among the elders to speak on the collection once it is brought out. The speeches by Matthew Lawrence, David Kadashan, William Johnson, Jessie Dalton, and Austin Hammond are examples of such speeches from the memorial for Jim Marks.

The patterns of use described here can be complicated further by interchanges among the Haida and Tlingit, where crests are often owned by the opposite moieties. Many crests that are Raven moiety in Tlingit society are Eagle moiety crests in Haida, and vice versa. As a recent example, a young Tlingit dancer of the Raven moiety was given a child-size Wolf Button Blanket as a gift by a Haida woman. The Wolf crest in Tlingit is a crest of Eagle moiety clans, but it is a Raven moiety crest in Haida. Therefore it is appropriate for the young Tlingit Raven dancer to wear the gifted blanket, because it is a Haida Wolf of the Raven moiety, and not a Tlingit Wolf of the Eagle moiety. On the surface it may appear as an inappropriate crest, and would in fact be if it were a Tlingit Wolf, which the young Raven girl would have no traditional right to wear. In other words, the important thing is not the object itself, but the object as contextualized through the kinship system.

The concept of at.óow is difficult for people outside the tradition to grasp, but it is an extremely important dimension of Tlingit social and ceremonial life, and of Tlingit oral literature—especially of oratory, which is inseparable from the ceremonial context in which it is presented. This final context is of at.óow in action, an aspect that will be treated later, in the discussion of "Levels of Mediation in Tlingit Oratory," where the visual art, oral literature, social structure, and ceremonial practice converge.

III. SOCIAL AND CULTURAL SETTINGS FOR ORATORY

The speeches in this book were collected in performance in a wide range of social contexts. Only the two speeches recorded on wax cylinder during the Harriman Expedition of 1899 were collected for the sole purpose of collecting. Two other speeches were composed into tape recorders, but for the purpose of posthumous or in-absentia delivery. All other speeches were taped in performance in natural social settings, ranging from informal gatherings to more formal banquets, conventions, and elders conferences; including traditional and contemporary dedications of clan houses and totem poles; and two traditional post-funeral memorials—the Forty Day Party; and the larger ceremonial known as k̲oo.éex' in Tlingit and most popularly called "Potlatch" in English.

Informal settings include home meals, where table graces and speeches are made, and a variety of other impromptu situations. Such speeches and situations are more personal and less public than other settings and tend to have a smaller audience. The style of these speeches is generally more direct and less complicated than those delivered at larger and more formal gatherings. We classify in this category the short speech by A. P. Johnson, delivered spontaneously in an informal classroom setting, where he and fellow elders were gathered to discuss matters of Tlingit orthography. The speech by Tom Peters welcoming Nora Marks Dauenhauer back to Teslin belongs in this category of informal oratory because it was delivered privately to one person. Jennie Thlunaut's Raven House prayer for and speech to her apprentices fall in this category. Depending on the size of the gathering, one could also consider as informal certain funeral speeches delivered in a small group, gathered intimately around the casket of the deceased, in contrast to a much larger, more public funeral or in contrast to speeches delivered at a Forty Day Party or Memorial Ceremony. The boundary line between formal and informal is perhaps somewhat arbitrary; in setting and oratorical style the differences are more of scale or degree than of basic structure or substance. In other words, the social structure and group dynamics, as well as the style of oratory, are as much intact in a small, informal setting as in a larger context.

In the category of ***formal contemporary settings*** we place speech events such as the Alaska Native Brotherhood Convention, church socials such as the banquet at St. Michael's Cathedral in Sitka on St. Michael's Day (no examples included in this book), the Sealaska Elders Conference, and the bi-annual Sealaska Heritage Foundation Celebrations. The speeches delivered here are often traditional, although the settings and situations which give rise to the speeches are not. The speech by Emma Marks from "Celebration 82" and the invocation by David Kadashan are good examples, and the entire set of speeches by Charlie Joseph and his contemporaries entitled "Because We Cherish You" illustrate a traditional kind of speaking generated

Lillian Hammond, Marie Olson, and David Light sample traditional foods (seaweed and herring eggs) at the Haines ANB Hall dedication, May 1974. Note the use of traditional foods during the Western-style part of the dedication. Note also the women's bracelets and the ANS and ANB sashes called koogéinaa in Tlingit.

by an innovative setting. Jennie Thlunaut's farewell speech at Klukwan probably belongs in this category because it was delivered following a banquet sponsored by the Klukwan Alaska Native Sisterhood in honor of her and her apprentices.

Traditional Dedications were and continue to be one of the main occasions for ceremonials and oratory. These are most commonly held to dedicate a new clan house or totem pole. The Tlingit term for house dedication is hít wóoshdei yadukícht, meaning "solidifying the house by dance." Part of the ceremony includes a ritual for making peace with the trees that were used to build the house posts, screen, and house itself. Because Tlingit people understand trees to be living things, and because when people cut them down, they inflict pain and finally death, it is important to make peace with the spirits of the trees. Examples in this book from totem pole dedications are speeches from the Kake totem pole raising of 1971, and the Fairbanks totem pole raising of October 1988. A house dedication may be done as a separate ceremony or may be combined with a memorial for a deceased elder. For example, the speech by Thomas Young in this book was delivered at a combined ceremonial in Klukwan, partly in memory of the deceased elder Tom Jimmie, and partly to dedicate the new Thunderbird House. The younger generation of leaders was invested as part of the event, with host Joe White choosing the stewards to take his place after he is gone.

Traditional dedications are very important in Tlingit ceremonial life, and the range of events today has been expanded. We would like to describe a few other examples, although speeches from these events are not included in this book. In May 1974, Austin Hammond and others hosted a ceremonial for the dedication of the new hall of the Alaska Native Brotherhood (ANB) in Haines, for which he and his family were major contributors of money and labor. It was an interesting and even ironic event because the ANB was overtly dedicated in 1912 to the abandonment of Tlingit language and culture, yet sixty years later, their meeting hall was accorded a traditional ceremony with oratory in Tlingit as well as English, indicating how many traditional practices were not abandoned but were combined, adapted, and syncretized into the protocol of the ANB and other organizations.

Another example of a traditional dedication is Austin Hammond's hosting of a traditional ceremonial in October 1974 to

Austin Hammond, wearing Sockeye Chilkat Robe, facing singers of various clans gathered at Chilkoot Lake, August 1980, during the filming of *Haa Shagóon*. To his right are Charlie Jimmie and David Andrews. Singers, L to R, are Rosita Worl in Chilkat Robe, Elena Topacio in button blanket and contemporary Raven headdress, Nathan Jackson wearing carved wood Raven hat, Nora Dauenhauer wearing button blanket and headband with silver pin (from Grouse Fort), Kathy Dennis wearing spruceroot hat, Ida Kadashan, Unident., Dixie Johnson drumming, Unident., Lillian Hammond. At far right is Mrs. Joseph James wearing button blanket and "Aleut style" hat. Nora Dauenhauer's silver pin was made for a Kaagwaantaan memorial at Grouse Fort in the late 19th Century. This is the only one left from a number of pins belonging to a woman of the Lukaax̲.ádi named S'aatál'. Nora inherited the pin from Jennie Marks. Photo by R. Dauenhauer.

commemorate the repair and rededication of Raven House in Haines and to acknowledge and reward those who worked to restore the clan house. Austin Hammond also hosted an appropriate ceremonial for the dedication of the new clan smokehouse on the beach across the road from Raven House. An excellent example of Tlingit oratory available on film is *Haa Shagóon* (Kawagey 1981) which documents a Chilkoot peace ceremony of 1980. It features subtitles as well as voice-over translation. We highly recommend this film as a supplement to the present volume.

As an economic outcome of the Alaska Native Claims Settlement Act (ANCSA) legislation of 1971, village corporations were formed and many of them became involved in modern hotel operations. Many of these facilities, as in Hoonah and Sitka, were dedicated with traditional clan house ceremonies, as was the Beaver House, a new community house in Saxman, dedicated on October 3, 1987. These dedications have ranged in size and intimacy from more private, clan-centered events such as the Thunderbird House dedication to larger, more public and community oriented dedications as of the Haines ANB Hall and commercial facilities in Sitka, Hoonah, and other communities. The Kake and Fairbanks totem raisings involved the entire region and state.

Alaska Native Brotherhood

Because of its importance in twentieth century Tlingit cultural history and because it is a primary setting for contemporary oratory, a few words about the Alaska Native Brotherhood (ANB) are in order here, before discussing the major traditional ceremonial settings. In almost every biographical sketch in this book, some reference is made to the Alaska Native Brotherhood or its parallel organization founded shortly thereafter, the Alaska Native Sisterhood (ANS). The ANB was founded in 1912 in Sitka by ten men who had been students at Sheldon Jackson School, including nine Tlingit and one Tsimshian. The standard history of the brotherhood movement is by Drucker (1958).[3]

The association of the founding of the ANB with Sheldon Jackson School and the Presbyterian church is widely known and well documented, but the organization also had roots in the

Orthodox Brotherhoods of Sitka and other Tlingit communities around the turn of the century. For example, ANB co-founder Paul Liberty of Sitka was a church reader and was active in the brotherhood movement at St. Michael's Cathedral. He was also a composer of new musical settings for traditional Orthodox hymns, most notably the festal matins hymn, "Glory to God in the Highest," popularly known as the "Paul Liberty Song." As a Tlingit composer of liturgical music, Paul Liberty remains without equal. Eli Katanook, another of the original ANB founders, taught various secular subjects in the St. Nicholas Parochial School in Juneau, and was also active in the church brotherhood.[4]

The ANB was founded on the model of western social and service clubs as well as on the model of the Orthodox brotherhoods and Protestant church sodalities. The fundamental purpose of the ANB was the material, political, and social advancement of the Native people of Southeast Alaska. To this end, certain policies were established, perhaps most important of which was that English would be the official language. The use of Native languages was discouraged or prohibited, not only to encourage development of English language skills for social and political advantage when communicating with outsiders but also to facilitate communication among the Tlingit, Haida, and Tsimshian membership. However, Kan (personal communication, 1989) reports that Tlingit was used in some early ANB meetings and functions as well. The ANB language policy follows the "English only" policies established by Presbyterian missionaries and educators S. Hall Young and Sheldon Jackson in the 1880s. Whereas bilingual education had been the norm during the Russian period in Alaskan history, bilingual education was outlawed in the American period, with insistence on English only.[5] In 1912 when the ANB was founded, the Native languages and cultural traditions were still very strong, so much so that they were perceived as detriments to education and as barriers to assimilation and advancement. The English-only policy of American education was so effective that by the 1980s and probably as early as the 1940s the situation was the reverse, with English being the dominant or exclusive language of the majority of the Native people in Southeast Alaska. In 1987 the ANB initiated the practice of each speaker introducing himself or herself in Tlingit, giving names and genealogy. In this sense, the ANB is now a primary advocate of contemporary Tlingit oratory in the Tlingit language, an important and ironic grass roots effort at restoring Tlingit identity eroded in the last seventy-five years of ANB practice.

But in the 1910s and 1920s, Tlingit language and cultural identity were still strong, despite the language policies of the government schools. The Native people of Southeast Alaska were involved with other socio-political issues; they campaigned for citizenship, for integrated schools, and for laws prohibiting discrimination in public places; they fought against the use of fish traps in commercial fishing. These were challenges to physical and economic survival greater than anything experienced during the Russian period. Many people are unaware that Native Americans were not granted United States citizenship until 1924 and that schools and public facilities such as restaurants and theaters in Alaska were segregated until 1945. Denied citizenship, Natives were thereby also denied participation in the legal processes for staking mining and homestead claims—the motive for and basis of establishing civil law in Alaska through the Organic Act of 1884. Thus, during the gold rush and cannery eras and the generation following, Native land was literally taken from around and underneath them. Europeans and European Americans moved steadily into Indian territory, displacing the Native populations, disenfranchising them politically, and establishing policies of segregation.

The ANB worked steadily toward addressing these issues. Intensive lobbying and the support of Governor Gruening from 1941 to 1945 finally resulted in the Anti-Discrimination Bill of 1945, which outlawed segregation in public places, and Roy and Elizabeth Peratrovich, two of the prime movers, were among the first Native couples to dance in the integrated ballroom of the Baranof Hotel in Juneau. Tlingit historians consider the 1929 ANB Convention in Haines to be the official beginning of the land claims suit. There the campaign was set into motion. After forty years of struggle it would culminate in the Alaska Native Claims Settlement Act of 1971 (ANCSA), federal legislation designed to compensate Alaska Natives for land taken without permission or recompense.

The ANB and ANS remain important in Tlingit life today. With seventy-five years of history, they are well-established institutions in the Tlingit community. Now, as then, Tlingits remain famous (some would say infamous) for their mastery of

Sitka ANB Hall, Camp #1, photographed at high tide in June 1971. Typical of many buildings in Southeast Alaska, the hall is constructed on pilings over tide land. The small boat harbor is in the background. The Alaska Native Brotherhood was organized in Sitka in 1912 as a Native fraternal and civil rights advocacy organization. The ANB Hall was constructed in 1914. Among other community activities, this is the home of the Sitka Native Education Program, where Charlie Joseph instructed the G̱ajaa Héen Dancers in the 1970's and 1980's and where most of his autobiography was taped. This is the site of many Forty Day Parties and memorials. Charlie Joseph delivered his December 1972 speech here, and the memorial for him was held here on October 10, 1987. Photo by R. Dauenhauer.

and delight in Robert's Rules of Order, a contemporary manifestation of traditional concern with protocol. The organization remains nonsectarian but has a strong religious base. "Onward Christian Soldiers" is its marching song. In many situations—such as death—ANB serves as a secular religious body, absorbing, paralleling, and taking the place of some of the functions of traditional ceremonial life and conventional Christian worship. These organizations are changing to meet changing times. For example, some of the wording of the Preamble, regarding Native people "taking their place among the civilized nations of the world," has become controversial among younger membership. With the erosion of traditional language and culture, the ANB has become increasingly supportive of local heritage programs. The G̱ajaa Héen Dancers and the Sitka Native Education Program, around whom the oratory in the third section of this book centers, are based in the ANB Hall in Sitka.

Forty Day Party

In most Tlingit communities today, the Forty Day Party, a postfuneral ceremonial, is the most common setting for traditional oratory. The clanspeople of the deceased host the opposite moiety and community at large and thank them for services performed at the funeral and during the time of grief. The favorite foods of the deceased are served, and sometimes, but not usually, gifts or money are distributed. A variety of speeches are delivered, first by the hosts, then by the guests. Forty Day Party oratory by the guests is characterized by humor, usually self-deprecating, in which the speakers tell of a funny personal experience. A main function of the humor is to cheer up the hosts, who have lost a clan member. On the other hand, some elders report that they have heard objection to the use of humor so soon after a funeral service, arguing that such usage would be in good taste months later. Such objections may reflect changing attitudes and Christian influence. Perhaps, on the psychological side, the compromise or loss of dignity and face risked or sacrificed by the guests helps to balance the loss of a relative's life by the hosts. The hosts are vulnerable because of their grief; the guests share in this by making themselves socially vulnerable through self-deprecating humor. Humor may also solidify the community through reaffirmation of joking relationships, which in Tlingit tradition depend to a large extent on genealogical relationships between the joking partners. The speeches at Forty Day Parties create social and spiritual balance through humor, whereas most oratory in other settings tends to be serious. In their serious aspects, the Forty Day speeches often clarify the relationship of the deceased to the speaker and others present, with the intent of reaffirming kinship and community ties. Charlie Joseph's 1972 speech illustrates this.

The origins of the Forty Day Party (considered by many elders to be a recent trend) remain unclear. There are two opposing theories and one middle position. Most Tlingit elders believe that the Forty Day Party was not originally Tlingit but was a relatively recent innovation imported by the Russians, even though non-Orthodox communities follow the tradition today. Some middle-aged and older Tlingit people have commented that, in their youth, only the Orthodox Tlingit held Forty Day Parties; they say the idea spread from there. In Orthodox tradition the requiem service, called Panikhida, is also observed as a memorial service forty days after death; it may be repeated on other dates significant in the life of the deceased. The fortieth day observance parallels, on the individual level, the Feast of the Ascension of Christ forty days after Easter. It was the custom of the early Christian Church to celebrate the third, ninth, and fortieth days after death with religious services. In most Orthodox parishes the fortieth day is still observed. The formal word for this in Greek is mnemosynon (from "memory") while a popular term is ta seranta, literally "the forty." An older name in Russian for the service is "Sorokoust," deriving literally from the Russian words for "forty" and "mouth." The basic definition of the word is "prayers said for the dead on the fortieth day after death." The meaning is also extended to the food served on the fortieth day. It is also the custom in Arabic Orthodox Christian communities to observe the fortieth day with a memorial service and "mercy meal," at which special foods are served. The name of the "mercy meal" derives from the Arabic "Allah yorhamu," God have mercy.

The opposing opinion states that the Tlingit people have always had a small ceremony or feast observed forty days after death. The middle position holds that some kind of a smaller event (as opposed to the larger memorial a year or more after death) was observed in precontact time, but was reinforced and set at forty days under Russian influence. Kan (1987a) favors this position.

Certainly ceremonialism involving the serving of food was and is an important part of Tlingit social and spiritual life, as it was all along the Northwest Coast. It is impossible to know for certain whether the Forty Day Party is of Tlingit or Russian origin. If originally Tlingit, it was clearly reinforced by Russian Orthodox tradition and liturgical practice; if originally Russian, it caught on quickly, reinforced by Tlingit custom, and became part of the existing pattern of postfuneral ceremonials. Cultural reinforcement from Russian Orthodox Christianity may also have contributed to the funereal emphasis in Tlingit ceremonial tradition. The forty day tradition may have been in part a Russian missionary effort to replace traditional ceremonials. If this was the original strategy, in the final analysis it did not replace a pre-Christian ceremonial, but was added to the existing pattern of postfuneral ceremonials. Kan (personal communication, 1989) believes that the Tlingit themselves played an active role in incorporating the Orthodox forty day observation into the indigenous memorial cycle.

The traditional Tlingit spiritual significance of the event is that it marks the time of the departure of the soul or spirit of the departed from the community of the living. Traditional belief is that the soul or spirit of the departed lingers with his or her family and in familiar places for forty days after death. In some households, places are set at the table for the departed. After forty days, the spirit departs for the spirit world. The same idea exists in Greek popular thought (Mousalimas, personal communication, 1989).

In Greek Orthodox and some Russian Orthodox traditions, a wheat and honey dish is shared at the memorial, but in other Russian communities and in most Russian Orthodox communities in Alaska, rice decorated with raisins and often seasoned with honey is served. This is interesting because rice is grown neither in Russia nor Alaska, although it has become a very important dish in the modern Tlingit diet. (Rice was also served by early coastal traders to Tlingits who came aboard their ships.) The funeral dish is called kutiyá in Russian, even when it consists of rice. The special Russian Christmas dish also called kutiyá is usually made of wheat, but in Alaska, it is sometimes of barley mixed with honey, poppy seeds and nuts. A candle is usually inserted into the memorial kutiyá, and it is also a common practice to light candles in memory of the departed at home and in the church during the forty days. At Forty Day Parties in some Tlingit communities, food is put into a fire for the spirits of the departed. The Tlingit term for this is gan ka s'íx'i, meaning "dishes over the fire," and this will be discussed below. In all Forty Day Parties, the sharing of food is essential, and a large banquet is always involved. The traditional Tlingit belief is that food shared among the living is also shared with the spirits of the deceased. (See the "Glacier Bay Story" by Amy Marvin in *Haa Shuká*, especially page 277 lines 306-330, and the note to those lines on page 425.) It is also interesting to note that in Orthodox parishes in Southeast Alaska a memorial service is traditionally offered at the cemetery on the first Sunday after Easter. Families prepare the rice dish, sharing some with the living and leaving the rest on the graves, in the same way that flowers are left on Memorial Day.

Forty Day Parties are ideally held forty days after death, and the larger memorial is held one year after, but latitude exists for both observations. Recently, for example, one deceased man's fortieth day fell in the middle of the Christmas holidays. Knowing that this would present problems for hosting a large community banquet, the family decided to postpone it until January; nonetheless, wishing to mark the fortieth day, they invited a small number of people from the Orthodox Church to dine at their home. As the family was Orthodox, and as the Alaskan Diocese was still on the old (Julian) calendar, this did not interfere with community celebrations. In late January, after Old Calendar Christmas and Theophany, about eighty days after death, the larger, "official" Forty Day Party was held at the ANB Hall, with the family and clan of the deceased hosting the community at large.

Because of the size of the gathering, both the Forty Day Party and the larger memorials are now usually held in community halls, such as the ANB hall; but traditionally they were, and sometimes still are, held in clan houses.

Traditionally, the family and clan of the deceased, with support from relatives and others of the moiety of the deceased, host the opposite moiety. Those of the guest moiety are seated; those of the host moiety stand at the edges of the room and prepare and serve food. This traditional structure is evolving, especially in Juneau, into a co-moiety, community-based event, no longer strictly following clan and moiety lines. Married couples and their children often sit together. Thus, seated guests include people of both moieties. The event typically incorporates a variety of religious traditions. Many Forty Day Parties in Juneau now begin with the St. Nicholas Orthodox Church choir singing "The Lord's Prayer" in Tlingit, "Holy God" in Tlingit, English, or Slavonic, and "Memory Eternal" in English or Slavonic. Later in the program, various religious groups often sing gospel music in English and Tlingit. Some of the oratory also reflects this new community focus and the changing relationship of hosts and guests. Joe Hotch, one of the speakers at the Forty Day Party for Alfred Widmark, March 12, 1989, opened with the words, "Children of God, you who are sitting here." The function remains essentially the same, food and oratory are featured, but the structure of the event no longer strictly parallels traditional Tlingit social structure.[6]

K̲oo.éex'

By the terms "memorial" or "ceremonial," we refer to the major postfuneral ceremony held approximately one year after death. In English, this event is commonly called "potlatch," a term well established in popular speech as well as anthropological literature, but one for which we do not particularly care, although we also use it at times for clarity. Sometimes the combination "memorial potlatch" is also heard. Probably "party" is the most common English term used in Tlingit communities. Sometimes "payoff party" is heard. The general Tlingit term is k̲oo.éex', deriving from the Tlingit verb stem "to call" or "invite." The word "potlatch" reputedly entered English from Chinook jargon, which borrowed it in turn from the Nootka word for "giving." Many knowledgeable Tlingit people consider the term both misleading and not authentic for describing Tlingit culture. One highly respected Tlingit elder, Walter Soboleff, advised us to "take this word and sink it in the deepest water." Alternatively, he advised us to "take this word far down the beach and bury it." Accordingly, we will use the word from time to time, sparingly, and most often when reviewing the anthropological literature on the subject; but when writing from our own point of view we will use terms more acceptable to the Tlingit community.

As noted above, the ideal timing for the k̲oo.éex' is one year after death, but this is flexible. In actual practice today, and no doubt in the past as well, the ceremonial may be held many years after a person's death because of the time, effort, and expense of hosting such a memorial. Conversely, some have been held less than a year after death, especially if the surviving elders feel they may not live long enough to fulfill their obligations to the dead. Also, the event may be a combined ceremonial in memory of more than one person, with several elders and their families joining efforts. The preferred time for the ceremonial is late fall or early winter, after the summer foods have been put up and after fall fishing, when people have time to focus on ceremonial life and have food and goods to distribute.

In Tlingit, the word k̲oo.éex' may also be used to designate a Forty Day Party. This somewhat complicates the problem of terminology, but despite its changing structure, the Forty Day Party remains for the most part distinct in size, structure, and timing from the major ceremonial popularly called "potlatch" in English. Also, the Forty Day party remains essentially a banquet with public speaking. In contrast to the memorial, money or gifts are almost never distributed at a Forty Day Party, and Cry Ceremonials are not performed. These are all characteristic of the larger memorial.

The institution of potlatching has captivated the minds of many generations of observers of Northwest Coast culture; it remains a popular subject of analysis to the present day. Our main intent in this book is to provide new primary data rather than to enter into dialogue with the existing studies on potlatch, but we would like to review briefly some of the main points raised in these studies, and how they relate to the speeches in this volume.

As suggested by their titles, some of the best known anthropological studies of the potlatch focus on rivalry and emnity: *Fighting With Property* by Helen Codere (1950), and *Feasting with Mine Enemy* by Rosman and Rubel (1971). While we are not in a position to dispute the accuracy of their analyses of traditions other than Tlingit, these descriptions of the Northwest Coast Potlatch do not seem to fit Tlingit practice. We tend to agree with those anthropologists who note the northern (Tlingit) orientation developing historically more toward funereal cycles. Swanton suggested that "regard for and respect for the dead" were the main "motive" of the Tlingit potlatch. He noted that, "among the Haida, on the other hand, the social idea quite overbalanced the religious" (1970*a*:434). We maintain that Tlingit community tensions are not ritualized through the feasting in the same way as they are described for groups to the south, although these other Northwest Coast groups may have been oriented this way, and this may have also been true for earlier periods of Tlingit. Tlingit tradition also includes a type of potlatch known as sh daatx̲ k̲ux̲'awdlig̲oo, "wiping the mouth from the body," to address defamation of character. In this type of potlatch, the host aggresively tries to wipe the slate clean where he or she has been the target of character assassination. We agree with Kan's suggestion (1986a and personal communication, 1989) that there was some competition between individuals and between kinship groups, but that it was masked by and couched in the rhetoric of love and respect.[7] It may also be that such explicit cultural concern with respect indicates deeper anxiety over treachery.

Traditional oratory follows the exchange patterns of other goods and services, including marriage, as described by structuralists such as Rosman and Rubel (1971). One of the editors has also indicated (R. Dauenhauer 1975) that Tlingit social structure is reflected in the style, content, and delivery of Tlingit oral literature. This is especially true of oratory. But we also emphasize the extent to which the content of Tlingit "potlatch" oratory focuses not on rivalry, but on healing. This is certainly true for the speeches in this book delivered at the Jim Marks memorial in Hoonah (1968) and those delivered at the Sitka Elders Conference of 1980.

Popular understanding and many scholarly treatments have tended to interpret potlatch as a demonstration of wealth and prestige, and have tended to emphasize economic aspects such as the distribution of goods. These aspects are certainly present to some degree in Tlingit memorials, but we feel that there are more important spiritual and healing dimensions that have often been overlooked, ignored or denied. Thus, we disagree with Olson's claim that "Tlingit ceremonies . . . bear little relation to the supernatural world" and that "their linkage with the memories of the dead and the spirits of the deceased is only nominal" (1967:111). This element of healing is demonstrated in the oratory and is our focus here.

IV. THE GENERAL STRUCTURE OF A TLINGIT MEMORIAL

A typical memorial (k̲oo.éex') is described here to illustrate in detail the principal context in which some of the most important traditional speeches are delivered. For example, the speeches in this book from the 1968 Memorial for Jim Marks in Hoonah are from the Cry ceremonies of section IV of the outline at the beginning of the introduction. Most of our examples come from Hoonah, but our outline is compiled from notes of memorials in other communities as well. This basic structure as outlined serves in a sense as a framework for all memorials, but affords much flexibility and latitude for variation. Local, clan, and family custom may differ. The four main sections of a memorial always follow this sequence, but within the third section much flexibility remains. Some of the distribution may overlap. Also, some of the dances which we have grouped together for convenience in the outline and discussion may also be done in conjunction with bringing out money. A collective Tlingit term for activity pertaining to various parts of the memorial is yoo koosgítk, which translates as "doing different things," or "to perform a ceremonial." Most of the photographs in this book are of Chookaneidí memorials in Hoonah and Lukaax̲.ádi memorials in Haines. They are intended to illustrate the activites depicted regardless of the moieties involved.

Preliminary Activities and Group Dynamics

As with a traditional American Christmas or Thanksgiving dinner, the consumption of the meal is but a small part of the total activity. For a Tlingit memorial, planning and preparation may take years. The most popular time to hold a memorial is in the fall, so that summer and fall fishing, berry picking, and deer hunting will provide traditional food, and income from commercial fishing can provide cash for other gifts. On the morning of

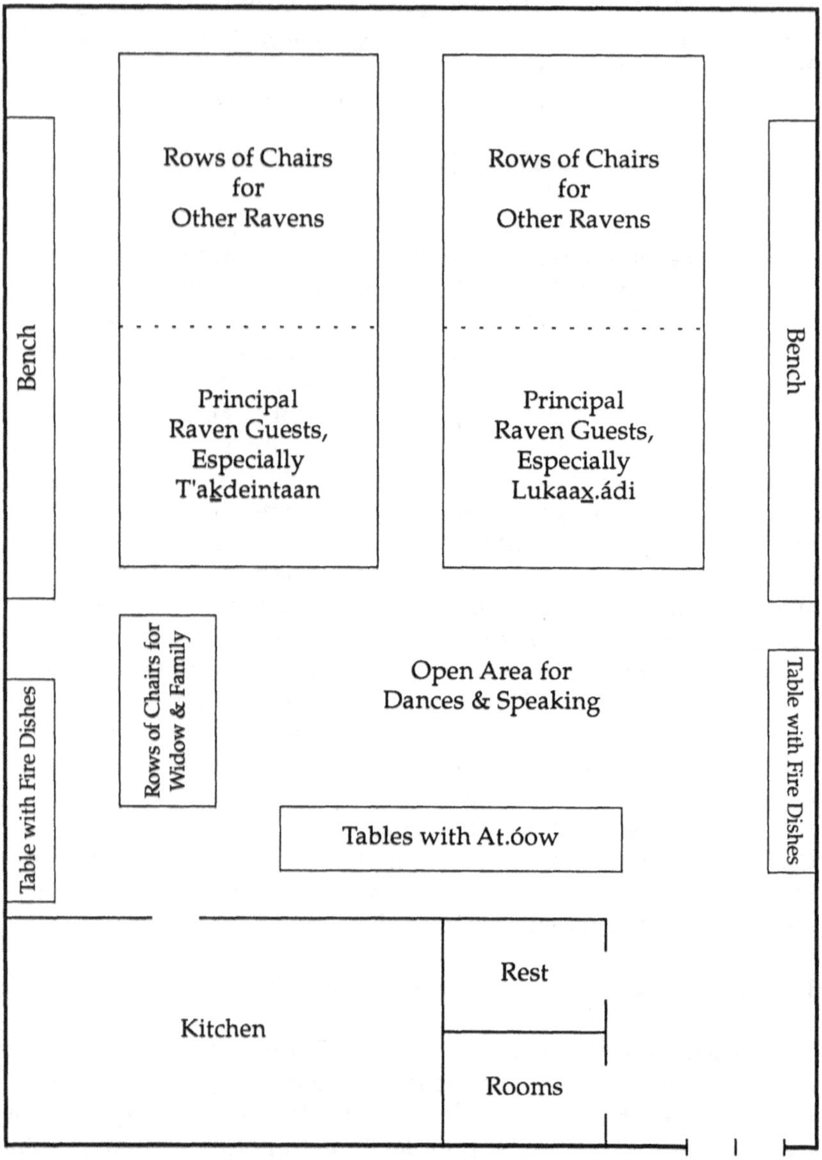

Seating Chart for Chookaneidí Memorial

Hoonah ANB Hall
October 1988
Figure 2. Not to scale.

the event, as one walks the streets of a village such as Hoonah, one can savor the aromas of various foods being prepared.

Typically, the hall slowly begins to fill about an hour or two before the official start of the ceremonial. Members of the host moiety and clan arrive bringing food they have prepared and a variety of gifts to be distributed. Within a short time, the main hall or adjacent store rooms are piled high with gifts. At an October 1988 Chookaneidí memorial in Hoonah, the ANB hall was piled four to six feet high around the front and side walls with boxes of apples, oranges, bananas, soft drinks, pilot bread ("hard tack"), boxes of towels and blankets, and buckets of berries. Front and side tables were spread with special gifts ("fire dishes," to be described below) and more were still in boxes. The kitchen was filled with food, and Coleman stoves were used to supplement the existing facilities for cooking and warming food.

Traditionally, the guests are seated, and the hosts remain standing or seated along the front and side walls. Some seating is in groups; other seating is at random. The widow and her family are seated in a special place, usually to the left of the hosts, as are various elders of the host clan. If the survivor is a woman, her children will be the same moiety as the guests; if the survivor is a male, a widower, his children will be of the host and not the guest moiety. The guests tend to seat themselves in clan groups, so as to be close together for the singing and dancing throughout the night. For example, at the 1988 (Eagle) Chookaneidí Memorial, the (Raven) Tak̲deintaan singers grouped themselves on the left side of the hall, and the (Raven) Lukaax̲.ádi sat on the right. In both cases, many of these people were Chookaneidí yátx'i—children of the host clan. Other members of the Raven (guest) moiety were seated to the rear of these groups.

Traditionally, no tables are used except at the front by the hosts, for gathering of gifts and display of at.óow; but where there is room, tables are becoming more common. Memorials in Sitka usually involve seating at tables, although this was not done for Charlie Joseph's in 1987. For most Hoonah memorials, guests are not seated at tables. At an October 1988 memorial in the Juneau ANB Hall, where there was sufficient space, the guests were seated at tables; but where there is not enough room, guests are seated in rows of folding chairs or on benches facing the hosts at the front. Between the rows of guest seating and the chairs and display tables of the hosts, there is usually as much open floor space as possible, in which hosts and guests will assemble for singing, dancing, and oratory.

Honored guests are escorted to their places. In the setting of a traditional clan house, honored guests are seated at the base of the clan house crests, if there are any. These are usually on the wall opposite the front door. The Tlingit term for this is diyeedéi—which translates loosely as "to the back wall."

As the time for the start of the ceremonial nears, the hosts remove their at.óow called l s'aatí át—"the masterless or ownerless things" from foot lockers and arrange them on the front tables.

Hosts robing up before the Chookaneidí memorial, Hoonah ANB Hall, October 1988. Co-host Mary Johnson, widow of William Johnson, is in the center. Note the l s'aatí át displayed on the table, and the cases of soft drink in the rear. The empty boxes piled on the stairs will be used by guests to carry home their food and gifts. Photo by R. Dauenhauer.

Other at.óow of both the hosts and guests remain in storage chests and will be worn or held later. Traditional Tlingit concepts of display differ from those of European and American practice. Whereas in Western tradition art and other valued objects are commonly displayed on walls and in showcases, Tlingit at.óow are normally kept in chests, out of sight. They are only displayed in action—in spiritual and ceremonial contexts or in dance performances. In Western tradition an owner's pride, appreciation, and custodial care are demonstrated through maximum public display; in Tlingit tradition, however, these values are demonstrated through restricted or minimum public display. In recent years some Native organizations, such as Sealaska Corporation, one of the Native Corporations created as a result of the Alaska Native Claims Settlement Act (ANCSA), have begun to display traditional art as a corporate collection, but this is a new concept. The context is also different because it is a display of a corporate art collection not used ceremonially, in contrast to the display and simultaneous use of family and clan at.óow. This could be said of most museum artifacts, and a parallel situation is the display of icons in museums, whereas in Orthodox Christian tradition they are used in action, in spiritual contexts of prayer and veneration.[8]

An important activity that begins before the memorial starts and continues throughout the evening is the passing of money from guests to hosts. Members of the host clan will eventually bring out money for distribution to guests, but an important group dynamic in Tlingit society is the support of the hosts by their friends and relatives of the opposite moiety. Guests quietly and discreetly pass money to the hosts. Usually these are small amounts—one or two dollars. In the case of closer family or friendship, it may be five or ten dollars, or even more. What is important is not the amount, but the show of support. By giving small amounts, guests show support to many relatives and friends in the the host clan. In this way, sizeable amounts of money can be generated in the course of a memorial, and each host is able to bring out more money than he or she could without the additional support. The hosts receiving such money usually put it in a special envelope and keep a list of each individual and the amount of money given. This list will be publicly announced later.

Taking Up the Drum:
The Cry (The Hosts' Cry and the Widow's Cry)

The Tlingit memorial (k̲oo.éex') always begins with the ceremony known in Tlingit as ***Gaaw Wutaan, "Taking up the Drum,"*** (or, "to pick up the drum," or "to bear or carry the drum"). This ceremony is also called "the Cry." The general Tlingit word for this is G̲áax̲, "cry," but there are also variations and elaborations on the basic term, such as g̲áax̲ kát anák̲ (people are standing on the cry), wudanaak̲ (standing), or kei gax̲dunáak̲ (people will stand), all of which translate loosely as "standing for the cry." The "Cry" or "Taking up the Drum Section" of the memorial consists of two parts. The first part, called K̲áa eetí gaax̲í ("The Cry for Someone") is conducted by the hosts; it consists of speeches and four songs of mourning. The second part, L S'aatí Sháa G̲aax̲í ("The Widow's Cry," literally "the cry for a leaderless woman") is performed by the opposite moiety (the guests), who respond with a ceremony to remove the grief of the hosts. It, too, consists of speeches and songs. The term l s'aatí sháa gaax̲í also applies to a widower.

The Gaaw Wutaan (G̲áax̲, or Cry) Ceremony is traditionally performed approximately one year after a person's death, as the opening part of the k̲oo.éex' in his or her memory. Tlingit elders maintain that this ceremony is much older in Tlingit tradition than the Forty Day practice, which, although of more recent origin, has become more common. Elders often say of the memorial, "Aan haa wdudliyéx̲," ("This is the one we were created with"). Forty Day Parties are almost always observed, but the memorial, because of its size and expense, in many cases is not, and most often a group will host a memorial for more than one relative.

The memorial (k̲oo.éex') proper always begins with the hosts' part of the "Cry Section," in which the hosts formally open the evening with a few words of welcome. Amy Marvin opened the Chookaneidí (Eagle) memorial in Hoonah in October 1988 by thanking the guests for coming, and by welcoming them to their fathers' land. The guests were of the Raven moiety, whose fathers would be Eagle; many of them were children of Chookaneidí.

After these words of welcome, the hosts begin to put on their at.óow. Usually persons of the opposite moiety are selected from

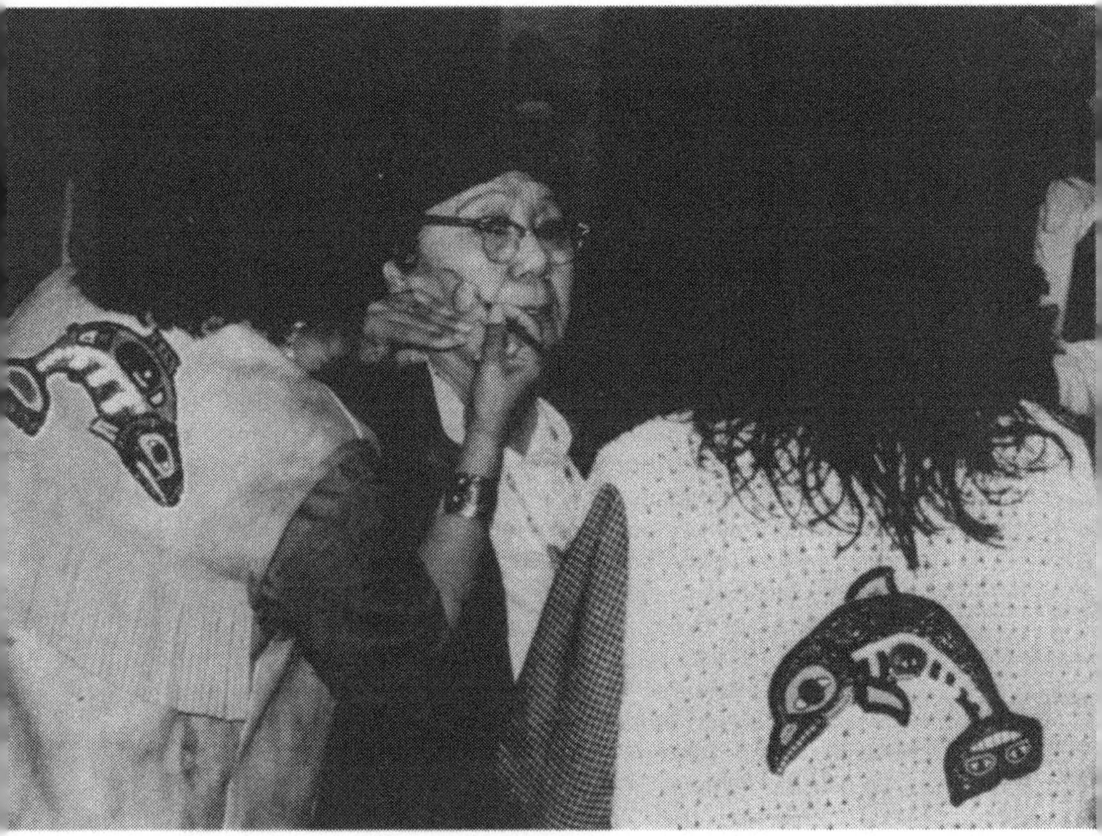

Face painting. Nora Marks Dauenhauer (back to camera, wearing contemporary moosehide vest with sockeye design beaded by Emma Marks) paints a bear paw design on the cheek of Eva Davis prior to the start of the Chookaneidí memorial, Hoonah, October 1988. Nora was requested to do this as a child of Chookaneidí. The woman with her back to the camera wears a contemporary vest with a porpoise design, one of a set beaded by Emma Marks and given as gifts to the clanswomen of her departed husband Willie Marks before his memorial in 1981. Photo by R. Dauenhauer.

among the guests for the honor of placing the at.óow on the hosts. The Tlingit term for this part of the ceremony is l s'aati át tóodei nagútch, literally meaning "stepping into the masterless things." The host literally steps into the inheritance, usually a robe or other significant object of which he or she is now the steward. Another term for this is k̲aa néixi k̲aa daadéi duyéesh, referring to the moment when objects or clothing are draped on those who have inherited them. Before this happens, the person who places the at.óow on the inheritor usually makes a speech. In Hoonah, in October 1988, guest Austin Hammond (Raven; Lukaax̲.ádi) spoke briefly before placing a robe on one of the hosts. In the event that no single person is designated as the inheritor, especially of a leader, or when there is no individual steward, the objects may be displayed on a table and not worn. Alternatively, many different objects of tribal ownership, usually hats and robes, are placed on several different people.

While putting on their robes and other at.óow, soot or black paint is applied to the faces of the hosts, as a sign of mourning. Often the design is a simple set of parallel black streaks on the cheeks. At other times, more elaborate designs may be applied. Often hosts will ask a special guest to do this, as at the 1988 Chookaneidí Memorial in Hoonah, when they requested Nora Marks Dauenhauer, as a child of their clan, to paint their faces; she designed and painted black bear paws on their cheeks.

When the hosts are robed in their at.óow, they begin the *G̲áax̲* or *Cry* with their cry for the departed. Usually four mourning songs are sung by the hosts, but under certain conditions only two are sung, or as many as eight. These are among the most sacred songs of the clan, and people usually prepare themselves before singing them. Preparations include avoidance of seafood. In recent years, with the proliferation of dance groups of younger people, some elders have expressed concern over the increasing secularization of such songs, which are now being performed outside of the traditional ceremonial context.[9] The major cause of anxiety expressed in the speeches in this book from the 1980 elders conference in Sitka was that the songs and dances performed by the young people would have traditionally been performed in the supportive context of the cry or some other part of a traditional ceremonial. Because they were performed in a secular context in the elders conference, and not in a traditional context, extra steps had to be taken by the guests to recreate an acceptable spiritual context. (Although these songs were sung in their entirety during the memorial for Jim Marks and at the 1980 elders conference, we have not included the song texts in this book, but have simply noted them here.) Each clan has its own set of songs. For example, Chookaneidí memorials almost always begin with the songs of their migration from Glacier Bay. These may be accompanied by speeches of encouragement to those in grief, or by historical explanation, as in Jim Marks' recording of the Xwayeenák song. At the end of the hosts' lamentation, someone from the guest group usually asks for permission to speak, and the hosts turn the floor over to the guests, who will conduct the Widow's Cry.

L S'aati Sháa Gaaxí, the Widow's Cry conducted by the guests, the opposite moiety of the hosts, consists of songs, speeches and display of at.óow for the removal of grief. The speeches in this book from the memorial for Jim Marks are from the Widow's Cry. These and other speeches in this book illustrate how the visual art is linked to the verbal art, and both to concepts of the spirit world. The guests are of the same moiety as the surviving spouse, the opposite moiety of the deceased and the hosts. They are often of the father's and grandfather's clan. In the speeches of the Widow's Cry, the guests perform a ceremony to remove the grief of the hosts, to whom they are usually related through marriage or paternity. The speeches of the Widow's Cry are to remove the sorrow and grief of those left behind, reminding them that, just as a living grandfather, a father, or a father's sister would be concerned when a young grandchild or small child or brother's child is in tears, the same emotion applies to the spirits after death. The paternal ancestor's spirits come to console the grieving survivors. As noted above, the term "Widow's Cry" applies to a man or woman, widow or widower, although the Tlingit and English terms sháa and widow are both female.

Acknowledging the depths of the loss of the host clan member related to the guests through marriage or as a father, the guests display their own clan treasures and invoke the appropriate spirits for help in removal of grief.

This interaction in the Widow's Cry can be confusing at first to people outside of Tlingit tradition, because the removal of grief is directed not toward the surviving spouse, who is also of the guests' moiety, but by the survivor's clan toward the clan of

The Widow's Cry. The sons of Willie Marks stand in blankets during the Widow's Cry of the memorial for Willie Marks, Hoonah, October 1981. L to R: Jim Marks wearing Diving Whale, Peter Marks wearing Raven Robe and Paul Marks wearing Diving Whale. Photo by R. Dauenhauer.

the departed! The speeches are directed not primarily or exclusively to the widow and her clan and moiety, but by her relatives to the family and clan of the deceased. This is not to minimize the grief of the widow (or widower), after whom this part of the ceremony is named, (and who is of the same moiety as the speakers), but to maximize the consolation offered across moiety lines to a clan of the opposite moiety who has lost a member. This member, though of the opposite moiety, is also a child and a paternal grandchild of the clans who are represented by the (guest) orators chosen to speak for the removal of grief. It is important to remember that this is not only personal (as in western culture) but is also structural and genealogical. This is a classic example of the "balance" and "reciprocity" of which we have been speaking—the underlying philosophy of Tlingit tradition and social structure. When people are in grief, others come to console them by telling them of their own losses. The at.óow displayed by the guests communicate the loss of relatives shared through the kinship system by hosts and guests. The message of consolation is first expressed immediately after someone's death, and culminates later in the Cry ceremony. First in word and then in ritual action, the guests are saying, "Put your spirit against mine. I have lost your paternal aunt." This is another example of "balance" or reciprocity through the "bracing" or mutual supporting of each other and of spiritual forces.

At the end of the Widow's Cry, the floor is returned to the hosts, who formally conclude the Cry Section of the memorial with speeches of gratitude to the guests. In Hoonah in October 1988, after the Ta<u>k</u>deintaan and Lukaa<u>x</u>.ádi displayed their at.óow and offered songs and speeches to the Chookaneidí hosts and then returned to their seats, the hosts made brief speeches thanking them. A typical speech was that by Annie Dick of Sitka, one of the host moiety, who thanked the guests for their display of at.óow and expressed how she had been feeling sick in body and spirit, but gained strength through the at.óow of her opposite clans. With this thanking of the guests, the mourning section of the memorial is brought to a close.

Now, as the elders commonly say, "it tips over to joy." The atmosphere of mourning changes immediately to an atmosphere of joy, and the remainder of the memorial will be conducted in a spirit of gaiety. Songs of mourning are replaced by love songs;

the atmosphere of grief and death replaced by joking and flirting between the opposite moieties, especially with the spouses of clan children. For example, the female Chookaneidí yátx'i (children of Chookaneidí) may flirt with the Chookaneidí men and give them money to bring out. The hosts remove their ceremonial robes, and many of the at.óow are packed away. In their place one often sees comical costumes and hats, but in general the rest of the memorial is conducted in everyday streetwear or sometimes with felt or hide vests with beadwork designs. In either case, the main point is that most of the at.óow are now retired to storage. Their role in the memorial and the removal of grief is over.

The Cry Ceremony consisting of lamentations by both hosts and guests is very important in Tlingit culture. According to traditional Tlingit belief, prolonged grieving is physically and spiritually unhealthy for the community and the individual. Therefore, prolonged grieving for the dead is taboo. The traditional belief is that if sadness lingers over the death of a relative, especially that of matrilineal kin, it will invite the death of another matrilineal kin. It is said that the cries of a relative endanger the life breath (daséigu) of the living. The breath of a family member may flow with the tears. The Tlingit expression for this is k̲aa daséigu t'éix̲ yaa kdugáx̲ch, "the cry behind the breath," or adaségu t'éix̲ yakawdigáx̲, "washing one's life away with tears." Cries loosen the hold on life of a kin, making him or her vulnerable. By crying, the breath of a family member is weakened, thus making him or her vulnerable to death and the spirit world. For this reason, the performance of the G̲áax̲, the Cry for the departed, is important to all, because it formally marks the end of mourning, of crying, and of the period of grief.

The same spiritual forces that can be negative during prolonged mourning can also be positive, especially when rallied during the Cry Ceremony, at which time the spirits of the departed and other spirits can be called through oratory and the accompanying display of at.óow to help in removal of grief. In Tlingit oratory delivered during the Cry Ceremony, the spirits of the departed are treated as if no boundaries exist between the living and the dead. The spirits of the departed are brought to the world of the living by words, especially when their kin are overcome by grief, particularly the child or grandchild on the

Eagle guest Eva Davis holds and speaks on G̱eesán tunic, formerly owned by Bert Dennis, addressing host Austin Hammond at the Raven House rededication, Haines, October 1974. Her husband George, also of the host moiety, stands at Austin's right. Eva explains the history of the tunic, who is about to put it on, and why. Photo by R. Dauenhauer.

father's side. This is why the father's side is also important in Tlingit kinship, social structure, and ceremonial life, especially in the ritual of the Widow's Cry.

To summarize and emphasize what was explained above: in the spirit world as in the world of the living, the father or paternal grandfather can be disturbed by the cries of distress of an offspring. In the same way as the father or grandfather in the land of the living may try to relieve the pain or injury of a child or grandchild, spiritual ancestors also come to the aid of their offspring, brought by words of speeches and songs, and by the display of at.óow to soothe and give them comfort. During times of crisis, especially grief, the spirits can become present in the world of the living to soothe those who are in pain. When those in grief cry out, the departed as well as the living come to their aid and give comfort. This relationship is not limited to a deceased biological father, but extends to any deceased member of the father's clan, even though the biological father may be living.

The close relationship between the living and the dead is also reflected in other aspects of the ḵoo.éex'. The memorial is for the recently deceased as well as for all the spirits of the departed. At a memorial, food, money, material goods, and speeches are given. In one action, there are two simultaneous destinations for these: distribution among the living present in memory of the departed, and, through them, to the spirits of the deceased, both immediate and in general. When the community of the living is cared for and comforted, the community of the departed is cared for and comforted as well.

Food, Gifts, Songs, and Dances

The order of events in this part of the memorial is flexible, usually beginning either with a meal or with the distribution of "fire dishes," followed by the first meal, depending on whether it is meal time, and how many meals are to be served. After the "fire dishes," other gifts may be distributed in various order, and in some cases simultaneously, according to local custom and specific needs. At the 1988 Hoonah memorial, to fit in with a 4 a.m. ferry departure of many of the guests from this island community accessible only by air and water, most of the gifts were distributed simultaneously; at Charlie Joseph's Memorial in Sitka in 1987, they were distributed in sequence.

Gan ka s'íx'i — "Fire Dishes" or ***"Dishes for the Fire."*** In memory of the deceased, gifts called "fire dishes," containers with contents especially prepared for individuals (as opposed to general distribution) are presented. Originally, food was actually placed into a fire and consumed by the flames, through which the spirits of the departed were fed. In some communities, food is still put into a fire to feed the spirits of the departed. This is the older practice, but is rare today. Most often, the "dishes for the fire" are distributed to the guests, instead. Prepared beforehand and labelled with the names of those for whom they are intended, these are usually small containers with packaged food and candy. The containers may be cups, bowls, dishes, baskets, rice bowls, plastic buckets, plastic jars with lids, even baking tins and colanders. The contents are usually snacks, candy, suckers, potato chips, fruit, packaged fruit juices and small souvenirs and party favors. When the fire dishes are assembled, the names of the clan departed are called out over them in remembrance, in the formula " ____ x̲'éidei" — "for ____" or, literally "to the mouth of ___." These are then distributed by the hosts as gifts to specially designated guests, usually close "affines"—spouses of the deceased or children of the deceased if the deceased was a man.

Guests assist the host in such distributions, helping to deliver items to the persons designated. To coordinate this and other activities, a ***naa káani*** is appointed by the hosts. The term translates as "in-law of the clan or moiety," and refers to a person of the guest moiety who is related by marriage to the hosts. A naa káani may be male or female. The naa káani helps to invite the other guests, and serves as "master of ceremonies" at the ceremonial. He or she also helps with the distribution of gifts.

Throughout the ceremonial, ***announcements*** are made by both hosts and guests. These are often "thank you" speeches, introductions explaining a kinship connection, and announcements about who contributed food and gifts. These might be called utilitarian speeches, because they convey information and confirm group relationships. They are not characterized by any of the complex rhetorical devices used in the formal speeches, such as the speeches for the removal of grief.

Meals. As mentioned above, the memorial for the departed is conducted with the idea that everything which is done is for the deceased as well as the living. Another term for the k̲oo.éex' or memorial for the dead is k̲aa naawu x̲'éix̲ at teex̲, "the feeding of a dead relative." When someone comes from another village to host a memorial for the dead, it is often said of him du naawu x̲'éit at yaawax̲áa, "he came to feed his dead." Thus, food is very important in Tlingit ceremonials, and several meals will be served in the course of the evening, ranging from light snacks to main meals. Traditional memorials usually begin in the late afternoon and last all night, often until midmorning the following day. Usually at least two main meals are served, one soon after completion of the Cry Portion of the memorial, and another later on, often while the money is being counted and sorted by those appointed to be record keepers. If the memorial lasts all night, breakfast will be served.

Fire Dishes assembled for distribution at the Raven House rededication, Haines, October 1974. Photo by R. Dauenhauer.

In addition to the main meals served and eaten hot, other food is distributed at a memorial. This may be consumed on the spot, or taken home. There is a special word in Tlingit, ***éenwoo,*** the food one takes home from a memorial. The éenwoo ranges from pilot bread (hard tack) to additional helpings of the main courses, especially boiled potatoes, pieces of meat and fish, and sometimes hardboiled eggs. Often salmon salad sandwiches are served.

Of the two main meals served, a pattern seems to be emerging that the first is of food not native to Alaska, and the second is traditional Tlingit subsistence food. Subsistence foods are especially valued and are saved for ceremonial distribution in memorials. In most cases, special hunts are undertaken by the men as part of the preparation for a memorial. The distinction between traditionally "Native" and "non-Native" food is our own categorization, based on observations at many memorials, noting the historical origins of which foods are served when. It is not meant to be rigid or dogmatic. Contemporary Tlingit cuisine is eclectic, with subsistence foods prepared in new ways. There is considerable influence of Chinese and Filipino cooking; for example, sweet and sour venison tenderloin with freshly killed deer meat, and venison adobo with older meat. These dishes also make the meat go further. Seal meat chop suey was served at a Forty Day Party in one village in the 1970s, and one of Nora Dauenhauer's favorite recipes is fresh seal meat baked with garlic cloves and potatoes, served with sauerkraut. Boiled potatoes seem to pattern with Native food, and mashed potatoes with non-Native food (although Willie Marks liked mashed potatoes with his deer steak). Rice and canned corn are served with both.

At the 1988 Chookaneidí memorial in Hoonah, the first meal consisted of ham, turkey, pork adobo, mashed potatoes, rice, and dressing. It was served mostly by children and teenagers of the host moiety. The second meal, served during the counting of the money, was Native food: deer stew, smoked seal meat, dryfish and various smoked fish, halibut, potatoes, rice, and corn. The Native food was served first as a plate to be eaten immediately; later, take-home boxes were distributed of additional seal meat, fish, and boiled potatoes.

The same pattern was followed at a recent combined L'uknax̱.ádi and Lukaax̱.ádi memorial in Juneau. The first meal was of turkey, mashed potatoes, gravy, dressing, dinner roll, and corn. The second meal, served during the counting of the money, was of Native food: a plate of various boiled fish, boiled potatoes, seal oil, seaweed, and salmon egg soup. Likewise, at the memorial for Charlie Joseph in Sitka, October 10, 1987, the first meal was of fried chicken and similar foods which are not originally Tlingit, but which are popular and common in the diet today. Many of these foods of more recent origin are served because traditional subsistence foods are increasingly more difficult to obtain and may be scarce or illegal at certain times, but they are also served because they were favorites of the deceased. Several years ago, one village flew in *Kentucky Fried Chicken* from Juneau as part of a ceremonial meal. The memorial for Charlie Joseph lasted all night and well into midmorning of the following day. Accordingly, several meals were served, including two main hot meals and several distributions of sandwiches, berries, cake and ice cream, and traditional food which could be eaten on the spot or taken home as éenwoo. The Native food meal consisted of boiled dryfish, deer stew, boiled potatoes, and frybread. Many families have special pots, often inherited, for preparing ceremonial foods. At Charlie Joseph's memorial, the cooking pot for the deer stew is worthy of note: it was two-feet high and three-feet in diameter!

The best explanation for this ritual distribution of food is offered by Amy Marvin of Hoonah, in her "Glacier Bay History," featured in *Haa Shuká*. This point is so important to an understanding of Tlingit ceremonial life that we will quote directly from Amy Marvin's story. Kaasteen, a young woman, has elected to remain with the clan houses, and be crushed by the rapidly advancing ice; the people have left her in Glacier Bay, after surrounding her with food and clothing. Amy Marvin explains:

> For whomever is mourned, people relinquish the ownership of things in their memory. Only after this do we feel stronger. And 'for her to eat,' is also said. Only if the food which is given is eaten with another clan can it go to her. This is when she will have some, the relative who is mourned. When the opposite clan takes a bite, she will also eat some. This is the reason we call it 'invitation to feast.' A feast is offered to remove our grief. Only when we give to the opposite clan whatever

> we offer, only when we know it went to her, only when this is done does it become a balm for our spirits. Because of her, Kaasteen. And whatever we relinquish our ownership to, for Kaasteen, when we give them to the opposite clan, only after this do our spirits become strong. It's medicine, spiritual medicine. Because of the things that happened to Kaasteen; this is what informed us. (Page 277, lines 307-330.)

In other words, out of the experience at Glacier Bay comes the spiritual covenant for ritual distribution of food and other gifts. Only through bonding with the living can one achieve spiritual bonding with the departed. When gifts such as food and blankets are given for the physical and spiritual warmth of the opposite moiety, they pass spiritually to comfort the departed. Through these acts of giving, the living hosts are also comforted with what Amy Marvin calls "spiritual medicine," or "a balm for our spirits." Her Tlingit term is haa tuwunáagu, and we have taken it and the looser translation "for healing our spirit" as the title of this book.

Songs and Dances are performed throughout the evening, usually with hosts and guests taking turns. The hosts often dance while the guests are eating, and the guests usually dance after eating. At spontaneous intervals throughout the evening, the guests will gather in small groups to sing and dance for the hosts, thanking them for the food and gifts. The mourning and cry ceremonies are now over, and the tone of the evening has changed to joy, so these are happy love songs, often involving humor, and directed to the opposite moiety, who are most often addressed according to their fathers' group. For example, the (Eagle) Chookaneidí hosts in Hoonah sing to the guests as Chookaneidí yátx'i—children of Chookaneidí. The guests are of the Raven moiety, mostly of the T'aḵdeintaan, Lukaax̱.ádi and L'uknax̱.ádi. Songs and dances may be performed at any of the traditional ceremonials, such as house dedications. Although they are generally not done at Forty Day Parties, songs and dances are an integral part of the larger ceremonials such as a memorial, where oratory, visual art, song, and dance are inseparable. These are the "regular" dances which everybody is expected to do when invited. No special training is required to perform these "regular" dances.

Raven guests singing and dancing during the joyous part of the memorial for Willie Marks, Hoonah, October 1981. L to R: William Johnson, John Marks (drumming) Austin Hammond (partially obscured) Richard Sheakley, Ron Williams, Jim Marks, Richard Bean (partially obscured) and Peter Marks. Nora Dauenhauer, kneeling, below drum. In foreground are two great-grand daughters of Willie Marks, Marissa and Andrea Florendo. Note dance posture and absence of traditional regalia, which has been returned to storage chests. Photo by R. Dauenhauer.

Jim Marks performing the "Love Song" or "Haida-type Dancing" during the ANB Hall dedication, Haines, May 1974. He wears a moosehide Raven tunic given to him by Austin Hammond, a Chilkat Robe, and shakee.át (dance frontlet).
Photo by R. Dauenhauer.

Jim Marks and his daughter Josie resting between dances at the Haines ANB Hall dedication, May 1974.
Photo by R. Dauenhauer.

Shakee.át (headdress) or Yéik utee (imitating the spirit) dancers, performing behind a blanket during the Raven House rededication, Haines, October 1974. L to R: unidentified, wearing Frog Headdress; William Johnson, wearing Raven and King Salmon Headdress, and George Davis, wearing Tlaxanéis Nóow (Kingfisher Fort) Headdress. Photo by R. Dauenhauer.

In addition to the ongoing "regular" joyous songs and dances, ***special songs and dances*** are performed at certain times. These include the ***yarn*** or ***motion dances*** (yoo koonáḵk dances) performed by the hosting women, and the ***shakee.át*** (headdress) or ***yéik utee dances*** performed by men wearing dance frontlets behind a blanket held by two people. These two types of spirit dances, important in the speeches in this book, are different in style from other Tlingit dancing, such as the style that accompanies the "love songs" exchanged between the moieties. Another distinctive type of dance is the ***Deikeenaa*** or ***Haida style*** dance performed with a headdress and Chilkat robe.

Motion or ***Yarn Dance*** is one of the joyous styles, and is sometimes also called the "sway dance." It is danced to yéik (spirit) and other songs. In Tlingit, two terms for this style of dancing are mentioned by Charlie Joseph in his speech at the 1980 elders conference: yoo kuwahangi yéik (singular) meaning literally "spirit who sways" (CJ 206) and yoo koonáḵk, literally "standing and swaying in place," (CJ 122) plural of above. This type of dancing to spirit songs is done by women, and is characterized by the swinging of yarn bundles attached to headbands and hanging in front of the ears. The yarns accentuate the swaying motion of the dance. The origin of the style is uncertain.

Yéik utee — Imitation of the Spirit, or "imitating the yéik." The yéik utee or shakee.át dances are usually done during the counting of the money, and are sometimes referred to as "dancing behind the money."[10] The term refers to a style of song and dance in which the dance is performed with an ermine headdress (shakee.át) behind a blanket, with only the bobbing headdress showing. For example, the yéik utee dance for the Cháatl ḵuyéik, the Halibut Spirit, depicts a halibut being caught on a wooden hook. The songs sung to such a dance are songs revealed or composed by spirits. In these yéik utee songs, the spirits speak a spirit language other than Tlingit, so the song texts are very different, and people don't understand them. This language seems in some cases to be a human foreign language, such as Haida or Tsimshian (songs were widely traded and otherwise exchanged among the Tlingit, Haida, and Tsimshian) and, in other cases, to be an unknown spirit language revealed to the shaman, who learned and passed on the song. Here is an example of a yéik utee song of the Chookaneidí clan:

Tsaal g̲anha
Tsaal g̲anha haa
ho, hi yei kwshigé.

The words are not intelligible to speakers of Tlingit. Lines 134 and 140 of Charlie Joseph's speech in this book refer to yéik utee daa sheeyí (yéik utee songs; spirit imitating songs). For more discussion by Charlie Joseph about yéik utee dances, see the video tape, *K̲aal.átk'* (Ostyn 1981). In contrast to the yéik utee songs, other songs, including other yéik or spirit songs, are usually sung in Tlingit, although some songs include words and phrases from other languages, such as English and Southern Tutchone. As the above examples of yarn and headdress dances suggest, much Tlingit dancing imitates animals: raven, bear, wolf, sea gulls and others. Tlingit scholar Walter Soboleff observes (personal communication, 1989) that dances are often anthropomorphic and may be thought of as people, too, as in the example of the K̲aaksateen Image Dance mentioned in Charlie Joseph's speech.

In addition to the yarn and headdress dances, songs and dances called ***Deikeenaa (Haida style)*** dance songs are commonly performed at house dedications and memorials. The origin of the term "Haida style" is unclear. The songs are love songs by Tlingit composers, and the dancers perform with a shakee.át (headdress) and Chilkat robe or button blanket. In contrast to the skakee.át dances described above, the Deikeenaa or Haida style dances are not performed behind a blanket, and are not imitative of animals.

Singing, dancing, and distribution of food and gifts are often accompanied by what might be called traditional ***dramatics***. These are most often imitations or dramatizations of at.óow. The general Tlingit term for this is yikteiyí. This is an older term, and in older practice often included magic acts and optical illusion. A contemporary example is when the "Sea Gull Ladies" (in Tlingit K̲'eik̲'w Sháa; variously called Tern Women, Sea Pigeon Women, Kittywake Women, and Sea Gull Ladies—terms to be discussed later in this introduction), women of the Hoonah T'ak̲deintaan, imitate birds at the rookery. They may be startled into flight by a drum beat or may swoop down on food. The people of the Chookaneidí stamp their feet rapidly, imitating the rumble of glaciers. One of the most delightful interchanges at Hoonah ceremonials is of the T'ak̲deintaan "Sea Gull Ladies" being startled up by the rumbling of the glacier ice enacted by the Chookaneidí men. At one time, riddles (in Tlingit, gáax'u) were enacted at ceremonials, but these are rare today. The clues to traditional riddles were often acted out. In the film *Haa Shagóon* (Kawagey 1981), George Davis poses a verbal riddle.

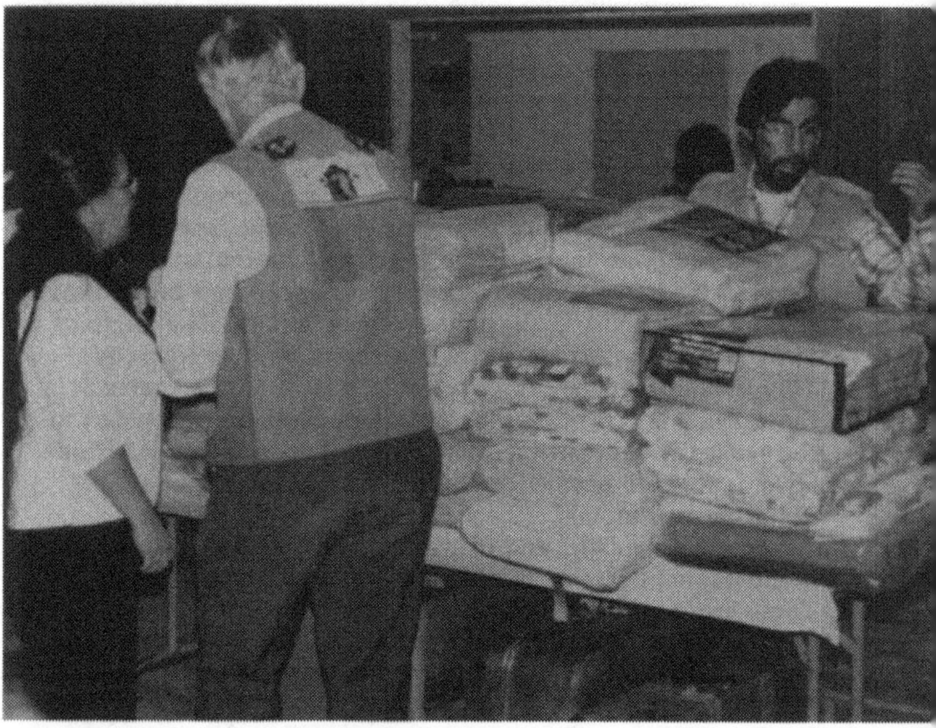

Chookaneidí co-host Ernie Hillman (back to camera) consulting with his wife Lillian (Takdeintaan) prior to the distribution of his blankets during the Chookaneidí memorial, Hoonah, October 1988. The beadwork on his vest represents the Glacier Bay History, Kaasteen sitting, with the ice coming over her. Suitcases under the table contain at.óow, now put away. Facing camera is Richard Dalton, Jr., grandson of Jessie Dalton. Photo by R. Dauenhauer.

After the first meal is served and the "fire dishes" are given out, ***other gifts*** are distributed during the remainder of the evening. All food is a gift, but not all gifts are food. The general pattern in distributing of special gifts is for the host to tell the naa káani who the gift is for; the naa káani then shouts out the name of the recipient, who responds "haadéi!"—"Here!" The response "haadéi" is used when accepting fruit, money, and other specially designated gifts, but not when accepting fire dishes. The Tlingit term for calling the recipient's name is k̲aa eedéi at dul.óowx'.

Dry Goods are distributed to the guests, either generally, or to special guests individually. These include clothing, (shirts, neckties, socks) blankets, wash cloths, towels, kerchiefs, pot holders, and other cloth objects. Sometimes whole bolts of cloth will be unwound around the guests, each of whom cuts off the section behind his or her back. The distribution of major gifts such as ***blankets*** usually involves a dedication of the pile of blankets before individual distribution to special guests. In the dedication of the pile of blankets, the names of the departed are called out in the pattern "___kaadéi" — "for ___", literally "to go on so-and-so." In the same manner in which food shared with the opposite moiety is shared spiritually with the departed, so the blankets distributed for the warmth of the guests will also warm the spirits. As with most other aspects of the ceremonial, there is simultaneous social bonding among the living and spiritual bonding with the departed.

Distribution of Berries is one of the most eagerly awaited moments of a memorial. Wild berries (usually blueberries and salmon berries) are given to the guests, who traditionally bring a bowl, jar and spoon to receive and eat such gifts. Berries are usually distributed by ladle from a large bucket or bowl. Bowls range from modern stainless steel to antique flow blue. Commonly called "potlatch bowls," these entered the northwest coast in the late nineteenth and early twentieth centuries and have been popular ever since. Some may date back to the fur trade era. Some of the berries are delivered to a person called out by name, and shared with those around him or her. In a joyous scramble imitating the feeding frenzy of birds, the guests transfer the berries from the host's delivery bowl into their own jars and bowls. When the serving bowl is emptied, the group of guests joins in a shout while lifting the bowl high. The "Sea Gull

Ladies" join in their characteristic bird cry when they are served. Other groups of women engage in similar dramatics; these include the Ts'axwéil Sháa (Crow Women) of the Lukaax̱.ádi and the Kax̱átjaa Sháa (Herring Women) of the Kiks.ádi, mentioned in the speech by George Davis.

Distribution of Fruit is handled in the same way as berries, and the same Tlingit term, ḵaa x̱'éidei at kadunáa, literally "taking round objects to a person's mouth," is used for both. Bowls of fresh fruits are given by name to special guests and those seated around them, and, in the meantime, cases of apples, oranges, bananas and sometimes other fruit such as grapes are distributed systematically around the room in the same way as the soft drinks.

The empty serving bowl raised high during the memorial for Ivan Gamble, Angoon, October 1988. L to R: Daniel Johnson, Sr., wearing a seal vest, Richard George holding the bowl, Mike Fred leaning over, Peter Demmert at right, holding bowl. Photo by Peter Metcalfe, courtesy of Kootznoowoo, Inc.

Cases of ***soft drinks*** are assembled by the hosts and their supporters, and are distributed to the guests, usually a can or two at a time. Members of the host moiety, usually in pairs, walk along the rows of seated guests distributing the gifts, one person holding the case or box, the other person handing out individual items. They go around the room repeatedly until all the cans of soft drink are distributed.

In a similar manner, but usually on a smaller scale, commercial ***canned goods***, usually fruit, and home-made preserves (salmon, deer meat, seal oil, berries, jam, jelly, etc.) are distributed.

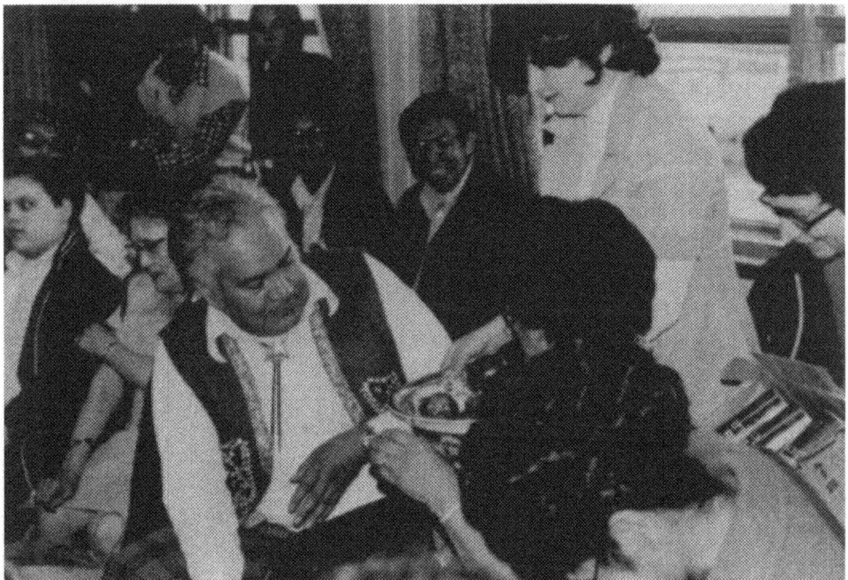

Marilyn Cesar Wieting delivering a bowl of fruit to Willard Jones and those around him during the Haines ANB Hall dedication, May 1974. Photo by R. Dauenhauer.

Eagle guests Willie Marks and his daughter-in-law Kathy Dennis during the distribution of food at the Raven House rededication, Haines, October 1974. Her daughter Josie Marks (back to camera) and mother Marion Dennis are to her left. Photo by R. Dauenhauer.

Distribution of ***miscellaneous small gifts*** continues throughout all of this. These gifts include combs, cosmetics, party favors, cookies, snacks, peanuts, candies, crackerjacks, bubble gum and chewing gum, cigarettes, etc. In some memorials, the distribution is done one item at a time, but most often wave after wave of hosts moves along the rows of seated guests giving each person a gift. Some of these gifts have cultural significance; for example, the Chookaneidí sometimes distribute bowls of small gifts as symbolic pieces of ice, in connection with their history in Glacier Bay. Bowls of tootsie rolls, lemon drops and other small wrapped candies, peanuts in shells and popcorn represent bowls of crushed ice. As the evening progresses, guests amass overflowing bags and boxes of gifts under and in front of their chairs. The Tlingit term for this general gift giving is k̲aa x̲óodei at kadulgéikw, meaning "distributing things among people."

An ***intermission*** is usually called at this point in the memorial, when all the gifts other than money have been distributed, to give people a chance to stretch, and to repack their food and other gifts. Most often, local guests take their gifts home at this point; therefore, having been filled to overflowing with gifts, the hall looks empty by contrast when people return and the last part of the memorial gets underway.

Money

The final sequence of the memorial deals with the handling of money. As with the Cry section, this follows a set order. In the first phase, ***money is brought out***. Individual members of the host moiety (the principal hosts, members of their extended family, and others of the same clan and/or moiety) line up and contribute their money to the common bowl located at the front table. Sometimes the hosts keep some at.óow such as a hat, tunic, or blanket on the table near the bowl. A record is kept and announcements are made by the naa káani as to how much is being put up by each individual, including how much was given to him or her as contributions by others. As described above, a very important aspect of the bringing out of money is that members of the guest moiety, especially in-laws, children, and members of the hosts' fathers' clan, can give money to individuals of the host moiety. In this way, community support is

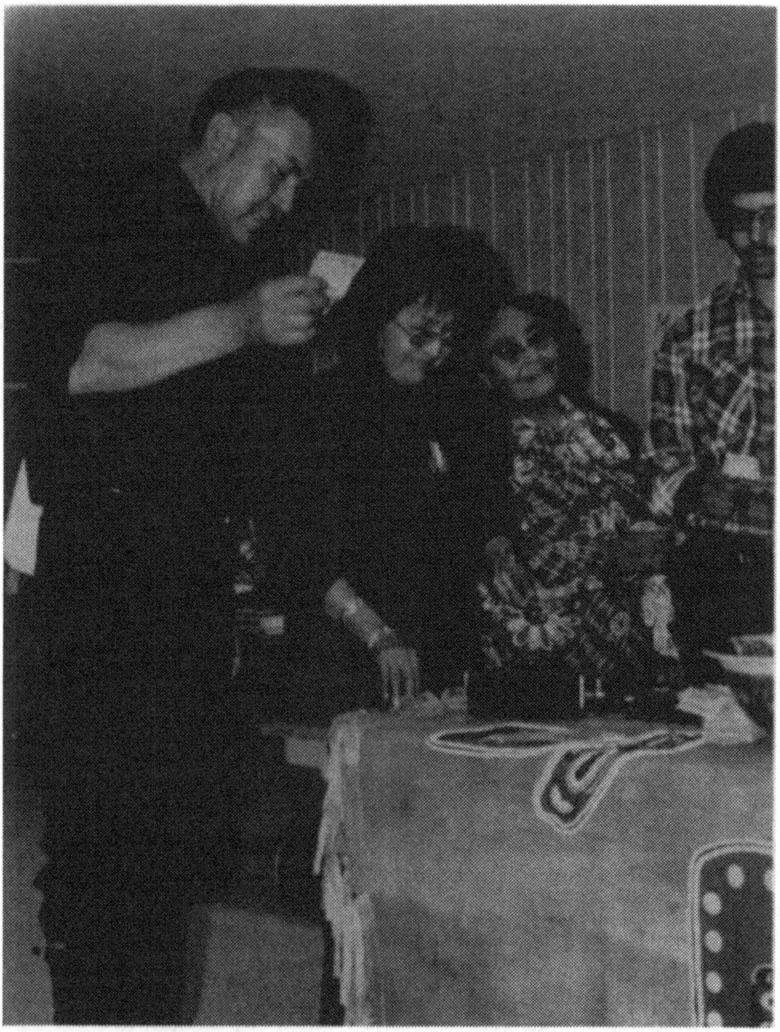

Nora Dauenhauer bringing out money during the Raven House rededication, Haines, October 1974. At the left is Jeff David. As Naa Káani, he holds up the money and announces who is presenting it. Next in line are Emma Marks and Aussie Hammond. Photo by R. Dauenhauer.

reinforced through a large number of small contributions, and fairly large totals of money can be brought out.

Characteristically, members of the host moiety who bring out money will designate their own contribution and then will identify, by name and amount, those of the opposite moiety who supported them. After making their deposits to the bowl at the front table, individuals of the host moiety usually address the guests directly, thanking them by name and kinship term, and reading off the list of people who supported them, including dollar amounts. The usual pattern is that after all members of the host moiety who wish to bring out money have done so, the principal hosts themselves will bring out their money. Depending on the size of the memorial, all of this can last several hours. At the October 1987 memorial for Charlie Joseph in Sitka, it took almost five hours for the money to be brought out and counted. The Tlingit term is dáanaa daak wootee, "bringing out money." Another term is dáana wuduwaják̲, meaning "money was killed." According to Hyde (1983:9) the Haidas use this term also, calling it "killing wealth" in general. There is some speculation as to whether this term is a carry-over from an era in which slaves might have been killed.

After being gathered and counted, the ***money is dedicated*** in memory of departed ancestors. The entire sum of money brought out by all of the host moiety is gathered in the bowl—usually an antique flow blue bowl. The bowl with the money is held, and dedicated with the calling out of names of the clan departed in the formula "__ kaadéi" — "for so-and-so", or "on so-and-so."

Once the money is brought out and dedicated, other ceremonies may take place in the combined presence of the money and the guests. Guests and hosts alike are witnesses to these events, and this aspect of the ceremonial serves as a "notary public" in traditional oral society. For example, ***adoptions,*** if any, and ***giving of names*** are usually done at this time. Also the ***bringing out of new at.óow*** is done at this time. In the naming process, clan elders select names to be passed on, and individuals to whom they will be given. The name is called out by a naa káani or other person of the guest moiety, and the name is repeated four times by all present as money is held or rubbed on the forehead of the person being named. Instead of or in addition to money, robes or other at.óow may also be held or rubbed on the forehead of the person being named. At this time the host can also confirm existing names and give additional names to his or her grandchildren (the children of their sons) to recognize and elevate them. In the case of new at.óow, one of the guests is selected by the host clan for the honor of putting the new blanket or other at.óow on a designated host—one of the host moiety, ideally a grandchild of the host clan. One of the important steps in the "life history" of any at.óow is that it be presented at a ceremonial and that money be brought out in its name. As Cecilia Kunz, one of the clan elders and hosts in a recent (November 1988) L'uknax̱.ádi memorial in Juneau explained to the younger hosts and guests, "You have to bring out money on it at a party before you can use it when people are in sorrow." In both naming and bringing out of new at.óow, the guests are witnesses, thereby validating the events.

When bringing out of new persons or at.óow is completed, the ***distribution of money*** begins. This is done both individually and generally. The first money taken from the bowl goes to the widow (or, as the case may be, the widower). A long line of individual hosts presents her (or him) with gifts of money. Specific persons are then called out by name and are rewarded for special services and help to the hosts during their time of grief. For example, pall bearers and others who helped significantly are rewarded. In smaller communities, where burials are less commercialized, members of the opposite moiety who dug the grave are also rewarded at this time. Individual hosts usually make gifts of money to certain individual guests, and the rest is left for general distribution. After designated individuals are paid, the remaining money is distributed among all of the guests. The hosts and/or naa káani make repeated circuits of the room giving small amounts to each guest until all the money is distributed. It is important to note that the money is generally recycled. For example, in a two-week period in October 1988, three memorials were held—two in Hoonah and one in Juneau. Thus, Ravens who received money in an Eagle memorial were soon giving it in a Raven memorial.

When all of the food, gifts, and money have been distributed, the evening is brought to a joyous close and ***exit***. In Hoonah, this is usually done by the hosts dancing with the upturned empty bowl, and the guests dancing out of the hall in a line-dance in which all of the hosts and all of the guests eventually dance with one another.

Dedication of money during the Raven House rededication, Haines, October 1974. Naa káani Jeff David holds the antique bowl and repeats in a loud voice the names of the departed being recalled by Austin Hammond and John Marks.
Photo by R. Dauenhauer.

V. SIMILE AND METAPHOR IN TLINGIT AND ENGLISH LITERATURE

Before going into culture-specific detail on the style of Tlingit oratory, it may be helpful to the general reader to review some of the common features of poetry and public speaking found in traditions around the world, including Tlingit. Traditional Tlingit speeches can be difficult to understand—even for people who speak and understand the Tlingit language well. The language of the speeches is often popularly described as "old time Tlingit," which might be called "classical" Tlingit. It is poetic language, especially employing simile and metaphor. While normally simile and especially metaphor are rare in Tlingit story telling, they are fairly common in songs (especially simile), and they are at the heart of Tlingit oratory.

Four common figures of speech are found in Tlingit oratory. Keeping technical terms to a minimum, we will illustrate them here with more familiar English terms and examples before moving to Tlingit examples in the final sections of this introduction.

Simile is a comparison using "like" or "as." We find examples in everyday speech as well as in traditional literature, such as the Bible.

> It's pretty as a picture.
> They are like a lion eager to tear,
> as a young lion lurking in ambush.

Metaphor is a comparison saying that one thing actually *is* something else. Again, we find examples in popular speech as well as formal tradition.

> That guy's a real turkey.
> The Lord is my shepherd.

Both similes and metaphors can be ***extended*** by adding more description. Extended similes are often called ***Homeric similes*** after the ancient Greek poet Homer. In the Bible many of the parables of Jesus are extended similes. For example, Matt 13:24, "The kingdom of heaven may be compared to a man who sowed good seed on his field," or Matt. 13:31 "The kingdom of heaven is like a grain of mustard seed." An extended or Homeric simile often concludes with a restatement or recapitulation of the initial comparision, as in this passage from Book Twenty-two of Homer's *Odyssey* (Fitzgerald translation; 1963:421) describing how the bodies of the enemies of Odysseus are piling up like fish dumped from a net:

In blood and dust
he saw that crowd all fallen, many and many slain.
Think of a catch that fishermen haul in to a halfmoon bay
in a fine-meshed net from the white-caps of the sea:
how all are poured out on the sand, in throes for the salt sea,
twitching their cold lives away in the sun's fiery air:
so lay the suitors heaped on one another.

Metaphors can also be extended, expanded, or developed. The Twenty-third Psalm is a good example of an extended metaphor: everything follows from the initial equation of the Lord and the shepherd. Much to the frustration of his audience, many of the parables of Jesus are more like riddles, in which the comparison is not given directly, either by simile or metaphor, but must be guessed. Many of the parables in the Bible are extended metaphors. Jesus comments in Matt. 13:9, "He who has ears, let him hear."

The metaphor in the magnificent opening lines of Shakespeare's tragedy *King Richard the Third* provides a good comparision to the complexity of Tlingit oratory:

Now is the winter of our discontent
made glorious summer by this sun of York.

These lines offer an excellent comparison to the use of metaphor and cultural allusion in Tlingit oratory. To understand these two lines of Shakespeare requires understanding of the poetic use of metaphor, appreciation of the English climate, and some knowlege of English history. There is a basic comparison of winter and summer to bad times and good, war and peace, defeat and victory. Linked to the idea of seasons, the "sun of York" is a pun on the word "son" and on the use of the sun as a badge or heraldic emblem by King Edward IV, the Son of York. In the Wars of the Roses, a struggle for the English crown, in which one side used as a crest the white rose, and the other side a red rose, the House of York has triumphed over the House of Lancaster, and the kingdom was at peace. Thus, these opening lines of the play tell the audience much about the situation as the story opens. But to understand what is happening, we must appreciate the metaphor and how it is based on historical and cultural background.

In its complexity of simile and metaphor, the style of Tlingit oratory may also be compared to English metaphysical poetry, for example to John Donne's "Goodfriday, 1613. Riding Westward," or "A Valediction: forbidding mourning," or to Andrew Marvell's "To His Coy Mistress." Whether of Ravens or Roses, both in Tlingit and English literature, metaphor and simile transform the physical into the metaphysical. Readers familiar with English language, culture, poetry, and history can appreciate and savor such passages as the opening of *Richard the Third*. Likewise, elders steeped in Tlingit tradition and social structure appreciate and respond to the metaphor and cultural allusions in the oratory of Jessie Dalton and others included in this book. But for those less familiar with the traditions, little or no shared cultural background may be assumed. Therefore, we have included detailed annotations which accompany the individual speeches, explaining the specific cultural references.

There are also Tlingit terms for these figures of speech. In Tlingit, simile is referred to as at ashoowatán, "to compare one's words to things." Metaphor is referred to as x'aakaanáx̲ yoo x̲'atánk, "speaking over a point of land." A term for comparison in general is awliyaak̲w. Riddles are called gáax'u and parables at kookeidí. Discussing a well-composed speech, one might ask, Daat yáx̲ sáyú wóoshi awas'áx'w? — "What did he put it together like?" A well-delivered speech may be described as tíx' yaa jikanagudi yáx̲ wootee, "like a rope running overboard."

VI. THE GENERAL STRUCTURE OF TLINGIT ORATORY

Most traditional Tlingit oratory is delivered in a "chanting" style, with the voice dramatically projected and pitched several notes higher than normal speech. This is partly in order to be heard without the use of microphones at a large gathering, but it also creates a characteristic delivery style unique to oratory and quite different from narrative performance such as story telling. Increasingly, as the events are being held less often in community houses and more frequently in larger community halls, there has been a move to microphones. Because of the size of the halls, it is often impossible to hear most of the elders without some kind of public address system, especially during the Widow's Cry when they are facing the hosts and may have their backs to the rest of the guests whom they are representing.

Most oratory delivered in the context of a ceremonial is, as stated above, addressed to the opposite moiety. Accordingly, most speeches begin with a genealogical catalog, in which the speaker addresses his or her relatives of the opposite moiety, usually paternal aunts, paternal uncles, in-laws, fathers (plural—addressing not only biological fathers but clan fathers, i.e. by extension all men of the opposite moiety) and grandparents of the opposite moiety.

The opening catalog is sometimes followed by a brief statement of the kinship ties between the speaker and the bereaved. Grief is often expressed at this point, and gratitude is expressed for gifts of food, materials, or services. A short speech could end at this point, often with another closing genealogical catalog, or, according to the situation, the speech may continue. If it is developed, at this point an image will normally be introduced. The image is usually from nature, from Tlingit oral literature or culture, or from a crest design, hat, blanket, robe, or other at.óow. The image may be simple or complex, depending upon what the situation calls for. If complex, the image may be expanded by simile and/or metaphor. A complicated speech may involve variations, or a series of images may be presented.

Sometimes the usual order may be inverted for special effect. For example, Jessie Dalton opens her speech in this book with a rhetorical question about death, followed by the genealogical inventory in which she addresses the grieving hosts. She then develops her speech through metaphor, extended metaphor, simile, and extended simile based on genealogy and at.óow. Her speech is examined in detail in the following section of this introduction, where examples of her metaphor and simile will be found. Her fellow speakers, especially Kaatyé and Daanawáak̲ (David Kadashan and Austin Hammond) use a similar style.

The speaker usually finishes with expressions of grief, gratitude, and reaffirmation of the kinship ties. Throughout all of this there is typically audience response, with people expressing agreement and approval, acknowledging references to them or their relatives. The general Tlingit term for making such responses is yoo x̲'ayakdudlisheek, "they respond to him or her."

The floor is usually open to anyone who wishes to speak. Sometimes individuals will speak in random order, and at other times a pre-arranged set of speeches will be delivered. The speeches composed, published, and recorded in performance at the October 1968 memorial for Jim Marks in Hoonah are a fine example of rhetorical style and content in a prearranged formal sequence. The central speech is by Jessie Dalton—Naa Tláa. Her fellow orators work together to establish a dramatic context for her, opening the way, building up to her speech and then diminishing after it—creating an overall structural unity to the set of speeches. Matthew Lawrence sets the stage with a very short speech. He is followed by David Kadashan, who delivers a longer speech, in which he develops the image of an uprooted tree floating downriver to the sea until it ends on a sandy beach. Sustaining the level of intensity reached by David Kadashan, William Johnson then delivers a short speech and turns the floor over to Jessie Dalton, the main speaker. This, the longest and most complicated speech, is the oratorical climax of the set. It is followed by a shorter speech delivered by Austin Hammond who begins what in drama is sometimes compared to the downward curve of the "horseshoe" design. As the key image in his speech, he expresses his sorrow and inadequacy by wishing that his priceless Chilkat robe were a simple and utilitarian towel that could wipe away the grief of the hosts, who are his father's people, mourning for his stepfather. Matthew Lawrence, who opened the set of speeches, now closes it with a brief but marvelous speech of resolution.

The speeches transcribed and translated in this collection are outstanding, but not unusual. We say this not to minimize in any way their genius and creativity and imagination—but rather to emphasize the quality of oratory composed perhaps not by every Tlingit individual, but certainly by a large number of elders who have studied and fostered the art through careful listening and lifelong practice. Public speaking is common in Tlingit gatherings, and depending on the occasion, much of it is still characterized by outstanding humor or skillful use of rhetoric based on various appropriate images or at.óow.

An example of this is ***a recent funeral***. On June 11, 1987, as we were drafting this introduction, we attended the funeral of Steve Perrin, a Tlingit carver and in many respects an average member of the community. He was Eagle moiety, of the

Kaagwaantaan, and a child of (the Raven) Lukaax̱.ádi. The service was a small affair, held in the social hall of the Episcopal church in Juneau. It was Bahai, with Bahai prayers and various testimonials and eulogy, but the service was also uniquely Tlingit.

Speeches were given in Tlingit and English by several elders of the Kaagwaantaan, including George Dalton of Hoonah and Edward Kunz of Juneau. As a central image in his speech, Edward Kunz noted the American flag on the coffin of the deceased, who was a war veteran. He commented that this is a sign of honor and respect, and the flag, by being given to the family, will become like a traditional Tlingit at.óow, through which the deceased will in a sense continue to live among us. This is a characteristic Tlingit response to the inter-ethnic setting and changing times in which most of us live, and the style of the speech was also very traditional. Use of the flag as an at.óow is also documented in many historical photographs of the last one hundred years.

At funerals such as this, people wear conventional American dress, not Tlingit ceremonial regalia, which are reserved for special occasions. Contemporary Tlingit dress, such as beaded vests, are worn by many people at Forty Day Parties, but the traditional regalia (at.óow) are usually not present until the memorial. So, although there was little visible evidence to show that a funeral such as Steve Perrin's was Tlingit, it was traditionally Tlingit in oratory and group dynamics. Readers interested in this aspect of Tlingit culture should refer to Sergei Kan, "Memory Eternal: Orthodox Christianity and the Tlingit Mortuary Complex" (1987a).

When the floor was turned over to the guests who wished to speak, several answering speeches were made by Ravens of various clans, including Jessie Dalton and Paul Marks. These were speeches for the removal of grief addressed to the family and clan of Steve Perrin, but were modest by design, on a small scale, appropriate to the immediate funeral, in contrast to the elaborately stylized speeches delivered at memorials. The short speech by Paul Marks, a young Raven of the Lukaax̱.ádi, child of Chookaneidí, who had been studying oratory with his clan leaders Horace Marks and Austin Hammond, is a good example. He began with a brief genealogical catalog, addressing the opposite moiety who had lost one of their members. The deceased was child of Lukaax̱.ádi; his father was Lukaax̱.ádi. Therefore the Lukaax̱.ádi at the funeral, including Paul Marks, despite his being much younger than the deceased, were considered parents of the deceased. The Lukaax̱.ádi men who were in attendance (and who, as members of the opposite moiety had been requested by the Kaagwaantaan to be pall bearers—Austin Hammond, Horace Marks, Peter Marks, Paul Marks, and others) are, in a tribal sense, fathers of the deceased. He then presented his central image: Raven, noticing sap running from an axe mark in a tree, comments, "You're crying, too." This is a paradigm for consolation—that all creation somehow shares in grief, that the Ravens share in the grief of the Eagles, and that the Lukaax̱.ádi mourn the loss of their son.

These two speeches by Edward Kunz and Paul Marks illustrate Tlingit oratory in what we have called an "informal situation." Although more intimate, less formal and less public, this does not mean that any less care or attention is given to language or style. Words are carefully chosen and delivered; figures of speech are carefully thought out. The speeches are structured around the genealogical context, selecting an appropriate image or at.óow, and developing it through simile, metaphor, parable, and/or riddle. They differ from the longer speeches in this book only in scale and level of formality, as determined by the setting. The point is that they are structurally the same in style and function. These speeches from the two sides of the genealogy of the deceased (the Eagle Kaagwaantaan and the Raven Lukaax̱.ádi) are also examples of balance and reciprocity.

VII. AT.ÓOW IN ACTION: LEVELS OF MEDIATION IN TLINGIT ORATORY[11]

Some dictionaries suggest that the English word "religion" derives from the Latin word "religio," referring to the bond between humans and the gods, and that this word in turn is possibly related to the Latin word "religo," meaning "to tie" or "fasten." In this sense, many aspects of Tlingit ceremonials may be considered religious, because they attempt to mediate, bind, or connect the world of humans and the spirit world. Nowhere is this more evident than in the oratory, and we will illustrate this here with analysis of the "Speeches for the Removal of Grief" delivered by the guests during the Widow's Cry of the memorial for Jim Marks in Hoonah, October 1968. Particularly in the speech by Jessie Dalton, we will show how she uses grammatical and poetical binding of words in her oratory to create bonding on community and spiritual levels. She achieves ultimate social and spiritual mediation through mediation first on syntactic, rhetorical, and stylistic levels, specifically through the devices of simile and metaphor.

An orator such as Jessie Dalton is selected to speak because of his or her sensitivity, and the orator is compared in Tlingit to someone who brings a very long pole into a house. In handling words, as in handling a pole, a speaker must be careful not to strike or hit anyone's face, or to break anything by accident. Referring to oratory during an interview, her own words were, "It is difficult to speak to someone who is respected. It is very difficult." Delivered carelessly, words can be dangerous and detrimental. But when delivered carefully, oratory can be a soothing medicine, a healing power and balm to one who is in pain. It can give spiritual strength. In Tlingit one says, k̲aa toowú kei altseench, "people gain spiritual strength from it," or toowú latseen k̲aa jeex̲ atee, "it gives strength to the spirit." The effect of words in a good speech is described as yándei kdusyaa yáx̲ yatee du yoo x̲'atángi, "his words were like cloth being gently spread out on a flat surface."

Elders educated in the tradition of oratory also describe a well-delivered speech as a supportive wedge which keeps those who are in grief from falling into danger or harm: in Tlingit, ax̲'aax̲ wujix̲eeni yáx̲ yatee du yoo x̲'atángi, "his words are as if they have fallen between two things." "Between" refers to the space between death and the person who is in grief, between the grieving survivor and the abyss of his or her grief itself. The image is of oratory being inserted like a beam being put into place and securing a structure. These sayings illustrate the delicacy and care with which oratory is traditionally performed, and its power if handled correctly. This is the stage onto which Jessie Dalton steps, after the scene has been elaborately set, first by the hosts of the opposite moiety, and then by her fellow guests and kinsmen. This has been described briefly above, but a few more words about this setting are in order here. Much of the following information will add specific detail to the general concepts and structures outlined in earlier sections of this introduction, and will connect one set of speeches to the general background already provided.

To bid his last farewell to his departed older brother, Willie Marks (Kéet Yaanayí) hosted the memorial or k̲oo.éex' for Jim Marks (K̲uháanx') with the support of other Eagle moiety clans, especially the Wooshkeetaan and Kaagwaantaan. Jim Marks was known as a "Lingít tlein," a "big person," or leader of the Brown Bear House (Xóots Hít) of Hoonah. He had died approximately one year before. Although Jim Marks had not lived in Hoonah for years, it was appropriate that his younger brother host the ceremonial there. It was conducted in the Wolf House (G̲ooch Hít) of the Kaagwaantaan clan because the deceased and his brother Willie Marks, although they were both Chookaneidí, were also both grandchildren of Kaagwaantaan.

The memorial began about five p.m., with the arrival of the hosts and guests, and lasted until about five o'clock the following morning. The hosts were seated at the front of the house, by the door, facing the guests and the back of the house. The guests who delivered the speeches in this book were seated along the back wall, facing the hosts. This is the traditional position of honor, under the clan crest of the house. Jessie Dalton delivered her speech from the right rear corner.

Between the guest-speakers and the hosts the other guests were seated. All of the seating around the edges of the house and in the middle was on benches. The "orphans"—the children and family of the deceased—were seated at the front in the first rows. These were the children and in-laws of the deceased, and were of the same moiety as the guests and the opposite moiety of the hosts.

The "Sea Gull Ladies" (or "Tern Women" or "Sea Pigeon Women") who sang several songs were seated by the wall to the hosts' left. As noted earlier, the "Sea Gull Ladies" (K̲'eik̲'w Sháa) are women of the T'ak̲deintaan, and figure prominently in Hoonah ceremonial life. They take their name from one of their major clan crests, variously called tern, kittywake, sea pigeon, and sea gull in English. (See the glossary entry k̲'eik̲'w for an explanation of the Tlingit word and various English translations.) At many points in the ceremonial they imitate the sounds and flight of terns. Jessie Dalton is the designated Clan Mother

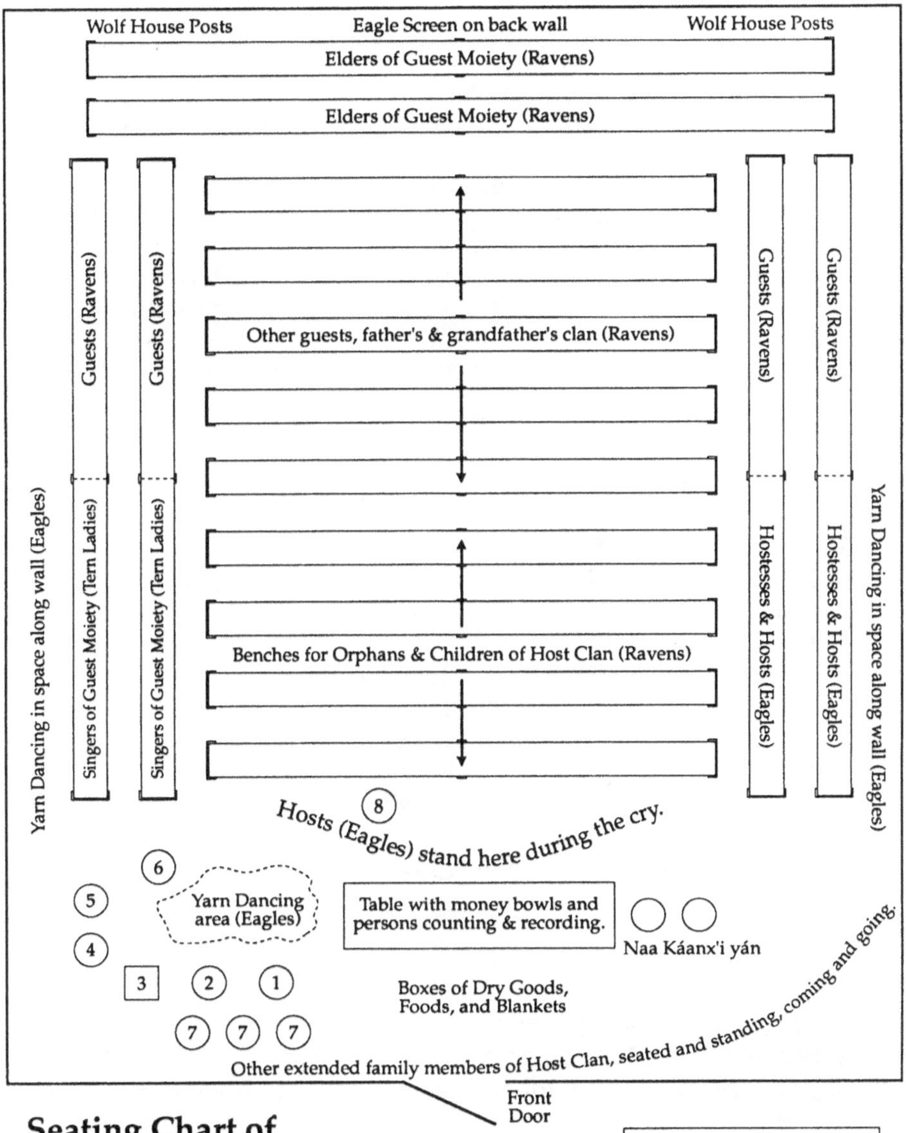

Seating Chart of Jim Marks Memorial in the Kaagwaantaan Wolf House

Figure 3. A similar arrangement was used in Kawdliyaayi Hít (House Lowered from the Sun) in Klukwan, setting for the speech by Thomas Young. This is the general relationship of hosts and guests in most memorials, although people are usually in motion and hosts may be seated at the other end of the table. In larger halls, chairs and even tables are used for guest seating.

Key

1. Host (Eagle)
2. Host's Daughter-in-Law
3. Stove
4. Widow (Raven)
5. Sister-in-Law (Eagle)
6. Drummer
7. Extended Family of Host
8. Song Leader (Eagle)

Opposite page: The Sea Gull Ladies, K̲'eik̲w Sháa, in front of the teachers' housing in Hoonah, prior to 1944. At the left stands Yuwáakw Eesh (Rainer McKinley) organizer of the group. Although now associated with the women of T'ak̲deintaan, the original group as photographed here includes some Raven women of L'uknax̲.ádi and Lukaax̲.ádi. Clan names are abbreviated: T = T'ak̲deintaan; L = Lukaax̲.ádi or Lukaax̲ Sháa; L' = L'uknax̲.ádi or L'uknax̲ Sháa. The English names of the houses are: Tax̲' Hít Taan, Snail House; Yéil Hít Taan, Raven House; Kaashaayi Hít Taan, Head House; T'ak̲dein Hít Taan, T'ak̲deintaan House; X̲'áakw Hít Taan, Sockeye House; Teet Hít Taan, Breaker House; Yéil Kudei Hít Taan, Raven Nest House. The editors thank Emma Marks, Mamie Williams and Katherine Mills for their help in identifying the women. Photo courtesy of Evalee Azar.

Top Row, *Left to Right*
1. Shaagí Tláa, Mrs. Lawrence, T, Tax̲' Hít Taan
2. K̲us.een, Jennie Marks, L, Yéil Hít Taan
3. Kaatyé Tláa, May Moy, T, Kaashaayi Hít Taan
4. Gunak̲áaaxwsayeidí, Mrs. Morgan, T, T'ak̲dein Hít Taan
5. Ms. Ridley (teacher), T
6. Xéetl'ee, Fanny McKinley, T, Teet Hít Taan
   (branch of X̲'áakw Hít Taan)
7. Yeidikáx̲, Mitchell Martin's mother, from Kake
8. Mrs. Ross, L'
9. X̲aawk'u Tláa (Aandeik), Jim Austin's grandmother, T,
   Yéil Kudéi Hít Taan
10. Tlék̲w Tsáayi, Mrs. Jim Young, L, X̲'áakw Hít Taan

Middle Row
1. K̲eiyákw, T, X̲'áakw Hít Taan
2. Lx̲éis, Mrs. Moses, T, Tax̲' Hít Taan
3. Shéix̲', Mrs. Charlie Bevins, T, X̲'áakw Hít Taan
4. Syaanjín, Mrs. Max Lindoff, T, Tax̲' Hít Taan
5. K̲eiyawjeewu.á, Wm. Johnson's mother, T, Yéil Kudéi Hít Taan
6. S'eistaan, Mrs. Harry Marvin, L'
7. Geesheix̲, Mrs. Karteedi, T, Tax̲' Hít Taan

Front Row
1. K̲aatuwdu.oo, Katherine Grant, T, Tax̲' Hít Taan
2. Tsax̲ Yádi, Helen Williams, T, X̲'áakw Hít Taan
3. Kawdusx̲á, Lilly Fawcett, T, Tax̲' Hít Taan

of the T'a<u>k</u>deintaan, and one of the major images in her speech is the tern.

People wearing the at.óow referred to in the speeches stood randomly among the guests in the center of the room. The only tables were at the front, on which the gifts, dry goods, and money to be distributed were assembled.

When the house was full, the hosts blackened their cheeks, signifying death and mourning. At the beginning of the memorial, the *Gaaw Wutaan,* or *"Taking Up the Drum,"* also called *<u>G</u>áax* or *"Cry"* Ceremony, was conducted by the Eagle hosts. It was performed by the matrilineal relatives assisting Willie Marks and by the biological family on the maternal side of the deceased. In the absence of biological kin, the closest to the biological kin participate.

The hosts' Cry for Jim Marks consisted of four songs, the last of which was the song in memory of Xwaayeená<u>k</u>, performed by Jim Marks before his death, recorded by John and Horace Marks, and played at this part of the ceremony on a tape recorder. The recording included his history of the song. We mention this because its use here was innovative; he sang the song before he died, with the request that it be played at his memorial as one of the four Cry songs.

There was singing with a drum, but no dancing at this point. Raven guest David Kadashan assisted the hosts by drumming on the Bear Drum of Jim Marks, and song master Seikdul<u>x</u>eitl' (David McKinley; Eagle; Wooshkeetaan) guided host Willie Marks and his co-hosts through the Cry. They sang the mourning songs, at the end of which the matrilineal family of the deceased and the widow of the deceased cried their last cry for <u>K</u>uhaanx'.

Upon completion of the Cry by the hosts, Matthew Lawrence formally requested that the floor be turned over to the guests. The ceremonial does not end without proper involvement of those of the opposite moiety who are formally designated to speak for the removal of grief. As described in section IV of this introduction, the ceremony performed by the guests that removes grief or crying from the bereaved hosting family and clan is called *L S'aatí Sháa <u>G</u>áa<u>x</u>í (the Widow's Cry)*. The grief is removed by guests who are the matrilineal relatives of the widow and who are also the father's clan of the deceased. Sometimes the ritual is also performed by the grandparent clan on the mother's father's side. Jim Marks, the deceased, was Eagle moiety, Chookaneidí, child of Lukaax̱.ádi, and grandchild of T'ak̲deintaan. His widow, Jenny Marks, was Lukaax̱.ádi, child of Kaagwaantaan, and grandchild of Shangukeidí. Thus, based on the rules of protocol, kinship and social structure, the responsibility fell to the Lukaax̱.ádi and T'ak̲deintaan, both of the Raven moiety. The ritual was performed by the Lukaax̱.ádi, who are the widow's clanspeople as well as the parents and grandparents of the deceased through the father's paternal line and by the T'ak̲deintaan, who are the grandparent clan of the deceased through the mother's paternal line. As Ravens, depending on their relationship, they had lost a father, a son, or a grandson. This cooperation reveals the strength of the extended family in Tlingit tradition.

Prior to making their speeches, the T'ak̲deintaan had clothed their younger clan members in at.óow and placed l s'aatí át in their hands. The speakers then address various aspects of the spiritual images depicted on the at.óow, including reference to the former owners, whose spirits also now accompany the at.óow. Central to the oratory, these objects include the following, which we have listed in the order of appearance in the text of Jessie Dalton's speech with line numbers in parentheses. Some of these had already been mentioned by David Kadashan, but Jessie gives the complete inventory. In conversational speech, some may have possessive suffixes that are not necessary when the names are used as titles of at.óow.

1. Shaatuk̲wáan Keidlí — Mountain Tribe's Dog (19): a wooden hat carved by Willie Marks representing a yéik or spirit image.

2. Geesh Daax̱ Woogoodi Yéil [K'oodás'] — Raven Who Went Down Along the Bull Kelp [Shirt] (27): a felt shirt, black appliqué on red, based on an image in the Raven Cycle; artist unknown. We understand this to be the same shirt referred to later in the speech (lines 82 and 87) as the shirt of Weihá.

3. Lyeedayéik X'óowu — Lyeedayéik's Robe (29): a button blanket, felt, in the older style with buttons around the edges, but with no image in beads or buttons on the blanket; application of such beaded or button designs seems to be of relatively recent origin in Tlingit tradition.

4. S'igeidi X'óow — Beaver Robe (32): a Chilkat robe with the image of a Beaver, belonging to L'utáḵl, (Jim Lee in English),

a T'akdeintaan man of Hoonah, Kaagwaantaan yádi, from Raven Nest House, who lived in Klukwan.

5. K'eik'w X'óow — The Tern Blanket (48): a beaded button blanket with the image of Terns from the rookery at Gaanaxáa; also identified as the blanket of Saayina.aat (46-47).

6. Gaanaxáa [X'óow] — Gaanaxáa [Blanket] (55): a button blanket with the beaded image commemorating the original village of the T'akdeintaan and the tern rookery; this is a copy of an older blanket.

7. Yeilkudei Hít X'óow — Raven Nest House Blanket (100): a beaded button blanket commemorating the Raven Nest House of the T'akdeintaan.

8. Yaakaayindul.át [X'óowu] — Yaakaayindul.át's Blanket (103): a button blanket, plain, without design.

9. Xíxch'i S'áaxw — The Frog Hat (151): a wooden hat from Taku with the image of a frog; carved by David Williams.

10. Kageet Kuyéik [S'áaxw] — The Loon Spirit [Hat] (196): a spirit design.

11. Gagaan L'axkeit — The Sun Mask (207-208): image of the sun.

12. Géelák'w Shakee.át — Small Mountain Pass Headdress (212): a carved dance frontlet, trimmed with ermine; named for a part of Tsalxáan, Mt. Fairweather. The same motif also appears on Tsalxáantu Sháawu S'áaxw — Mt. Fairweather Women Hat, a wooden hat carved by Willie Marks representing a yéik or spirit image. The headdress is mentioned by name, but it is unclear if the hat was also physically present in 1968, though it is almost always brought out.

Some of these T'akdeintaan at.óow are replicas carved by Jim Marks, Willie Marks, and their nephew David Williams after the originals were lost in 1944, when a fire destroyed most of Hoonah. As noted earlier, according to Tlingit tradition, a clan commissions individuals of the opposite moiety to execute its designs. This adds a special dimension to this particular ceremonial display of the at.óow, because the work of the deceased and host are called upon by the guests and owners to give comfort and strength to the artists who created them.

As noted above, the Widow's Cry in the memorial for Jim Marks consisted of six speeches (included in this book) and two songs, performed by the guests. While their clans-people were still wearing or holding these at.óow, the orators began. The

Yeilkudei Hít X'óow, the Raven Nest House Blanket being worn by guests during the Widow's Cry of the memorial for Willie Marks, Hoonah, October 1981. At the left rear Austin Hammond speaks. Jacob White (L'uknax̱.ádi) stands at right rear. Photo by R. Dauenhauer.

Opposite page: Tsalxáantu Sháawu S'áaxw, the Mt. Fairweather Women Hat, depicting the Tsalxáantu Sháawu, the Women inside Mt. Fairweather. The Tsalxáantu Sháawu spirit was a vision of the T'akdeintaan Shaman, Shkík. This is an important at.óow of the Hoonah T'akdeintaan, and is significant in oratory and ceremonial display. It was carved by Willie Marks. Photo by R. Dauenhauer.

Above: Men of the Raven moiety (primarily T'akdeintaan) wearing at.óow during the Widow's Cry of the memorial for Jim Marks, Hoonah, October 1968. One of the rare photographs available from this event, it shows the physical setting in which the at.óow were presented and became departure points for the speeches for the removal of grief by Jessie Dalton and her fellow orators. L to R: the Raven Shirt, Raven Nest Robe, Robe of Yaakaayindul.át (plain, with buttons) and Raven Who Went Down Along the Bull Kelp Shirt. Photo by Rosita Worl.

Below: William Johnson (R) speaking on the T'aḵdeintaan at.óow during the Widow's Cry of the memorial for Willie Marks, Hoonah, October 1981. L to R: David Williams, Jr. and Melvin Williams, who holds the shirt of Weihá, Géesh Daaḵ Woogoodi Yéil, the Raven Who Went Down Along the Bull Kelp Shirt. Behind William Johnson, partially obscured, are Nora Marks Dauenhauer and Elena Topacio. Photo by R. Dauenhauer.

Opposite page: Táx̱' Hít, the T'aḵdeintaan Snail House, Hoonah, was named after a dike built to hold back a rising river and save a house from flooding. The dike was built in the shape of an arrow point or > in front of the house. Later, when a new house was being built, the snail was adopted for the name of the house. Táax̱' means "snail" and "dike," and also the platform which runs around the central fire pit in a traditional house. The screen on the house front begins at the top with the Mt. Fairweather motif. The top figure is the part of the mountain known as G̱éelák'w, pictured with two ears and an animal figure for the mountain. The second group of figures depicts Raven and his crew

when he tricked the spring salmon into coming in. The side panels are Táx̲' Gáas', Snail Posts, with motifs of snails and floral designs depicting snails hanging on flowers. The house was built by the older K̲aajeesdu.een (not the younger John K. Smith) of the T'ak̲deintaan. The house in this picture is older than the one that was standing in the 1940's and destroyed in the Hoonah fire of 1944. The central screen on that house was bordered by snail posts added after this picture was taken. Although physically lost as a place of residence, the Snail House remains important in genealogy and in T'ak̲deintaan cultural history. Photo courtesy of Peter Corey, Sheldon Jackson Museum.

first speaker was Matthew Lawrence, a man of the T'aḵdeintaan, and of Taẋ' Hít (Snail House) who asked that his group of orators be given time to speak for the removal of grief. In so doing, Matthew Lawrence formally asked the hosts for time to conduct the L S'aatí Sháa G̱aaxí, the Widow's Cry, (customarily done by leaders of the grandparent or father's clan of the deceased). The second speaker was David Kadashan, also of the T'aḵdeintaan and the Snail House, who spoke and played a tape of two songs performed by his deceased maternal uncles: Xíxch'i S'áaxw Daasheeyí (the Frog Hat Song) and Shaa Tuḵwáan Keidlí S'áaxw Daasheeyí (Mountain Tribe's Dog Hat Song). This use of the tape recorder was also innovative.

The third speaker was William Johnson, T'aḵdeintaan, who also acted in the role of naa káani, the "emcee" or assistant to the hosts from the guest side. William Johnson mentioned that the Clan Mother Jessie Dalton would be making the main speech. Jessie, also T'aḵdeintaan and of the Raven Nest House (Yeilkudei Hít), followed him as the fourth speaker with her "keynote" speech. The fifth speaker was Austin Hammond, Lukaax̱.ádi and stepson of the deceased. The final speaker was Matthew Lawrence, who opened the set of speeches, and who spoke again in closing it.

As explained above, the speeches of the Widow's Cry are offered to remove the sorrow and grief of those left behind. Members of the opposite moiety, especially the paternal grandparents, do this by reminding those in grief that, just as a living father, paternal aunt, or paternal grandfather would be concerned when a child, niece, nephew, or grandchild is in tears, the same emotions apply to spirits after death. The spirits of paternal ancestors come to console the grieving survivors. This is accomplished through oratory and the use of at.óow.

The speeches begin by confirming the kinship relations, and then turn to the objects being worn by the clan's grandchildren, clarifying in turn the relationship of the owner of the at.óow to the speaker and the hosts. This is the setting of the "Speeches for the Removal of Grief" delivered during the Widow's Cry of the memorial for Jim Marks.

We will now analyze Jessie Dalton's speech in detail as an example of "at.óow in action." One way of studying and understanding her speech is to view it in terms of an underlying structure of oppositions or contrasts operating on many levels at the same time. It is important to remember that these contrasts are not in conflict, but are separate parts of a larger whole, and are ultimately complementary. The basic division of Tlingit society into two moieties or halves is one example; the contrast of the living and the departed is another. Through the gift of human speech, Jessie Dalton will attempt to close or bridge these distances, and bring things together in harmony poetically, socially, and spiritually. She opens her speech to members of the opposite moiety with a rhetorical question about life and death, beginning with the harsh reality that has torn them apart, yet has also brought them together for the events of the evening:

> Does death take pity on us?

and she answers her question in line 5:

> It doesn't take pity on us either.

Her use of the word "either" (tsú in Tlingit) is reinforced by her clan's bringing out for display the at.óow of their own departed relatives. A literal translation of the opening line is "Does it take pity on us?" The context is death, and we make this more explicit in English translation. (The original Tlingit texts are not included in this introduction, but may be consulted in the main body of the book.) We understand Jessie to be referring to all the things that have happened, including the blow that death has struck. The purpose of her speech is to help the community come to grips with death, and to help resolve the grief brought by death. She is aware of the enormity of her task, and at one point, referring to the list of names of all the departed and their at.óow, she asks:

> Can I reach the end?
>
> . . . .
>
> Can I reach the end? (123, 126)

She is also aware of the limited ability of mortals and metaphor to resolve such things, and expresses skepticism and inadequacy in line 172:

> not that it can heal you.

Nevertheless, she undertakes the steps of healing, the ritual imitation of her ancestors ("only imitating them"—178) even though her actions may be imperfect and incomplete. She begins by mentioning her departed ancestors as represented by their younger living descendants who are wearing or holding the at.óow. In so doing, the speaker begins a twofold linking, or bringing together, or mediation of opposites: the living and the departed are brought together, and together they face the grieving hosts of the opposite moiety. She tells of her own personal loss by invoking her departed relatives, the former owners of the at.óow, and she calls upon them to join her and her living clanspeople in helping to remove the grief of their hosts.

All of these at.óow capsulize the history of the T'ak̲deintaan people and others in the community to whom they are related. They anchor the people in place (G̲aanax̲áa, G̲éelákw, Mt. Fairweather), recall physical and spiritual events that happened on the land (the Tern Blanket, the Mt. People's Dog Hat, etc.), and remember the ancestors to whom things happened and to whom the at.óow belonged. By focusing on an at.óow while addressing the people present, the speaker metaphorically conveys her listeners to the place the at.óow represents and gathers them among the ancestors and spirits who are there. The community is thus made complete: its members are together. Jessie Dalton does this when she focuses on the Gaanax̲áa Blanket, which she turns to first. Through this blanket, physically present in the room, she will eventually bring all of the living people present, as well as the spirits of the human departed, and various other disembodied spirit powers, to the rookery at G̲aanax̲áa. This at.óow, (the blanket and the design on it) becomes the place to which the speaker gathers people, both physically and spiritually. In all of this, we are reminded of the serious word play in English: the connection of the words "heal," "whole," and "holy," and of the words "re-member" and "remember."

Jessie begins to gather the community and to mediate between the spiritual and the physical by remembering the spirits of the departed—the original owners of the at.óow—and recalling them to the present time and place by means of the at.óow. At first, she refers to their disembodied voices which were heard on the tape recording played by David Kadashan in conjunction with his speech.

> Which is why you hear their voices like this. (7)

She then gives motivation for the spirits of the former owners of the at.óow to appear, a reason for her departed relatives to come out. As explained above, they come to the natural world in response to the tears of their children, grandchildren and in-laws:

Lest your tears fall without honor
that flowed from your faces.
For them
they have all come out this moment,
your fathers
have all come out.
They are still present
is how I feel
about my grandparents. (9-17)

At this point in her speech, Jessie introduces the various at.óow. Some of these are simply mentioned and alluded to without further comment, while others become the subject of poetic elaboration.

Having assembled the living and the departed of her own clan, Jessie now turns to the living hosts, the members of the opposite moiety, and summons them on her metaphorical journey to G̱aanax̱áa.

A person who is feeling like you
would be brought by canoe,
yes,
to your fathers' point,
G̱aanax̱áa.
That is when
the name would be called out, it is said,
of the person who is feeling grief. (50-57)

At this point, Jessie begins to call out the names of those present who are feeling grief. This is a catalog or inventory of approximately 60 lines in the speech, in which she identifies the hosts by name and kinship term. Each person responds to the orator with the word "áawé!" which is almost impossible to translate, but is something like "amen," or "that's it." It is more of a function or process word used by the hosts to acknowledge and accept the recognition of the speaker. The Tlingit term for this is x̱'ayawulishee, meaning "a verbal agreement at the correct moment."

Now that she has brought the grieving hosts to G̱aanaxáa, the site of an ancestral village of the T'aḵdeintaan, and has laid the groundwork by introducing each of the at.óow, she describes each at.óow as showing its face at G̱aanaxáa. She continues to introduce her relatives and the at.óow "as if they are revealing their faces" or "as if they have come out for you to see." The entire community is now metaphorically assembled at G̱aanaxáa —the grieving hosts and their departed, the guests and their departed, and their at.óow. In addition to recalling or evoking the spirits of the human ancestors who were original or former owners of the at.óow, the speaker also calls to the present time and place the spirits the at.óow depict. At this point Jessie now begins her most elaborate mediation.

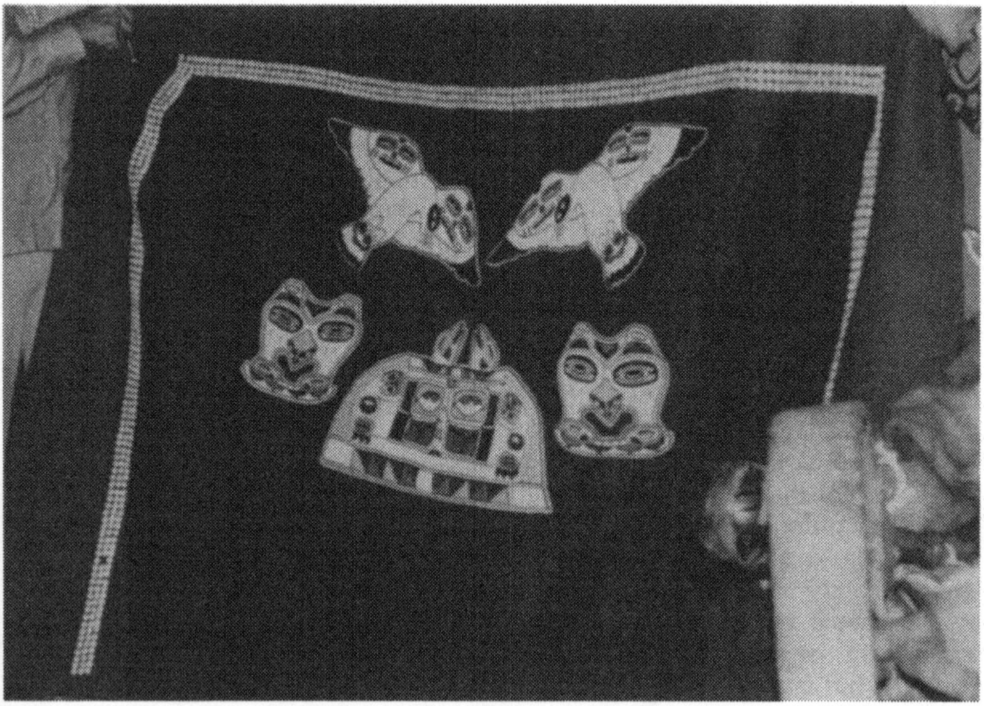

Ḵ'eiḵ'w X'óow, the Tern Blanket, an important at.óow of the T'aḵdeintaan and a central image in Jessie Dalton's speech of 1968, photographed here during the memorial for Willie Marks, Hoonah, October 1981. Photo by R. Dauenhauer.

Such mediation between the spirit world and the human world is handled through metaphor and simile. Metaphorically, the blanket representing G̱aanaxáa becomes the place it represents. In other places, there is simile, especially involving animation and personification of at.óow. As elder Walter Soboleff emphasizes, the Tlingit world is anthropomorphic, and the at.óow often become as people. Jessie Dalton's speech includes four examples of the animation of at.óow: The Mountain Tribe's Dog Hat, The Tern Blanket, The Frog Hat, and The Sun Mask.

Richard Bean wearing Xíxch'i S'áaxw, the Frog Hat, during the memorial for Willie Marks, Hoonah, October 1981. An important at.óow of the T'aḵdeintaan, the hat is a major image in Jessie Dalton's speech of 1968. It was carved by David Williams. Photo by R. Dauenhauer.

The poetic transformations of these at.óow are varied, but can be reduced to a general formula:

1. The at.óow is literally presented to the audience.
2. Simile or metaphor is employed.
3. Animation or personification takes place as the orator extends the simile or metaphor and uses the at.óow to remove grief.
4. There is restatement of the simile or return to the physical at.óow.

This is the basic structural pattern. In actual performance, the parts can be inverted or repeated, and the pattern may be augmented. The following examples show not only the basic pattern, but how complicated the variations can be. Describing the Mountain Tribe's Dog Hat, Jessie Dalton begins with physical and material reality, and moves through simile to spiritual reality.

> Here someone stands wearing one,
> this Mountain Tribe's Dog.
> It is just as if
> it's barking for your pain is how
> I'm thinking about it. (18-21)

This image is compound: she is referring not only to the visual image of the hat, but to one of the songs played by David Kadashan as well.

Likewise, she describes the Terns, in one of the most beautiful, moving, and memorable passages of her speech. She begins by calling attention of those present to the Tern Blanket, an at.óow of the Hoonah T'ak̲deintaan, of the Raven Nest House, formerly the blanket of Saayina.aat. She then develops the image of the blanket poetically, returning to the image of the terns at the rookery.

In this passage, Jessie Dalton alludes to down, an important symbol of peace in Tlingit and other Northwest Coast Tlingit cultures. In the words of Walter Soboleff, "Down is a symbol of peace, love, and welcome—a great feeling, yet landing so lightly" (personal communication, 1989). Down is placed in ermine headdresses to symbolize peace when dancers entertain a visitor, shaking down from the headdress. During peace dances, in which a special person is ritually designated as "hostage" or "peacemaker," down is put on the peacemaker's head before the final ceremony. He or she in turn places down on those invited to dance. Down was also used by shamans. In Jessie's speech, the paternal aunts represented in the at.óow use their down as a gesture of welcome to the spirit world. Down is a gentle image, and in the speech by Jessie Dalton the images of down leave the grieving hosts in spiritual peace after the ritual.

> The Tern Robe . . . .
>
> . . . .
>
> These Terns I haven't yet explained,
> yes,
> these Terns.
> Your fathers' sisters would fly
> out over the person who is feeling grief.
> Then
> they would let their down fall
> like snow
> over the person who is feeling grief.
> That's when their down
> isn't felt.
> That's when
> I feel it's as if your fathers' sisters are flying
> back to their nests
> with your grief. (48; 127-140)

She describes the Frog Hat in a similar way.

> The Frog Hat . . . .
>
> . . . .
>
> During the warm season
> this father of yours
> would come out.
> That's when
> I feel it's as if your father's hat
> has come out for your grief.
> Yes,
> your grandparent's hat.
> With your grief
> he will burrow down,
> with it,
> with your grief he will burrow down. (151; 160-171)

Alluding to the speech by David Kadashan, she also describes the Sun Mask.

> And here,
> yes,

is the one this brother of mine explained a while ago:
how that tree rolled for a while on the waves.
Then when it drifted to shore,
the sun would put its rays on it.
Yes.
It would dry its grief
to the core.
At this moment this sun is coming out over you,
    my grandparents'
mask.
At this moment
my hope is that your grief
be like it's drying to your core. (198-211)

Shaatukwáan Keidlí, the Mountain Tribe's Dog Hat, an important at.óow of the T'akdeintaan, displayed during the memorial for Willie Marks, Hoonah, October 1981. This is a replica carved by Willie Marks. The original was burned in the Hoonah fire of 1944. This hat is an important image in the set of speeches from 1968. The Shaatukwáan Keidlí spirit was a vision of the T'akdeintaan Shaman, Shkík. Photo by R. Dauenhauer.

In this pattern, the at.óow is animated, and grief is removed through some kind of appropriate action: the dog barks, the terns gather grief into their down and fly away, the frogs burrow back into hibernation, and the sun evaporates grief. The world of nature is brought to life in human terms in the world of Tlingit at.óow and iconography.

We should emphasize here that this use of simile and metaphor is not limited to this speech by Jessie Dalton in Hoonah twenty years ago, but is basic to formal Tlingit oratory for the removal of grief. Some twenty years later, in October 1988, speaking as a guest during the Widow's Cry section of a L'uknax̱.ádi memorial in Juneau, Anna Katzeek, an Eagle woman of the Shangukeidí, spoke about the blanket she was wearing depicting the Sun Children motif. She expressed her wish that her blanket would be like the sun for the grieving hosts, and evaporate their grief.

But to return to the memorial for Jim Marks, Jessie has recalled and recreated the traditional land and ancestors of the T'akdeintaan, who lived at G̱aanax̱áa, at the base of G̱éelák'w and Mt. Fairweather. The deceased ancestors who were the former owners of the at.óow are now spiritually present, along with their living descendants who are the stewards today. They are all there—even the sun.

The concluding image of Jessie Dalton's speech mediates and binds on several levels at once, because it offers resolution to all of the themes in her speech, and provides resolution for those to whom it is directed. It is a striking finale:

> G̱éelák'w Headdress,
> yes.
> Your fathers' sisters
> would reveal their faces from it,
> from G̱éelák'w,
> yes. (212-217)

The headdress representing the mountain has become the mountain. The headdress is an at.óow of the T'akdeintaan, as is the mountain itself (Tsalx̱aan, Mt. Fairweather) and the part of it known as G̱éelák'w (Small Mountain Pass). This is also the name of a T'akdeintaan clan house. From within the mountain the spirits of the deceased female side of the clan, especially those associated with the tern crest, look out, or show their faces. Among these would be the spirits of Lyeedayeik and

Yaakaayindul.at, both of whom are the former owners of blankets mentioned in the speech, and also the spirit of Saayina.aat, the former owner of the tern blanket central to Jessie Dalton's speech. Referring to the G̱éelák'w Headdress, Jessie concludes:

> That's the one there now. Someone is standing
> there with it,
> this headdress,
> my grandfather's headdress. (218-220)

She has transformed the headdress into the mountain, and now it is again turned into the headdress, but only after verifying that the spirits of the T'aḵdeintaan women reside there, and only after confirming that the terns have flown away with the grief of the hosts. When the headdress is poetically returned to its present form, and the ceremony returns to the physical and temporal present, the grief has been removed.

At first impression, Jessie Dalton's conclusion may seem abrupt. But Willie Marks' (Kéet Yaanaayí's) response indicates that it is not. According to Tlingit protocol, for each oration there must be adequate response. The speech concludes not with the orator, but with those to whom her speech is addressed; the grieving host who is feasting the memory of his older brother signifies that the oratory has functioned. Throughout the speech, there is also ongoing audience response, indicating audience understanding and approval. The speech has been delivered by the orator and received by her audience, in all its complexity, understood and appreciated in form and function by Willie Marks, who completes it on behalf of the hosts with a simple Gunalchéesh, "Thank you."

As noted above, Austin Hammond and Matthew Lawrence follow Jessie Dalton with shorter speeches that bring the ritual to a close. At the end of these speeches the hosts also respond with expressions of understanding, approval, and gratitude. Again, the hosts have the final word in the oratory of the guests, and again it is "thank you."

Jessie Dalton's goal as an orator is to restore peace of mind to Willie Marks and his grieving co-hosts. She works toward this by binding, or uniting on at least three levels: rhetorical, spiritual, and social. The rhetorical level is the way her words are put together grammatically and poetically, especially using simile and metaphor, which are devices to link unlike things.

Rhetorical Level

images of material world	images of the spiritual world
literal images	change by simile and metaphor

Spiritual Level

physical at.óow	spirits of former owners
physical at.óow	spirits represented
tape recording	voices of deceased
living participants	departed participants
descendants	ancestors
Hoonah	G̱aanax̱áa
duplicate at.óow	burned originals

Social Level

orator	audience
guests	hosts
Raven Moiety	Eagle Moiety
Raven Moiety Clans such as T'aḵdeintaan	Eagle Moiety Clans such as Chookaneidí
older generations	younger generations

The spiritual level is what the words say, the way in which the speaker invokes spiritual reality, including traditional spirits and the personal spirits of the departed and brings them ritually to a gathering of the living. The social level is what the words do, how they affect the community of the living.

One might view the speech in terms of many sets of interacting pairs or oppositions operating on the social, spiritual, and rhetorical levels. The orator is bringing unlike but complementary things together on three levels at once.

Her first level of mediation is on the level of grammar and involves poetic and rhetorical style. As described above, the devices of simile and metaphor are used to compare unlike things, and link them together through human imagination. In simile the distinction between the two differing objects is retained, but in metaphor the two unlike things are joined, and one thing is made into another. Personification and animation are types of metaphor, but in Tlingit oratory they often operate within a larger context of extended simile—a metaphor within a simile. Whether simile or metaphor or a combination, the rhetorical devices act to initiate the removal of grief. Once the words and images are put together as a speech, the speech begins to combine unlike things at other levels. The speech creates mediation on the spiritual level, linking the world of the living with the spirit world. The words of spiritual mediation lead to mediation on the social level, combining the "opposite" moieties and "opposite" clans, and this social mediation reaffirms the

The Sun Mask and other T'aḵdeintaan at.óow being displayed during the Widow's Cry in the memorial for Jim Marks, Hoonah, October 1968, at which they became particularly important images in the oratory of David Kadashan and Jessie Dalton. Jacob White holds the Sun Mask; the Beaver Robe is worn by Alice Hinchman, and the Frog Hat by Ms. Hanlon, grandchildren of T'aḵdeintaan. G̱éelák'w Headdress is at the far right. Photo by Rosita Worl.

oneness and solidarity of the Tlingit people. There is spiritual and social bonding—communion as well as communication.

At the same time as her oratory functions for the removal of grief, the speaker strengthens kinship ties between the two clans of the opposite moieties, the T'akdeintaan and the Chookaneidí, and by connecting her speech with that of Austin Hammond of the Lukaax̱.ádi, she also strengthens her clan and personal relationship with another clan of the same moiety.

At the same time as she ritually mediates between the living and the dead, the speaker of the older generation also directs much of her attention to the younger generation of the living. By involving them, she encourages the descendants of her clan to continue tradition. Jessie is instructing the younger generation and helping them become responsible stewards by publicly acclaiming the deceased owners of the at.óow the younger people are wearing and of which they will eventually become caretakers. She gives a verbal history of the at.óow and also provides a model for ceremonial performance. In this way, the speaker also becomes a mediator between the generations, between the grandparents and the grandchildren.

This section has been in part a conceptual and theoretical analysis of how words are put together in Tlingit oratory, and why. But it should come as no surprise that the rhetorical and anthropological theory corroborate what Amy Marvin expressed in her telling of the "Glacier Bay History," when, explaining the basic concept of feasting in Tlingit ceremonials, she says that only if food is given and eaten with an opposite clan can it go to the relative who is mourned.

> Only when we give to the opposite clan . . .
> does it become a balm for our spirits.

This is the same mediation we see in the oratory: the binding of Raven and Eagle clans, the binding of the physical and the spiritual, the binding of the living and the dead. Jessie Dalton and the other orators do this with words, and their words follow the same pattern of distribution of food and gifts described by elder Amy Marvin. Words, too, go to the opposite moiety; words, too, are a gift. They are given with care because, once spoken, they cannot be taken back. Words are shared, and through the words, and through the shared revelation and display of treasured at.óow, the power of the at.óow is also shared as a priceless gift to the opposite moiety. As we take care of the living, we also take care of the departed. If we take care of the living, the living will take care of us. If we take care of the departed, the departed will take care of us.

At some point, the question may arise, "Are the spirits considered to be really present, or is all of this only symbolic?" Such a question is rooted in western dualism, which goes further than contrasting categories of material and spiritual and posits an almost unbridgeable gulf between them. It parallels the question of "real presence" in the Christian sacrament of communion. It may be helpful here to quote the Orthodox Christian theologian Fr. Alexander Schmemann, who, when asked about the Orthodox position on the question of "real presence," responded with the counter question, "Is there such a thing as an unreal presence?" Many spiritual observers have commented that a great cultural tragedy of contemporary Western civilization is the rise of its dualistic thinking and corresponding loss of vision (and faith) in poetry and metaphor. Tlingit oratory is exciting because it operates artistically and poetically at the boundaries of three worlds, and three levels of reality: the material, the spiritual, and the verbal. It demonstrates the power of human vision and speech to bind and heal.

VIII. TREATMENT OF SPIRITS IN TLINGIT ORATORY

In the previous section, we focused on one set of speeches featured in this book to illustrate how simile and metaphor are used in Tlingit oratory. We now focus[12] on another set of speeches, delivered at an elders conference banquet, to illustrate the attitude of Tlingit tradition bearers toward the images of spirits invoked in oratory. We have selected each set of speeches to illustrate specific features of Tlingit oratory, but we emphasize that both sets use simile and metaphor, and both address a range of spirits. Figures of speech also abound in the oratory at the elders conference; images of spirits are also plentiful in the speeches at the Jim Marks memorial. Both groups of speeches achieve social and spiritual bonding. The feature distinguishing the two sets is that the speakers at the memorial for Jim Marks make no spoken or explicit reference to "balance," answering speech for speech and song for song, whereas it is the central theme articulated in the speeches from the elders conference.

We believe the reason for this is the context. The speeches for the removal of grief were delivered as part of a traditional ceremonial: in their speeches during the memorial for Jim Marks in 1968, the elders exemplified the act of balancing. They were putting theory into practice through ritual action. In other words, they were doing it without talking about it. The guests were balancing the hosts. But the speeches delivered by the guests at the Sealaska Elders Conference in 1980 were in a very different setting: it was innovative and secular, and the elders had no firm idea of how many in the audience really understood what was happening. Therefore, the elders made things explicit that would normally have been tacitly assumed. Some of the most expert tradition bearers in Tlingit culture used the situation as an opportunity to teach in ways they had never instructed before. For this reason, the set of speeches from the elders conference offers a fortuitous example of the articulation of traditional values combined with actual practice.

On May 29, 1980, Sealaska Corporation (an acronym for Southeast Alaska), one of the regional corporations constituted under the Alaska Native Claims Settlement Act of 1971 (ANCSA, popularly called the "Land Claims Act"), sponsored an elders conference in Sitka, with the theme "Sealaska Elders Speak to the Future." The purpose of the conference was to provide an opportunity for elders to share their concerns over the current situation and fate of the languages and cultures of Southeast Alaska, and to suggest what actions might be taken to prevent the ongoing loss. Tlingit and Haida elders attended. An eventual outcome of the conference was the formation of Sealaska Heritage Foundation, a nonprofit corporation given the mandate to work for the preservation of the language, culture, and heritage of the Native people of Southeast Alaska. An immediate outcome was a group of speeches, delivered in a modern physical and social setting, but with a traditional spiritual context and style. Ten of these speeches are included in this book.

The conference was held in the Shee Atika Lodge in Sitka, a new hotel constructed and owned by Shee Atika Corporation, the ANCSA local corporation for Sitka. As a welcoming gesture, the G̱ajaa Héen Dancers of the Sitka Native Education Program gave

Travelling troupe of the G̱ajaa Héen Dancers, on the stage of the Sitka ANB Hall, mid 1970's. L to R, top: Marla Kitka Marshall, Janice Williams, Nancy Eddy, Judy Brady Lindoff, Alice Kitka, Ethel Williams, Ruth Farquhar (front) Cynthia Williams (rear) Dorothy Lord, Janice Johnson (front) Laura Joseph Castillo, Sharon Frank, Marlene Thomas, Lillian Nielsen Young. Bottom: Donna Lang Howard (drumming), Ethel Makinen, Tim McGraw, Larry Garrity, Mike Spoon, Maria Thiemeyer, Charlie Joseph, Isabella Brady.
Photo courtesy of the Sitka *Daily Sentinal*.

a performance of Tlingit singing and dancing following the conference banquet. K̲aal.átk', Charlie Joseph, one of the most knowledgeable elders of Sitka, the teacher and leader of the group, narrated his students' program in a powerful and dignified manner.

In his opening speech, Charlie Joseph elaborated on the clan ownership of the songs, the villages where they were composed, and the composers' relationships to the students and the audience. One of his most moving statements describes the value traditionally placed on grandchildren: "We cherish them. Even those things we treasure, we used to offer to them." Charlie honored this tradition with his life, and in the work of his later years, especially his teaching of the young people. To his fellow elders at the banquet he explained in detail the grandchildren's rights to use grandparents' songs or "the things they used to say."

In 1980, the concept of a community-based dance group composed of members from a variety of clans was relatively new to all of the elders, but an innovation in which most of them would eventually become involved. Until recently, most songs and dances were performed only in traditional ceremonial settings (such as the memorial for Jim Marks) and by members of a single clan that also owned the songs and dances. The new problem was in establishing the right of the larger community-based group, made up of members of many clans, to use collectively the songs and dances of various clans, because of the right of individuals within the group to use them separately.

Charlie Joseph also set a precedent by including yéik (shaman spirit) songs in his program. Ordinarily these songs would only be sung on solemn and highly formal ceremonial occasions, such as a memorial for the deceased, where they would be part of the ceremonial and would be responded to in a traditional manner by the guests. They would not be sung in the context of a secular public performance. As described earlier in this introduction, the new context created new problems, and these were addressed directly by the elders who responded to Charlie Joseph and the young dancers.

Following the last song, the elders in the audience responded to Charlie's presentation, as the protocol of the Tlingit and Haida cultures dictates and provides. Even though the setting was nominally new and secular, the elders slowly transformed the structure to meet their spiritual needs. The elders were concerned for the youth who had sung the yéik (spirit) songs, because these songs are the most delicate and powerful in Tlingit tradition, and must be treated accordingly. It is important that the songs and the spirits they invoke be matched and "balanced" by the guests. The elders began to respond to the songs of the hosts—the young dancers—with their own songs, spirits, and words to ensure the safety of the dancers and conference participants, that they would be cleansed of any unattended spirits lingering in the air. The elders cleansed by way of oratory, alluding to spirits of their own.

As noted above, Charlie Joseph spoke first, introducing and explaining the songs and dances, which the young dancers then presented. This was followed by a set of speeches in return, with George Davis speaking first and assuming the role of master of ceremonies for the sequence of speakers. In these speeches, the elders expressed their concern that, in order to prevent harm, the spirits first evoked by the songs and dances of the hosts must be matched or balanced with spirits of the guests. The host speaker, Charlie Joseph, was of the Eagle moiety and Kaagwaantaan clan, and many of the spirit songs performed by the young people were from clans of the Eagle moiety (Kaagwaantaan and Chookaneidí). Three of the major speakers among the guests (George Davis, William Johnson, and Charlie Jim) were of Raven moiety clans (Deisheetaan and T'ak̲deintaan), so that their speeches and the images with which they responded also followed the traditional pattern of reciprocity between the moieties: Ravens and Eagles "balance each other." Additional spirits were addressed more indirectly through reference to grandparent clans, according to protocol.

The elders were concerned lest the spirits evoked by the young people wander aimlessly, floating in space unanswered, unattended. Jessie Dalton also alludes to this situation in her lines "It is like the saying 'They are only imitating them, lest they grope aimlessly'" (178-179). "They" refers to the spirits wandering unanswered. Such a situation would be dangerous, creating a potential for accidents or harm, possibly even sickness and death. The Tlingit word for this concept is jinaháa, a term used by George Jim in line 68 of his speech. Catharine McClellan comments (personal communication, 1989) that the neighboring Southern Tuchone are also "very specific about the spiritual power of words if used by those physically as well as cognitively too young."

To avoid this situation, various responses are effective. As a basic gesture, a non-verbal response, people of the opposite moiety can extend their hands when spirit songs are being sung. This act creates a physical as well as spiritual support or "brace," for the spirits, meeting and balancing spirits coming from the other side. Beyond this, people can respond with words, in the form of songs, or in this case, speeches alluding to images and evoking spirits of their own clans. There is a range of images one can summon for bracing or balance, and at least three kinds of evocation are used in these speeches: calling of spirits of departed ancestors, calling of shaman or other disembodied spirits (yéik), and calling or displaying various kinds of physical at.óow and, by extension, the range of spirits they depict.

A few lines from the opening speech by Charlie Joseph, in which he introduces the dancers and describes the program, will serve to summarize his presentation.

It may seem as if they have combined all
these songs their grandparents
left for them,
yes,
when they use them.
Even from long ago
we have placed our grandchildren
high above ourselves.
Yes.
We cherish them.
Even those things we treasure
we used to offer up to them,
to those who are our grandchildren.
That is why now
we made these songs their vision.
If they're not right, or if they go against
your feelings, please forgive them.
— (Charlie Joseph 44-59)

This is Charlie Joseph's argument for teaching the young and passing the songs on to them as individuals and as a group. But to do this makes the elders vulnerable. They must part with things that are precious and must take the risk of sharing them with youth, but this is the tradition and is well documented in history and myth. Raven stories describe grandparents sharing, and there are many examples in the clan histories of old people going under the glaciers to explore for the young, or going on board trading ships when they first came. For the elders, there is always the risk of losing their own lives and treasures, but this is part of the risk and process of transmission of culture.

The problem in the modern world is that traditional society is much more fragmented. Tlingit people no longer live in a world that is totally or even predominantly Tlingit. The community is increasingly multi-ethnic. Many of the elders speak very limited English, and their grandchildren now usually speak no Tlingit at all. The generation gap is extreme; this increases the sense of alienation and risk felt by the elders, who fear that the traditions may be abused or desecrated. Also, as the speeches indicate, the elders fear that the learners risk bringing danger upon themselves and others by not knowing how to use the songs and their accompanying spirits correctly. Charlie Joseph points out how the group has combined all the songs left to various individuals by their grandparents. He closes the passage by asking for understanding and forgiveness from his fellow elders if any mistakes are made. Walter Soboleff (personal communication, 1989) describes this passage as an example of "Tlingit courtesy at its best."

The spirits of the ancestors come alive through the performance of the young dancers. Charlie Joseph explains:

> It seems as if the spirit helpers
> of my grandparents
> are joining in this,
> and now they will be heard from
> their grandchildren's lips.
> — (Charlie Joseph 96-99)

Two kinds of spirits will be heard from the grandchildren's lips: the spirits of the human departed, and the spirits (shageinyaa) that revealed themselves to the ancestors long ago, and that have become at.óow. This is understood and appreciated by elders in the audience. For example, William Johnson replies:

> The at.óow
> of my maternal grandfathers:
> here this
> G̱aanax̱áa,

it is as if
these children
right now
have come out in view from the place I came from.
We're losing
our culture,
we're losing it.
How very proud we are
that you have brought them out
for us to see, my father's maternal nephew.
— (William Johnson 41-54)

William Johnson is clarifying that through their performance, the dancers have made present (re-presented) the spiritual homeland of the T'aḵdeintaan (the place called G̱aanax̱áa) as well as the spirits of his ancestors. These are not shaman spirits (yéik) but are the spirits of the human departed and spirits of place. He also expresses a sense of cultural and spiritual continuity: it is as if the children dancing have just stepped into this world from the spiritual homeland of his clan.

There is comfort and delight in this experience, but there is danger as well. Through their song and dance, the youth have not only evoked the pleasant spirits of the departed and the spirits of place, but they have also summoned forth the ambiguous spirits, the spirits called yéik. Most of these spirits do not seem to be intrinsically evil, although some may be, but, as with handling fire and loaded firearms, caution and skill must be employed. Certainly their spiritual presence is a cause for anxiety for the elders, so we must conclude that the spirits are not generically benevolent, and are probably ambiguous at best. George Davis expresses this concern and sets a theme for his fellow guests in his response to Charlie Joseph.

Of all the songs they sang
there are two among them
that are sensitive
and cannot be sung without a reply
before people take leave.
That's the way
our ancestors lived it.
— (George Davis 1:32-38))

George Davis is following Tlingit tradition here, and is also setting the stage for a series of responses, in which the guests

deliver speeches to the hosts. The pattern is one of reciprocity and healing—in this case "preventive medicine." Especially in this case, if tradition and proper protocol are observed, the danger of using spirit (yéik) songs can be neutralized.
Elders often use the term "respect" as a synonym for such protocol, as when Charlie Jim says,

> We who are Tlingit,
> our respect for each other has emerged.
> — (Charlie Jim 112-13)

Reciprocity is an important part of this respect, and William Johnson reiterates the concern raised by George Davis.

> This song
> cannot just be left lingering in the air.
> . . . . .
> The song that you sang
> that belongs to our fathers,
> this spirit
> cannot echo in the air.
> . . . . .
> In reply to it, a song is usually lifted.
> — (William Johnson 22-23; 31-35)

William Johnson continues, comparing the reciprocity to an image of clasping hands:

> With this grandfather of ours
> . . . . .
> they are clasping hands
> and with the song of the Eagle Hat
> they are clasping one another's hands.
> — (William Johnson 36-43)

Throughout William Johnson's delivery, Charlie Joseph responds with expressions of gratitude and agreement, thanking the speaker for his words. A major concern of the elders is that so few people seem to understand the importance of this reciprocity and respect; but without the balance and interaction, there is both immediate spiritual danger and the chronic danger that the culture will disintegrate. Balancing represents and reinforces the social structure; not balancing releases the spirits of social disintegration. All of the speeches delivered in response to Charlie Joseph's speech and the dancers' presentation express these dangers. Here we focus not on the problem of loss of culture, certainly a major theme in itself in the speeches of the elders, but on those images dealing directly with neutralizing the danger of unattended spirits. The speeches present a range of methods according to which people can respond.

As noted above, the first of these methods is simply to raise one's hand during the singing of spirit songs by the opposite moiety. Charlie Jim describes this:

> People would raise their hands to it, it is said,
> toward it,
> . . . .
> so that it does not cause harm.
> — (Charlie Jim 85-88)

A few lines later, he recapitulates his intention:

> That it doesn't cause harm
> is why
> I'm thinking this.
> — (Charlie Jim 105-107)

The raising of hands is described in detail by George Jim. The point has already been made by William Johnson and Charlie Jim, but George Jim considers it so important that he also discusses it, repeating it not only in Tlingit, but also in English for extra emphasis and clarity.

> The hosts would stand up in the back when the guests sang their spirit songs.
> Spirit.
> That's a spirit song.
> And the entire opposite moiety
> would stand
> with their hands raised
> to ward off the spirit
> with the heel of the hand.
> — (George Jim 72-80)

The Tlingit text of these lines, in which George Jim supplies his own translation, is:

> Yéik.
> Spirit.
> That's a spirit song.
> And the opposite tribe on that side,
> they have to stand up
> and hold your hands up. . . .
> — (George Jim 73-78, Tlingit)

In addition to raising one's hand in response to spirit songs being sung by the opposite moiety, a person may deliver a speech in return, in which specific spirits and other at.óow of his or her clan are called upon for support. The following spirits are called upon or addressed in the speeches by Charlie Jim and George Jim:

K'óox K̲uyéik	Marten Spirit	(Charlie Jim, 95)
Kéidladi K̲uyéik	Sea Gull Spirit	(Charlie Jim, 96)
L'ook K̲uyéik	Coho Spirit	(George Jim, 31)
G̲ooch K̲uyéik	Wolf Spirit	(George Jim, 42)

David McKinley and Mary Johnson raise their hands in response to spirit songs being sung by the guests during the memorial for Jim Marks, Hoonah, October 1968. Note soot of mourning on the cheeks. David McKinley (Wooshkeetaan) was song leader for the mourning songs. Photo by Rosita Worl.

Like William Johnson, Charlie Jim imagines these spirits clasping hands with the spirits called through song by the G̱ajaa Héen Dancers. George Jim does not simply mention the Wolf Spirit, but he develops the image poetically. Such language is one of the characteristics and delights of Tlingit oratory, by now familiar to readers of this introduction.

We are cautious
when the spirits
are used.
In order that
it does not cause harm
because they danced to this spirit song,
this Wolf Spirit
is lapping it up from among them,
he is lapping up potential trouble
    from among them
that things do not cause harm for them
and for those who are sitting here.
— (George Jim 60-70)

The Tlingit terms used in this passage are yéik (spirit; shaman spirit) yéik x̱'asheeyí (spirit song) and G̱ooch Ḵuyéik (Wolf Spirit). This use of the Wolf Spirit by George Jim is interesting because he is calling on it, not as one of his own (he is Eagle and Wooshkeetaan), but as one of his grandfather's spirits, an at.óow of the Kaagwaantaan. In a sense, he is not calling on a new spirit to accompany one already invoked, but rather he is elaborating on the presentation of the dancers, balancing not so much with a new spirit as with new words about the already existing. He describes in poetic detail how he imagines the Wolf Spirit taking pity on the children, and taking action to remove danger and keep them from harm.

In addition to calling upon the spirits (yéik), whether of one's own clan or another (such as a grandparent clan) to which one has some genealogical connection, an orator can call upon the spirits of his or her departed relatives.

Those who left me behind,
yes, now it's as if
I will lead them out is how it seems to me,
these fathers of mine.

. . . . .

I don't want to have it lie unattended.
— (George Jim 26-29; 32)

The total context of this passage is too complicated to discuss here. Simply stated, the speaker is calling on the spirits of his departed relatives on his father's side. He imagines them coming out now, to balance or attend the appropriate spirit, in this case the Coho Spirit, L'ook K̲uyéik.

Finally, in addition to shaman spirits (yéik) and spirits of their human ancestors, speakers can use a variety of other at.óow to balance the oratory and songs of the opposite moiety. Charlie Jim introduces the Raven Robe (Yéil X'óow). He does not have it physically present, as he would at a traditional ceremonial, but simply to mention its existence is enough. Oratory and poetry do the rest.

I now have in my care the Raven Robe.
It is as if I will use it as a brace,
I will use it as a brace to the song
so that it doesn't cause harm.
— (Charlie Jim 108-11)

His lines embody the pattern that is now familiar: the mention of at.óow and, through simile (as here) or metaphor, employing it for the support of the opposite moiety. A similar passage by George Jim also summarizes the situation:

I am expressing to you
my appreciation
yes, for the songs of my fathers
that I heard from your lips.
Yes,
that they do not linger in the air
I am raising my grandparent's spirit in return
and these that I see draped on their shoulders.
This Dogfish Robe that was made for me
is the one I'm using to brace the Frog Robe.
I'm bracing it,
yes.
— (George Jim 115-26)

The passage affords an excellent illustration of a person replying to a host, thanking him for the songs, expressing concern for the safety of the singers and the entire assembly, and calling on his own spirits and at.óow to balance or accompany those already present: in the words of the speaker, to "brace" the other spirits and thereby brace the singers and the host. The Tlingit text is interesting. We have supplied the word "songs" in English translation. The literal Tlingit is a<u>x</u> éesh hás aayí, "the thing (or things) of my fathers." The Tlingit of line 121 is a<u>x</u> léelk'w du yéigi, "my grandfather's shaman spirit." This is the possessive form of yéik. The robes are X'átgu X'óow and Xíxch'i X'óow for Dogfish Robe and Frog Robe. The word implies a felt robe or blanket, such as a button blanket, as opposed to a woven robe or blanket, called naaxein in Tlingit.

Two other at.óow are also used by the orators: clan houses and land. As noted above, the elders conference and banquet were held in the Shee Atika Lodge, a new hotel constructed and owned by Shee Atika Corporation, the ANCSA corporation for Sitka. One of the dining areas of the hotel is named after <u>K</u>udatan Kahídi, the Salmon Box, alluding to the story of how Raven brought the salmon run to shore, making it accessible to the average person as a continuing source of food. To "balance" the spiritual presence of the house they are in, namely the Shee Atika Hotel, seen here as a community house, Charlie Jim calls up images of the traditional clan houses of his own community.

And also this building,
the house we're sitting inside of,
Shee Atika,
yes,
the houses of my older brothers,
Deishú House,
Raven House,
so that it doesn't cause harm for them
it's as if they are sitting against it
    is what becomes of them in my hands,
yes,
that it becomes good fortune in our hands.
— (Charlie Jim 118-28)

Again, the speaker wishes all the best for his hosts, and uses his own at.óow to work for their enrichment and well being. The pattern is traditional even though the setting is contemporary. Another example of the use of at.óow to support the host of the opposite moiety spiritually is the mention of land. In lines 41-54 (cited earlier in a different context) William Johnson mentions <u>G</u>aana<u>x</u>áa, the traditional and spiritual homeland and village of the T'a<u>k</u>deintaan.

Our discussion here is limited to "primary images," in which the various speakers use language to achieve specific spiritual and social goals or explain certain spiritual and social concepts. But their speeches also contain many additional references to traditional practice and belief regarding shamans. For example, George Jim (line 43) refers to the practice of fasting and chanting to prepare for and call on shaman spirits. (There is, however, no guarantee that the spirits will come and reveal themselves; the spirits seem to choose the shaman, not the other way around. The individual contributes to the process by attempting to keep in a state of spiritual readiness.) Charlie Jim (lines 175-180, 211 ff., 215, 219) George Jim (lines 29-31) and William Johnson (lines 36-40) make further references to shamans and other shaman spirits. These are not fully developed in their speeches, but are a kind of oral literary allusion, which the traditionally educated listener will identify and understand. These are references to stories about shamans and shaman spirits, and events in the lives of shamans. These are additional levels of complexity not covered in this introduction, but which we hope to address in future work.

IX. VOCABULARY OF THE TLINGIT SPIRIT WORLD

We find the most helpful method of sorting out the abstractions of the Tlingit spiritual world to be that of sorting out its vocabulary. We began by limiting ourselves to the terms used in the oratory itself, but have added other terms where suggested by patterns or images. For example, the Tlingit word for the spirit of a deceased human being never appears in the texts, although references to the spiritual presence of the deceased abound. We also begin this section with a general disclaimer: we are attempting to work from the Tlingit concepts outward, sorting out hierarchies, distinctive features, and mutually exclusive categories. There are many problems to deal with, not the least of which is the problem of definitions and synonyms in English as well as Tlingit. For example, we are still not prepared to address the definition of "spirit." We leave much of this to be refined at a later stage of the work, and present for now the following as work in progress and tentative, as we make our way from exegesis and explication of traditional texts presented in this book to analysis of their underlying world view.

We have benefited greatly here from dialogue with colleagues, especially Walter Soboleff, who helped us sort out some of the Tlingit world view, and Soterios Mousalimas, whose systematic look at southern Alaskan shamanism and whose categories of analysis in neighboring traditions (Mousalimas 1987, 1988) have suggested concepts for us to examine in Tlingit. Comments by Lydia Black, Sergei Kan, and Catharine McClellan on this part of the manuscript were extremely helpful in advancing it to this stage. As noted above, what follows should be taken as work in progress.

People

íx̱t' — shaman. In Tlingit tradition a man or woman with the gift of healing, telepathy, and prophecy, sometimes called "Indian doctor" in English. The shaman would characteristically go on a quest to possess yéik, a supernatural power that would become his or her vision. This vision, in addition to being a supernatural power, would also be a song. Although it is dangerous to generalize, it is safe to say that ideally and in theory, the Tlingit íx̱t' was a positive figure, who attended to the physical and spiritual well-being of the Tlingit people. A good definition of the ideal form of "what is a shaman?" is offered by I. M. Lewis (in Hoppál 1984:9):

> A shaman is an inspired prophet and healer, a charismatic religious figure, with the power to control the spirits, usually by incarnating them. If spirits speak through him, he is also likely to have the capacity to engage in mystical flight and other "out-of-body experiences."

Simply stated, shamanism in Tlingit tradition was ideally devoted to physical and spiritual healing, and to other positive forces in the community, such as telepathy. Tlingit shamanism in theory and practice, and in its spiritual range, was explicitly opposed to the forces and powers of sorcery and witchcraft, although the two are frequently confused by the general public. But there are indications that, in practice, the ix̱t' was also a source of anxiety because of the tremendous power in his or her hands—spiritual as well as economic and socio-political power. There is little doubt that shamans could harm deliberately or by accident, though this is not the cultural ideal. Observations and conclusions by Mousalimas (1988b:328) about southern Alaskan shamans seem to apply to Tlingit as well.

> As a class, shamans were morally ambiguous: a shaman might act benevolently or malevolently. However, their primary social tasks (those tasks most frequently associated with them) were beneficial. Those tasks were: healer, hunting facilitator, and seer. Shamans acted through extraordinary contacts with spirits which the shamans influenced and by which the shamans were influenced. As for the spirits, while some were psychological phenomena, others were intelligent beings. In this sense, regarding spirits, southern Alaskan cosmology was like Russian cosmology, and both were like early Christian cosmology.

Shamans have been popularly stereotyped as negative figures, especially by Protestant missionaries; but there is also the danger of stereotyping them as benevolent. The truth probably lies in between, and is inseparable from the personality of each shaman. Until more lives of individual shamans can be researched, much of the discussion of Tlingit shamans will remain in the realm of generality at best, and stereotype at worst.

Shamanism as a religion is no longer viable in Southeast Alaska. There are no practicing shamans of whom we know, although there were some as recently as the 1930s. All of the orators included here are members of various Christian churches, and none should be construed as being a shaman. It is fair to say, however, that their speeches illustrate and present a coherent, traditional world view characterized by evocation of traditional spirits who, in turn, operate in traditional relationships for social and spiritual healing.[13]

Nakws'aatí — witch, sorcerer. Literally, "master of medicine," more loosely, "medicine man." The nakws'aatí is traditionally a negative and evil figure, the opposite of íx̱t'. We are advised by colleagues that the terms witch, sorcerer, and medicine man are not synonymous in the professional literature, but we are not prepared to address this level of complexity at present. See also de Laguna (1987) for additional terms regarding negative spirits. Many writers avoid using the term "medicine man" because whites in nineteenth century Alaska used the term to refer to íx̲t' (shaman).

K̲aa shagóon kanéegi — a person who fortells the future with cards or a crystal ball.

K̲ulnuk s'aatí — one who heals by feeling. It could be for a baby that is in a wrong position in the womb, for setting broken bones, or even drawing out bad blood or pus from infections. This was a woman's profession, but patients included both men and women.

Spirits

Yéik — spix̲it; "shaman" spix̲it. This is the word for a disembodied spirit or supernatural power that reveals itself to a shaman and comes to the shaman as a helper. Sometimes we have used the English term "shaman" spirit, but we are not totally satisfied with the term. "Spirit" is probably the safest term; perhaps "yéik" is the best. The term also refers to songs sung by the spirits. As stated above, it is our understanding that most of these yéik are not intrinsically evil, though some may be; certainly all are powerful and ambiguous at best, and not generically benevolent. Hence, the anxiety expressed in all the speeches studied here. This word is not used for the spirit of an animal or departed human, or for the spirit of other natural objects. It is, however, the basic stem for other words pertaining to different kinds of spirits. The word appears in both possessed and unpossessed forms:

yú yéik	that spirit	(George Jim 80)
has du yéigi	their spirit	(Charlie Jim 93)

K̲uyéik — The spirit of some thing, usually of certain animals. This prefixed term derives from yéik and is used in conjunction with animal names, for example:

G̲ooch K̲uyéik	Wolf Spirit	(George Jim 42)
K'óox K̲uyéik	Marten Spirit	(Charlie Jim 95)
Kéidladi K̲uyéik	Sea Gull Spirit	(Charlie Jim 96)
L'ook K̲uyéik	Coho Spirit	(George Jim 31)

Yakwg̲ahéiyagu — The spirit of a deceased person; the supernatural self that separates from the physical body at death. The etymology is "spirit that moves around." Yakw- is a contracted form of yéik. We have not yet noticed the word in a traditional text, but in speech it seems to be obligatorily possessed, i.e., it always appears with a possessive pronoun. This word is also used for Holy Spirit in translation of Christian scripture: Loolitóogu ḵáa yakwg̱ahéiyagu. This is also a term for the spirit of a human ancestor, and a general term for "ghost."

Ḵáa Kinaa Yéigi — a personal spirit helper, like a guardian angel, in contrast to shageinyaa, which could be personal or a group guardian spirit.

S'aagi Ḵáawu — the spirit of a dead person. Plural: s'aagi ḵáax'u.

Yahaayí — Image; the image of a spirit; a reflection in a mirror; a photograph; the incarnation of someone. The *Tlingit Noun Dictionary* (Naish and Story 1976) glosses this as "soul," but we are not sure of this meaning. The meanings of the word seem to have something to do with coming to life again, with a separate but parallel or reflected life. The word appears to be obligatorily possessed:

íx̱t' du éet góot du yahaayí (Charlie Joseph 219)
when her image came to the shaman

McClellan (1975:334 ff.) mentions the difficulty in defining this term for Inland Tlingit. Also, see McClellan (1975) for many additional terms not covered here.

Léikwayi — strength; the power of the spirits. Naish and Story (1976) gloss this as "fighting spirit."

Shageinyaa — guardian; personal spirit helper; also the spirit helper of an entire clan or group, to which the individual also has access (Charlie Joseph, line 98). The word is also used frequently in the film *Haa Shagóon* (Kawagey 1981). Literally, it means "spirit above." Some elders indicate that it may be immediately above one's head; i.e., not necessarily far above in a distant spiritual realm. It is unclear to us whether any hierarchy is involved, but it does not seem to us at present that shageinyaa implies a spirit power superior to any other spirit power.

Ḵwáani — This word is used as a combining form for the various communities of spirits in nature, or inhabiting spiritual realms. For example:

aas ḵwáani — spirit(s) of the trees; people of the trees
teet ḵwáani — spirits (or people) in the waves; the sea
Daḵaa kinaa ḵwáani — the spirits above Inian Island.

The word has also been used by de Laguna (1972) and McClellan (1975) as a general English term for such spirits. We are not satisfied with this as an English term, but we have no alternative to offer. The problem is that the word is bound to others, and is a possessed form, meaning something like "spirits of." The distinctive feature seems to be the sense of community of spirits. The word derives from ḵwáan, meaning "people of," but which is always used in combination with a place name. For example: Xunaḵwáan — Hoonah ḵwáan — the people of Hoonah.

This human form is not possessed, following the Tlingit grammatical rules for absence of possessive suffixes with human body parts and kinship terms. In contrast, the term aas ḵwáani has the possessive suffix -i, indicating a nonhuman or disembodied state.

The Lands of the Dead

In Tlingit tradition, the spirits of the deceased reside in one of three places. Although these are not mentioned by name in the speeches in this book, everything Tlingit people traditionally did at a memorial was with and for the spirits in Haayee, Keewa.áa, and Daḵanḵú. In contemporary memorials, the term Daḵanḵú is most commonly used; Haayee and Keewa.áa are rarely heard.

Haayee — "Under Us." The resting place of the drowned. This may also appear as Haayee Aaní, the Land Under Us.

Keewa.áa — "Place Above." The resting place of those who have died by violence or accident, including slain warriors and those who have been murdered. When the northern lights come out, they are sometimes referred to as Keewaḵáawu—the people of Keewa.áa. People who are mentally retarded are sometimes referred to as Keewaḵáawu yahaayí, the image or spirit of a person of Keewa.áa.

Daḵ.aanḵú (or Daḵanḵú) — "Land Far Back," or "Land Beyond the Forest," or "Land in the Forest." The resting place of those who die of natural causes.

S'aagi Ḵáawu Aaní — Land of the Dead; a general term, synonymous with Daḵanḵú. The etymology is unclear. When a person dies, he or she is transformed into a s'aagi ḵáawu and enters s'aagi ḵáawu aaní, where he or she remains and participates in a supernatural, spiritual culture. The social structure, kinship systems, and traditions adhered to in the supernatural world parallel the world of the living. The families of the living are there, and the interrelationships or behavior of a family are the same. In other words, in the Tlingit world view, the total family and community consists not only of the physically living but also of the departed, who are spiritually alive. A traditional cemetery with its grave houses replicates the village of the living.

X. CONCLUSION: THE PAST, PRESENT, AND FUTURE OF TLINGIT ORATORY

We conclude this introduction on the form and function of Tlingit oratory with a review of its documented history, some observations on Tlingit public speaking in the context of other Native American traditions, and with some final comments on the viability of Tlingit oratory.

The Paper Trail: The Written Record of Tlingit Oratory

Oratory is a major genre in Tlingit and other Native American oral literature, but documentation of Tlingit oratory in the writings of nineteenth century Russian and American observers has been spotty at best. Still, some written records exist as examples of oratory from the past, and it is interesting to compare them to contemporary speeches recorded in performance. We are especially grateful to Richard Pierce and Lydia Black for their help in locating some of these nineteenth-century accounts. The first written record of Tlingit oratory—and among the fullest—is a speech delivered by a Tlingit man shortly before his execution on 11 July 1802 on board the *Globe* out of Boston under the command of Captain William Cunningham following the first Battle of Sitka, in which the Tlingits attacked and destroyed the Russian settlement. The full history of the episode remains incomplete and must be put together from various sources, all of them fascinating but beyond the scope of this book. It will be handled in greater detail in our forthcoming volume in this series on the Battles of Sitka, 1802 and 1804, from the Tlingit, Russian, and Anglo-American points of view.

The highlights, as they pertain to the written history of Tlingit oratory, are as follows. William Sturgis, sailing from Boston at the age of 17, arrived on the Northwest coast in 1799. He kept a journal, which includes a word list of English, Haida and Tlingit. In an appendix to his journal for the year 1802 (Jackman 1978), Sturgis describes in very general terms the Tlingit destruction of the Russian settlement at Old Sitka and the hanging of a Tlingit presumed to be one of the attackers. As far as we know, Sturgis was not an eye-witness to these events; his knowledge was second hand, and we are uncertain how he came by the information. At present writing, it appears that Sturgis, in command of the *Caroline*, may have met Captain Cunningham in Canton in September 1802. Sturgis deplores the hanging of the Tlingit captive, calling it "repugnant" and "a transaction which attaches a very considerable share of blame to some of my countrymen" (Jackman 1978:123). He claims that the Tlingit leaders, who had approached the ship in peace and with a desire to trade, were fired upon and that one of the leaders was seized and executed. He shares the Tlingit point of view that the Tlingits were not hostile to the Americans, but only to the Russians, and that there was no reason for the Americans to take reprisals against the Tlingits. At any rate, it appears that one Tlingit was in fact hanged by American captains. According to William Sturgis, he gave the following speech before his execution. We have changed the use of dashes in the original to modern punctuation, but otherwise give the speech as presented by Sturgis, noting puzzling phrases:

> What crime have we been guilty of to justify this wanton attack on our liberty and lives? Have we in any instance violated the harmony hitherto existing between us? Did we not on a late occasion nicely discriminate between our commercial friends and our invaders and cruel oppressors? When we sacrificed the one to our just resentment, the other we protected, supported, and on the first opportunity, restored to their countrymen. And is this the proper return for such conduct? You say 'tis to revenge the massacre of the Russians and release the prisoners that this attack is made. The Americans have heretofore declared that the Russians were a distinct Nation with whom they had no closer connections than with us. If that is the case, by what right do you interfere in the quarrel

> betwixt us? When the Russians took numbers of our Tribe and carried them into captivity, no one offered to rescue them. Your countryment [sic], tis true, reprobated the measure and insinuated that we ought to take every precaution to prevent the Russians from establishing themselves among us. This led us, rather, to view you as friends from whom we might expect assistance, that [sic] as enemies who would oppose us. If you persist in your present conduct, all friendly intercourse with us is at an end, for who will ever dare place any confidence in people who have so grossly abused, as you have in the present instance? (Jackman 1978:125).

Sturgis notes that "this speech had no effect and the man was executed." The text of the speech as presented by Sturgis raises many questions about how he acquired it. As noted above, our research to date indicates that Sturgis was not present, but is reporting second hand. Sturgis gives only an English text. Who was the translator? If the speech is legitimate (and not made up or modified by Sturgis or someone else along the way), then it must have been heard and transmitted by the orator's fellow Tlingit leaders, who were later released, or by a bilingual Aleut survivor, some of whom had been rescued by Captain Henry Barber on the *Unicorn* and may have been present. The speech may have passed into oral tradition. It could have been retold and passed on to Sturgis, in the course of his linguistic fieldwork, by a Tlingit, an Aleut, or even by one of the American sailors who had jumped ship or had been put ashore and had gone to live with the Tlingits rather than the Russians. (There were, in fact, Americans sailors from Boston on both sides of the 1802 Battle of Sitka.) Schuhmacher (1979) suggests that the prisoner was taken from Barber's *Unicorn* to the *Globe*, commanded by Captain Cunningham, for the hanging, in which case there were probably no Tlingit or Aleut witnesses present, but only the Americans who had been living with the Tlingits for several years. If Sturgis and Cunningham were both in Canton in autumn 1802, Sturgis may have learned about the hanging there. We can only speculate about the chain of delivery. In style the English translation is clearly more Sturgis and late eighteenth or early nineteenth century English rhetoric than it is Tlingit.

No accounts of Tlingit oratory appeared in the decades following that of Sturgis, but Yuri Lisianski (1812, 1947), describing the events of 1804 and 1805, makes frequent reference to discussions and negotiations with the Tlingit; he notes what appear to him as seemingly endless sessions of singing and dancing, but he includes no samples of formal speech making as such. Baron Friedrich Heinrich von Kittlitz, on an expedition commanded by F. P. Litke [Lütke], arrived in Sitka in June 1827 and cites (1987:144) brief remarks by "one of the chiefs to a Russian governor." In the 1830s Veniaminov (1984:437) refers to greetings conveyed by the Stikine people and mentions many informal conversations and discussions, but cites no formal speeches although his journals may contain such. In 1862, however, Heinrich Holmberg, a Finn travelling in Russian America in 1850 and 1851, describes Tlingit oratory in somewhat more detail. In a paper delivered 3 February 1862 (Holmberg 1985:69-70) he paraphrases a short "speech of a Tlingit chief" negotiating with and granting Russians permission to look for coal in the "vicinity of Khutznov" [Xootsnoowú: Angoon —eds.]. The speaker is not identified.

The first known detailed description of Tlingit oratory in Russian sources seems to be in the letters of Captain P. N. Golovin (1863: Vol. 5, 101-82; Vol. 6, 275-340) describing events of December 1860. Despite Golovin's attitude toward the Tlingits, parts of his account are worth repeating here. We are grateful to Lydia Black for pointing out and translating these passages. Golovin first refers to oratory when he and Active State Councillor Sergei Kostlivtsev arrive in Sitka in December 1860. The leader of the Sitka Tlingits, so recognized by the Russians, whose Christian name was Mikhail, arrives to greet the Russians who find him a comical figure, "overdressed," baptized, but not a speaker of Russian. A description of the costume, apparently an early nineteenth-century naval uniform or variation thereof, including a navy officer's sword, follows. Through the interpreter, the dignitaries inform Toion Mikhail that he and all of the Indians can come to them with any business. Golovin writes:

> He responded that he is happy about our arrival, that he will transmit our words to the Indians, and that they shall consider if they have any requests, as it is not

> proper to bother such important persons with stupid speeches (Golovin 1863:179-180; 1983:82-83).

Golovin's second description of oratory is from mid-December 1860:

> Just recently we were notified that the Tlingit toions or elders desire to see us. We set a date, this past Wednesday, December 14, at 11 o'clock in the morning, and about thirty toions appeared at the club. In the hall, chairs were set out for them, in a single row; on the opposite side near the other wall, on a rug, were placed three velvet chairs for Kostlivtsev, myself and Furuhjelm [the governor —eds.]. On this occasion the Tlingit were in their festive costumes; i.e., the Russian Toion Mikhail in the jacket of a navy skipper, the three Tlingit amanats in blue dinner jackets and pantaloons with a red seam stripe. The rest of the toions had, over their shirts [tunics], festive blankets, blue in color, with red edgings all around and decorated with silver pieces of small size, which formed a sort of trim /galoon. The costumes were completed with boots or slippers, a luxury the Tlingit permit themselves but rarely, on special occasions. They wear no headgear, as their hair keeps them warm enough: thick, long, black as tar. All sat in silence awaiting our entrance, with elbows on their knees and their chins in their hands. Some looked very picturesque in their costumes, so cleverly draped in the blankets: bronzed faces, shining coal-dark eyes, wide shoulders and muscular limbs—all witnessed to their energy and strength. We came in and sat in the armchairs.
>
> The toions raised their heads, but did not stand. This is not their custom. Through the interpreter, it was declared that we came to converse with them, in accordance with their wish, and that if they had anything to say, they should do so, not all at once, but each one in turn; we are listening. The toions nodded, without changing their postures. The silence continued for several minutes. Each deemed it unseemly to begin too soon. Finally, one old toion raised his head, folded his arms, and, with appropriate emphasis and intonation, delivered the following speech.

> "Russians and those Tlingit who are christened believe in God and Jesus Christ who are in Heaven. . . . When the weather continues foul too long, they pray and ask God to send them good weather. And they pray for a day, sometimes, or two and three, and finally God hears their prayer and sends them good weather. We are not christened, but we also believe in God who is in Heaven and we pray to God, too. And we prayed not a day or two, but several days, and God heard our prayer and permitted us to meet you, and thus the sun has risen for us and good weather came, as if we cannot see the Liege Lord himself, the powerful and mighty one, but we can see you who were sent by our Liege Lord to meet us, to converse with us, and we are joyful and thank God. I have spoken."
>
> The rest of the toions nodded their heads in silence to express their approval. Some were smacking their lips in approval. After a brief silence we answered that we are glad to meet them. (Golovin 1863:282-84; 1983:95-97)

This speech is interesting because it illustrates the basic structure of Tlingit oratory (now familiar to readers) adapted to a new context. The speaker begins by establishing the kinship connection, here through God, Orthodoxy, and citizenship. Any person who was baptized was recognized as a child of God and citizen of the Empire. He then presents a central image, the bad weather, and develops his comparison: as God sends the sun, a brilliant light but less than God, the Emperor has sent these representatives. The speaker concludes with expressions of joy and gratitude. This is the same pattern as can be observed in traditional Tlingit oratory recorded in performance today. Likewise, the pattern between the speeches appears to be the same. We omit here the response by Kostlivtsev and Golovin to the speech and continue with Golovin's account of the next Tlingit speech, in which the speaker alludes to the Battles of Sitka of 1802 and 1804 and the subsequent peace. It is unclear whether this is the same leader or a different man speaking, but in either case the oratory sustains the level of the previous speech, and offers resolution.

> Again, after several minutes of silence, one of the toions responded. "There was a time when the Russians,

> having settled in our land, offended us, shed our blood, and we took vengeance, blood for blood, as is our custom handed down from our forefathers. But the Russians began to establish friendship with us and we began to be friends with the Russians and now we live in peace. True, there are from time to time quarrels; when wine makes heads hot, they quarrel, they fight among themselves, and make peace again, and all is well. If we are offended, we petition, but we do not execute vengeance ourselves for the offense. Thus, we live in peace and we shall live in peace in the future, because this is good."
>
> Afterwards, some of the toions presented to us written certificates issued to them by various chief managers to the effect that they are devoted to the Russian [cause] and have given us various services. The Tlingit treasure such certificates and they pass from father to son (Golovin 1863:284; 1983:97).

Golovin may be in error in his last assumption; the certificates probably passed from maternal uncle to sister's son, following conventional patterns of transmission of clan property.

In 1898 a set of speeches enters the record in U.S. Government documents. Ted Hinckley (1970) offers a retrieval of this moving Tlingit oratory in his article *"The Canoe Rocks—We Do Not Know What Will Become of Us": The Complete Transcript of a Meeting Between Governor John Green Brady of Alaska and a Group of Tlingit Chiefs, Juneau, December 14, 1898.* Hinckley's work is based on archival documents, primarily the transcription of the English translation at the meeting, and is a good example of what can be done with the "paper trail" of Native American oratory. We disagree with some of Hinckley's analysis and interpretation, but he is due great credit for calling these speeches to the attention of the reading public. The texts are too long to include here, but we will describe them briefly. We direct interested readers to Hinckley (1970) or directly to his sources in the National Archives (1898).[14]

The meeting took place in the government school in Juneau, with George Kostrometinoff as translator. The first speaker was Chief Kah-du-shan from Wrangell. He protested the taking of land and petitioned for the return of creeks and hunting grounds. (His Tlingit name in modern spelling is K̲aadasháan; it is unclear if he is Lukaax̱.ádi, or if the name was being used as a surname, regardless of clan. We have not attempted to transliterate the names of most of the other speakers because they are not intelligible.) The second speaker was Chief Johnson, Yash-noosh, of Juneau, Chief of the Takou [sic] tribe. He repeated the first speaker's theme, and focussed on love and friendship. The third speaker was Chief Koogh-see [K'oox Sée?] from Hoonah, who also agreed with the others, emphasizing the impact of the disruption of hunting. He presented a well argued speech, commenting that Lituya Bay had been closed to them, and that if whites take the land, they should pay for it. The fourth speaker, Kah-ea-tchiss of Hoonah, described a medal given to his ancestors by the Russians, and produced a document dated July 23, 1840. He stressed his desire to be at peace, but emphasized the need for payment for land. He described the depletion of game at Lituya Bay. The fifth speaker, Chief Shoo-we-kah [Shuyeeká?] from Juneau described the need for payment. He is the only one who used figures of speech, and Hinckley's title derives from his most striking comparision: "We are like a certain man in a canoe. The canoe rocks; we do not know what will become of us" (1970:278). A second passage is unclear: "I have been in the dark. Very dark now. Give me light...so that I can see" (1970:279). Chief Ah-na-tlash from Taku [probably Aanyaalaháash] spoke sixth and complained that American treatment of the Tlingits was worse than that of the Russians. Charley, of Juneau, spoke seventh and complained about the Treadwell mine claiming streams on Douglas Island. The eighth and final speaker, Jack Williams of Juneau, using Fred Moore as translator, described the loss of hunting grounds and requested a reserved area or reservation for Indians.

As noted above, there is little "poetic language" in this oratory. Few figures of speech are used. The speeches are direct. They are well argued, well-balanced, and well-paced. The speakers are eloquent and moving in their unanimous concern with land. Although never articulated directly, land as at.óow is the cultural concept underlying the entire set of speeches. But Governor Brady missed this point. In his reply to the Tlingit leaders he argued, illustrating his speech with various charts and diagrams, that the Tlingits had "wrong notions of how much land they own" (1970:285-286). Brady essentially denied the problem. He reminded the Tlingits of how bad they were, of what poor workers they were, and of how well off they were under the Americans as compared with the Russians. Brady offered them a choice: "to be put on an island and not abandon your old customs," or "be citizens of the United States and have their protection;"—to be on an island with "agents over them to keep them straight" or to "obey white men's laws; have all the privileges that he has" (1970:286). Following Governor Brady, a Mr. Frank Grygla addressed the Tlingits, telling them they are "almost equal to the white men," but must "decide whether you want to be American citizens or want to live in your old customs" (1970:289).

The speeches documented in "The Canoe Rocks" are similar to other Native American oratory of the nineteenth century in their concern for cultural and economic survival in the face of increasing encroachments of European Americans upon Indian land. "The Canoe Rocks" is a very eloquent and powerful presentation, but unfortunately the speeches fell on deaf ears. Despite Hinckley's assertion that "in truth, Alaska's Natives never had a better friend" (1970:267), Governor Brady goes down in history as particularly unsympathetic regarding Tlingit land use and possession. Contemporary documents (Oleksa 1987:322-26; Kan 1985:132-36; Kan 1986b) indicate that Brady personally seized Tlingit land and directed the building of a road through the center of the Tlingit burial grounds in Sitka, with the result that some of the streets of Sitka are paved, literally, with Tlingit bones. In 1897 ten Tlingit Orthodox chiefs of Sitka petitioned the president of the United States regarding this and other abuses, and in the same year seventy Orthodox citizens of Sitka petitioned the Imperial Russian ambassador to Washington for protection. The pattern of exploitation and usurpation objected to by the Tlingit elders in their 1898 meeting with Brady are but one example of patterns of seizure of Native American land and resources that characterized the westward expansion of the United States—patterns of behavior repeatedly protested in Native American oratory.

Swanton (1970*b*:372-89) offers some examples of Tlingit oratory, but all of it is ultimately speculative because the speeches were never actually given, but are explanations of what might be said in a speech. They are framed with such phrases as "He will perhaps speak as follows," or "might rise and speak as follows," or "so the speaker begins, perhaps thus." The samples include some very nice images based on clan crests and show the interaction of the moieties. The oratory in Swanton is authentic, in that it comes from the lips of orators telling Swanton what would, could, or might be said in a given situation, but unlike the oratory in the present volume or the "paper trail," the speeches in Swanton were not recorded "in performance."

Tlingit and Other Native American Oratory

Although individual speeches such as (Nez Perce) Chief Joseph's "Surrender Speech" have become widely known and anthologized, and although oratory has received some attention in popular anthologies such as Astrov (1945; 1962), Vanderwerth (1971), Bierhorst (1971), and others, Native American oratory has not been studied in detail as much as other genres such as narrative and song. What follows is a bit academic, but it is important because only two other Native American oratory traditions have been described to date.

In what Donald Bahr (in press) appropriately calls "the rather uncrowded field of Native North American public speaking scholarship," the studies of Iroquois tradition by Chafe (1961), Bierhorst (1974), and Foster (1974a,1974b) stand out on the one hand, and Bahr's (1975) and Underhill's (1979) Pima and Papago research on the other (1979). For comparative purposes, the most interesting and important are Underhill (1979) and Foster (1974a). Before turning to these in some detail, we will survey the others.

In the published studies and collections of Native American oratory, the closest comparison to Tlingit seems to be the Iroquois Ritual of Condolence described in Bierhorst, *Four Masterworks of American Indian Literature* (1974:107-83). The Tlingit and Iroquois traditions of oratory are both set in a context of social relationships and mourning and both rely heavily on kinship and figures of speech. However, the Tlingit and Iroquois traditions are quite different. Specifically, Tlingit oratory is not memorized or fixed like a liturgical text, and none of the Tlingit oratory is a set "ritual poem" recited or handed down more or less verbatim over generations. In this respect, Tlingit oratory also seems unlike other widely studied Native American traditions such as the Navajo Chantway which have been described as myth and stories performed in a set ritual pattern (Spencer 1957) and as script for ritual drama (Bierhorst 1974). In contrast, the pattern or model for Tlingit speeches is traditional, but Tlingit oratorical tradition dictates that each speaker compose anew according to the context of each ceremonial, with specific details and poetic images appropriate to the new situation, but composed in accordance with traditional patterns and structure. Tlingit oratory is probably best described as having a set structure filled by details composed in performance and determined by the specific genealogical and iconographic contexts.

Whereas the Iroquoian condolence oratory described by Bierhorst (1974) seems somewhat comparable to Tlingit in its concern with mourning, the Pima tradition described in Bahr, *Pima and Papago Ritual Oratory* (1975) provides a sharp contrast. The Pima oratory documented there is connected with rituals of warfare, whereas the Tlingit is associated with peacemaking and mourning, house dedications, and similar celebrations. Still, some of the dynamics are similar. For example, Bahr observes that "these speeches could equally be called 'orations' to a live audience or 'prayers' to a distant spirit" (Bahr 1975:6). Underhill (1979) is much closer to Tlingit, and will be described below.

Also, the Tlingit texts come to us in a different manner. Whereas the Iroquois condolence speeches were first transcribed over 100 years ago and are partly reconstructed by Bierhorst and others, and the Piman texts were transcribed between forty and seventy years ago and have been reworked by Bahr and others, the Tlingit texts featured in this book were all recorded in "live performance" within the last ninety years. Most were collected on audio and video tape within the last twenty years, but two speeches on wax cylinders date from 1899.

The present volume on Tlingit may be joined with studies of oratorical traditions from two other Native American culture areas to create an interesting triangle, with points of comparison in the rain forests of the Pacific Northwest, the desert Southwest, and the Northeast woodlands of New York State and Ontario, Canada. The oratory in all three traditions shares some features of style and composition, but fundamental differences seem greater to us at this point than the similarities.

Underhill (1979) is based on texts gathered by Ruth Underhill in the 1930s and supplemented by recent fieldwork by Donald Bahr and three Papago co-authors. The book is a detailed study of Papago oratory, presenting texts, facing translations, and analysis. The speeches and ceremonials are part of the yearly ritual cycle, intimately connected with life in the desert of southern Arizona and northern Sonora, following the seasons of rain, ripening of cactus, and journeys for sea salt.

There are clear differences between Papago and Tlingit oratory, but also some conceptual similarities. The most obvious difference between Tlingit and Papago is that Tlingit has no fixed calendar of ritual celebrations. Bahr suggests that journeys of one kind or another underly the structure of all of the Papago oratory, but the extent to which journeys are important in Tlingit speaking remains to be demonstrated. Journey themes are clearly present in Tlingit oratory: Tlingit orators and audience travel to the site of a memorial, and within the speeches there is metaphorical travel of the living and the departed.

Many of the underlying oratorical concepts are the same, although the specific surface details are culture-specific and different. Papago oratory, as Tlingit, draws its metaphors from the physical and spiritual environment. The hosts' round house is deified through rhetoric (Underhill 1979:32). Likewise, all oratory involves some kind of host-guest relationship in general, but the specific details are determined by the social structure of each group.

Theoretical contributions advanced by Bahr apply to the study of other traditions as well. Bahr makes the very important point that Native and Christian historical traditions are both active in total contemporary religious practice, and that this fact should be accepted by scholars without prejudice. Bahr writes (Underhill 1979:10) "that most Papagos are as seriously involved in the one side as in the other. They derive benefits from both traditions and find it possible to believe in both. A full account of Papago religious life must treat both." There are also public and private settings for religious practice, so that the total Papago religous context is a four-way interface of Native and Christian, public and private, of which the oratory he analyzes is from the overlap of the Native and public domains. This religious framework applies to Tlingit and other traditions as well, as does Bahr's observation (Underhill 1979:11) that in oratory, words move in two directions: toward the spirits and toward the participants.

The most detailed study of a single Native American oratorical tradition is the Iroquois research by Chafe (1961) and Foster (1974a) in speeches from Thanksgiving rituals—(not to be confused with the American Turkey holiday in November). Chafe notes that the Thanksgiving Speech, "the most ubiquitous of all Seneca rituals, opens and closes nearly every ceremony. The only exceptions are the Funeral Ceremony and the Dance for the Dead" (1961:2). Accordingly, much of Tlingit tradition, with its focus on postfuneral oratory, has little in common with the Seneca Thanksgiving Rituals studied by Chafe (1961). Not all Tlingit oratory is funereal, but we feel that its greatest achievements are in memorial contexts different from those settings described for Iroquois. Foster (1974a) continues and expands the study of the Iroquois Thanksgiving Ritual, and his approach offers many interesting points of comparison and contrast with our Tlingit work. Foster's book is valuable for its method (the study of texts in the context of social structure and world view), its description of the group dynamics of oratory, and its discussion of oral composition theory. Although on the content level Tlingit and Iroquois Thanksgiving oratory could not seem more unrelated, the study of context and group dynamics suggests many similarities, and the comparison helps to distill what is unique to each tradition.

Foster's discussion of context (including longhouse seating diagrams by sex and moiety) treats concepts immediately familiar to students of Tlingit oratory. He observes that "longhouse speaking is a highly formalized dialogue...between the moieties" (1974a:29) and emphasizes that "longhouse dialogues are not so much two-party events as three-party events" (1974a:29) with two sets of speakers and an audience listening to both. He describes the public stance of the speaker as one of humility, stressing the fact that he has been appointed to speak, and making a formal apology for any errors (1974a:31). This is in keeping with Tlingit protocol. Much of the moiety interaction described by Foster also applies to Tlingit. In a given ritual exchange there is a leading side and a respondent side; one side leads, and the other confirms (1974a:123). People are brought together in a ceremonial "scene" that may be defined not only as a physical setting, but also as a psychological setting (1974a:123). Within this setting there is oratory and the distribution of food. Foster describes a uniting of the moieties similar to that of Tlingit ceremonial. Where we have described "levels of mediation" in this introduction, Foster speaks of "horizontal" and "vertical" dimensions (1974a:127). Horizontal refers to the uniting of moieties, and the vertical to the relationship between human beings and the creator. As with Tlingit, oratory is a key factor in the unification.

Foster describes the Thanksgiving oratory as hierarchic speeches providing a key to longhouse cosmology as well as a key to the rich ceremonialism associated with Iroquois subsistence activities (1974a:108). While the calendrical nature of Iroquois ceremonies is different from Tlingit, Foster's detailed study of the relationship of the speeches to the ceremonies parallels our interests here, as well as his description of oratory as "speech events whose context and structure are the most explicit expressions . . . of the spirit forces in contemporary . . . religion, now that the art of myth-narration has fallen into disuse" (1974a:3). Like Tlingit, the Iroquois speeches include "inventories" of the spiritual forces (1974a:131) although the nature of the spirit forces is quite different in Tlingit and Iroquois tradition.[15]

For serious students of oral literature, one of the most valuable sections of Foster's book is his discussion of the oral composition process in Chapters VII, VIII, and IX (1974a:169-253). In-depth treatment of the subject is beyond the scope of this introduction, but we would like to review some of the principal concepts, and focus on the main theoretical points as they apply to Tlingit. Foster reviews the shift in folklore research from emphasis on text to concern with performance—folklore as event. Text is what the speaker composes; performance is how he or she composes. Part of this shift involves focus on the speaker's perspective and the demands of oral composition in "live performance" or "real time." Important in the evolution of this approach is the work of Milman Parry and Albert Lord on the composition of Homeric epics and Yugoslavian narrative songs. Based on Lord (1960), Foster reviews the main points: such composition is oral; there is no written guide or time to revise. It is conservative; originality and innovation are not goals. There is a sense of urgency—the need to find the next line in an oral performance.

The most important contribution of Parry and Lord was the concept of formulaic composition: the theory that oral epics are not memorized and repeated verbatim, but are composed anew with each performance according to building blocks called formulas. (These formulas are the repetitions that readers immediately notice when reading oral literature.) One of Foster's important contributions is a suggested adaptation of the concept and definition of "formula" to Native American composition.

Foster maintains that "the Longhouse situation is in many respects analogous to the Yugoslavian situation" (1974a:187). There is a certain thematic hierarchy (based on conceptions of the cosmos) that is never violated; on the other hand, there is much flexibility and variety in the way words and phrases are put together to build individual lines. The creativity in oral literature lies in the unique way the tradition bearer selects and combines these words and phrases on each occasion. These words and phrases are the formulas, which Foster describes as the "molecular units of oral composition" and the "lexicon of the composition process" (1974a:185). Foster's discussion of discourse and section rules and of what constitutes a line (Chapter VIII) are also of theoretical importance for Tlingit research, but are too technical to review here for the general reader. The most important concept here is the formula.

Parry and Lord were working primarily with Classical Greek and contemporary Serbian epics. These epics are composed in metrical "feet;" each line has a fixed number of total syllables arranged in a set pattern of alternation of long and short or stressed and unstressed vowels. Like building blocks of varying size, words and phrases may be combined in different patterns to make up the total length. For example, Athena may be called "Athena," "the Goddess Athena," "gray eyed Athena," or "the gray eyed Goddess Athena" depending on how much of the line the composer needed to fill out. A hero may mount a "horse" or a "milk white steed" depending on the syllable count. Measuring (or meter) is very important in European epic tradition, and is a key factor in the original definition of a formula as "a group of words . . . regularly employed under the same metrical conditions to express a given essential idea" (1974a:201).

Foster emphasizes that "the Longhouse speech line has no such arithmetical requirements" (1974a:203-204). Neither does the Tlingit speech line. We agree with Foster that much work remains to be done on rhythm in Native American oral traditions, but we also endorse his statement as it pertains to the Tlingit: "At the moment I will stick to the position that metricality in the strict sense used by Parry and Lord does not play the same constitutive role in [Iroquois] speech line formation as it does in Yugoslavian epics" (1974a:205). We also agree with his suggestion that the original Parry and Lord definition of a formula "is still highly serviceable, even in a tradition as different from the Homeric and Yugoslavian as the Longhouse speaking tradition" (1974a:202). This leaves students of Native American oral literature with the theoretical problem of whether to abandon the European-based definition, or modify it to fit different bodies of data such as Iroquois and Tlingit. We find Foster's solution very practical and worth quoting here.

> It is obvious that the intial definition is going to have to be modified because very different traditions are involved. This seems to be the only alternative to scrapping the idea of oral-formulaic composition altogether. In such cases as the black sermon and the Longhouse speeches there is clearly a use of conventionalized phrases; there is also an organizing scheme for the whole discourse; and there is the fact that each performance is in some sense unique. It would seem justified to modify the definition in order to retain Parry and Lord's deeper insights about the oral composition process. We are more interested in the spirit than in the letter of the definition. (1974a:202-203)

In an attempt to capture the essence of Parry and Lord while modifying their ideas to fit the Longhouse data, Foster proposes a modified definition suitable to the Iroquois speeches. "The formula is a recurrent phrase expressing a conventionalized idea and capable of multiple combination with other such phrases in the discourse" (1974a:203). At the present state of our research, this modification seems important not only for Iroquois studies, but for the study of Tlingit and other Native American oral traditions as well.

Foster concludes that what emerging tradition bearers are learning is "not a set of memorized texts but a pattern of performance" (1974:a251). This applies to Tlingit as well. Foster demonstrates that the speeches are not memorized and repeated verbatim, but are created by formulaic composition. Still, in contrast to Tlingit, the examples in Foster's study suggest that Iroquois tradition operates from some sense of a fixed or anticipated text; a certain hierarchic sequence (based on and articulating Iroquois cosmology) is expected, although there is latitude regarding the precise way in which words are put together. The main point of comparison is that Tlingit rhetorical tradition does not share this sense of a fixed or anticipated text. There is no specific, obligatory, sequential content as in the Iroquois speeches. There is in Tlingit a fixed sense of rhetorical structure, but the details of content are flexible and are conditioned by social context, especially the genealogies and at.óow of the participants in relationship to the deceased. Although the sense of content is different, Tlingit composition, like Iroquois and much other documented oral composition, is highly formulaic in the terms adapted and defined by Foster for Native American tradition.

These are some of the points that become clear through comparison to other Native American oratorical traditions. Tlingit has no fixed annual cycle of calendrical rituals. House dedications, pole raisings, peace ceremonies, and similar events can be held at any time of the year. As noted above, fall is the preferred time for "potlatching," but only because people are free then, and all the food has been gathered, so that it can be shared: fish, berries, deer, etc. But the events at which oratory is delivered are occasional and individual, not calendrical. (We should note here that the Iroquois condolence speeches are also not calendrical.) Also, Tlingit oratory has no fixed or memorized text. Even with the understanding of formulaic composition as applied in non-metrical situations, there still seems to be a sense of fixed or expected text in Papago and Iroquois, but not in Tlingit. (Perhaps this is due to the differing nature of the cosmologies upon which the oratory is based.) One would expect a Tlingit speech from fifty or one hundred years ago to have the same structure, but different particulars. The structure is traditional, but the specific images are not. Unfortunately, we have no longitudinal studies of a single orator, but one would expect similarity in structure, favorite turns of phrase, but different figures of speech according to the situation.

The absence of shared cosmology in Tlingit tradition is also interesting. Paradoxically, what is shared is the concept of not sharing. Each clan brings its own spirits to the feast, so to speak,

Some Major Differences Between Tlingit Oratory and Some Other Native American Oratory

Iroquois (Foster) & Papago (Bahr)	Tlingit
1. Annual calendrical ritual cycle	No fixed annual cycle. Occasional, such as house dedications, post funeral ceremonials
2. Set or fixed text passed from generation to generation (not necessarily verbatim, but "formulaic" as modified for Native American metrics)	No fixed text. Text is variable and depends on specific social context. Structure is traditional (kinship address, regalia, metaphor & simile, conclusion)
3. Shared "national" cosmology	No shared cosmology. Each clan has its own set of spirits (at.óow) connected with its ancestors. The spirit world is very "genealogical" and "ancestral." The structure and system are shared, but not the specific components.
4. Moieties may or may not be involved, depending on social structure. Some kind of host-guest relationship is involved.	Oratory is generally delivered across moiety lines. Two halves make the whole. In a sense, each clan is "fractional," and combined in ritual interaction, they make the whole.

and they "balance" each other. The social structure and belief system are shared, but not the specific components. Bahr (personal communication 1989) suggests the concept of a polarity between the "monolithic" Longhouse speeches at the one pole and the Tlingit spirituality of at.óow at the other. Tlingit cosmology, like Tlingit social structure, is reciprocal and complementary. Tlingit focus is on the kinship of the living and the dead. The symbols and frame of reference of Tlingit oratory are within the kin group, and serve to reaffirm the unity of the kin group, the unity of the consanguines and affines, or, in less technical terms, the unity of those related by blood and those related by marriage.

It seems to us that a distinctive feature of Tlingit culture and oral literature is the absence of common spirit powers shared by the entire tribe or nation. Instead, spirits (yéik) are revealed to individual shamans of each clan, and become clan property—part of that clan's heraldic system and inheritance (at.óow). Clan spirits are at the heart of Tlingit oral literature and traditional world view. Songs are often the revelations, if not the manifestations, of the spirits themselves, and they evoke the spirits when sung. Oratory employs the spirits in ceremonial use, especially for healing, removal of grief, and prevention of harm. Narratives form the foundation of the entire system, recalling how the spirits were historically revealed, and Tlingit oral literature is rich in accounts of acquisition of shaman spirits by the ancestors of various clans. Unlike ordination into a pre-existing religion, each shaman receives personal spirits. Key elements in Tlingit social structure and oral literature are the clan ownership of these spirits and reciprocity or "balance" among the clans when they evoke their spirits in ceremonial practice. As noted at the beginning, Tlingit society is divided into two moieties, each of which consists of many autonomous clans. Thus, each clan is a fraction of the whole, and each moiety is a half. When the clans come together, especially in rituals for healing, a social and spiritual whole is created.

Viability of Tlingit Oratory

Oratory, the art of public speaking, called in Tlingit *ḵaan kik' eetx' yoo x̱'atánk,* meaning "speaking in public" and characteristically in formal settings to people of the opposite moiety, is one of the shining gems of Tlingit oral literature. The Tlingit term may derive from "speaking around the fire" and reflects its ancient and ceremonial origins. Paradoxically, Tlingit oratory may be the most viable genre of Tlingit oral literature, and yet at the same time the most endangered. It is most alive because Tlingit oratory is by definition and practice composed and delivered or "published" only in performance, although usually thought out well in advance.[16] In contrast to the continuing and relatively little changed social setting for oratory, what some folklorists call the "tale telling situation" has changed radically for Tlingit narrative. Most if not all Tlingit stories told today in Tlingit are told into a tape recorder to a collector. Few that we know of are told in the traditional settings that the elders and story tellers describe from their childhoods. It is very difficult to hear a Tlingit story in a traditional setting; in contrast, it is almost impossible *not* to hear Tlingit oratory in a traditional or contemporary setting involving a speaker-audience relationship, although the style, language, and content of delivery will vary according to the situation.

As seen in this book, modern variations of traditional practice have evolved where hospitalized elders have tape-recorded speeches to be played at memorials they were unable to attend, and some elders have taped speeches to be played posthumously at their own memorials. But the speeches are always composed with an audience in mind, particularly people of the opposite moiety, and even the taped speeches are eventually played to that audience, even with the composer in absentia or deceased.

Traditional Tlingit oratory is also endangered for a number of reasons: the language itself is moribund; the elders are dying, and as they pass away, the younger generations have fewer models of language and style to follow; finally, the situations in which the most traditional speeches are delivered are becoming increasingly rare. Memorials, the principal cultural and spiritual context of the most sublime oratory, are still common, but Forty Day Parties are much more frequent, and are always held, even if Memorials are not. With few people under the age of forty speaking or understanding Tlingit, it is clear that the ranks of orators and audience who can engage in traditional oratorical reciprocity are now diminished. The roles of speaker and audience are interchangeable and neither is passive, because hosts and guests make speeches and responses to each other, maintaining the "balance" and protocol that the elders call "respect." Even fluent speakers of Tlingit comment frequently that they don't know "old time Tlingit." "Old time Tlingit" does not refer to archaic grammar or vocabulary (although they may be part of it) but more to matters of form and rhetorical style—specifically the ability to use metaphor and simile with reference to visual art and the spirituality it represents. For all of these reasons, we do not expect traditional oratory in the Tlingit language as represented in this book to survive in the future.

Younger orators are acutely aware of the limitations they face, not only regarding their ability to use metaphor, simile, and riddles as the elders did, but their ability to speak Tlingit. It is possible and probable that the oratory will survive using the English language. Regardless of the language used, the ability to use metaphor and simile is important. Because the metaphor and simile are based on the kinship system, history, traditional belief system, and at.óow, it is important for speakers to be thoroughly grounded in visual art (or iconography), history, genealogy, literature, and spirituality. Moreover, according to the elders, this knowledge must not be theoretical, but must be lived. A violation of Tlingit traditional practices would in former times disqualify one from becoming an orator, and some elders maintain that even today one whose conduct violates acceptable behavior ought not to speak in public or seek to be a leader or occupy a position of influence. As one elder emphasized, if such unqualified persons do speak, they are "never heard."

Traditional Tlingit oratory thus illustrates a combination of training in Tlingit language, rhetoric, and the entire range of Tlingit culture for orator and audience alike. It is important to remember that oratory involves not only a competent speaker, but a competent audience. There must be "balance" for Tlingit oratory to work. When any of these factors changes, the nature of the oratory changes. The speeches in this book are fine examples of differing combinations of these elements.

Interesting things happen when the language of oratory changes. In the early 1970s Charlie Joseph spoke at a Forty Day Party in Sitka. In deference to the many people in the audience who did not understand Tlingit, he spoke in English. It was interesting to note his frequent apologies for his inability to express what he really wanted to say. He kept apologizing for his poor and limited English. In fact, his English was not poor at all. His English was limited not by his own ability but because the English language itself simply does not have the words to express the basic Tlingit social concepts Charlie Joseph wanted and needed to communicate. Later, he spoke again in Tlingit, delivering one of the speeches included in this book.

We fully expect that in coming generations, much general knowledge of the Tlingit language and culture will be lost, and the traditional world view, history, and spirituality will change, becoming more westernized and secularized. The tradition of oratory will change accordingly. But it is possible that a new synthesis of traditional Tlingit spirituality and Christianity will emerge. This process is already well underway in the ANB memorial services.

On the positive side, we anticipate that Tlingit oratory will not only survive, but will thrive in coming generations, although in the English language and with a different world view. Tlingit oratory of the future, without a doubt, will express different concepts and will take place in different social settings. But we are optimistic that Tlingit oratory can and will continue in English, if for no other reason than Tlingit people's fondness for public speaking. People jokingly comment that public speaking is second only to basketball as the Tlingit national sport.

NOTES

1. Tlingit is pronounced Klínk-it in English, and Lingít in Tlingit, with a voiceless "L".

2. The word is pronounced utt-oow (the "a" as in "America" and the "oow" as in "coo" or "two") and is a compound noun from át ("thing") and the verb stem -.oo or -.oow ("to buy, own, or possess"). The period (.) signifies a glottal stop and shows that at.óow contrasts with the word atóow, "he/she is reading it" or a tóo "inside it." The acute accent (´) indicates high tone. The word may also be pronounced "at.óowu," with the possessive suffix -u, but we use the short form for convenience.

3. A locally written history by a descendant of one of the founders is Andrew Hope, III, *Founders of the Alaska Native Brotherhood* (1975), but this book is unfortunately no longer in print.

4. We emphasize the Orthodox heritage of the ANB here only because it has been less publicized than the Presbyterian connection. It was recently documented by Sergei Kan (1985).

5. For more background on this, see Dauenhauer (1982) *Conflicting Visions in Alaskan Education.*

6. Our discussion of the Forty Day Party is intended mainly to provide the general reader with some background on one of the main cultural contexts of contemporary oratory. Persons interested in a more detailed treatment should consult the work of Sergei Kan (1983, 1987a) and others listed in his bibliography.

7. Catharine McClellan (personal communication, 1989) reports that the healing emphasis is confirmed by her experience too. Nora Marks Dauenhauer discusses this at length in her paper "Levels of Mediation in Tlingit Oratory," (1975, 1976), updated and revised as Section VII of this introduction. Her main thesis is that Tlingit oratory mediates and binds on three levels: the rhetorical, the social, and the spiritual. Our own subsequent work on the subject (1988) is also incorporated in this introduction. Newer research on Tlingit potlatch, notably that of Sergei Kan, has also moved in this direction, and away from the earlier focus on rivalry, as is suggested in the title of his Ph.D. dissertation *"Wrap Your Father's Brothers in Kind Words:" An Analysis of the Nineteenth-Century Tlingit Mortuary and Memorial Rituals"* (1982) and his article, "Words that Heal the Soul: Analysis of the Tlingit Potlatch Oratory" (1983). See also Kan,

"The Nineteenth-century Tlingit potlatch: a new perspective" (1986a). Both articles make outstanding theoretical contributions and include detailed discussion of secondary literature on the subject. Kan's most recent work (1989) is *Symbolic Immortality: Tlingit Potlatch of the Nineteenth Century.* For a general background on the potlatch see *Under Mount Saint Elias* (de Laguna 1972:611-12). For a concise and recent overview of traditional Tlingit culture, including potlatching, see the contributions by de Laguna (1988a, 1988b) to Fitzhugh and Crowell, *Crossroads of Continents* (1988). The book also includes many articles that show Tlingit art and culture in the wider context of peoples of the Northwest Coast, Alaska, and Siberia. Catharine McClellan (1954) also discusses in detail many points touched upon in this introduction, including reciprocity, the role of the father's clan, and regalia. Potlatch as a public payment is described in detail and is contrasted with other ceremonialism such as "feasting" and "peacemaking." This distinction is also supported in analyses by Tlingit scholars. Walter Soboleff (personal communication, 1988), points out that "feasting" and "peacemaking" are specific segments of larger ceremonies. He also suggests that the English term "feasting," while far superior to "potlatch," still detracts from the dignity associated with Tlingit ceremonies. The subject of potlatch is complicated, but is inseparable from the study of Tlingit oratory, although with the exception of our work and Kan's, little or no attention has been given to the role of oratory in the potlatch (although Codere does support her thesis with illustration of the repeated references to war in Kwakiutl potlatch songs and speeches). For a new perspective on the subject, see Irving Goldman, *The Mouth of Heaven* (1975) and Stanley Walens, *Feasting with Cannibals: An Essay on Kwakiutl Cosmology* (1981). For a recent discussion of potlatch and oratory in the adjacent Tsimshian tradition, see Margaret Seguin *Interpretive Contexts for Traditional and Current Coast Tsimshian Feasts* (1985). For the most current survey of literature on the Haida potlatch and its relationship to oral literature and social structure, see Marianne Boelscher, *The Curtain Within: Haida Social and Mythical Discourse* (1989). These studies and their bibliographies will provide the interested reader with ample opportunity for further directions in theoretical analysis. For a less theoretical approach with excellent photographs, Ulli Steltzer, *A Haida Potlatch* (1984) offers readers graphic insights into the potlatch as a setting for oratory. Ruth Kirk, *Tradition & Change on the Northwest Coast* (1986) provides excellent background on the history, culture, and physical environment of the Northwest Coast. Kirk does not describe the Tlingit or their immediate neighbors, the Haida and Tsimshian, but the settings of the groups in British Columbia and Washington are quite similar, and readers unfamiliar with Southeast Alaska will get a general feel for the Northwest Coast. As noted elsewhere, no attempt is made here at a definitive bibliography or history of literature on potlatch. Our notes and references are intended as a starting point for interested readers, and as a reference point for the context of our work.

8. For more on this, see Nora Dauenhauer, "Context and Display in Northwest Coast Art" (1986).

9. This is also discussed in Kan, "Potlatch Songs Outside the Potlatch" (1987b).

10. Etymologically, the morpheme u- is irrealis (designating incompleted or nonexistent action), and the stem -tee means "to be." So the word yéik utee may be analyzed literally as "not to be" or "spirit that is not." One might compare this concept to European poetic traditions attempting to describe manifestations or appearances of something else, to represent in words or visual art the larger and intuitive reality that lies beyond the symbol. This tradition includes Byzantine hymns about "pre-eternal God" and "holding Him who cannot be held," or "seeing Him who cannot be seen," and extends through the symbolist movement of the late nineteenth and early twentieth centuries. On the other hand, this may be stretching things too far. As Leer points out (personal communication) the irrealis actually functions as a thematic prefix in Tlingit verbs and nouns, far beyond its more restricted use of indicating the negative or situations contrary to fact.

11. This section is based on material first presented by Nora Dauenhauer at the Alaska Anthropology Association meetings at the University of Alaska-Fairbanks, 1975, and in revised form at the Simon Fraser University Northwest Coast Conference, Burnaby, B.C., 1976. It is published here for the first time.

12. Most of this section first appeared as a professional paper prepared by Nora and Richard Dauenhauer for the 12th International Congress of Anthropological and Ethnological

Sciences, Zagreb, Yugoslavia, July 1988. The paper was published in Hoppál and von Sadovszky (1989:317-329).

13. We have limited our discussion here to those aspects of shamanism addressed directly in the speeches. Shamanism in general and discussion of the lives of shamans, the revelation of spirits, visions, journeys and the acquisition of at.óow are beyond the scope of the present volume. Readers seriously interested in Tlingit shamanism may wish to research the subject further in de Laguna (1972), McClellan (1956, 1975), and in recent articles by de Laguna (1987), and Kan (1983, 1986, 1987a, 1987b). Readers may also wish to consult works on shamanism by Eliade (1964), Grim (1983), Hoppál (1984), Hoppál and von Sadovszky (1989), Michael (1963), and Siikala (1978).

14. Hinckley's source is NA 1898. National Archives, Interior Department, Territorial Papers, Alaska; Microfilm 430, Roll 5, Frame 651 ff.

15. Foster (1974a:114) also offers terminology which we have not yet systematically applied designating the term "ceremony" as an entire religious occasion, whereas the term "ritual" is used to designate a bounded segment on that occasion. In these terms, memorial would equate to ceremony, and cry to ritual.

16. Foster (1974b) touches on this aspect of Iroquois oratory in his essay "When Words Become Deeds: An Analysis of Three Iroquois Longhouse Speech Events" (in Bauman and Sherzer 1974; 1989:354-367). He describes the distinct grammatical forms of Iroquois oratory and notes that although performance of ritual oratory may be brief, it requires long and careful training and preparation.

Speeches from Various Occasions

Ch'a uwayáa du yoo x̱'atángi
haa séix̱ aawayeeshée yáx̱ yatee
yá x'óow,
tuwulatseen x'óow.
— G̱ooch Oox̱ú

It is as if his words
are like a robe
pulled over our shoulders,
a strength-giving robe.
— *Richard King,*
Welcoming Address, Celebration 1988

Ix̱t'ik' Éesh
Sheet'ká, 1971

Lingít áyú yéi yanaḵéich
"Yee eedéi x̱'akḵwatáan."
Ḵaa yoo x̱'atángi
héen yíx̱ kei nagut ḵáa yáx̱ yatee,
k'éx̱'aa teen.
Héen wánx̱ oowax'agi x̱áat áyú
du k'éx̱'ayi a kát ax̱'eilhaashch.
Ag̱ak'éx̱'ín ch'a yóo kaawahayi x̱áat
du eenx̱ nasteech.
Yéi áwé yatee ḵaa yoo x̱'atángi.
Ch'a yóo kaawahayi yoo x̱'atánk
du eenx̱ nasteech.

First Unidentified Speaker
Sheet'ká, 1899

Wéit yinági ax̱ x̱oonx'í
yee eedéi x̱'akḵwatáan.
Ha yáa yeedát táakw
aadéi haa toowú kawlig̱éiyi yé.
Adaat yee eedéi x̱'akḵwatáan.
Tlax̱ wáa sá haa toowú kawlig̱éi.
Ldakát yéidei haa toowú sigóo
T'aakú aanḵáax'u haadéi gax̱du.ix' nóok.
A tuwáatx̱
haa toowú litseeni yé,
ayáx̱ wootee
ḵa yá Kaagwaantaanx̱ haa sateeyí.
Yá haa léelk'w hás ádi
ch'a ldakát
gagi yéi wtusinéi s du waḵshiyéex'

A. P. Johnson
Sitka, 1971

A person will often say
"I am going to speak to you."
Public speaking
is like a man walking up along a river
with a gaff hook.
He lets his gaff hook drift
over a salmon swimming at the edge of the river.
When he hooks on it, the salmon way over there
becomes one with him.
This is the way oratory is.
Even speech delivered at a distance
becomes one with someone.

First Unidentified Speaker
Sitka, 1899

You who are standing there, my relatives,
I will speak to you.
Well, this last winter
how proud we were.
I will speak to you about it.
How very proud we were.
We were happy in many ways
when the Taku aristocrats were invited here.
How much strength of mind
we gained
because of it,
and because we are Kaagwaantaan.
We took all
the things of our grandfathers out
for these Taku aristrocrats

yá T'aaḵú aanḵáax'u.
Has du waḵsheeyee yéi wtusinéi
haa toowú klag̱eiyí ch'a wáa sá.
Yá T'aaḵóotx̱ haat ḵudu.éex'
tlél wáa sá wootee.
Haa toowú wlitseen.
Ch'a ldakát yéidei
aan yátx'ix̱ haa siteeyi yé
gákx' yéi wtusinéi ḵa hás tsú aadéi aan yátx'i has siteeyi yé.
Tlél daaḵw lingit'aaní tuḵwáani sá
haa yáx̱ gug̱atée, ḵa hás
aadéi haa toowú litseeni yé
yú dáanaa aadéi woonaawu yé
aadéi yakoogeiyi yé;
yá Sheet'káx'
aadéi ḵut wooxeexi yé
yú xíxch'i daatx̱
Xíxch'i Hít yeet ḵuwdu.éex'i.
Ách áyú tlél tsu
a kináa yéi at utée.
Xíxch'i Hít dzeidí g̱al'éex'
aadéi haa toowú yateeyi yé.
Ldakát lingit'aaní
ḵoonóogu kináax' yéi wootee,
yóo ḵoonóok
yú Sheet'káx
yú L'uknax̱.ádi aanḵáawu haat ḵu.éex'
aan yátx'i.

Second Unidentified Speaker
Sheet'ká, 1899

Haa tlax̱ wáa sá haa tuwáa sigóo
yá táakw,
haadéi yaa ḵukdu.éex'.
Yú haa yaḵaax'u yán
has du eeg̱áa anagóot
tlél wutoox̱éx'wx̱.

to see.
How very much we showed them
how proud we are.
When they were invited here from Taku,
everything went smoothly.
We gained strength of mind.
In all kinds of ways
we showed where we are noble
and how they are noble too.
No other people in the world
will be like us, and them
the way we had strength of mind,
how much money was brought out,
how much there was;
how much was brought out
in Sitka
for the frog
when people were invited to the Frog House.
This is why nothing else
can surpass it.
How bad we felt
when the steps of the Frog House broke.
The event
at Sitka,
surpassed all other events
in the world
when that L'uknax̲.ádi aristocrat invited
the nobility here.

Second Unidentified Speaker
Sitka, 1899

Yes, how very much we wanted
to invite those people here
this winter.
We couldn't sleep
when our people went to invite
those opposites of ours.

Tsu ch'u ldakát haa aankwéiyi tu.aasí
woosh gunayaadéi s'eenáax̱ sitee.
Ách áyú uhaan tsú haa toowú ayáx̱ wootee.
Tsu yá dleit ḵáa aanḵáax'u
haa éet wudishée.
Ch'a ldakát át haa jiyís yéi s awsinei.
A tuwáadáx̱ ḵu.aa
haa toowú wlitseen.
Ch'a ldakát yéidei
ḵustí yéi wtusinei.
Tléil haa tuwáa ushgóowun.
Haa wáa sá kaawahayi táakw áyá haat ḵudu.éex'
haa tuwáa wsigóo.
Ách áyá ch'a ldakát át
adaatx̱ yawtuwanáḵ.
L ushik'éiyi át
toowú kaxeel
tlél haa tuwáa wushgú.
Haat ḵuwdu.éex'eech ḵu.aa
yá haa tl'átgi kát ḵuwdu.éex'eech
haa toowú wlitseen.
Há yáa yeedát
tlax̱ wáa sá haa tuwáa sigóo
yá haa léelk'w has eetéex̱ yawtooḵeiyéech.
Ách ayáx̱
haa léelk'w hás ádi
has du waḵshiyeex' kéex' yéi wtusinei.
Ách áyá haa toowú wlitséen.
Haa toowú
tlax̱ wáa sá wook'éi
yá aanḵaax'u yán teen
haa toowú.

Even all of our flag poles
were different kinds of light.
This is why we too felt the same.
Even the white aristocrats
helped us.
They did all kinds of things for us.
Because of this
we gained strength of mind.
We did
all kinds of things.
We never wanted it.
But how we enjoyed it
when the people were invited here this winter.
This was why we stood back from
all kinds of things.
We didn't want
bad things,
or worries.
But because people were invited here,
because people were invited to our land,
we gained strength of mind.
Now at this moment
we want it very much
because we are sitting in place of our grandfathers.
Because of this
we brought out our grandfathers' things
for them to see.
This is why we gained strength of mind.
We felt
so good
with these aristocrats,
so good.

G̲ooch Éesh
K̲éix̲', 1971

Yéi áwé yanak̲éijin
ax̲ léek'w
yéi duwasáagu
áx̲ léek'w
Naakil.aan.
Hú áwé yéi yanak̲éijin
du x̲ánt uwak̲ux̲u k̲áa
"Yaanáx̲ x'wán
haanaanáx̲."
I yeex̲ kawdliyáas' i aat tléin.
Asx̲ánin áwé
du x̲ooni yádi.
Yéi áwé,
yéi áwé, yee yakk̲wasak̲áa yeedát,
haat k̲ayeeyteení ldakát,
ax̲ sani hás,
ax̲ aat hás.
Yóo áwé yee yakk̲wasak̲áa.
L aa yee x̲wlisaag̲i yé
yee ya.áakx̲ áwé shwudliyéx̲
yee aat tléin
k̲a yee sáni
Hinkwéix'.
Yáax' haa daat nág̲i k̲u.oo áwé.
Yeedát yee een x̲waasáakw
has du hídi tsu s yee een x̲waasáakw:
X̲'áakw Hít
yee sáni hídi
tsu yee sáni hídi
K̲utis' Hít
tsu yee sáni hídi
Kóoshdaa Hít
tsu yee sáni hídi
Wandaa Hít.

Johnny C. Jackson
Kake, 1971

This is what my grandfather
used to say,
my grandfather
whose name was
Naakil.aan.
He was the one who used to say
to someone coming to him by canoe,
"Please come this way,
come closer."
Your great paternal aunt has made a lap for you.
She used to love
the children of her relatives.
This is all,
this is all I will say to you now,
now that you have all arrived here,
my paternal uncles,
my paternal aunts.
That is what I will say to you.
Your great paternal aunt,
has transformed herself
into a place where you can rest,
and your paternal uncle
Hinkwéix'.
They are the people who stood by us.
I'm naming them to you now.
I'm also naming their houses to you:
Watermarked Salmon House
your paternal uncle's house,
and another paternal uncle's house,
Looking House,
and another paternal uncle's house,
Land Otter House,
and another paternal uncle's house
Around the Edge House.

Yéi áwé yee yax̱wsiḵáa
"Gunalchéesh!"
haat yee kawdak'éet'i
áx' eeshan déin haa wooneiyí yé áwé.
Haa tóodáx̱ ḵugax̱yisaháa
tl'áx̱'wkwx̱náx̱ áyá haa ya kawusóosin.
Yeedát ḵwá
yee ḵ'asagoowú tóonáx̱ áwé
    (Unidentified) *Yéi yís áwé!*
yadax̱ ya gax̱tudaxóon.
Yéi áwé.
Gunalchéesh.
Yóo yee yax̱wsiḵáa
"Ḵwáaḵt tsé aanéi x'wáan
yeewháan."
Yéi áwé.
Yándei tugax̱tula.áat
yée jiyís.
    (Unidentified) *Gunalchéesh á!*
Yéi áwé
yee eet x̱'ax̱waatán.
    (Unidentified) *Gunalchéesh á!*
Yeedát ḵwá
haa kaani yán a x̱oox' yéi yatee
ḵa haa sani hás tsú ax̱oowú.
Haa kaanx'i yán
yóo toosáaych uháanch.
Ách áwé yeedát
has du jeedéi áayax̱ gugatée.
Has áwé
has du léelk'w hás
aadéi neilx̱ ḵuteeyi yé
áwé yéi s agux̱sanéi.
    (Unidentified) *Gunalchéesh.*
Al'eix̱ áwé.
    (Unidentified) *Gunalchéesh.*
Gunalchéesh.

I am saying
"Thank you" to you
for coming here
where a sad thing has happened to us.
You will remove the sadness
from our faces that fell in the mud.
But now,
with the help of your joy,
we will lift our faces.
    (Unidentified) *That is what it's for.*
This is all.
Thank you.
I am saying to you,
"Please don't let anything happen
to any of you."
This is all.
We will think good wishes
for you.
    (Unidentified) *Thank you, indeed!*
This is all
I am saying to you.
    (Unidentified) *Thank you, indeed!*
And now,
our brothers-in-law are among you,
and our paternal uncles are also among you.
Our brothers-in-law
is what we call them.
This is the reason now
we will turn this ceremony over to them.
They themselves
will do things in the same way
as their grandparents
once received guests.
    (Unidentified) *Thank you.*
There will be ceremonial dancing.
    (Unidentified) *Thank you.*
Thank you.

Wóochx̲ Kaduhaa
K̲éix̲', 1971

Ch'a áwé yéi át át koodayáaych.
Ch'a áwé yéi át koodayáaych.
Yá yeedát áwé
yéi haa yatee.
G̲una aan k̲wáani
yá X'aalkweidí
Aangóonx'
chúch x̲óodei s awdisáa
yá xáanaa kát.
Ách áwé yéi,
haa toowú kg̲watee uhaan tsú
aaa,
yá xáanaa kát
K̲éix̲'
a jiyís.
Yee jín gax̲tulat'áa.
Chá ldakát yéix' áwé
k̲áach koo.aak̲w nooch
eex̲ k̲a ch'u héen
héen teen
wooch x̲oo ayax̲sadaayéet tutée nooch eex̲.
Tléil k̲áach áwé woonadlách,
yéi yan kawdayaayí.
Yá yeedát x̲á yá X'aalkweidí aaní
káx' x̲á yéi haa woonei
yá yeedát.
Ch'a tléix'
wooch x̲oox' x̲á yéi haa wditee
yá xáanaa kát.
Tléil daat sá kwshí wé
wooch x̲oo yagux̲dadáa.
Yá xáanaa x̲áa wé yilatín
aadéi wooch x̲oox' yaa shundaxíx yé
haa k̲usteeyí yá xáanaa kát.

Jimmie George
Kake, 1971

This is how things come about.
This is how it comes about.
This is what is happening to us
right now.
Angoon selected
X'aalkweidí
of another village
to be among them
this evening.
This is the reason
we will feel this way too,
yes,
throughout this evening,
for
Kake.
Let us warm your hands.
In many places
men have constantly tried
blending together oil
and water—
oil and water.
No one has succeeded
in making it happen.
But now on this X'aalkweidí land
it has really happened to us
at this moment.
Just as one
we have come together
this evening.
There is nothing
that will blend them together.
Yet this evening surely you can see
the way our lives this evening
are flowing together as one.

Tléil daatnáx̲ sá kwshí
yéi yándei kagux̲dayáa.
Wooch isx̲án
ch'a tléix' tí
ach asgíwé
wooch x̲oo yakagux̲dadáa haa k̲usteeyí
(Unidentified) *Yéi á!*
yá Southeast Alaska káx' yéi haa teeyí
(Unidentified) *Yéi á!*
káx' yéi haa teeyí.
Lingit'aani tuk̲wáani
yáax' woosh kaanáx̲ yee yawdahaayí,
"Gunalchéesh aa"
yéi x̲'ayax̲aká
x̲át tsú
yá ax̲ sáni hás du daa yoo x̲'áx̲atángi
yá xáanaa kát.
(Unidentified) *Hó, hó!*
Yéi yá kg̲wagéi yeedát
áx̲ yoo x̲'atángi.
Gunalchéesh!

K̲aajeetg̲uxeex
Tlákw.aan, 1972

Ax̲ tuwáa sigóo
x̲át tsú x̲'ank̲adataaní
ax̲ hunx̲u hás.
Aaa
ldakát yáat yinág̲i,
yá yées k̲áax'wx̲ siteeyí aa
áwé a kaax̲ ax̲ toowú klig̲éi
x̲át tsú
yáa yeedát.
Yá yee jeet wuduwateeyi át
a daadéi yee yagux̲sataagí,
yá yee tláa kaak hás at.óowu
ax̲ éesh hás yáat yinág̲i

There is nothing
that can force this to happen.
Love for each other,
being one
perhaps that is what
will blend our lives together,
  (Unidentified) *That's right!*
we who live in Southeast Alaska,
  (Unidentified) *That's right!*
we who live here.
You people of the world,
who are gathered together here,
"Thank you indeed"
I too
am saying
in speaking about my paternal uncles
this evening.
  (Unidentified) *Hó, hó!*
This will be enough for now
of my speech.
Thank you!

Thomas Young
Klukwan, 1972

I would like
to speak too,
my older brothers.
Yes,
all of you standing here,
you who are young men,
are the ones I too
am proud of
right now.
These things that were given to you,
that you will care for,
these at.óow of your mother's maternal uncles,
you my fathers who are standing here,

áwé a kaax̱ ax̱ toowú kligéi.
Tlei dahéen áyú
dutláakw,
yéi sh kalneek
ax̱ éesh hás.
Áwé yéi kdunéek
yú taan.
Du déinx̱ áyú ḵuyawdudlijáḵ.
Aag̱áa áwé
teet jinax̱satánín áwé yú.á.
Tle akaax̱ héent usgeetch
wé du káak hás eejí.
Wáa nanéi sdágáawé yú.á
ch'a áa ng̱waanaawu yéidei kát áwé
yayát uwagút,
yá shaa yá daadéi.
Wáa nanéi sáwé
a yáa uwagút wé x̱'eis'awáa.
Aag̱áa áwé
ash x̱'eiwawóos'
"goodéi sáyá yaa neegút?"
"Ch'a áa x̱at nag̱waanaayí yéidei áyá
yaa nx̱agút."
X̱ach du léelk'w áwé wé x̱'eis'awáa.
"Yóo ax̱ tlaa kaak hás eejí
tle a kaax̱ héent x̱at usgeetch.
Yá ḵutí ax̱ kayáanáx̱ yatee."
"Haagú! Chx̱ánk'! Haagú!"
Aag̱áa áwé ash yík aawaxóo yú.á.
X̱'eis'awáach áwé yik uwaxóo yú taan.
Aag̱áa áwé yux̱ ash kaawanáa.
Goosá wé aax̱ héenx̱ latéedi yéeyi
tle tléix' áwé át uwagút
yú du tláa káak hás
eejí kaadéi.
Yú x̱'eis'awáa yík wuxoowóoch áwé
tlél a kaax̱ héent wusgeet.
Ách áwé
ch'u yaa yeedátdei
yeeytéen aan.
Ḵushtuyáx̱ wáa sá teet jiwustaaní

this is what I am proud of.
My fathers,
a story is told;
they tell
about a certain time.
They tell about
the sea lion.
This was while,
they say, the waves were rolling.
He would fall into the sea
His relatives were all killed off.
from his mother's maternal uncles' reef.
At what point was it, they say,
he began climbing
to the face of that mountain,
to a place where he could just die.
At what point was it
he came across a ptarmigan.
This is when
the ptarmigan asked him,
"Where are you going?"
"I'm going
to a place where I can just die."
Here, the ptarmigan was his grandparent.
"I keep falling off into the sea
from my mother's maternal uncles' reef.
The weather is stronger than I am."
"Come here! Grandson! Come here!"
That was when he put rocks inside of him, they say.
Ptarmigan put rocks inside the sea lion.
This was when he told the sea lion to try again.
Where he used to get washed into the sea,
he went up just once
onto the reef
of his mother's maternal uncles.
Because the ptarmigan had put rocks inside him,
he didn't fall off into the sea.
This is why
you can see it
even today.
No matter how the waves pound,

a káa ganúkch.
Yéi yá yee kgwatée
yá yee léelk'w hás yá diyeet ḵin aa.
Has du yoo x'atángeech áwé oowayaa
yee yik has aawaxuwu yáx̱ gugatee.
Ách áwé   60
tlél 'x'wán
a kaax̱ héent aa wusgeedéeḵ
yá yee tláa kaak hás toowú.

Yeilnaawú
Tás Tlein, 1972

X'éigaa
ax̱ toowóo yak'éi
áyá yeedát.
Áyá guna aandáx̱
haa x̱óot has uwa.át.
Tlél tsu has du éex̱ ḵutoojeeyí áyá yáax'
haa x̱oot has uwa.át.
Ha haa x̱oonx'í
áyá mtusiteen.
Tlax̱ x'éigaa,   10
aak'é ḵu.oo áyú yéi yatee.
Ha haa toowú tlax̱ daat yáx̱ sá a kaax̱ yak'é.
Aadáx̱ óosh
ch'a tlákw
ch'a yei yiguwáatl'
yei woosh toostínch
ḵa woosh yáx̱ kei tutudatánch,
aaa
áyá yei woosh toostínji.
Ha ch'a tlax̱ á yáanáx̱ áyá   20
tlél tsu aa sá yéi tusatínch.
Shayadihéin wé Lingít.
Áyá Gunanaa yoo tsú aa dax̱duwasáakw, de ch'as á áwé.
Ha tlél yá haa yáx̱ yoo x'ali.átgi aa.

they sit there.
This is how you will be
with your grandparents sitting in the back.
Their speeches will be
as if they are putting rocks inside you.
This is why
don't ever let
any of you fall off into the sea
away from the wishes of your mothers' maternal uncles.

Tom Peters
Teslin, 1972

I feel
really fine
at this moment.
They came here to us
from another country.
We didn't ever think it could be them;
they came here to us.
We have seen
our relatives.
They are truly
fine people.
We feel very happy because of them.
Even if only
once in a while
just for a short time
we can see each other
and our spirits be lifted,
yes,
when we see each other.
For too long now
we haven't seen anyone.
There are many Native people.
Some are also called Athabaskan; they're the only ones we see.
But none who speak like us.

Adax̱ hás ḵwá yéi yeedát yá haa x̱oo yéi s yateeyi aa ḵwá ch'u tle
tle x'éig̱aa
haa aani ḵwáni yáx̱ áhé s yatee
yá aadéi haa x̱'éináx̱ yoo s x̱'ali.atgi yé.
Ha ch'áakw
áyú ch'áakw
ch'áagu ḵáawu
ha yei áyá woosh wuskóowun.
Haa aaní yáx̱ téeyin yú éil' ká.
Á yoo a.átgin.
Haa yá x̱át ax̱ niyaanáx̱ a yá ax̱ x̱oonx'í.
Aaa, ḵa yá
yá Yanyeidí yoo dax̱duwasáagu aa,
ḵaa aaní yáx̱ téeyin.
Aax̱ áyá mdoodzikóo.
Ha yáadáx̱
hé Southi niyadéi
áyá Lingít
dax̱tuwatéen.
Tlél tsu haa x̱'éináx̱ yoo has x̱'éil.átk.
Ḵa yáadáx̱ North
down the Yukon River
tlél tsu has x̱'atoo.áx̱x̱.
Ch'a g̱óot has du yoo x̱'atángi ḵudzitee.
Adax̱ yéi yeedát yáax' haa x̱oo yéi s yatéeyi aa ḵu.aa,
ch'u shúgu haa yoo x̱'atángí tlél tsu daaḵw aa sá tsu missx̱ ustí.
Ha ch'a goosá,
tle wáa yei koowáat' sá tlél has du kaadéi haa sakwg̱wax'aaḵw.
Aaa
ha yéi áyá
woosh x̱ánx̱ da.aadín
áyá woosh x̱ang̱aa ḵáa,
aaa, át woosh sanast'ánjin
áyá ch'áakw
dax̱ḵustéeyi aa Lingít.
Adax̱ áyá yeedát áhé yées nawáadi
tlél yéi ootí.
Tle ch'as yú Dléit Ḵáa yinaadéi yáx̱ litseen
has du tundatáani.

But now they, they who are among us,
truly
they are like people of our land,
how they can speak our language.
This is how long ago,
the people from long,
long ago,
used to know each other.
It used to be like part of our territory on the ocean.
People used to go out there.
Those relatives on my side
yes, and those
those who are called Yanyeidí.
It was like their land.
This is where we know them from.
From here
on the southern side,
we can see
people from there.
They don't even talk our language.
And to the north of here
down the Yukon River
we can't even understand them.
They have a different language.
But those people who are here among us now,
it's our very same language; there's nothing missing.
No matter where,
no matter how long, we won't forget them.
Yes,
this is how
we used to visit each other,
those related to each other,
yes, they used to get lonesome for each other,
the Tlingits
who lived long ago.
But the new generation now
is not like that.
Their thinking
is strong only toward the white folks.

Ka yá ch'áagu ádi has du een kaduneegí
tlél ayáx̱ yoo aa tukwdatánk.
Tlél ák' has ooheen
áyá ch'áakw aadéi ák' aduheeni yé.
Tle oowayáa x'úx' kaax̱
dutóow át yéi áyá téeyeen ch'áakw.
Áyá k̲aa k̲usteeyí áyá Lingít   70
yá Lingít'aaní.
Aaa,
akáax' áyá wooshdáx̱ wuskóowun k̲á woosh yaa awudanéiyin.
Ha,
ha de hóoch' áwé.
Gunalchéesh.

K̲aal.átk'
Sheet'ká, 1972

Gunalchéesh áwé
yáax' yeeydanaagí
yáa yeedát
Kaagwaantaan yátx'i,
Kadakw.ádi yátx'i, gunalchéesh,
Chookaneidí yátx'i.
Aaa.
Yá ax̱ kéilk'
oowayáa toowú latseen
áwé du jeet yeeytée.   10
Dziyáak adaat x̱'ax̱ditaan
yáanáx̱ kawdi.ayí yá aas yátx'i.
Aaa.
Yá yeehwaan
Kiks.ádix̱ yee sateeyí,
áwé yanax̱ kayeeytee
yá du kaak hás x'aakeidí.
Yeedát áwé yeeytéen
du tóonáx̱ kanas.á áyá ldakát yaa daak wu.aadín.
Kichgaawch áwé wliyéx̱.   20
Has du sákw

And when they're told about the old ways
they don't think about them properly.
They don't believe
the way people believed long ago.
The way things were long ago
is like something read from a book.
This was the Tlingit way of life
in this world.
Yes,
from this the people knew each other and respected each other.
Well,
there is no more.
Thank you.

Charlie Joseph
Sitka, 1972

Thank you
for standing up here
now,
children of Kaagwaantaan,
children of Kadakw.ádi, thank you,
children of Chookaneidí.
Yes,
it is as if you have given
strength of mind
to this nephew of mine.
A while ago I spoke about
the little trees standing here.
Yes.
Those of you
who are Kiks.ádi
planted
the seed for his maternal uncles.
Now you can see
all those who have their roots in him have come out here.
Kichgaaw is the one who made them.
Their ancestor,

has du léelk'wx̲ wusitee.
Ách áwé gunalchéesh
yóo yee daayax̲ak̲á
yáa yeedát, du yáx̲ yeeydanaag̲í.
Aaa.
Tléix' yateeyí yéix'
tléil k̲aa daa yaa k̲ushusgé.
Yá x̲át L'uknax̲.ádi yádix̲ x̲at wusitee.
Yá du tláak'w hás Kiks.ádi yádix̲
has wusitee.
Ch'a aan áwé, "ax̲ éek'" yoo ax̲ yáx̲
x̲'awdliyoo.
Yáadu k̲u.a áwés
ách yéi yan kawsiyayi át.
Dáx̲náx̲ áwé wootee
du shatx'i yán, Kichgaaw.
Shux'áa aayí
G̲ooch Hít Taan sháawu áwé aawasháa,
shux'áanáx̲.
Du saayí k̲wa k̲utx̲waag̲éex'.
Aax̲ yá G̲ooch Hít Taan sháawu
du nák̲ nanáa áwé
awdligein
Kichgaaw.
Aag̲áa áwé aax̲ aawatee yá ax̲ tláa, du shát,
Katsóosgu Tláa.
Katsóosgu Tláa
du tláa eetee yéi natee áwé yá has du tláa,
yá ax̲ dlaak',
yá haa nák̲ woogoodi aa.
Aag̲áa áwé,
tle ayát x̲'awdliyóo.
Du tláa eetéex̲ ayawsik̲áa,
"atléi."
Ách áwé du tláax̲ wusiteeyi aa.
Du éesh yádix̲ x̲át sateeyéech
x̲át tsú tle ax̲ yát x̲'awdliyóo,
"ax̲ éek'."
Du éek'x̲ x̲át wusitee.
Áx' ch'a wooshdag̲akóot diteeyi yéix'
haa shá,

he was their grandfather.
This is why
I am saying "thank you" to you
for standing up to face him now.
Yes.
We are one but
some people don't understand.
I am child of L'uknax̱.ádi.
These maternal aunts of his
were children of Kiks.ádi.
But still she would address me
with the kinship term, "my brother."
And here is why
things came out this way.
Kichgaaw
had two wives.
The first one he married
was a woman of the Wolf House,
the first one.
But I've forgotten her name.
From when the woman of Wolf House
died,
Kichgaaw
looked for a wife.
This is when he took my mother for his wife,
Katsóosgu Tláa.
Katsóosgu Tláa
took the place of her mother, their mother,
of this sister of mine,
this one who has departed.
At that time
she adopted her
as her mother, calling her
"mother."
This is how she became her mother.
Because I became the child of her father,
she also adopted me, calling me
"my brother."
I became her brother.
Even though our ancestors
were different,

yá aadéi yan has kawdiyayi yéich ku.aa
tle tléix'x̱ haa wusitee.
Ách áyá yáax̱ has yawsix̱éi yá ax̱ kéilk',
x̱a tsu yóonáx̱
yáax' daak woogoodi aa.
Tsu hú du aayí du tláa tsú ch'u yéi ax̱ yáx̱ x̱'alyoowún
Ḵaax̱'ashtuk'áax, "ik'."
Hél x̱wasax̱ú á ku.aa.   70
Hu tsú tsu ch'a góot yéináx̱ x̱udzitee
du éesh hás.
Ha, yá du tuwánt áa
ch'a ax̱ yáx̱ áhé kwdayéin.
Ax̱ éesh kéilk' áyá yaax'
ax̱ tuwánt áa.
Hú tsú tsu du éesh kéilk' áyá
du tuwánt áa yáax'.
Du sáni
yáax' du yaa wdihaan.   80
Ha yá du aat hás
ku.a wés tlél yáadei aax̱wsateen.
Ha, gunalchéesh,
yéi yeedát
tsu ch'u yéi gugéink'
x̱unáax̱ daak at kawuneek teen
yéi wusneiyí.
Ch'u oowayáa aan x̱'adushugu yáx̱ áyá yatee
yéi yóox̱ x̱'alyoowú, "ax̱ káak,"
uncle.   90
Of course we have a space in between
us
yéi yanax̱éich dleit x̱áa
haa káak teen.
Ch'a aan x̱wás yóox̱ x̱'alyoo.
Ha yá naná x̱u.a yá yéi yan at kawsiyáa.
Yáax' daak uwagút yá ax̱ aat'asháa.
Tsu ch'u yéi áyá yan has kawdiyáa.
Shux'áanáx̱ yá, has du éesh,
aaa,   100
Dax̱l'awshaa aawasháa.
Yá Dax̱l'awshaa nanaa ítdáx̱ áyá tsá.
Yá has du tláa sákw aax̱ aawatee.

because of the way things happened to us,
it made us one.
This is why my maternal nieces and nephews are all sitting here,
and the one who came out
over here.
His mother too, Kaax'ashtuk'áax,
also used to call me "brother."
But I never learned why.
Her fathers
come from a different place.
Now, the person sitting next to him
is like me.
This is my father's maternal niece
sitting next to me.
He too, his father's maternal niece
is also sitting next to him here.
His paternal uncle
stood up to face him here.
But now
I didn't see any of his paternal aunts.
Thank you,
now,
for including
an explanation,
even just a little.
It was as if people were laughing at his words
when he said, "ax káak,"
maternal uncle.
Of course, we have space between
us,
as the white man would say,
about our mother's brother.
But we still address them as our kin.
It was death that did this.
My wife's sister's husband came here.
This also happened to them.
First their father,
yes,
married a woman of Dakl'aweidí.
After this woman of Dakl'aweidí died,
he took her for their mother.

Ách áwé du húnxux sitee
yóodáx, yóox' dziyáak daak uwagoodi aa.
Yéi áyá kudayéin
haa kusteeyí
Lingítx haa sateeyí uháan.
Ha, gunalchéesh
yáa yeedát
ch'a yéi gugéink'
kunáax daak at kawuneek teen
yéi wusneiyí.
Yéi áyá.

Keet Yaanaayí
Mt. Edgecumbe Hospital, 1976

Aaa,
ha yáat yikeení
ax kaani yán,
ax léelk'w hás,
ldakát yéidei ax ée yee kawaháa.
Ax tláa aat hás,
ax toowú yanéekw,
yá yee ya xoot l axulgeiní.
Ách áyá ch'a ax sé gay.aaxéet áyá,
yéi wdudzinei ax jiyís yá át
ch'a yee éet x'akataan kayaa.
Aaa.
Yá át aadéi ax tóoch waliyaagu yé
yá haa chooní,
yá haa wlichuni ku.oo,
yá du daa yéi jitooneiyí.
Gunalchéesh haat yeey.aadí.
Aaa.
Wáa yoo kganein sáwé
yá ax tlagu kwáanx'i
du eeti káawu yéi ayanaskéich,
"Sheenú!
Neechx naxtookoox."

This is why he is an older brother to him,
the one who came out over there.
This is the way
our culture is,
those of us who are Tlingit.
So, thank you
now
for letting me give
this little
explanation.
This is all.

Willie Marks
Mt. Edgecumbe Hospital, 1976

Yes,
you who are sitting here:
my brothers-in-law,
my grandparents,
you are related to me in many ways.
My mother's paternal aunts,
I am grieved
that I can't look among your faces.
That is why, so you can at least hear my voice,
this recording was made for me,
that I might in some way speak to you.
Yes.
This is how I compare
our wounds,
these people who wounded us,
those for whom we are doing these rites.
Thank you all for coming.
Yes.
At what point
would this ancestor of mine
say to someone who is to succeed him,
"Wake up!
Let's go along the beach by boat."

Wduskóowun áyú yá haa shuká tlein,
aagáa ígee yéi teexi yé yá xóots
ayayeedéi áwé xdutsáaych wé ḵaa kéilk'íx siteeyi ḵáa.
Aagáa áwé shaadanookch.
Gunéi uḵooxch.
Yá áa shadudziteeyi yéix'.
Tliyéi yei ngatéen áwé wé yaakw,   30
yóox gwáa wé yeiḵ nagút.
(Yá yee sáni tlein.)
Aagáa áwé áa jikanduḵéich wé ḵaa eeti ḵáa
"Góok!
I jeegáa woogoot," yóo.
Awu.óoni áwé, tléik',
ch'as choondéin
dáḵdei nashíxch.
"A ítnáx yei eeshéex," yóo yan dusḵéich.
A ítnáx yei gagúdín áwé tsu haat ugootch.   40
"Tléik', tlél akáx kuxwashee," yu.á.
"Ch'as x'áal' áhé kíndei aawas'él'."
Xach du chooní x'eis
du chooní yís áwé kínde as'éil'
wé x'áal' ḵu.aa
yú yatseeneit.
Aagáa áwé akáax' áwé yagagútch.
Yá du chooní x'éidei al.aat nooch
wé x'áal',
ách asdéex' wé óonaa eetée.   50
Yéi áyá ax toowóoch wuliyaaḵw
yá yixwsateení,
yá x'áal' yáx áyá ax jee ḵuwdi.oo.
Yáax' neil yeey.aadí yá yee yadook xoot axwalgeiní,
yá ax chooní x'éidei áwé kḵwatée.
Gwál akáax' yax yakḵwahaanán.
Ha yéi áyá s gugwatée shákdei yee aat hás.
Has du chooní x'éidei s aguxla.aat.
Yá yee ḵ'asagoowú.
Yéi áyá sh tugaa xat ditee.   60

It was known when this great ancestor of ours
this brown bear, would come down to the beach.
A man, a person's nephew, would be asked to lie in wait for it.
That is when he would get out of bed.
They would begin paddling
to where it was expected to appear.
When the boat stopped
it was coming down over there.
(This immense uncle of yours.)
That's when he'd say to the man who would succeed him
"Go ahead!
It's walking into your hands!" he'd say.
After the nephew shot it—no!—
only wounding it—
it would run into the forest.
"Go chase it!" his uncle would tell him.
Having followed it, he would return.
"No, I didn't find it," the nephew would say.
"It had only torn up some skunk cabbage."
They were for his open wounds,
the animal
was tearing up the skunk cabbage
for his wounds.
Then with their help he was able to walk.
He put the skunk cabbage
on his open wounds,
plugged his gunshot wounds with them.
This is how I compare it.
You whom I see here
have become like skunk cabbage in my hands.
Looking among the faces of you who have come here,
I will apply them to this open wound of mine.
Perhaps with this help I will be able to stand again.
Now perhaps this is how your paternal aunts will be.
They will apply some of your kindness
to their open wounds.
This is why I'm grateful.

Kaatyé
X̲'agáax'i
Xunaa, 1976

Lord Dikée Aank̲áawu
wáa gunalchéesh sá
wooch x̲áni yéi haa wdateeyí
yá ANB Hallx'
aatx̲ yá haa t'aak̲x'í
ldakát yéitx̲ yáa yéi wootee.
Wa.é k̲u.aa
aan ix̲'usyeet x̲waagút
toowú k̲'anashgidéix̲ satí een.
Aáa,
akáa daak jisataan x'wán
aantk̲eení g̲isak̲ée Jerusalem káx'.
Aatx̲ áyú yiysik̲ee
yú keijín táawsan yéi yá koogeiyi aantk̲eení.
Aatx̲ áyá
sakwnéin yeex̲oox̲, k̲óox̲.
I jeet áyú wduwatee
yú sakwnéin k̲a yú x̲áat.
Aax̲ áwé wóosht alwáal' áwé shawahík
wé s'u k̲ákwx'.
Ldakát yá aantk̲eení xoox áwé yakawdudligáa
k̲a yá x̲áat.
Aáa, atóonáx̲ áwé
ldakát k̲áa áwé shaawahík.
Yéi x'wán has nag̲atee yá haa t'aak̲x'í.
Aax̲ kei has akg̲watée
i daa dleeyéex̲ siteeyi át,
has du eenx̲ inastí.
Has du káa daak jisataan.
L wáa sá haa uteeyí
k̲a yá yageeyi tóonáx̲.
Amen.

David Kadashan
Invocation for the ANB Convention
Hoonah, 1976

Lord Dikée Aanḵáawu,
how much gratitude there is
that we are together
in this ANB Hall,
and that these brothers and sisters of ours
have all come here from everywhere.
And now to you
I come to your feet
poor in spirit.
Yes,
just extend your hand out over us,
as when you seated the multitude in Jerusalem.
Then you seated
the multitude that numbered five thousand.
And then
you asked the people for bread.
The bread and fish
were given to you.
When they were broken they filled
the grass baskets.
Through all the crowd it was distributed,
and the fish.
Yes, from this
all the people were fed.
Let it be this way for these brothers and sisters of ours.
When they take up
that which is your flesh,
please be with them.
Extend your hand out over them.
Let nothing happen to us
throughout the day.
Amen.

Seigeigéi
Dzantik'i Héeni, 1982

Aaa, ax t'aakx'í
tléix' Dikaankáawooch yaax' tl'átgi káa yan haa uwatée.
Aaa, yú Book of Life yoo duwasáakw Bible haa jéex'
ldakát uháan.
Chácht yoo too.átgi haa ée dultóow.
A káx' áyú yei x'ayaká
Dikaankáawu s'e "Shux'áanáx."
Ach áyá ax toowú yéi yatee
yá yeedát.
Aaa, ax Aankáawu
du ée axahéen
yá diyéex'.
Ch'a uwaayáa yá tl'átgi káx'
haa xoo yaa woogoodi yéx haa xoowú a
haa Aankáawu.
Haa téix' du yinaadéi téeyee
awsikóo tlek'gaanáx haa teeyí
haa tundatáani wáasá yatee.
Ka yá du x'úx'u káa yéi yatee
wóoch káx' x'anáx tudagáax'
aagaa áyá yéi haa kgwanéix,
ka wóoch gaxtoosxán.
Tláx wáa yak'eiyi átx sá sitee du aaní káx'
yá haa Aankáawu.
Aaa,
yá
aax haat xat kawdiyayi yé xát,
Aalséix áyá aax haat xat kawdiyáa.
Aantkeeneex áyú haa satéeyin
yóo yú kduneegéen.
Ax léek'wch
yéi xat gusageink'í
tlél xat oolgé
Kuchéin yóo dusáagun

Emma Marks
Juneau, 1982

Yes, my brothers and sisters,
God put us here on this land as one.
Yes, we have the Bible called the Book of Life
all of us.
Going to church, we are taught.
There the voice of the Lord
said, "Put me first!"
This is why I feel like this
today.
Yes, I believe
in my Lord
down here.
It is as if
our Lord
is still among us as he walked the earth before.
When our hearts are toward Him,
He knows each one of us
and what our thoughts are.
And in His book it says
that we should pray for each other
then we will be saved,
and we should love one another too.
How very fine it is in his land,
our Lord's.
Yes,
this
place where I come from,
I come from Alsek.
It is said
we were many people.
My grandfather
when I was a child,
still very small,
(his name was K̲uchéin)

yú ax̱ léelk'w
ax̱ tláa du éesh
hú áyá du x̱'éidei x̱a.áx̱jin.
Aaa, yei kwdzigeiyi aa
at yátx'i yax̱ haa wooskeich.
Sh kakgwalneegí
tlél aadéi gunéi aa ux̱ jixeexi yé uháan.
Áyá yáa yeedát
ax̱ yátx'i tín kux̱a.aagu yóo x̱'ax̱la.átgi,
T.V. dultínch.
Uháan tlél yéi haa wootee.
Tlél,
akáa wtudahaan
haa léelk'w haa éen sh kalneegí.
Áyá yáa yeedát
ax̱ daat áyá ḵaa shoowaxíx.
Ch'as ax̱ yátx'i áyá s du een ḵux̱dzitee,
yá Lukaax̱.ádi,
yú haa dusáagu
yá Alséix̱dáx̱.
Aaa
yá haa kahídi
Tsalx̱aan Hít yoo aa wduwasáa
ḵa Shaaka Hít.
Aaa, Tsalx̱aan X̱'éen
tsu a yee yéi téeyin
yá haa kahídi.
Aaa
ax̱ tuwáa sigóo
tsu yá anax̱ ḵux̱dziteeyi yé
kx̱waneegí.
Ax̱ éesh du léelk'w
áyá yéi dusáagoon
Yaandu.ein,
Kaagwaantaan.
Yá ax̱ éesh du éesh ḵu.aa áwés
Ḵaawus.aa
yóo duwaasáa.
Dax̱ aa du saayí,
Ḵusán
yóo duwaasáa.

my grandfather,
my mother's father,
he is the one I heard this from.
Yes, we smaller children
would sit in a row.
When he was going to tell stories
none of us could get up and run.
But now,
when I try talking with my children
they watch T.V.
We were not like that.
No,
we didn't get up
during our grandfather's storytelling.
Today
my relatives are all dead.
There are just my children whom I survived with,
the Lukaax̱.ádi,
we who are named
from Alsek River.
Yes,
one of our houses
was named Mt. Fairweather House,
and Canoe Prow House.
Yes, the Mt. Fairweather Screen
was also inside
this house of ours.
Yes,
I would like
to tell
about my origin, too.
My father's grandfather's
name was
Yaandu.ein,
a Kaagwaantaan.
My father's father
was named
K̲aawus.aa.
His second name
was also
K̲usán.

Áhé ax̱ léelk'wx̱ sitee,
yáax' daak x̱at wusigút
ax̱ léelkw hás eetée.
Aaa, has tsu dei yei s shunax'ix
yá ax̱ léelk'w
yá Yaakwdáatdáx̱.
Ax̱ éek'x̱ tsú sitee.
Aaa, ch'a haa shagóon áyá wooshkaadáx̱ yóot kawdzi.áa.
Ach áyá yá
yóox' yoo x̱'eiwatani aa tsú ax̱ éek'x̱ sitee.
Aaa, yáat'aa,
yáat.
Ax̱ kéek' áhé.
Ax̱ éesh du kéilk'
du sée áhé.
G̱anáḵt'
yóo dusáagoon.
Ḵa ax̱ toowu yak'éi
yáa yeedát
x̱át tsú yee x̱óo ax̱walg̱einí
ḵa yá ax̱ aani ḵwáani
has du x̱óo x̱at kawuhaayí.
Aaa, first time ḵu.a áyá yoo x̱'ax̱aatank
yéi yateeyi yéix'.
Yei at duwasáakw
at kux̱laḵéiyin áyú.
Aa ḵushayadiheini yé tléil ax̱ tuwáa ushgú ax̱ ya x̱wagoodí.
Dleit ḵáach yéi yasáakw "shy."
Tléil school yóo x̱wagoot ch'á ax̱oo aa ḵwa x̱wsikóo.
Aaa,
tsú kakḵwanéek
ya ax̱ tláa yinaanáx̱ ax̱ léelk'w yinaanáx̱.
Ax̱ tláa du tláa saayéex̱ áyá x̱at sitee.
Seig̱eig̱éi
yóo wduwasáa
ax̱ tláa du tláa.
Ax̱ tláa ḵwá Leetkwéi yú duwasáa.
Áyá yá ax̱ saayí ḵu.a áyá Teiḵweidí yádix̱ wusitee,
Yaakwdaat aa.
Ax̱ tláa ḵu.a hés
Shangukeidí yádix̱ wusitée.

This is my grandfather
who brought me out,
my grandparents' descendant.
Yes, they too are fast passing away,
these my grandparents
from Yakutat.
He is also my younger brother.
Yes, our ancestors' lives branched off from each other.
That is why this one
who spoke over there is my brother, too.
Yes, this one
here.
She is my younger sister.
She's the daughter
of my father's nephew.
His name was
G̱anáḵt'.
And I am feeling happy
at this moment
that I too look among you
and these my people
that I am among them.
Yes, I'm speaking for the first time
on an occasion such as this.
I was what is called
being shy.
I didn't want to pass by where there are a lot of people.
In English they call it "shy."
I did not attend school, but I do know a little English.
Yes,
I will also explain
my mother's lineage, my grandmother's lineage.
I am my mother's mother's namesake.
Seigeigéi
was her name,
my mother's mother.
But my mother's name was Leetkwéi.
My namesake was a child of the Teiḵweidí
of Yakutat.
But my mother
was a child of Shangukeidí.

Ax̲ éesh k̲u.a áwé
Naag̲éi yóo wduwasáa,
Yéil Éesh.
Nás'k
du yáa wootee.
Kinaadak̲een.
Yéi áyá kdulnéek
yú haa aaní.
Ax̲ áat áyú x̲áan sh kalnik noojéen.
Yú dak̲kaadéi
Aalséix̲ yík
tulatsak̲ g̲anugún.
Aaa, g̲il ayu akaanáx̲ yan kaawa.áa yu.á
ya Aalséix̲.
Tlél a tayeenáx̲ shaa; kaanáx̲ áyá x̲too.átch.
Yú yaakwx' anáx̲ g̲atula.átch.
Yaax' áwé k̲úx̲dei haa yakwdaháaych.
Ya sít' tayeenáx̲ yóo áwé yaa haa ax̲sagúkch,
yaakwx'u yíkt.
A tayeenáx̲ yaa haa g̲asagug̲ún áwé
lk'wáa aan g̲unein áwé ayée ktudanák̲ch
wé yaakw,
al'eix̲.
At dushée nuch.
Yéi áwé x̲wsikóo.
Aaa, yá ax̲ yátx'i
yáat han áa yá ax̲ sée.
Jilk̲áatnáx̲ áhé k̲uwaháa du léelk'w.
Jak̲wteen yóo dusáagun yá du léelk'w
wé has du léelk'w,
yá ax̲ x̲án.aa du éesh.
Xunaanáx̲ k̲u.aa awés sháawat dú léelk'w
k̲u.aa áwé
Táx̲' Hít Taan yádix̲ wusitée, ach wuskóowu yáadu.
Táx̲' Hít Taan yádix̲ áwé wusitee hú k̲u.aa.
A tóodei áhé has k̲uwaháa
yá Xunaa tóodei tsú,
k̲a Jilk̲áat.
Yéi áwé has kaawahaa ax̲ yatx'i.
Ha, ax̲ tuwóo yak'éi

My father's name
was Naaḡéi,
and Yeil Éesh.
He had three
names.
Kinaadaḵeen.
This is the way it's told
about our land.
This is the way my paternal aunt would tell it to me.
We would pole our way
up the Alsek River
to the Interior.
Yes, a cliff of ice ran across this river
the Alsek River.
We did not go under; we went over the mountains.
We would carry our boats over.
At this point we would return.
We would float down underneath the glacier
in the boats.
When we floated out from underneath,
when nothing had happened to us we would stand
in the boats
and dance.
We would sing.
This is the way I know it.
Yes, these children of mine:
the one standing here is my daughter.
Her grandfather is from Chilkat.
Her grandfather's name was Jaḵwteen,
their grandfather,
my husband's father.
Their grandmother, however, is from Hoonah.
And
she was a child of the Snail House;
 there are people here who know this.
She was a child of the Snail House.
They are related
to both Hoonah
and Chilkat.
These are my children's relatives.
Now, I'm happy

x̱at tsú ch'a yéi yiguwáatl'
gaaw ax̱ jeet yeeyteeyí.
Tlél yéi ḵoox̱wají
yá yeedát yáa wóosh kaanáx̱ ḵugawdahaayi
yáax' yoo x̱'akḵwtaaní.
Ha "Gunlchéesh" yóo ḵwa
daayax̱aḵá hé ax̱ léelk'w
x̱at wusaayí.
Yéi áyá kakḵwalagéi.
Gu.aal kwshé Dikaanḵaawu haa eenx̱ wusteeyiḵ tsu
next year yís.
Yéi awé.
Sh tug̱áa x̱at ditee.

Shax'saani Kéek'
Deishú, 1985

Ax̱ tuwáa sigóo
yee éen at kax̱waneegí
ax̱ sisdees.
Ax̱ toowú yak'éi,
aaa,
hóoch'i gaawú
yaa kunax̱laséin
(x̱at yeeytéen)
aax̱ yá gaaw
yee tuwaá sigóo yeeysakoowú
yá aan x̱at kawdudlix̱edli át.
Tléil yaa ux̱shagé.
Ax̱ tuwáa sigóo g̱oot ḵaach wuskoowú.
Aaa, shux'áanáx̱
ax̱ tláa,
Sitgeedáx̱ áwé,
ax̱ éeshch uwasháa
Tlákw.aandéi.
Ax' áwé ḵux̱dzitee.
Ax̱ aat hás jeedáx̱ atwuskú áyá.
Yá gaaw

that you allowed me
some time too.
I didn't think
that I would speak here
today where we are all gathered together.
And I say, "Thank you"
to this grandfather of mine
for calling me.
This will be the extent of my speech.
My hope is that God will be with us again
next year.
This is all.
I am thankful.

Jennie Thlunaut
Haines, 1985

I would like
to tell you something,
my sisters.
I am happy,
yes,
as I am coming close
to my final hour
(you can see my condition)
that at this time
you want to learn
this weaving I was blessed with.
I don't want to keep it to myself.
I want someone else to learn.
Yes, to begin with,
my father married
my mother,
who was from Sitka,
and they moved to Klukwan.
I was born there.
This is the art of my paternal aunts.
My father's sister

yá blanket
ax̱ éesh dlaak'
yéi dusáagun
Deinḵul.át.
Dú jeedáx̱ atwuskú áyá
ax̱ jee yéi wootee.
Tlél aan ḵukin x̱at x̱'eití.
Ax̱ tuwáa sigóo
ax̱ x̱ooni ḵáach wuskoowú.
Ha yá gaaw
gunalchéesh.
Yéi yoo yee kayasheik ax̱ x̱ándéi.
Aaa,
aadéi shtug̱áa x̱at ditee.
Áyá ax̱ Aanḵáawooch aan x̱at kawlix̱étl
yá yéi jiné.
Aaa,
yá gaaw ḵu.aa,
tlél ch'a koogéiyi.
Ch'a yéi x̱at gusagenk'idáx̱
ax̱ cháchi
áa x̱at shukawajeis' ax̱ tláa,
ḵa ax̱ éesh;
Wednesday ḵa Sunday
yaa x̱at jigatánch cháchdei.
Aax̱ yá gaaw
yá aan x̱at kawdudlix̱etli át.
Gunalchéesh,
yee tuwáa sagoowú.
Ha gu.aal kwshé
Dikaanḵáawux' yan tuytán x'wan,
aa yan nax̱yidlaaḵ.
Aaa Yáat'aa
dei du ée at x̱alatóowun.
Haa yá gaaw áwé
gunalchéesh yéi ax̱ toowú yatee,
ax̱ x̱ándei yéi yee kasheigí.
Aaa, Dikaanḵáawu éex̱ ḵwá gayisg̱áax̱
yanax̱ yidlaag̱í
yá akáx̱ haat ḵayeeytini át.

at the time
of that blanket
was called
Deink̲ul.át.
This is the art from her
that was passed to my hands.
I'm not stingy.
I would like
someone like me to learn it.
Now at this time
thank you.
You have experienced hardships to be with me.
Yes,
I'm grateful for this.
God gave his blessing to me
for this work.
Yes,
and I want to tell you now
none of this was by accident.
From when I was little
my mother
and my father instructed me
on where my church was;
Wednesday and Sunday
she would take me by the hand to church.
From that time to this
I have been blessed with this weaving.
Thank you
for wanting it.
My hope is
you will have faith in God,
that you will learn.
Yes,
I have been teaching her already.
Now, at this time,
I feel thankful
that you have experienced hardships to be with me.
Ask our Lord above
to learn
what you came for.

Yéi áwé ax̲ tundatáani yatee yáa yagiyee,
 aadéi sh tug̲áa x̲at ditee.
Aaa, ax̲ g̲aawú uwayáa yaa kunayach'i yáx̲ yatee.
Shux'áanáx̲
1901
áwé ax̲ tláa
ax̲ éeshch áwé akaa k̲oowak̲éi.
Ax̲ tlaak'w yéi duwasáakw,
Saantáas'.
Áwé
yéi wé dulgeis'ín:
fifty dollars
one blanket.
Yéi áwé x̲'alatseenín.
A jeet awatée
wé fifty dollars ax̲ tláak'w jeet.
Aag̲áa áwé ax̲ tláa ee awlitúw.
1901.
Tlél yeedadi yáx̲.
Shaax'sáani
át luwugook̲ ch'áakw.
Gwál ch'a x̲át giwé yéi x̲at wuduswáat.
"Haagú!"
Any time you start it.
"Haagú!"
Áyá du déix̲'i k̲anúkch.
I am watching what they're doing.
1908 áwé woonaa ax̲ tláa.
Aag̲áa áwé yan akawsinéi yóot'aa yáx̲,
black and yellow.
All mine.
Ax̲ éeshch
ax̲ jeet uwatée.
Dei k̲wá x̲ashigóok.
I know how to weave.
Aanáx̲ áwé
ax̲ léelk'w
ax̲ éesh du tláa
hooch áwé
shux'áanáx̲ ax̲ ée awlitúw.
1908,

This is how I feel today, I'm grateful for this.
Yes, my time seems to be getting short.
In the beginning,
in 1901,
my father paid
for my mother's instruction.
My maternal aunt was named
Saantáas'.
Then,
they used to pay this much for it:
fifty dollars
for one blanket.
This was the dollar value.
He gave
the fifty dollars to my aunt.
This was when she taught my mother.
1901.
It wasn't like now.
The young girls
didn't run around long ago.
Maybe it was only me that was raised this way.
"Come here!" they'd say
every time they began weaving.
"Come here!"
I would sit behind her.
I'd watch what they were doing.
My mother died in 1908.
This is when she finished weaving it, like that one,
black and yellow.
All mine.
My father
gave it to me.
I already knew how to weave.
I knew how to weave.
After this
my grandmother,
my father's mother,
was the one
who first taught it to me.
in 1908,

Porcupine gold mine-ix' tle all summer áwé
yan kax̱wsinéi,
tléix' ḵutaan.
Yawdi.aa wéit'át; it's a slow job.
Ax̱oo aa yú lingít
two years x̱'áak aksané.
Aa yei gax̱yisatéen aadéi lich'éeyag̱u yé.
Aax̱ yan néi
yéi áwé
wududzigéy fifty dollars.
Déix̱,
I got two twenty
and one ten,
gold.
Aag̱áa áwé
shux'áanáx̱ ax̱ x̱án.aa
"take good care of that money.
Don't use it."
Yéi wooyáat' aag̱áa
ax̱ jee yéi wooteeyi yé,
wé naaxein yeidí.
Aaa, yáa yeedadi ḵáawu dáanaa yaa ayakanadláḵ.
They spend it right away.
Ha yéi sh kadulneek á yahaayí ḵudzitee dáanaa.
Sh tóon yoo diteek ḵóodáx̱
l áyáa ayaduneiyí.
Ách áwé
tsu x̱wahooní
ax̱ naaxeiní
I keep the money for two, three months
or four months.
Ách áwé yeedát tlél k'anashgideix̱ x̱at ustée.
Aaa,
ax̱ éesh hás,
ax̱ aat hás jeedáx̱
atwuskú áwé.
Ách áwé ayaa awux̱aanéi.
Ha yá gaaw ḵu.aa ax̱ tundatáani ax̱ x̱'agáax'i yéi yatee,
ch'a aadooch sá yan gadlaag̱í
yáa yéi daax̱ané át.
Kanay.aaḵw yee Aanḵaawoox' yan tuytán

at Porcupine gold mine I weaved all summer
and finished it
in one summer.
Those things take time; it's slow work.
It takes some people
two years to weave one.
Now you'll all see how slow it is.
When it was finished
it was bought
for this much: fifty dollars.
Two,
I got two twenties
and one ten,
gold pieces.
This is when
my first husband said to me
"Take good care of the money.
Don't spend it."
I kept the money
for a long time then,
the money from the naaxein.
Yes, people of today, as soon as they make the money
they spend it right away.
Well, they say money has a spirit.
You can offend it
if you don't respect it.
That's why
when I sold
my naaxein
I kept the money for two, three,
or four months.
This is why I'm not a poor person.
Yes,
this art
is from my fathers
and my paternal aunts.
Because of this I respect it.
And now at this time my thoughts are, my prayers are,
that someone master
the things that I do.
Try to concentrate on your Lord

aa yanax yidlaagí.
Yéi áwé
áwé aadéi yoo kawaneiyi yé wé naaxein.
Tlákw.aannáx áwé kuwdzitee.
Gaanaxteidí yóo
s duwasáakw ax éesh hás.
Hásch áwé s aawasháa
Tsimshian woman.
Yéi áwé
du saayí tlél du káx xat seix'aakw.
Yéi áwé wduwasáa
Hayuwáas Tláa.
I remember the name.
Hayuwáas Tláa jeedáx atwuskú áwé
first in Tlákw.aan.
Kux has akawsikéi
wé naaxein.
Ch'u yeedát áwoo á.
They got it.
Martha Willard got it,
that blanket.
First blanket from a Tsimshian.
Áwé kux has akawsikéi.
Ch'as ax aat hásx siteeyi áach áwé
has awshigóok.
Yaax' áwé s du kaani yán ee s awlitúw, yá uhaan.
Yanwaa Sháa ee s awlitúw.
Ách áwé yéi duwasáakw
Jilkáat Blanket.
Tlél tsu Sitka,
tlél tsu Hoonah,
tlél tsu goox' sá yéi daaduné.
Only Tlákw.aan.
That's why they call it Jilkáat Blanket.
Ha yéi áwé yee tóo yéi kgwatée.
I don't know why they lost the art
wé Tsimshian ku.aa.
Tlél yeedát
I don't see
somebody make it like that.
Aaa

so that you'll master it.
This is the way
it happened with the naaxein.
It came through Klukwan.
My fathers are called
G̱aanax̱teidí.
They were the ones who married
the Tsimshian woman.
This is why
I don't forget her name.
Her name was
Hayuwáas Tláa.
I remember the name.
This is art from Hayuwáas Tláa
first done in Klukwan.
They unraveled
the naaxein.
It's still there now.
They have it.
Martha Willard has
that blanket.
The first blanket from a Tsimshian.
They unraveled it.
Only those who were my paternal aunts
learned it.
Then they taught it to their sisters-in-law, to us.
They taught it to the Yaanwaa Sháa.
That is why it's called
Chilkat Blanket.
It wasn't made in Sitka,
or Hoonah,
or anywhere else.
Only in Klukwan.
That is why it's called Chilkat Blanket.
This is what you will keep in mind.
I don't know why the Tsimshians
lost the art.
I don't see
anyone now
making them like that.
Yes,

yá gaaw k̲u.aa ax̲ toowú yak'éi,
yee tuwaa wusgóowu.
Ax̲ x̲'agáax'i yéi yatee ch'a aadóoch sá yawudlaag̲í.
Aaa
yéi áwé.

Shax'saani Kéek'
Deishú, 1985

X̲'agaax' k̲wa yéi kk̲wasanéi.
Haa Aank̲áawudéi tunaydataan.

Lord, Dikaank̲áawu,
ax̲ s'aatí,
gunalchéesh yá s'ootaat
ax̲ yéi jineiyí aan x̲at kaylax̲eidléen;
aatx̲ yá gaaw
ax̲ sisdees
k̲a ax̲ dachx̲anx'i sáani
hásch tsu sh too s akg̲waltóowu yá s'ootaatdáx̲.
Wa.éich has du yaa k̲oosg̲eiyí too yéi inati x'wán.
Dikaank̲áawu, ch'a daak̲w aach sá yan g̲adlaag̲í.
Yá yéi dax̲ane át
de aan guk̲wagóot, ax̲ Aank̲áawu.
Tléil k̲wa yaa ux̲shagé;
ax̲ x̲ooni k̲áach k̲wa g̲aax̲shagóogu
yá s'ootaat ax̲ x̲'agaax'i yéi yatee,
i yéet Jesus saayí tóonáx̲.
Amen.

but now I feel good
that you have wanted to do it.
My prayer is that someone learn it.
Yes,
this is how I feel.

Jennie Thlunaut
Haines, 1985

I will offer a prayer.
Lift your thoughts to our Lord.

Lord! God above,
my master,
thank you, this morning
for my work that you have blessed me with;
that now
my sisters
and my grandchildren
are also going to learn from this morning on.
Please have them keep you in their knowledge.
Lord above, let whichever of them learn.
This work that I do,
I'm going to go with it soon, my God.
But I don't want to keep it to myself;
instead, that someone like me learn it,
is my prayer this morning,
in the name of Your Son, Jesus.
Amen.

Shax'saani Kéek'
Tlákw.aan, 1985

Aḵ tuwáa sigóo
x̱'ax̱wdataaní.
Tlákw.aan Sisterhood,
gunalchéesh,
aadéi ax̱ éet yeeydishiyi yé,
aaa,
yee x̱ooníx̱ x̱at sateeyéech áwé.
Ax̱ toowú yéi wootee,
yee een sisterhood x̱at sateeyéech.
Yá xáanaa gunalchéesh,
aadéi ax̱ eet yeeydishiyi yé,
ḵa yá
haat ḵuwatini aa,
aadoo sá
yá naaxein yéi adaané.
X'oon gunalchéesh á.
Ch'a oowayáa tlél toox̱wanookw.
Tlákw x̱at yanéekw,
ḵa ekskóos yéi daax̱ané.
Ch'a aan áwé
has du tuwáa sigóo wé dleit ḵáa ḵu.aa
ḵoox̱latóowu wé át.
K'e yáa yeedát
Dikaanḵáawudei tux̱atán
yan ḵadlaaḵ.
Yá déix̱ yagiyee ux̱sayéx̱.
Yee eedéi sh tugáa x̱at ditee
ldakát all of you girls
aadéi ax̱ een yéi jiyne yé.
Aaa, yá xáanaa
aadéi
ax̱ daa yee tuwateeyi yé yáx̱ ax̱ een yéi jiyiné,
        Tlákw.aan Sisterhood.
Gunalchéesh.

Jennie Thlunaut
Klukwan, 1985

I would like
to speak.
Thank you,
Klukwan Sisterhood,
for the way you have helped me,
yes,
because I am your relative.
I feel this way
because I am in the Sisterhood with you.
Thank you, tonight,
for the way you have helped me,
and those
who have come here
who are doing
Chilkat weaving.
Many thanks.
It is as if I no longer feel sick.
I was sick all the time
and kept making excuses.
But still
the White people wanted me
to teach this.
For example, now
I keep my mind on the Lord
that I can finish teaching.
There are two more days to go.
I am grateful
to all of you girls
for what you have done for me.
Yes, this evening,
because of the way you feel about me,
you have done this for me, Klukwan Sisterhood.
Thank you.

Aaa,
yá tsu ax̱ naa.ádi,
yá kát aax̱ datéen,
yá ax̱ sgóonwaanx'i jeedáx̱ át.
Ax̱ jeet wuduwa.áx̱.
Aaa.
Ax̱ tundatáani yéi yatee,
Gunx̱aa G̱uwakaan.
        (Gunx̱aa G̱uwakaan) *Áawé.*
Aan daaḵ kuḵwagóot
i eedéi sh tug̱aa datí.
Wa.é i eenáx̱ yáa yeedát
yá yéi jiné ax̱ jee yéi wootee,
ḵa gunalchéesh.
Aaa.
Ax̱ yátx'u sáani,
ax̱ dachx̱ánx'i sáani,
gunalchéesh.
Oowayáa yeex̱wshakéeni.
Ḵa wa.é,
Joe Hotch,
ax̱ éek'átsk'u,
gunalchéesh
aadéi ax̱ daa yoo x̱'eeyatangi yé
yá xáanaa.
Aaa.
Tlél ax̱ tuwáa ushgú
yee aanídáx̱ ḵoo at x̱alatuw yéix'
yáat'át l ḵaa jeet wutooteeyí.
Yóo áwé a daa tux̱ditáan.
Ách áyá yeex̱wshikín,
ax̱ sistee.
Aaa, yeedát ḵu.aa
ax̱ toowú yak'éi.
Tlél waa sá ax̱ toowú utée,
tsu a ítx' waa sá x̱at wuneiyí.
Aaa, yá xáanaa
gunalchéesh, ldakát yeehwáan
yéi yee daayax̱aḵá
aadéi ax̱ een yéi jiyeeyneiyí yé
ḵa yá

Yes,
even the dress
that's on me now
is from my students.
It was given to me.
Yes.
Austin Hammond
has been on my mind.
        (Austin Hammond) *Áawé.*
I will enter the forest
with my gratitude to you.
Because of you now
this work has come to me,
and I thank you.
Yes,
my dear children,
my dear grandchildren,
thank you
for letting me impose on you.
And you,
Joe Hotch,
my dear little brother,
thank you
for the way you have been thinking of me
this evening.
Yes.
I didn't want
to teach something from your village
without our giving this dinner.
This is how I feel about it.
This is why I'm imposing on you,
my sisters.
Yes, but now
I feel good.
I won't feel bad about anything,
even if something happens to me after this.
Yes, this evening
I am saying
thank you to all of you
for what you have done,
for this,

wéit'át
yei gax̱dusteení.
Ax̱ toowú yak'éi.
Yáax' daak wus.eení ḵu.aa shákdéi wé yak'éi.
Tsu x̱at wunawú
yóox' yaa kanajux át
ldakát yeehwáanch
yáax' yoo x̱'ax̱atángi
ḵaach yei gux̱satínch.
Tsu x̱at wunaawú
tlél ax̱ kaadéi yisag̱wax'áakw
yéi áwé g̱watee wé ax̱ léelk'w hás ádi,
ax̱ een yáax'.
A yahaayí ldakát lingit'aaní tuḵwáaneech yéi gux̱sateen.
Ax̱ toowú yak'éi aadéi i tundatáani wooteeyi yé.
Yá Sítkax' ḵwa aag̱aa yak'éiyi
picture-x̱ gux̱satée
wéit'át.
Wé naaxein tsu.
Yax̱ shaysa.áx̱w.
Yéi daax̱aneiyéech áwé wé naaxein
yáat'áach haat yaawax̱áa
x̱áach yéi x̱wsineiyi aa.
Á tsú ax̱ tuwáa sigóo yá,
yá haa yahaayí teen
a káa yéi wooteeyí.
Yéi áwé.
Gunalchéesh.

this here,
that people will see.
I am happy.
Perhaps it it is best that your things be brought out here.
Even when I die
all of you
who are talking here
will see
that camera running out there.
Even when I die
you won't forget me.
This is how my grandparents' things will be
along with me here.
The pictures will be seen by people all over the world.
I am happy for the way your feelings are.
Then this
will be made in Sitka
into a nice film.
This Chilkat blanket, too.
Hang it over there.
Because I made this Chilkat blanket
she brought it here,
one that I made.
I would like it also
to be included with us,
as part of the picture.
This is all.
Thank you.

Daanawáaḵ
Fairbanks, 1988

Yáa yeedát
ax̱ tuwáa sigóo
x̱'ax̱wdataaní.
Aaa,
ha yá dziyáak áwé
i x̱'éit x̱wasi.áx̱,
Lyeḵwudusdéich,
i tundatáani
aadéi yateeyi yé.
Aaa,
tsu nisdaat áwé i eet x̱'ax̱waatán.
Yáa yeedát yáat naḵ aa hasch tsú s ag̱a.aax̱ít áwé tsu
    ax̱ tuwaa sigóo x̱'ax̱wdataaní adaat.
Aaa,
tleidahéen áwé yéi at wootee
yáa yeedádi yáx̱.
Yándei áwé yaa ḵunanéin.
Wé ḵoo.éex'x' al'eix̱í
sh daat ḵudushée.
Áwé wé ḵáa
tlax̱ áyú du toowú yak'éi
aadéi yándei yaa at nanein yé.
Yáax' áwé, du een kawduwaneek.
Du x̱ánt aawagút.
Aag̱áa áwé yéi yawdudziḵaa,
"I kéilk' áyá woonaa."
Aag̱áa yan tawdinúk.
Ldakát yá du een al'eix̱í áyá
wooḵéi.
Ḵaa tóot uwagás'.
Aag̱áa áyá ḵaa ya x̱oot awdlig̱ein,
ḵaa ya x̱oot awdlig̱ein yu.á.
Aag̱áa áwé yéi yaawaḵaa,
gadaháan,

Austin Hammond
Fairbanks, 1988

At this moment
I would like
to speak.
Yes,
a while ago
I listened to you,
Lyek̲wudusdéich,
and how
you were thinking.
Yes,
I also spoke to you last evening.
In order that these people standing here could hear it too,
I would like to say it again.
Yes,
at one time this happened
like now.
People were getting ready.
People were dressing
for a ceremonial, a dance.
And this man
was very happy
the way it was coming along.
This was when someone told him.
Someone came to him.
This was when someone said to him,
"Your maternal nephew passed away."
This is when he sat down.
All the dancers with him
sat down.
It pierced them.
This is when he looked among their faces,
he looked among their faces it is said.
This is when he said,
as he stood up,

"Góok! Góok! Sh daat kaydashéedéi,
sh daat kaydashéedéi.
Aan lushgoowu aan yádi nanáach."
Yei áyá i toowú wootee, Lyekwudusdéich.
Yáadei, yáat'át yakgwaxeexí
ch'a uwayáa yáadei yeeteeyi yax áwé wootee.
Ách áwé wé dziyáak
tlél yan kaysheeyí.
Aaa,
haa tuwáa sigóo
ha yá at shí
ch'a wtoosheeyí
ch'a haa x'éideix yi.aaxí.
Ha yéi áyá yá shí kei gaxtooshée.
"Shunliháash."
Handei yaynák! Handei yaynák!
Woosht yidanák!
Ha yá shí ax tuwáa sigóo
yan kaxwaneegí.
Ha yá kaa
kaa jee yux gugwagoodí—
Kélk'! Goosú wa.é?
Yaax' haagú ax kéilk'!—
Yáa yeedát áwé
ax tuwáa sigóo atx wxalayeixí
yá shí.
Yá yan yisineiyí
kootéeyaa,
haa éesh hás ádi
haa káani s ádi.
Aaa,
tlax áyá
Lingítch sh tóox isnóogun.
Yéi yateeyi át
tle kaa jikawdukaayí tsá
áx ashee.
Aaa,
yáa yeedát áwé ax tuwáa sigóo atx xwalayeixí yá shí
aaa,
yá aadéi yéi jeeyaneiyi yé.
Aaa,

"Continue! Continue! Keep on dressing,
keep on dressing.
When a village becomes boring a noble child dies."
This is how you felt, Lyeḵwudusdéich.
When we were to have this ceremony,
it was as if you put your mourning aside for this.
This is the reason awhile ago
you didn't finish your song.
Yes,
we would like
to sing
this song
just so you could hear it from us.
In this way we will sing this song.
"Shunlihaash."
Move closer! Move close!
Get close together!
Now I would like to explain
this song.
Now when this man
was going out to be killed—
Nephew! Where are you?
Come over here, nephew!—
At this moment
I would like to use
this song.
This totem pole
that you have completed
is our fathers' thing,
our brothers-in-law's thing.
Yes,
how very
awkward it was to a Tlingit.
Only when a person is commissioned
did we touch
a thing of this nature.
Yes,
at this moment I would like to use this song,
yes,
for your work.
Yes,

yaax' haat has koowatini aa,
ch'a uwayáa yá lingit'aaní tóotx áyá.
Aaa,
yáax' haat kuyawdiháa
i yéi jineiyí,
aaa.
Tlél kwas yá Lingít yinaanáx kawuhaayín
Dleit Káach ijikawukaayí.
Ách áwé kaa jee yux gugwagóot wé káa.
Aagáa áwé kei akakwgwashee nook áwé
wé shí.
Áa yaa gútch wé neil.
Yáax' áwé yéi yanakéich,
"Ho! Ho! Ho! Ho! Ho!"
Chush ya yeedéi
x'awusdaaych.
Aagáa áwé yéi yaawakáa,
"Góok! Yúx xát kanayhaakwdéi!
Yúx xát kanayhaakwdéi!"
Aaa,
áyá atx gaxtulayéix yeedát.
Ch'u uwayáa igeinyaax yux gukwagoodi yáx áyá
    sh tuxdinóok kélk'.
Hóoch'i aayí áyá xát
yú áa yéi xat teeyí yé.
Aaa,
gwál dei wéidu ách wusikoo káa
tsu yá shí.
Ách áwé kei gaxtoosheeyí,
kei gaxtooshée dei.

[Song: Shunlihaash]

A huwaa haa ei hei hu wei ya
A huwaa haa ei hu waa haa ei hei huwei ya
A huwaa haa ei ya hei hei hei hoowei hoowaa aa.

Yux xat kanayhaakw dei, hoo wei ya.
Yux xat kanayhaakw ax kaa-gee has-a.
Yee xoot angalgein-a, hei hei hei hoowei hoowa aa.

those who came here,
it is as if they are from all over the world.
Yes,
many people came here
for your work,
yes.
But it was not a tradition of our people
to have the white people commission someone.
This is why a man would go out to face the people's weapons.
Then, when he was going to sing
this song,
he paced around in the house.
Now and then he would say,
"Ho! Ho! Ho! Ho! Ho!"
He would cry out
in fear for his life.
Then he said,
"Begin! Cry me out now!
Cry me out now!"
Yes,
this is the song we will use now.
It's as if I'm going out in place of you is how I feel, nephew.
I'm the last one
from the place I'm living.
Yes,
maybe there are people who know
this song, too.
This is why we will sing it,
we will sing it now.

[Song: Shunlihaash, composed by Kul'ootl']

A huwaa haa ei hei hu wei ya
A huwaa haa ei hu waa haa ei hei huwei ya
A huwaa haa ei ya hei hei hei hoowei hoowaa aa.

Cry me out now, ei, hoo wei ya.
Cry me out now, my mother's brothers
Let me look among your faces, hei hei hei hoowei hoowa aa.

Shunlihaash-aa ei hoo wei ya.
Shunlihaash-aa ax̱adawoodli.
Ax̱ leel-ak'w has hidi aanaḵ yei nax̱dzeegeed-aa, hoowa aa.

Aaa,
yéi áyá ax̱ toowú yatee,
ax̱ éesh hás,
ax̱ kaani yán.
Hooch'in yís áyá,
yéi x̱at kawdiyaa.
Ax̱ léelk'wch áwé chush yeedéi kawdlishee,
Gunx̱aa G̱uwakaan,
chush ya yeet akawdishée.
Yéi yá x̱'ayaḵá,
"Dei héidei ḵwgóot yeenáḵ,
dei héidei.
X̱át áwé yoo x̱'ax̱atánk,"
yoo áwé x̱'ayaḵá.
Aaa,
yá shí áwé adaa yoo x̱'ayatánk.
Ách áwé yáa yeedát atx̱ x̱alayéix̱.
Waa sá yat'éex',
aaa,
sh daat ḵaa shuwuxéex.
Aaa,
ch'a yee waḵshiyeet áyá x̱waahaan,
ax̱ éesh hás,
ax̱ kaani yán,
tsú ax̱ aat hásx̱ siteeyi áa.
Aaa,
yá ax̱ kéilk'
yáat woogoodi,
aaa,
yéi áyá ax̱ toowú yatee.
Yéi.
Aaa
yáa yeedát áwé
ax̱ tuwáa sigóo tsú adaa x̱'ax̱dataaní.
Aaa.
Yá dziyáak

The end has floated out, ei hoo wei ya.
The end of my trouble has floated out
From my mother's ancestors' house I have done this,
  hoowa ei hoowa aa.

Yes,
this is how I feel,
my fathers,
my brothers-in-law.
This is for the last time
I'm doing this.
My grandfather sang this before he died,
Gunx̱aa G̱uwakaan.
He sang it before he died.
He said this,
"I'm already going from among you to the other side,
already to the other side.
It is me speaking,"
is what he said.
Yes,
the song is the one he is talking about.
This is why I'm using it now.
It is so difficult,
yes,
when your relatives have died off.
Yes,
I'm just standing around in your sight,
my fathers,
my brothers-in-law,
also you who are my paternal aunts.
Yes,
this nephew of mine
who is walking around here,
yes,
this is how I feel.
How I feel.
Yes,
and now
I would like to speak about this again.
Yes.
Awhile ago

wé gáanx'
aaa,
at wuduwashée.
Tléil yan shax̲wlahéek.
Aaa, yáa yeedát
yá gáannáx̲ yei k̲watsak̲ aa,
a ux̲taag̲áni x̲'áanáx̲ áwé wooshoo
wé s'áak̲.
Aaa.
Yaa gagóot wé k̲áa,
ax̲ satéen áwé du géidei yanashíxi
wé g̲ooch,
aag̲áa áwé du toowú yéi yatee,
aaa, atóo kei akawag̲íx' du óonayi.
Aag̲áa áwé ch'a altín.
Ch'a altín.
Tlél ayóo áyáx̲ ooteen.
Tlé wé dleit tóonáx̲ áwé yag̲as.éich, yu.á,
wé g̲ooch k̲u.áa.
Waananei sáwé tsu g̲unéi ushéexch du yinaadéi.
L áyáx yéi agoosteen áwé,
du óonayi yanáx̲ awlitsáak̲.
Yanáx̲ awlitsaak̲ du óonayi.
Aag̲áa áwé agéidei yatx̲ uwag̲út.
"Waasá kwshéi eewanéi cháa?
Waasá kwshéi eewanéi?"
Aag̲áa áwé sh yaadáx̲ x̲'awdli.áat.
Woosh yaatx̲ x̲'awli.áat.
Aag̲áa áwé awsiteen.
A x̲'aanáx̲ naashóo
du ux̲ x̲'áaknáx̲
wé s'áak.
Aag̲áa áwé yéi ayawsik̲aa,
"Tlél cháa eewunéi, cháa.
I eedéi k̲wadashée."
Aag̲áa áwé du lítayi aax̲ kéi aawatee.
"Yan ín!. Yan ín!"
Aatx̲ kei ayéesh áwé,
wé dleit kát áwé uwaxíx
wé s'áak̲.
Yéi kunaleiyi yéi yawjixíx

outside,
yes,
when people helped,
I didn't finish my part.
Yes, and now,
on this pole that will stand outside,
the bone
stuck out between the canine teeth.
Yes,
as that man was hunting,
when he saw this wolf
running toward him,
that's when he was thinking,
yes, he loaded his rifle.
This is when he just watched it.
He just watched it.
It didn't look right to him.
The wolf
would rub its snout into the snow, it's said.
At times it would begin running toward him.
When it began to look worse
he stuck his rifle in the snow.
Into the snow he stuck his rifle.
Then he started toward it.
"I wonder what has happened to you, brother?
I wonder what has happened to you?" he said to it.
That's when it dropped its jaw.
It dropped its jaw.
That's when he saw it.
The bone
was sticking out
between its teeth.
This is when he said to it,
"You have been hurt badly, brother.
I will help you."
This is when he took out his knife.
"Be ready for it! Be ready for it!"
When he yanked out
the bone
it dropped on the snow.
When the wolf

wé gooch,
aagáa áwé aax aawatee.
Aagáa áwé yei adaayaká,
"Aax kei kgwatée,
ch'a ax jee yéi kgwatée.
Xat ku.aa x'wán idashi."
Ách áwé yeedát,
aaa,
yá du uxx'áatx
kei wtuwateeyí át áwé
ch'a haa jee yéi kgwatée.
Aaa,
laxeitl atóonáx haa jee yéi wootee
yá gáannáx yéi kgwatsak
kootéeyaa.
Aaa,
yaandéi gaxtootee,
yá du ux x'aatx kei wtuwayishi aa,
haa jeex' laxeitl yáx nagateeyí.
Yéi áyá ax toowú yatee.
Aaa, tsu yá ax sáni
yá xóots.
Ldakát yéidei áyá
yeedát
yá dleit káach k'idein at wusi.áx.
Át gasa.aaxí
aadooch sá has du een kawuneegí.
Ldakát át yáx áwé
Lingítch woosikóo,
wudashée a éex wuduxooxú.
Aaa,
yá xóots
yaa kgagudín áwé
ch'a yéi kunaleiyi yéidei áwé.
Ax éesh hásx áwé sitee
xóots.
Aagáa áwé yéi daayaduká nuch,
"Eesháan xát! Ax atxaayí kax át xwaagoot."
Aagáa áwé kaa x'éit us.aaxch.
Ách adaa yóo x'axatangi át
ax sani hás.

had backed a short distance away from him
the man picked up the bone.
Then he said to the wolf,
"I'll take it.
I will just keep it.
But please help me."
This is why now,
yes,
we will just keep
this object pulled
from between the totem's teeth.
Yes,
this totem pole
that will stand outside
has brought us luck.
Yes,
we will keep
this bone pulled from between its teeth,
so that it can become good luck for us.
This is how I feel.
Yes, also my paternal uncle
this brown bear.
In many ways
now
the white people listen to this.
Let them listen
to whoever tells them.
We Tlingit know
every animal
when we ask them for help.
Yes,
this brown bear
when it ambles on,
only a short distance.
Brown bears
are my fathers.
This is when we ask them,
"Take pity on us. I'm here for my food."
This is when it would hear us.
This is the reason I'm talking about it,
my paternal uncles.

K̲aa x̲'éit us.aax̲ch
yéi daa yaduk̲aayí,
"X̲át tsú ax̲ atx̲aayi yá akax̲ át x̲waagoot."
Aag̲áa áhé k̲aanák tliyaadei awoodagóotch.
Yáa yeedát áwé yéi duwasaakw,
guk yik dagéix',
guk yik dagéix'.
Yáa yeedát áwé haa x̲'éit wusi.áx̲
dziyáagidáx̲.
Aadéi a daa yoo x̲'atuli.atgi yé
haa x̲'éit wusi.áx̲.
Aaa,
guk yik dagéix'
yóo toowasáakw,
aaa,
yá xóots.
Aaa,
ách áwé yeedát
yá a daa yóo x̲'ayla.átgi
ax̲ sani hás,
tlax̲ yeekaax̲ áwé ax̲ toowú dikeet yas.éin.
Aaa,
yáa yeedát áwé ch'áak'
wé ch'áak'
a saa a yát yeeyteeyi
ldakát uháan áwé kindax̲'ein yawtudixoon,
kindax̲'ein yawtudixoon
yee kaax̲ tuwu ké.
Aaa.
Haa yadaax̲ áwé yayeeyshée.
Aaa,
yéi áyá a daax̲ tuwatee,
yéi.
Gunalchéesh.
(Unidentified) *Gunalchéesh.*

They listen to us
when we say to them,
"I'm over here for my food, too."
This is when they turn away from us.
We call them
big ears,
big ears.
They are listening to us right now
from awhile back.
They are listening
to the way we have been speaking of them.
Yes,
we call them
big ears,
yes,
this brown bear.
Yes.
This is why now
when you speak about them,
my paternal uncles,
my feelings are lifted because of you.
Yes,
now this eagle,
this eagle
that you have given a name,
all of us have lifted our heads,
have lifted our heads,
being proud of you.
Yes,
you have cleansed our faces.
Yes,
this is how I feel about you,
this is how.
Thank you.
(Unidentified) *Thank you.*

Speeches for the Removal of Grief from the Memorial for Jim Marks, Hoonah 1968

Ch'a ya<u>x</u> at <u>g</u>wakú "a kayaa áyá s ootee
tla<u>x</u> kaawayíkt jeenaxée<u>g</u>aa."
— Naa Tláa

It is like the saying "They are only imitating....
lest they grope aimlessly."
— *Jessie Dalton*

...Robes to capture the passion of your tears....
— *Willie Marks, 1981*
Forty Day Party for his daughter Eva

Goox̱ G̱uwakaan
Xunaa, 1968

Aaa!
Héi Yaakwdáatdei áwé
kawdiyaa
wé haa x̱oodáx̱
Ḵ'aadóo.
Áx' áwé
du yee tl'átgi ḵuwdzitee.
Aaa.
Ách áwé
chush t'aḵkaadéi asawdihaa du kéek'.
Aadéi yaa ajiklaháa áwé
yá Ltu.áa watyeex'
yaakw du een héent wudik'ít'
naháayi.
Hú ḵu.aa áwé sh wudzineix̱.
Aag̱áa áwé ḵaa eeti sheex'í áwé kadulsheex̱,
ḵaa eeti sheex'í.
Yú ḵaa wanáak áwé áa g̱anúkch hú ḵu.aa,
wé aadéi x̱'ayaduḵa yé.
Ch'a ḵóodáx̱ sh nadlileyi yáx̱ áwé g̱anúkch.
Yan née áwé
ya ḵaa eeti sheex'í,
aag̱áa áwé x̱'awduwawóos',
aaa,
wé ax̱ léelk'w
Ḵ'aadóo.
Aag̱áa áwé yéi yawdudziḵaa
"Tleigíl ch'a wáa sá yakg̱eeḵaa
yá i kéek' eetéex' x̱á?"
"Yak'éi x̱á!
Ax̱ daadéi g̱unei y.á."
Chush daadéi áwé ḵuwdix̱oox̱.
Ách áwé du daadéi g̱unayéi a.áat.
Aadéi áwé kéi akaawashée wé shí,
awliyex̱i shí.

Jim Marks
Hoonah, 1968

Yes!
From among us
K'aadóo
went
to Yakutat.
It was there
he got his land.
Yes.
For that reason
he asked his younger brother to go with him.
While he was taking him there,
at the entrance to Lituya Bay
the canoe swamped with them,
these travelers.
But K'aadóo saved himself.
At that time memorial songs were composed,
memorial songs.
But he would sit away
from what people were saying.
He would sit as if he wanted to be far away from everyone.
When these commemorative songs
were finished,
that's when he was asked,
yes,
my grandfather
K'aadóo.
That's when they said to him,
"Aren't you going to say anything
to eulogize your younger brother? "
"Fine! Sure.
Come, gather around me."
He asked them to gather around him.
That's why they began to gather around him.
There he began to sing the song,
the song he had composed.

Kwéix' Éesh (1)
Xunaa, 1968

Ax̱ tuwáa sigóo x̱'ax̱wdataaní
ax̱ éesh hás,
ax̱ aat hás.
    (Unidentified) *Áawé.*
Tlákw áyú yéi kwdayéin.
Yáa yeedát
ax̱ kaani hás,
ax̱ éesh hás,
ax̱ aat hás,
    (Keet Yaanaayí) *Áawé.*
has ḵustéeyin yee éesh hás
yee yátx'i tsú has ḵustéeyin,
yáa yeedát
Keet Yaanaayí
ax̱ éesh
    (Unidentified) *Áawé.*
yáa yeedát
tlax̱ haa tukayeeysinúk.
Tléil áwé aadéi nax̱tudzigeedi yé ḵoostí,
yá i yátx'ix̱ haa sateeyí ḵa yá i dachx̱anx'i yánx̱ haa sateeyí,
yá
i aat hás
ldakát hás.
Ch'a yóo nax̱toosgeedí g̱óot áyá
i aat a daa s tuwli.aat
has du tuwáx' áyú sigóo
yéi yeeguwáatl' chance haa jeet yeeyteeyí.
    (Keet Yaanaayí) *Áawé.*
Yéi áyá.
    (Keet Yaanaayí) *Áawé. Yéi kg̱watée.*

Matthew Lawrence (1)
Hoonah, 1968

I would like to say something
my fathers,
my father's sisters.
        (Unidentified) *Áawé.*
It has always been this way.
At this moment
my brothers-in-law,
my fathers,
my fathers' sisters,
        (Willie Marks) *Áawé.*
your fathers were once alive
your children, too, were once alive,
at this moment
Keet Yaanaayí
my father
        (Unidentified) *Áawé.*
at this moment
how much we feel your stirring.
There is nothing we can do,
we who are your children, and we who are your grandchildren,
these
sisters of your fathers
all of them.
With nothing else for us to do
your fathers' sisters thought
they would like you
to give us a chance for just a little while.
        (Willie Marks) *Áawé.*
That's the way it is.
        (Willie Marks) *Áawé. It will be.*

Kaatyé
Xunaa, 1968

Ax̲ sani hás,
áwu tsú tléix' ax̲ kaani yán
(Keet Yaanaayí) *Áawé.*
tóox' áyá tuwanook
yee ée sh danóogu,
tóox'.
Ax̲ káak áyá x̲'akk̲watee
K̲áak'w Éesh du yéet
i yádi.
Tsalx̲aan G̲uwakaan,
(Tsalx̲aan G̲uwakaan) *Héiy!*
Yakwdeiyí G̲uwakaan,
(Yakwdeiyí G̲uwakaan) *Héiy!*
yee káani áyá x̲'akk̲watee.
(Unidentified) *Áawé.*
Ax̲ káani Keet Yaanaayí,
(Keet Yaanaayí) *Áawé.*
K̲aatooshtóow,
(K̲aatooshtóow) *Áawé.*
yee káani x̲'akk̲watee.
Gusatáan,
(Gusatáan) *Héiy!*
Yee yádi x̲'akk̲watee.
(Unidentified) *Gunalchéesh á.*
Ha de
yat'éex'i át áyá,
k̲a jiklidzée
yéi yateeyi át
k̲a kwlits'ígwaa.
A eetéenáx̲ áyá haa wootee
ax̲ káak hás.

Héen áyú gadéich,
héen.

David Kadashan
Hoonah, 1968

My fathers' brothers,
all my brothers-in-law,
    (Willie Marks) *Áawé.*
we are feeling
your pain,
feeling it.
I will imitate my mother's brother
son of K̲áak'w Éesh,
your child.
Tsalx̲aan G̲uwakaan,
    (George Dalton) *Héiy!*
Yakwdeiyí G̲uwakaan,
    (David McKinley) *Héiy!*
I will imitate your brother-in-law.
    (Unidentified) *Áawé.*
my brother-in-law Keet Yaanaayí
    (Willie Marks) *Áawé.*
K̲aatooshtóow,
    (John Wilson) *Áawé.*
I will imitate your brother-in-law
Gusatáan,
    (Harry Marvin) *Héiy!*
I will imitate your child.
    (Unidentified) *Thank you.*
Surely this is
a hard thing to do,
and it is difficult to handle
a thing like this,
and sensitive.
We are in need
of my mother's brothers.

The river would swell,
the river.

Yá héen yík
héen áyá, séew áyá a kaadéi daak ustaanch, yá áa.
Tóo hinyawudaayí áwé yá aas tayeex̲ áwé daak̲ kagadéich
yá héen.
Yá k̲útl'kw áwé aax̲ shalawal' nuch.
Aag̲áa áwé yéi tundatánch
k'e ng̲al'éex'.
Wool'éex'idáx̲ áwé, héen yíx̲ áwé yei klaháshch
héen yíx̲.
Yá lingit'aaní kaadéi áwé tundatánch.
Yá éil' tlein káx' áyá ulhaashch.
Aatx̲ áyá a káa ayax̲dateech.
(Naawéiyaa) *I x̲'éit wusi.áx̲ i kaani yán.*
A káa ayax̲datéex' áwé; g̲unayéi ulteetch
yak'éiyi l'éiwdei.
Át g̲alatídín áwé l'éiw
yan ulhaashch. Áa yan yoo latitgi nuch,
áa yan yoo latitgi nuch.
Yáax' áwé a yeetx̲ yaa kdawúx̲ch,
a yeetx̲ yaa kdawúx̲ch.
Áa yan utaanch.
S'ootaatx' áwé a kaadéi yaa akdagánch
s'ootáatx'.
Yá a kát awdagaaní áwé a daadéi yaa gaxúkch.
Gu.aal kwshé yéi yee wuteeyík̲
a ítdáx̲
ax̲ kaani yán,
ch'a aadéix̲ siteeyi aa.
(Naawéiyaa) *Gunalchéesh.*

X̲at yeeyliyéx̲, Chookaneidí.
X̲at yeeyliyéx̲.
Ách áyá x̲át tsú yee jiyís yéi sh x̲adinook.
Aaa!
Xwaayeenák̲ áwé yéi yatee.
(Keet Yaanaayí) *Áawé.*
Yá lingit'aaní g̲eix'
woosh jin toolshát yeisú.
Tléil sh tóotx̲ yoo tudateek uháan tsú haa nanéiyi.
Aaa,
yáa yeedát

In the river,
in the lake, the rain would fall on the water.
When the river had swollen, it would flow
under the tree.
The earth would crumble along the bank.
That's when it would think
of breaking.
When it had broken, down the river it would drift,
down the river.
It would think of going out into the world.
On this great ocean it would drift.
From there the wind would blow over it.
(Harry Marvin) *Your brothers-in-law are listening to you.*
After the wind would blow over it; it would begin to roll
with the waves to a fine sand.
When it rolled on the waves to the sand
it would drift ashore. It would be pounded there by the waves
it would be pounded there.
Here the tide would leave it dry,
would leave it dry.
It would lie there.
In the morning, sun would begin to shine on it
in the morning.
After the sun had been shining on it, it would begin to dry out.
My hope is that you become like this
from now on,
my brothers-in-law,
whoever is one.
(Harry Marvin) *Thank you.*

You created me, Chookaneidí.
You created me.
This is why I, too, feel for you.
Yes!
This is the way Xwaayeenák is.
(Willie Marks) *Áawé.*
In this world
we're still holding each other's hands.
Neither do we overlook our dead.
Yes!
At this moment

a kát adagánni, gu.aal kwshé a tóodei wuxoogóoḵ
yee yadaax̱ kaawadaayi aa.
(Keet Yaanaayí) *Yéi kg̱watée x̱á.*
Sagóox̱ nax̱satee yéi áyá yee jiyís tux̱datán.
(Naawéiyaa) *Gunalchéesh.á.*
Yeeysikóo yee kaani yán
yee aat hás.
(Keet Yaanaayí) *Gunalchéesh.*
(Naawéiyaa) *Gunalchéesh.*
Yéi áyá.
Aaa!
Yándei gax̱yeenáaḵ.
Yee sani hás, aadéi s ḵunoogu yé yéeyi
yéi koonax̱dayeinín
aaa,
yee tuwú daa oox̱lit'aayi átx'.
Yee yáx' yéi hás a daanéi noojéen,
aaa,
yá a eetée ḵux̱dziteeyi aa yeedát.
Yéi áyá.
(Keet Yaanaayí) *Gunalchéesh.*
(Naawéiyaa) *Gunalchéesh.*

(Wudlisáa.)

Ax̱ kaani yán
ax̱ sani hásx̱ siteeyi aa
(Keet Yaanaayí) *Áawé.*
ax̱ aat hásx̱ siteeyi aa
(Aan Káx̱shawustaan) *Áawé.*
ch'a a kayaa áyá yéi gax̱tusanéi.
Hél aadéi has yee daang̱waanéiyi yé.
Ha yeeytéen áyá a tóot hás náḵ.
Aaa,
kagax̱too.aaḵw.
Yéi áyá.

(Yáax' áyá Xíxch'i S'áaxw daasheeyí kei kawduwashée.
Dax̱.aa shí ḵu.aa Shaatuḵwáan Keidlí S'áaxw daasheeyí.)

when the sun shines on it, my hope is that it dries out
the flowing from your faces.
(Willie Marks) *It shall be.*
Let it turn to joy for you is my wish.
(Harry Marvin) *Thank you. Thank you.*
You all know your brothers-in-law,
your fathers' sisters.
(Willie Marks) *Thank you.*
(Harry Marvin) *Thank you.*
This is the way it is.
Yes!
You will stand.
The way your fathers' brothers used to do
when such things happened,
yes,
these are the things that might warm your feelings.
The people I'm living in place of now
yes,
used to bring these out for you to see.
This is the way it is.
(Willie Marks) *Thank you.*
(Harry Marvin) *Thank you.*

(The orator rests.)

My brothers-in-law,
those who are my father's brothers
(Willie Marks) *Áawé.*
those who are my father's sisters
(Mary Johnson) *Áawé.*
we will only imitate (our ancestors).
There is no way they can do anything for you.
You can see them wearing them,
yes.
We will try.
This is the way it is.

(At this point, two songs are sung, the Frog Hat Song, and Mountain Tribe's Dog Hat Song.)

Yéi áyá.
Yéi áyá.
        (Ḵaakwsak'aa) *Gunalchéesh.*
        (Keet Yaanaayí) *Gunalchéesh.*
        (Ḵaakwsak'aa) *Gunalchéesh, ax̱ éesh hás.*
        (Aan Káx̱shawustaan) *Gunalchéesh.*

Keewaax̱.awtseix̱ G̱uwakaan
Xunaa, 1968

Yee yadaax̱ kaawadaayi aa káx̱ áyá
ax̱ léelk'w yátx'i
ax̱ kaani yán
ax̱ éesh hás, ax̱ aat hás.
        (Unidentified) *Áawé.*
Hás áyá yáat.
Wáa yadali át yáx̱ sáyú nateech
haa jeex'
hé aa x̱'awdatáan.
Ch'a á yeeysikóo yéi yangaḵéinín
"Ḵáa yáx̱ i daa ax̱ tuwatee, dlák'," yóo.
A yáx̱ yatee ax̱ dláak'.
Yándei ashagux̱lahéek,
aaa, áyá ax̱ jiyís,
        (Keet Yaanaayí) *Áawé.*
ax̱ jiyís yándei ashagux̱lahéek.
I gu.aa yáx̱ x'wán, dlák'.
        (Naa Tláa) *Yéi kg̱watée.*
Has du yáa x'wán nalyaaḵw, i léelk'w hás
yáa x'wán.
Wéix̱ has yaawanáḵ, has du eetéedáx̱
ḵut ayawji.áak yáa yeedát,
i yátx'i
i káalk'w hás.

This is all.
This is all.
(David Williams) *Thank you.*
(Willie Marks) *Thank you.*
(David Williams) *Thank you, my fathers.*
(Mary Johnson) *Thank you.*

William Johnson
Hoonah, 1968

This is for what flowed from your faces
my grandfather's children
my brothers-in-law
my fathers, my father's sisters.
(Unidentified) *Áawé.*
This is them here.
What a heavy burden it is always like
for us
for them to speak.
You all know how it is when a person might say,
"You are like a man to me, sister."
My sister is like that.
She will complete this
for me, yes,
(Willie Marks) *Áawé.*
she will complete this for me.
Have courage, sister.
(Jessie Dalton) *It will be done.*
You will explain your grandfathers for them,
won't you?
They are standing there; from among them
one is missing now,
from among your children,
your brothers' children.

Naa Tláa
Xunaa, 1968

Eeshandéin ágé haa daa tuwatee uháan tsú
ax̱ káalk'w hás
(Keet Yaanaayí) *Áawé*
ax̱ éesh hás?
Ch'a tléix' ax̱ éesh hás.
Tléil eeshandéin haa daa tootí uháan tsú.
Yá wooteeyeit.
(Unidentified) *Yéi áwé.*
Ách áwé a yáx̱ has x̱'ayeey.áx̱ch
yee éesh hás,
tle tlax̱ ch'a nichkáx̱ aa wooxéexg̱aa ḵu.aa áwé
(Naawéiyaa) *Gunalchéesh.á.*
(Keet Yaanaayí) *Gunalchéesh.*
yee waḵhéeni yee yadaax̱ kawadaayi aa.
A káx̱ áwé
yáa yeedát yanax̱ yeiḵ kawdik'ít'
yee éesh hás
yanax̱ yeiḵ has kawdik'ít'.
(Naawéiyaa) *Hó hó.*
Ch'u yáadu sígé hás,
yóo áwé has du daa ax̱ tuwatee
ax̱ léelk'w hás.
(Keet Yaanaayí) *Gunalchéesh.*
Yáat a tóot ahan aa
yá Shaatuḵwáan Keidlí.
Ch'u oowayáa áwé
yee sh tudanóogu káx̱ ashaayi yáx̱ áwé daa yoo tux̱aatánk,
(Keet Yaanaayí) *Gunalchéesh.*
ax̱ éesh hás, ax̱ káalk'w hás
ax̱ aat hás,
aaa.
Yáadu áwé

Jessie Dalton
Hoonah, 1968

Does death take pity on us too
my brothers' children,
    (Willie Marks) *Áawé.*
my fathers?
All my fathers.
It doesn't take pity on us either,
this thing that happens.
    (Unidentified) *That's how it is.*
Which is why you hear their voices like this,
your fathers,
lest your tears fall without honor
    (Harry Marvin) *Thank you.*
    (Willie Marks) *Thank you.*
that flowed from your faces.
For them
they have all come out at this moment,
your fathers
have all come out.
    (Harry Marvin) *Hó, hó.*
They are still present
is how I feel
about my grandparents.
    (Willie Marks) *Thank you.*
Here someone stands wearing one,
this Mountain Tribe's Dog.
It is just as if
it's barking for your pain is how I'm thinking about it,
    (Willie Marks) *Thank you.*
my fathers, my brothers' children
my father's sisters,
yes.
Here

yá a shóodei han aa.

Geesh Daax̱ Woogoodi Yéil áyá.
Yáanáx̱ á a shóodei aa ahán.

Lyeedayéik x'óowu.
A áwé yáanáx̱ á. A shóodei ahán.
Aaa
(Naawéiyaa) *Gunalchéesh.*
(S'eilshéix̱') *Gunalchéesh.*
S'igeidi X'óow áwé
Jilḵáatdáx̱.
Naaxein.
(Unidentified) *Uhuh.*
(Keet Yaanaayí) *Gunalchéesh.*
Lutáḵl
yee éesh
du x'óowu yéeyi áwé
du naaxeiní yéeyi.
(Unidentified) *Hó hó.*
(Naawéiyaa) *Gunalchéesh.*
Yee kujéen áwé tsú
gági uwagút.
(Séi Akdulx̱éitl') *Hó hó.*
(Keet Yaanaayí) *Gunalchéesh.*
Aaa,
yáa yeedát áwé
ch'a ldakát áwé gági yawdixuni yáx̱ áwé ax̱ tuwáa yatee.
Yee aat hás
ax̱ tláa
Saayina.aat
(Unidentified) *Yéi á.*
(Unidentified) *Yéi áwé.*
du x'óowu
Ḵ'eiḵ'w X'óow.
Aaa.
(Unidentified) *Yéi á.*
(Keet Yaanaayí) *Gunalchéesh.*
Yá yee yáx̱ sh daa tuwditaani ḵáa áwé
aan áwé a yát yakw.uḵoox̱ch
aaa,

someone is standing next to it.

It's Raven Who Went Down Along the Bull Kelp.
Someone is standing closer, next to it.

Lyeedayéik's robe.
That is the closer one. Someone is standing next to it.
Yes.
(Harry Marvin) *Thank you.*
(Eva Davis) *Thank you.*
It's The Beaver Blanket
from Chilkat.
A Chilkat Robe.
(Unidentified) *Uhuh.*
(Willie Marks) *Thank You.*
Lutáḵl
your father
it was once his blanket,
once his Chilkat robe.
(Unidentified) *Hó, Hó.*
(Harry Marvin) *Thank you.*
Because of you
he came out.
(David McKinley) *Hó, hó.*
(Willie Marks) *Thank you.*
Yes
at this moment
all of them seem to me as if they're revealing their faces.
Your fathers' sisters,
my mother,
Saayina.aat
(Unidentified) *That's it.*
(Unidentified) *That's right.*
her robe
the Tern Robe.
Yes.
(Unidentified) *That's it.*
(Willie Marks) *Thank you.*
A person who is feeling like you
would be brought by canoe,
yes,

yee éesh hás x'aayí
Gaanaxáa.
Aagáa áwé
dusáaych áwé yú.á
yá eeshandéin sh daa tuwditaani káa,
aaa.
Eésh, Séi Akdulxéitl',
(Séi Akdulxéitl') *Áawé.*
aaa.
Ax léelk'w yéet
Koowunagáas',
(Koowunagáas') *Áawé.*
ax káalk'w yéet
Keet Yaanaayí,
(Keet Yaanaayí) *Áawé.*
aaa,
ax éesh kéilk'
Xooxkeina.át.
(Xooxkeina.át) *Áawé.*
Tlax wáa sáyú
yee tula.eesháani káx
gági yawdixún i aat hás,
Kálk'w
(Keet Yaanaayí) *Gunalchéesh.*
Kaatooshtóow,
(Kaatooshtóow) *Áawé.*
Kaakwsak'aa,
(Kaakwsak'aa) *Áawé.*
aaa,
ax éek' shát Aan Káxshawustaan.
(Aan Káxshawustaan) *Áawé.*
Aaa
tlax wáa sá
gági yawdixuni yáx has du daa yoo tuxaatánk
yee kaani yán.
Aaa
gági has yawdixún.
Weihá aayí k'oodás':
ch'a yeisú áwé
du daax'

to your fathers' point,
G̲aanax̲áa.
That is when
the name would be called out, it is said,
of the person who is feeling grief.
Yes.
Father! Séi Akdulx̲éitl'
(David McKinley) *Áawé.*
Yes.
My grandfather's son
Koowunagáas'
(Joe White) *Áawé.*
My brother's daughter's son
Keet Yaanaayí
(Willie Marks) *Áawé.*
yes,
my father's sister's son
X̲oox̲keina.át.
(Pete Johnson) *Áawé.*
How very much
for your grief
your fathers' sisters are revealing their faces,
My brother's son
(Willie Marks) *Thank you.*
K̲aatooshtóow,
(John F. Wilson) *Áawé.*
K̲aakwsak'aa,
(David Williams) *Áawé.*
yes,
my brother's wife, Aan Káx̲shawustaan.
(Mary Johnson) *Áawé.*
Yes
how very much it is
as if they're revealing their faces
is how I'm thinking about them,
your sisters-in-law.
Yes,
they are revealing their faces.
The shirt that belonged to Weihá:
it was only recently
we completed

yan yéi jiwtuwanéi.
Á áwé wéit.

Yeil K'oodás'.
(Keet Yaanaayí) *Gunalchéesh.*
Tsu hú áyá yáat yan x'ayeey.áx
Weihá.
Yá ax éek'.
Yá yee Guwakaaní,
hú du jeex' áwé yándei kwga.áax,
yá Weihá k'oodás'i.
(Unidentified) *Gunalchéesh.*
Áwé ch'a oowayáa yee wakshiyeex' gági gútxi
yáx áwé yatee yeedát.
(Keet Yaanaayí) *Aaa.*
Aaa.
Tlax wáa sá
aan
sh tuwaagáa kastéeyin hú tsú
yá yee káani.
(Unidentified) *Ha waa sá.*

Yeilkudei Hít X'óow.
Yáat a tóot hán yá yee aat.
Tliyaanax á aa ku.aa áwé
Yaakaayindul.át yee aat,
aaa.
Dei ch'a ch'áakw áwé has du ée antulaxáchch,
yá yee aat hás,
yee éesh hás.
(Unidentified) *Hó hó.*
(Unidentified) *Gunalchéesh.*
Aaa,
Geesh Daax Woogoodi Yéil K'oodás'
i éesh,
Kaadéik,
(Kaadéik) *Áawé.*
du k'oodás'i
á áwé.
(Unidentified) *I x'éit wusi.áx i káalk'w hás.*
Á áwé, tléil yéi a daa yoo tooxatánk kaawagaan áyá yóo.

the rites for him.
That's the one there.

The Raven Shirt.
    (Willie Marks) *Thank you.*
You heard him here also,
Weihá
this brother of mine.
This Peacemaker of yours:
this shirt of Weihá
will remain in his hands, in his care.
    (Unidentified) *Thank you.*
Now it's as if he is coming out for you to see.
    (Willie Marks) *Yes.*
Yes.
How proud
he too used to be
wearing it,
this brother-in-law of yours.
    (Unidentified) *How very much.*

The Raven Nest House Robe.
Here this father's sister of yours stands wearing it.
And on the far side
is Yaakaayindul.át, your father's sister,
yes.
We had long since given up hope of their return,
these fathers' sisters of yours,
your fathers.
    (Unidentified) *Hó, hó.*
    (Unidentified) *Thank you.*
Yes,
Raven Who Went Down Along the Bull Kelp Shirt,
your father,
Kaadéik,
    (Unidentified) *Áawé.*
it's his shirt,
that's the one.
    (Unidentified) *Your brothers' children are listening to you.*
That's the one there; I don't feel that it burned.

Aaa.
Ch'u shóogu á x̱áa wéix' aan i dayéen aan hán i sáni.
(Keet Yaanaayí) *Gunalchéesh.*
(Tsalx̱aan G̱uwakaan) *Gunalchéesh.*
Ách áwé
aaa,
Gusatáan
(Gusatáan) *Áawé.*
ch'a oowayáa ldakát yeewáan yee x̱wasaayí
ax̱ kaani yánx̱ siteeyi aa,

aaa.
A shunaayát ágé nḵwaagoot
ax̱ kaalk'w hás?
Aaa.
A shunaayát ágé nḵwaagoot?
Ya ḵ'éiḵ'w áyá tléil yan ux̱layaaḵwch,
aaa,
yá ḵ'eiḵ'w.
Eeshandéin tuwateeyi ḵáa káx' áwé daak koolyeechch
yee aat hás.
(Keet Yaanaayí) *Áawé.*
Aax̱ áwé
has du x̱'wáal'i a kaadéi
has a kooldánch
wé eeshandéin tuwateeyi ḵáa.
(Tsalx̱aan G̱uwakaan) *I x̱'éit wusi.áx̱ i káalk'u hás.*
(Naawéiyaa) *Gunalchéesh.*
Aag̱áa áwé tléil áwé too kwdunook nuch
has du x̱'wáal'i.
Aag̱aa áwé
yee tula.eesháani tín áwé
has du kúdi kaadéi
has ayakawdliyiji yáx̱ áwé has du daa ax̱ tuwatee yee aat hás.
(Naawéiyaa) *Gunalchéesh.á.*
Aaa.
Yáat ahan aa
yáat
ax̱ tláa du káak du s'áaxu.
Aaa,

Yes.
It's the same one in which your father's brother
is standing there in front of you.
(Willie Marks) *Thank you.*
(George Dalton) *Thank you.*
That is why,
yes,
Gusatáan
(Unidentified) *Áawé.*
it will be just as if I will have named all of you,
those who are my sisters-in-law,

yes.
Can I reach the end,
my brothers' children?
Yes.
Can I reach the end?
These terns I haven't completely explained,
yes,
these terns.
Your fathers' sisters would fly out over the person
who is feeling grief.
(Willie Marks) *Áawé.*
Then
they would let their down fall
like snow
over the person who is feeling grief.
(George Dalton) *Your brothers' children are listening to you.*
(Harry Marvin) *Thank you.*
That's when their down
isn't felt.
That's when
I feel it's as if your fathers' sisters are flying
back to their nests
with your grief.
(Harry Marvin) *Thank you indeed.*
Yes.
Here someone stands,
here,
my mother's mother's brother, his hat.
Yes,

T'aaḵú wátdei áwé yú á wooḵoox̱
aag̱áa yú s'áaxw,
du léelk'w hás x̱oodéi
du léelk'w hás x̱oodéi.
Aaa,
aax̱ áwé du jeet kawdiháa yú.á yá Xíxch'i S'áaxw.
A t'aḵkát áwé uwawúḵ
yá Weihá jeedáx̱ aa k'oodás'.
(Tsalx̱aan G̱uwakaan) *Yéi á.*
Aaa,
tsu T'aaḵóonáx̱ háhé haat kawdiyáa.
Ách áwé
gunalchéesh yóo x̱'ayax̱aḵá
yee dayéen aan has nág̱i yáa yeedát.
(Keet Yaanaayí) *Gunalchéesh áwé.*
Aaa,
yá ḵut'aayg̱áa
gág̱i ugootch
yá yee éesh.
Aag̱áa áwé
yee tula.eesháani káx̱ áwé gág̱i uwagudi yáx̱ ax̱ tusitee
yá yee éesh du s'áaxu.
Aaa,
(Naawéiyaa) *Gunalchéesh á.*
yee léelk'w du s'áaxu.
Aan áwé
yanax̱ daaḵ gug̱anóok,
aan
yee tula.eesháani teen áwé yanax̱ daaḵ gug̱anóok.
(Tsalx̱aan G̱uwakaan) *I x̱'éit wusi.áx̱ i kaalk'u hás.*
A yát sh g̱ayisnoogóot ágé
ax̱ kaalk'u hás ax̱ éesh hás,
(Unidentified) *Gunalchéesh.*
ax̱ aat hás
ax̱ kaani yán.
Ha yáa yeedát
aaa,
ch'a yax̱ at g̱wakú "a kayaa áyá s ootee
tlax̱ kaawayíkt jeenaxéexg̱aa"
(Tsalx̱aan G̱uwakaan) *Gunalchéesh á.*
yá yee léelk'w hás aadéi x̱'ayaḵáayi yé.

to the mouth of Taku he went by boat
then for that hat,
to his grandparents,
to his grandparents.
Yes,
From there it's said he acquired the Frog Hat.
Along with it came
the shirt from Weihá.
    (George Dalton) *That's it.*
Yes,
it also came from Taku.
That is why
I keep saying "Thank you"
that they're standing in front of you at this moment.
    (Willie Marks) *Thank you.*
Yes,
during the warm season
this father of yours
would come out.
That's when
I feel it's as if your father's hat
has come out for your grief.
Yes,
    (Harry Marvin) *Thank you indeed.*
your grandparent's hat.
With your grief
he will burrow down,
with it,
with your grief he will burrow down.
    (George Dalton) *Your brothers' sons are listening to you.*
Not that it can heal you
my brothers' children, my fathers,
    (Unidentified) *Thank you.*
my fathers' sisters
my sisters-in-law.
And now
yes,
it is like the saying "They are only imitating them
lest they grope aimlessly,"
    (George Dalton) *Thank you indeed.*
the way your grandparents said.

Ách áwé
a yáa has wudli.aadi yáx̱ has yatee
yee éesh hás.
Yáadu aa.

Yáadu aa.
Yáat a tóot ahan aa.
Yáa ax̱ léelk'w
Yooḵis'kooḵéik du s'áaxu.
(Unidentified) *Hó hó.*
Yee dayéen
yanax̱ wudihaan hú tsú.
Aaa.
(Unidentified) *Hó ho.*
I éesh du s'áaxu
Koowunagáas'
(Koowunagáas') *Áawé, gunalchéesh áawé.*
yee dayéen yanax̱ wudihaan,
(Keet Yaanaayí) *Gunalchéesh.*
(Unidentified) *Gunalchéesh.*
aaa
Kag̱eet Ḵuyéik.

Aaa.
Yáax' áwé
aaa,
yá dziyáak yá ax̱ éek'ch wuliyaag̱u aa:
yaa gax̱latídín yú aas.
Aag̱áa áwé yan g̱alaháshín
g̱agaanch áwé a kát x̱'us.utsóowch.
Aaa.
Du tóodei áwé yaa gaxúkch
du tula.eesháani.
Yáa yeedát áwé yee káx' gági yawdzi.áa yá g̱agaan
ax̱ léelk'w hás
l'ax̱keidí.
(Unidentified) *Yéi á.*
(Unidentified) *Gunalchéesh.*
(Unidentified) *Hó hó.*
Yáa yeedát
gu.aal kwshé yee tóodei wuxoogu yáx̱ wooteeḵ

That's why
it's as if your fathers
are guiding them.
Here is one.

Here is one.
Here someone stands wearing one.
The hat of Yook̲is'kook̲éik,
this grandfather of mine.
    (Unidentified) *Hó, hó.*
He too has stood up
to face you.
Yes.
    (Unidentified) *Hó, hó.*
Your father, his hat
Koowunagáas'.
    (Unidentified) *Thank you, indeed.*
He has stood up to face you,
    (Willie Marks) *Thank you.*
    (Unidentified) *Thank you.*
yes,
the Loon Spirit.

Yes.
And here,
yes,
is the one this brother of mine explained a while ago:
how that tree rolled for a while on the waves.
Then when it drifted to shore
the sun would put its rays on it.
Yes.
It would dry its grief
to the core.
At this moment this sun is coming out over you, my grandparents' mask.
    (Unidentified) *That's it.*
    (Unidentified) *Thank you.*
    (Unidentified) *Hó, hó.*
At this moment
my hope is that your grief

yee tula.eesháani.
(Tsalx̱aan G̱uwakaan) *Yéi ḵgwatée.*
(Keet Yaanaayí) *Gunalchéesh, yéi ḵgwatée.*
G̱éelák'w Shakee.át,
aaa.
A tóonáx̱ áwé daak woodaxoonch
yee aat hás
G̱éelák'w tóonáx̱,
aaa.
Á áwé yáa yeedát wéit. Aan ahán,
yá shakee.át
(Unidentified) *Gunalchéesh á.*
ax̱ léelk'w du shakee.ádi.

(Keet Yaanaayí) *Gunalchéesh.*

Daanawáaḵ
Xunaa, 1968

Ax̱ tuwáa sigóo
x̱át tsú x̱'ax̱wdataaní, ax̱ sani hás, ax̱ aat hás.
Aaa!
Tlax̱ wáa sá
x̱át tsú eeshandéin ax̱ toowú yatee,
aaa, yáax' haat x̱at kawdayaayí
aaa, l ch'u yee waḵshiyee ḵwaasháadi át.
Ha yáa yeedát
yáax' aan
daak uwagút.
(Unidentified) *I x̱'éit wusi.áx̱ i sani hás.*
Ldakát yéidei yéi yee ngatéenín áyú yoo x̱'atángi noojéen
aaa, yá K'eedzáa.
Yáadu du x'óowu, yáat aan hán.
(Keet Yaanaayí) *Áawé.*
Tlax̱ wáa sá yoo x̱'atángeen a daax'
yéi at nagatéenín ḵa du aat hás x̱oot nagaldléigún.
Yáa yeedát áyá a eetéenáx̱ haa yatee.

be like it's drying to your core.
    (George Dalton) *It shall be.*
    (Willie Marks) *Thank you. It shall be.*
G̱éelák'w Headdress,
yes.
Your fathers' sisters
would reveal their faces from it,
from G̱éelák'w,
yes.
That's the one there now. Someone is standing there with it,
this headdress
    (Unidentified) *Thank you indeed.*
my grandfather's headdress.

    (Willie Marks) *Thank you.*

Austin Hammond
Hoonah, 1968

I would like to speak
also, my father's brothers, my father's sisters,
Yes!
How very much
I too feel grief,
yes, and even that being here,
indeed, I am with nothing to show you.
At this moment
he came out
here with it.
    (Unidentified) *Your father's brothers are listening to you.*
In many ways, when you were like this,
yes, K'eedzáa always used to speak.
Here is his robe, here he stands with it.
    (Willie Marks) *Áawé.*
How much he used to speak of it
when things were like this and when he expressed affection
    among his father's sisters.
At this moment we are in need of him.

Ḵa yáanáx̱ á a shóodei han aa
yá Kaatyé
tsu hú.
Ax̱ káak du x'óowu Tsagwált,
aaa,
du eetéetx̱ ax̱ jee yéi wootee.
(Keet Yaanaayí) *Áawé.*
Ḵa yá tléix' yateeyi aa
(Tsalx̱aan G̱uwakaan) *Gunalchéesh.*
yá tléix' yateeyi aa.
Aaa,
ch'a kḵwalayaaḵw.
Tléil yáa yéi wootee.
Ax̱ éesh
Keet Yaanaayí!
(Keet Yaanaayí) *Áawé.*
Yá yee káani yee daat x̱'ayanash.ákjeen.
(Keet Yaanaayí) *Gunalchéesh.*
Yá haa jee yéi yatee Naatúxjayi
yee tula.eesháani káx̱ hú tsú
tsú yáax'
(Keet Yaanaayí) *Gunalchéesh.*
aaa
yee tóodáx̱
kei ag̱atee.
(Unidentified) *Gunalchéesh.*
Ḵa yáa yeedát wé x'óow
aaa, ch'a oowayáa jig̱wéinaa yáx̱ ax̱ jee ḵuwda.oowú.
Yéi áyá x̱át tsú ax̱ toowú yatee,
ax̱ aat hás.
(Unidentified) *Gunalchéesh.*
(Unidentified) *Gunalchéesh.*
(Unidentified) *Gunalchéesh.*

And on this side, someone is standing next to it,
Kaatyé
he too.
My mother's brother Tsagwált, his robe,
yes,
I own it in place of him.
　　(Willie Marks) *Áawé.*
And there is one thing,
　　(George Dalton) *Thank you.*
there is one thing
yes,
I will just explain.
It's not here.
My father,
Keet Yaanaayí!
　　(Willie Marks) *Áawé.*
This brother-in-law of yours would speak proudly of you.
　　(Willie Marks) *Thank you.*
This Naatúxjayi whom we have,
he too
has also come here for your grief,
　　(Willie Marks) *Thank you.*
yes,
to remove it
from you.
　　(Unidentified) *Thank you.*
And now, that blanket:
indeed, it's just as if it has become a towel in my hand,
　　to wipe away your tears.
This is how I feel too,
my fathers' sisters.
　　(Unidentified) *Thank you.*
　　(Unidentified) *Thank you.*
　　(Unidentified) *Thank you.*

Kweix' Éesh (2)
Xunaa, 1968

Aaa,
gunalchéesh áyá
ax̱ éesh hás,
ax̱ kaani yán.
Yá gaaw
ch'a yéi yiguwáatl'
ax̱ tuwáa sigóo
x̱'ax̱wdataaní.
Yan ashawlihík yá haa tláach.
Ha tlax̱ wáa lax̱éitlx̱ sá haa wootee
yá haa x̱oox' yéi teeyí
yá haa tláa.
Haa káx̱ háni
yáx̱ yatee.
Ax̱ tuwáa sigóo yáat'aa x̱walayaag̱ú
yá at wuduwateeyí,
yá s'áaxw.
Yee tula.eesháani
áyá aan gug̱agóot.
    (Keet Yaanaayí) *Áawé.*
    (Tsalx̱aan G̱uwakaan) *Gunalchéesh.*
Tsalx̱aan tóodei aan ayagux̱dagóot
yee toola.eesháani.
    (Ḵaatooshtóow) *Áawé.*
Yee yadaanáx̱
kawduwatl'oog̱u aa,
aan gug̱agóot
    (Keet Yaanaayí) *Gunalchéesh.*
yee éesh hás shaayí tóodei.
    (Unidentified) *Yéi á.*
    (Unidentified) *Gunalchéesh.*

Matthew Lawrence (2)
Hoonah, 1968

Yes,
this is in thanks
my fathers,
my brothers-in-law.
At this time
I would like
to speak
for just a short while.
This mother of ours has completed everything.
And what a great gift we have
that this mother of ours
is among us.
It is as if
she's standing for us.
I would like to explain
this thing we have been holding,
this hat.
It will go
with your grief.
(Willie Marks) *Áawé.*
(George Dalton) *Thank you.*
It will go back into Mt. Fairweather
with your grief.
(John Wilson) *Áawé.*
With those tears
which fell from your faces
it will go
(Willie Marks) *Thank you.*
into your fathers' mountain.
(Unidentified) *That's right.*
(Unidentified) *Thank you.*

"Because We Cherish You . . . :" Sealaska Elders Speak to the Future

(Selected Speeches from the First Sealaska Elders Conference, Sitka 1980)

Even from long ago
we have placed our grandchildren
high above ourselves....
Even those things we treasure
we...offer up
...to those who are our grandchildren.
— Charlie Joseph

We don't like to see words go to waste.
We lay our at.óow
for the words to fall on.
This is when the opposite clan
knows that its words
have been received.
— George Jim (Interview) 1989

Ḵaal.átk' (1)
Sheet'ká, 1980

Yoo x̱'akḵwatáan
tlél ch'a g̱óot át x̱'éináx̱
ch'a aadéi ḵwá yéi x̱at x̱'agax̱yi.oo
        tsu aadóo sás tlél x̱at x̱'ay.áx̱ji.
Aax̱ yáa ax̱ dachx̱anx'i yán
yáax' yee waḵshiyeex' neildéi has gug̱wa.áat.
Aadáx̱
yá shí
átx̱ has agux̱layéix̱
yá Jilḵáatdáx̱
yei wduwasáa Kwáal
has du léelk'w.
A x̱'asheeyí áyá a kát yaa s gug̱wa.áat
yóo tliyaanax̱ aadáx̱
yáa anax̱ neildéi agug̱wa.áat yéidei
Kwáal x̱'asheeyí kát.
Aax̱
sh yáa awudanéix'i yáat yiḵeení
aak'é ax̱ dachx̱anx'i yán
tsu l ayáx̱
woosh kát has wudanaag̱í xwan ch'a aadéi yéi s nay.oo.
Aaa.
A ít
neildéi s gug̱wa.áadi ḵu.aa wés
x̱áa s aklihéin yá shí
yá Xunaadáx̱
yá ax̱ káak
Keitóoḵ
du x̱'asheeyí kát áyá neildéi agug̱wa.áat.
Aaa.
A shóodei áwé tsu s aa kakg̱washée tsu déix̱ shí.
Yéi áyá yaa s ayagux̱saxéex
yáa yeedát.

Charlie Joseph (1)
Sitka, 1980

I will speak
in no other language,
so please forgive me, whoever doesn't understand me.
Soon these grandchildren of mine
will come in here for you to see.
Soon
they will use
this song
of the man from Chilkat
called Kwáal,
their grandfather.
It is on his song they will enter
from over there,
where they will enter
to the song of Kwáal.
Then
you people of honor seated here,
even if they don't
move correctly, please forgive them,
my fine grandchildren.
Yes.
Following
their entrance
they will continue with the song,
this song that is said to belong to me,
the one from Hoonah
from my maternal uncle
Keitóok.
Yes.
Following this they will sing two songs.
This is how they will present them
now.

1. Kwáal x̱'asheeyí; T'aḵdeintaan
2. Keitóoḵ x̱'asheeyí; Kaagwaantaan

Sh yáa awudanéix'i
ch'a ldakát yéidei áyú kawdlixwás'
has du ḵusteeyí
yáax' neil uwa.adi ax̱ dachx̱anx'i yán
tsu yá Kaagwaantaan tóodei
L'uknax̱.ádi tóodei
Chookaneidí tóodei
Deisheetaan tóodei.
Ldakát yéidei
shula.át has du ḵusteeyí.
Ach áyá
yá has du léelk'w hás
a náḵ ḵutx̱ shuwaxeexi yá át
ch'a oowayáa woosh x̱oo has ayakaawajeli yáx̱ yatee
aaa
átx̱ has alyeix̱í.
Ch'u tlákwdáx̱
haa dachx̱án
haa kináa kei wtusinúk.
Aaa.
X̱'atulitseen.
Tsu ḵushtuyáx̱ daa sá yaa tushigéiyi át
du jeedéi yatx̱ g̱atooteeyín
haa dachx̱ánx̱ siteeyi ḵáa.
Ách áyá yáa yeedát
s du waḵshiyeex̱ tulayéx̱x̱.
Tsu l ayáx̱ yee tugéit has yawuḵaayí ch'a aadéi yéi s gax̱yi.oo.
Aaa.
Shaawát G̱uwakaan x̱'asheeyí áyá a kát has akg̱wal'eix̱.
A ítnáx̱x' áwé kakg̱waháa
Ḵáataan aayí.
Is that right?
Yéi áwé.
Hwói.

3. Shaawát G̱uwakaan x̱'asheeyí; T'aḵdeintaan

1. Kwáal Song; T'ak̲deintaan
2. Keitóok̲ Song; Kaagwaantaan

People of honor,
the lifelines
of these grandchildren of mine who entered here
strand off in many directions—
into Kaagwaantaan
into L'uknax̲.ádi
into Chookaneidí
into Deisheetaan.
Their lives point
in many directions.
That is why
it may seem as if they have combined all
these songs their grandparents
left for them,
yes,
when they use them.
Even from long ago
we have placed our grandchildren
high above ourselves.
Yes.
We cherish them.
Even those things we treasure
we used to offer up to them,
to those who are our grandchildren.
That is why now
we made these songs their vision.
If they're not right or if they go against your feelings, please forgive them.
Yes.
They will dance to Shaawát G̲uwakaan's song.
Following this will be
K̲áataan's.
Is that right?
That's it.
Hwói.

3. Shaawát G̲uwakaan Song; T'ak̲deintaan

Aax̲ yá yáa yeedát kei s akakg̲washee aa
has du léelk'wx̲ áyá sitee
tsu hú tsú.
A x̲oox̲ áyá aa yaawanák̲ shayadihéin T'ak̲deintaan
aaa.
Yáa yeedát kei has akakg̲washee aa
K̲áataan
yá Aan Eeg̲ayaa Hítdáx̲
aaa
aag̲áa x̲'óon x'áat'i daadáx̲
yá
at délich yaa s yaksanáak̲
aax̲ ajinák̲ k̲ut has galas'ées.
A ítdáx̲
yax̲ wunateeyán
akawlisheeyi shí áyá.
Áyá yeedát
kei has akg̲washée.
Tsu has du léelk'wx̲ sitee hú tsú
hú tsú
aaa.
Áyá a x̲'asheeyí kei has akg̲washée.
Hwói!

4. K̲áataan x̲'asheeyí; Kaagwaantaan

Ax̲ t'aak̲x'í
yáa yeedát átx̲ has alyex̲ aa
aax̲ k̲u.aa áyá yeedát
hú tsú
yá a tóo yéi haa yateeyí
yá woosh teenx̲ istí.
Ch'u oowayáa a tóot uwagudi yáx̲ yatee
ax̲ léelk'w hás
has du shageinyaa
áyá yeedát has du x̲'éidei gax̲du.áax̲
aaa
has du x̲'éidei gax̲du.áax̲.
Yá dziyáak
yéi kwdzigeyi aach wooshee tsu.
Aaa.

The song they will sing now,
he again was also
their grandfather.
Many T'a<u>k</u>deintaan stand among them,
yes.
The one they'll be singing now
<u>K</u>áataan
from Down The Beach House,
yes
is from the time at the fur seal island
when
the guard was chasing them
and they were blown off course by the wind.
After that,
when things settled down
this is the song he composed.
And now
they will sing it.
Again, he is their grandfather too,
he too,
yes.
This is his song they will sing.
Hwói!

4. <u>K</u>áataan Song; Kaagwaantaan

My brothers and sisters,
the one they will sing now
from now on
he too
was in this membership we share,
relatives of each other.
It seems as if the spirit helpers
of my grandparents
are joining in this,
this is what will be heard from their grandchildren's lips,
yes,
they will be heard from their lips.
A moment ago
the children also sang it.
Yes.

Ch'a tléix' at shí yáx̲ gíyáa
yaa kg̲washée
ch'a tléix'.
Ch'a wáa kawuháax' sá tléil has du tuwáa ushgú yax̲
has ashalaheegí.
Ch'a aadéi k̲wá yéi has gax̲yi.oo.
Hwói!

5. Yéik x̲'asheeyí; Kaagwaantaan

Change-íx̲ has agux̲layéix̲.
Yeeysikóo
shayadihéini aa yeewáan yáat yik̲éen
gwál ax̲ shaawu yánx̲ aa sitee k̲a ax̲ aat hás
aax̲ yee yéi jineiyí yéeyi áyá
yee wak̲shiyeex' yéi has agux̲sanéi.
Gwál tle daax'oon jinkaat táakw wanáax'
tlél tsu k̲wasatínch
yá l'eix̲.
Aaa.
Yéi wduwasáa
"yoo koonák̲k."
Aaa.
Ha ch'u déix̲
dax̲yeekaadéi a g̲óot yatee.
Shux'aa aayí "g̲áax̲ kát nák̲" k̲udzitee.
Aax̲ áyá "kindachóon aawanaak̲" yóo wduwasáa.
Aaa.
Sagóodei áayax̲ wujix̲ín.
Áyá yeedát has akg̲watee.
Dei x'óon yeekaadéi sá
yatee yá shéex'.
Ayáx̲ átx̲ has alyéix̲
yéik utee daasheeyí, Deikeenaa x̲'asheeyí
ldakát yaa has ayaksaxíxch.
Yáa yeedát
aan héidei has ashug̲watan aa
has du léelk'w hás
Chookaneidí aayí.
Yéik utee aayí yá aan héidei has ashug̲watáan
yá s du k̲unéegu.

Maybe they will sing as one song,
when it's sung,
as one.
Why is it they don't like to complete the song?
But please forgive them.
Hwói!

5. Spirit Song; Kaagwaantaan

They will be doing a change of clothing.
You all know,
many of you who are seated here,
maybe some who are my sisters and paternal aunts,
they will enact for you
some of the songs that are yours.
I have not even seen
this dance
for maybe over forty years.
Yes.
It is called
"sway dance."
Yes.
There are two,
two different kinds.
The first one is "standing for the cry."
The next one is called "standing upright."
Yes.
The singing tips over to joyous ones.
This is what they will imitate now.
How many kinds
of these songs there are.
They'll be using them accordingly.
The Spirit Imitating Song, Haida type singing,
they perform them all.
Now
the one they will begin with
belongs to their grandparents
of the Chookaneidí.
They will begin with the "imitating the spirit"
ceremony.

A niyaadéi áwé yándei has akgwatée
tsu has du léelk'w Kaax'achgóok aayí
a x'asheeyí.
Yéi áyá.
Hwoi!

6. Yéik utee daasheeyí; Chookaneidí

Kaa x'éix' áyá yaa shukaktookéijin
yá kconéek yéi daatoone ganúgún
yáa yeedát kwá tle yéi áyá yaa has akgwashée.
Tsu yá s du léelk'w aayí
Kaax'achgóok aayí kei akakgwashée yáa yeedát
aaa
aax yóo l duwatini yéit agutáan
yú x'áat' káx' akawlisheeyi shí
has du x'éidei gaxdu.áax.
Góok!

7. Kaax'achgóok aayí; Kiks.ádi

Yáa yeedát kei has akakgwashee aa
aaa
yá Jilkáatdáx
yá ax daakanóox'u
Sakuyei
a x'asheeyí yá kei has akakgwashée
Deikeenaa x'asheeyí
aaa.
Has du kusteeyí áyá
ldakát yéidei kadlixwás'
aaa
ch'u yéi tsú hás yatee.
Aaa.
Yáa yeedát
a tóo haa kaawahayi kustí
ách
a x'éidáx has ash kaawashéet'
has du léelk'w hás aadéi kunoogu yé.
Yeedát áwé ch'u oowayáa yú gaaw du.áxji

Following this they will place
the song
of another of their grandfathers, K̲aax̲'achgóok.
This is all.
Hwói!

6. Imitating the Spirit Song; Chookaneidí

We used to call out each person's name to sing
when we performed these songs,
but now they will just sing them one after the other.
Again the property of a grandparent,
they will now sing the one of K̲aax̲'achgóok,
yes,
the song he composed on that island,
from when he was blown off course to the place
no one has ever seen
you will hear from their lips.
Go!

7. K̲aax̲'achgóok Song; Kiks.ádi

Now they will sing one,
yes,
from Chilkat,
my outer shell
Sak̲uyei,
this is his song they will sing,
a Haida type song
yes.
These lifelines of theirs
strand off in all directions,
yes,
they in turn are also the same.
Yes.
And now
this way of life we are in
is the one
that displaced from their mouths
the ceremonies their grandparents used to do.
And now they seem just as if

a káa wduwach'ini káa yáx
has yatee
a kayaadéi
yóo has shayagíx'k
has du léelk'w hásx has sateeyí.
Ách áyá átx has aguxlayéix á tsu.
Áyá.
Góok.

8. Sakuyei x'asheeyí; Jilkáat

Ch'áak' Hít.
Ách áyá
Kaagwaantaan dachxanx'i yán a tóo shayadihéin
yáat nák
aaa.
Ách áyá s du x'éidei gaxdu.áax
has du léelk'w hás
s'áaxw daa sheeyí.
Aaa.
Yéi áyú has oosáayjin
tlax aatlein sh kalneek ku.aa áyú a díx'náx áa yéi yatee
Ch'áak' Tláa
yóo áyú s oosáayjin yú ách kawlisheeyi káa
aaa
Ch'áak' Tláa x'ayáx á.
Hwói!

9. Ch'áak' Tláa x'asheeyí; Kaagwaantaan

Yáa yeedát
kei s a kakgwashee aa
yá shí
L'uknax.ádi aayí áyá.
Hóoch'i aayíx has aguxlayéix.
Yéi wduwasáa yá shí
"Yoo Kuwahangi Yéik."
Yéi yá sh wudisáa.
Ha déix yeekaadéi áyá s aséix noojéen
yá ax éesh hásch
yá shí.

they are like the man
whose hair was tied into the sound of the drum
kind of keeping beat with their heads
toward those
who are their grandparents.
Again, this is why they will use this one.
Now
go ahead.

8. Sak̲uyei Song; Chilkat

Eagle House:
the reason for this
is that there are many grandchildren of Kaagwaantaan
standing here among them,
yes.
This is why you will hear this song from them,
the song
for their grandparents' hat.
Yes.
Great is the story behind it.
Her name was
Ch'áak' Tláa,
the name of the person who composed the song,
yes,
just like Ch'áak' Tláa said it, indeed.
Hwói!

9. Ch'áak' Tláa Song; Kaagwaantaan

Now
the ones they will sing,
these songs,
belong to L'uknax̲.ádi.
These are the last ones they will do.
These songs are called
"The Spirit Who Sways."
This is what it named itself.
These songs
usually were called two ways
by these fathers of mine.

Aadé duwasaagu yé
K̲aaksateen yahaayí.
Dax̲.aax̲ sitee
yá K̲aaksateen yóo wduwasayi shaawát.
Hú áyá yá l'ook áx̲ jiyaak̲uwdlig̲át.
Áyá ux̲ kei uwatée.
Á áyá kei s akakg̲washée
kei
íx̲t' du éet góot du yahaayí.
Góok.

10. K̲aaksateen x̲'asheeyí; L'uknax̲.ádi
11. K̲aaksateen yahaayí; L'uknax̲.ádi

Kichnáalx̲ (1)
Sheet'ká, 1980

Gunalchéesh.
Aaa
ax̲ éesh eeti g̲aneix̲
dziyáak áwé
ch'a kaawayídei áwé dag̲átch
i yoo x̲'atángi.
    (K̲aal.átk') *Haa wáa sá.*
Tléil áwé ách woonax̲lisheeyi k̲áa k̲oostí.
    (K̲aal.átk') *Yéi yatee, yítk', yéi yatee.*
Yá gaaw áwé
kaax̲ áwé shawjix̲een
haa k̲usteeyí, haa Lingítx̲ sateeyí
aadéi yéi jinéiyi yé
shux'áa aayí
aaa
ax̲ éesh eeti g̲aneix̲
aaa.
Dziyáak áwé has du x̲'éit x̲wasi.áx̲ yú haa yátx'i
yéi áwé s at shí.
"Yéi áyá k̲aa jín du.ús'kw,"
yú.á

K̲aaksateen's Image
was what it was named.
The second one is
this woman who was named K̲aaksateen.
She was the one who offended the coho salmon.
Then it turned bad for her.
These are the ones they will sing,
sing
when her image came to the shaman.
Go.

10. K̲aaksateen Song; L'uknax̲.ádi
11. K̲aaksateen Image Song; L'uknax̲.ádi

George Davis (1)
Sitka, 1980

Thank you.
Yes,
my father's surviving relative,
a moment ago..
your words
only fell into space.
    (Charlie Joseph) *Indeed.*
There wasn't a person present who could grasp them.
    (Charlie Joseph) *That's how it is, son. That's how it is.*
At this time
the cover has fallen away
from our culture, our Tlingit identity,
the way our predecessors
used to do things,
yes,
my father's surviving relative,
yes.
A moment ago I listened to those children of ours,
to how they sang.
"This is how one's hands are washed,"
it is said,

"yéi áwé k̲aa jín du.ús'kw." 20
Yisikóo
yá yéi at kunax̲dayéin áwé
aaa
yaa kdus.ínjin áwé x̲á wé s'íx'.
Aaa.
Neil wuduwateeyi aa jín du.ús'gun.
Ch'u yéi áwé a daa tux̲ditaan.
Yá dziyáak
yá s du x̲'asheeyí
aadéi s ashutan yé 30
aaa
yá ldakát yáx̲ has ayawlishiyi shí
a x̲oox' áwé déix̲ aa k̲udzitee
kulits'ígwa aa áwé
áwé tléil ch'a aadéi ch'a neechx'
kei kawduwashiyi yéix' gándei oongaa.aadi yé.
Yóo áwé
haa shagóon k̲udzitee.
        (K̲aal.átk') Gunalchéesh áwé.
Yáat'aa á
ách áwé 40
yei k̲ugwastée
aaa
yei k̲ugwastée
dáx̲náx̲ has gugwatée
yá haa daat
yóo x̲'atánk yóodei s akgwatee aa
aaa.
X'úx' káx' áwé yéi s aya.óo
yáa yeedát
yáax' 50
yáax'
haa tóot has k̲oowatini aa
aaa.
Haa Lingít x̲ sateeyí áwé
kaax̲ yéi shukgwashx̲éen
a k̲usteeyí.
        (K̲aal.átk') Gunalchéesh áwé.
Dei haa jeex' áwé
a káa yáa haa jinalsák̲

"This is how one's hands are washed."
You all know,
when things like these were happening,
yes,
they used to carry in a basin, you see.
Yes.
The hands of the one who is taken in would be washed.
This is just how I'm thinking about them.
A while ago,
they way they directed
these songs of theirs,
yes,
of all the songs they sang
there are two among them
that are sensitive
and cannot be sung without a reply
before people take leave.
That's the way
our ancestors lived it.
(Charlie Joseph) *Thank you.*
That is why
there will be
this person,
yes,
there will be,
there will be two of them,
the ones
who will respond for us,
yes.
They have written some into books
already
here
here
those who have joined with us,
yes.
For those of us who are Tlingit,
the cover will slide off
from our culture.
(Charlie Joseph) *Thank you.*
Even now our grip
is weary from holding on to it,

yáat
haa Lingítx̱ sateeyí.
Naaléi áwé aadéi yéi aa kandutax̱'w yé haa jináḵ.
Áwé a shú áwé tulashát
áwé yáa yeedát áwé tlax̱
ax̱ toowóo
sh kax' x̱'awdigáx'
yá Sealaskach a daa wdahaaní.
Aan át haa x̱'awdagáax'in
yáx̱
haa léelk'w hás
aadéi yéi s jinéiyi yé.
Át ax̱wdishée haa Aanḵáawoo has du éet wudasheeyí
has du jín kée awulsháadi.
Aag̱áa tléil ḵut kei kag̱waxeex haa Lingítx̱ sateeyí.
L yéi yei s jeenaneinín ḵu.aa áwé
x'úx' áwé at has akg̱watée
a kaadáx̱ áwé a akg̱watóow.
Dei ch'áakw áwé wduwatíḵ'
haa Dleit Ḵáax̱ sateeyí yá haa x̱oonx'ích
haa Lingítx̱ sateeyí;
á áwé a kaadéi s akg̱walg̱éen.
Áwé ch'u l yéi unaneijí áwé.
Aaa,
gunalchéesh x̱á
aaa,
adaanáx̱ has wudanaag̱í
yá ḵustí yá haa Lingítx̱ sateeyí.
(Ḵaal.átk') *Gunalchéesh.*
Aaa
aadéi sh tug̱áa haa ditee
aaa
aadóo ḵu.aa sá kwshí shux'aanáx̱.
Wa.é gé?
Aaa, yáadu yá ax̱ kéek'
Keewaax̱.awtseix.
Yoo x̱'atánk yei agux̱sanéi.

here,
on to our Tlingit identity.
It is very deep to where most of it has sunk from our grip.
We are just clutching the very tip
but this moment though, how
my silent
prayer continues
that Sealaska would rise to it.
It was as if
we went and begged to have someone do it
the way our grandparents
used to do things.
My hope is that our Lord will assist them
and lift their hands.
Then, our Tlingit identity will not vanish.
But if they don't do this
they will only be carrying books around with them
that they can read this from.
Our Tlingit identity
has long been misunderstood
by our relatives who are white.
This is what they will be looking at.
This is to prevent this from happening,
yes.
Thank you,
yes,
for rising
to this culture, to this Tlingit identity.
    (Charlie Joseph) *Thank you.*
Yes,
we are grateful for this,
yes,
but I wonder who will be the first.
Is it you?
Yes, here is this younger brother of mine
Keewaax̱.awtseix̱.
He will make a speech.

Keewaax̱.awtseix̱ G̱uwakaan
Sheet'ká, 1980

Gunalchéesh.
Át ḵoowaháa yáa yeedát
(Unidentified) *Gunalchéesh.*
ax̱ éesh kéilk'.
(Ḵaal.átk') *Aaa.*
Ldakát át yádix̱ áyú x̱at wusitee
naa yádi.
Wooshkeetaan ax̱ éeshx̱ wusitee shux'áanáx̱
a ítdei áwé Kaagwaantaan
a ítdei áwé Chookaneidí.
Ách áwé tléix' ax̱ aat hás.
Kaagwaantaan jeedéi áyá g̱uwakaanx̱ x̱at wusitee
yá Xunaax'.
Hóoch'i aayí Keewaax̱.awtseix̱
yú Jilḵáat
yú shaa kaax̱ áwé x̱at wuduwasáa
yá ax̱ éesh kéilk'
has du aaní.
Dei ldakát yéidei áyú yoo x̱at kawsitée
yá haa ḵusteeyí
át ḵoowaháa yáa yeedát
haa Lingít ḵusteeyí
a káx̱ yáax' haat ḵuwtuwatín.
Yá shí
tlél áyá aadéi ch'a kaawayíx̱ woog̱axeexi yé.
Gidaan kélk', haa gú!
Át ḵoowaháa
kélk'.
I káak hás eetéet eehán.
Áx̱ nas.aax̱.
Haa eetéex' yaa yakg̱ila.áat
i káak hás aaní.
Áyá yá kei kayeeyshée yá shí
yá haa éesh hás aayí

William Johnson
Sitka, 1980

Thank you.
The moment has come
(Unidentified) *Thank you.*
my father's maternal nephew.
(Charlie Joseph) *Yes.*
I became the child of many clans,
a child of each clan.
To begin with my father was Wooshkeetaan,
after that Kaagwaantaan
and after that Chookaneidí.
That is why my paternal aunts are one and all.
I became a peace maker to the Kaagwaantaan
in Hoonah.
Lastly Keewaax̱.awtseix̱
of Chilkat,
these nephews of my fathers
named me for the mountain,
for their land.
This culture of ours
has tried me in many ways,
the moment has come
in our Tlingit culture
for which we came here.
This song
cannot just be left lingering in the air.
Stand, maternal nephew, come here!
The moment has come,
maternal nephew.
You are standing in the place of your maternal uncles.
Listen to them.
You will steer
your maternal uncles' land in place of us.
The song that you sang
that belongs to our fathers,

yá yéik
tlél áyá aadéi kawayíkx wooxdzi.aaxi yé.
(Kaal.átk') *Ha wáa sá. Gunalchéesh xáawé.*
A yáax' áyú kei aa dustaanch.
Ha yá haa léelk'w
X'eijáak'w
aan áyá woosh jín alshát
ka yá Ch'áak' S'áaxw daa sheeyí
aan áyá woosh jín yéi s alshátch.
(Kaal.átk') *Gunalchéesh áwé.*
Ax léelk'w hás
has du at.óowu
yáat yá
Gaanaxáa
ch'u oowayáa
gági has wu.aadí yá aax haat kuwtuwatini yé
ha yáa yeedát
yá at yátx'i.
Tlax wáa sá haa toowóo kligéi
haa kusteeyí
kut kei ntoogíx'
kut kei ntoogíx'
yáa yeedát haa wakshiyeex'
yóo ysaneiyí xá ax éesh kéilk'.
(Kaal.átk') *Ha wáa sá.*
Gunalchéesh.
(Kaal.átk') *Gunalchéesh áwé.*
I ítnáx gunéi kgwa.áat
(Kaal.átk') *Gunalchéesh.*
i ítnáx gunéi kgwa.áat
yáat keen.

Tóok'
Sheet'ká, 1980

Ákwshéiwé
tsú aadáx kawdzixát ax kusteeyí
xát tsú hé Deisheetaanx xat sateeyí

this spirit
cannot echo in the air.
(Charlie Joseph) *Yes indeed. Thank you.*
In reply to it, a song is usually lifted.
With this grandfather of ours,
X̲'eijáak'w,
they are clasping hands
and with the song of the Eagle Hat
they are clasping one another's hands.
(Charlie Joseph) *Thank you indeed.*
The at.óow
of my maternal grandfathers:
here this
G̲aanax̲áa,
it is as if
these children
right now
have come out in view from the place I came from.
We're losing
our culture,
we're losing it.
How very proud we are
that you have brought them out
for us to see, my father's maternal nephew.
(Charlie Joseph) *Indeed.*
Thank you.
(Charlie Joseph) *Thank you.*
People will begin to follow your example
(Charlie Joseph) *Thank you.*
people will begin to follow your example,
those who are sitting here.

Charlie Jim
Sitka, 1980

Didn't my life
also stem from there,
from Chilkat,

Jilk̲áatdáx̲.
Áyá yá haa éesh hás
yéi áyá has x̲'ayak̲áa noojéen
"Aaa
át kadikékwt
yee éesh hás aaní."
Áyá yeedát yá ax̲ húnx̲w
x̲at x̲'akawunáayi.
Dziyáak
yá at yátx'i yoo koonák̲wgoo áwé a daa yoo tux̲aatánk
haa Lingítx̲ sateeyí aadéi yateeyi yé.
Á áwé tsá
k̲aa shagóon yan akooneekch.
Yóo áwé sh kalnik noojéen haa káak hás
haa léelk'w hás.
Aaa.
Yáa yeedát yáat x̲aháni áwé
aaa.
Ax̲ húnx̲w
Kichnáalx̲
du kéek' áwé yéi wduwasáa
Yéil Hít daa yéi s jine nóok
Yéilk'.
Aag̲áa áwé yéi s yaawak̲aa
"Tléil tsu du t'ak̲káx'yei aa gax̲dusaa Yéilk'
ax̲ kéek'," yóo.
Á áyá
héench yéi wsinei.
A ít áwé
aaa, kuk̲astée áwé
x̲at wuduwax̲oox̲
"Haat yisanú haa kéek'."
Aag̲áa áwé yoo x̲'atánk
yéi s anasnéi áwé.
"Hú áyá yáadoo
Yéilk'.
Tléil tsu k̲áa du t'ak̲káa yéi gax̲dusaa."
Aaa, k̲áax̲ yaa x̲at gasatée ax̲ een yóo x̲'ali.átk Kichnáalx̲.
Aag̲áa áyá yéi x̲at yawsik̲aa ax̲ húnx̲w
"Ee een naa yádi jeedéi áwé tsá kg̲eetée yá saa."
Yóo áwé

mine too, who am Deisheetaan?
These fathers of ours
used to say
"Yes,
the land of your fathers
untangles things."
This is it here now, when my older brother
told me to speak.
A while ago
when these children were dancing that was what I thought
of the way our Tlingit identity is.
It is this
that ultimately reveals one's ancestry.
This is what our maternal uncles used to tell us,
our grandfathers.
Yes.
Now that I am standing here,
yes.
My older brother
Kichnáalx̱,
his younger brother was named
Yéilk'—Little Raven—
when they were building the Raven House.
This is when they said
"No one beside my younger brother
will be named Yéilk'."
But
the water did him in.
After this,
yes, when I was born,
they asked for me,
"Bring our younger brother over here."
And then
they made speeches.
"This is him, here,
Yéilk'.
No other man beside him will be named this."
Yes, when I was becoming an adult Kichnáalx̱ instructed me.
This is when my older brother said to me,
"Give this name only to a fellow clan child."
That is how

yan x̲at yawsik̲áa.
Aaa.
(Unidentified) *Ha wáa sá.*
Ax̲ shagóon aadéi yoo shukawsixixi yé
ax̲ tláanáx̲
aaa,
Wooshkeetaan dachx̲ánx̲ áyá x̲at wusitee.
Á áyá nax̲awóos' áwé
ax̲ léelk'w
k̲aju Yuwáak'w dachx̲anx'i yánx̲ áwé haa wsitee
ax̲ tláa yinaanáx̲.
Aaa.
Ch'a x̲át yá ax̲ éesh yinaanáx̲ k̲u.aa wés
(ax̲ éesh
Daalkoowoox̲' Éesh yóo áwé wduwasáa)
Deisheetaan
áwé chuchgadachx̲ánx̲ áwé x̲at wudzitee.
Aaa, yá gaaw áwé a daa yoo tux̲aatánk
ax̲ káak hás k̲usteeyí
aaa.
Yá yáadei
ax̲ káani K̲aal.átk'
(K̲aal.átk') *Áawé.*
lax̲éitlx̲ áwé ax̲ jee sitee.
(K̲aal.átk') *Ha wáa sá.*
Aaa.
Lax̲éitlx̲ ax̲ jee sitee, ax̲ léelk'w Yuwáak'w
tsú ax̲ léelk'w
ax̲ kaani yán
haa yátx'i
Anaxóots
k̲a yáat aa aa Aangóon
Deisheetaan yátx'i.
G̲uneit
Deisheetaan yádix̲ wusitee.
Áyá yáat has k̲éen.
Aaa.
Has du yinaanáx̲ kei jikawsixixi yáx̲ áwé tsú yáat'aa ax̲ léelk'w
Keik̲óok'w, léelk'w

he instructed me.
Yes.
(Unidentified) *Indeed.*
The way my ancestry took its course
through my mother,
yes,
I became a grandchild of Wooshkeetaan.
When I asked my grandfather
about this
we had been the grandchildren of Yuwáak'w all along
through my mother's side.
Yes.
But through my father's side,
(my father's name
was Daalkoowoox̱' Éesh)
I became my own grandchild
of Deisheetaan.
Yes, this is what I am thinking now
of my maternal uncles' way of life,
yes.
Here and now
my brother-in-law K̲aal.átk'
(Charlie Joseph) *That's it.*
it is becoming good fortune in my hands.
(Charlie Joseph) *Indeed.*
Yes.
It has become good fortune in my hands,
my grandfather Yuwáak'w
also my grandfather
my brothers-in-law
our children
Anaxóots
and these people from Angoon,
children of Deisheetaan.
G̱uneit
became a child of Deisheetaan.
It is they who are sitting here.
Yes.
It is as if the strand surfaced from their side too,
these grandfathers of mine.
Keik̲óok'w, grandfather

yáa yeedát áwé
(Keik̲óok'w) *Áawé.*
aaa.
Yáat x̲a.aayí
yá yéik.
Aag̲áa áwé kei jidultsóowch áyú yú.á
a yinaadéi
haa Lingítx̲ sateeyí
ux̲ kei utéeg̲aa.
Ax̲ tundatáani áwé kei jiwlitsák̲
aaa
yéi tutídáx̲ áwé
ax̲ hunx̲w hás
has du yéigi
aaa
K'óox K̲uyéik,
Kéidladi K̲uyéik.
Yáa yeedát áwé ax̲ tundatáani yéi yatee
aan woosh jín has alshát.
Yá xáanaa
(K̲aal.átk') *Ha wáa sá.*
ax̲ tundatáani áwé yéi yatee.
K̲a tsú yá Ch'áak' Tláa
aaa
du x̲'asheeyí tu.áx̲ji áwé, ch'a g̲óot yéidei tsu
haa tundatáani yatee.
(K̲aal.átk') *Gunalchéesh.*
Lax̲éitl á
lax̲éitl á yóo áwé ax̲ tundatáani yatee.
(K̲aal.átk') *Gunalchéesh.*
Ách áwé
ax̲ tundatáani yéi yatee
ux̲ kei utéeg̲aa.
Ax̲ jeet áwé áx̲ yáa yeedát yú Yéil X'óow.
Oowayáa a yaadéi shakk̲walagáas'
a yaadéi shakk̲walagáas'
ux̲ kei utéeg̲aa.
(Unidentified) *Gunalchéesh.*
Lingítx̲ haa sateeyí
wooch yáa awudané áyá yatx̲ uwaxíx
yá yeedát

at this moment
    (George Jim) *Indeed.*
yes.
While I was sitting here
I thought about this Spirit.
People would raise their hands to it, it is said,
toward it,
those of us who are Tlingit,
so that it does not cause harm.
My spirit raised its hands,
yes,
from thinking this way,
the spirit
of my older brothers,
yes,
Marten Spirit,
Sea Gull Spirit.
This moment I'm thinking that they're clasping hands
    with one another
this evening
    (Charlie Joseph) *Yes, indeed.*
this is what I'm thinking.
And also this Ch'áak' Tláa,
yes,
as we listen to the song about her, it stimulates our thoughts.
    (Charlie Joseph) *Thank you.*
What a good fortune indeed,
what a good fortune indeed is what I'm thinking.
    (Charlie Joseph) *Thank you.*
That it doesn't cause harm
is why
I'm thinking this.
I now have in my care the Raven Robe.
It is as if I will use it as a brace,
I will use it as a brace to the song
so that it doesn't cause harm.
    (Unidentified) *Thank you.*
We who are Tlingit,
our respect for each other has emerged
now

yá gaaw
aaa.
K̲a tsú yá hít
yá a yeet tuk̲in aa yá hít
Shee Atika
aaa
ax̲ hunx̲w hás hítx'i
Deishu Hít
Yéil Hít
ux̲ kei utéeg̲aa áwé yáa
adookt has yaawak̲iyi yáx̲ áwé ax̲ jee k̲uwdi.oo
aaa,
lax̲éitl aax̲ haa jee nax̲satee.
Yá xáanaa áwé sh tug̲áa x̲at ditee
(Unidentified) *Gunalchéesh.*
sh tug̲áa x̲at ditee
aaa.
Shux'áa kei x̲at gawáat áwé x̲a.áx̲jin
aaa
ax̲ hunx̲w hás x̲'éidei
Jilk̲áat een áwé woosh kik'i yánx̲ wudzitee
aaa.
Yá adaax' yoo x̲'ax̲aatangi yé
yá gaaw
Deishu Hít yeedéi
á x̲á tlax̲ lax̲éidli aax̲ sitee aadéi took̲in yé yá xáanaa.
Aaa, shayawdihaa
has du dachx̲anx'i yán.
Aaa, a daax' áwé yéi s jeewanéi
Deisheetaanch.
Á áyá yáat aa áa.
Yá ax̲ húnx̲wx̲ sitee
T'aawchán
Walter Soboleff.
Gwál ax̲ ítx' Dleit K̲áa x̲'éináx̲ sh tóog̲aa gux̲datée.
Daat yáx̲ sáyú has du léelk'w hás
has du daa yéi jeewanei.
(K̲aal.átk') *Gunalchéesh.*
Aaa.
Yeeysikóo yá ax̲ húnx̲w

at this time
yes.
And also this building,
the house we're sitting inside of,
Shee Atika,
yes,
the houses of my older brothers,
Deishú House,
Raven House,
so that it doesn't cause harm for them,
it's as if they are sitting against it is what becomes of them
    in my hands,
yes,
that it becomes good fortune in our hands.
This evening I am gratified
    (Unidentified) *Thank you.*
I am gratified,
yes.
Early in my life, while I was growing up, I used to hear,
yes,
from my older brothers' lips,
how they were younger brothers to Chilkat,
yes.
The way we are sitting tonight is surely good fortune for us,
this of which I am speaking,
this moment
inside Deishú House.
Yes, there were many
who were their grandchildren.
Yes, the Deisheetaan
treated them well.
There is one sitting here.
He is my older brother,
T'aawchán,
Walter Soboleff.
Perhaps, he will express his gratitude following me in English.
How fine their grandfathers
treated them.
    (Charlie Joseph) *Thank you.*
Yes.
You all know this older brother of mine,

Samuel G. Johnson yéi dusáagun
Yeilnaawú
aaa.
Du ít áwé k̲ux̲wdzitee.
Ch'a aan áwé daat yáx̲ sáwé ax̲'awlitseen
du léelk'wx̲ x̲at sateeyí
yá Deishu Hít yeedáx̲.
Yá xáanaa áwé
áa yoo s x̲'asatángin
áa yoo s x̲'asatángin yú aa yéi s k̲éech yá aan.
Ách áwé yáa yeedát
sh tug̲áa ditee Xutsnoowú.
(Unidentified) *Gunalchéesh.*
Sh tug̲áa ditee Xutsnoowú.
Ax̲ toowú yak'éi.
Aaa.
Tsú yá atx̲á áwé.
Haa Lingítx̲ sateeyí áyá át k̲uwaháa
yá atx̲á
aaa
wáa yá gaaw sáwé Lingít wooch g̲aax̲da.éex'ín
a daat yoo x̲'atánk yóox̲ xeex.
Wáa ng̲aneen sáwé ch'a kalk'átl'gináx̲ aag̲áa áwé anawóos'ch
"Aadóo sákwshí yéi x̲at wusinei?"
Wáa ng̲aneen sáwé yéi yandusk̲éich
"I káani áwé,
i dachx̲án áwé."
Yá xáanaa áwé
yá atx̲á tsú aax̲ sh tóogaa tsú x̲at ditee.
Gunalchéesh
sh yáa awudanéix'i
yóo áyá x̲'ayax̲ak̲á
(Unidentified) *Gunalchéesh.*
ax̲ aat hásx̲ siteeyi aa
Ho, ho!
Ho, ho!
(Unidentified) *Gunalchéesh.*
Át tleinx̲ áyá haa jee wsitee.
Kag̲ax̲toonéek x̲á
k̲ux̲ k̲utudatínni
aadéi haa daat yee yateeyi yé

Samuel G. Johnson was his name,
Yeilnaawú,
yes.
I was born after him.
Even then he valued like nothing else
that I was his grandfather
from Deishú House.
This evening
the dancers gave it voice,
they gave it voice where they sat in the village.
That is why at this moment
Angoon is gratified,
    (Unidentified) *Thank you.*
Angoon is gratified.
I feel fine.
Yes.
And this food, too:
The time has come for us to talk about our Tlingit tradition,
regarding food,
yes,
how at a time like this when Tlingits hosted each other
words would be said about the food.
Sometimes someone would ask quietly,
"I wonder who did this for me?"
Sometimes they would say to him,
"It was your brother-in-law," or
"It was your grandchild."
This evening
I am also grateful for this dinner.
Thank you,
people of honor,
is what I'm saying
    (Unidentified) *Thank you.*
to those who are my paternal aunts.
Hó, hó!
Hó, hó!
    (Unidentified) *Thank you.*
It has become valuable in our hands.
We will tell about it, you see,
when we get back home,
of how you were concerned for us,

aaa.
Tlax̱ oowayáa
kindachóon yaa g̱ax̱too.áat ḵúx̱dei.
Ha yéi áyá, sh tug̱áa x̱at ditee.
Gunalchéesh.
Ho, ho!

Kichnáalx̱ (2)
Sheet'ká, 1980

Yak'éi.
Aaa.
Dziyáak áwé i séit x̱wasi.áx̱.
Aag̱áa áwé anax̱ haat keeyaník
gaaw du.áx̱ji.
Yáa yeedát áwé
aaa
a káa haa jiwlisáḵ
yax̱ shawtulatsaag̱i haa Lingítx̱ sateeyí.
(Unidentified) *Gunalchéesh.*
Aaa
dei áx' haa jeex' tl'aadéin yáa naltídi áwé
yá Sealaska
anax̱ haat has uwanáḵ.
Aaa.
Gu.aakwshíl
dakdachóon has ayawutaaníḵ haa jeex'
(Unidentified) *Gunalchéesh.*
ch'oo l haa jeedáx̱ unatáx̱'wji
haa léelk'w hás aadéi x̱'ayaḵáayi yé.
Aaa.
Ách áwé x̱'éidáx̱ kandushéet' áwé
aaa
ch'a yú at tan yéix' ch'a áa sh wudigwaal
yú du gaawú
aaa
haa toowú áwé yéi téeyin dé

yes.
It is very much as if
we will be returning with our heads held high.
This is how it is, how gratified I am.
Thank you.
Hó, hó!

George Davis (2)
Sitka, 1980

It's fine.
Yes.
A while ago I listened to your voice.
You told us then
about the beat of the drum.
Now,
yes,
our grip has wearied
on our Tlingit identity that we were holding in place
        with a pole.
        (Unidentified) *Thank you.*
Yes,
it was rocking sideways in our grip under the pounding waves
when Sealaska
surfaced.
Yes.
My hope is
they will point what our ancestors used to say
into the waves
before it sinks from our grip.
        (Unidentified) *Thank you.*
Yes.
Because when they shoved him aside,
yes,
even while that drum of his
was lying there pounding,
yes,
that is how we felt,

aaa
ch'a a kayaadéi yoo shatoogíx'gin.
Áwé dziyáak i x̱'éidei x̱aa.áx̱ch
yá yoo x̱'atánk.
(Unidentified) *Haa wáa sá.*
Aaa
yáa yeedát ḵudzitee áx' yéi yatee du daat du shuká
yéi yoo x̱'ax̱aatángi aa
yú ax̱ léelk'w eetiganeix̱
hé Keiḵóok'
hú áwé yoo x̱'atánk
áwé yéi agux̱sanéi.

Keiḵóok'
Sheet'ká, 1980

Gunalchéesh áyá. Aaa,
Yuwáak'w
ax̱ léelk'w saayí, gidaan!
Has du waḵshiyeex' yan hán i éesh hás
wa.é tsú
gidaan.
Hél yoo x̱'akgeetaan áwé, x̱át áwé yoo x̱'akḵwatáan i jiyís.
De dleit yáx̱ x̱at shasitee.
Du shukáa x̱waagút yá Ḵaal.átk' aadéi yaa x̱at yanadlaḵ yé de,
yeedát ḵu.aa
wé i sée daaḵw aa sáwé?
(Daasdiyáa) *Daasdiyáa.*
Daasdiyáa.
Aaa.
Aan yátx'u sáani,
shakaḵáax'w,
yáat yiḵeení
yá ax̱ tláa léelk'wx̱ áyá has wusitee
yá Sheet'ká
Kaagwaantaan.
Ách áyá
tlél x̱'atukawushyaa ax̱ jee yéi utí.

yes,
kind of keeping the beat toward it with our heads.
A while ago I heard these words
from your lips.
    (Unidentified) *Indeed.*
Yes,
now there is someone following me; I'm speaking of
my grandfather's surviving relative,
Kei<u>k</u>óok',
who will make
a speech.

George Jim
Sitka, 1980

Thank you. Yes,
Yuwáak'w
my grandfather's namesake, stand up!
You too,
stand up,
stand in the sight of your fathers.
You will not be speaking, I will speak for you.
My hair is like snow now.
How far I've already aged beyond Charlie Joseph
    from how he gets the better of me; but now
which one is your daughter?
    (Ethel Makinen) *Daasdiyáa.*
Daasdiyáa.
Yes.
Children of noble people,
paddlers at the bow,
you who are sitting here,
the Sitka
Kaagwaantaan
are my mother's grandparents.
This is why
I have no fear of speaking.

Ax̱ léelk'w hás x̱aan wuliléelk'w hás
yá Ḵóok Hít yeex̱ has yawuḵeeyi aa
Shaanchg̱akeitl yátx'i á.
(Ḵaal.átk') *Gunalchéesh áwé, kík'. Gunalchéesh áwé, kík',*
aadéi yoo x̱'eeyatangi yé.
Aaa, ách áyá
yáa yeedát
ax̱ náḵ has wu.aadí
aaa, oowayáa
yáa daak has shux̱wa.aadí yáx̱ áyá ax̱ toowú yatee
yá ax̱ éesh hás
awulyeilí
yá L'ook Ḵuyéik.
Tléil áwé ax̱ tuwáa ushgú ch'a nichkát teení.
Shayadihéin áyá a tóodei ksixadi ḵáa
yá Sheet'káx'.
Ách áwé
ax̱ tuwáa sigoo
aaa
áyá akawuneegí.
Ax̱ léelk'w áyá awulyeilín
a tóot
awulyeilín
yú G̱ooch Ḵuyéik.
Aag̱áa áyú x̱'awux̱ekáx' aya.áakt at kag̱ashéenín áyú
Ḵaak'wx̱wán G̱ushkáx̱ áyú yeiḵ lugagúḵch
yú g̱ooch.
A yádi a x̱'éitx̱ kei kg̱agudín áwé du x̱'éitx̱ kei kg̱agudín,
ḵáa ítdei áwé kei u.éex'ch
yú aak'wátsk'u.
Aax̱ áwé kei shukanals'el'i yáx̱ natéech.
Yéi áwé ax̱ tusitee yeedát,
yáa yeedát
yáax'
wooch kanax̱ wutooda.aadí, aaa
yá G̱ooch
Ḵuyéik.
Yáax' has al'eix̱
yá ax̱ aat hásx'i sáani
ax̱ sani hás
yá haa dachx̱anx'i sáani.

My grandfathers became grandchildren with me
those who were within the Box House,
children of Shaanchg̲akeitl indeed.
(Charlie Joseph) *Thank you, younger brother. Thank you,*
younger brother, for the way you speak.
Yes, because of this
now
those who left me behind,
yes, it's as if
I will lead them out is how it seems to me,
these fathers of mine
who were enchanted
by the Coho Spirit.
I don't want to have it lie unattended.
There are too many people's life lines leading into it
into Sitka.
Yes,
that is why
I want to
say something in return.
It was my grandfather who was enchanted
enchanted
by
the Wolf Spirit.
Even as he fasted and was chanting to prepare for it,
those wolves
ran out on K̲aak'wx̲wán Ridge.
While they were all running, and their mother
began to outrun them,
her little ones would begin howling after her.
They would sound like roots ripping from the ground.
That's how it seems to me now,
now
that we have gathered
here, yes,
this Wolf
Spirit.
These young paternal aunts of mine,
my paternal uncles
these grandchildren of ours
danced here.

Ux̱ kei aa utéeg̱aa
sh tóodei katudzi.éi
yá yéik
atx̱ dulyeix̱í.
Ách áwé
ux̱ kei aa utéeg̱aa
yá yéik x̱'asheeyí kát has al'eix̱í
has du x̱ootx̱ áwé kei anatlét'
yú G̱ooch Ḵuyéikch.
Has du jinaháayi áwé has du x̱oodáx̱ kei anatlét'
ux̱ kei aa utéeg̱aa
ḵa yá neilt ḵin aa.
Aaa.
Kei dunáḵch áyóo diyeenáx̱ kei kawdusheeyí
yéik.
Spirit.
That's a spirit song.
And the opposite tribe on that side
they have to stand up
and hold your hands up
chuch kaax̱ áyá kakg̱idachóox
yú yéik.
Aadéi ḵut kei ntugix' yé haa ḵusteeyí.
Ach áyá yeedát a daa yoo x̱'ax̱aatánk.
Shayadihéini át áyá a tóonáx̱ kaawaháa haa ḵusteeyí.
Wooch isx̱án áyá a tóonáx̱ kaawaháa.
Wooch yáa awudané tsú a tóonáx̱ kaawaháa.
Daa sá yá yaa yanaxíx yeedát
ḵaa yáa awuné áyá
yáat tooḵeení.
Aaa.
Tsú yá dléigu ldakát uháan áyá s haa ladléigu
yá haa dachx̱anx'i sáani
aaa.
Ḵusax̱án
yaadachóonx̱ satí
yaadachóon yoo x̱'atánk.
Haa Lingítx̱ sateeyí
ḵut kei naxíxi.
Dleit Ḵáach óo at wulituwu aa
l haa x̱'eiya.áx̱ji aa

That it does not cause harm for them,
we are cautious
when the spirits
are used.
In order that
it does not cause harm
because they danced to this spirit song
this Wolf Spirit
is lapping it up from among them,
he is lapping up potential trouble from among them
that things do not cause harm for them
and for those who are sitting here.
Yes.
The hosts would stand up at the back when the guests
sang their spirit songs.
Spirit.
That's a spirit song.
And the entire opposite moiety
would stand
with their hands raised
to ward off the spirit
with the heel of the hand.
How much we are losing our culture.
This is why I'm speaking about it now.
Many things come from our culture.
Love for each other comes from it.
Respect for each other also comes from it.
Whatever is in progress now,
we are sitting here
out of respect for each other.
Yes.
Also these lullabies that cuddle all of us,
these grandchildren of ours,
yes.
Love
is honesty,
speaking honestly.
Our Tlingit identity
is being lost.
To those who were educated by the white men,
the ones who don't understand us

yá gaaw yoo x̱'ax̱atángi.
Tammmmmmmmmmmmmmmmmmmmmmmmmmmmmm
yéi áwé duwa.áx̱ch has du shantóox'
yeedát.
Aaa.
Tléil ḵwá aadéi has du káa kḵwasiháayi yé.
Aaa.
Of course tléil áwé haa x̱'ei.áx̱ch.
X̱át tsú yéi áwé x̱at nateech.
Lidzee yú at ḵug̱ahéin
yú yoo s x̱'ala.atk g̱anúgún.
Yéi áwé du.ax̱ji nuch ax̱ shantú.
Gwál ax̱ húnx̱w tsú yéi áwé du.ax̱ji nuch du shantú.
(Ḵaal.átk') *Yáanáx̱.*
Haa
aaa
yáat'át gunalchéesh
yóo áyá yee daayax̱aḵa
aaa, yá ax̱ éesh hás aayí
yee x̱'éidei x̱wa.aax̱í.
(Unidentified) *Gunalchéesh.*
Aaa
kaawayíkt unaxéexg̱aa áwé
ax̱ léelk'w du yéigi áyá x̱wsihaan
ḵa yá has du náadei x̱aatini aa.
Yá ax̱ jiyís yéi wdudzineiyi yá X'átgu X'óow
áwé a yát shux̱waatán yá Xíxch'i X'óow.
A yát shux̱waatán
a a a
ax̱ léelk'u hás
a tóodáx̱ woo.aadí.
Ax̱ jiyís yan yéi wdudzinéi.
Ax̱ tláa léelk'w
Keiḵóok'w
ldakát hás áyá Kaagwaantaan dachx̱anx'i yánx̱ has wusitee.
Ách áwé ax̱ jiyís yéi wdudzinéi wé G̱ooch
aaa.
Yá gaaw áwé
aaa
sh yáa awudanéiyi ḵáa yáx' kei kḵwateech

while I'm speaking at this time,
Tammmmmmmmmmmmmmmmmmmmmmmmmmmmmmmmm
is how it's sounding in their heads
right now.
Yes.
But there's no way I can blame them.
Yes.
Of course there's no understanding.
This is the way I am, too, at times.
It's difficult at times
when people speak to me.
That's the way it sounds in my head.
Maybe that's how it sounds inside the head
    of my older brother too.
    (Charlie Joseph) *On this side.*
Now,
yes,
I am expressing to you
my appreciation
yes, for these songs of my fathers
that I heard from your lips.
    (Unidentified) *Thank you.*
Yes,
that they do not linger in the air
I'm raising my grandparent's spirit in return
and these that I see draped on their shoulders.
The Dogfish Robe that was made for me
is the one I'm using to brace the Frog Robe.
I'm bracing it,
yes.
My grandfathers
left them behind.
One was made for me.
Keik̲óok'w,
my mother's maternal grandfather,
all were Kaagwaantaan grandchildren.
That is why the wolf was made for me,
yes.
At this time,
yes,
I will show it with pride to a person of honor,

ldakát yá x̲aan aax'w hás ax̲ kéek' hás
aaa.
K'e yá ax̲ húnx̲w
yeedát
(K̲aal.átk') *X̲át tsú i kéek' áyá.*
aaa
i léelk'u geig̲í x̲áawé wa.é
aaa.
Ách áwé
aaa
tlél aadéi át x̲at x̲'awoonax̲ji.áagi yé.
Oowayáa ax̲ shayéenaa yáx̲ a daa ax̲ tuwatee
ax̲ káak hás
ax̲ jeex' a nák̲ has woo.aat.
Tóos' K'oodás'
ax̲ jeewóo.
Has du shakee.ádi tsú ax̲ jeewóo á.
(Unidentified) *Gunalchéesh, gunalchéesh.*
Ch'eet Wootsaag̲áa tsú ax̲ jeewóo á.
Ldakát yeewáan yáa daak yeey.aadí
yee yát áwé shax̲wligás'
ux̲ kei aa utéeg̲aa
yee yoo x̲'atángi ch'a kaawayíkt unaxéexg̲aa.
(Unidentified) *Gunalchéesh.*
Aaa.
Yáa yeedát aadéi sh tux̲dinoogu yé.
Aaa.
Gunalchéesh
ax̲ aat hás.
Aaa.
Tleidahéen áyá
yáat'aa k̲wá ch'a yándei shukk̲watée
aaa
héen x̲ukáx' áyú kei uwax'ák yú áyú tóos', aaa.
Aag̲áa áwé
"Héinráx̲ haagú," yóo ayawsik̲aa.
A t'áat uwagut yú du aat
ax̲ sáni.
"Haagúk' haagú," yú áwé.
Aag̲áa áwé
"Ik̲asháat áwé yándei ix̲waax̲oox̲."

all those with me, my younger brothers,
yes.
For example, my older brother
now
    (Charlie Joseph) *I'm also your younger brother.*
yes,
you are surely your own grandfather,
yes.
That is why,
yes,
in no way can I talk aimlessly.
It is as if my maternal uncles are my anchor
is how I think of them,
that they left these behind in my care.
The Shark Tunic
is in my care.
Their ermine headdress is also in my care.
    (Unidentified) *Thank you, thank you.*
A Murrelet Staff is also in my care.
I am bracing
all of you who came out here
so that it doesn't cause harm,
so that your words not linger in the air.
    (Unidentified) *Thank you.*
Yes.
That's the way I feel now.
Yes.
Thank you
my paternal aunts.
Yes.
But now I will end with this:
one time
yes,
this shark surfaced on the ocean, they say, yes.
And then
"Come over this way," Raven said to her.
My paternal uncle
had come to the beach by his paternal aunt.
"Come here, come here, honey," he said.
And then he said,
"I'm calling you to the beach so I can marry you."

"Ha tlél x̲áawé áyáx̲ utí yá ax̲ xáas'."
"Ch'a iyakas.éini káx̲ áwé," yú.á
(Unidentified) *Gunalchéesh.*
Aaa
yéi áyá
aaa
yá ax̲ sháawu
yá ax̲ sáni hás
ax̲ aat hásx̲ siteeyi aa,
yee gukáa kx̲anéek.
Aaa.
Yéi áyá.
Yéi yá kakg̲wagéi.
Gunalchéesh.
Gunalchéesh.
X̲at wulix̲éitl.
(K̲aal.átk') *Gunalchéesh aadéi yoo x̲'eeyatangi yé.*
Yú aax̲ haat k̲ux̲waatini yé
yú ax̲ léelk'w hás atx̲ has x̲at wus.aayí yee x̲oodéi
tlél shákdéi wé s x̲at yawuwóok̲.
Ch'a l yei x̲wagoodí kát k̲u.aa áwé ax̲ daséigu tóot
g̲waxeexín x̲áa.
Yeedát k̲u.aa wé sh tóonáx̲ kei kax̲wdijél.
Xwéi.
(Applause; audience laughter.)

Kichnáalx̲ (3)
Sheet'ká, 1980

Aaa.
Yáa yeedát
a xaat' [...]
aaa
héidei yoo kdayeik nóok
dei kawtuwa.áx̲ áwé
haa léelk'w hás aadéi s x̲'ayak̲áayi yé
aaa,
gáas' k'éedei áwé

"Not with my skin the way it is," she said.
"It was just for the way you held your head," he said.
(Unidentified) *Thank you.*
Yes,
this is all,
yes,
I tell about this sister of mine,
for you to hear,
my paternal uncles,
those who are my paternal aunts.
Yes.
This is all.
This is all there will be.
Thank you.
Thank you.
I am fortunate.
(Charlie Joseph) *Thank you for the way you're speaking.*
In the place I came from
perhaps those grandfathers of mine who chose me to join you
had faith in me.
But if I had not arrived, it would have remained in my breath,
you see.
But now I have brought out everything from myself.
Whew!
(Applause; audience laughter.)

George Davis (3)
Sitka, 1980

Yes,
now
when the sound,
yes,
kept fading,
of what we heard faintly
of the way our grandparents used to say things,
yes,
it was as if

gáas' t'éidei áwé
oowayáa
a yayeex̱ atoolg̱einín
áwé yáa yeedát áwé
aaa
aaa
yáat
a tóox'
yatx̱ has awuteeyí
aaa
ḵáa toowóo shaysinúk.
Aaa.
Ldakát át áwé aadéi yaa shukaneelx̱úx̱
aaa.
Akax̱wshiwóo.
Aaa.
Kaagwaantaan yádit
shukeelx̱óox̱
ch'a ax̱ tuwóo áwé jiwdlix̱wál ax̱ yat'ákwx'.
Aaa.
Aadéi yáax̱ x̱at wooxeexi yé áwé.
Ch'a aadé x'wán yéi x̱at nay.oo.
(Ḵaal.átk') *Gunalchéesh. Gunalchéesh, yítk'. Gunalchéesh.*
Aaa.
Yáa yeedát,
aaa,
aaa,
yáa yeedát
wéidei
yidahaaní,
aaa,
aanáx̱ haat ḵukawdiyayi yé
á áwé
át shukax̱dulx̱úx̱ín áwé
aadóo sá du éet shukawdudlix̱úx̱u áwé
jeelx̱wálch du yat'ákwx'.
Aaa
g̱unéi uhaanch a kát.
Aaa.
A yádi áwé

we were looking for a place to bury it
under a house post,
in the back of a house post,
but now,
yes,
yes,
here
when you brought it out
from within,
yes,
you reawakened our feelings.
Yes,
the way you sang to the children of all the clans.
Yes.
I was reluctant.
Yes.
When you sang
to the child of Kaagwaantaan,
it was only my mind that rattled its hand beside its temple.
Yes.
This is how I have weakened.
Please forgive me.
    (Charlie Joseph) *Thank you. Thank you, son. Thank you.*
Yes.
Now,
yes,
yes,
now
that you have stood up
there
yes
from where a person's father's people originated
whenever
the words of a song are just for a person according to
    his father's clan,
whoever the words of a song are for
would then rattle his hand beside his temple.
Yes.
He would begin to move to its beat.
Yes.
When the words of a song are sung

du ee shukawdudlix̱úx̱
aanáx̱ áwé woosh has uskóowjin
aaa
aadóo yádix̱ sá ḵusateeyí.
Áwé yáa yeedát áwé yayeeysixeex.
Aaa.
Gunalchéesh x̱á.

Kichnáalx̱ (4)
Sheet'ká, 1980

Yak'éi.
Yak'éi, kík', yak'éi.
        (Unidentified) *Gunalchéesh.*
        (Kawóotk') *Gunalchéesh.*
Aaa.
Ch'a yéi gugénk' áwé a kaax̱ shukaylis'úx̱
haa tlagu ḵwáanx'i aadéi s ḵunoogu yé.
Áwé
yáa yeedát
aaa,
ch'a ayáx̱ sh g̱ayisnoogóot ágé
aaa
yei tunook yee kát wugoodéen ax̱ éesh hás eetig̱aneix̱?
        (Ḵaal.átk') *Ha wáa sá.*
Yáax'
á áwé
yáa yeedát áwé ch'a i tóo kawtuwatlex̱u yáx̱ áwé
        haa tóo wjix̱een.
        (Ḵaal.átk') *Yak'éi.*
Ách áwé
yéi x̱'ayaḵá yee yátx'i
        (Ḵaal.átk') *Gunalchéesh.*
aaa
yáax' aadéi yéi jeeyaneiyi yé tlél haa tuwaa ushgú
        ch'a kawayíx̱ yawus.aax̱í, haa léelk'u hás
aadéi yéi s jineiyi yé áwé.
De áa awtulixaaji át áwé

for one's clan child,
from there they begin to know each other,
yes,
whoever's child a person is.
That is what you have performed.
Yes.
Thank you, indeed.

George Davis (4)
Sitka, 1980

Fine.
Fine, younger brother, fine.
    (Unidentified) *Thank you.*
    (Paul Henry) *Thank you.*
Yes.
We have uncovered only a tiny portion
of the way our ancient people used to do things.
This
now,
yes,
is it only to soothe the pain,
yes,
of what befell you, my father's surviving relative?
    (Charlie Joseph) *Indeed.*
Here
it is this,
now we're just trying to calm your thoughts
    is how it came to mind.
    (Charlie Joseph) *Fine.*
That is why
your children say
    (Charlie Joseph) *Thank you.*
yes,
we don't want what you did here to only echo in the air,
    how our grandfathers
used to do things.
We had given up hope of seeing

áa haa waḵkeeyaḵaa.
Ách áwé
kakawtuwakél'.
Aaa.
Dei kawtoo.aag̱óon áwé x̱á
aaa
haa tláa léelk'w hás, haa tláa káak hás
has du ḵusteeyí
has du yoo x̱'atángi.
Dei áa awtulixaaji át áwé
haa jiyís.
Aaa.
Haa jeex' kakeeyakél'.
Ách áwé tsu héidei shugax̱tootáan
yá yaaḵoosgé daakeit
haa jeex' a náḵ has kawdik'éet'.
    (Ḵaal.átk') *Yak'éi, yak'éi.*
Haa káak hás
ḵa haa léelk'w hás
yáa yeedát áwé
yáadoo.
Aaa.

Kichnáalx̱ (5)
Sheet'ká, 1980

Dziyáak áwé yoo x̱'atánk yóodei kḵwatée yáat'át a shukát.
Aaa.
Yáax' shadaḵéex̱in, ax̱ léelk'w hás.
Aaa.
Áwé yoo x̱'atánk yéi s agux̱sanei g̱anúgún áwé
yéi at gug̱aneiyí
aaa
Kax̱átjaa Sháa áwé kei kawdzix̱át.
Yéi áwé woonei
dziyáak ax̱ toowóo
aadéi yaa ḵugaháa yáat.
Aaa.

what you told us to look at.
That is why
we unwrapped it.
Yes.
We had tried already, you see,
yes,
the culture,
the language
of our mothers' grandparents, our mothers' maternal uncles.
We had given them up
for ourselves.
Yes.
You have unwrapped it for us.
That is why we will open again
this container of wisdom
left in our care.
(Charlie Joseph) *It's fine, it's fine.*
Our maternal uncles
and our grandparents
now
are here.
Yes.

George Davis (5)
Sitka, 1980

A while ago I was going to offer some words even before this.
Yes.
My grandparents used to waken over here.
Yes.
Just then, when they were about to make speeches,
when a ceremony was to begin,
yes,
the Splattering Women would shatter the surface of the sea.
That was what happened
to my mind a while ago
when the moment approached.
Yes.

Kax̱átjaa Sháa áwé
Yaaw Teiyí yaanáx̱ kei kadutl uwaxíx.
Tliyaadéi áwé ax̱ yáa kadutl naxíx.
Yóo áwé a daa yoo tux̱aatánk.
Yáat'át shukát áwé yóodei kḵwatee
át áwé a geinyaax̱ x̱'ayax̱wditán.
Tléil áwé ax̱ tuwáa ushgú
aan yá gándei x̱wagoodí.
Aaa.
Hóoch'i aayí sákw áwé joke áwé kakḵwalaneek.
Yéi áyú wduwasáa
there was a man
his name Dr. Johnson.
You all know him.
Taakw K'wát'i
and there's no man walked on the sea.
You all know it
that's the salt water out there.
But this is the man that walked
on the sea.
Roy
Peratrovich
have to bear witness to watch
his uncle
had walked on the sea.
He looked at it.
Aaa.
Haa sáni tlákw eexwéi dziyáak.
Ách áwé
chuch yáax' áwé.
Aaa.
Ḵa wé Mister Brown.
Aaa.
Tlákw haa sáni
haa yáx̱ shaysi.áx̱w.
Cha ch'a yee sáni áwé tsá héen x̱ukáx̱ yaawagút.
Aaa.
Taakw K'wát'i.
Yéi áwé yan shoowatán. Gunalchéesh.
Thank you very much.

The Splattering Women
came up in a cluster by the Herring Rock.
The cluster rolled away.
This is what I am thinking.
I was going to say this before
but my words got side tracked.
I don't want to
leave without saying it.
Yes.
For the last, I'll tell a joke.
There was a man.
His name was Dr. Johnson.
That's what they call him.
You all know him.
Taakw K'wát'i.
And there's no man who ever walked on the sea.
You all know
that's the salt water out there.
But this is the man that walked
on the sea.
Roy
Peratrovich
will have to bear witness
that he watched his uncle
walk on the sea.
He saw it.
Yes.
You made remarks about our paternal uncles a while ago.
That's why
I'm retaliating.
Yes.
And that Mr. Brown.
Yes.
They're dangling our paternal uncles
in front of us.
It was finally your paternal uncle that walked on the surface
of the sea.
Yes.
Taakw K'wát'i.
This is how it will end. Thank you.
Thank you very much.

Ch'a yéi k̲u.aa wé yatee
haa Lingítx̲ sateeyí.
We can't cut it short.
And still we made it.
We cut it short.
Because
Roy and
Mr. Brown want to step out tonight, you know.
(Audience laughter)
We can see it on his face
so we cut it short.
(Applause)
Thank you very much.

K̲aal.átk' (2)
Sheet'ká, 1980

Ax̲ tuwáa sigóo x̲át tsú,
aaa.
Ax̲ dachx̲án áyá yáa yei téeyin.
Dimitry
yóo dusáagoon.
Hú áwé yéí x̲'ayak̲áayin.
Yú yées k̲áax̲ x̲at satéex'
I used to listen to him
and he
used to say that
one way love
tleiyeekaadéi k̲usax̲án
gug̲anáa.
(Kichnáalx̲) *Haa wáa sá.*
Woosh géidei
k̲usax̲án k̲u.aa wés
for long living
yei k̲ukg̲wastée.
(Kichnáalx̲) *Yéi á.*
Yéi áwé ax̲ toowóo yatee.
(Kichnáalx̲) *Gunalchéesh.*

But that is how
our Tlingit culture is.
We can't cut it short.
And still we always do.
We cut it short.
Because
Roy and
Mr. Brown want to step out tonight, you know.
(Audience laughter)
We can see it on his face
so we cut it short.
(Applause)
Thank you very much.

Charlie Joseph (2)
Sitka, 1980

I also want to speak again,
yes.
My grandchild used to live here.
He was called
Dimitry.
It was he who used to say this.
When I was a young man
I used to listen to him
and he
used to say that
one way love
one way love
will die.
(George Davis) *Indeed.*
But love
for each other
will live
for a long time.
(George Davis) *That's how it is.*
That's how my feelings are
(George Davis) *Thank you.*

Yá haa jeedéi yatx̱ yiytiyi
yee k̲usax̲áni   20
        (Kichnáalx̱) Haa wáa sá.
a yee daak̲ k̲ashee
chuch tóo neil k̲adatee x̱áach tsú.
        (Kichnáalx̱) Gunalchéesh á.
Gunalchéesh áwé.
Gunalchéesh áwé
i éesh hás shageinyaa
ách yéi x̱'ayeek̲á
ax̱ dachx̱anx'i sáani yáax'
aan has wudinaagi
aaa.
Yéi k̲wá a daa ax̱ tuwatee   30
aaa
ax̱ léelk'w hás shageinyaa
Alaska Native Brotherhood tóot uwagút de
        (Unidentified) Gunalchéesh.
Alaska Native Brotherhood tóot uwagút.
Hú tsú
Shee Atika a tóowoo hú
a tóot hán.
Aaa.
Ách áyá yáatx̱
ch'a wáa yéi kuwáat'dei sá s k̲udzitee   40
átx̱ has agux̱layéix̱.
Tsu has du nák̲ yú dáak̲dei nx̱agútni
ch'a aan has du x̱'éidei gax̱du.áx̱ch.
Gunalchéesh áwé
aadéi haa daat yeeysheeyi yé
yá has du yéi jineiyí.
Ch'a oowayáa kéex' kei s yiytée.
Gunalchéesh
yéi áwé yee daayax̱ak̲á
has du jiyís   50
yá ax̱ dachxanx'i yán.
Tlax̱ wáa koogei át sá.
Tléil ax̱ tuwáa ushgú
shux'áanáx̱.
Gidaan yítk'.
Johnson

These things you handed up to us,
your love,
(George Davis) *Indeed.*
let me put out my hand
that I too may receive them into my soul.
(George Davis) *Thank you.*
Thank you.
Thank you
to your fathers' spirit helper
that made you say these words
when my little grandchildren here
stood with them,
yes.
But I feel this way about it,
yes,
the spirit helper of my grandfathers
has already joined the Alaska Native Brotherhood.
(Unidentified) *Thank you.*
He has joined the Alaska Native Brotherhood.
He also
is within Shee Atika,
standing within it.
Yes.
That is why from now on
no matter how long they live
they will use it.
Even when I enter deep into the forest from them,
even then it will be heard on their lips.
Thank you
for how you have treated us
for their achievements.
It is as if you have elevated them.
Thank you
is what I am saying to all of you
for them,
these young grandchildren of mine.
How valuable this is.
I didn't want it
in the beginning.
Stand, my son.
When Johnson

ax̱ x̱ánt góot
yá at yátx'i
has du ée at ḵalatóowoot
tlax̱ ch'u oowayáa du géidei ḵux̱lagawu yáx̱ wooti.
Hél ax̱ tuwáa ushgú a tóo yéi x̱at teeyí.
And one reason
"Yaa sh ḵ'analyél
he's lying.
He not telling the truth.
He not doing right."
The reason why.
But now
I thank you
all you
delegates
and all these officers.
Thank you very much.

approached me
that I instruct
these children
it was very much as if I fought against it.
I didn't want to join them.
For one reason,
they'll say, "He's lying,
he's lying.
He's not telling the truth.
He's not doing it right."
That was the reason why.
But now
I thank you,
all of you
delegates
and all these officers.
Thank you very much.

Notes to the Speeches

Notes to the Speech by A. P. Johnson

Transcribed by Nora Marks Dauenhauer, Sitka, June 1971.
Translated by Nora Marks Dauenhauer.

This speech was collected at the First Tlingit Language Workshop, Sheldon Jackson College, Sitka, June 1971. Mr. Johnson delivered the short, impromptu speech to his fellow workshop participants during a class discussion. A few minutes later, during a break, Nora Dauenhauer re-elicited the speech, and wrote it down in Tlingit from Mr. Johnson's dictation. It was first published in Tlingit in *Doo G̱oojée Yeenaa-déi / Tlingit Language Workshop Reader* (April 1972). The Tlingit text here is revised and corrected. This is the first publication of the English translation.

This is Tlingit "meta-oratory," or "meta-rhetoric." The speech explains the function of speech; it is a speech about speech, about the importance of using language carefully and accurately. The opening lines show how we literally connect ourselves to the person or people we are talking to. The next lines develop the simile of speech being like a man with a gaff hook: even though a person is at some physical distance, the words have the power to connect, when there is mutual understanding. Although it is not stated directly in the speech, the correct use of kinship terms is one of the technical skills involved, and when people address each other by kinship terms, they both know they are one.

The speech is a good example of extended (or "Homeric") simile in Tlingit oratory: the comparison is made using "like" or "as," then elaborated on with description, and finally recapitulated.

Because of its style and subject matter, and because it is a good example of careful speech about speech, it seemed an appropriate one with which to begin the book.

Grammatically, the speech is also a good one for students to begin on, containing a range of noun and verb forms: occasional (lines 1, 7, 9, 12) future (2) attributive (4, 6, 8, 11) and contingent (8). The attributive suffix -i does not appear in the form in line 4 (kei nagut k̲áa) because of the classifier used here, the "zero" form of the "A" classifier, called "B extensor" in Story and Naish (1973:357, 369 ff.). The stem "hook" appears as a noun in line 5 (k'éx̱'aa) a possessed noun in line 7 (du k'éx̱'ayi) and as a verb in line 8:

a	-	g̲a	-	k'éx̱'	-	ín
direct object		aspect prefix		stem		suffix for contingent

Compare English: hook, his hook, he hooks.

In lines 3 and 10, the expected tone on k̲áa is "stolen" by the following words. It is also stolen from the attributive in line 6 by the noun following.

3, 10, 11. We have translated yoo x̱'atánk as "speech," "oratory," and "public speaking."

11. Tlingit has no indefinite article. This line can be translated "speech" or "a speech," with different poetic nuances.

Notes to the Sitka Speeches from 1899

Collected on wax cylinders in Sitka in 1899 during the Harriman Expedition, these two speeches are the oldest known recordings of the Tlingit language. They were presumably collected in mid June, 1899. The Sitka *Alaskan* for Saturday, June

17, 1899, and Wednesday, June 21, 1899, has articles on the visit of the expedition. One describes a dinner party at Governor Brady's where the visitors were "entertained by a number of well-known Natives, who sang some of their war songs, records of which were taken by a phonograph for future reference." No note is made of recording oratory, but elsewhere the newspaper comments that some visitors "have spent considerable time in the Indian village."

The original recordings of these speeches are in the Harriman Expedition Collection, acquired by the Heye Museum of the American Indian, housed in the Indiana University Archives of Traditional Music. The technical data are: Indiana University Archives of Traditional Music; Cylinder Project; Accession # 83-908-F; North America; United States; Alaska; Eyak and Unknown Indians; Collector uncertain, possibly George Byrd Grinnell or Edward H. Harriman; 1899; A copy of EC 10" #501; Item 1, Cylinder #6038, Strip A. This contains the two speeches transcribed here, and the start of a third speech, but the needle was stuck in the cylinder or record, and the third speech could not be transcribed. Item 2, Cylinder #6039, Strip A, contains another short speech introducing a song, but the speech and song are too damaged to transcribe.

Anthony Seeger of the Smithsonian Institution Office of Folklife Programs brought these wax cylinders to the attention of Dr. Michael Krauss of the Alaska Native Language Center, University of Alaska-Fairbanks, who received a copy in 1985, identified the language as Tlingit, called them in turn to our attention, and passed on a cassette copy to Nora Dauenhauer, who transcribed and translated the speeches. We are grateful to Anthony Seeger and Michael Krauss for locating and identifying this valuable contribution to the history of Tlingit oral literature.

The speeches present no grammatical problems, but are difficult to annotate with any certainty. They raise many interesting questions that we leave for future researchers to explore. But, based on internal evidence, we can make some observations, and on the basis of other research and contemporary documents, we can make additional suggestions.

The first speaker is a man of the Kaagwaantaan praising the social achievements of his relatives. We do not know who the speaker is, by name, although we can tell from his voice on the tape that he is a man, and from line 12 that he is a man of the Kaagwaantaan, an Eagle moiety clan of Sitka. But we do not know for sure who the people from Taku are. A contemporary observer, Fr. Anatolii Kamenskii, writing in 1901 cites a local newspaper article referring to "a big potlatch...three years ago...given by the Sitka L'uknax̱.ádi in honor of the Taku Indians." (Kamenskii 1985:117; see also Appendix 9, pp. 117-22.) We do not know if this is the same event or not, and we would prefer not to guess.

The style of the first speech is very straightforward; there are no rhetorical devices such as comparison by simile or metaphor. He speaks very rapidly, with many false starts, and with only the slightest of pauses where we have indicated line turnings.

8, 16. Aanḵáax'u. Literally "men of the land or town," or "lords," we have translated this as "aristocrats."

8, 19, 33, 42. The Tlingit verb stem used in these lines is ḵu-.eex' meaning "to invite to a ceremonial." This, as we note in the introduction, is the Tlingit term for what is popularly called "potlatch" in English. For readers interested in the Tlingit language, this example shows how a given stem appears in the context of different prefixes and suffixes. This is like English: invite, invit-ed, invit-ing, invite-s, invit-ation, un-invited (an uninvited guest), un-invit-ing (an uninviting place), I am inviting, I am invited, etc. The Tlingit forms are: gax̱du.ix' nóok, ḵudu.éex', ḵuwdu.éex'i, and ḵu.éex'. The noun form is ḵoo.éex'. Such variations on underlying stems are pointed out in many of the notes in this book, but we do not go into as much detail as in this note.

12. Kaagwaantaan. Sometimes popularly called the "Wolf" or the "Brown Bear" clan, this is one of the Eagle moiety groups in Sitka.

14. Things. (Tlingit, line 13.) The "things of our grandfathers" are the clan crests, or at.óow. These are the art treasures of a clan and are brought out for display on ceremonial occasions. See the speeches for the removal of grief from the Jim Marks memorial for some examples.

23, 43. Aan yátx'i. Literally, "children of the land or town." The term "aan yádi" ("child of the town") refers to a person of social standing in the community. We have translated this with such words as noble, nobles, nobility, but these are not adequate.

Again, for those interested in language, the forms of the words differ according to use. Line 23 has the suffix -x̱ because the word is a predicate nominative here. Singular is "aan yádi."

28, 31. Two Tlingit verbs are used here, which we have translated as "was brought out." In line 28, the Tlingit is literally "died" and in 31 "perished" or "was lost." These are important verbs in Tlingit ceremonial life, and are used to describe the money or other items assembled and distributed in memory of a person or an event. The money is said to be "killed." To put out money is to "kill" it.

42. L'uknax̱.ádi. Popularly called in English "Coho," this is one of the Raven clans of Sitka.

The second speech is impossible to annotate with certainty. We presume that his speech refers to the same events as the first speaker, but there is no way we can be certain. The text gives no clues as to the genealogy of the orator. The references to grandparents' things could possibly suggest that he is also Kaagwaantaan, if he is referring to the same "things" as the first speaker, but it is impossible to know for sure. He could be a grandchild of the opposite moiety, and, in fact, his attitude toward the at.óow suggests that he is of the opposite moiety; but, we emphasize, it is impossible to know for sure. The second speaker has a good speaking voice, and his delivery is much slower and more evenly paced than the first speaker. Where the tone of the first speech conforms to the stereotype of Northwest Coast pride in rank and display, the second speaker touches on common themes in Tlingit oratory—how the younger generations are always moving into the positions of departed grandparents, and how one gains strength of mind from the display of at.óow.

3, 18, 25, 26. The Tlingit verb stem here is ḵu-.eex', "to invite." See also the notes to this stem in the first speech.

4, 37. The plural marker yán is phonetically wán on the recording, because of the vowel "u" immediately preceding.

6. Opposites. In Tlingit, yaḵáawu (singular; line 4 is plural, with stolen stress). The word can mean the equal, opposite number, or trading partner of a person. Here it also seems to refer to the opposite moiety. If we are correct in guessing that the Kaagwaantaan were invited, this reference further suggests that the speaker is L'uknax̱.ádi.

7, 8. The image of the lights and flagpoles is unclear. Possibly he is poetically emphasizing how hard it was to sleep, as if the flagpoles were bright lights burning. They may have literally hung lanterns on the poles.

17. We never wanted it. This line is unclear to us.

29, 31, 36. On the recording tlax̲, ayáx̲, and tlax̲ are tleix̲, ayéx̲, and tleix̲, respectively. We have standardized them here.

32-34. This passage touches on a common theme in Tlingit oratory: how one gains strength through display of at.óow.

Notes to Johnny C. Jackson and Jimmie George

The set of speeches by Johnny C. Jackson and Jimmie George was recorded on video tape in performance during the totem raising ceremonies in Kake, Alaska, on September 30, 1971, by the Tlingit and Haida Central Council, who provided an audio cassette copy for Nora Marks Dauenhauer, who transcribed them in Tlingit and translated them into English.

The speech by Johnny C. Jackson was delivered as a welcoming address to the visitors who traveled to Kake to participate in raising the world's tallest totem pole, 136 feet, on September 30, 1971. Johnny C. Jackson was one of the principal hosts and officials, as was his maternal uncle K̲'a.oosh, Tommy C. Jackson. The speech is characteristic of Tlingit oratory in its use of kinship references to bind the community and visitors socially and spiritually. The speaker thanks the guests for helping to uplift community spirits.

Some important concepts of Tlingit social structure underlie the speeches. Johnny C. Jackson is a Raven, and resident of Kake, and he is welcoming members of the Eagle moiety. He is their father, and they are his father. He is speaking to the guests as a whole, and at the same time to Jimmie George in particular, who will speak as a representative of the guests and of the opposite moiety, as a child of the people of Kake, and as a naa káani, or brother-in-law to the clan.

Jimmie George and his wife Lydia George of Angoon were invited by the Kake people to assist the hosts in welcoming the guests. Lydia describes how they and other people brought gifts for the occasion, "scarfs, hankies, and socks, and many other things. When it was being raised, the scarfs, hankies, socks and others fell from it. Anything that fell by you was yours." Because of such gifts, and because of some of the crests or at.óow carved on the pole, many of the guests share an attachment and special sense of ownership to the pole. This relationship to the pole and the Kake community is also created through kinship, as expressed in specific lines of the speech.

5. Naakil.aan. This is also one of Johnny C. Jackson's names, a name his clan shares with the L'uknax̱.ádi.

10; 20-21. Paternal aunt . . . lap. This is a complicated image. The guests are the paternal relatives of the speaker, and the speaker and his people are the paternal relatives of the guests. By extension, the Kake community is compared to a paternal aunt who makes room for all her nieces and nephews, all her relatives of the opposite moiety. This may also be a reference to a K̲aach.ádi at.óow of Kake. It remains unclear to us.

23. Hinkwéix'. Maternal uncle of the speaker, and deceased clan leader. A K̲aach.ádi name, this was also one of Johnny C. Jackson's names. See also the biography.

27-34. The speaker is using a traditional pattern of invoking at.óow (clan possessions) to give comfort and support. The speaker is naming various clan houses of the Raven moiety. X̱'áakw Hít (Red River-Salmon or Watermarked Salmon House), K̲utis' Hít (Looking House), Kooshdaa Hít (Land Otter House), and Wandaa Hít (Around the Edge House) are all K̲aach.ádi Raven moiety houses, houses of the paternal uncles of the guests, who are being welcomed to their "fathers' land."

38. Sad thing. Reference is to the tragic crash of an Alaska Airlines jet on the approach to Juneau on September 4, 1971. The worst disaster in Alaska aviation history, the crash took the lives of 111 people, including four residents of Kake. Finally, the line may be understood more generally, as referring to the cumulative results of a century of contact during which the village of Kake was destroyed by the U.S. military (1869) and the village cut down its totem poles (1912) in a community effort to modernize and westernize in response to pressure from the missionaries. Two generations later, in 1971, they are proudly raising a new pole.

43a. Response. It is common in Tlingit oratory for members of the audience to make responses, most commonly thanking the speaker for kind references to their families, or responding when their names or kinship terms are called. This is the first such response in this book, but many more will follow. In page format, the responses are indented and set in italics, and the speakers are identified in parentheses where known. Responses are not included in the line count.

55-56. In-laws and paternal uncles. These are the relatives of the opposite moiety of the speaker.

60. Turn ceremony over. According to Tlingit protocol, at a given point in any ceremony, the floor is turned over to the guests, who deliver oratory of their own in response to the words of the hosts.

The speech by Jimmie George was delivered in response to Johnny C. Jackson, with Jimmie George speaking on behalf of the guests. He speaks as their son, and as a child of the opposite moiety. Jimmie George and his wife Lydia both expressed their gratitude for the honor of being invited to participate.

6. X'aalkweidí. A Raven moiety clan that relocated from Angoon to Kake, with the result that the communities are related.

16. Warm your hands. To "warm" a visitor's hands is to invite him or her for food—a welcome dinner with oratory following. The speaker is also emphasizing the importance of helping each other out. This is an example of what the elders often refer to as "respect" or "balance."

19-42. Oil and water. In this comparison the speaker marvels at the blending, through reciprocal love, of the opposite moieties as one community, and the many communities as one nation. By extension, the comparsion applies to all the people, regardless of ethnicity, gathered to join in this common effort and event.

The editors thank Mr. Thomas Jackson, Mr. and Mrs. Jimmie George, the Office of the City of Kake, the Tlingit and Haida Central Council, Clarence Jackson, and Gordon Jackson for their help in researching the notes to these speeches.

Notes to the Speech by Thomas Young

Recorded by Nora Marks Dauenhauer, Klukwan, May 5, 1972. Transcribed and translated by Nora Marks Dauenhauer.

The speech was delivered in Klukwan, May 5, 1972, at ceremonies combining the dedication of the Shangukeidí house "The House Lowered from the Sun," and a memorial feast for the deceased Shangukeidí John Abbot, Tom Jimmie, and Anita Marks. During the ceremonies, hosted by Joe White and his family, new leaders were introduced, young men designated to inherit and pass on the tradition. The young men to whom Joe White transferred the Shangukeidí at.óow were David Katzeek (Juneau), Willie Lee (Klukwan), Frank See (Hoonah), and Tom Abbot (Klukwan). The at.óow included "The House Lowered from the Sun," and all the house posts and art pieces in the Shangukeidí ownership.

In his speech, Thomas Young gives encouragement and advice to the young Shangukeidí men who were to become the stewards of the Shangukeidí at.óow, which he mentions using this term in line 12. This is a very traditional type of Tlingit public speaking. It was very common in the past, but has now become increasingly rare for older relatives to give speeches of instruction, encouragement, and advice to younger men as they advance into positions of greater responsibility. Thomas Young is Shangukeidí yádi—child of Shangukeidí. His father was the maternal uncle of the host Joe White. The "mother's maternal uncles" referred to in the speech include Thomas Young's father.

Thomas uses the parable of the sea lion and the ptarmigan to warn the young Shangukeidí men, the inheritors of ancient tradition, that a sea of foreign culture will try to wash them from their maternal grandfathers' reef (the at.óow). But the speeches of the guests, who are the clan grandfathers and grandmothers of Joe White and the other Shangukeidí hosts, are metaphorically the rocks that were put inside the sea lion by the ptarmigan for ballast. This was to strengthen them to keep their maternal grandfathers' at.óow, lest they sell or otherwise lose them to the rising sea of foreign culture and conflicting, alien world view.

Of his speech, Thomas commented some fifteen years later, while helping us with the preparation of this book, "The coming of the white man is like a heavy sea, but your grandfathers' words will be your ballast, that you won't sell your at.óow." He commented that the T'a<u>k</u>deintaan clan, also among the grandparents of the young men, had also offered words of encouragement and guidance.

13. My fathers. The speaker is addressing those present. Because the young men are of the speaker's father's clan, they are also his fathers.

20-59. The parable of the sea lion and ptarmigan. The orator tells the parable, and at the end ties everything together: "Their speeches will be / as if they are putting rocks inside you." The guests and their oratory are compared to the ptarmigan, and the sea lion to the hosts. The comparison is further developed in the closing sentence, in which the reef is metaphorically identified with the mind, desire, and/or wishes (the Tlingit word means all three) of the maternal uncles and other ancestors of the clan from whom the young men now inherit position and at.óow.

43. Nouns are also used in the Tlingit original, for extra clarity and emphasis. As noted frequently in *Haa Shuká, Our Ancestors,* pronouns are more common in these positions in Tlingit narrative, and it is often necessary to supply nouns for clarity in translation.

45. Tlingit, latéedi yéeyi. This is a decessive in the dependent clause, indicated with the word yéeyi instead of the suffix -in or -un.

56-57. Grandparents . . . in the back. As guests, the grandparents were sitting at the rear of the clan house.

58. Their speeches. The speeches of the guests.

62. Tlingit wusgeedée<u>k</u>. Optative perfective. Literally, don't let yourself to have fallen.

Notes to the Speech by Tom Peters

This speech was delivered privately in Teslin, Yukon, on September 8, 1972, to Nora Marks Dauenhauer, who recorded, transcribed, and translated it. This is the very first thing Tom Peters wanted to record with Nora. The speech is straightforward, with little rhetorical embellishment. Tom Peters expresses his feelings—his delight at receiving a visit from a Coast Tlingit, namely Nora Marks Dauenhauer, and Richard Dauenhauer. He reaffirms the traditional relationship of the Coast and Inland Tlingit, emphasizing that her language is the same as his, whereas Tlingit is distinct from the speech of his immediate neighbors, who are Athabaskan. He also recalls the traditional contact between the interior and the coast, a pattern which shifted after the construction of the Alaska Highway during World War II. For more on the Yukon Native people, see McClellan et al. (1987). Tom Peters indirectly expresses his sense of personal alienation and isolation, not only because his group is different from its neighbors, but also because of the widening generation gap within his own culture, characterized most dramatically by loss of language and traditional world view.

During this visit, Tom Peters also recorded the story of "The Woman Who Married the Bear," which is featured in *Haa Shuká, Our Ancestors* (Dauenhauer and Dauenhauer 1987). In 1973 we returned to Teslin and read back to Tom Peters the published transcription of his story. He was thrilled to hear it, and his excitement prompted us to think for the first time, "How does it feel to *be* the story teller in a community? Who tells *you* stories?"

1. X'éig̱aa. Some speakers pronounce the word x̱'éig̱aa (with x̱').

3. Áyá. Phonetically, Tom Peters pronounces this áyéi at certain times, including here.

9. Mtusiteen. This is interior dialect, the most striking characteristic of which is "m" in some positions where coast dialects have "w". See also the notes to his story in *Haa Shuká.*

13, 25. On the tape there is a contrast between the conjunctions aadáx̲ and adax̲. A more literal translation is "then" or "from this."

15-16. This could also be transcribed as one long line; several false starts have been edited out here, and the line set as two.

20-21. For too long. . . . This sentence could also be translated with a positive phrase: "It's been too long since we've seen anyone."

22-23. This is a difficult passage to translate. Lingít means a person, a human being, an Indian, or a Tlingit in particular. We take his sense in this context here to mean Native people and not strictly Tlingits, because he goes on to emphasize that although they, too, are Native, they have different languages, whereas Tom Peters and Nora Dauenhauer speak the same language, with only minor dialect variation. The lines could also be interpreted, "There are many Tlingits; there are also the Athabaskans." G̲unanaa is the Tlingit word for Athabaskan.

23. Dax̲duwasáakw. The dax̲- is a distributive prefix, and appears more frequently in Tom Peters' speech than in others. It also appears in the verbs in lines 37, 43, and 59.

33. Like our country (or land). He is referring to the coastal origins of the Inland Tlingit. In the Tlingit text of this line, yú is pronounced long on the tape—yóo.

35. My side. His moiety and clan, the Raven (called "Crow" in Yukon) and Tuk̲.weidí, historically part of the Deisheetaan.

37. Yanyeidí. A clan of the Eagle moiety (called "Wolf" in Yukon) and Tom Peters' father's clan. See the biography of Tom Peters in *Haa Shuká* for more detail. See also McClellan et al. (1987) for more on Inland Tlingit clans and social structure.

40-48. South and north. The neighbors of the Inland Tlingit are Athabaskans. To the north and northwest are the Northern Tutchone, Southern Tutchone, and Tagish. To the south and southwest are the Kaska and Tahltan. See McClellan et al. (1987) for more on the Yukon Native languages.

60. On the tape, áyá is pronounced áyéi.

70. K̲usteeyí. We have translated this word as "way of life;" it may also be translated as "culture." Notice this stem

also in line 59, where it is an attributive form of the verb. The basic meaning of the stem is "life" or "to live."

75. No more. The ending is ambiguous. Hóoch' áwé can be translated as "There is no more," or "This is the end," or even "All gone." In any case, it is ambiguous whether the phrase refers to the end of his speech or the end of traditional way of life, or both.

Notes to the 1972 Speech by Charlie Joseph

This speech was delivered in early December 1972, at the Forty Day Party for Susie (Susan J.) Paul (July 4, 1882-November 1, 1972) held at the ANB Hall in Sitka. It was recorded in performance by Nora Marks Dauenhauer, who transcribed it in Tlingit and translated it into English. Susie Paul, Náats'i, was the mother of Patrick Paul. Her father was named Kichgaaw. When Susie's mother died, her father married Charlie Joseph's mother, Katsóogu Tláa. This made Susie and Charlie sister and brother, and Charlie and Patrick Paul uncle and nephew. Náats'i had a younger sister named K̲aax̲'ashtuk'áax, not mentioned in the speech.

This is an important kind of speech, and typical of much Tlingit oratory in its concern for explaining kinship ties that might not be immediately apparent. The speaker explains genealogical connections and reaffirms community relationships so important in traditional Tlingit society. On the one hand, the speech is fairly simple and straightforward, with the metaphor of the Christmas tree being its only figure of speech; its purpose is only to explain the kinship relationships. On the other hand, it becomes very difficult because the kinship terms and relationships are complex. Other speeches in this book are far more complex in simile and metaphor, and assume understanding of the kinship ties as the basis for development of figures of speech. This speech is interesting because it makes the kinship ties explicit. It allows readers to sort out some of the complexities of Tlingit social structure without also having to sort out complex metaphors.

1-6. Charlie Joseph, a Kaagwaantaan of the Eagle moiety, is addressing the Ravens according to their fathers' clans.

10. Nephew of mine. Patrick Paul, son of the departed Susie Paul and maternal nephew of Charlie Joseph through the relationship he is about to explain.

12. The little trees. Earlier in the ceremony, Charlie addressed the guests in English. Later, he decided to give his speech again, in Tlingit. Throughout his English speech he apologized for his "poor English," and was frustrated by his inability to express himself. The problem was not Charlie's English, but rather that the kinship terms and concepts are not the same for Tlingit and English. It was not that Charlie didn't know the proper words; rather, the words do not exist in English. The Forty Day Party was held during the Christmas season, and the central image of Charlie's speech in English was the set of tiny Christmas trees used as table decorations. This is a pun in Tlingit, aas yátx'i meaning baby trees and children of trees, or tree children. Thus the image works in two senses, as a literal family tree with branches, and a little forest of trees on every table.

12, 16. Tlingit. Language students might be interested in the minimal pair here with yáanáx̲ (through here) and yanax̲ (put down, or plant).

15-17. Kiks.ádi planted seed. The maternal uncles would be of the opposite moiety of the father's clan. The Raven Kiks.ádi are the father's clan, planting seed for the Eagle Kaagwaantaan. This is an important concept in Tlingit social structure. Although an individual follows his or her mother's line, it is the opposite moiety through the father as well that contributes to the population of a clan. Each moiety is dependent on the opposite moiety for life and continuation of its own line.

19. Come out. In the social setting for such speeches, the people the orator is talking about are generally asked to stand as a group while the orator explains the relationship to the general audience.

20. Kichgaaw. A Kiks.ádi man. When his wife died, he married Charlie Joseph's mother, the stepmother of Susie Paul (the deceased, and mother of Patrick Paul).

21. Ancestor. We have paraphrased here. The Tlingit word "sákw" is more literally "ingredients," "raw materials," or "makings for."

25. Standing up to face him. Charlie is thanking the guests who rose to face and thank the hosts, especially Patrick Paul.

29. Child of L'uknax̲.ádi. Charlie is Kaagwaantaan, of the Eagle moiety; his father was L'uknax̲ádi ("Coho") of the Raven moiety; this makes Charlie L'uknax̲.ádi yádi or child of L'uknax̲.ádi.

30-31. Maternal aunts . . . children of Kiks.ádi. This is a complicated image. The maternal aunts are Kaagwaantaan, of the Eagle moiety, but their father, Kichgaaw, is Kiks.ádi and of the Raven moiety. Charlie's father was of a different Raven moiety clan, the L'uknax̲.ádi. Although they are of the same clan (Kaagwaantaan) their fathers are of different Raven clans. This is a recurring theme in the speech.

36-37. Kichgaaw had two wives. His first wife was a woman of the Wolf House Kaagwaantaan (G̲ooch Hít) and the second was Charlie's mother, Katsóosgu Tláa, also a woman of the Kaagwaantaan.

48-51. Charlie's mother, Katsóosgu Tláa, took the place of her (Susie Paul's) mother, in place of their biological mother, who had died. The recently departed Susie Paul thereby becomes Charlie's stepsister; accordingly, Charlie Joseph becomes the maternal uncle of Patrick Paul, and Charlie's mother becomes the grandmother of Patrick Paul.

53. She adopted her. Susie Paul accepted and adopted Charlie's mother as her mother. Through adoption Charlie's mother becomes Susie Paul's mother. The punctuation is different here between English and Tlingit because we have translated more loosely here. Literally, the Tlingit is, "in place of her mother she called her 'mother.'"

57. Child of her father. This is a complex image. "Her mother" is Eagle; therefore, "her father" is Raven; therefore, the "child of her father" is also Eagle, not Raven. Susie and Charlie are both Kaagwaantaan, but from different houses. Susie is from the Wolf House, and Charlie from the Box House. Susie adopted Charlie as her brother.

59. My brother. The Tlingit term ax̲ éek' is used by or of women referring to a brother of any age.

61-64. Even though . . . it made us one. This is a complex image. The ancestors of the children are different, because their fathers are of different clans, Charlie's being L'uknax̲.ádi and

Susie's being Kiks.ádi. Yet they are one by being Kaagwaantaan, and because of the adoption and step-sister-brother relationship.

65. Maternal nieces and nephews. The Tlingit term is kéilk', and could also be translated as "my sister's children." The Tlingit kinship system has two separate terms for nephew and niece. One (kéilk') refers to the son or daughter of a man's sister. The other (káalk'w) refers to the son or daughter of a woman's brother. Both terms cross sex lines, but one term (káalk'w) crosses moiety lines, and the other (kéilk') does not. This is because in Tlingit, the children of a woman's sister or a man's brother are considered sons and daughters, not nieces and nephews. Because of the matrilineal system, a man's children are traditionally never of his own moiety and clan (but they may be his patrilineal uncles and aunts if they are of his father's clan), likewise, a woman is traditionally never the same clan and moiety as her brother's children. This is one example of the different concepts underlying Tlingit and English kinship terms, and suggests why Charlie had difficulties explaining the Tlingit concepts and relationships in English words. Charlie is referring to the Kaagwaantaan hosts.

75-78. "Sitting by someone" in Tlingit, in noun and verb forms, refers to marriage or a spouse. Here, Charlie is talking about his wife and Patrick Paul's wife indirectly, using this phrase, and kinship terms. His wife was literally sitting next to him but the word x̱án.aa is a spouse. A person's spouse is traditionally of the opposite moiety. In older Tlingit tradition, marriage to one's father's sister's child, or one's father's maternal niece, would be a proper and even a very desirable marriage for a number of social and political reasons. This runs contrary to European tradition, which frowns on first cousin marriages. The relationship need not be biological, but can also be a clan relationship; i.e. a man might marry a woman of his father's clan.

90. Uncle. Patrick Paul called Charlie maternal uncle because his mother considered Charlie her brother.

96. Death . . . did this. Presumably the death of Kichgaaw's first wife. His second marriage created the step-sibling relatonship explained in the speech.

97. The Tlingit term aat'asháa refers to people who are married to siblings.

97-108. Such relationships through adoption are common in Tlingit. We do not know precisely who Charlie is referring to in these lines, but the concept is the same regardless of the specific genealogy. Charlie's point is to clarify this, and emphasize the oneness of the community and extended family. Because Susie Paul adopted Charlie's mother as her mother, Charlie and Susie became siblings, even though their fathers are of different clans (Kiks.ádi and L'uknax̱.ádi). Although they were already considered brother and sister according to the Tlingit kinship system, the marriage strengthened the relationship. Through this Patrick Paul and Charlie Joseph become one.

Notes to the Speech by Willie Marks

This speech was delivered on October 3, 1976, at Mt. Edgecumbe Hospital. Because he was hospitalized and unable to participate in person as a clan leader and orator at a memorial that his clan was hosting in Hoonah, Willie Marks delivered his speech in absentia. It was spoken into a tape recorder operated by his daughter, Nora Marks Dauenhauer, who transcribed and translated the speech, and who later carried the tape to Hoonah, where she played it at the memorial. Because of his illness, he spoke in a weak voice, with very slow delivery. As one of the hosts, Willie Marks is speaking to Raven guests. Willie was a House leader (Hít S'aatí) of the Hoonah Brown Bear House, succeeding his departed elder brother Jim Marks in that position. Because her husband was not able to be physically present, Willie's wife, Emma, distributed gifts in his name: sets of earrings she had beaded for the Raven women.

1-2, 7-8. These lines could also be transcribed as single long lines. There is only a slight pause at the end of each.

1-5. In the opening lines, the Eagle moiety speaker establishes his relationship to the audience, especially his in-laws and grandparents of the Raven moiety.

6. Mother's paternal aunts. These would be Raven women of the T'ak̲deintaan clan. Willie's mother, Eliza Marks (Tl'oon Tláa) was Chookaneidí, and child of T'ak̲deintaan; her father was also a deceased steward of the Snail House (Tax̱' Hít).

7-11. He can't look among their faces because he is in the hospital. Therefore, he is making the tape recording. As he gets into his speech, he gradually shifts this point of view, and begins to address the audience directly, as if he were there.

13-16. Compare . . . wounds . . . rites. He is setting up the extended comparison in his speech, developed in the body of the speech and recapitulated at the end. Survivors are compared to the wounded bear; persons in grief over the death of a loved one are viewed as having been wounded by death. Survivors are left in pain, with open wounds that can be soothed only by the comfort and support of each other.

20-21. Ancestor of mine . . . someone who is to succeed him. The image is of a maternal uncle and a nephew. K̲aa tlagoo k̲wáanx'i is the general Tlingit term used for deceased relatives.

24-25. Great ancestor of ours . . . brown bear. The brown bear (*Ursus arctos*) is an at.óow (clan crest) of the Chookaneidí. For more on this concept, and for more on bear stories of other clans, see *Haa Shuká, Our Ancestors: Tlingit Oral Narratives*. It is interesting to note that in these lines Willie Marks uses the term haa shuká, from which the title of that book derives.

32. Immense uncle of yours. This line is spoken as an aside to the Raven audience, including the collector, establishing their relationship to the bear and the speaker. Also, this is an indirect reference to the brown bear, who is addressed by kinship term.

42. Skunk cabbage. (*Lysichitum americanum*). These grow exceptionally tall in Southeast Alaska, sometimes even overhead, and are common in wet areas of the forest. The leaves are used by people for wrapping and cooking. Here the animal uses it as a compress or medicine.

44. Animal. In Tlingit (line 46) yatseeneit. A term reserved for bear only, this is another indirect reference to bear.

54-59. The simile of the bear and the skunk cabbage is recapitulated here. We can safely claim that the simile in lines 52-53 ("you . . . have become like skunk cabbage") is unique in world literature. Culturally, the speaker is saying, "You have become like salve." This is an outstanding example of culture-specific images in Tlingit literature, much the same as Shakespeare's "sun of York" metaphor is bound to English history and culture. The speaker's point here is that the presence of the opposite moiety is soothing to the hosts' open wound of grief. At the same time as he directly compares the opposite moiety to skunk cabbage, he compares himself indirectly to the wounded bear, using an appropriate clan crest (at.óow).

57. Your paternal aunts. These would be Eagles, the clan sisters of Willie. They too, as Willie, will draw strength and comfort from the Ravens. As the presence of the Ravens soothes the speaker in his grief, so too will their presence soothe and heal his grieving sisters, the paternal aunts of the guests.

Notes to the Invocation by David Kadashan

This prayer was offered at the opening of the Hoonah Convention of the Alaska Native Brotherhood (ANB) and Alaska Native Sisterhood (ANS) in October 1976. It was recorded in performance, transcribed in Tlingit and translated into English by Nora Marks Dauenhauer. It was to be David Kadashan's last public speech.

Nora Dauenhauer made the following notes in her Journal. "As he was leaving the ANB Hall, he asked me, 'Did you get it?' I answered, 'Yes.' He said, 'Good,' and walked away toward the door. I went to see him two days later to continue working with him, but he wasn't feeling well. So I told his wife, Ida, I'd come back when he felt better. Not even an hour passed when he lost consciousness, and they took him to Mt. Edgecumbe Hospital in a plane. He regained consciousness only briefly during the next few days, and then we lost him."

This speech is an example of a contemporary Tlingit table grace. When compared with David's memorial speech in this collection, this prayer illustrates the ease with which he and most of the older generation elders operate in both traditional and Christian contexts, anchored firmly in the spirituality of both worlds. For most of the elders, the conflict is not between Tlingit and Christian spirituality, but between a spiritual world view and a secular world view that denies spiritual reality.

1. We have tried to reflect the power of David's use of both languages by not translating the opening line. Dikee Aank̲áawu

is the Tlingit word for God, or more precisely, Lord; literally "Man of the Land (or Town) on High."

9-24. Poor in spirit . . . people were fed. David draws his imagery here from the Gospels, taking some of his language from the Sermon on the Mount (Matt. 5:3-12 and Luke 6:20-26), and his central simile from the miracle of the loaves and fishes (Mark 6:30-44, Matt. 14:13-21, Luke 9:10-17, John 6:1-13).

12, 13. The Tlingit grammar is interesting. G̱isaḵée in line 12 is sequential; it is characterized by its position in the dependent clause, the "A" form of the classifier, the long, high vowel, and the conjugation prefix (in this case -g̱a-). In line 13, yiysiḵée is perfective, indicative, and in the main clause. In both forms, the "s" classifier is used to make the verb causative: not "you sat down," but "you seated them" and "as you seated them."

Notes to the Speech by Emma Marks

This speech was delivered in Juneau at the Tlingit and Haida Community Center during Sealaska Heritage Foundation's "Celebration 1982." It was recorded on video tape, and was first transcribed and translated by Paul Marks, Ḵinkaduneek, the son of Emma Marks. Paul's draft was substantially edited and annotated by Nora and Richard Dauenhauer.

Emma was introduced by Paul Henry (Kawóotk'), L'uknax̱.ádi of Yakutat, who wanted her to speak and explain the kinship connection between Emma and the Juneau Lukaax̱.ádi on the one hand, and the Yakutat people on the other, both of the Lukaax̱.ádi and L'uknax̱.ádi. This speech is an example of the importance of personal names and genealogy in Tlingit culture, and the role of names as at.óow. Paul Henry introduced Emma Marks in the following words:

Gunalchéesh.
Ha áyá
ax̱ t'aaḵx'í,
yáat'aa, Emma Marks.
Ax̱ tuwáa sigóo ch'a yei yiguwáatl' yee éet x̱'awutáani hú tsú.

Thank you.
This,
my siblings,
is Emma Marks here.
I would like for her, too, to speak to you for a little while.

1-24. These lines are an expression of Emma's world view. She is witnessing for the Lord. She has dedicated her life to witnessing. As with many elders of her generation, her life is a synthesis of Christian and traditional Tlingit values.

34. K̲uchéin. A Shangukeidí, child of L'uknax̲.ádi, he was Emma's grandfather, her mother's father, from the Italio River, called Aakwéi in Tlingit. His English name was Frank Italio. He was one of the elders with whom Frederica de Laguna worked on her Yakutat research, and he is pictured in plate 215 of *Under Mount Saint Elias* (de Laguna 1972:1144-45). Their clan house was the Thunderbird House, which Frank Italio (K̲uchéin) and his younger brother George Frances (Naag̲éi) later built in Yakutat when Emma Marks was a child. The screen from this house is now on display at the Alaska State Museum in Juneau.

52-54. Lukaax̲.ádi . . . Alsek. The Lukaax̲.ádi from Alsek are also known as G̲unaax̲uk̲wáan.

58. Canoe Prow House. Literally "At the Bow House." This was one of three community houses on Cannery Creek near the old cannery site on the north shore of the mouth of the Alsek River at Dry Bay. A second house was called Mt. Fairweather House. Emma does not remember the name of the third house. Canoe Prow House was built between 1915 and 1925 by Seitáan (John Williams), brother of Seig̲eig̲éi, the mother of Leetkwéi and grandmother of Emma Marks, whose Tlingit name is also Seig̲eig̲éi. The house had a Frog Screen brought there by K̲aawus.aa. See also de Laguna (1972:81, 83).

59. Mt. Fairweather Screen. This screen was from the Lukaax̲.ádi Mt. Fairweather House at Dry Bay, not to be confused with the Shangukeidí Thunderbird Screen from Yakutat, now at the Alaska State Museum.

68, 72, 75. Yaandu.ein . . . K̲aawus.aa . . . K̲usán. Yaandu.éin is the great or great-great-grandfather of Emma Marks, depending on how one does the genealogy. Yaandu.éin, a man of the Kaagwaantaan, was the father of K̲aawus.aa, also known as K̲usán and Dry Bay George. K̲aawus.aa married Shtulkaalgéis', a woman of the Shangukeidí, and was the father of K̲uchéin and Naag̲éi. K̲uchéin, known in English as Frank Italio, was the father of Leetkwéi, who married Naag̲éi, her paternal uncle, her father's younger brother. This is an acceptable marriage pattern in Tlingit tradition. Leetkwéi (Katy Dalton) and Naag̲éi were the parents of Emma Marks. Naag̲éi also had the Tlingit names Yéil Éesh and Kinaadak̲een. His English name was supposed to have been Frances George, but the name was confused on the records and transposed to George Frances. It is a common problem in Tlingit names that missionaries and government officials gave different names to biological brothers, so that while Frank Italio and George Frances are actually brothers, the family names do not reflect the relationship. The name K̲aawus.aa was also given by their father to Emma's brother Ernest Frances, following the tradition of a man's giving his father's name to his son. More recently, Emma gave the name K̲aawus.aa to her great-grandson Ronaldo Topacio.

76. My grandfather. Reference is to Paul Henry, L'uknax̲.ádi, and one of the traditional leaders of Yakutat, who introduced Emma and asked her to speak. Emma's grandfather K̲aawus.aa was also L'uknax̲.ádi, so Emma addresses Paul Henry as her grandfather.

82. Younger brother. Because both are Raven, Emma Marks also refers to Paul Henry as her brother.

85, 88. Brother . . . younger sister. Emma is indicating persons of the Raven moiety in the audience whom we cannot identify at this time.

92. G̲anák̲t'. A man of the Shangukeidí who was Emma's paternal uncle and the nephew of Emma's father. She is explaining how people in the audience, although they may not realize the connection, are related through grandparents in Yakutat.

109. Seig̲eig̲éi. The name of Emma Marks and also her maternal grandmother, her mother's mother. Her grandmother was Lukaax̲.ádi and child of Teik̲weidí.

112. Leetkwéi. Emma Marks' mother, a woman of the Alsek Lukaax̲.ádi, also known as G̲unaax̲uk̲wáan; child of Shangukeidí.

117-122. Father's name, etc. Naag̲éi, Yéil Éesh, and Kinaadak̲éen are all Shangukeidí names from the Italio River. The same names appear in Klukwan and other communities.

127. Alsek River. One of the great rivers of North America, the Alsek rises in Yukon and flows through B. C. and Alaska, entering the sea at Dry Bay. The Alsek flows through and in places forms the northern boundary of the Glacier Bay National Park and Preserve areas. This is an area of active glaciation. In general, the glaciers to the south in Glacier Bay are retreating, but in the north, in the Russell Fiord area, they are advancing. In 1986, the Valerie Glacier, a tributary of the Hubbard, advanced at rates of up to 130 feet per day. The Hubbard Glacier advanced one mile, closing off Russell Fiord. The Alsek River cuts through the middle of this massive ice field and sections of the river above the confluence with the Tatsenshini are not navigable, and require helicopter portage. The two major river routes to the interior were the Alsek and the Alsek-Tatsenshini which the editors had the opportunity to float in August 1989. See de Laguna (1972:57-106) for a detailed description of the areas mentioned in Emma's speech.

139. Dance. During Celebration 1988 the G̱eisán Marks Trail Dancers performed the Alsek River canoe songs and dances Emma is referring to in these lines.

143-144. Daughter . . . grandfather from Chilkat. Reference is to Nora Marks Dauenhauer.

145. Jaḵwteen. Lukaax̱.ádi; Father of Emma's husband, Willie Marks; also the name of her son Jim Marks.

148. Grandmother from Hoonah. Reference is to Eliza Marks, Tl'oon Tláa, Chookaneidí, T'aḵdeintaan yádi, mother of Willie Marks and grandmother of Emma's children.

150. Child of the Snail House. Eliza Marks, a child of T'aḵdeintaan, was a child of the Snail House, one of the prominent T'aḵdeintaan community houses in Hoonah.

Notes to the Welcome Speech by Jennie Thlunaut

This speech was delivered by Jennie Thlunaut at Raven House in Haines, Alaska on February 26, 1985, to her apprentice weavers, who had travelled to Haines and gathered for a Chilkat Weaving Workshop (February 26 - March 8, 1985) sponsored by the Institute of Alaska Native Arts, and coordinated by Jan Steinbright and Julie Folta. The speech (here transcribed and translated by Nora Dauenhauer) was video taped by Suzanne Scollon as part of the documentation of the workshop by her and Nora Dauenhauer, sponsored by Sealaska Heritage Foundation, with the main grant support coming from the Alaska Humanities Forum, and with additional support from Judson Brown. Part of this footage has been edited and is now available on a video tape entitled *In Memory of Jennie Thlunaut* (Dauenhauer and Scollon 1988).

The women who participated in the workshop and are the charter members of the Shax'sáani Kéek' Weavers' Guild (named in honor of Jennie) are, in alphabetical order: Delores Churchill, Nora Dauenhauer, Anna Ehlers, Ernestine Hanlon, Clarissa Hudson, Tanis Hinsley, Edna Jackson, Edith Jaquot, Irene Jimmie, Vesta Johnson, Rachel Dixie Johnson, Geraldine Kennedy, Ida Kadashan, Clara Matson, Maria Miller, Mary Ann Porter, Phoebe Warren.

Maria Miller and Anna Brown Ehlers have many major pieces to their credit. Several others have completed samplers and are at work on larger projects. Ernestine Hanlon (who has also completed a large piece of weaving) and Delores Churchill are primarily known for their basketry. Chilkat weavers are few in number, and two non-Tlingit artists should be noted here: Dorica Jackson, wife of Tlingit artist Nathan Jackson, is an accomplished Chilkat weaver, with many pieces to her credit. She was not involved with the workshop, but Cheryl Samuel, a well-known non-Tlingit weaver and author of a book on the subject did visit the workshop.

Jennie delivered this speech seated on the couch in the living room of Raven House, sitting next to Nora Dauenhauer, who was acting as interpreter. The speech is characterized by a very slow, and sometimes weak delivery—even feeble and fragmented in places. This is reflected in the style of the speech, and we have taken some syntactic liberties in English translation in an effort to make some of Jennie's implied connections more explicit. Where significant, these places are indicated in the notes. The weak and slow delivery of this speech, delivered from the seated position, contrasts dramatically with the speed and energy of her prayer of the following day, delivered standing, also included in this book. Jennie gained strength and enthusiasm during the course of the workshop, in which she delivered many informal speeches and much personalized instruction as she moved from apprentice to apprentice in the living room of Raven House, which was filled from wall to wall with looms. Her energy was contagious, so much so that one young woman who simply dropped in to see what was going on began to learn the techniques by weaving on a mop head!

In this speech, Jennie touches on two themes: that she is not stingy with her knowledge, but wants to pass it on; and that she is happy the younger generation is taking over. For Jennie, the transmission of her knowledge involves not only the passing on of technique, but the ongoing cultural history of Chilkat weaving. Much of this introductory speech is devoted to how the weaving was brought to the Chilkat area, and how she came to learn it, and to be in the position to pass it on to her apprentices. From the point of view of genre theory, this speech overlaps to a large degree in style and content with narrative and suggests that the boundary between oratory and narrative is vague at times.

The most fascinating aspect of this speech is Jennie's personal history of the art of Chilkat weaving. This history is well documented by outsiders, including Emmons (1907, 1916), Jonaitis (1986), Kaplan and Barsness (1986), Samuel (1982) and others, and in historical photographs by Case and Draper, Winter and Pond, and others; but Jennie was personally connected to all of this, and her life illustrates the all-important cultural context of the art. Her speech is a part of the living tradition in which she and the younger women share. She experienced this history as a child and young woman. She lived the life of Chilkat art as a learner, a master, and a teacher. For her students and apprentices, she was a living connection to the past, and in this speech she invites the younger women to join in this process and relationship.

For more on Jennie see Worl and Smythe (1986) "Jennie Thlunaut: Master Chilkat Blanket Artist" in Suzi Jones (1986) *The Artists Behind the Work*. The article includes maps and many photographs.

1-10. There are some problems with syntax here. The main verb is in line 4, and the dependent clause is completed in line 10. Jennie seemed very weak at this time, and this shows up in this section of the speech, where we have translated more freely.

3. Sisdees. A loan word from English, "sisters," referring to the Alaska Native Sisterhood relationship as well as clan and weaving guild relationships.

11. Weaving. This word is supplied in translation. The Tlingit is literally "this thing."

16-17. Mother . . . Sitka. Jennie's mother was a Kaagwaantaan woman of the Wolf House in Sitka. Thus Jennie's life is connected not only to important events in Klukwan, but in Sitka as well.

20. Paternal aunts. Women of the Raven moiety and G̱aanax̱teidí clan.

21-25. Father's sister . . . that blanket . . . Deink̲ul.át. In these lines Jennie introduces a number of themes she will develop later in her speech. "That blanket" refers to the famous history of the Tlingit women learning the technique by unravelling a Tsimshian apron to see how the stitches were done. Deink̲ul.át was one of Jennie's teachers, so Jennie is also establishing here the line of transmission for her apprentices. Jennie identified the weaver in Winter and Pond photograph 87-197 (Wyatt 1989:130) as her paternal aunt Deink̲ul.át (Mrs. Benson).

26-30. Stingy, etc. As well as establishing her line of transmission, Jennie emphasizes that she is not stingy with her art, but wants to pass it on to the younger generation.

36-37. God . . . blessing. Jennie emphasizes her belief that her work and talent are gifts of God. This is a very traditional and very conservative expression of faith, recognizing and taking pride in one's personal talent, but also humble in the awareness of its spiritual sources. Lines 36-61 in general emphasize the spiritual aspect of her work.

39-40. This time . . . not by accident. This is a puzzling phrase, and difficult to translate, partly because of the conjunction "k̲u.aa" and partly because of Jennie's fragmented delivery here. We understand these lines to emphasize Jennie's belief that her talent is not coincidental or accidental, but is part of her upbringing and is and directly connected to her early training by parents who were believers in God. They taught her that if she believed, she would achieve. It is also possible that she is admonishing her apprentices not to weave carelessly. Alternative translations are "not by chance," "not haphazard," "not any old way," or "not carelessly."

42. Chách is a loan word from English "church" and is the common Tlingit word for a Protestant church. Kaneisdi Hít, literally meaning "cross house," is often used for an Orthodox church, "kanéist" being a borrowing of the Russian "krest'."

44. Where my church was. This is a bit awkward in Tlingit as well as in English. Jennie is emphasizing her religious education.

46. Jigatánch. This is a good example of how Tlingit verbs are constructed. The stem is -tán, generally meaning "to handle an empty container." The stem is surrounded by affixes, including the nominal prefix ji- meaning "hand," and the conjugation prefix -ga-. used in combination with the occasional suffix-ch. The direct object is x̲at. All of this translates into English as "would take me by the hand."

52. Dikaank̲áawu is a contraction of Dikee Aank̲áawu, meaning "Lord above," or "God."

55. Teaching her already. This particular reference is to Nora Marks Dauenhauer. Jennie had helped Nora rip back several incorrect rows of weaving the night before, and was already teaching her the proper technique.

62. Tlingit. sh tóog̲aa and sh tug̲áa are both heard, and both are correct.

63. My time. This is a transition point in the speech. Jennie recapitulates the idea from lines 6 and 7 that she feels close to death, and is happy to have someone to whom she can pass the tradition on. The rest of her speech explains the history of Chilkat weaving and how she learned it.

66. Ax̲ tláa. This line is possibly a false start which Jennie corrects in the next line. It is difficult to tell for certain, due to the fragmentary delivery here. If this is a false start, and were deleted, the translation would read, "It was my father who paid for it." If the line is left in, the literal translation is something like, "Speaking about my mother—it was my father who paid for her to learn." We have left the line in, and loosely translated "my father paid for my mother's instruction," which is the point she is making here.

68-69. Saantáas' was Jennie's maternal aunt, her mother's sister, a woman of the Kaagwaantaan. Jennie explains (lines 64-78) how her (Raven) father commissioned his sister-in-law (Jennie's maternal aunt) to teach Jennie's mother. Jennie learned by watching them, an interesting example of the method of learning by observation. Jennie tells about how each time her relatives wove they would make her sit and watch them. This passage also illustrates the tradition of commissioning the opposite moiety for services.

79-81. Tlél . . . ch'áakw. In Tlingit, we understand the negative "tlél" to apply to both phrases, and we have translated somewhat freely here to convey Jennie's point.

86. K̲anúkch. (I would sit.) This is an uncommon form, a first person singular occasional. The underlying form is g̲a-x̲a-núk-ch. The subject pronoun -x̲a- and the conjugation prefix -g̲a- contract to -k̲-.

88-93. When Jennie's mother died in 1908, her father gave her the unfinished blanket to complete.

89, 103, 107, 109. The Tlingit text contains some interesting forms of the verb "to weave." (The morphemes are separated by hyphens.)

89.	yan	a-ka-w- si-néi	she finished weaving it (perf)
103.	yan	ka-x̲-w-si-néi	I finished weaving it (perf)
107.		a-k-sa-né	he/she weaves it (imperf)
109.	yan	néi	when it was finished (sequential).

The verb stem is -néi, meaning "to make or do." Combined with the nominal prefix ka-, referring to a round object, and the -s- classifier, it means "to weave with string-like object." The prefix "yan" means "to completion." The form "yan néi," without the nominal prefix and classifier refers to finishing something in general, as opposed to a weaving.

89-90. That one, black and yellow. The video tape shows Jennie sitting on the couch, pointing to a blanket in progress by Nora Dauenhauer, whose loom was closest at hand. Black and yellow are the traditional colors for Chilkat weaving. The term also indicates progress, the black and yellow rows being the top two rows of border, which must be completed, and the corners turned, before the weaver can begin on the central designs.

94-95. Already knew. Jennie had already learned by sitting behind the weavers and watching them.

96-100. After this . . . my grandmother . . . taught it to me. This passage is unclear to us. Perhaps it refers to her first formal teacher, in contrast to her having looked on as a child and learning by observation. Also, one learns different techniques from different people. Jennie mentioned at one point that she learned the technique of dividing strands from her mother-in-law. Her paternal grandmother would have been a woman of the G̱aanax̱teidí.

102. Porcupine. A mining camp about twenty-six miles northwest of Klukwan, where Jennie and her husband spent the summer.

106. Some people. In Tlingit, Jennie uses the word "lingít," meaning a person or a Tlingit.

108. You'll all see. She is addressing her apprentices, emphasizing how difficult and how slow it is to weave. The Tlingit (gax̱yisatéen) is second person plural future, relatively uncommon in texts.

110-111. On the video tape, Jennie raised the five fingers of one hand to emphasize her point.

125. Money has a spirit. In Tlingit, the word used for spirit is "á yahaayí." The line could also be translated as "It is said that a spirit exists in money," or "There is a spirit for money." The values Jennie is explaining here are shared by other elders of her generation. Emma Marks also describes how she was taught to keep money for a while "so it gets used to you."

130. Naaxein. This is the Tlingit word for Chilkat Blanket or Chilkat Robe, and, at the suggestion of some weavers, we have tried using it here. The "x" is like the German "ich," the "aa" like English "father," and "xein" rhymes with English "vein."

133. Poor person. This line is the culmination of Jennie's comments on money. Jennie was not "needy" or ever in want, and she attributes her material success to her traditional treatment of God, Church, and Tlingit spiritual things, including money. If a person offends the spirits of natural objects, they can turn against the offender, and cause harm. Therefore, one traditionally takes care to have respect for the spirit world and the spiritual side of the material and physical world. See the introduction and notes to the last set of speeches in this book for more on the treatment of spirits. This is an excellent example of the synthesis of Christian faith and traditional world view.

135. Ax̱ eesh hás. (English, 136, my fathers.) This is possibly a false start, corrected in the next line, but can also be understood as intended, because the art is from her father's moiety, and would include her fathers as well as her paternal aunts.

142. Yan tuytán. Second person plural imperative. The combination of stem (tan) nominal prefix (tu) and directional

prefix (yan) means to place an empty container, namely the mind, in one spot and not move it; i.e., focus, concentrate, or keep your thoughts on something. The form is also interesting because -tan is a singular stem, and one would expect the plural stem with the plural subject pronoun—something like "yan teeyla.á."

147-148. My fathers . . . G̱aanax̱teidí. A clan of the Raven moiety. They are the keepers of the Frog House in Klukwan. Jennie's father came from this house.

150-154. Tsimshian woman . . . Hayuwáas Tláa. Jennie is alluding here to the history of a Tsimshian woman named Hayuwáas Tláa, who was married to a man of Jennie's father's clan, the G̱aanax̱teidí. She is credited with bringing the first Chilkat weaving to Klukwan, where the local women learned the technique by unravelling it, and then putting it back together. As she explains in subsequent lines, the style became associated with the Chilkat area, and Klukwan became a center for the art, while it declined among the Tsimshian. Although the term "blanket" is often loosely used as a generic term, the weaving they unravelled was actually a dance apron. This history is also covered in Worl and Smythe (1986:137-140).

160-164. It's still there. The weaving still exists in the community.

166. Only . . . paternal aunts. At first only the G̱aanax̱teidí women knew the technique.

168. To their sisters-in-law, to us. To the Kaagwaantaan and other women of the Eagle moiety, with whom the Raven moiety, G̱aanax̱teidí women shared the technique.

169. Yanwaa Sháa. "Navy Women." This is an important group in Tlingit ceremonial life. It seems to have been composed originally of the Kaagwaantaan women, but today Eagle moiety women of other clans also participate. For historical reasons, (but presumably for the taking of a life or for an unpaid debt) the Kaagwaantaan women have for generations claimed the U.S. Navy uniform as a crest, and wear parts of it at memorials. For many years, Jennie was the "Commodore," or ceremonial leader of the Yanwaa Sháa, and therefore ceremonial leader of all the Kaagwaantaan women. See also Worl and Smythe (1986:134) for more on Yanwaa Sháa and photographs.

188. The transcription of Jennie's speech ends here, but the setting was informal, and flowed naturally into a discussion and question and answer session, with Nora Dauenhauer translating.

Two points were clarified. First, Jennie repeated a main point: "Deinkul.át and her side unravelled it. Those who were my paternal aunts were the ones who unravelled it. But the Tsimshian woman was their sister-in-law."

Nora Dauenhauer asked, "What was the name of the Chilkat weaving, the one they unravelled?" Jennie replied, "It is called S'igeidí K'ideit. It's still there now, but it's getting worn out."

Jennie also went on to explain that a few months before the workshop she didn't want to teach because she didn't feel strong enough. She wanted to be excused. But she emphasized her desire to teach, and her gratitude that the younger women are excited about learning.

Notes to the Prayer by Jennie Thlunaut

With this prayer, delivered on February 27, 1985, Jennie Thlunaut opened the second day of the Chilkat Weaving Workshop held at Raven House in Haines, Alaska February 26 - March 8, 1985. The speech was recorded on video tape by Suzanne Scollon as part of the documentation of the workshop, and was transcribed and translated by Nora Marks Dauenhauer. (See the notes to the previous speech for more details.) On the first day, Jennie delivered a welcome speech to her apprentice weavers. The balance of that day and evening was devoted to preparing wool and other materials. Jennie began her actual weaving instruction on the second day, and prior to the instruction, she addressed the workshop. She began with a short speech, delivered standing, in which she commented that she would be ninety-five years old in May. She shared with the women her sense of impending death. The speech culminated in the prayer included here, and lines 1 and 2 actually mark the end of the speech and the beginning of the prayer. Jennie's delivery was very rapid, as is suggested in the long lines.

3. Dikaankáawu is a contraction of Dikee Aankáawu, "Lord above," or "God."

8-9. Sisdees is the English word "sisters." Reference is to other Kaagwaantaan women, and more generally other Eagle women. The term "grandchildren" covers those of the Raven moiety present.

15-16. Keep it to myself . . . learn it. This is a major theme not only in this opening prayer, but in Jennie's welcome speech. She is happy that younger women are taking up the traditional art of Chilkat weaving.

After Jennie's prayer, Austin Hammond, steward of Raven House and host of the Chilkat Weaving Workshop, addressed the apprentices in English. Austin made the point that he also made in the *Haa Shagóon* film (Kawagey 1981) and again on the video tape *In Memory of Jennie Thlunaut* (Dauenhauer and Scollon 1988) that as the Chilkat weavers weave at.óow they are also weaving the history of the people: "We wear our history." At one point Austin said, "What you are going to weave now—I have blankets in that box, Chilkat Blankets—that's our history that you are going to start, what you're going to put on it, what kind of design. My grandfather told me, 'Whatever you have, don't sell it.' What they meant was what I got there. 'Don't sell it; it's your history. How are you going to get it back?' "

Notes to the Klukwan Speech by Jennie Thlunaut

On March 6, 1985, toward the end of the Chilkat Weaving Workshop at Raven House, with "two more days to go," as Jennie says in her speech, a banquet for her and the weavers was hosted by the Klukwan Alaska Native Sisterhood at the ANB Hall in Klukwan. After the dinner, Daisy Phillips spoke, introducing members of the Sisterhood and Jennie's relatives and descendants. Gifts of flowers and plants were given to Jennie, after which she moved to the front of the hall and delivered the speech included here.

In many respects, this may be considered Jennie's public farewell speech. There is a strong tone of "unfinished business" in this speech. Although she was to live for another year, Jennie was preparing to die, and spoke eloquently on this. Feeling herself near death, she thanks those around her and talks about their place in history, as well as her own. There are many poignant lines in this speech. It is also an excellent example of the importance of public expression of gratitude in Tlingit tradition. (For example, there is no single word for "please" in Tlingit, but there is a word for "thank you," and the culture is exquisitely structured around ceremonials and other public occasions for expressing gratitude.) As in other speeches in this book, the importance of at.óow and the protocol surrounding their display are emphasized.

Her delivery was in a strong and powerful voice, slow, deliberate, evenly paced (as reflected in the short lines in the transcription and translation) but not weak. A few lines were delivered much more rapidly, and this is reflected in the longer lines. There were a few false starts, and these are indicated in the notes.

3. Klukwan Sisterhood. The Klukwan "Camp" of the Alaska Native Sisterhood.

19. Tlingit. Ekskóos; the English word excuse. Elsewhere Jennie mentions that she declined to teach at first due to poor health.

20. White people. Reference is to Jan Steinbright of IANA (Institute of Alaska Native Arts) and Julie Folta, who coordinated the business end of the workshop.

35-38. Dress . . . given to me. Jennie is joking here, and the audience responds with laughter. There are two references here. One is to the "official" T-shirt of the Chilkat Weaving Symposium, designed by Clarissa Lampe Hudson, one of the apprentices. It is beige, with a blue-green Chilkat design. Jennie's daughter Agnes Bellinger was holding the T-shirt up in front of Jennie. Her apprentices also gave her a dress.

37. Sgóonwaanx'i is from the English "school man." The -x'i is plural possessive. A false start between 36 and 37 has been edited out, and 37 is partially obscured by laughter.

38. Wuduwa.áx̲ is a good example of Tlingit verb structure and the use of a classificatory stem. It is perfective (wu-) with the 4th person or impersonal pronoun (du) usually translated into English as passive voice. The classifier is -ya- but appears in its -wa-form because it follows the vowel -u-. The stem -áx̲ means "to

handle cloth." The phrase translates literally as "my hand-to an unspecified person moved cloth."

41. (Tlingit) Gunx̲aa G̲uwakaan is one of Austin Hammond's Tlingit names. He is on her mind in the present context because he is the host of the Chilkat Weaving Symposium at Raven House, and the steward of Raven House, where Jennie lived when her second husband was steward. Austin is also her son-in-law, his first wife being Jennie's daughter Katherine, who died in 1940.

41a. Austin responds, acknowledging the speaker.

42-43. I will enter the forest with my gratitude for you. This is a magnificent passage, a euphemism for death. She is saying, "I will carry my thanks to you to the grave." The passage could also be translated in different ways. Daak̲ is a directional prefix meaning "inland, upland, into the forest," or "inland from the beach"—all in contrast to daak, the directional prefix indicating "out to sea," or "seaward from the beach."

43. Stolen stress on sh tug̲aa.

44-46. Because of you. . . . Jennie acknowledges Austin's important role as an organizer and prime mover. "This work" refers to the Weaving Symposium at Raven House.

48-49. Children . . . grandchildren. Biologically or through clan relationship, Jennie is the mother and grandmother of many of the ANS hosts of the banquet.

51. Impose. The passage is difficult to translate. Expressing her gratitude for their hard work, Jennie is apologizing for any imposition arranging the banquet may have caused. Although it is technically a separate sentence, we have combined it in translation with the preceding sentence. The Tlingit, more literally is, "It seems I am imposing on you," or "It seems (to me) as if I am imposing on you." A false start between 50 and 51 has been edited out.

53-54. Joe Hotch, my dear litle brother. As a fellow Kaagwaantaan, Joe Hotch is Jennie's clan brother, younger in age. Their fathers were both G̲aanax̲teidí. His father was the steward of Whale House until he died.

60. Your village. Klukwan, historical home of Chilkat weaving.

66-68. Feel good . . . won't feel bad . . . if anything happens. Jennie is reaffirming that everything is fine, and that even if she were to die soon, everything is now in order.

73-74. A false start between 73 and 74 has been edited out.

75. That people will see. From here to the end of her speech, Jennie alludes to the video tape being made, and their place in it.

77. Things be brought out here. It would be customary to put the at.óow on Jennie's coffin, and to display them at her memorial. Jennie is confirming her pleasure to be associated with these treasures of her clan while she is still alive, in the presence not only of those assembled for the banquet, but of those who will see the video in the future, even though they were not present in time and place when the speech and display of at.óow happened.

78-84. Even when I die . . . see . . . camera . . . you won't forget me. This is a very poignant passage, in which Jennie again expresses her comfort at the thought of being remembered. We have supplied "camera" in English translation; the Tlingit is literally "that thing."

85-87. How my grandparents' things will be with me here. Pictures will be seen . . . all over the world. Again, Jennie is expressing how happy she feels to be remembered in this total context, along with her ancestors' at.óow.

90-91. Sitka . . . film. The video was actually edited in Haines and Juneau. Some of the footage shot by Suzanne Scollon and Ross Soboleff has been edited and is now available as the video *In Memory of Jennie Thlunaut* (Dauenhauer and Scollon 1988). Other footage is still being edited.

93. Hang it over there. Jennie had hoped to see the original apron of Hayuwáas Tláa included with the other at.óow, and was under the impression that it was present. Unfortunately, the steward was not available during the period of the workshop and banquet, so the weaving was not brought out.

94-96. Because I made it. Jennie is referring here to the Wolf Blanket woven for and worn by her daughter Agnes Bellinger. It is prominent in the video recording.

98. Included. To the at.óow that are Jennie's ancestors' things brought out by Joe Hotch and Richard King, Jennie adds one of her own making. This illustrates a basic concept of folklore—that tradition is both conservative and dynamic; at the same time as a tradition bearer, such as Jennie, follows tradition, she also creates and contributes to it.

Jennie's speech was followed by a presentation by the Kaagwaantaan, who displayed and spoke on their at.óow. The texts of these speeches are not included in this book, but we hope to see them included in a separate publication on Jennie Thlunaut and Chilkat weaving. For now, we will limit ourselves to commentary on some highlights.

After Jennie's speech, Daisy Philips spoke first, emphasizing the uniqueness of Chilkat weaving, and how it is more complicated and time consuming than other Tlingit art. She also mentioned that Jennie's birthday was coming up ("May 18, she'll be ninety-five years old") and that her birthday was to be officially designated as Yanwaa Sháa Day. (See the biography of Jennie Thlunaut for more on this.) She concluded her speech with introductions of the hosts and Jennie's family. After Daisy Phillips, Jennie's daughter Agnes Bellinger spoke briefly, expressing her thanks.

Joe Hotch spoke next, first in English, then in Tlingit. He welcomed the weavers, expressing how the community was uplifted by their visit. "ANB and ANS will be strengthened by your presence," he said. He then turned to the difficulty of understanding traditional culture because of the erosion of Tlingit language and culture. "English entered our lives and our minds, and is confusing our cultural understanding," he said. He emphasized the importance of each younger generation, including his own, to know the culture and heritage. "Our elders used to say, 'There's going to be a time when we'll be gone from amongst you.'" He stressed the importance of being able to understand and speak publicly about at.óow. With the passing of the elders, this becomes a responsibility of the next generation. The apprentice weavers are the ultimate inheritors of this knowledge, which is as important as the technical skills of weaving. At one point, Joe Hotch addressed Jennie, saying, "What good will it do for me to bring out our at.óow on your coffin, sister? This is why I brought them out here, so that you can see." Reference is to the practice of bringing out at.óow on the coffin of a deceased relative.

After Joe Hotch, Austin Hammond spoke about his fathers' at.óow. These were on the head table at the back of the hall, covered with a cloth. Austin explained the protocol involved in talking about at.óow. Because the Kaagwaantaan at.óow would be presented, it would be important for him to speak of at.óow from the Lukaax̱.ádi side as well, to balance out the spirits. He explained that he would mention Naatúxjayi, a tunic woven by Jennie. Although not physically present, it would be enough just to mention it. (See the notes to the last set of speeches in this book for more on this.)

At this point, the at.óow were unveiled. Joe Hotch spoke briefly about Tom Jimmy, an elder who died in the 1970's, and then Richard King spoke. "All our elders have gone," he began. He expressed the sense of loss with the death of elders, and how, regardless of age, "we are reaching . . . to learn our . . . culture." He then addressed the apprentice weavers, "I am proud to look among you people, and thank you for what you are doing." He compared the situation to flood conditions, and imagined his people standing in the reeds, with water over their feet. "Who will rescue us?" he asked, and continued, with an indirect but implied comparison to the apprentice weavers who are carrying on the tradition, "I'm glad the water is going down, and we can stand on solid ground."

At this point, the Kaagwaantaan displayed and spoke on their at.óow. Among the at.óow were a giant spoon, staff, dagger, hat, dance frontlet (shakee.át), ground squirrel robe and button shirt. Austin Hammond, a child of Kaagwaantaan, spoke with great strength, pride, and joy regarding his father's people's at.óow. Joe Hotch commented "We fight for our fathers' community." Annie Hotch, the mother of Joe Hotch, spoke in Tlingit on the at.óow, and Jennie Thlunaut spoke again, this time on the wolf blanket that she wove and which her daughter Agnes Bellinger was wearing.

These speeches embody the importance of public speaking in conjunction with the display of at.óow, and the importance of display as part of significant cultural events. The speeches over the Kaagwaantaan at.óow show how, for the Tlingit people, the technical skills involved in weaving, as important as they are, are only a small part of Chilkat weaving; the social and spiritual contexts make up the rest, and these, by definition of at.óow as well as tradition, involve more than one generation.

We are reminded here of the Russian poet Boris Pasternak's image (in the poem "Night") of the artist as "hostage of eternity, a prisoner of time." Less poetically stated, we live in a given moment, but we belong to eternity. Or, as the American writer Wendell Berry says, "we live in eternity while we live in time. It is only by imagination that we know this." (1983: 90). In the Tlingit sense, the artist as "hostage" is also a peacemaker between eternity and time, spiritual reality and the material world. Jennie Thlunaut knew this, and lived this in her weaving and her words.

Notes to Austin Hammond, Fairbanks

This speech was delivered in Fairbanks, on Friday, October 21, 1988, as part of the ceremonies for the raising of the Eagle Kaagwaantaan Totem Pole at the University of Alaska Museum on the campus of University of Alaska-Fairbanks. The speech was recorded on video tape by the University of Alaska Museum, and a copy was made available to Nora Dauenhauer who transcribed and translated it. The raising of the totem pole was the culmination of a series of public programs sponsored jointly by The University of Alaska Museum and the Institute of Alaska Native Arts (IANA) with support from the National Endowment for the Arts. The other events included the actual carving of the pole and panel discussions regarding the process.

The pole was carved by Nathan Jackson, a Tlingit from the Chilkat area now living in Ketchikan, and his apprentice Lee Wallace. At the top is the Eagle looking down; below this is the Wolf with a splinter of bone stuck between its teeth. Below the wolf is a Brown Bear. All of these images are important in Austin Hammond's speech.

The totem pole raising took place just outside the Museum at sunset on a clear early winter subarctic afternoon. The temperature had dropped to -5°F, and the ground was frozen. This was an unusual setting, as most Tlingit totems are raised in Southeast Alaska where it doesn't get this cold in October! The totem raising generated much interest, and approximately 600 people of mixed backgrounds came to observe, including participants of the Alaska Federation of Natives Conference. Several Tlingit clan leaders were invited from villages from Southeast Alaska to officiate in the raising and dedication.

Oratory was first delivered outside. The pole was then carried to the pit by random volunteers from among the observers.

Ropes were tied to the pole and volunteers pulled the pole into the hole with a fanfare of Tlingit drumming. All present could hear and feel its end hit the frozen bottom of the pit. As the pole stood up it came to life. Following the outdoors oratory the splinter of the bone between the teeth of the figure of the wolf was pulled out by Austin Hammond. This action symbolizes the removal by the guests of the pain of grief suffered by the hosts because of the recent death of one of their members.

After the totem was raised everyone went inside the museum for the last half of the ceremony, the dedication. Again, oratory was given by the hosts, guests and observers. In all, three songs were sung, two from the Eagle side and one from the Raven side. The pole was given the name "Everyone's Ancestor" by George Dalton. Gifts were passed to guests and observers at the ceremony by the wives of the Kaagwaantaan men. IANA provided souvenir scarfs for the totem. Food was served, including pizza. It was different to eat pizza at a totem pole dedication, but culturally acceptable, with local businesses contributing to the ceremony. Even though pizza is not a traditional Tlingit ceremonial food, the group dynamics of community involvement followed the tradition of a host community receiving outside guests.

Each clan member who came from Southeast Alaska took part in the raising and dedication. George Dalton, along with fellow Eagle leaders Charlie Joseph and Daniel Johnson, acted as the hosts. Austin Hammond and the other (Raven) Lukaax̱.ádi acted as the major guest group along with the rest of the Ravens. Just before the totem was raised, oratory was delivered by leaders of both the host and the guest groups. All of this follows the group dynamics of traditional Tlingit ceremonials, in which clans of the opposite moiety interact with each other.

Among those of the Eagle moiety attending were Kaagwaantaan: George Dalton (Hoonah), Richard King, Alfred Widmark, and Richard Warren (Klukwan); Daḵl'aweidí: Judson Brown (Klukwan); Teiḵweidí: Daniel Johnson, and Charlie Joseph (Angoon); Chookaneidí: Ernest Hillman (Hoonah); Shangukeidí: Rosita Worl and Sandra Samaniego (Juneau), and Carmen Plunkett (Anchorage). Of the Raven moiety were T'aḵdeintaan: Richard Dalton (who served as naa káani, or traditional master of ceremonies) and Jessie Dalton (Hoonah); Lukaax̱.ádi: Austin Hammond and Nathan Jackson (Haines),

Nora Dauenhauer and Paul Marks (Juneau), Linda Dugaqua (Fairbanks) and James Jackson (Anchorage); Deisheetaan: Cyril George and Verna Johnson (Angoon); L'uknax̱.ádi: Albert Davis (Sitka).

When an art object is dedicated, songs to fit the occasion are sung by the Eagle and Raven groups. The participants from all over the state helped support their clan leaders. For example, eight members of G̱eesán Dancers sang for Austin Hammond's portion of the ceremony: Austin Hammond, Sandra Samaniego, Linda Dugaqua, James Jackson, Nathan Jackson, Paul Marks, Nora Dauenhauer and Rosita Worl. Likewise, the Tlingit dance group from Anchorage led by Carmen Plunkett supported Charlie Joseph with his song.

Most of the traditional oratory was delivered in Tlingit, with Walter Soboleff interpreting. Much of it was of extremely high quality, and we are hoping to transcribe and translate these speeches eventually, either in book or video tape format. The event was too late for us to include as much as we would like in this book, not only because of the time involved in transcription and translation, but in researching notes and biographies.

Austin's speech is a good example of traditional Tlingit ceremonial process in a contemporary and innovative setting with non-traditional group dynamics. At one point he addressed the problem of conflict between traditional Tlingit protocol and contemporary western, explaining how traditionally such a pole would be commissioned by a clan, not an organization such as as museum.

As a sample of another speech, we include here a response to Austin's speech given by Charlie Joseph, Teik̲weidí of Angoon. (This is a different Charlie Joseph than the man from Sitka whose speeches are included in the main body of this book.)

Speech by Charlie Joseph, Eagle, Teik̲weidí of Angoon
(translated by Walter Soboleff)

I will say thank you
to Austin Hammond
for the words he gave us.
They will not lie here.
His speech

will echo to Angoon.
When a brown bear
is killed
this is when
a person would walk around
in the direction of the setting sun.
I am thinking now
about the words
of my father's brother
I say thank you to him.
(Austin Hammond) *Thank you.*
We will not stand
in the spirit of sadness.
We will be returning
with good feelings.
I say thank you
to all of them.
This is all.

Speech by Charlie Joseph of Angoon
(Tlingit transcription)

Gunalchéesh yóo áwé yakk̲wasak̲áa
yá Daanawaak̲
aadéi yoo x̲'atánk haa jeet aawateeyi yé.
Tlél yaa yándei kg̲atee.
Aangóondei áwé gug̲was.áax̲
du yoo x̲'atángi.
Xóots áyú
k̲aa jeet nag̲atéen,
aag̲áa áwé
g̲ag̲aan yaa naxíxi yáx̲ áyú du daa yaa agagútch.
Yáa yeedát áwé yéi a daa ax̲ tuwatee
du yoo x̲'atángi
ax̲ sáni.
Gunalchéesh yóo áwé daayax̲ak̲á.
(Daanawaak̲) *Gunalchéesh.*
Tlél x̲a toowunéekw teen
yándei gax̲toonaak̲.
Toowulak'é teen áwé

k̲úx̲dei yaa k̲ugax̲tudatéen.
Gunalchéesh yóo has yax̲wsik̲aa
ldakát hás.
Yéi áyá.

7. Lyek̲wudusdéich. Charlie Joseph, a Teik̲weidí elder from Angoon. He was accompanied by Daniel Johnson, a fellow Teik̲weidí elder of Angoon. The brown bear is an at.óow of the Teik̲weidí. They are present because one of their at.óow is depicted on the pole.

14-39. At one time this happens. . . . Austin compares Charlie Joseph to the man in his story. Charlie's relative, a Teik̲weidí, had just passed away, but Charlie put his grief aside to travel to Fairbanks for the totem pole raising because he felt it was too important an occasion to miss. Austin's story is an extended simile or parable. He recapitulates his point in line 37, "This is how you felt, Lyek̲wudusdéich," and explains it further in lines 38-39, "When we were to have this ceremony, it was as if you put your mourning aside for this."

36. Village . . . boring. This is a proverb. Austin explained to us that, "People wake up when someone dies." When someone in the community or family dies, awareness is increased, and the survivors' sense of their own mortality is heightened.

40-41. Reason . . . you didn't finish. It is customary to sing only part of a song when there has been a death in the family that has not yet been resolved with a memorial.

48. Shunlihaash. This is a Lukaax̲.ádi song composed by K̲ul'ootl', a man who was about to be killed in payment for the death of another man. He was going to be killed according to the Tlingit law that a person of equivalent status must pay with his life for the life of a person who was killed, even if he was not necessarily personally responsible for the killing. The song was performed between lines 103 and 104 of Austin's speech, where we have included the text and translation. The words describe how the composer felt at the moment. The second verse refers to a house he was building when it was time to die. Austin and his fellow Ravens are offering this Lukaax̲.ádi song for the removal of Charlie Joseph's grief, and in answer to the display of the bear at.óow on the totem pole. Also in payment of his kinsman's carving the pole. See below.

55. Nephew. Austin interrupts the flow of his explanation to call his nephew to his side. The nephew is Nathan Jackson, Yéil Yádi, a Lukaax̱.ádi carver who was one of the carvers of the Eagle-Wolf pole being raised.

62-63. Thing. The Tlingit word is ádi, the possessive form of át, meaning "thing," as in the compound noun "at.óow." Reference is to the Eagle as an at.óow of the Eagle moiety clans, and the wolf as an at.óow of the Kaagwaantaan. Both Austin and Nathan are children of Kaagwaantaan.

66-69. Awkward . . . Tlingit . . . commissioned . . . touch . . . thing of this nature. Austin is explaining the complexity of the commissioning of an at.óow according to traditional Tlingit protocol. The present pole was commissioned not by a Tlingit clan of the opposite moiety, but by the University Museum and the Institute of Alaska Native Art. It was traditionally awkward for or embarrassing to the owners of an at.óow for someone other than the clan itself to commission a pole unless it was in payment for some kind of a debt. This is not the case here; no clan debt is involved, but to avoid any misunderstanding, Austin is explaining how different cultural assumptions may be in conflict. His speech attempts to resolve this situation, offering words and song in payment, and addressing the wider contemporary setting. In the lines following, 71-82, Austin addresses this wider setting, with people from all over the state and from different cultures participating in this event. Although the event itself is innovative and not traditional, he and his fellow elders act in traditional ways to "adopt" and adapt to the new situation.

84. Face the people's weapons. Reference is to the "stand-in," the man going to be killed. A group of men from the community would be gathered to share in the execution.

97. Last one. Austin is the last of his generation of clan elders physically residing in Raven House in Haines.

110-111. My grandfather . . . Gunx̱aa G̱uwakaan. Reference is to Austin's grandfather Gunx̱aa G̱uwakaan, James Klanott, one of the Lukaax̱.ádi elders, who sang this song in his old age at the memorial for K'eedzáa, Alfred Andrews, in Juneau, about 1956. Other singers were Austin's mother Jennie Marks, Emma Marks, Nellie Willard, Jessie Kasko, Jim Marks, Florence Marks, Peter Marks, and Horace Marks. James Klanott was among the first to be recorded by his family members Horace and John Marks. Other songs were recorded at the same time, and through this taping, the Marks Trail Dancers also remember and sing the song of K'eedzáa, "Waasa haa kg̲watée."

114. I'm going . . . to the other side. To the land of the dead, Dak̲ank̲ú.

116. It is me speaking. The voice of K̲ul'ootl' is Austin's.

130. Nephew. Again, reference is to Nathan Jackson.

140. Outside. Austin is referring to the first part of the ceremony, held outdoors, when and where the pole was raised. He is now speaking indoors during the continuation of the event.

149. Hunting. The Tlingit text is literally "walking," an indirect reference to hunting.

150. When he saw the wolf. Reference is to the origin of the Kaagwaantaan at.óow, which he will now explain. In the story that follows, Austin explains the significance of the bone splinter that was placed in the teeth of the totem, and which Austin extracted. This action symbolizes the removal by the guests of the pain of grief suffered by the hosts because of the recent death of a clan member.

201. Also my paternal uncle. Reference is to the Chookaneidí at.óow. Austin is also a nephew and child of Chookaneidí, whose at.óow include the brown bear crest. Austin's father, Jim Marks, was of the Brown Bear House.

210. Ask for help. Reference is to the Tlingit tradition of talking to animals in general and mammals in particular, especially brown bears when one is in their territory.

Notes to the Speeches for the Removal of Grief from the Memorial for Jim Marks

This set of speeches was recorded in performance in Hoonah, October 1968, on audio cassette by Rosita Worl. The speeches were transcribed in Tlingit and translated into English by Nora Dauenhauer. This set of speeches is extremely important because it is, as far as we know, the first and only published set of speeches recorded in performance from a Tlingit memorial. It is certainly the first set collected in performance, transcribed, translated, and annotated by a scholar for whom Tlingit is a first language. The Tlingit texts were first published in *Doo G̲oojée*

Yeenaa-déi / Tlingit Language Workshop Reader in 1972. A revised transcription, accompanied for the first time by facing English translation and annotations, was distributed in a limited, field test edition by Sealaska Heritage Foundation, February 1984. Annotated English versions of three speeches appeared in *The Alaska Quarterly Review* (N. Dauenhauer et al. 1986:105-31). The Tlingit transcriptions and English translations have been substantially revised for this book and the set of speeches is also accompanied in this book by a glossary, first distributed in limited field test format October, 1984. It, too, is substantially revised and published here for the first time. We hope that this combination of text, translation, notes, and glossary, accompanied by the biographies of the orators, will encourage multiple use of the speeches in teaching Tlingit language, literature, and culture.

General Background Notes

Approximately one year or more after a person's death, his or her clans-people, with the support of members of other clans of the same moiety, and with indirect support from relatives of the opposite moiety, host a memorial called k̲oo.éex' in Tlingit. The memorial for Jim Marks was held in October 1968 in Hoonah, hosted by his younger brother Willie Marks, with the support of relatives and friends of the extended family. It took place in G̲ooch Hít, the Kaagwaantaan Wolf House in Hoonah, starting about 5 p.m. and lasting until about 5 o'clock the following morning. During the course of this memorial, the speeches in this section were delivered, as part of the ceremonial effort by the guests to remove the grief of the hosts.

About 5 p.m. people started arriving. The hosts were seated at the front, facing the guests and the back of the house. The guests who delivered the speeches in this section were seated along the back wall, facing the hosts. Jessie Dalton delivered her speech from the right back corner. Between the hosts and the guest-speakers the other guests were seated. The "orphans"—the children and family of the deceased—were seated at the front. The "Sea Gull Ladies," an important group of T'ak̲deintaan women who sang several songs, were at the left front wall.

The people wearing the at.óow referred to in the speeches stood randomly among the guests in the center of the room. The only tables were at the front, on which some of the gifts, dry goods, and money to be distributed were assembled. The naa káanx'i (naa kaanx'i yán; naa káanis), George Davis and William Johnson, stood at the end of the table. At the table were seated persons (usually three or four) recording the gifts of money.

When all of the important guests had arrived, the hosts blackened their cheeks, signifying grief, and began the Cry ceremony. There was singing with a drum but no dancing at this point. David Kadashan drummed on the Bear Drum which had belonged to Jim Marks. (For a photo of this drum, see *Haa Shuká*, page 490.) At this part of the ceremonial, either four or eight songs are traditionally sung by the hosts, and these are usually the most serious and sacred of the clan songs. They are very sensitive, and people prepare themselves before the singing of such songs. Preparations by the hosts include avoidance of seafood. David McKinley of the Wooshkeetaan was the song leader for the mourning songs.

In this case, four mourning songs were sung, the last of which was on a tape recording by the deceased, prepared before his death, in anticipation of his memorial. The song was preceded by the history included here by Jim Marks about the composition of the Xwaayeenáḵ song. The tape ended with the song itself, the text of which is not included here.

After the hosts' Cry, the guests ceremonially requested permission to speak, and time to conduct the l s'aati shaa g̱aax̱í—the Widow's Cry, and the activities were turned over to the guests. At this point the rest of the speeches included in this section began: the speeches delivered by the guests Matthew Lawrence, David Kadashan, William Johnson, Jessie Dalton, Austin Hammond, and ending with a second speech by Matthew Lawrence. The central speech is by Jessie Dalton, and her fellow orators cooperate to set a context for her, building up to her speech, and settling down again after it, creating an over-all dramatic structure similar to that of traditional European drama. The speeches of the guests are delivered in response to the mourning songs of the hosts.

It may be helpful for readers to see in tabular form the principal clans involved in the oratory:

Guests	Hosts
(Raven Moiety Clans Children of the Host Moiety)	(Eagle Moiety Clans)
Lukaax̲.ádi	Chookaneidí (main hosts)
T'ak̲deintaan	Wooshkeetaan (song leader)
	Kaagwaantaan (grandchildren
	Shangukeidí of the hosts)

The house groups of the hosts and guests are also important. The following are those which appear most frequently in the speeches and notes.

Chookaneidí Houses (Eagle)

Brown Bear House	Xóots Hít
Brown Bear Nest House	Xóots Saagí Hít
Upper Inlet House	Naa Naa Hít
Yellow Cedar House	X̲áay Hít

The Brown Bear Nest House was also known as X̲'aak Hít "Center House," or "Middle House," because of its central location in the village.

T'ak̲deintaan Houses (Raven)

Snail House	Táx̲' Hít
Raven Nest House	Yéil Kudei Hít
Head House	K̲aa Shaayi Hít

Snail House is also known as Mount Fairweather House, or Tsalx̲aan Hít.

Notes to the Narrative by Jim Marks

The history of the Xwaayeenáḵ song was tape recorded by Jim Marks before his death while he was still strong enough to record, with the intent that it be played at his memorial during the Cry by the hosts. He recorded it because there were few people alive who knew the song. His stepson Horace Marks did the recording at their home at Marks Trail in Juneau. The delivery is very slow and measured, with significant pauses between the lines. The history is of his maternal ancestors Ḵ'aadóo and Xwaayeenáḵ, two brothers whose canoe swamped near Lituya Bay. Ḵ'aadóo and Xwaayeenáḵ were both from Xoots Saagi Hít. Ḵ'aadóo was one of the names given to Willie Marks at a memorial.

The tape was made by Jim Marks and his wife Jennie Marks (the mother of Horace Marks and Austin Hammond) because the song composer Ḵ'aadóo was Jim's ancestor two generations back—his maternal grandfather. Jim Marks and his wife made the tape so that others would know that Ḵ'aadóo and Xwaayeenáḵ were the grandfathers of Jim Marks (Gooẖ G̱uwakaan) and his brother Willie Marks (Keet Yaanaayí). Even if they are not biological grandparents, they are considered grandparents because they are of the same house group. Xwaayeenáḵ was also the Tlingit name by which Willie Marks called his son-in-law Richard Dauenhauer.

Jim Marks was a house group leader of Brown Bear House, and was the last traditional leader of the group. He inherited the position and house from his maternal uncle Willis Hammond, and later married his widow. The Brown Bear House burned during the Hoonah fire of 1944 and Jim and his brother Willie were the last of the traditional lineage of the house group. Although the house itself was lost in 1944, other members of the family still live in Hoonah, and are caretakers of the clan at.óow. Among these are Eva Davis, Mary Johnson (the widows of George Davis and William Johnson) and Jennie Lindoff.

Although brief, the speech by Jim Marks is important, not only because of its content of the song of mourning and history of its composer, but because it ceremonially prompts or cues the guests. The speeches that follow by the guests are offered in response to the mourning songs and speeches of the hosts.

1. Yes. (Aaa.) This word is commonly used in Tlingit oratory and narratives to start, end, or link a phrase. It is used elsewhere in this speech, and throughout the other speeches. Its meaning and function varies. Sometimes the word seems to be used as a rhetorical agreement with oneself. At other times it seems to signify emphasis, as in the English "indeed." These stylistic uses should not be confused with the English word "uh" used as a filler or break when speaking (although in some places the orators may in fact be using the word also as a filler).

2. From among us. From Hoonah, and from his Chookaneidí relatives from Brown Bear Nest House.

7. He got his land. K'aadóo had land in Yakutat.

10. He wanted his younger brother to go with him. K'aadóo asked his younger brother Xwaayeenák to go with him to Yakutat.

11. While he was taking him. While they were on their way to Yakutat. The journey is on the open sea along a coast with no harbors except Lituya Bay.

12. At the entrance to Lituya. At the entrance to Lituya Bay their canoe capsized and everyone drowned except K'aadóo. "Lituya" is the anglicized version of Ltu.áa, meaning "Lake at the Point." Lituya Bay is a very dangerous place, especially in the winter. It is difficult and at times impossible to enter or leave. See *Haa Shuká* for stories and historical notes about Lituya Bay.

14. These travelers. In the time of K'aadóo, people traveled by canoe. Most Tlingit canoes were built to travel on the ocean.

15. But K'aadóo saved himself. K'aadóo managed to make it to the safety of the beach. His younger brother Xwaayeenák drowned. A search was conducted, but the body was never found. We have supplied the name in the translation; the Tlingit text has "he" saved himself.

16. Memorial songs. When a person of high esteem died, memorial songs were composed. People gathered to compose and sing memorial songs for Xwaayeenák.

18-31. K'aadóo would sit away from the group, alone, not joining in the group that was composing songs. When the others had finished composing their memorial songs, they asked K'aadóo if he was going to compose or sing a song.

25. My grandfather. The narrator is speaking of Kaadóo, as his maternal grandfather. The relationship need not be biological, but applies to an ancestor of the same house group.

31-35. All the while K'aadóo was by himself he had been composing a song, and now he asks the group to gather around him so he can sing it. At this point in the tape recorded narrative, Jim Marks and his wife Jennie Marks sing the song, and at this point in the memorial for Jim Marks, the tape recorded song was played. Thus K'aadóo's song in memory of Xwaayeenák, sung by Jim Marks in memory of his ancestors, becomes a song in memory of Jim Marks. In the Tlingit of line 31, the word written separately as "y.á" is connected in speech with the word in front of it, "gunei."

Notes to Matthew Lawrence (1)

1-9. Of all the speeches, this is the most difficult to hear on the tape recording. The orator's voice is very faint, and lines 1-9 are especially obscured by other noise in the room. These lines are partly reconstructed on the basis of the fragments that are audible. From midway in line 9 to the end, the speaker's voice is very clear. This is the first speech by the guests in the Widow's Cry. This and the following speeches are all from the Widow's Cry.

2. My fathers. The speaker is addressing the Chookaneidí clan, of which his father was a member. This kinship address is a very common one in Tlingit oratory and is also very important. People to whom the oratory is addressed must be addressed first. Here the speaker, as a guest, is addressing the host clan. Such kinship terms are used throughout the speeches, both to establish the relationship between the orator and the audience, and as terms of respect to the father's clan. Those who are addressed should always respond.

3. My father's sisters. This could also be translated, with a more technical tone, as "my paternal aunts." The speaker is addressing the women relatives of his father, the Chookan

Sháa, the women of the Chookaneidí people. He is especially addressing three women who are close relatives of the deceased and the host Keet Yaanaayí (Willie Marks):
Aan Káx̱shawustaan (Mary Johnson, the wife of William Johnson), S'eilshéix̱' (Eva Davis, the wife of George Davis), and Aanshéix̱' (Jennie Lindoff).

3a. Áawé. This is a response by a person or persons being addressed by the speaker. The format we use sets all such responses in italics, and the name of the speaker, if known, in parentheses. Here, the responses are by the hosts, who are being addressed by the guests. There is no exact English translation for the word "áawé," so we have left it in Tlingit. It means something like "That's it" and functions as a response as something like "Amen," or "You're right."

4. Always . . . this way. The line is unclear, but probably refers to the cycle of death and mourning, and memorials for the removal of grief.

6. My brothers-in-law. A general term for men of the opposite moiety, in this case the Eagle men. The speaker, of the Raven moiety and T'ak̲deintaan clan, is also addressing the Eagle moiety men who are married to women of the T'ak̲deintaan clan. Thus they are his clan brothers-in-law. Conversely, they are also his in-laws because he, as a Raven, is married to an Eagle woman.

8a. Keet Yaanaayí. Keet Yaanaayí, Willie Marks (1902-1981) was the brother of Jim Marks and the principal host of the memorial. Here the speaker is addressing Willie Marks and the Chookaneidí as his fathers, and Willie is acknowledging this through his response.

9. Your fathers were once alive. The speaker is referring to men of the father clan of the hosting group who are now dead. Because the hosts are Eagles, the father clans of the hosts would all be Ravens, as are the guests. This genealogical reference further establishes the relationship between the host and guest groups. Matthew Lawrence is addressing especially the children of T'ak̲deintaan, as Austin Hammond addresses the children of Lukaax̱.ádi.

10. Your children, too, were once alive. The children of Chookaneidí would be Ravens, as are the guests, and many of the important guests are children of Chookaneidí. The speaker is establishing the relationship of the children of the Chookaneidí

clan who were his (Matthew Lawrence's) relatives who are now deceased.

12-13. Keet Yaanaayí my father. The speaker, Matthew Lawrence, is a child of Chookaneidí, meaning that his father was Chookaneidí, and that by extension the host, Keet Yaanaayí, (Willie Marks) is his father also. It is important to remember that these terms of kinship are used to designate clan relatives as well as biological relatives.

14-15. At this moment how much we feel your stirring. Reference here is to the pain from grieving for a departed relative.

16. Nothing we can do. A theme in this speech and others is the feeling of inadequacy of the guests to remove grief, but that they will do their best.

17. We who are your children . . . your grandchildren. Reference again to the children of Chookaneidí, i.e. those of the Raven moiety whose fathers are of the Chookaneidí clan, and the grandchildren of the host clan (grandchildren of Chookaneidí) who are among the guests.

19. Sisters of your fathers. This could also be translated as "your paternal aunts." Reference is to the women of the T'a<u>k</u>deintaan. The paternal aunts or father's sisters of the Eagle Chookaneidí (members of which clan are Eagle because they follow their mothers' line and not their fathers') would be Raven, and in this case the Ravens of the T'a<u>k</u>deintaan clan. By extension, all women of the Raven moiety are considered father's sister or paternal aunt regardless of clan. This term of address further establishes the relationship between the grieving hosts and the guests.

22-24. Your fathers' sisters . . . chance . . . for a while. Here both the fathers and the aunts are plural. The Raven women, paternal aunts of the hosts, want the hosts to give the guests an opportunity to speak. This is a formulaic or ritual requesting of the floor according to protocol. The main purpose of the first speech by Matthew Lawrence is to request permission for his group to speak. Essentially, he is preparing the way for David Kadashan, who will deliver the first major speech.

25b. It will be. The principal host, Willie Marks, formally gives permission for the guests to continue.

Notes to the Speech by David Kadashan

David's delivery is very slow, evenly paced, well articulated, and almost musically chanted, sometimes with stresses evenly spread over all syllables of words. He makes very long pauses between most lines, so much so, in fact, that the speech could have been set in double-space type to emphasize this.

1-2. My father's brothers, all my brothers-in-law. Following protocol, the speaker is establishing a kinship relationship between himself and the hosts, whom he addresses as his brothers-in-law and paternal uncles. David Kadashan is a Raven of the T'akdeintaan clan, and a child of Shangukeidí. Among the hosting Eagles he is addressing, along with Willie Marks and his relatives, are Tom Jimmie and Joe White, who are members of the Shangukeidí assisting their fellow Eagle Chookaneidí hosts. Tom Jimmie is a child of Lukaax.ádi (as are the host and deceased) making him a brother, and Joe White was a co-clan child of Jim and Willie's mother making him a maternal uncle to Willie Marks. Moreover, Emma Marks, the wife of the host Willie Marks, is also a child of Shangukeidí, as is the speaker, David Kadashan. Also, David's wife, Ida Kadashan (Kaashtináa) is a woman of Shangukeidí, which makes the Shangukeidí men, and by extension other Eagle men such as Keet Yaanaayí his brothers-in-law. Thus the speaker is addressing the hosts with these kinship terms as prescribed by tradition. Men can be addressed as paternal uncles (father's brothers) or brothers-in-law regardless of their ages.

3-4. We are feeling your pain. The guests include people who are related to the host and deceased. The speaker is expressing sympathy for the bereft family.

6. I will imitate my mother's brother. Reference here is to the maternal uncle, who is traditionally the most important figure in the education of a Tlingit male child, and a role model in his life. (Because a child is not of the same clan and moiety as his or her father, clan traditions pass from maternal uncle to nephew.) The education given to a sister's son was usually

according to the role the male child would play in his future life. He would be trained in hunting, fishing, art, and/or leadership. This line contains the first of many references to "imitating." The present generation of elders is following the actions of their departed ancestors.

7. K̲áak'w Éesh is a Kaagwaantaan name. The son of K̲áak'w Éesh is J. C. Johnson, a Raven of the T'ak̲deintaan clan, child of Kaagwaantaan and maternal uncle of the speaker—the mother's brother referred to in the previous line.

8. Your child. As a Raven, David's maternal uncle is a clan child of the male Eagle hosts.

9-10. Tsalx̲aan G̲uwakaan and Yakwdeiyí G̲uwakaan are Eagle Moiety, Kaagwaantaan, and are considered the maternal uncles of K̲aak'w Éesh. Thus they are the maternal uncles of the father of the speaker's maternal uncle. Through the use of these names and kinship terms, the speaker is establishing his various (and complex) relationships with the opposite moiety. This set of speeches is an excellent example of the Tlingit kinship system in operation, and of how kinship is inseparable from the oratory.

9. Tsalx̲aan G̲uwakaan (English name George Dalton) is a Kaagwaantaan peacemaker for the T'ak̲deintaan. He inherited this position from his younger brother (Jim Martin) who is now deceased. The term g̲uwakaan, literally "deer," means "hostage" or "peacemaker," and derives from the image of the deer as a gentle and peaceful animal. A person is chosen to be taken as a hostage and occupy the position of peacemaker, or g̲uwakaan for life. With the title of peacemaker goes a number of responsibilities, one of which is that a person is peacemaker for life. In this case, whenever there is a dispute in the T'ak̲deintaan clan, he can intervene and defuse or resolve it. This personal name has two parts: Tsalx̲aan (Mt. Fairweather in English) is an at.óow of the T'ak̲deintaan, and G̲uwakaan is "deer."

9a, 15a. Héiy! This is another word used by a person to respond to the speaker. As individuals are recognized by the speaker either by their personal names or kinship titles, the individuals acknowledge the speaker by responding. The word has no exact English translation, but is something like "yo" or "yes" or "here I am." The speaker is addressing the hosts, who respond.

10. Yakwdeiyí Guwakaan. A peacemaker of the Wooshkeetaan clan, David McKinley. He inherited the title after the death of Louie Hanson. After David McKinley's death Eli Hanlon inherited the position. Yakwdeiyí is a place name in Lituya Bay and means "Canoe Trail." It is a place where boats can take refuge when there is a storm on the Gulf of Alaska. David McKinley was the song leader for the Cry Songs of the hosts.

11. I will imitate your brother-in-law. He is addressing the men who are married to children of Kaagwaantaan, referring again to his maternal uncle, their brother-in-law.

11a. Unidentified. Probably David McKinley replying.

12. My brother-in-law Keet Yaanaayí. David Kadashan is now directing his speech to Keet Yaanaayí, Willie Marks, the host, who is the younger brother of the deceased. Keet Yaanaayí is Chookaneidí, Lukaax̱.ádi yádi, and of X̱'aak Hít ("Center House" or "Middle House" of the village) also known as Xóots Saagí Hít (Brown Bear Nest House).

13. Ḵaatooshtóow. His English name was John F. Wilson, a Chookaneidí clan member but from a different house group (X̱aay Hít, Yellow Cedar House); Tax̱' Hít Taan yádi (child of the Snail House People). Ḵaatooshtóow is also Chookaneidí dachx̱án, a grandchild of Chookaneidí. His father was a child of Chookaneidí (Chookaneidí yádi). He was like a maternal uncle to Ḵuháanx' (Goox̱ Guwakaan—Jim Marks) and Keet Yaanaayí (Willie Marks) because the mother of Goox̱ Guwakaan and Keet Yaanaayí was also Tax̱' Hít Taan yádi, (child of the Snail House) making her and Ḵaatooshtóow tribal house brother and sister. (Their fathers came from the same house—Tax̱' Hít—Snail House.) He is also the brother-in-law of Ḵáak'w Éesh du yéet (the son of Ḵáak'w Éesh), J. C. Johnson, whose wife was also from X̱aay Hít (Yellow Cedar House).

14. I will imitate your brother-in-law. Again, reference is to Ḵáak'w Éesh du yéet, J.C. Johnson. David Kadashan is imitating his maternal uncle, who was the brother-in-law of the hosts. The speaker is assuming the position of his mother's brother. By imitating his maternal uncle, he is presenting him to the grieving brother-in-law Keet Yaanaayí and his relatives. The orators make frequent reference to "imitating." We understand this to mean taking ritual action following a traditional ceremonial pattern.

15. Gusatáan. Harry Marvin. Kaagwaantaan; T'aḵdeintaan yádi; Ḵóok Hit Taan—child of T'aḵdeintaan, of the Box House. (In Tlingit, note how the tone on hít is also stolen by the low tone on Taan.) Gusatáan is named as part of the hosting family because he is a grandchild of Chookaneidí. (His father was a child of Chookaneidí.) Gusatáan is present to support Keet Yaanaayí and the departed Ḵuháanx'. His name was also Naawéiyaa, the Tlingit name by which we identify him in the responses. (See line 37a.) He died in the mid 1970's while dancing with the Hoonah Mt. Fairweather Dancers during a performance in Juneau for the First Americans Emphasis Week. He was featured at various times in *Alaska Magazine* and in the *Alaska Geographic* Book on Southeast Alaska.

Harry Marvin wearing the Noble Killer Whale Hat (Kéet Aanyádi S'áaxw), an at.óow of the Kaagwaantaan. Copyright © 1973, The Alaska Geographic Society, Box 4-EEE, Anchorage, Alaska 99509. Photograph by Lael Morgan.

16. I will imitate your child. Again, reaffirmation of the genealogy to the hosting group completes the foundation of the oratory. Reference is again to the orator's maternal uncle, identified as the child of Gusatáan.

16a. Unidentified. Probably Harry Marvin replying.

17-21. Surely . . . and sensitive. In these lines the speaker expresses how difficult it is to make a speech of this kind. When he speaks, he remembers all of his clan's departed relatives who are related to Keet Yaanaayí, and also the speaker's grief for his maternal uncle K̲áak'w Éesh du yéet, the child of K̲áak'w Éesh, is renewed every time he mentions his name in this kind of speech.

22-23. We are in need of my mother's brothers. Were the maternal uncles of the speaker (and others) alive and present, they would be the ones making this speech. The idea is that when one tells a grieving family about one's deceased relatives it is soothing, because everyone has deceased relatives, and the survivors can draw support from each other. This is also a transition point in the speech. The orator completes his "catalog" of kinship by emphasizing how much they need their departed ancestors. This theme of inadequacy will be repeated after he turns to the central image of his speech, the uprooted tree.

24-44. The river would swell, etc. This begins an elaborate, multi-layered extended simile comparing the death of Xwaayeenák̲ and his song, and the departed Jim Marks and his song, and the surviving mourners to the tree uprooted by the swollen river, buffeted by the stormy seas, and deposited on a sandy beach. The uprooted tree is compared both to the grieving survivors as well as to the deceased. Through death, both are deprived of roots and connections. With the kinship relationships established by the first speaker and reconfirmed by David Kadashan, David, the second speaker, can now begin to make even more complicated connections, and tie the various elements together. The general style of the oratory now moves from the opening genealogical inventory or catalog into the extended use of simile and metaphor. In Tlingit, the bottom of a tree, where it anchors to the ground, is also called "ancestors."

32-33. Breaking . . . broken. In Tlingit and English this is a good example of "terrace" — a feature of narrative style in which the opening of one line builds on the closing of the previous.

37a. Naawéiyaa. Harry Marvin: Kaagwaantaan; T'a<u>k</u>deintaan yádi; <u>K</u>óok Hít Taan (Box House). Harry Marvin also had the name Gusatáan, by which he is called by the orator earlier in the speech. See note to line 15.

45-52. It would lie there . . . whoever is one. The log would lie on the sandy beach. This is another simile, comparing the mourners who have been stricken and are filled with grief to the soaked log. The sun will shine on the log and dry it out, warming it to the core. The speaker expresses his wish that his brothers-in-law, the grieving hosts, will be like this. The sun is metaphorically the Sun Mask to be presented in the speech by Naa Tláa (Jessie Dalton). The Tlingit of line 52 (aadéi<u>x</u>) is unusual. Aadoo<u>x</u> is more common for "who."

53-54. You created me, Chookaneidí. This is a beautiful passage, expressing a concept fundamental to Tlingit social structure and to Tlingit oratory. David Kadashan is a grandchild of Chookaneidí. David's father <u>K</u>aalgei was a co-clan child with <u>K</u>uháanx' and Keet Yaanaayí, all being Lukaa<u>x</u>.ádi yátx'i. Thus, although he is not a member of that clan, he was created or given life by that clan. Such relationships bind the entire community. As he says in the following line, this is why he feels such sympathy for the family. David's grandfather was <u>K</u>aadasháan, a Lukaa<u>x</u>.ádi who was a close relative of Ja<u>k</u>wteen, the father of the deceased. The name Kadashan derives from the Lukaa<u>x</u>.ádi name <u>K</u>aadasháan from the Chilkat area.

57. This is the way Xwaayeená<u>k</u> is. David now connects several oratorical threads, reaffirming that the drowned Xwaayeená<u>k</u> is like the log, and recapitulating the simile of the log.

58-60. In this world . . . our dead. These lines reconfirm the relationship between the two groups, the Chookaneidí and the T'a<u>k</u>deintaan: how the two clans both care for their dead by holding memorials for the departed, and how they support each other in these ceremonials by caring for each other. The speaker is emphasizing that his clan, like the hosts, are also traditional in their care for the departed, and that they also value the sense of balance and reciprocity so important in traditional Tlingit society. This is a difficult passage to translate. Focus does not seem to be on "we" but on the departed. Alternate translations are "We don't overlook our dead either," or "We also don't overlook our dead."

62-64. At this moment . . . faces. These lines are a restatement of grief turning to happiness, of a beginning for new life. The lines are a metaphor for the sun mask, in which the mask physically present is compared to the sun it represents, evaporating grief of the mourners, who are compared to the log. David is very traditional in this passage, talking around the topic at hand. He doesn't make a direct connection to the mask, but leaves it up to the audience to make the connection.

64a. This response, and many of the others, actually overlaps some of the words of the speaker. Although in actual performance these coincide or come before the end, we have placed this and some of the other responses at the end of the speaker's phrase or sentence for clarity and ease of reading. A more technical ethnopoetic transcription would use a system indicating the overlaps.

65. Joy for you. This was difficult to translate. Three elements are present: joy, wish, and you. An alternative (and our earlier translation) is "Let it turn to joy is my wish for you."

66-67. You all know your brothers-in-law, your fathers' sisters. The speaker is referring to people who are standing in their at.óow, waiting for Naa Tláa to speak about them: hats, shirts, tunics, masks, headdresses, Chilkat robes and button blankets.

70. You will stand. The speaker is now addressing his fellow guests who are already standing or who now stand up. They will remain standing, and their at.óow will become the basis of Jessie Dalton's speech.

71-74. The way . . . used to do . . . when such things happened . . . are things that might warm your feelings. What the ancestors (the paternal uncles) would do when there were ceremonials for the deceased. Through the ceremonial display of their at.óow, the guests (clanspeople of the speaker) bring good will and comfort to the grieving hosts. Reference is also to the sun.

75-77. The people . . . for you to see. The speaker's ancestors would show the at.óow both to the living hosts and to the ancestors of the hosts. "You" refers both to the very people who are hosting, and to their departed ancestors as well. This is the way Tlingit tradition is. This passage capsulizes the ritual process of the ceremony.

79. Brothers-in-law, etc. Again, a restatement of the kinship bonds between the speaker and the hosting family and clan.

81a. Aan Káx̱shawustaan. Mary Johnson. Chookaneidí; Lukaax̱.ádi yádi; wife of William Johnson, the next speaker. She is the maternal niece of the deceased and the host, and is a main hostess. The speaker addresses her as his paternal aunt.

82. We will only imitate our ancestors. The guests will imitate their ancestors who are deceased. Note the blend of the living and the deceased here and in the following speeches. The living people present are imitating their ancestors, from whom many of them inherited the at.óow in which they are standing. In this way the departed are made spiritually present. We have supplied "our ancestors" for clarity in translation; Tlingit has "them."

83. There is no way they can do anything for you. The speaker is expressing the feelings of inadequacy caused by death, and the survivors' inability to solve the problems of death and grief.

87a. The Frog Hat Song and Mountain Tribe's Dog Hat Song. The first song was played on a tape recorder; the second sung "live." The concept of at.óow extends to songs as well as visual art. The visual art often has songs to go with it.

88-89. This is all. This signals that the speech is over. The phrase also means "Thus it is" or "This is how it is," or "This is the way it is," and we have used that translation for line 87.

89a. K̲aakwsak'aa. David Williams: Chookaneidí; T'ak̲deintaan yádi. Biological maternal nephew of Willie and Jim Marks, and one of the hosts. The name was inherited from his maternal uncle, John Marks, brother of Jim and Willie Marks.

Notes to the Speech by William Johnson

William Johnson's delivery is very rapid. The tape is clear, except for lines 16-19, where he speaks rapidly and the responses of the hosts overlap his lines. Although we have arranged the responses sequentially, many are simultaneous in the actual performance.

1. This is for what flowed from your faces. Reference is to the tears of grief flowing on the faces of Keet Yaanaayí and his co-hosts.

2-4. My grandfather's children, my brothers-in-law, my fathers, my father's sisters. Again, terms of respect and kinship are used in addressing the hosts of the opposite moiety. Protocol requires that the relationship of the speaker to the hosts be established. The speaker is also establishing his relationship to the at.óow that have been brought out and will be described by Jessie Dalton. Following David Kadashan, the main function of this short speech by William Johnson is to reconfirm the shared grief and to introduce Jessie Dalton, who will deliver the central speech for the guests.

5. This is them here. Reference is to the guests who are younger T'ak̲deintaan or grandchildren of T'ak̲deintaan who are standing robed in their at.óow for Naa Tláa to speak about in the following speech. These are the guests standing for the tears of the hosts, the image with which William opened his speech.

6-8. What a heavy burden . . . to speak. Reference is to the difficulty of speaking to people in grief.

9. When a person might say. The "person" would usually be a maternal uncle.

10. You are like a man to me, sister. The speaker is addressing Naa Tláa, Jessie Dalton, who is his clan sister. Both are T'ak̲deintaan. Jessie Dalton will be delivering the central speech to the hosts on behalf of the guests. His comment is prompted because such oratory in the past was more commonly done by a man. Here and in following lines, the speaker is expressing his and Jessie's fellow clanspeople's absolute support of and confidence in her and her abilities as an orator.

11. My sister is like that. The speaker's clan sister, Naa Tláa, is like one of his maternal uncles.

12. She will complete this. The stage is now set for Naa Tláa to complete the efforts of the guests by delivering the central and culminating speech.

15. Have courage, sister. He is giving her encouragement for the difficult task ahead.

15a. Jessie Dalton replies that "it will be done."

16. You will explain your grandfathers for them. William Johnson is asking Jessie Dalton to explain the T'ak̲deintaan at.óow of their ancestors to the grieving hosts.

18. They're standing there. Reference is to the grandchildren of T'ak̲deintaan standing, waiting for Jessie to begin explaining the T'ak̲deintaan at.óow to the hosts. Most of those standing are T'ak̲deintaan; some are Lukaax̲.ádi, and some L'uknax̲.ádi.

18-19. From among them one is missing now. The missing one is Weihá (Jim Fox), one of the T'ak̲deintaan grandchildren who was to have been among those standing, but who died before the memorial. He was former owner of the Raven Who Went Down Along the Bull Kelp Shirt and also a very good friend of Jim Marks. See also the text and notes to lines 83-85 of Jessie Dalton's speech. The Tlingit verb is interesting and loses much in translation; more literally, it means "one has staggered away," having been dealt a staggering blow, namely death, which impacts both the hosts and the guests.

20-21. Your children, your brother's children. Addressing the hosts and referring to the guests, William again reconfirms the relationships between host and guest. To the extent that the guests standing are children of Chookaneidí, they are tribally the children and paternal nieces and nephews of the hosts. More generally, all the Ravens standing are children of Eagle men. Jessie's own, and her sisters' children are also Raven; but her brothers' children follow their mothers' lines (the lines of the brothers' wives) and are Eagle.

Notes to the Speech by Jessie Dalton

Jessie Dalton delivered her speech in the strong, loud, and powerful voice of a traditional Tlingit orator. One of our earliest drafts was typed entirely in capital letters in a graphic attempt to express this remarkable quality of voice. The setting of her speech has been established by those who spoke before. Many of her fellow guests were asked to stand by David Kadashan, and they are still standing when Jessie begins. She will now elaborate on the at.óow they are wearing.

1. Does death take pity on us? Jessie opens her speech with a rhetorical question. In the Tlingit text, "death" is not explicitly mentioned, but is implied. The Tlingit is literally "does it take pity on us," in which the "it" is death. We have translated more freely here. This is a personification of death. She asks if death takes pity on us. She answers her question in line 5: "It doesn't take pity on us either." Her speech is to remove grief and somehow come to grips with the impact of death.

2. My brothers' children. She is addressing her paternal nephews and nieces. These would be of the opposite moiety, i.e. Eagle, following their mothers' lines and not the line of their Raven fathers.

3. My fathers. She is addressing the men of the Wooshkeetaan, her father's clan.

4. All my fathers. She is addressing all men who are of the Eagle moiety that is hosting. The Eagle hosts include Chookaneidí (principal hosts), Wooshkeetaan, Kaagwaantaan, and Shangukeidí.

6. This thing that happens. Again, the reference is to death.

7. Why you hear their voices like this. Reference is to the tape recording played earlier by David Kadashan in conjunction with his speech. The recording was of the voices of the T'a<u>k</u>deintaan singing the Mountain Tribe Dog Song.

8. Your fathers. This line is directed to the children of T'a<u>k</u>deintaan, who are Jessie's paternal nephews and nieces. These would be men and women of the hosting Eagle clans, whose mothers would have been Eagles, but whose fathers would have been Raven of the T'a<u>k</u>deintaan. More generically, she is addressing all the Eagle hosts, whose fathers are Ravens.

9. Tears . . . without honor. Reference is to the traditional period of mourning, and the taboo of mourning beyond that. The relatives of the deceased mourn for approximately one year, until someone does the ritual for the purging of grief—the ceremonial at hand.

9a-9b. On the tape, lines 9a and 9b overlap with 10.

10. That which flowed from your faces. Reference is to the tears shed during the cry by the hosts.

12. They have all come out at this moment. Two things are happening in this line: the speaker is referring to the living clan

members present who are wearing at.óow; and not only are the living T'a<u>k</u>deintaan assembled for the tears of the hosts, but the T'a<u>k</u>deintaan spirits are gathered as well. Physically, there is a group of guests wearing at.óow, and the orator will now speak on each piece in turn, poetically transforming it.

13-14. Your fathers have all come out. Jessie is speaking metaphorically now, as well as in the literal sense of clan relationships. The clan regalia, called at.óow in Tlingit, are physically present in the room; the at.óow have been brought out and are worn by the T'a<u>k</u>deintaan grandchildren. The departed fathers of the hosts are made spiritually present.

14a. Hó hó. This is another untranslatable response, emphasizing enthusiastic gratitude. This is the only occurrence of the sound ó in Tlingit. The word also commonly appears in the phrase "Gunalchéesh, hó, hó."

15. They are still present. The deceased relatives are thought of as still present through the at.óow.

16-17. That is how I feel about my grandparents. Reference is to the feeling about Tlingit at.óow, and how it is regarded as the grandparent because it was once owned and worn by the grandparent. Some of the at.óow were carved by the host Willie Marks, his deceased brother Jim Marks, and their nephew David Williams as tribal commissions by the opposite moiety.

18. Here someone stands wearing one. This is a refrain running throughout Jessie Dalton's speech, and refers to the grandchildren wearing the at.óow. She will refer to them one by one through the rest of her speech.

19. Mountain Tribe's Dog. This is a carved hat, the image of a dog, a very important piece of T'a<u>k</u>deintaan tribal art, and a very significant at.óow. It is the image of one of the T'a<u>k</u>deintaan yéik or spirits that appeared to Shkík, an í<u>x</u>t'. The original hat was lost in the Hoonah fire of 1944. Jim and Willie Marks were commissioned to carve the replica or replacement. (It is Tlingit tradition to commission artists of the opposite moiety to make clan regalia.)

20-21. It is just as if it's barking for your pain. The bark is the song of the hat, played by David Kadashan. This is the first of many poetic comparisons Jessie will use. In this simile, the Mountain Tribe's Dog Hat embodies the spirit of a real dog acting in an appropriate way in response to the grief of the hosts. The at.óow of the guests "speak" to the hosts. Through this visual display of at.óow in action, the spirit depicted is recalled.

22. My fathers, my brothers' children. As in the opening lines, a refrain showing both respect and her relationship to the hosts. She refers to her father's people, the Wooshkeetaan, and to her paternal nephews and nieces of various Eagle clans who are the children of T'a<u>k</u>deintaan.

23. My father's sisters. Jessie is addressing the women of the Wooshkeetaan clan, her paternal aunts. Jessie Dalton's speech shows the importance of knowing one's own genealogy, the genealogies of other persons involved, the meaning of tribal art, and the relationship of the tribal art to genealogy—and the art of tying it all together through the protocol and rhetorical devices of public speaking.

26. Someone standing next to it. The "it" is the at.óow she described earlier. Now she is moving on to the next. Using this refrain for each transition, she lets her audience know that she is talking about the people standing with the T'a<u>k</u>deintaan at.óow. On the tape, there is a pause between lines 26 and 27, during which the orator moves or turns to the next person before continuing her speech.

27. Raven Who Went Down Along the Bull Kelp. In Tlingit, Geesh Daa<u>x</u> Woogoodi Yéil. Reference is to a shirt one of the T'a<u>k</u>deintaan is wearing, formerly owned by Weihá, Jim Fox. The motif is taken from an episode in the Raven cycle in which Raven went down along the bull kelp to obtain a sea urchin to bounce on the Tide Lady's hind end, to make her get off the spot which controls the sea. As long as she stays in one place, the sea doesn't move. If she gets off, the tide will go out. Raven bounces the spiney sea urchin on her butt, forcing her to move, thereby giving tide to the people. Use of this shirt is a good example of the connection between visual art, verbal art, ceremony, and the kinship system. Tribal art is worn or brought out by certain people at certain times; the art usually quotes, commemorates, or otherwise alludes to songs, stories, or history. All of this is happening here, and in turn provides the basis for another generation of verbal art—the speech composed and delivered by Jessie Dalton. See also the notes to lines 82-84, on the shirt of Weihá.

29. Lyeedayéik's robe. Continuing down the line of persons wearing at.óow, the speaker comes to this one. Lyeedayéik (her

English name Eliza Lawrence) was a woman of the T'akdeintaan. When she died, a relative inherited the robe. Again, Jessie is making the deceased spiritually present through the presentation of her former regalia.

31a. Naawéiyaa. Harry Marvin: Kaagwaantaan; T'akdeintaan yádi. He is thanking the speaker, because he is T'akdeintaan yádi—child of T'akdeintaan.

31b. S'eilshéix. Eva Davis: Chookaneidí; Lukaax.ádi yádi, sister of Mary Johnson and wife of George Davis. She is responding to the speaker's reference to the Beaver Robe (which Jessie has indicated but not yet named) because of her connection to Chilkat and Lutákl.

32-34. Beaver Blanket. Reference is to the Beaver Robe from Klukwan.

35-36. Lutákl your father. Again, a deceased former owner or custodian of tribal regalia is made present through the at.óow. His English name was Jim Lee, a T'akdeintaan man of Hoonah, Kaagwaantaan yádi, from Raven Nest House, who lived in Klukwan. Four people respond to the orator, of whom three are identifiable on the tape recording. Two have a special relationship to Lutákl, who was T'akdeintaan and Shangukeidí yádi (child of Shangukeidí). These are Naawéiyaa (Harry Marvin: Kaagwaantaan; T'akdeintaan yádi) and Séi Akdulxéitl' (David McKinley: Wooshkeetaan; T'akdeintaan yádi; from Head House). The voice of Willie Marks is also identifiable in response here.

44. Your fathers' sisters (or paternal aunts). The orator is addressing the Raven moiety, referring to the Eagle women, presenting now the Tern Robe according to the owner's genealogical relationship to the hosts.

46. Saayina.aat. Irene (Mrs. Jim) Young: T'akdeintaan; Chookaneidí yádi. Biological mother of William Johnson and clan mother of Jessie Dalton.

48. The Tern Robe. Jessie is now introducing the Tern Robe, on which she will build one of the most beautiful, intricate and powerful metaphors of her speech. The following lines begin the metaphor, after which she will move to other at.óow, and then return to the Tern Robe later in her speech.

54. Gaanaxáa. This is the beginning of an extended metaphor by which the next several people are brought to the peninsula or point of land, where their names are called out.

G̲aanax̲áa is a point near Lituya Bay. It is also a tern rookery. The speaker will now continue, calling out the names of the hosts who are in grief, transporting them metaphorically to G̲aanax̲áa, the spiritual homeland of the T'ak̲deintaan. At the same time, through the blanket, G̲aanax̲áa is literally and figuratively present and brought into the room where the people are standing.

59. Father, Séi Akdulx̲éitl'. David McKinley: Wooshkeetaan; T'ak̲deintaan yádi. Because Jessie Dalton is child of Wooshkeetaan (Wooshkeetaan yádi), according to protocol, she can address him as "father." Metaphorically she is calling him to G̲aanax̲áa, where later she will call the terns to fly out over him for the removal of grief. See also the text and note to David Kadashan, line 10, where David McKinley is addressed by a different name (Yakwdeiyí G̲uwakaan). It is common in Tlingit culture for people to acquire names throughout their lives; therefore, it is not unusual for a person to be referred to by various names.

61-62. My grandfather's son Koowunagáas'. Joe White: Shangukeidí; T'ak̲deintaan yádi. Koowunagáas' was also like a maternal uncle to Keet Yaanaayí because his mother and Koowunagáas' were considered brother and sister because the fathers of both were from Tax̲' Hít (Snail House). See also the note to David Kadashan, line 13. On the tape, yéet of line 61 is phonetically wéet.

63-64. My brother's daughter's son Keet Yaanaayí. Willie Marks, brother of the deceased and host of the memorial. Keet Yaanaayí's mother, Eliza Marks, was a child of T'ak̲deintaan, a child of one of the speaker's clan brothers. The mother of Keet Yaanaayí was a paternal niece of Jessie Dalton.

66-67. My father's sister's son X̲oox̲keina.át. Pete Johnson: Wooshkeetaan. Jessie Dalton's father was also Wooshkeetaan. X̲oox̲keina.át was also adopted as a brother into the Chookaneidí clan by Goox̲ G̲uwakaan (Jim Marks).

70. Your fathers' sisters are revealing their faces. This line is directed to the Eagles, the children of T'ak̲deintaan and Lukaax̲.ádi. The fathers' sisters (their paternal aunts) are T'ak̲deintaan women whose crest is the tern (sometimes also called Sea Pigeon or Sea Gull). Metaphorically, the fathers' sisters (or paternal aunts) become the terns, and are revealing their faces at the rookery to which the mourners have been

called by the speaker. G̲aanax̲áa is the tern rookery where the terns would sit on the cliffs.

72. K̲aatooshtóow. John F. Wilson: Chookaneidí; T'ak̲deintaan yádi. He is also one of the survivors of the people who are the original people of Kaasteen (of Glacier Bay—see *Haa Shuká* for more on this). He is a paternal grandchild of Chookaneidí.

73. K̲aakwsak'aa. David Williams: Chookaneidí; T'ak̲deintaan yádi. Maternal nephew of Goox̲ G̲uwakaan. His father was T'ak̲deintaan of the Raven Nest House (Yéil Kudei Hít).

75. My brother's wife Aan Káx̲shawustaan. Mary Johnson: Chookaneidí; Lukaax̲.ádi yádi. She is a maternal niece of Goox̲ G̲uwakaan and married to William Johnson, a clan brother of Jessie Dalton, and the orator who spoke just before Jessie.

78. As if they are revealing their faces. The G̲aanax̲áa extended metaphor ends here with a simile, in which terns (metaphorically the paternal aunts at the rookery) are imagined as revealing their faces.

79. Your sisters-in-law. This line is addressed to Aan Káx̲shawustaan (Mary Johnson) and her sisters.

82. Shirt of Weihá. Reference is to the Raven Who Went Down Along the Kelp Shirt. (See Note to line 27.) Weihá: Jim Fox; G̲aanax̲.ádi from Taku; Yanyeidí yádi.

83-85. It was only recently we completed the rites for him. The rites for Weihá are also mentioned by William Johnson in his speech, lines 18-19.

88. You heard him also here. Reference is to the Frog Hat Song that was played earlier on a tape recorder by David Kadashan.

90. This brother of mine. Weihá is in the English language sense Jessie Dalton's cousin, but in the Tlingit sense her brother because both are Raven. Their fathers are of the Wooshketaan and Yanyeidí.

91. This Peacemaker of yours. Reference is to William Johnson (Keewaax̲.awtseix̲ G̲uwakaan; T'ak̲deintaan; Wooshkeetaan yádi) one of Jessie's fellow orators and who is Kaagwaantaan's peacemaker.

92-93. This shirt of Weihá will remain in his hands, in his care. The shirt of Weihá went to the care of William Johnson.

94. It is as if he is coming out for you to see. Again, a simile comparing the regalia to the deceased owner or custodian. Each time the shirt comes out it will be as if Weihá is coming out.

96-98. How proud he used to be wearing it. Weihá felt proud when he wore the shirt.

100. The Raven Nest House Robe. There was a T'akdeintaan clan house in Hoonah named Raven Nest House (Yéil Kudei Hít) which was destroyed along with all the other clan houses in the Hoonah fire of 1944. The robe (a button blanket) was made to commemorate the house.

103. Yaakaayindul.át your father's sister. Metaphorically referring to the deceased owner of the Robe. Through the blanket Yaakaayindul.át is present. This robe is one of the older ones and does not have a motif on it; it has only buttons and felt. Yaakaayindul.át was a woman of the T'akdeintaan; she was Jessie Dalton's maternal aunt and Bertina Peterson's great-grandmother; Bertina Peterson, mother of the late Evalee Azar, also has this name.

105. We had long since given up hope of their return. The former owners of all the T'akdeintaan at.óow are deceased, but are still referred to as being present and merged with the at.óow. The line can be understood to have two meanings. Literally, they are dead and will not return; figuratively, they are suddenly back, even though people had given up hope of their return.

107a, 107b. Again, these simultaneous responses are put on paper at the end of the phrase.

110-112. Your father, Kaadéik, it's his shirt. The speaker is addressing Kaadéik (George Dalton), a man of the Kaagwaantaan, reaffirming that it is his father's shirt. Kaadéik, George Dalton, is the orator's husband, whom she addresses here by a different name than the one used by other orators.

114. I don't feel that it burned. The original shirt of Kaadéik was in fact destroyed in the 1944 fire. Along with many other at.óow, it was replaced by a newer duplicate, but the orator expresses her belief that the replica has the same force as the original.

116. It is the same one in which your father's brother (i.e. paternal uncle) is standing there in front of you. Kaadéik's father is merged with his shirt.

119. Gusatáan. Another name for Naawéiyaa. Harry Marvin: Kaagwaantaan; T'akdeintaan yádi; Chookaneidí dachxán (grandchild of Chookaneidí). One of the host group.

120. It will be just as if I will have named all of you. She is naming both the grieving Eagle hosts present and the departed T'akdeintaan who are former stewards of the at.óow. The speaker has been relating persons of the guest and the host groups to each other. Here she expresses that she will be unable to name all the living and deceased individually, but this gesture is as if she had named them all.

123-126. Can I reach the end? After a slight pause, she says this because there are too many of her deceased to recall them all.

127. These terns I haven't completely explained. The speaker is now leading up to her final images of the terns, returning to and completing the image she called up earlier.

129-140. These terns. Your fathers' sisters would fly out over the person who is feeling grief . . . etc. A metaphor within an extended simile, this is one of the most striking images of the speech. The terns are identified with women of the opposite moiety, and with the spirits of the T'akdeintaan paternal aunts of the hosts who are feeling grief. The terns would fly out over the person who is feeling grief, and let their down shower like snow over him or her. The down is soothing; it is not felt. The extended simile concludes with the speaker saying that she feels as if the terns are removing the grief by absorbing it into their down and flying back to their nests with it.

136a. There is a response on the tape here, the beginning of which is too obscure to transcribe. It ends with the phrase "i kaani yán, "your in-laws."

142-155. Here . . . Frog Hat . . . from Taku. The speaker presents and gives a history of the Frog Hat, showing one way an item is acquired and becomes at.óow.

157. I keep saying thank you. Jessie is thanking the hosts for letting them bring out their ancestors' at.óow, for the opportunity to display their at.óow in ceremonial context.

160-171. During the warm season . . . burrow down. In another metaphor and simile, the Frog Hat is described as a real frog, and its deceased owner is made present. Both are identified as a man of the opposite moiety and father of the hosts, who as former owner of the hat, comes out in response to the grief. The spirit of the departed appearing in the human world is compared to a frog coming out of hibernation in the spring. It removes the grief from the mourners, and burrows back down with it.

168-169. There are some false starts, rare in Jessie's delivery, in this passage.

178. It is like the saying. The following phrase is a Tlingit saying, and the speaker is reiterating two themes: the group is ritually imitating their ancestors, and the purpose is that the spirits do not go unanswered.

179. Lest they grope aimlessly. Lest the Xwaayeenáḵ song and other songs of the hosts resonate without response; lest the words of the grandfathers resonate without response. The verb in Tlingit is singular, but we have translated it as plural to avoid the gender distinction (he-she-it) required by English but not conveyed in Tlingit. Also, the sense of the line is plural. "They" refers to the spirits in general, but especially of Xwaayeenáḵ and Ḵ'aadóo. Jessie refers here to responding to the spirits, as discussed in the introduction and notes to the third set of speeches in this book. It is very important in the Tlingit system of balance and reciprocity that words and songs be answered. The guests' speeches here are delivered in response to the mourning songs of the hosts. (See also the notes to the next sequence of speeches in this book, where the orators make this concern even more explicit than Jessie does here.) Also, myth and ritual provide models for human behavior. Without them, people also grope aimlessly.

180. The way your grandparents said. The particular grandparent referred to here is Ḵ'aadóo, the composer of the Xwaayeenáḵ song in Goox̱ G̱uwakaan's explanation played posthumously by the hosts.

182-183. It's as if your fathers are guiding them. As if Keet Yaanaayí's ancestors are leading the at.óow, the oratory, and songs.

187-188. The hat of Yooḵis'kooḵéik, this grandfather of mine. This is the beginning of the metaphor based on the Loon Hat. Yooḵis'kooḵéik (Leonard Davis: T'aḵdeintaan; Kaagwaantaan yádi) was a custodian of a model of Táx̱' Hít (Snail House). The custom is that members of the same house group will refer to an older generation of the group as a grandparent generation. This is why Jessie Dalton calls him grandfather. Yooḵis'kooḵéik was the biological father of

Koowunagáas' (Joe White: Shangukeidí; T'a<u>k</u>deintaan yádi), and the speaker is now establishing this relationship to him. Joe White's father was the custodian of Tá<u>x</u>' Hít that burned in 1944.

196. The Loon Spirit. A spirit helper that appeared to a shaman (í<u>x</u>t'). In a previous line, the speaker says that the spirit "has stood up to face you." In some narratives the spirit will stand up in the path of a candidate. The spirit stands up before him (or her) before it enters to give strength and assistance. The orator speaks about the at.óow giving healing spiritual powers to the hosts in grief.

198-200. Here is the one this brother of mine explained awhile ago. Reference is to the log and sun images in David Kadashan's speech.

201-203. How that tree rolled on the waves. This is a metaphor that works two ways. The uprooted tree is compared both to the grieving survivors as well as to the deceased. The deceased are looked at as someone carried by a storm. This is an especially appropriate comparison because the body of Xwaayeená<u>k</u> was never found. The survivors are also thought of as someone who has lost his or her homeland, someone who has also been uprooted. In Tlingit, the bottom of a tree, where it anchors to the ground, is also called "ancestors." Jessie Dalton recapitulates the essence of David's final comparison: the sun would put its rays on it, and would dry its grief to the core. The Tlingit verb in 203 is interesting. Where the English has a metaphor of sun beams, the Tlingit stem -tsoow means "to place something upright" also "poke into." The nominal prefix <u>x</u>'us refers to feet. Literally, the sun puts its feet on it.

207. At this moment this sun is coming out over you, my grandparents' mask. Jessie has been leading up to the presentation of the Sun Mask. The sun that is drying the grief is again the at.óow. The Sun Mask belonged to <u>K</u>aajeesdu.een (no English name), then to Kichxit'aa of the Head House (<u>K</u>aa Shaayi Hít) also before the time of English names. It then passed to <u>K</u>aa<u>k</u>w Daa Éesh, the father of Joe White. From then it passed to S'e<u>k</u>yatóow (Frank Wilson). It then passed to Shaa<u>k</u>wlayéi<u>x</u> (Leonard Davis). (Like many Tlingits, Leonard Davis has many ceremonial names.) The mask is now in the care of Katherine Mills' son, George Mills, also named <u>K</u>aa<u>k</u>w Daa Éesh.

210-211. My hope is that your grief be like it's drying to your core. This is the line Jessie has been leading up to. This is the line that extracts the sorrow. This is the way Tlingit people traditionally cope with death. This gives a person the feeling that he or she is not alone at times of loss or grief.

212. G̱éelák'w Headdress. An ermine headdress made in the image of the frontal screen of Tsalx̱aan Hít (Mt. Fairweather House), better known as Táx̱' Hít (Snail House). See the following note for more detail.

214-216. Your father's sisters would reveal their faces from it, from G̱éelák'w. This passage is a metaphor of how the spirits of Mt. Fairweather, who are women, would appear and come to a shaman to heal those who are ill.

G̱éelák'w is another name for Tsalx̱aan, Mt. Fairweather. Specifically, the name G̱éelák'w is an image of the part of the mountain where it separates into two peaks. While the name G̱éelák'w refers specifically to the "V" made by the two peaks, the name is also generally synonymous with Tsalx̱aan in referring to Mt. Fairweather as a whole. G̱éelák'w is the part of the mountain where Goox̱k', the little boy who became a one horned goat climbed, taking all the animals with him. The One Horned Goat transformed into a powerful spirit for the T'ak̲deintaan shaman and is an at.óow of the T'ak̲deintaan. A retelling of this story is included in Samuel's *The Chilkat Dancing Blanket* (1982:50-51) and a version by David Kadashan will be featured in a forthcoming volume in this series.

There was a frontal screen on the Tsalx̱áan Hít (Mt. Fairweather House) in Hoonah. The base of the screen rested on the floor of the porch, and the top reached above the second story windows. The screen was about two feet wider on each side than the door. There was a hole in the bottom center of the screen for the entrance to the house. The G̱éelák'w headdress (dance frontlet) is made in the image of the frontal screen for the house. As the headdress is displayed, the spirits are metaphorically made present. Mt. Fairweather is a powerful spiritual ground and is one of the important at.óow for the T'ak̲deintaan.

There is also another at.óow, a hat, representing these same spirits of Mt. Fairweather. Metaphorically the women spirits of the Mountain, who are also among the shaman spirits, are carved into Tsalx̱áantu Sháawu (The Mt. Fairweather Hat) carved by

Willie Marks. On this hat, a woman appears from the crown. Tsalx̱aantu Sháawu S'áaxw, the Mt. Fairweather hat, was James Grant's, then John K. Smith's, then passed to Leonard Davis, then Matthew Lawrence, and is now in the care of Richard Sheakley. It is possible that Jessie Dalton at this point is alluding to the hat as well, although she mentions only the dance frontlet specifically.

220. My grandfather's headdress. Jessie ends her speech with the image of the G̱éelák'w headdress, and the women coming out on Keet Yaanaayí, the hosts, and the guests. This headdress was Frank Wilson's, and was held, not worn, during the memorial. Jessie ends her speech with the image of Mt. Fairweather and the spiritual power residing there. Willie Marks thanks her.

Notes to the Speech by Austin Hammond

2. My father's brothers. This could also be translated, with a more technical tone, as "my paternal uncles." Austin is laying the foundation of his speech. He is the stepson of Goox̱ G̱uwakaan—Jim Marks—in whose memory the ceremonial is being held. In Tlingit tradition, there is no difference between an adopted child and a biological child, and the kinship terms are the same. Here the speaker is addressing Keet Yaanayí—Willie Marks—and other men of the Eagle moiety. "My father's sisters" could also be translated as "my paternal aunts." Here he is addressing the women of Chookaneidí, and all the Eagle women. Austin is a biological child of Kaagwaantaan and also child of Chookaneidí.

4-5. How very much I, too, feel grief. Austin is expressing the sharing of grief for his father, the brother of the hosts. He is also speaking on behalf of the Lukaax̱.ádi clan, the parent clan of Jim Marks, as Jessie Dalton spoke on behalf of the T'ak̲deintaan.

6-7. That being here, I haven't even got anything to show you. Reference here is to clan at.óow. The speaker is powerfully expressing his sense of utter helplessness in the face of grief. Also, in the overall dramatic structure of the sequence of speeches, Austin begins the winding down of the speeches. In contrast to the dazzling array of T'ak̲deintaan at.óow in Jessie's speech, Austin will focus on fewer pieces of art. But for now, rhetorically and dramatically, he is looking in vain for a single at.óow with which to support the hosts, his father's people. He will return to the theme of regalia at the close of his speech, where he will rhetorically depreciate a magnificent Chilkat weaving, implying that it is nothing in contrast to the grief and loss the host clan is feeling, but he hopes that it will act in some small way to remove the grief.

8-10. At this moment he came out . . . with it. At the moment when the orator was feeling this helplessness, someone, a grandchild of Lukaax̲.ádi, came out with a woven robe.

11-12. In many ways . . . K'eedzáa used to speak. K'eedzáa was a man of the Lukaax̲.ádi, the father's clan of Jim and Willie Marks, and the clan of their wives, Jennie and Emma Marks; his English name was Alfred Andrews. In the past, when one of Keet Yaanaayí's relatives died, K'eedzáa used to speak to them with words of comfort. But K'eedzáa, Austin's maternal uncle, and also Goox̲ G̲uwakaan's paternal uncle, is now deceased. The orator is emphasizing his inadequacy in comparison to the departed elders.

13. Here is his robe. . . . The robe is the Sockeye Chilkat Robe that Austin's mother, Jennie Marks, inherited at the death of K'eedzáa, and which Austin would eventually inherit from her. Jennie Marks, the widow of Jim Marks, was alive at the time of the memorial, and was the custodian of the robe. It was woven by Saantaas', aunt of Jennie Thlunaut.

16. In need of him. In need of K'eedzáa and his affection for his paternal relatives in this time of grief.

18. Kaatyé. David Kadashan, a grandchild of Lukaax̲.ádi, who delivered the second of the guests' speeches.

20. My mother's brother Tsagwált, his robe. This could also be translated as "maternal uncle." Tsagwált, whose English name was Jack David, was Austin Hammond's biological maternal uncle. Austin inherited the Naatúxjayi tunic from him.

22-24. These lines overlap on the tape.

23, 24. There is one thing. Austin is preparing to discuss Naatúxjayi for the grieving hosts to draw encouragement from.

27. It's not here. The Naatúxjayi at.óow was not physically present at the memorial for Austin to show to the grieving

family, so he will just explain about it. The line could also be translated "It didn't come," or "it didn't get here."

28-29. My father Keet Yaanaayí. Keet Yaanaayí, Willie Marks, is Austin's paternal uncle and clan father, and in turn Austin is a paternal uncle of Keet Yaanaayí, who is a child of Lukaax̱.ádi.

30. This brother-in-law of yours. . . . Tsagwált (Jack David) was very proud of his brother-in-law Keet Yaanaayí (Willie Marks). Keet Yaanaayí's wife (Emma Marks) is Lukaax̱.ádi, as is Austin Hammond, and as was Austin's mother, Jennie Marks. Because of flu and smallpox epidemics of the early twentieth century, most of the female line of the Haines area Lukaax̱.ádi had died out. Emma Marks was one of the few Lukaax̱.ádi women left. This verb is difficult to translate. Literally, it means "stagger," and refers to being at a loss for words, or having difficulty finding the right word. It is spoken in a positive sense here, implying that Tsagwált would be at a loss for words to express how proud he was of his in-laws.

31. Naatúxjayi. Naatúxjayi is an image of a Lukaax̱.ádi spirit woven by Jennie Thlunaut into a Chilkat tunic for her husband's clan brother, Jack David, Tsagwált. The spirit appeared as a helping spirit to the Lukaax̱.ádi shaman G̱éek'ee. See also the frontispiece and caption.

32-33. He, too, has also come here for your grief. Austin personifies the shaman spirit Naatúxjayi, whom he is rhetorically calling to the present time and place to assist in the removal of grief.

35. To remove it. The shaman spirit Naatúxjayi will remove grief in the same way that it acts through a shaman to remove illness.

37-38. That blanket . . . as . . . a towel. . . . This is a simile to remove Keet Yaanaayí's grief. It is as if the blanket becomes a hand towel, to wipe away the tears. The term x'óow is somewhat unclear here; literally, it refers to a blanket, and strictly speaking, Naatúxjayi is a tunic, and not a blanket. We assume that Austin is speaking generically here, and is referring not to the Sockeye Blanket which was present, but to the tunic which was not present. After considerable thought and discussion, we finally reinstated "to wipe away your tears" in the English translation. This phrase was present in the earliest drafts from the early 1970's, but was deleted as being too free a translation. This is certainly Austin's intention here; the thought is implied in the Tlingit, but not stated in words.

39. This is how I feel too. The speaker is expressing his grief for his father and sympathy and sharing of grief with his father's brother and his paternal aunts.

Notes to Matthew Lawrence (2)

Matthew's voice is soft, and his delivery rapid.

3. My fathers. The speaker is again addressing and thanking the Chookaneidí hosts. The speaker is a child of Chookaneidí. In this short speech, the man who opened the set of oratory by the guests now brings it to a close. Where his first speech functioned primarily to request the floor, now, in this brief but eloquent closing speech, he will combine many themes and bring final resolution to the oratory for the removal of grief.

4. My brothers-in-law. A general term for men of the opposite moiety. The speaker, a T'a<u>k</u>deintaan and child of Chookaneidí, is addressing those among the hosts who are married to women of the T'a<u>k</u>deintaan and other Raven clans.

9. This mother of ours has completed everything. Reference to Naa Tláa, Jessie Dalton, the "Clan Mother" of the T'a<u>k</u>deintaan, who delivered the primary speech on behalf of the T'a<u>k</u>deintaan.

13-14. It is as if she is standing for us. A simile which describes her position and refers to her ability at speech making.

16,17. This thing we have been holding, this hat. The speaker is referring to the hat named "The Mountain Tribe's Dog Hat"—Shaatu<u>k</u>waan Keidlí S'áaxw.

18-25. It will go with your grief, etc. This dog will go with your grief. In the metaphor of the Mountain Tribe's Dog Hat, the speaker capsulizes the final removal of grief. The spirits associated with the hat will return to Mt. Fairweather with the grief of all the hosts. The hat is spoken of as if it were alive; rhetorically and spiritually it becomes the live dog, appearing for the removal of grief, and returning with the grief and tears of the Chookaneidí clan and the other Eagle co-hosts to the mountain which is the spiritual homeland of the T'a<u>k</u>deintaan.

The final line, "into your fathers' mountain," completes the spiritual purging of grief, confirms the social relationships, brings comfort to the hosts, and resolution to the set of speeches.

24a, 25a. Thank you. That's right. These final responses by the hosts thank the speaker and all the speakers, and reconfirm the ritual purging and removal of grief.

Notes to Charlie Joseph (1)

On May 29, 1980, Sealaska Corporation sponsored its first elders conference, with the theme "Sealaska Elders Speak to the Future." The conference was held at Shee Atika Lodge in Sitka, and as a welcoming gesture, the G̱ajaa Héen Dancers of the Sitka Native Education Program gave a performance of Tlingit singing and dancing following the banquet.

Charlie Joseph, K̲aal.átk', the teacher and leader of the group, introduced and narrated his students' program in a very powerful and dignified manner. He elaborated on the clan ownership of the songs, the villages where they were composed, and the composers' relationships to the students and the audience.

One of the moving statements Charlie made was how "even from long ago we cherish our grandchildren; no matter what we value, we offer it up to them." He was honoring this tradition in practice in his teaching of the youth group, and in explaining the grandchildren's rights to use a grandparent's song or "the things they used to say." He added to these traditions a new precedent by including yéik (shaman spirit) songs in the program. Ordinarily they would only be sung on solemn occasions such as during a memorial for the deceased.

For Charlie, all of this involved a certain amount of risk. The concept of a group of young people of various clans joining together to learn and sing songs of different clans was relatively new, and Charlie did not know how this presentation would be received by his peers in the elder generation. There was also risk on the spiritual plane, which the elders soon addressed.

Following the last song, the elders in the audience joined in his presentation, and became part of it through their response as only the protocol of the Tlingit and Haida cultures can provide. The elders expressed their joy at hearing the old songs. Some expressed surprise at hearing songs they never expected to hear again, because they hadn't been sung since the death of the older generation. For some elders, it was as if their departed ancestors were again made present through the young people dancing. But the elders were also gravely concerned for the youth that were singing the yéik songs because these songs are the most sensitive and must be treated accordingly. Such spirit songs need to be "balanced" with spirits from the opposite moiety.

The elders began to treat the songs with their own songs, spirits, and words to ensure the safety of every one of the dancers and all participants of the conference, that they would be cleansed of any unattended spirit powers lingering in the air. They cleansed by way of oratory.

George Davis acted as master of ceremonies for the guests, and introduced the speakers as they took their turns, some speaking in English, but most in Tlingit. The following persons made speeches, and are listed here in alphabetical order, along with their Tlingit or Haida names.

John Bell	Aank'ix̲oo Éesh
Isabella Brady	Yeidikuk'aa
George Davis	Kichnáalx̲
Eli Hanlon	Yuwáak'w
Paul Henry	Kawóotk'
Charlie Jim	Tóok'
George Jim	Keik̲óok'w
Annie Joseph	Aanáanáx̲ Tláa
Charlie Joseph	K̲aal.átk'
A.P. Johnson	Ix̲t'ik' Éesh
William Johnson	Keewaax̲.awtseix̲ G̲uwakaan
George Lewis	Sa.áat'
Ethel Makinen	Daasdiyáa
Clara Natkong	T'aawl.ilt'gaat
Patrick Paul	Anaxóots
Walter Soboleff	K̲aajaak̲wtí
Frank O. Williams	Xwaats

Of their twenty-one speeches published in *"Because We Cherish You..." Sealaska Elders Speak to the Future* (Dauenhauer and Dauenhauer 1981) ten have been excerpted for this book, accompanied here for the first time by a complete set of cultural annotations. The English translations have been substantially revised in places, reflecting in part our increased understanding of the speeches gained in working with the texts over nine more years. For the complete set of speeches, see *"Because We Cherish You."* All of these speeches were delivered on May 29, 1980, and were recorded on audio tape by students of the Sitka Native Education Program, who made copies available to Nora Marks Dauenhauer, who transcribed and translated the speeches, and wrote the annotations.

We also thank the orators themselves for their help. Charlie Joseph assisted Nora Marks Dauenhauer, who read the transcription of his speech to him. Charlie supplied commentary on many names, and background on some unclear passages. George Jim and Charlie Jim also assisted in explaining references in their speeches. Unfortunately, some textual problems came to our awareness only after the deaths of Charlie Joseph and Charlie Jim, and some points that might have otherwise been clarified remain unclear.

Charlie Joseph, K̲aal.átk', was for about a decade from the mid 1970's to the mid 1980's the dance and song instructor for the Sitka Native Education Program, physically located in the Alaska Native Brotherhood Hall in Sitka. Young people of all ages came, and continue to come, weekdays after school and on weekends to be involved with Tlingit culture. The focus was primarily on singing and dancing, and the dance group, called G̲ajaa Héen Dancers, has won national recognition and has travelled widely.

Charlie was Kaagwaantaan (Eagle moiety) of the Box House (K̲ook Hít Taan) and a child of L'uknax̲.ádi (his father was L'uknax̲.ádi, X'at'ka.aayí of Sitka).

1-3. Charlie Joseph opens his speech announcing his intent to speak in Tlingit, his Native language, and "not in another language" (or, in no other language) i.e. English. He follows with an apology to those who might not understand. The audience was primarily of Tlingit elders, but included many younger Tlingits and persons of Tlingit ancestry who do not speak or understand the language. Also present were a number of non-Native guests, and Tsimshian and Haida elders, whose cultures are in many ways similar to Tlingit, but whose languages are different. He prefers to speak in Tlingit not only because his command of Tlingit is greater than his command of English, but because many of the concepts he and the other elders will be expressing are not found in European-American social systems and are therefore difficult to express in English.

4. These grandchildren of mine. Charlie Joseph refers to the G̱ajaa Héen Dancers as his grandchildren not only as a term of affection, but because the group includes members of many clans from different localities who are, according to Tlingit social structure (popularly called the "clan system,") his clan grandchildren.

5. Will come in here for you to see. Charlie Joseph is introducing the dancers, who are about to enter the room and perform for the elders.

7-10. They will use this song . . . Kwáal. Charlie Joseph is now introducing the composer and origin of the song the group will perform as they enter. The verb "use" is significant in Tlingit because songs are considered property and are not just casually sung, especially in public. Care is given to indentify the composer and how he or she is related, thus establishing the right to sing or "use" the song.

11. Their grandfather. Here the speaker is establishing the relationship of the singers to the composer, according to the Tlingit clan system.

17. People . . . seated here. Charlie Joseph, as a host, is now addressing the dinner guests. In the following lines he asks them to be patient and forgiving of the young dancers if they don't do things correctly. "People of honor" is a traditional term of respect referring to someone who respects him or herself, and who is respected by others.

22-28. Following . . . Keitóok̲. Charlie Joseph also announces the first song they will sing following their entrance, a song composed by his maternal uncle, Keitóok̲ of Hoonah. The song originally belonged to Keitóok̲, a man of the Box House Kaagwaantaan of Hoonah. One of his other Tlingit names was Kashkéin. When Keitóok̲ died, Charlie Joseph inherited the song. In these lines, the speaker is giving an example both of the concept of clan owership of Tlingit songs, and of the laws of inheritance. It is important to note that Charlie Joseph does not simply state directly that this is his song, but acknowledges its history as his maternal uncle's song from Hoonah, thus keeping the greater sense of the ownership intact.

1-31. Tlingit future tenses. Because of the nature of Charlie Joseph's speech, which is to introduce what is going to happen next, there is a very high frequency of future forms in his speech, as demonstrated in these opening lines, in contrast to Tlingit narrative and much oratory in general, where perfective and occasional forms are most frequent. Because of the relative rarity of future forms in Tlingit texts published to date, we will comment briefly on the futures here, in hope that they will be of interest and use to students of the language. Readers not interested in Tlingit language can ignore this and similar notes on grammatical analysis.

1. x̲'akk̲watáan	I will speak
8. has agux̲layéix̲	They will do (use) them
5, 12. has gug̲wa.áat	They will come in
23. gug̲wa.áadi	(After) they (will have) have come in
14, 28. agug̲wa.áat	They will come in (on it)
30. kakg̲washée	They will sing
31. s ayagux̲saxéex	They will present them

At this point, readers should consult the charts that are part of the glossary in this book. The future is characterized by use of the irrealis, the conjugation prefix -ga-, the aspect prefix -g̲a-, and the "a" form of the classifier. Unfortunately for learners of Tlingit, the future is a good example of what linguists call morphophonemics, which means that the theoretical forms often appear in other forms. For example, the irrealis may be "w," the conjugation prefix "-ga-"may appear as -k-, and the -g̲a- may appear as -x̲-. Most of these changes are because a series of three open syllables (syllables ending with a vowel) before the verb stem is unstable. If the vowel in the second syllable is short, it often falls out. The consonants that are now next to each other change. For example, the underlying form in line 8:

a-gu-g̲a-la-yéix̲ becomes
a-gu-g̲- la-yéix̲ which becomes
a-gu-x̲- la-yéix̲.

32a, 32b. At this point, the dancers enter, and present the two songs indicated. We have not included the song texts here. Some of these songs are included in the Sitka Native Education Program video tape on Charlie Joseph entitled *K̲aal.átk* (Ostyn

1981). The sense of clan ownership of Tlingit songs is very high, and runs as a theme through Charlie Joseph's speech, in which he explains the genealogical connections which give members of the G̱ajaa Héen group the right to sing certain songs. In his speech, most of the songs are identified by composer, and the owning clans are indicated.

34-36. Lifelines . . . strand off in many directions. Charlie Joseph is speaking about kinship, and the Tlingit clan system. Traditionally, each individual has members of many clans as part of the extended family. These lines go in all directions, but Charlie Joseph is emphasizing here the variety of grandparent clans of the singers and dancers—how the ancestry of each member of the group may stem from many clans. Therefore, there are many grandparent clans present, and the dancers represent and embody many clans.

37-40. These are some of the "directions," the clans, mentioned by name. Kaagwaantaan and Chookaneidí are of the Eagle moiety; L'uknax̱.ádi and Deisheetaan are of the Raven moiety. The concepts of moiety and clan are basic to Tlingit social structure, and are well covered in the anthropological literature on Tlingit (where the term "sib" is often used, and the names may be in a technical or scientific orthography).

44-48. Combined all these songs their grandparents left (behind) for them . . . when they use (sing) them. Each individual singer has a number of ancestors, and brings their songs to the group, and the whole group joins in the singing. This makes for a very complicated pattern.

49-51. Even from long ago we placed our grandchildren high above ourselves. Charlie Joseph now works toward his main point, the time honored love and respect that Tlingit people show for their grandchildren—not only biological grandchildren, but clan grandchildren as well. He says in line 53, "We cherish them."

54-56. Things we treasure . . . offer . . . to their grandchildren. Because people cherish their grandchildren, they offer their treasures to them. In these lines, Charlie Joseph makes his main point to the assembled elders: the children in the dance group have every right to use these songs for two important reasons—because of the traditional love and generosity of the elders for their grandchildren, and because they have a genealogical right according to the Tlingit clan system.

Especially because of the generation gap created by English language schooling and European-American culture, the traditional sharing may now involve emotional risk for the grandparents. Will the children take care of the "treasures?" Will they use the power and knowledge correctly? Will the knowledge harm them? This concern is addressed by the guests, who speak after Charlie. (The motif of grandparents offering treasures to grandchildren is also common in creation myths of the Northwest coast, in which Raven "cons" his grandfather out of the sun, moon, and stars, among other things.)

This issue also requires some extra commentary. In principle, there is no problem with grandchildren inheriting from the elders. In practice, however, a serious problem has arisen in many Tlingit and other Native American communities. Increasingly, the youngest generations have been raised in the English language, and educated in public and government schools. For much of the twentieth century, Tlingit children were educated in boarding schools, where they were away from their families and communities nine or ten months a year after the seventh grade, so that very little transmission of language and traditional cultural information and values could take place. In fact, most of the values taught in school were directly and openly opposed to the continuation of Native language and culture. These generations of students, bilingual themselves, began to raise their children in English.

Therefore, many elders now lament that the children are in some sense no longer Tlingit because they do not speak the language, and do not know the culture. With the death of elders, some immediate families lost the ability to pass the information and values on. For Charlie Joseph and many other elders in a number of communities, the solution was to move from the immediate family or even clan level to the community level, and organize community dance groups made up of children from various clans. This was a new concept in the Tlingit community, and posed new problems. One problem was over rights to the songs sung by a group of people, who, on the surface, might appear to have no rights to use a song. Another problem was in passing spirit power on to people who do not completely understand it—like playing with fire or with a loaded gun. In Charlie Joseph's opening speech, and in the speeches that follow, we see the assembly of elders working out solutions.

58. We made these songs their vision. This is a difficult line, and a difficult concept. A paraphrase would be "That is why we who are the elders are passing the vision of the ancestors along to the grandchildren so that it will be their vision also." Based on our understanding of the line, we have supplied the word "songs" in English translation. As we understand it, "them" refers to the "treasures" and songs mentioned above; "their" is the grandchildren's; "vision" means the spirit helper called léikwayi in Tlingit. The spirit gives vision to a shaman. The vision is to give spiritual strength (for healing, and positive works in the community). This line is very important and pivotal in the speech, because Charlie Joseph, having established the right of the young people to share in the tradition, is now passing the power on to the youth, making the visionary spiritual songs of the older generation also the vision of the youth. He is not doing this singlehandedly, but uses the pronoun "we" (tu-) as a spokesman for his generation. This is because not all of the songs are his exclusive property, but the property of many interrelated clans, as he explained above. Also, in some cases, there is no living grandparent to pass the songs on to the younger generation. The verb is in the imperfective (or "present"), indicating that the action is somehow still going on—namely, through the teaching that Charlie Joseph and other elders have been doing. The Tlingit spelling yéx̱x̱ may look unusual, but is a combination of the stem -yéx̱ and the durative suffix -x̱, conveying a sense of repeated or habitual action carried out over a period of time. It could also mean "We are doing it repeatedly in their sight."

59. Please forgive them. The apology is characteristic of Tlingit understatement. The line is very important because Charlie Joseph is not only asking his fellow elders for their understanding and forgiveness for any technical shortcomings as may appear in the singing or dancing, but he is also asking for their cooperation in the entire concept of passing the songs on to the grandchildren. Also, Charlie realizes they are presenting the songs out of traditional context, and he asks forgiveness for doing so. Traditionally, they would be performed as part of a memorial, such as the one described for Jim Marks. Here, the dancers are perfoming as after dinner entertainment.

61, 66a. Shaawát G̱uwakaan. The name means "Woman Deer" or "Woman Peacemaker" and derives from the time the name bearer, a man named Jackson became a peacemaker. Thus, even though the word "woman" appears in the name, it is a man's name. Mr. Jackson had inherited the song, and when he died, James Grant inherited the song. The song is now Marlene Johnson's (who is a member of the Board of Directors of Sealaska Regional Corporation). The song belongs to the T'ak̲deintaan, a major clan of the Raven moiety in Hoonah.

63, 73, 89a. K̲áataan. This is the name of a Kaagwaantaan man from Aan Eegayaa Hít (Down the Beach House) a clan house of the Sitka Kaagwaantaan. The name K̲áataan was given to Joe Judson.

67-89a. Again, we see the general pattern of Charlie Joseph's speech to the elders: he identifies the song, tells about it, and points out the genealogical connection of the singers as grandchildren of T'ak̲deintaan or Kaagwaantaan.

76-80. Fur seal island . . . blown off course. According to Charlie Joseph, a revenue cutter was stationed at the fur seal island. When K̲áataan and his crew came to hunt in their traditional hunting ground, the revenue cutter began to chase them. The Tlingit men were then blown off course. The song probably dates from the period known as "Navy Rule." From the U.S. purchase in 1867 to the Gold Rush of 1884, there was no civil law in Alaska, which was ruled first by the Army, then by the Navy. Katherine Mills comments that when her grandparents still lived out at Lituya Bay, the *Jamestown*, the principal U.S. Navy ship in Alaska, was stormbound there and ran out of food. Katherine Mills' grandparents gave them food and saved them from starvation. They were repaid with blankets and other dry goods. It is possible that the ship that chased K̲áataan and his crew was the *Jamestown*, but we do not know for certain. A valuable research project would be to examine the Navy logs from the period, as well as the Army records for Sitka, Haines, and other communities impacted by military occupation.

90. Brothers and Sisters. Charlie Joseph is now addressing his co-members of the Kaagwaantaan. He was a recognized clan leader.

93-94. He too . . . membership. This passage is ambiguous. We take it to mean the Kaagwaantaan clan. "He" is the composer of the song. But the passage also admits a wider range of possibilities. At the most literal is membership in organizations such as the ANB, Tlingit & Haida, Sealaska, Shee

Atika, etc. At the other end of the spectrum is the more traditional sense as used by St. Paul and Wendell Berry—spiritual communion or membership in a spiritual body or community: we are members of each other.

99. Heard from their . . . lips. The Kaagwaantaan Spirit Song will be sung by the group, and through the young people the spirits of the ancestors will be heard.

108. Don't like to complete the song. Traditionally, this type of song is not completed during a memorial, especially if there are more departed to be feasted. After all of the clan departed are remembered in memorials, the song may be completed. In line 109, Charlie Joseph begs the pardon of the elders who are aware of this tradition, because his group will be singing the spirit song in its entirety as part of the performance for the gathering of elders.

111. Change. The young people have left the room for a costume change. The remainder of the program is of spirit songs, and part of the change in regalia includes the addition of ear yarns (guk l'éinxw—"ear fringe") which are hung from a head band to accentuate the motion of the dances. See also the note to line 122.

114. Sisters and . . . aunts. Traditionally, Charlie Joseph or any person speaking as host would be addressing only his paternal aunts, i.e. his father's sisters—people of the opposite moiety. Because the elders' conference is a mixed gathering, and a contemporary one, the guests also include members of his own clan and moiety.

116. Yours. Charlie is announcing that the dancers will be performing songs owned by various clans who are present, beginning with a song of a shaman of the ancestors of the Chookaneidí.

122. Sway Dance. This could also be translated "Motion." The Tlingit word is yoo koonáḵk, literally "to be standing" (plural form, because it refers to the whole group; -k is a durative suffix). The singular, for one dancer, but rarely used, would be yoo koohánk, as in the term yoo koowahangi yéik, the spirit doing the motion or sway dance. The dance is also called ḵus'áas' referring to the sliding movement of the feet. It is usually done by women, who dance with ear yarns on the sides of their heads, (hanging from a head band) and sway to the songs in time with the drum. It is often done in a ceremony for the

dedication of a house. It is also done during the happy part of a memorial, following the ending of grief. See also the note to line 206.

126. Standing for the cry. Charlie uses the term "G̱áax̱ kát nák̲." Another Tlingit term for this is wudanaak̲. It refers to the sad or grieving part of a memorial for the departed.

127. Standing upright. This is the term for the ending of grief, the happy part of a memorial for the departed. The Tlingit term is kindachóon aawanaak̲.

129. Tips over to joyous ones. This expression is used to describe the point in a memorial when the feast ends the grief and turns to new life. The tone of the memorial changes from the singing of very "heavy" songs of mourning to "lighter" songs of joy. Comedy typically enters the celebration here, and some people wear funny hats or costumes. Love songs are typically exchanged between hosts and guests.

134. Spirit Imitating . . . Haida type. The Spirit Imitating songs (yéik utee daasheeyí) are traditionally believed to be composed or revealed by the spirits of a shaman, and passed to the shaman. Haida type songs (Deikeenaa x̱'asheeyí) are songs composed imitating the style of Haida songs.

138-139. Grandparents . . . Chookaneidí. Again, Charlie Joseph is identifying the clan owners of a song, and indicating that among the dancers are young grandchildren of Chookaneidí, a major Eagle moiety clan of Hoonah, with members also in Sitka.

147. Call out . . . to sing. In traditional ceremonial settings, the song leader would call out the name of the person who would sing or dance to the next song. Each person would be called to sing his or her song. He or she would answer "Héiy!", a form of saying "Yes." The song leader would then tell him or her that it is now his or her turn, and give words of encouragement. The singer would then answer "Thus it is" or "It shall be thus," and would be told by the song leader that what the ancestors used to say will now be heard from his or her lips. At the end of the sentence, Charlie Joseph is again indicating a point of departure, at least for the evening, from traditional style. Here, not in a ceremony, the whole group will sing all songs.

The verb form shukaktook̲éijin is decessive occasional. The underlying form is: shu-ka-ga-tu-k̲aa-ch-in. The occasional is marked by the conjugation prefix (ga, contracted to k-) and the suffix (ch, here changed to j between vowels). The decessive operates throughout the Tlingit verb system, and its marker is the suffix -in.

148. The verb g̲anúgún is contingent. In contrast to the suffix for the decessive in the line above, which has the opposite tone of the stem, the contingent suffix is always high, sometimes creating two high tones in the same word, as here. This construction is very interesting because the affixes are on the helping verb nook and not the main verb.

150-155. Grandparent . . . K̲aax̲'achgóok, etc. Following his pattern, Charlie introduces another composer and his relationship to the singers. K̲aax̲'achgóok is an ancestor of the Kiks.ádi of Sitka, who composed this song when he was blown off course, ended up somewhere in Asia, and returned home. This story is featured in *Haa Shuká, Our Ancestors: Tlingit Oral Narratives*. See also *K̲aal.átk'*, a video tape featuring Charlie Joseph (Ostyn 1981).

160, 161. Outer shell. In Tlingit, ax̲ daakanóox'u, the term refers to a person of one's mother's father's clan, if that person is of other than one's own father's clan; i.e. one's mother's father could be any clan of the opposite moiety, not necessarily the same clan as the father of the speaker. Sak̲uyei is the man's name.

171-174. This way of life . . . that displaced . . . the ceremonies. Reference is to Western, European-American culture, schools, acculturation, and other cultural impacts on Tlingit tradition that have resulted in displacement of Tlingit traditions.

175-180. Seem . . . like the man . . . whose hair was tied into the sound of the drum, etc. Reference is to the story of a shaman who foresaw that his helper, who beat a drum for him, would be shoved or forced away from the drum. To prevent his drummer from losing control over beating the drum, the shaman tied the hair of his helper around the sound of the drum. Thus, even when the helper was physically shoved away from the drum, he kept beating it with his head, by bouncing or sharply nodding his head toward the drum. Charlie Joseph compares his young students to the shaman's helper. They have been forced away from the drum, and have only the beat. The young people are learning the songs, but do not speak the language in which the songs are sung. They are apprentices learning the tradition, and are beating the drum, but from a distance they are working to close. They are trying to keep the beat of their grandparents, their ancestors. This is an important image, to which other speakers will subsequently allude.

184. Eagle House. Charlie Joseph is now introducing a new topic, the Eagle House of the Sitka Kaagwaantaan.

185-187. The reason . . . grandchildren . . . among them. Among the dancers are many grandchildren of Kaagwaantaan, including descendants of the composer of the song Charlie Joseph is beginning to describe. This is why they are doing a Kaagwaantaan Eagle song.

193-196. The story . . . Ch'áak' Tláa . . . who composed the song. Ch'áak' Tláa (Eagle Mother) was a Kaagwaantaan woman who composed the song about an eagle she adopted as a pet, because small pox had wiped out her family. See the video tape *K̲aal.átk'* (Ostyn 1981). The song is used in memorial feasts by the Kaagwaantaan and Kaagwaantaan grandchildren.

198. Just . . . indeed. The children will sing the words just as Ch'áak' Tláa composed them.

203. Belong to L'uknax̲.ádi. The last songs the group will sing are of the L'uknax̲.ádi, a clan of the Raven moiety, popularly called "Coho," Charlie Joseph's father's people.

206. The Spirit Who Sways. In Tlingit, Yoo Kuwahangi Yéik. This is the dance performed by the women wearing yarns hanging by their ears while the male dancers stand in place, pounding ceremonial dance staffs in time with the drum. The dance is performed at memorial feasts and house dedications, and is sometimes referred to as "yarn dancing." See also the note to line 122.

207. Named itself. The spirit revealed its own name and identity.

210. These fathers of mine. Charlie Joseph's father was L'uknax̲.ádi. By extension, men of this clan are his clan fathers.

211. K̲aaksateen's Image. This is a medley of two songs, K̲aaksateen's Song, and K̲aaksateen's Image Song. They are usually sung in this order at a memorial or house dedication.

215. Offended the Coho. The girl, K̲aaksateen, unintentionally offended the Coho People, who then took her away, never to return. Someone dreamed of her later (hence, the "Image" song). It is important in Tlingit tradition to have respect for all living and nonliving things, lest the spirits of these things be offended. It is a common motif in Tlingit oral

literature for people who offend other forms of life to be taken by them, either for a short period of time, or forever. See, for example, the stories in *Haa Shuká* about the man and woman who married the bear, and the woman in the ice at Glacier Bay. For a similar story of the Kiks.ádi, see versions 99 and 100 of Swanton (Swanton 1970:301-320).

219. Her image came to the shaman. The song and "sway dance" (yoo kuwahangi yéik) commemorate the moment when the image (spirit, or "ghost") of K̲aaksateen revealed itself to the L'uknax̲.ádi shaman as the Coho Spirit.

Notes to George Davis (1)

3. My father's surviving relative. A kinship term, directed toward Charlie Joseph, because George Davis' father and Charlie are both Kaagwaantaan. According to Tlingit tradition, men and women of the same clan are considered siblings.

5-6. Your words only fell into space (or, just went into the air). This is a euphemism for few people in the room truly understanding or really hearing Charlie's words.

6a. Charlie's response indicates that he and George Davis understand each other and the situation. From this point on, the oratory continues with audience response, and becomes traditional in style, with interaction between orator and audience.

7. Person . . . who could grasp them. George Davis is exaggerating slightly, but not much, emphasizing how few people in the room really understand what is happening at the moment. Only a handful of elders in the room understand the dynamics of what is unfolding. No one present in the gathering could respond to Charlie, partly because it was a new kind of ceremony, the first of its kind, and therefore it became awkward in places. Usually when someone is explaining about a song or introducing a song, there would be a response from the individual who is being called to sing. See also Charlie Joseph (1) lines 147-149.

9-10. The cover has fallen away from our culture. It is as if the traditional culture is being uncovered, being revealed in the young dancers and explained in the responses of the elders. Traditional oratory takes over, and overrides the contemporary setting in which the evening began. George's image is of the cover of a box or container falling off.

10. Our culture, our Tlingit identity. Two separate terms are used in the Tlingit of line 10: haa ḵusteeyí (our culture) and haa Lingítx̱ sateeyí, which is more difficult to translate. Literally, it means "we who are Tlingit," the -x̱ being a predicate nominative suffix. But it can also be translated more loosely as "our way of life" or "our identity." After much deliberation, we have decided to translate this as "our Tlingit identity" in most places. It is a refrain throughout this set of speeches. In some places, we have translated it as "those of us who are Tlingit."

12. Used to do things. Tradition in general; perhaps more seriously and specifically, ritual and the ceremonial "balance" of oratory.

18, 20. How one's hands are washed. This line introduces an extended simile. The performance of the dancers is like washing the visitors' hands in a gesture of welcome.

32-35. Of all the songs . . . two . . . are sensitive, and cannot be sung without a reply. These are the yéik (shaman spirit) songs. Traditionally sung only at memorials for the departed and at house dedications, they cannot be sung without proper treatment. The traditional belief is that when they are sung, they have the power or are the power or embody the power of the spirits associated with their composition or revelation. One way or another, the songs invoke the spirits. Therefore, the songs have the power to be harmful if not "neutralized" or somehow "balanced." This is done by an equal song from a clan of the opposite moiety. The spirits of the opposite moiety act as a supporting post for the spirits lingering among the people. If a person or group who does not own a song sings that song, especially one of the opposite moiety, it can become especially dangerous and harmful. Like firearms or explosives, songs and the spirits associated with them have great power and can be dangerous in the hands of those who do not know how to handle them. Much of the oratory from this point on is directed at balancing and defusing the spirit power (thus protecting the performers, hosts, and guests) by responding properly to the potential danger.

37-38. That's the way our ancestors lived it. Reference is to how the ancestors practiced protocol, ritual, and reciprocity. In line 38a, Charlie, the host orator, is appropriately thanking George Davis for his act of reciprocity.

44. Two of them. George Davis will ask two speakers to respond, to balance out the two yéik songs. Other speakers will also rise to the occasion, but he is designating two to begin with, first William Johnson, then Charlie Jim.

48-52. Books . . . joined with us. Reference is probably to Richard Dauenhauer in particular, who is related to Tlingit through marriage, but George is also referring in general to earlier field workers who have written about Tlingit. The concern of George and other elders is that until recently, little had been written about Tlingit by Tlingits, describing the culture from within. As an elder and co-founder of Sealaska Heritage Foundation, he also liked the idea of being presented in his own words, rather than being paraphrased. George and others took the opportunity of the elders conference to offer explicit instruction in aspects of culture usually learned by observation and participation.

55. The cover will slide off. The elders will begin to spearhead the documentation of Tlingit culture from a Tlingit point of view, for the benefit of the younger generations, as well as interested and sympathetic persons around the world who are interested in Tlingit culture. George senses that the time has come for the elders to explain things, so that things can be done correctly.

57-73. Even now our grip . . . will not vanish. These lines are a powerful description of the sense of loss of culture—the grip is weary, as the clan elders are clutching at the very tip of what is left, hanging on by a tiny corner. The image is of a boat sinking. Once it fills with water, it is impossible to save. Rescuers can only hold on to a corner of it. The Sealaska Elders Conference in general, and the dynamics of the oratory ongoing at the present moment in particular, are examples of the clan elders holding on to a small tip of the traditional culture before it goes under, sinks, and is lost. He is praying that Sealaska Corporation will rise to the challenge to assist the elders.

74-76. If they don't do this, they will be carrying books . . . read from. George Davis is arguing that culture should be learned by living it, not from books. Even if totally accurate and faithful, books are a "last ditch effort" at learning about culture.

George and other elders fear that the living connection with the past will be lost, leaving only books.

77-79. Tlingit identity . . . misunderstood . . . by . . . white. George Davis and other Tlingit elders are often suspicious of and disappointed with books written about Tlingit, because they often do not reflect the Tlingit point of view. Some are blatantly racist and factually incorrect, others are questionable regarding theory. Even those non-Tlingit writers most sympathetic and closely related can easily and often misunderstand. His concern is that if books are to be written, they must be done correctly, or children of future generations will have only the unsatisfactory books to fall back on. He argues for more aggressive or assertive teaching of the traditions to the young, as exemplified in Charlie Joseph's work, and for the documentation of the tradition in an acceptable manner from the Tlingit point of view.

80. This is what they will be looking at. This line is ambiguous; "this" and "they" are unclear. The line can be understood or paraphrased in two ways: 1) This present ceremony is what the writers will be looking at; 2) The future books are what readers will be looking at. We take the line in both senses, each stressing the importance of describing things correctly and explaining from the elders' point of view.

81. This is to prevent this. This (forthcoming explanation) is to prevent this (such misunderstanding) from happening. George Davis is emphasizing that what he and his fellow elders are about to make explicit has never been described before (the cover is being removed) and they are explaining it so people will understand why the elders follow tradition in this manner.

92-94. Acting as a traditional master of ceremonies, George Davis introduces and turns the floor over to William Johnson, his tribal younger brother, who will deliver a speech.

Notes to the Speech by William Johnson

3. My father's maternal nephew. These words of kinship are directed to Charlie Joseph, the instructor and leader of the G̱ajaa Héen Dancers. William Johnson's stepfather was Kaagwaantaan, therefore the clan maternal uncle of Charlie. In

these opening lines, the speaker is establishing his relationship to Charlie. William himself is T'a<u>k</u>deintaan of the Raven moiety.

4. The child of many clans. Through his mother's marriage, and through his names, William acquired fathers in many clans, and is therefore the child of many clans: Chookaneidí, Kaagwaantaan, Wooshkeetaan.

6-8. Wooshkeetaan, Kaagwaantaan, and Chookaneidí are Eagle moiety clans historically closely related to each other.

9. Paternal aunts. Through the Tlingit clan system, the speaker has paternal aunts (or fathers' sisters, i.e. women of the opposite moiety) in many clans.

10-11. Peacemaker to Kaagwaantaan in Hoonah. William and two other men of Kaagwaantaan, Jim Martin and Jacob Pratt, were peacemakers in Hoonah, and William was a peacemaker for the Kaagwaantaan.

18. Tried me in many ways. Reference to his experience as a peace emissary. Because of this and other experiences, William was highly regarded as a a tradition bearer.

22-23. Song . . . lingering. William takes up the theme introduced by George Davis that the songs cannot be sung without a reply. Speakers after William will also return to this as the central theme of the evening. This is a difficult image to translate. The idea is that words can't be left unattended, floating, spinning, tossing, or tumbling. Elders also compare this to a spinning knife.

24-27. Stand, maternal nephew . . . place . . . of your maternal uncles. William is addressing Frank O. Williams in these lines, identifying him as his maternal nephew. Frank O. Williams is also T'a<u>k</u>deintaan, therefore a clan nephew of William Johnson. He is a biological nephew of Matthew Lawrence, one of the other speakers represented in this book. William's point here is that the younger men must take over the responsibilities of the departed elders.

28-30. Listen . . . steer . . . land . . . in place of us. In this metaphor, the land is compared to a boat, and the nephew will become the captain and navigator, taking the leadership position of the present generation of elders who are approaching death.

31-34. The song . . . our fathers . . . echo. In these lines, William addresses Charlie Joseph, who responds in line 34a. Reference is probably to the Eagle Hat Song, which would be a song of the Eagle fathers of the T'akdeintaan. An important song such as the Eagle Hat Song requires a song in return.

35. In reply . . . a song is . . . lifted. William reiterates George Davis' concern here.

36-40. Grandfather . . . X'eijáak'w . . . clasping hands. This is a nice image of the reciprocity the elders are talking about. The Eagle Hat Song is "holding hands" with a song or response lifted from the "other side" or opposite moiety. Rather than actually singing a song in return, William only mentions the shaman X'eijáak'w, whose spirit helper's song this was. X'eijáak'w was a well-known shaman (íxt') of the T'akdeintaan, a Raven moiety clan of Hoonah. By mentioning his name, William is joining the hand of this yéik to that evoked by the singing of the Kaagwaantaan Eagle Hat song. The image is also of literally standing with one's right arm extended during the singing of yéik songs. See also Charlie Jim lines 85-88 and George Jim lines 72-80.

41-42. The at.óow of my maternal grandfathers. In Tlingit, William uses the term at.óow. Reference is to the T'akdeintaan clan of Hoonah, and to the spirits William is now mentioning and thereby invoking in return. He is bringing out T'akdeintaan at.óow in the form of names and other references to clasp hands and "balance" the Kaagwaantaan spirits evoked by the Eagle Hat song. X'eijáak'w was from the Snail House, and William Johnson from Raven Nest House, both clan houses of the Hoonah T'akdeintaan. See notes to the speeches from the Jim Marks memorial for more on the Hoonah houses.

44. Gaanaxáa is a point of land in the Cape Fairweather area, a traditional village site of the T'akdeintaan people. Its English name is Salmon Beach. See the speech by Jessie Dalton for further references to Gaanaxáa.

45-48. As if these children have come out. In this simile, William Johnson is saying it's as if his ancestors from Gaanaxáa have come out or been made present through the songs of the Gajaa Héen Dancers, or that the dancers have made Gaanaxáa physically present. This is a very traditional use of rhetoric, and this type of response from William and the other speakers transforms the tone of the evening from secular to ceremonial. The elders explain how the songs have a different meaning for them than for the children, who may not fully understand their spiritual impact.

49-50. We're losing our culture. William now takes up another recurring theme of the elders—that the culture is not being practiced, the language is not being spoken, and that both are therefore being lost.

52-54. How . . . proud . . . brought them out . . . see. "Them" is the at.óow, the songs. The elders are proud of the young dancers. Through the performance of the G̱ajaa Héen Dancers, the elders can see that there is hope, that all is not lost, and that with Charlie's instructions the young people can sing and dance. William Johnson is thanking Charlie Joseph for showing the elders that it is possible to maintain this segment of the culture. He is thanking Charlie for demonstrating what can be done.

56. People will begin to follow your example. Other elders will follow Charlie's example and teach the young people of their villages. Since 1980 the movement has been growing, as manifested in the strong performances by many village groups at such events as the Sealaska Heritage Foundation Celebrations of 1982, 1984, 1986, and 1988. These impressive public performances are made possible only by long hours of practice and instruction at the community level. In the mid and late 1970's, Charlie demonstrated a new way to cultivate traditional songs and dances, when the traditional channels of training and transmission had been broken due to social upheaval. On a grand and highly organized scale, the G̱ajaa Héen Dancers moved the instructional relationship from the house and clan level to the community, multi-clan level. See also Charlie Joseph (2) lines 56ff. and notes for more on this.

Notes to the Speech by Charlie Jim

After the speech by William Johnson, the complete set of transcriptions includes two more speeches by George Davis in his role as master of ceremonies, between which Ms. Clara Natkong, a Haida woman from Hydaburg delivers a speech thanking Charlie for his efforts and for including the Haida people. At the end of her speech she makes a money contribution to the dance group. Please see the complete texts of "*Because We*

Cherish You..." for these and other speeches not reprinted here. The set of excerpts in the present volume now resumes with a speech by Charlie Jim.

1-4. Don't . . . Deisheetaan. Charlie opens with a rhetorical question introducing his genealogy and his connection to the songs and dances that were performed, and to which he is responding. Deisheetaan is a clan of the Raven moiety.

8-9. The land . . . untangles. The saying is a metaphor: if you understand genealogy, especially on your father's side, things become clear. In Tlingit tradition, the mother's side is more immediately obvious, because children follow that moiety and clan line, and are identified by those names and clan crests. The father's line is less visible, and needs to be recognized. Charlie uses the quote specifically to explain that everyone is related and a part of Chilkat, however unclear it may seem at first, but that everything is made clear when in Chilkat.

10. Older brother. George Davis, a clan brother of the Deisheetaan.

16. Reveals one's ancestry. This is a nice passage about the role of singing and dancing in Tlingit society. One of his points is that people are related, but often do not understand how and why, and therefore tend to forget it, or overlook the bonds that unite the Tlingit people of various communities.

22-29. Older brother Kichnáal<u>x</u> . . . Yéilk'. In Tlingit tradition, names are recycled. In this passage, Charlie Jim goes into the history of two names. Kichnáal<u>x</u> is also the name of George Davis. The Orthodox Church records for Killisnoo indicate that this was also the Tlingit name of the leader known in the American records only as "Saginaw Jake," who was the maternal uncle of George Davis. His "church" or baptismal name was Nikolai, and the church documents refer to him as "Toion (leader) Nikolai" and "Kichnalk," and describe him as a "sound supporter of Orthodoxy" who converted in the 1880's. We thank our colleague Dr. Lydia Black for calling to our attention the church recording of this name. Yéilk', meaning Little Raven, was the name first given to Charlie Jim's brother at a house dedication (Raven House) then later given to Charlie.

31. Water did him in. The original Yéilk' drowned.

53, 58. Yuwáak'w, Daalkoowoo<u>x</u>' Éesh. As of this writing, we have no further information on these names, beyond what is in the text. Yuwáak'w is Charlie Jim's grandfather of the

(Eagle) Wooshkeetaan. Daalkoowoox̲' Éesh is Charlie's father's name, of the (Eagle) Dak̲l'aweidí.

59. English, 60. Tlingit. My own grandchild . . . Chuchgadachx̲án. This is a complicated and very "high class" Tlingit genealogical relationship, according to which one's own clan is the same as one's grandparents on the father's side. See also George Jim 21, 143.

65. K̲aal.átk', Charlie Joseph, is addressed as his brother-in-law because he is of the opposite moiety, Charlie Joseph being Eagle and Charlie Jim Raven.

66, 68. Good fortune. The songs and dances presented by the dancers are becoming good fortune or enrichment to Charlie Jim.

71, 75. Anaxóots and G̲uneit are (Eagle) children of Deisheetaan. Anaxóots is a Kaagwaantaan name, and the Tlingit name of Patrick Paul, who was the formal master of ceremonies for the Western protocol at the banquet, opening and closing the entire event. Patrick Paul turned the program over to Charlie Joseph for the traditional dancing. After the presentation of the dances and during the traditional speech making, George Davis acted as master of ceremonies.

79. Strand . . . from their side. He is recognizing his kin from the opposite moiety, mainly George Jim.

80. Keik̲óok'w, grandfather. Charlie Jim is addressing George Jim, who responds in line 81a. Even though they are of the same generation and approximate age, George Jim is Charlie Jim's clan grandfather through name and social structure. The details of the genealogy are not clear to us as of this writing.

84. This spirit. Reference is to one of the spirit songs; we do not know for certain which one, but probably song #5 in the dance presentation, the Kaagwaantaan Spirit Song.

85-88. People . . . raise . . . hands . . . not cause harm. During the singing of a spirit song, members of the opposite clan raise their hand to the people singing, as a "brace" to neutralize the potentially dangerous spirits. One yéik is used to balance or neutralize another yéik.

95-96. Marten spirit, sea gull spirit. This is another example of the concern with balancing out the songs by replying in kind. Charlie responds by calling up the marten and sea gull spirits.

97. Clasping hands with one other. He brings the yéik into a position of clasping hands with each other—the ones he is calling up, and those called up through the song.

108-110. Raven Robe . . . brace . . . to the song. He will use another at.óow, the Raven Robe, to brace the song of Ch'áak' Tláa and keep "jinaháa"—accident—from the dancers, so that things don't turn bad or cause harm for the young people. A variety of at.óow may be used to "balance." Here a blanket is used. It is not physically present, but merely alluded to, and the yéik depicted is thus invoked. See also George Jim, line 68, where the noun "jinaháa" is used.

113. Our respect for each other has emerged. The proper protocol is being displayed. When the proper protocol is used, there is no danger when the yeik songs are used. The elders often use the English term "respect" to cover a range of protocol.

119. Shee Atika. (Pronounced "she attica") The hotel in Sitka, owned by the Sitka Village Corporation. Many communities invested in hotels and other tourist related businesses as part of the economic reorganization under ANCSA (Alaska Native Claims Settlement Act). In a sense, the Shee Atika Hotel is a modern clan house, the property of all the clans of Sitka. The Elders' Conference took place there. The word is a slightly anglicized pronunciation of Sheey.atiká, meaning "located on the outside of Baranof Island," from which the word Sitka derives.

122-123. Deishú House (House at the end of the Road) and Raven House are significant for art commissioned by ancestors. The clan name Deisheetaan derives from Deishú Hít Taan, the people of End of the Road House. Charlie Jim is mentioning these clan houses of Angoon as at.óow to "brace" Shee Atika.

143. Treated them well. The ancestors trained the generation to follow them well. Charlie Jim is leading up to his introduction of Walter Soboleff, a man of the (Raven) L'eineidí clan and grandchild of Deisheetaan, whom he invites to speak.

146-147. T'aawchán is the Tlingit name of Walter Soboleff, a Tlingit elder respected and well-educated in both Tlingit and Western tradition. He is an ordained Presbyterian minister and a Tlingit educator, and often serves as an interpreter because of his eloquence in both Tlingit and English, and his ability to explain the intentions and references of each party that might otherwise be overlooked or misunderstood. Charlie is hoping that Walter will speak in English, so that those who do not understand Tlingit might understand what is happening. The name T'aawchán is admired and respected, one of the many delightful names deriving from different aspects of the Raven; t'aaw is "tail feather" and chán is "fragrant." Walter Soboleff's speech is No. 11 in *"Because We Cherish You..."*.

153-154. Samuel G. Johnson, Yeilnaawú. The name translates as "Death of the Raven" and was also the Tlingit name of Tom Peters of Teslin, featured in *Haa Shuká*, and one of the orators in this book.

158. Grandfather. The title is used for the namesake of a person's grandfather, even if the person who bears the name is younger than the person addressing him.

164. Angoon is gratified. Charlie Jim is also speaking on behalf of Angoon (in Tlingit, Xutsnoowú—Brown Bear Fort) and is expressing his gratitude that he was given an opportunity to speak and respond to Charlie Joseph.

168-180. Food . . . dinner. Charlie Jim explains the protocol of thanking hosts for the food they have provided and shared.

184. Paternal aunts. The paternal aunts, women of the opposite moiety, are usually addressed according to protocol both at traditional ceremonials and at banquets such as that in which he was participating.

185, 186, 196. Hó, hó! This word is "extra-systemic" in Tlingit, having the only occurance of the vowel "o" in the language, and used only as a reply or expression of extreme gratitude.

193. Heads high. People will return home proud and inspired from now on.

Notes to George Davis (2)

5. The drum. Reference is to Charlie Joseph (1) lines 175-180 and the image of how the shaman's helper pounded the drum by keeping beat with the nodding or bobbing of his head. See also note to line 20, below.

8-18. Grip . . . grip. The image here is of Tlingit culture likened to a boat or canoe in stormy water, being held in place only by a pole. In the metaphor, Tlingit culture is the canoe, and Western culture is the storm. The grip of the elders is weary from holding on, trying to anchor it so that it doesn't float away in the storm or capsize.

12. Sealaska. Sealaska Corporation (an acronym for Southeast Alaska) one of the Regional Profit Making Corporations created under ANCSA—Alaska Native Claims Settlement Act. In 1980 George Davis, William Johnson, and other elders moved for Sealaska Corporation to create the Sealaska Heritage Foundation, a non-profit organization with a mandate to foster the Native languages and cultures of Southeast Alaska. In this image in the speech, Sealaska is seen as coming to the rescue. This is an interesting mixture of traditional and contemporary images. George Davis was always "up to date" at the same time as being firmly rooted in tradition. George and his fellow elders realized the need for new methods of fostering preservation of culture and heritage. They recognize the different kinds of resources available to the corporation on the one hand, and the families and communities on the other. Charlie's dancers are an excellent example of preservation of living tradition at the community level—young people learning from elders. This is the only way the traditions will survive. The production of books (such as this) using corporate, public, and foundation resources is an example of "non-living" preservation through documentation.

16-18. Point . . . into the waves before it sinks. In this metaphor, "what our ancestors used to say" (culture, tradition, ritual, protocol, etc.) is compared to the boat or canoe being swamped, and Sealaska the crew setting into the waves before it sinks.

20-27. Shoved him aside . . . heads. Again, reference is to the image of the shaman's helper pounding the drum by the bobbing, bouncing, or nodding motion of his head. The helper was pushed away from the drum; he couldn't keep beat with his hand and drumstick, but only by nodding his head from a distance. The comparison is that Tlingit people, especially in the twentieth century, and especially children of all generations born after 1920, have been pushed away from the traditional culture by force, and can only relate to it from ever increasing distances. The drum is still lying there, pounding, resonating from the nodding of the head of the helper.

32-33. My grandfather's surviving relative, Keiḵóok'. This is a kinship term referring to someone who is still alive from one's grandfather's clan or house group. Reference is to George Jim, (also known as Yaanashtúk̲) of the Wooshkeetaan clan of Angoon, whom George now invites to speak.

Notes to the Speech by George Jim

2-3. Yuwáak'w, my grandfather's namesake. Yuwáak'w is the Tlingit name of Eli Hanlon from Hoonah, one of George Jim's clan grandfathers. Eli Hanlon's namesake was George Jim's father's father. The speaker is asking him to stand up and be recognized as a relative.

7. Speaking. It is common in Tlingit protocol for one person to speak on behalf of someone else. The Tlingit verbs are first and second person singular future, an unusual combination in the same sentence. The stem tones are different, one low and one high, for reasons we do not understand.

8-9. My hair . . . I've aged. It is common for children of a clan to joke with each other, which George Jim is doing with Charlie Joseph in these lines. Charlie is older than George Jim, but his hair was still fairly black, whereas the speaker's is like snow. Both men, while they are of different Eagle moiety clans, are L'uknax̲.ádi yátx'i, children of L'uknax̲.ádi, popularly known as the "Coho" clan. The verb x̲at shasitee is interesting because of the nominal prefix sha- (head) used with the classifier -si- and the stem -tee (to be). It translates more literally as "Like snow I am of the head."

10. Your daughter. The question is directed to Charlie Joseph. Ethel Makinen, Charlie's daughter in question, responds, giving her Tlingit name, Daasdiyáa, which the speaker repeats in line 11. Ethel Makinen is one of the instructors of the G̲ajaa Héen Dancers.

13. Children of noble people (Aan yátx'u sáani) is traditionally a very respectful way to address one another in public speaking.

14. Paddlers at the bow. A metaphor for the elders from various groups present.

16-18. Sitka Kaagwaantaan . . . my mother's grandparents. In these lines, the speaker is reaffirming his kinship ties with

Charlie Joseph, who is Kaagwaantaan. George Jim is explaining that his mother's grandfathers were Sitka Kaagwaantaan.

21. My grandfathers became grandchildren with me. This is a very complicated and very "high class" Tlingit genealogical relationship, according to which one's own clan is the same as one's grandparents on the father's side. See also line 143 of this speech, and line 59 (Eng) and 60 (Tl) of Charlie Jim. The Tlingit sentence is very interesting because the stem for "grandparent" or "ancestor" is used both as a noun and a verb. Ax̱ léelk'w hás (my grandparents) is the noun form, and the verb form is

wu	-li	-léelk'w
perfective	classifier	grandparent

literally, as in English "they grandparented." In line 16 the word appears as a predicate nominative with the suffix -x̱.

22. Within the Box House. Specific reference is made to the Box House, or Ḵóok Hít, the clan house of the Sitka Kaagwaantaan from which Charlie Joseph comes. (Note the important difference in Tlingit between Ḵóok Hít, meaning Box House, and Kóoḵ Hít, meaning Pit House. The difference between the two words is very difficult for non-speakers to hear, and has caused some confusion among the younger generations.)

23. Children of Shaanchg̱akeitl. As of this writing, we have no further information on this name.

23a. Thank you, younger brother. Charlie Joseph is thanking George Jim for his recognition of the relationship, and is addressing him as his younger brother.

26. Those who left me behind. His departed Kaagwaantaan relatives.

27-28. It's as if I will lead them out. He will lead out or bring back the departed relatives and Kaagwaantaan ancestors by mentioning their at.óow, or clan crests. This is a central rhetorical device and spiritual concept in Tlingit oratory and ceremonial. See also the speeches from the Memorial for Jim Marks.

29-31. Fathers . . . enchanted . . . by the Coho Spirit. This is a complex image, and refers to Ḵaaksateen's male relatives, her brothers, men of the L'uknax̱.ádi who were enchanted or captured by the Coho Spirit—their sister's spirit. Ḵaaksateen was a woman shaman of the L'uknax̱.ádi. Her shaman spirit was the yoo kuwahangi yéik. George Jim is a child of the L'uknax.ádi, the "Coho" clan. The verb awulyeilí, which we have translated as translated as "enchanted" can also mean captured, and is most literally "raven-ed!" The same stem in Tlingit means both "raven" and "to lie" or "deceive," depending on the prefixes.

a	-wu	-l	-yeil	-í
obj	perf.	clas.	stem	participial

The verb appears in lines 39 and 41 in the decessive, implying a brief or temporary state. The analysis is the same, except for the addition of the decessive suffix -n: a-wu-l-yeil-í-n.

32. Lie unattended. The speaker wishes to respond to the L'uknax̲.ádi yeik. He is bringing out his relatives to neutralize the potentially dangerous íx̲t'i yéigi (shaman spirit) lest it harm the guests, or, above all, the young dancers.

42. Wolf Spirit. In discussing these lines, George Jim explained that the G̲ooch K̲uyéik (Wolf Spirit) was the spirit helper of his grandfather Tl'oog̲u Tsées, a shaman of the Wooshkeetaan. Other spirit helpers that came to him were Tóos' yéik (Shark Spirit), Keitl K̲uyéik (Dog Spirit) and X'aayayik K̲áa (Eagle Spirit). The name means "voice over the point" which refers to a place in the air where eagles congregate.

43. Fasted and was chanting. To prepare or make one's self receptive to spirits, the shaman would fast, and then chant to invite the spirits to come.

44-54. Wolves . . . Wolf Spirit. The speaker is using the image of the wolf, a major clan emblem or at.óow of the Kaagwaantaan. He compares the image of the mother wolf running along a ridge and her pups falling behind and crying to the young dancers who have been separated from the mother language and culture. The sound of their howling after the mother is compared to the noise roots make when being ripped out of the ground—like a chain reaction, with the sound of a series of breaking stems. This sound is compared to the voices of the singers. The passage is typical of the use of analogy and metaphor in Tlingit oratory, based on natural images and clan emblems, and linked to the genealogies of those present, and delivered for the removal of grief in a context of reciprocity such as the host-guest relationship.

43, 46. The verbs kagashéenín and kei kg̲agudín are contingent.

44, 61. Notice the contrast in the Tlingit words:

44.	yeik̲	out along (directional prefix)
61.	yéik	shaman spirit (noun)

48. Tlingit. Shu-ka-na-l-s'el'-i. The underlying base is li-s'eil' "tear up" or "pull up roots." The verb is in the dependent clause (participial progressive) with nominal prefixes shu- and -ka- and the conjugation prefix -na-.

49. Tlingit. The verb is tu-si-tee, literally "my mind is" with the nominal prefix tu-. Compare this to line 8, sha-si-tee, with the nominal prefix sha-.

55-56. Young paternal aunts . . . uncles. The speaker is referring to the young people in the Ḵajaa Héen group who are singing and dancing to the opposite tribe's song, specifically the L'uknax̱.ádi youth singing their song.

59-69. Not cause harm . . . we are cautious . . . the Wolf Spirit is lapping . . . so it does not cause harm. This passage capsulizes the anxiety shared by the elders: that spirit songs must be used with caution, that when spirits are mentioned, they must be balanced or neutralized or accompanied by spirits of clans of the opposite moiety. The counterbalancing spirits are evoked, and poetically remove the danger. This passage might be considered an example of the entire set of speeches "in a nutshell." Compare this passage to the structurally similar removal of grief in the speeches from the Memorial for Jim Marks. "The wolf spirit is lapping . . ."(66-67) is a good example of metaphor, with the wolf removing danger (line 68, jinaháa, "accident", potential trouble) in a naturally or physically appropriate manner. See also Charlie Jim 108-110 and notes.

72. Stand up in the back of the house. Guests are usually seated at the back of the room facing the hosts who are in front.

73-80. Yéik. Spirit . . . yú yéik. Linguistically, an example of "code switching" or changing languages. To be sure everybody understands, and to emphasize his main point, he clarifies how those of the opposite moiety should stand and raise their hands in response to the singing of a yéik song. This point has been mentioned by William Johnson and Charlie Jim, but it is so important that George Jim repeats it in English for extra emphasis.

90. Lullabies that cuddle . . . us. (Or, "the cradle songs that cradle us.") In Tlingit, the same stem is used for the noun (yá dléigu) and the verb (haa la-dléigu). Reference is made to the songs performed by the group, and that Charlie and his singers presented the songs of many clans out of respect for all of the

guests, and to give all of them comfort. Thus, George Jim refers to the songs as "lullabies." The songs and clans include:

1. Kwáal	T'akdeintaan
2. Keitóok	Kaagwaantaan
3. Shaawát Guwakaan	T'akdeintaan
4. Káataan	Kaagwaantaan
5. Yéik song	Kaagwaantaan
6. Yéik song	Chookaneidí
7. Kaax'achgóok	Kiks.ádi
8. Sakuyei	Chilkat
9. Ch'áak'	Kaagwaantaan
10. Kaaksateen	L'uknax.ádi

96-105. Identity . . . lost . . . educated . . . blame them. George Jim is not blaming, but sympathizing with the younger generations who no longer speak or understand Tlingit, saying that he has the same trouble with English, and often doesn't understand what people are talking about. It sounds like so much ringing in the ear. Language loss is the most obvious symptom of the "generation gap" in many Native American communities. More subtle are differences in world view, with the younger generations increasingly adapting Western thought and understanding less and less of traditional Tlingit intellectual culture. The process of language abandonment and loss is complex, but boarding schools were a major impact.

99, 102, 111, 112, 118. Students of Tlingit may be interested in the different forms of the verb stem -.aax, meaning "to hear, listen, understand, sound" (depending on the prefixes).

99.	x'eiya.áxji aa	the ones who don't understand
102.	duwa.áxch	it sounds
111.	du.axji nuch	it sounds
112.	du.axji nuch	it sounds
118.	xwa.aaxí	that I heard

101. Tammmmmmmmmmm. George Jim uses this sound effect, a humming like sound, to indicate confusion, the way a foreign language sounds to a non-speaker.

110. Tlingit. X'ala.atk ganúgún. The form is contingent, with the affixes on the helping verb.

112, 112a. Maybe . . . older brother too . . . on this side. George Jim and Charlie Joseph, as children of the same clan, are joking with each other again in these lines. After poking fun at himself, George Jim pokes some fun at Charlie Joseph, who responds in kind, indicating which side of his head is buzzing, or on which side of his head English makes no sense. Such self deprecating humor is very common at certain times in Tlingit oratory, especially in speeches given at forty day parties to cheer up those in grief. Humor may also be directed at others according to social structure. On the tape, George Jim is chuckling as he speaks line 112.

117. Songs of my fathers. Reference is to the songs of the L'uknax̲.ádi. We have supplied "songs" in translation; the Tlingit is aayí, "one's own."

118a. On the tape there are many more unidentified "thank you's," too confusing to sort out and transcribe.

120. Do not linger. The song has to be balanced out by another song or piece of art so that it doesn't float, wander, or resonate unanswered in the air. See William Johnson 22-23 and other speakers as well.

121. Raising my grandparent's spirit in return. Reference is to the Wolf Spirit he talked about earlier, the K̲aaksateen yéik. The Tlingit term is du yéigi.

122-124. And these . . . Dogfish Robe . . . to brace this Frog Robe. Again, the speaker is using his clan emblems to "balance" those of the opposite moiety. In this case, the Dogfish, referring to a small shark, is used to respond to the Frog.

124, 125. Bracing it. The image is of bracing something with a pole. The Tlingit verb stem used, -taan, is a good example of the classificatory verb for handling a pole-like rectangular object.

130-133. Keik̲óok'w, my mother's . . . grandfather . . . all . . . Kaagwaantaan grandchildren . . . wolf made for me. This is an important passage in many ways. The speaker is identifying his namesake, his mother's maternal grandfather, as well as others of that generation, as grandchildren of Kaagwaantaan. Once again, George Jim is clarifying his relationship to the Sitka Kaagwaantaan. Finally, he is explaining the traditional use of clan art and music by grandchildren of the clan. Thus, while George Jim is Wooshkeetaan and not Kaagwaantaan, he is entitled under certain ceremonial conditions, to use the at.óow of his grandparent clan, in this case the Kaagwaantaan. Use of at.óow by grandchildren of the clan is a very important concept in traditional Tlingit ceremony, oratory, and spirituality.

137. A person of honor. The term is singular in this sentence, but more commonly appears in the plural.

140, 141a. My older brother . . . your younger brother. George Jim's reference to Charlie Joseph as his older brother, and Charlie's playful response about being his younger brother as well are part of their joking relationship, and artful manipulation of the Tlingit kinship system.

143. You are surely your grandfather. George Jim continues the ongoing banter and repartee over kinship terms, and chuckles while delivering this rejoinder. This line is both serious and joking. On the serious side, George Jim is doing the proper thing by pointing out that Charlie Joseph, as a grandchild of Kaagwaantaan, is also his own grandfather. This is considered a "high class" or prestigious relationship. In traditional Tlingit social conduct, it may be considered abrasive if the status is pointed out by one who is not properly related. In this case, the line is also done jokingly, by the same class of people, asserting co-membership because of their genealogy and joking relationship. See also George Jim line 20, and Charlie Jim 59-60.

147. Tlingit. X̱'awoonax̱ji.áagi yé is potential attributive, an unusual verb form. The underlying stem is -.aa "to be delayed in speaking" when used with the nominal prefix x̱'a (mouth). The underlying form is:

x̱'a	u	na	g̱a	ji	.áa	k	i
NP	IR	CP	AP	CL	ST	S	S

148-158. Maternal uncles . . . air. George Jim now alludes to the at.óow of his own people, the Wooshkeetaan. He expresses the feeling that his maternal uncles are his anchor, having left in his care various items of clan art and regalia, including the Shark Tunic, the ermine headdress, and a Murrelet Staff. As with the at.óow previously mentioned, he is using these to balance out the songs so that nothing turns bad. Eagle moiety at.óow of clans related through the person of the speaker are named to respond to the Raven moiety at.óow of the songs and dances. As elsewhere in this set of speeches, "words not float aimlessly" refers to the words of the songs that are otherwise unattended, ignored, or not responded to by the opposite moiety.

156. Tlingit. In shax̱wligás', which we translate as "brace," the stem is -gaas', "to prop up by placing a long object underneath." The same stem appears in noun form meaning "house post."

166-177. One time . . . hold your head. After addressing serious content, George Jim now begins to close his speech with humor, and turns to a kind of genealogical "in-joke" very characteristic of Tlingit oratory, the humor relying on relationship. The shark in line 168 is his clan crest, Wooshkeetaan, on the Eagle side. "Raven" in line 170 is supplied in translation; the Tlingit is simply ayawsiḵaa—"he said to her" or "she said to him," depending on context. "My paternal uncle" in 171 is Raven, being a man of the opposite moiety of the speaker. "His paternal aunt" in 172 is the shark, being a woman of the opposite moiety of Raven. "Honey" of line 173 is supplied in translation, to correspond to the untranslatable use of the diminutive suffix on the imperative verb form in Tlingit, "Haagúk'" as contrasted with the normal "haagú," (a contraction of haa-t gú). The joke about Raven courting the Shark again reinforces the mutually supportive relationship of the clans of the opposite moieties. Humor is very difficult to translate, and we have paraphrased this passage and rearranged lines in places in translation.

177a. An unidentified speaker, presumably of the Raven moiety, thanks the speaker for the joke, and for expressing the reciprocity through humor.

181, 183, 184. "This sister of mine" (181) is the shark; the paternal uncles and aunts (183-184) are those in the audience who are Raven moiety. In these lines, the speaker caps his joke.

188-190a. Thank you. The speaker thanks the hosts, and Charlie Joseph in turn thanks the speaker for responding with his at.óow.

191-192. Place I came from . . . faith. Reference is to Angoon and the elders who selected the speaker to represent the community.

194-196a. Breath . . . brought out everything. The speaker ends on another bit of self deprecating humor, much appreciated by the audience. As most of his other humor, this passage has a serious as well as a playful side. As well as "getting it out of his system," the passage shows profound insight into the creative act, the concepts of the unspoken word, the unsung song, and the connection between creativity and breath. The audience response is appropriate to the non-traditional setting of the elders conference, but would not happen in a traditional ceremonial.

Notes to George Davis (3)

3. Brackets and ellipsis points indicate where the tape is too unclear to transcribe. We have reconstructed the English translation here.

10-12. Place to bury . . . post. Reference is to the Tlingit tradition of placing cremated ashes into niches in the backs of mortuary totem poles and house posts. George states (5-7) that the way their grandparents used to do things had almost died out, and was moribund to the point where they were looking for a suitable burial spot, when Charlie's dancers revived it.

17, 20. Brought it out . . . reawakened. Charlie's dancers have rekindled the tradition by singing songs the elders considered extinct or almost extinct.

24-28. Reluctant . . . child of Kaagwaantaan . . . mind that rattled. Most songs are directed to people, usually of the opposite moiety, identified not by their own clan, but according to their fathers' clan, as children of "x." George Davis is Deisheetaan and child of Kaagwaantaan, so songs are addressed to him not as Deisheetaan, but as a child of Kaagwaantaan. When one is identified or called out this way in a song, protocol requires that one stand and dance in recognition of his or her father's clan. The dance posture is characterized by a trembling, quavering, or wiggling of the hand by the temple, as if shaking a rattle. George Davis confesses that he was weak, and only did this mentally rather than by actually standing, as he should have done.

40. Where . . . originated. We have paraphrased here, inserting "father's people" for clarity in translation. The Tlingit is literally "where a person originated."

41-44. Whenever . . . temple. George Davis describes what he referred to in lines 24-28: when a person's father's clan is called, he or she stands and responds by dancing, as a child of that clan. Money is often brought out also, in honor of one's father's people, and in gratitude to the singers. There is a special verb for this in Tlingit, used in lines 42, 43, and 49. We have translated this as "words are sung for." The underlying dictionary form is shu-ka-dli-x̲oox̲ and is defined as "call forth response from opposite clan, by means of song."

42.	shu-ka-x̲-du-l-x̲úx̲-ín	contingent
43.	shu-ka-w-du-dli-x̲úx̲-u	participial, perfective
49.	shu-ka-w-du-dli-x̲úx̲	perfective

48-57. Words . . . clan child . . . know each other. A person's clan and mother's clan are obvious from one's personal name and regalia, but a person's father's clan is not obvious, and must be acknowledged. Through this recognition, people begin to know each other and learn the genealogies.

55. Thank you. George Davis' speech continues, introducing the next speaker. See *"Because We Cherish You..."* for the complete text.

Notes to George Davis (4)

At the end of the previous speech (George Davis 3), the speaker introduces Dr. Walter Soboleff, calling him by the name K̲aajaak̲wtí, who spoke in English, explaining to the non-Tlingit speakers how moving it was for the elders to hear the most sacred songs of Tlingit culture, songs they had almost given up hope of ever hearing again from a younger generation, and how the elders wanted to respond. Walter then offers his Dog Salmon at.óow in balance and appreciation. See also the notes to Charlie Jim, lines 147-148.

Following Dr. Soboleff, Mr. Paul Henry, L'uknax̲.ádi from Yakutat offered a speech of gratitude directed to Charlie Joseph, explaining how he relates to Charlie, the dancers, and the songs. He opened with humor about waiting for the coho salmon to begin to swim. This is a joke about his clan crest. See *"Because We Cherish You..."* for the texts of the speeches by Walter Soboleff and Paul Henry. The present set of texts continues with another short speech by George Davis in his role as master of ceremonies.

2. Younger brother. George Davis is addressing Paul Henry, a fellow Raven.

9. Soothe the pain. Reference is to a death in Charlie's family. The connection here is the ongoing theme of the richness

of Tlingit tradition in using words to heal, but the growing awareness of how much of the healing tradition has been lost.

14. Calm your thoughts. This is a metaphor, with thoughts compared to salmon. In seining, a salmon plunger is used to keep salmon from getting riled up and jumping out of the seine. The underlying dictionary form is ka-ya-tleix̲w, "cause fish to move, especially salmon, when seining."

22. What you told us to look at. Reference is to the songs--looking back at and to traditional music—how the songs were and are used, who composed them, who owns them. George is thanking Charlie for urging and even insisting that people keep an eye on tradition. The speakers are all expressing how they are now again seeing and hearing things they had given up as lost.

23, 33. Unwrapped. Reference is to Charlie's teaching the dancers, thereby disclosing what people had lost sight of.

35. Container of wisdom. Reference is to the knowledge of Tlingit heritage and culture. In this passage George Davis confirms support of what Charlie started—to open up and pass on the traditional wisdom left in the care of their (the elders') generation. This is also a reaffirmation that it is possible for the younger generations to learn, given commitment and hard work by elders and learners.

37-40. Uncles . . . here. In a touching conclusion, George Davis reaffirms the presence of his ancestors, made present through at.óow—the songs and dances presented by the youth.

Notes to George Davis (5)

Speeches by George Davis and Annie Joseph (wife of Charlie Joseph) are omitted here. Please see *"Because We Cherish You..."* for the texts. The main point of Annie Joseph's speech is that she is happy to hear children perform songs that she had long since given up hope of hearing. She talks about kinship both through the traditional clan system and ANB/ANS, and makes a cash donation to the dancers.

3. My grandparents used to waken over here. Reference is to the Kiks.ádi clan, who are the clan of the father of George's father.

8-16. Splattering Women. This is a metaphor for the Kiks.ádi, and how the orator is being inspired by them. The image is of herring, and the Herring Rock. Kiks.ádi women are referred to as Herring Women, and the Herring Rock is a Kiks.ádi landmark in Sitka. He is comparing getting an idea to the splattering women shattering the surface of the sea water. There is a Herring Rock Chilkat Blanket belonging to the Kiks.ádi at the Visitors Center in Sitka. The Herring Rock is also in Swanton (1970*b*: 176-177; 299-300). George is also describing the traditional practice of people acting out their at.óow in a ceremonial, as described in the introduction to this book.

20. Leave without saying. The Tlingit is literally, "leave with it (still in my possession)" i.e. without sharing the image of the Herring Rock.

22-27. A joke . . . Dr. Johnson . . . Taakw K'wát'i. The rest of George's speech is an example of Tlingit humor and joking between opposite moieties. George is referring to Frank Johnson (featured in *Haa Shuká*) who is a "joking relative" of George Davis. His Tlingit name translates as "Winter Egg" and refers to raven eggs layed in the winter. We do not completely understand the reference to walking on water.

33-34, 44. Roy Peratrovich (1910-1989, Eagle/Naasteidí) and Mr. (Judson) Brown (Eagle; Dak̲l'aweidí) are of the opposite moiety from George, and George is now joking with his father's people or paternal uncles, or, by extension, any man of the opposite moiety, poking fun at them. Most people will do this at a banquet. Much of this humor is very difficult to appreciate outside of Tlingit culture, but within the culture such joking is a very powerful force for reaffirmation of the sense of community. This is a good example. Roy Peratrovich and Judson Brown have both served on the Board of Directors of Sealaska Heritage Foundation. Roy Peratrovich was Naasteidí, a little-known clan of the Eagle moiety. The clan had three houses: Kóon Hít (Flicker House), Ch'eet Hít (Murre House), and G̱ooch Hít (Wolf House). They were Koowyook̲wáan, people of Kuiu. After smallpox struck, there were only nine people left. They moved to Klawock. Influenza also struck the clan, either in the old village or after their move. The editors thank Evelyn Edenso, niece of Roy Peratrovich, for her help on this note.

40-42, 46. Paternal uncles . . . retaliating. Roy Peratrovich and Judson Brown had previously engaged in some joking comments about George's paternal uncles; now George is continuing the humor by retaliating with jokes about Roy and Judson. He will also use this as a light touch on which to end the serious part of the evening.

48. Your paternal uncle. With great economy, in a fine coup of Tlingit humor, based on genealogy and protocol, George uses his joking relative Frank Johnson, who is the paternal uncle of Roy and Judson, to get back at Roy and Judson for their jokes about George's paternal uncles.

59-60. Roy and Mr. Brown . . . step out. George Davis uses this joking with his fellow elders to wrap up the responses from the guests and conclude this portion of the speech making. This speech is a good example of the balance of the serious and the humorous. As in traditional ceremonial, after dealing with serious matters, the evening turns to the lighter side.

Notes to Charlie Joseph (2)

3-5. My grandchild . . . Dimitry. In Tlingit culture and genealogy, a person who may be biologically older, such as the old Dimitry when Charlie was young, may be referred to as generationally younger—and vice versa, such as an older person's calling a younger person his or her father or mother or grandfather. Charlie was of Dimitry's grandfather's clan—perhaps his namesake—thus making Dimitry his tribal grandson although biologically older. This is a difficult concept to grasp.

25, 32. Your fathers' spirit helper. The spirit helper of my grandfathers. Charlie uses the Tlingit term shageinyaa, which we translate as "spirit helper." It is a general term for spirits. Elders often explain shageinyaa as "God," a Tlingit pre-Christian intuitive understanding of a Creator not incompatible with Christian thought and concepts. Elders often make the point that Tlingits had the concept of God prior to the arrival of Christian missionaries.

33. Have joined the Alaska Native Brotherhood. This is a complex image. The ANB was formed in 1912 on the model of Western men's clubs and social service organizations and out of the experience of the Orthodox Church Brotherhoods and the Sheldon Jackson School. A main objective was to form an organization that would combine and transcend traditional clan organization, and become a political and social force in Sealaska. The ANB took the lead in the fights for American Citizenship for Native Americans, integrated schools and public facilities, and land claims suits, among others. (See Drucker 1958). Charlie implies that the traditional spirit helper or protector is now collectively owned by the ANB and its members. As with the individual clan dances and songs, where there are often not enough trained members of each clan to maintain the tradition, but the tradition can be maintained by combining forces, Charlie is suggesting that the spirit power which once guided individual clans, and the spirits that were claimed by separate clans because the spirits revealed themselves to individual members of those clans, now be shared collectively—but with the individual identity and owning clan still known and recognized. This is an extremely important concept being put forth by Charlie as an elder at the elders conference.

36. Shee Atika. The place name from which "Sitka" derives and the name of the hotel. Charlie is asserting that the traditional spirit power is also to be found in new places and new situations, like ANB and Shee Atika, and will continue to live with the Tlingit people. See also the note to Charlie Jim, line 119.

42. Deep forest. Euphemism for death.

43. It will be heard. The traditional helping spirits will still be heard in new and changed and changing times.

44-45. Thank you, etc. Charlie is expressing his gratitude for all the oratory directed toward him and the dancers.

46. Their achievements. The songs the dancers have learned of all the clans represented among the dancers.

55-56. Stand, my son . . . Johnson. Charlie is asking A.P. Johnson to stand. He addresses him as his son, because A.P. Johnson, who is Kiks.ádi, is also Kaagwaantaan yádi—child of Kaagwaantaan, meaning that his father was Kaagwaantaan. Because Charlie is of that group, he is by extension a father of A.P. Johnson. Mr. Johnson is represented in this collection by the short speech that opens the book, and he is featured in *Haa Shuká*.

56-67. When Johnson approached me . . . reason why. In this very powerful and moving passage, Charlie Joseph expresses in public his initial fear and reluctance to teach the children, when A.P. Johnson requested him to do so. Charlie would face extreme risk in teaching, because the concept was innovative. Rights to perform songs and dances in public are very rigorously maintained by the individual clans who own the songs, and they are normally performed by elders, not children. Yet the community concern was that children were no longer learning the songs and dances, not through their own fault or lack of interest, but because the traditional clan structure and community setting for natural and traditional learning had been eroded beyond the point of no return. The only solution would have to be innovative—a formal dance group for children of all clans who would learn and perform the songs and dances of all clans represented in the group. This constitutes a kind of "synthetic transmission" of culture, certainly unnatural in traditional times, but perhaps no longer, where all of American society is so conditioned by schooling. Being traditional himself, Charlie explains that he was not immediately in favor of the idea. Moreover, he could imagine only too well the hostility he might face in the community, either because of legitimate concerns over the altering of tradition, or simply because of petty rivalry and jealousy. People might accuse him of lying or doing things all wrong.

Fortunately, the experiment was a great success. Young people went to the ANB Hall after school and on Saturdays to practice and learn from Charlie. The group has won national recognition as one of the most accomplished dance groups of its kind, and has performed nationwide. Through the efforts of Charlie and the other elders who are his counterparts in different villages in Southeast Alaska, the concept of community dance groups for young people, or people of all ages, singing songs of various clans in the group and community, has won widespread acceptance, and many communities now have outstanding groups. The important point is that as long as the proper clan ownership is recognized, the maintenance of songs and dances is passing from the individual clan or clan house level to the community level, where it seems to be thriving. This set of speeches is a kind of "benchmark" documenting a point in the process where Charlie

Joseph demonstrated the results to his peers, who publicly responded with acceptance, emphasizing how no clan stands alone, but all are related and interconnected. The elders seized the opportunity to explain the culture in their own words.

In their speeches, Charlie's peers gave him and the young dancers full support. They expressed their gratitude and joy at hearing the traditional songs again, and they also expressed their concern for the risks being taken. The risks were social and spiritual. The speakers expressed their community support, and on the spiritual plane offered up spirits and other at.óow in traditional patterns of reciprocity. This concern and action is important because it demonstrates that the elders also accepted the songs in a traditional manner and took Charlie and the G̱ajaa Héen Dancers seriously. The elders not only endorsed Charlie, but actively joined in the teaching, using the Elders Conference setting to explain things in Tlingit, in their own words, so that the teaching would be the way they wanted it. In general, those elders with the greatest knowledge of Tlingit culture were also those with the most limited English. The elders often comment on this language barrier, as in the speeches here. We hope that the transcription, translation and annotation of this set of speeches will help remove some of the language barriers, and make the Tlingit elders' teachings more accessible to learners of all generations.

64. He's lying. At this point, Charlie switches to English for the remainder of his speech.

69-73. Thank you. Charlie Joseph, who opened the speechmaking of the traditional part of the evening with his introduction and presentation of the dancers, now closes his final speech by thanking people for their acceptance and support.

After Charlie's speech, the evening was concluded with four short speeches of gratitude in English by A.P. Johnson, Eli Hanlon, John Bell (the young man who was president of the dance group) and Isabella Brady, the director of the program. Interested readers will find these in *"Because We Cherish You...": Sealaska Elders Speak to the Future* (Dauenhauer and Dauenhauer 1981:68a-77a).

Glossary

This glossary is primarily the work of Richard Dauenhauer, arising from his interests and needs as a learner of Tlingit, and based on his experience as a high school and college learner of German, Russian, Finnish, Classical Greek, and other languages. The glossary is included as part of this book in hope that it will serve the needs of linguists and students of Tlingit everywhere, but especially the needs of community instruction programs in Southeast Alaska.

Glossaries (small dictionaries limited to a specific text or set of texts) have traditionally been a central component of sets of instructional materials at the beginning and intermediate levels of language learning. A glossary helps the student move from grammar study into literature in the original language. On the grammatical level, a glossary helps him or her bridge the often overwhelming gaps between an elementary grammar book such as *Beginning Tlingit* (Dauenhauer and Dauenhauer 1976) or a more technical reference grammar such as the "Appendix" to the *Tlingit Verb Dictionary* (Story and Naish 1973) on the one hand, and a full-sized dictionary (such as the *Tlingit Verb Dictionary*) on the other. On the literary level, a glossary helps learners take the major step between the limited text covered by the glossary and the limitless body of literature that awaits in the language at large.

Accordingly, our long range goal over the last 20 years has been to develop a full range of instructional and cultural resource materials. This includes a grammar, spelling book, and this glossary on the one hand, and collections of oral literature (including the speeches in this book) on the other. It has been our long range goal to collect and transcribe classics of Tlingit oral literature and make them more accessible to students of Tlingit language and culture. The language of the stories and speeches has provided much of the base for the instructional materials, and the instructional materials are designed to lead into the literature. It is sad to note that every year there are fewer people for learners of Tlingit to speak with, as the elders pass away, but the written record of the oral literature is increasing, and stories and speeches may be read in memory of the elders who composed them. Specifically, this glossary accompanies the six speeches for the removal of grief delivered by the guests at the memorial for Jim Marks, Hoonah, 1968. Our hope is that students of Tlingit can use this glossary not only to read the one set of speeches in the original, but, through using the glossary, to become more familiar with the larger, more technical *Tlingit Verb Dictionary* and use it to expand into reading more of the Tlingit texts in this book and in *Haa Shuká* in the original language.

Every word used in the set of speeches is included in the glossary, alphabetized by underlying stem and then listed in the theoretical underlying format used in the *Tlingit Verb Dictionary*. Each word is presented as it appears in the text and is analyzed according to its underlying form. Through this analysis, we hope that students will learn how Tlingit words, especially verbs, are put together in a complicated but orderly system of prefixes and suffixes combining with a stem. Native speakers of Tlingit do this automatically "by ear," but for people who do not already speak or understand Tlingit, it is one of the most difficult languages in the world to learn. Once a student gets some insight into how the system of the language operates, he or she can then use the larger Naish-Story Dictionary and the texts in the *Classics of Tlingit Oral Literature* series to continue the study of Tlingit language and literature. Because this glossary is a reference tool, it includes no instruction in grammar. For details on grammar we direct readers to our *Beginning Tlingit* and especially to the "Appendix" of the *Tlingit Verb Dictionary* by Constance Naish and Gillian Story (1973). For additional technical studies, see the theses by Naish (1979) and Story (1979), and Story's most recent (1990) analysis of a Tlingit text.

Work on the glossary started on file cards in 1972, and a limited, field test edition of the working draft was circulated in October 1984. The present version is still very much a draft of work in progress, but it seems preferable to make it more widely available, despite its shortcomings, than to delay publication in light of the most recent advances in Tlingit linguistics, especially by Jeff Leer. It has been revised on the basis of comments on the field test version. We thank especially Dr. Heinz-Jürgen Pinnow for his careful review of that manuscript. We have incorporated as many of his suggestions as practical and possible for our purposes. More recently, Gillian Story (personal communication 1989) has shared her work in progress, and Jeff Leer (personal communication 1989) has made suggestions based on his current research in Tlingit. At this juncture in acknowledging the help and inspiration of others, lest we in any way misrepresent their work, we should clarify that in the interests of practical pedagogy we have not reflected all of their theoretical advances in the charts. Leer's research in progress will demonstrate a different hierarchical relationship in some parts of the verb system. What is presented here is intended as a practical tool, designed for entry into literature with no pretensions to advances in linguistic theory. The Verb System Chart in particular admittedly does not do justice in reflecting the actual complexity of the total system. It is intended as a "field guide to the verbs" rather than a model of ecological relationships.

We should emphasize here that our primary concern over the years has been Tlingit literature. In all aspects of Tlingit linguistics we acknowledge our debt to those whose knowledge and insights far exceed our own, notably Michael Krauss, Jeff Leer, Constance Naish, Gillian Story, and Heinz-Jürgen Pinnow. We have benefitted from their research, guidance, and encouragement over the years. In the same breath, we apologize to them for any shortcomings in the linguistic analysis presented in this glossary. We have tried to keep the non-technical learner in mind without falsifying or oversimplifying certain points of grammar, especially the morphophonemics. Our own understanding of certain points of Tlingit grammar is incomplete, and, on the other hand, much of the theory and terminology is still being resolved. We have attempted to synthesize the linguistic work over the years, especially Naish and Story and the latest research by Story (1990) and Leer. We have tried to keep our terms and analysis as close to Naish and Story as possible, with the notable exception that we use the traditional term "classifier" where they use "extensor," and we label the classifiers "I" and "A" according to their form rather than "A" and "B" according to their position on the chart.

For those readers interested in the technical details, the full range of the decessive may be misrepresented in the accompanying chart. Also, in Leer's words (personal communication 1989), "the progressive and customary superaspects constitute a separate dimension" and this is not reflected in the existing chart. Some of the allomorphs are not technically correct; for example, -woo- is not an allomorph of the perfective, but a contraction of wu-ya. Leer also points out that the "purposive -t is . . . a post-position which may optionally be preceded by the subjunctive i/u. It can therefore be eliminated." There is also some technical inconsistency in the chart: we have not listed all contracted forms of prefixes and allomorphs, although it has been revised to show -wa-, -a-, and -y- as allmorphs of the ya classifier. On a more trivial level, certain conventions of word division are still being defined in Tlingit orthography, especially involving personal names, compound nouns and some of the nominal prefixes in the verb complex (yakw and x̱'us, for example).

It is with great humility that we include this glossary here. We offer it as work in progress, understanding that some entries and certain features of the glossary, especially the Verb System Chart, are subject to revision. Both charts were revised shortly before going to press to reflect some of the most recent theoretical analyses and suggestions. Other features of the chart have been retained, even though they may no longer be technically accurate in light of the most recent research. For the time being, however, we have retained these on the chart, feeling that the redundancy or simplification may be helpful to learners. The glossary has helped us, and we hope it will help others. Even where the analysis is uncertain, it seems important to include the data rather than to omit them for fear of public error. Where this glossary is uncertain or in error, we hope that others can make better analytical sense of the data. We thank our colleagues and students for their help and suggestions, and we apologize for any errors of omission and commission the glossary may be found to contain. We hope that a new generation of scholars can join ranks and improve on it. We hope that even with its limitations, this glossary will serve as instructional material for self study and in classrooms, and that corrections and additions will be generated through its use.

How to Read the Glossary

A Tlingit verb dictionary can be confusing at first glance, but with a little experience it will become easy for a reader to use. In Tlingit, the most important part of a word is the ***stem***. For most nouns, this is the first part of the word, so it is easy to list nouns in alphabetical order in a Tlingit dictionary. Most nouns in this glossary are very straightforward, and require no further comment. But in Tlingit verbs, the stem is almost always at the end of the word, or buried in the middle, surrounded by prefixes and suffixes. The stem may also appear with a long or short vowel, and with high or low tone, depending on what is being said. In the dictionary and in this glossary, stems are listed long and low.

In this glossary, **STEMS** are listed in alphabetical order, **BOLDFACE**, and in **CAPITAL LETTERS**. Stems routinely appear with a variety of ***prefixes***, combinations of which are used to express a rich range of meaning. The most important sets of prefixes for the purposes of the specific glossary entry are listed below the stem, in **lower case bold face**. These are taken from the *Tlingit Verb Dictionary* and are the theoretical underlying forms that give the basic meanings of the verb. Abbreviations follow the *Tlingit Verb Dictionary*. The type of verb is indicated in parentheses: (in), intransitive; (st), stative; and (tr), transitive. Empty parentheses ( ) or (?) indicate uncertainty.

Then, marked with a bullet • the word is given in a phrase as it appears in the speech. The speaker and line number are identified. Below this, marked with an arrow < meaning "comes from underlying form" is the grammatical analysis. This line is especially important for showing the grammatical prefixes and suffixes that are not part of the underlying dictionary meaning of the verb, but which change according to what a person is saying. (For example, "I go," "she goes," and "he is going" are grammatical variations of the underlying word "go". Likewise, "sang" and "sung" are related to "sing," and "went" is related to "go.") Below the analysis, these parts of the word are identified. They are written out where space permits, otherwise abbreviated. Abbreviations are explained in two charts, one in alphabetical order, and one in grammatical order. In some cases, additional notes call attention to interesting, important, or unusual features of the entry. The purpose of all of this is to provide examples from Tlingit oral literature of how the Tlingit language actually operates.

A Typical Entry with Analysis and Commentary

.AAK̲W	STEM
ka-ya-.aak̲w (tr) try	**underlying form** and meaning
• kagax̲too.áak̲w we will try DK 86	• example from text, and line number
<ka-ga-g̲a-too-.aak̲w	< grammatical analysis
np cp ap sp stem future	identification of parts

Note the contraction of the conjugation prefix ga and the aspect prefix g̲a to gax̲. This is very common in the future 1st person plural. Ø or zero is the a form of the ya classifier.

Note on A and Á

"A" is often a difficult form, because it has many homonyms—words that sound alike, but have different meanings. It appears with low tone (a) and high tone (á). The most common forms and meanings of "a" are:

1. Possessive pronoun, 3rd person singular, inanimate (its), without focus on this person. Example: a koowú (its fin, plume). This form is commonly used in locative construction, such as: a daa-x' (about it) or a shóo-dei (next to it; toward the end of it).
2. Object pronoun, 3rd person singular, inanimate (it), without focus on this person, and animate, especially human. (him/her); for example: a-wu-si-teen (he/she saw him/her).
3. Subject pronoun, indefinite 3rd person, used with verbs of sitting, standing, and motion; for example: ahán (someone is standing).

The spelling convention is to write the possessive pronoun as a separate word, but to combine the object and subject pronouns with the stems; for example, du hídi (his house) a koowu (its fin) a daax' (about it) but awusiteen (he/she saw him/her/it) x̲ahán (I am standing) ahán (he/she is standing).

The form á has two common meanings:

1. Subject pronoun, 3rd person singular, with focus on this person (he, she, it, someone).
2. Locative; locative base, there; that place, it (indefinite or previously mentioned place). Sometimes, as in the phrase á áwé, it functions like a conjunction.

Also, á is the imperative stem of .aat (go):

ax̲ daa-déi g̲unei y.á	Come, gather around me. JM 31

Also, the form á is further complicated because it can appear with its high tone "stolen," (tone sandhi) so that it looks like "a". The following are easy to confuse in texts:

á	there
á	he, she, or it; that (3rd sing. with focus)
a	it, its, him, her, he, she (without focus)
aa	one; someone
aa-	combining form of á, with long vowel and low tone, as in aa-déi
áa	a variation of áx' (there)
áa	lake

The Tlingit Alphabet

The Tlingit Alphabet as arranged here generally follows the same order as English, with the following exceptions: DL, DZ, SH, TL, TL', TS and TS' are treated as separate letters, as are K, K', K̲ and K̲', X, X', X̲ and X̲'. But, W is treated as a "regular" letter; that is, KW, XW, X'W K̲'W, and so forth, are not treated as separate letters, which they technically are, but are alphabetized according to the variety of K or X, with the W following. The alphabetical order is thus:
A, CH, CH', D, DL, DZ, E, G, G̲, H, I, J, K, K', K̲, K̲', L, L', N, O, S, S', SH, T, T', TL, TL', TS, TS' U, W, X, X', X̲, X̲', Y.

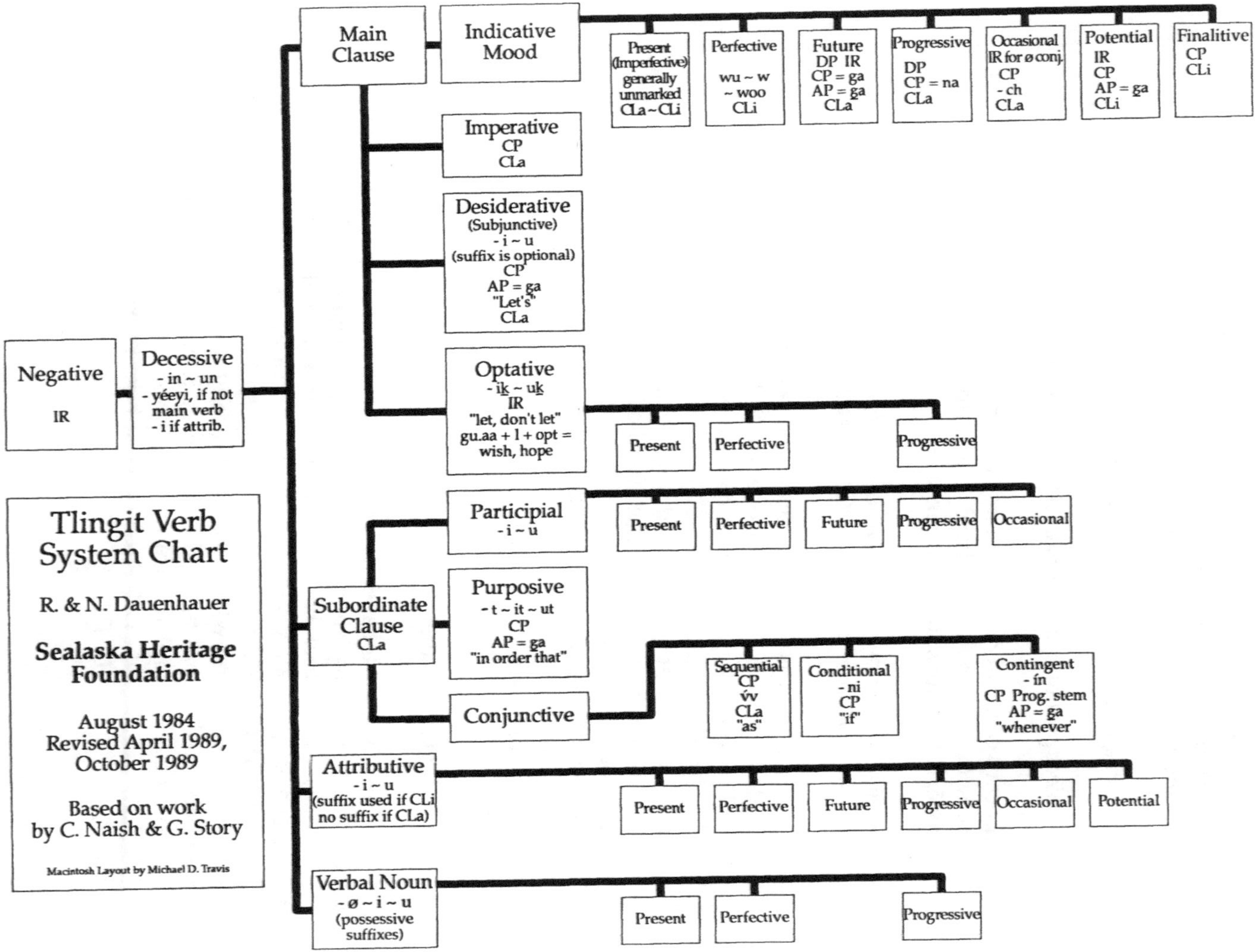

Tlingit Verb System Chart
R. & N. Dauenhauer
Sealaska Heritage Foundation
August 1984
Revised April 1989, October 1989
Based on work by C. Naish & G. Story
Macintosh Layout by Michael D. Travis
Negative
IR
Decessive
- in ~ un
- yéeyi, if not main verb
- i if attrib.
Main Clause
Indicative Mood
Present (Imperfective) generally unmarked CLa ~ CLi
Perfective wu ~ w ~ woo CLi
Future DP IR CP = ga AP = ga CLa
Progressive DP CP = na CLa
Occasional IR for ø conj. CP - ch CLa
Potential IR CP AP = ga CLi
Finalitive CP CLi
Imperative CP CLa
Desiderative (Subjunctive) - i ~ u (suffix is optional) CP AP = ga "Let's" CLa
Optative - ik ~ uk IR "let, don't let" gu.aa + l + opt = wish, hope
Present
Perfective
Progressive
Subordinate Clause CLa
Participial - i ~ u
Present
Perfective
Future
Progressive
Occasional
Purposive - t ~ it ~ ut CP AP = ga "in order that"
Conjunctive
Sequential CP v́v CLa "as"
Conditional - ni CP "if"
Contingent - ín CP Prog. stem AP = ga "whenever"
Attributive - i ~ u (suffix used if CLi no suffix if CLa)
Present
Perfective
Future
Progressive
Occasional
Potential
Verbal Noun - ø ~ i ~ u (possessive suffixes)
Present
Perfective
Progressive

Bound Adverb	Directional Prefix	RP	PL	Object Pronoun	Nominal Prefix	IR	CP	AP	Dist	Subject Pronoun	Classifier (extensor)	Stem	Suf-fixes
yéi yóo	ḵut ¦ yei ¦ yoo yaa ¦ yax̱ yeiḵ yan neil daak daaḵ kei kux̱ yoot yoox̱	wooch~ woosh chush	has	x̱at~ax̱ i haa yee ø~a- ash ḵu~ḵaa at aa sh	ji ¦ ya~ ¦ ka~ tu ¦ w ¦ k- x̱'a sa sha shu ḵ'a ḵu ḵi x̱i daa lu ta t'aa ga sha yee yakw	u oo	ø na~n ga~k g̱a~x̱ wu ~ woo ~ w	g̱a~x̱	dag̱a ~ dax̱	x̱a~x̱ i~ee ø tu~too y~yi~yee du~doo	see below	góot goot gút etc. 1,000 - 2,000 stems in Tlingit	see Suffixes

Classifier (extensor)

I	A
ya~ wa~ a~ y	ø
di	da
si	sa ~ s
dzi	s
li	la ~ l
dli	l
shi	sha ~ sh
ji	sh

Naish-Story	This Chart
A	I
B	A
Even	D

Tlingit Verb Complex Chart

Sealaska Heritage Foundation

Richard and Nora Dauenhauer

Based on work by Constance Naish (SIL), Gillian Story (SIL), and Jeff Leer (ANLC)

November 1983

Revised October 1984, April 1989 and October 1989

Macintosh Layout by Michael D. Travis

Conjugation System Overview

	Imperative	Future	Perfective	
	CP	DP	Stem Shape	
Zero	ø	ø	ø	v́v, v́c
Progressive	na	ø	Non - Zero	vv
Ascendant	g̱a	kei		vvc
Descendant	g̱a	yei		v́vc'

Suffixes

Aspectual	Inflectional	Post Positions
-x̱ -k~kw -ch -t -s' -l' -t' -x'~x'w Some take special directional prefix	**Main Clause** -in~un decessive -i~u subjunctive -ḵ~iḵ~uḵ optative eeḵ~ooḵ optative **Subordinate** -i~u participial -t~it~ut purposive -ni conditional -ín~ún contingent **Attributive** -i~u **Verbal Noun** ø~i~u possessive	-x̱ -ch -dax̱ -gaa -yáx̱ (and other post positions added to verbs)

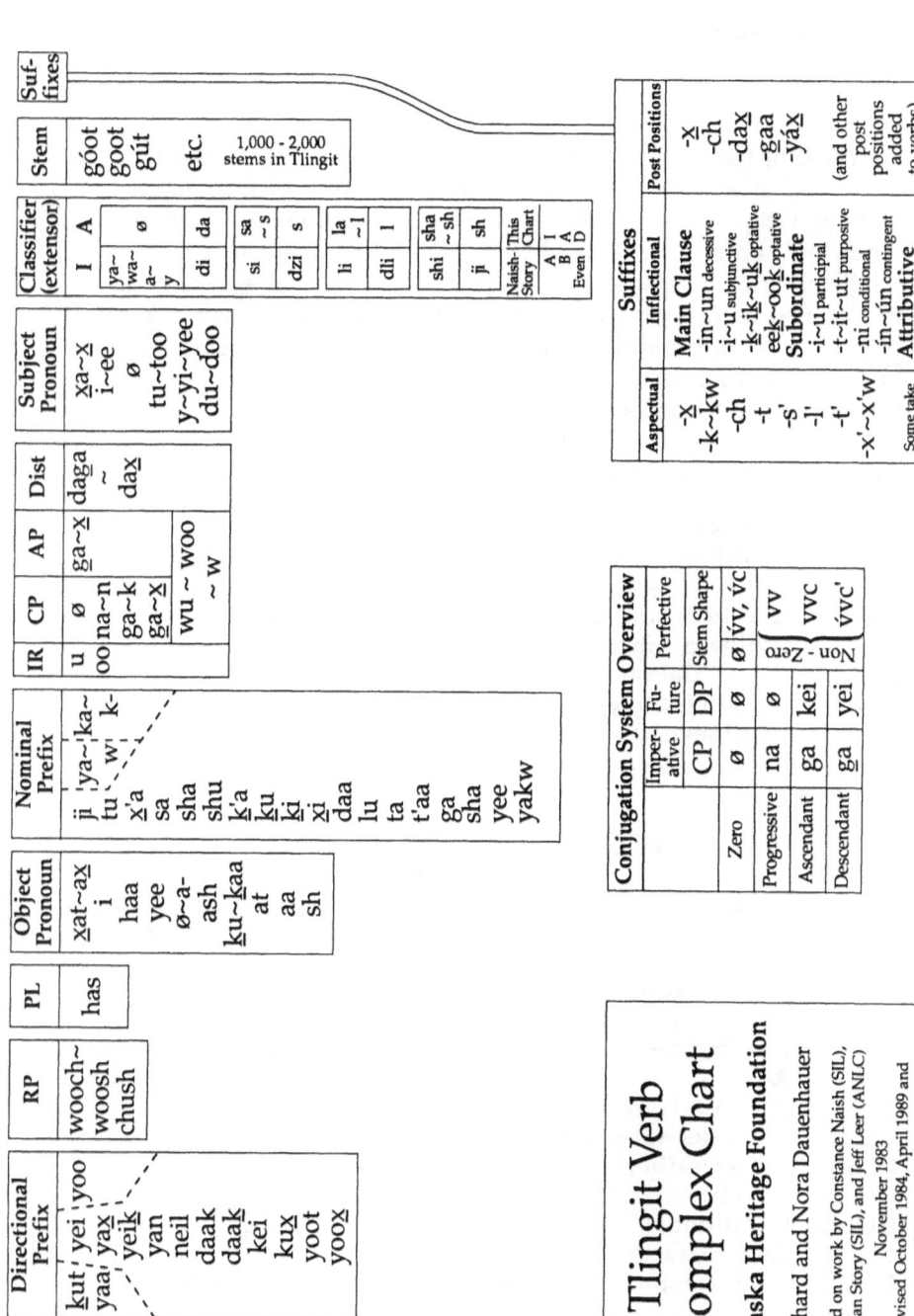

ABBREVIATIONS

Most of the abbreviations for syntax systems, tense, mode, mood and aspect are three letters, except for some of the conjunctive set, which are four. Most of the abbreviations for parts of verbs and sentences are two letters. The most distinctive features are listed after the name. AP is specified as -wu- or -g̲a- and CP is specified as -ga- or -na- where invariable. The English examples are only approximate. There are two sets of abbreviations here, the first listed in ALPHABETICAL order, the second in GRAMMATICAL order.

Abbreviations of the Orators

JM	Jim Marks
ML1	Matthew Lawrence, Opening Speech
DK	David Kadashan
WJ	William Johnson
JD	Jessie Dalton
AH	Austin Hammond
ML2	Matthew Lawrence, Closing Speech

General Symbols

~	or
<	comes from underlying form
-	-suffix
	prefix-
	-infix-

Abbreviations In Alphabetical Order

Abb	Name	Grammatical Feature	Approximate English Example
AP	Aspect Prefix		
AS	Attributive Suffix		
ATT	Attributive	-i~u	It's a going thing.
AV	Adverb		
BA	Bound Adverb		
CL	Classifier (also called extensor)		
CLa	"a" classifier		
CLi	"i" classifier		
COND	Conditional	CP -ni	...if he goes.
CONJ	Conjunctive		
CONT	Contingent	CP g̲a -ín~ún (always high)	...whenever he goes.
CP	Conjugation Prefix		
DI	Distributive Prefix		

DP	Directional Prefix		
DEC	Decessive	-in~un	It used to go.
DES	Desiderative (Sometimes called Subjunctive or Hortative)	CP g̲a -i~u	Let's go!
DUR	Durative	(suffix)	He goes (every day).
FUT	Future	DP IR ga g̲a	He will go.
HV	Helping Verb		
IM	Imperfective (or "present")	(unmarked)	He goes.
IMP	Imperative	CP	Go!
IND	Indicative		It goes.
IP	Independent Pronoun		
IR	Irrealis		
LO	Locative base; part-noun		
MAIN	Main clause		It goes. It's going.
N	Noun		
NEG	Negative	IR	It doesn't go.
NP	Nominal Prefix (also called Thematic Prefix)		
OCC	Occasional	CP~IR(Ø) -ch	He would go (now and then).
OP	Object Pronoun		
OPT	Optative	IR -ik̲~uk̲	Let it go. Don't let it go.
PAR	Participial	i~u	I know how it goes.
PER	Perfective	-wu-	He went.
PL	Plural	(hás)	
PO	Post Postition		
POT	Potential	IR CP g̲a	He can go.
PP	Possessive Pronoun		
PRO	Progressive	DP NA	He is going along.
PRS	Present (or Imperfective)	(unmarked)	He goes. I am going.
PS	Possessive Suffix		
PUR	Purposive	CP g̲a -t~it~ut	...in order to go
RP	Reciprocal Pronoun	(woosh)	
S	Suffix		
SEQ	Sequential	CP CLa	...as he was going.
SP	Subject Pronoun		
SS	Subordinative Suffix		
ST	Stem		
SUBO	Subordinate	-i~u	I'm happy that he's going.
VN	Verbal Noun		The going got tough.

Abbreviations in Order of Grammatical Hierarchy

Abb	Name	Grammatical Feature	Approximate English Example

Polarities Operating in Entire System

NEG	Negative	IR	It doesn't go.
DEC	Decessive	-in~un	It used to go.

Syntax System

MAIN	Main clause		It goes. It's going.
SUBO	Subordinate	-i~u	I'm happy that he's going.
ATT	Attributive	-i~u	It's a going thing.
VN	Verbal Noun		The going got tough.

Moods of the Main Clause

IND	Indicative		It goes.
IMP	Imperative	CP	Go!
DES	Desiderative (Sometimes called Subjunctive or Hortative)	CP ga -i~u	Let's go!
OPT	Optative	IR -ik~uk	Let it go. Don't let it go.

Moods of the Subordinate Clause

PAR	Participial	-i~u	I know how it goes.
PUR	Purposive	CP ga -t~it~ut	...in order to go
CONJ	Conjunctive	(see next 3 examples)	

Aspects of the Conjunctive Mood

SEQ	Sequential	CP CLa	...as he was going.
COND	Conditional	CP -ni	...if he goes.
CONT	Contingent	CP ga -ín~ún (always high)	...whenever he goes.

Aspects of ATT and VN, and of IND, OPT and PAR Moods

IM	Imperfective (or "Present")	(unmarked)	He goes. I am going.
PRS	"Present" (or Imperfective)	(unmarked)	He goes. I am going.
PER	Perfective	-wu-	He went.
FUT	Future	DP IR ga ga	He will go.
PRO	Progressive	DP na	He is going along.
OCC	Occasional	CP~IR(Ø) -ch	He would go (now and then).
POT	Potential	IR CP ga	He can go.
DUR	Durative	(suffix)	He goes (every day).

Parts of Verbs and Sentences

N	Noun
LO	Locative base; part-noun
PO	Post Postition
PP	Possessive Pronoun
IP	Independent Pronoun
AV	Adverb
BA	Bound Adverb
DP	Directional Prefix
RP	Reciprocal Pronoun (woosh)
PL	Plural (hás)
OP	Object Pronoun
NP	Nominal Prefix (also called Thematic Prefix)
IR	Irrealis
CP	Conjugation Prefix
AP	Aspect Prefix
DI	Distributive Prefix
SP	Subject Pronoun
CL	Classifier (also called extensor)
CLa	"a" classifier
CLi	"i" classifier
ST	Stem
S	Suffix
PS	Possessive Suffix
SS	Subordinative Suffix
AS	Attributive Suffix
HV	Helping Verb

A

A Pronoun (Subjective, Objective, and Possessive). It, its, him, her, he, she (without focus)

a dáa — about it ML1 22
a daa-x' — about it AH 14
a ká-t — on it DK 48
a yá-x̱ — like it JD 7
a yá-t — to its face JD 51
Ya a shóo-dei han aa — Someone is standing next to it. JD 26
Yáa-náx̱ á a shóo-dei aa ahán — Someone is standing there closer, next to it. JD 28
A shóo-dei ahán — Someone is standing next to it JD 30

- Ḵa yáa-náx̱ á a shóo-dei han aa. — And there, on this side, next to it, stands someone. AH 17
  á — there
  a — it
  aa — one; someone
- asawdihaa — he wanted him (to go) JM 10
  <a- sa- w-di-haa
  op np ap cl st — perfective

Á There, that place, it (indefinite or previously mentioned place) With á áwé it functions like a conjunction. In constructions with yé, aadéi often translates as "how" or "the way"; with negative it translates as "nothing" or "no-thing" or "no-how" or "no way." Á most commonly appears with the postpositions expressing location, usually as a long, low vowel.

á-x' áwé — it was there JM 6
á-a — (= áx') there DK 41, 42, 45; JM 8
aa-x̱ — along it; from it DK 30
aa-tx̱ — (= aa-dáx̱) from it DK 37
aa-déi — (to) there JM 11, 19
aa-déi has ḵunoogu yé — what (the way/how) they did DK 71
Tléil áwé aa-déi nax̱tudzigeedi yé. — There is nothing we can do. ML1 16
Hél aadéi has yee daang̱waanéiyi yéi. — There is no way they can do anything for you. DK 83

- K̲a yáa-náx̲ á a shóo-dei han aa. And there, on this side, next to it, stands someone. AH 17
  - á there
  - a it
  - a a one; someone

AA one, thing, someone

Yá tléix' yateeyi aa.	There is one more. AH 23
Yá a shóodei han aa.	One is standing next to it. JD 26
Á áwé yáanáx̲ aa.	That is the closer one. JD 30
Yáadu aa.	Here is one. JD 184, 185

.AA

ya-dzi-.aa (in) peer; peep; swim underwater, but with head emerging every so often

- Yáa yeedát áwé yee káx' gági yawdzi.áa yá gagaan ax̲ léelk'w hás l'ax̲keidí. This moment this sun has come out over you, my grandparents' mask. JD 207

<ya-wu-dzi-.aa
np ap cl st perfective

ÁA lake
yá áa this lake DK 27

AAA Yes. AH 3, 6, 7, etc.
Commonly used in oratory for emphasis and rhythmic and thematic balance; in most cases, we do not consider this to be like the English "uh" or mere pausing, although it does seem to function as such from time to time. In normal, informal conversation the word is pronounced aaá, but in oratory it is pronounced low.

AAG̲ÁA then, on that account, at that time

aag̲áa áwé	and then JM 16
aag̲áa yú s'áaxw	then, for that hat JD 147

.AAK

ya-ji-.aak ( ) stagger (of wounded animal or person); flounder (of wounded seal or exhausted fish)

- yá yee káani yee daat x̲'ayanash.ákjeen this your brother-in-law spoke proudly of you (literally–he was stumbling

about you in speech) AH 30
<x̲'a- ya- na- sh- .aak- ch- een
np np cp cl st occ dec
This is an occasional decessive: literally, he used to speak on occasion about you. Note the nominal prefix for "mouth", the na conjugation prefix and suffix ch for the occasional, and the decessive suffix -een. Sh is the "a" form of the ji classifier.

- k̲ut ayawji.áak yaa yeedát   one of them is missing now (someone has been struck a blow by death; wounded by death) WJ 19
  <a- ya-wu-ji-.aak
  op np ap cl st   perfective

.AAK̲W
ka-ya-.aak̲w (tr) try

- kagax̲too.áak̲w   we will try DK 86
  <ka-ga-g̲a-too-.aak̲w
  np cp ap sp stem   future
  Note the contraction of the conjugation prefix ga and the aspect prefix g̲a to gax̲. This is very common in the future 1st person plural. Ø or zero is the a form of the ya classifier.

AAN = á + (ee)n   with it

yáa-t aan hán	here he stands with it AH 13
aan gug̲agóot	it will go with it ML2 19, 24
aan ayagux̲dagóot	it will go back with it ML2 20
aan	with it JD 51, 158, 168, 170

AANKÁX̲ SHAWUSTAAN   Personal name (Mary Johnson); see annotations

AANSHÉIX̲'   Personal name (Jennie Lindoff); see annotations

AAS   tree
yá aas   the tree(s) DK 28

AAT   Paternal aunt; father's sister

ax̲ aat hás	my paternal aunts ML1 3; WJ 4; JD 23; AH 2, 40
yee aat hás	your paternal aunts JD 44

.AAT (1) (plural of **GOOT**)
Note: the numbers after the stem refer to categories in the Naish-Story *Tlingit Verb Dictionary.*
ya-.aat (in) walk, go, come in general

- ax̲ daa-déi g̲unei y.á Come, gather around me JM 31
  <g̲unei y- .á
  av sp st Imperative

- du daa-déi g̲unayéi a.áat they began to gather around him JM 33
  <g̲unayéi a- .áat
  av sp stem imperfective
  Note a as subject of a verb of motion without any prefix or subject marker

.AAT (2) (Plural of **TAAN**)
tu-li-.aat
A + tu-li-.aat decide, make up one's mind
a daa + tu-li-.aat think over, consider

- i aat a daa s tuwli.aat your maternal aunts thought it over/decided ML1 22
  <has tu-wu-li.aat
  pl np ap cl st Perfective; s is a contraction of has

li-.aat ( ) to guide; move plural objects in a controlled manner (Note: not attested in dictionary with this meaning)

- a yáa has wudli.aadi yáx̲ has yatee It's as if they are guiding them JD 182
  <a yáa has wu-dli-.aat -i yáx̲ has ya-tee
  op lo pl ap cl st s lo pl cl st
  This is attributive perfective. The main verb in the sentence is yatee, and wudli.aadi is in a dependent or subordinate clause, marked by the suffix -i. The t between two vowels changes to d; dli is the d form of the l classifier.

AATX̲ (= aadáx̲ = á + dáx̲) from it
aatx̲ from it DK 37

ÁAWÉ Rhetorical form of áwé, used by listeners to respond to orators. Translates loosely as "That's it." We leave this untranslated. AH 13a, 22a, 29a

AAX̱ then, after that, from there; (derives from á + x̱)
aax̱ áwé then JD 131
aax̱ áwé from there JD 151

.AAX̱ (1)
Note: the numbers after the stem refer to categories in the Naish-Story *Tlingit Verb Dictionary*.
si-.aax̱ (in) listen
A + si-.aax̱
ḵaa x̱'éi + si-.aax̱

- I x̱'éit wusi.áx̱ i sani hás. your paternal uncles are listening to you AH 10a
<i x̱'éi -t wu- si- .aax̱
pp n po ap cl st perfective
- I x̱'éit wusi.áx̱ i kaani yán your in-laws are listening to you DK 37a
- I x̱'éit wusi.áx̱ i káalk'w hás your brothers' children are listening to you JD 113a

The above are perfective forms. Note how many Tlingit perfectives translate into English present forms. Emphasis in Tlingit is not on the time of the action, but on the receiving of the sound as prior in time to the statement of listening. Literally "listening to your mouth."

ya-.aax̱ (tr) hear
x̱'a-ya-.aax̱ (tr) understand, hear with understanding

- ách áwé a yáx̱ has x̱'ayeey.áx̱ch that is why you hear them (their voices) like this JD 7
<a yáx̱ has x'a-yee-ya-.aax̱-ch
op pp pl np sp cl st dur imperative

This is a durative form, with the suffix -ch, indicating action enduring over a period of time. Note the contractions of the 2nd person plural pronoun yee-, and the classifier -ya-.

- yan x̲'ayeey.áx̲ you heard them JD 88
  <yan x̲'a-wu-yee-ya-.aax̲
  dp np ap sp cl st perfective
  Yan implies "you heard them out"; "you heard them to the end," or "completely." Note contractions.

.AAX̲ (2)
ya-.aax̲ (tr) carry, take cloth-like object;
lie (of cloth-like object)

- hú du jeex' áwé yándei kwg̲a.áax̲ it will remain (lie) in his hands JD 92
  <hú du jee-x' áwé yán-dei u -ga-g̲a-.aax̲
  ip pp lo po lo po ir cp ap st
  This is 3rd person sing. future. Note the contraction of the irrealis and conjugation prefix. Yándei conveys a sense of "it will completely lie"; literally, "to reach the end or shore."

AAYÍ Thing, property (possessed form)
Weihá aayí k'oodás' Weihá's shirt JD 82

ÁCH And so; that's why (á + ch)
ách áwé that is why JD 117
ách áyá this is why DK 55

ÁGÉ Interrogative particle, like an English question mark. In Tlingit and many other Alaska Native languages, questions are not marked as much by word order or tone of voice as in English, but by insertion of a question marking word in the sentence.
Eeshandéin ágé haa daa tuwatee Does it take pity on us? JD 1
A shunaayát ágé nk̲waagoot Can I reach the end? JD 123

ÁT Thing
Wáa yadali át yáx̲ sáyú nateech. What a heavy burden it is always like. WJ 6
Yat'éex'i át áyá. This is a difficult thing. DK 18
Yéi yateeyi át A thing like this DK 20
Yee tóowu daa oox̲lit'aayi átx'. These are the things that might warm your feelings. DK 74

l ch'u yee wak̲shiyee k̲waasháadi át you AH 7	with nothing to show

ÁWÉ That is; it is

This word has two important uses in Tlingit:

1) Like a verb in English: Hít áwé. That's a house.
2) As a phrase boundary marker, like a pause, comma, or period in English. Used this way, it is a word to show the beginning or end of a phrase. Here is an example and literal translation from JM 1-5.

Aáa	Yes
héi Yaakwdáaatdei áwé	to this Yakutat it was
kawdiyaa	went
wé haa x̲oodáx̲	this from among us
K̲'aadóo	K̲'aadóo

This use of the word áwé is often not translated literally into English. There are a number of possible translations:

Yes	Yes	Yes
it was to Yakutat	to Yakutat it was	K̲'aadóo
that this K̲'aadóo	that K̲'aadóo	went
went	went	from among us
from among us.	from among us.	to Yakutat.

ÁWU There are there (á + loc. post position -u)

AX̲ My. Possessive pronoun.

ax̲ tuwaa sigóo	I want to ML1 1; AH 1
ax̲ sani hás	my paternal uncles AH 2
ax̲ éesh	my father AH 28
ax̲ éesh hás	my fathers ML1 2
ax̲ jee	in my hand AH 38
ax̲ toowú yatee	it seems to me (it is in my mind) AH 39
ax̲ aat hás	my paternal aunts ML1 3

ÁYÁ This; this is. Commonly functions as a phrase boundary marker in Tlingit oratory and narrative, in which case it is usually not translated; for example: yáa yeedát áyá (AH 16). See discussion under áwé.

Héen áyá, séew áyá, a kaadéi daak ustaanch. The rain would fall on the water. DK 27

AYÁX̲ and thus; that's how (á + yáx̲)

ÁYÚ That; that is. Commonly functions as a phrase boundary marker in Tlingit oratory and narrative, in which case it is usually not translated. See discussion under áwé.

Yéi yee ng̲atéenín áyú	When you were like this AH 11
Héen áyú gadéich	The river would swell DK 24

CH

-CH Agent marker. The ending -ch shows that the noun marked is the do-er of the action.

Yá haa tláach	this mother of ours ML2 9
Yá ax̲ éek'ch	this brother of mine JD 200

CHOOKANEIDÍ A clan name; a clan of the Eagle moiety, meaning "people of the grass" from chookán. This clan is especially associated with Glacier Bay and Hoonah. DK 53

CHUSH himself; herself JM 32

CH'

CH'A Just; else; Ch'a also acts as an intensifier.

Ch'a kk̲walayaak̲w	I will just explain it. AH 26
Ch'a oowayáa	just let it resemble AH 38
Ch'a yeisú áwé	it was just/only recently JD 83
Ch'a yéi yiguwáatl'	for just a short/little while ML2 6

Ch'a yóo nax̲toosgeedí g̲óot áyá without anything else to do ML1 21

CH'ÁAKW long ago JD 105

CH'U Even; still; exactly; just

L ch'u yee wak̲shiyee k̲waasháadi át. I can't even find anything to show you; I don't even have a thing to show you. AH 7

Ch'u yáadu sígé hás	they are still present JD 15
Ch'u oowayáa áwé	It is just/exactly as if JD 20

D

DAA around; about; on; for

a daa-x'	of it AH 14
du daa-x'	about him; for him JD 84
yee daa-t	about you AH 30
ax̲ daa-déi	(to) around me JM 31
du daa-déi	(to) around him JM 33
a dáa	about it ML1 22
a daa-déi	around it DK 48
haa daa	on us (about; dealing with) JD 1
has du daa	about them JD 16, 78
Geesh daa-x̲	along the Kelp JD 27
yee yadaa-x̲	along your faces WJ 1, DK 64, JD 10

DAA

ya-daa (st) flow (of water, tide); flood; water (of eyes)

- héen áyú gadéich the river would swell DK 24
  <ga-daa-ch
  cp st occ occasional
  Note change of daa to dei. This is a common pattern in Tlingit verbs. Note pattern of occasional suffix used with conjugation prefix.

- tóo hinyawudaayí áwé when the river had swollen DK 28
  <héen ya-wu-daa-i
  np np ap st s subordinate participial perfective
  This is an unusual form. Tóo means "within;" héen is contracted to hin, and joined with the verb. The main verb is in the next line, so this form is a subordinate form in a dependent clause. The suffix is the indicator of the participial, and indicates that the verb is not a main verb. In English, "when" is used to mark a dependent clause.

ka-ya-daa (st) flow; run (nose) bleed

- daak kagadéich   it would flow (out) DK 28
  <daak ka-ga-daa-ch
  dp np cp st occ   occasional
  Note the use of the directional prefix, and the required combination of the occasional suffix and the conjugation prefix. Note also the alternation of the daa stem to déi.
- yee yadaax̲ kaawadaayi aa (káx̲ áyá)   this is for that which flowed from your faces WJ 1, JD 10, DK 64
  <yee yadaa-x̲ ka-wu-ya-daa-i (aa káx̲ áyá)
  pp n pp np ap cl st s one for it is
  Note the contraction of the nominal prefix, the wu-perfective aspect prefix and the ya classifier. This is a common pattern in Tlingit verbs. The vowel of the nominal prefix lengthens, and the y of the classifier changes to w because of the u vowel in front of it. Ya-daa is a compound noun.

DAAK   out from shore; into the open
daak uwagút   he came out AH 10
séew...daak ustaanch   the rain would fall DK 27
daak kagadéich   it would flow (out) DK 28

DAAK̲   into the interior; out of sight
yanax̲ daak̲ gug̲anóok   He will burrow back JD 169

DAAL
ya-daal (st) be heavy (usually of inanimate things); (fig.) be weighty, important (of abstract things)
li-daal (st) be heavy (usually of live creature)

- wáa yadali át yáx̲ sáyú nateech   how it is like a heavy burden WJ 6
  <ya - daal - i
  cl stem s   attributive

DAAN
ya-ka-ya-daan (st) snow heavily

- has a kooldánch   they would let fall like snow JD 133
  <ka-u- l -daan-ch
  np ir cl st occ   occasional

Note the use of the irrealis instead of the conjugation marker for the Ø conjugation verb (because it has no conjugation marker other than the Ø or "zero") with the occasional suffix. Note also the l classifier used here as a causative: they would cause their down to snow. This is a very powerful verb in Tlingit, and difficult to translate into English. The speaker is comparing the terns dropping their soft down on the mourners to snowfall. She uses the verb "to snow heavily."

DAANAWÁAḴ
Personal name (Austin Hammond); see annotations.
<dáanaa + waaḵ   silver (dollar) + eye

DACHX̱ÁN   grandchild
Ḵa yá i dachx̱anx'i yánx̱ haa sateeyí   and we who are your grandchildren ML1 17
<dachx̱an - x' - i yán - x̱
   x'   plural marker
   i   "peg vowel" between words
   yán   plural marker
   x̱   predicate nominative marker
Note "stolen stress"

DANÓOGU   See NOOK

-DAX̱   from; after; when; (See also TX̱)
yee tóo-dáx̱	from inside you AH 35
haa x̱oo-dáx̱	from among us JM 4
ḵóo-dáx̱	away from people JM 20
has du eetée-dáx̱	from among them WJ 18
wool'éex'i-dáx̱	when it had broken DK 332
a ít-dáx̱	from this DK 50

DAX̱.AA   second; second one
dax̱.aa shí   the second song DK 87b

DAYÉEN   facing
i dayéen   facing you (singular) JD 116
yee dayéen   facing you (plural) JD 158

-DEI to, toward (locative; takes opposite tone of stem)
way, road (noun)

a shóo-dei	next to it; toward the end of it AH 17
ldakát yéi-dei	in all ways AH 11
Yaakwdáat-dei	to Yakutat JM 2
t'ak̲kaadéi	to beside JM 10
ax̲ daa-déi	to around me JM 31
du daa-déi	to around him JM 33
Tsalx̲aan tóo-dei	to inside Mt. Fairweather ML2 20
a kaa-déi	on it DK 27
a daa-déi	around it DK 48
a tóo-dei	to inside it DK 63
ya a shóo-dei han aa	someone is standing next to it JD 26
du léelk'w hás x̲oodéi	to among his grandparents JD 148, 149
yán-dei ashagux̲lahéek	she will complete this WJ 12
ch'a aa-déi-x̲ siteeyi aa	whoever is one DK 52

DEI ~ DE Truly; for sure; emphasize
Ha de surely, for sure; truly DK 17
Dei ch'a ch'áakw áwé has du ée antulaxáchch. We had long since given up hope for their return. JD 105

DEI (See **DAA**)
kagadéich DK 28 See **DAA**

DU His; her. Possessive pronoun.

du x'óow-u	his robe AH 13, 20
du aat hás	his paternal aunts AH 15
du eetée-tx̲	from in place of him AH 22
du kéek'	his younger brother JM 10
du daa-déi	to around him JM 33
has du tuwáx' áyú sigóo	they want ML1 23

DL

DLÁK' A man's sister WJ 10
Dlák' is the form or term used for direct address, when a man is talking to his sister. The term of reference, when a person is talking about a man's sister, is dláak'.

DLÁAK' A man's sister

A yáx̱ yatee ax̱ dláak'. My sister is like that. WJ 11

DLÉIGOO

li-dléigoo (tr) pat, gesture to express affection

- nag̱aldléigún when he expressed affection AH 15

<na-g̱a- l- dléigoo- n

cp ap cl stem contingent

The contingent takes the -n suffix plus the aspect prefix g̱a and the conjugation prefix. It is in the subordinate conjunctive system, meaning that the action expressed is always connected to other action in the main verb. The contingent and decessive suffixes are similar in form, but the contingent ending is always high, whereas the decessive is the opposite of the stem.

DZ

DZEE

li-dzee (st) be hard (in abstract) be very difficult, almost impossible

- ḵa jiklidzée and difficult to handle DK 19

<ji-ka-li-dzee

np np cl st imperfective

This is an interesting form because of the two nominal (or thematic) prefixes. Ji means "hand" and implies handling something; ka refers to a round or general object, but is virtually meaningless in this context. It seems that ji- may be replaced by ji-ka- with little or no difference in meaning. This is picked up in the translation "difficult to handle." The verb could also be translated "difficult".

DZIYÁAK Just now; a little while ago JD 200

E

EE = I You; your

(2nd pers. sing. subject, object and possessive pronoun)

I kéek' your younger brother JM 29

I kaani yán your brothers-in-law DK 37a

ÉE For. An "empty base" on to which endings may be put, this is a relational noun (locative) plus post position: ée = ée+x'.

has du ée antulaxáchch we have/had given up hope for their return JD 105
yee ée sh danóogu your feelings; your pain DK 4

ÉEK' A woman's brother
ax̱ éek' shát my brother's wife JD 75
ax̱ éek'-ch wuliyaag̱u aa the one my brother explained JD 200
(Note -ch ending; agent marker)

EEN With
du een with him JM 13

ÉESH Father
ax̱ éesh my father AH 28
ax̱ éesh hás my fathers ML1 2
ax̱ éesh Keet Yaanaayí my father K. Y. AH 28

EESHANDÉIN grief
(eesháan + déin; déin = noun maker; like English wide-width)

X̱át tsú eeshandéin ax̱ toowú yatee. I too feel grief. AH 5
Eeshan déin ágé haa daa tuwatee uháan tsú? Does it take pity on us too/either? JD 1
Yá eeshan déin sh daa tuwditaani ḵáa the person who is feeling grief JD 57
eeshan déin tuwateeyi ḵáa person who is feeling grief (grieving) JD 130, 134

EETÍ in place of; imprint or aftermath; place where it was

Du eetée-tx̱ ax̱ jee yéi wootee. I own it in place of him. AH 22
ḵáa eetisheex'í memorial songs; songs in place of a person JM 16
yá i kéek' eetéex' x̱á? in place of your younger brother JM 29
has du eetéedáx̱ from among them WJ 18
yá a eetée ḵux̱dziteeyi aa yeedát the people I am living in place of now DK 77

In the pattern eetéenáx̲ ___ yatee, it means "to need"
Eetée-náx̲ haa ya-tee. We need. AH 16

G

GAAN

ka-di-gaan (st) shine, produce light by burning

- a kaadéi yaa akdagánch [the sun] would begin to shine on it DK 46
  <a-ga-da-gán-ch
  op cp cl st progressive occasional
  The "k" here is a contraction of the conjugation prefix.
- yá a kát awdagaaní áwé after the sun had been shining on it DK 48
  <a-wu-da-gaan-i
  op ap cl st participial perfective
- a kát adagánni when the sun shines on it DK 63
  <a-da-gán-ni
  op cl st conditional

ka-ya-gaan (st) burn; cremate; scorch

- kaawagaan it burned JD 114
  <ka-wu-ya-gaan
  np ap cl st perfective

GAAW Drum, time
yá gaaw (at) this time ML2 5

GÁGI out
gági uwagút he came out JD 40
ch'a ldakát áwé gági yawdixuni yáx̲ áwé all of them seem (to me) as if they are revealing their faces JD 43

GEESH kelp; bull kelp
geesh daax̲ woogoodi yéil áyá it's raven who walked (down) along the kelp JD 27

GEET

dzi-geet (in) A + dzi-geet   do; act (often in relation to instruction, public opinion, law or custom)

- Tléil áwé aadéi nax̲tudzigeedi yé k̲oostí   There is nothing we can do ML1 16
  <na-g̲a-tu-dzi-geet-i
  cp ap sp cl st potential
- Ch'a yóo nax̲toosgeedí g̲óot áyá   just without anything to do; with nothing else for us to do ML1 21
  <na-g̲a-too-s- geet-i
  cp ap sp cl st desiderative

GOO

si-goo (st)
k̲aa toowáa + sigoo = want, like, desire
k̲aa toowóo + sigoo = be happy, glad
Ax̲ tu-wáa si-góo.   I want. AH 1; ML1 1
has du tuwa-x' áyú sigóo   They want ML1 23

GOOT   (singular; see also .aat)

ya-goot (in) walk, go, come
gági + ya-goot   to appear

- aan gugag̲óot   it will go with it ML2 19, 24
  <u-ga-g̲a-góot
  ir cp ap st   future
- aan ayagux̲dagóot   it will go back with it ML2 20
  <a- ya- u- ga-g̲a-da-góot
  op np ir cp ap cl st   future
  Note the contractions: irrealis and conjugation prefix combine; and the vowel of the aspect prefix drops, causing the change of g̲ to x̲. Such contractions are typical of Tlingit verbs, especially in the future.
- Daak uwagút.   He came out. AH 10
  <wu-ya-gút
  ap cl st   perfective
  Note the contraction of the classifier and aspect prefix. This is common in the perfective.
- gági uwagút   he came out JD 40
  (See analysis above.)

- geesh daax̱ woogoodi yéil áyá It's Raven Who Walked (down) along the Bull Kelp JD 27
  <woo-goot-i
  ap st attributive
  This is an attributive perfective, modifying yéil. Tone on the suffix is stolen by the noun following.
- gági gútx̱i yáx̱ áwé yatee It is as if he keeps coming out JD 94
  <gút-x̱- i
  st s participial durative
  The suffix x̱ is durative, expressing action taking place over a period of time. This is a participial durative. The durative is part of the present or imperfective system in Tlingit, but it is translated more freely here as future.
- a shunaayát ágé nḵwaagoot Can I reach the end (of it) JD 123
  <u- na-g̱a-x̱a-ya-goot
  ir cp ap sp cl st potential
- gági ugootch it would come out JD 161
  <u-goot-ch
  ir st occasional
  Note the irrealis used with Ø conjugation verbs.
- yee tula.eesháani káx̱ áwé gági uwagudi yáx̱ as if he came out for your grief JD 164
  <wu-ya-gut-i
  ap cl st participial

GOOX̱ Slave
Goox̱ G̱uwakaan Personal name of Jim Marks.
See annotations.

GU.AA
I gu.aa yáx̱ x'wán have courage WJ 16
This is an idiomatic expression, possibly related to gu.aal (hope) and to the verb stem .aa (have courage, be calm).

GU.AAL hope
gu.aal kwshé my hope is DK 49, 63; JD 210
This is a particle, possibly derived from gu.aa l; possibly related to gu.aa kwshél and gushé.

GUSHÉ I don't know; idiomatic expression

GUNALCHÉESH Thank you AH 23a, etc.

GUSATÁAN Personal name (Harry Marvin); see annotations. DK 15, JD 119

G̱

-G̱AA For, in order to obtain
wooxéex-g̱aa in order not to fall (so that they do not fall for nothing) JD 9
yá ḵut'aay g̱áa during the warm season JD 160
sh tuwaa g̱aa kastéeyin proud; pleasing to his feeling JD 98
The suffix -gaa often appears in constructions such as "sh tuwaag̱áa" "to one's own liking." Example:
sh tuwaag̱áa ditee or sh tug̱áa ditee
it is to his own liking

G̱AANAX̱ÁA Place name; see annotations

G̱AGAAN Sun
yá g̱agaan the sun JD 207
- g̱agaan-ch áwé the sun JD 203
<g̱agaan-ch
stem agent marker

G̱ÉELAK'W Place name (part of Mt. Fairweather); see annotations. JD 212, 216

G̱EI Location within a circle or enclosure
- yá lingit'aaní g̱eix' in the world DK 58
<g̱ei - x'

G̱ÓOT Without
ch'a yóo nax̱toosgeedi g̱óot áyá without anything else we can do; with nothing else for us to do ML1 212

G̱UNAYÉI Begin to; (See also G̱unei)
- g̱unayéi a.áat they began to gather JM 33
Note "a" as the subject marker of the verb of motion "áat"; the verb is used without any other prefix or subject marker.

• g̱unayéi ultéetch it would begin to roll DK 39
<u- l- teet-ch
ir cl st occasional

G̱UNEI Begin to; (See also G̱unayéi)
ax̱ daa-déi g̱unei y.á gather around me JM 31

G̱UWAKAAN Deer; peacemaker; hostage. See notes, introduction, and Charlie Joseph's biography for more on this concept.
yá yee G̱uwakaaní this peacemaker of yours JD 91
Goox̱ G̱uwakaan Personal name of Jim Marks

H

HA Now; well. Interjection; conjunction.
ha yáa yeedát and now JD 176
ha yeeytéen áyá a tóot hás náḵ you can now see them standing in these DK 84
ha yáa yeedát at this moment AH 8

HAA Us, our, we. 1 person plural object and possessive pronoun; also functions as subject pronoun in objective verbs.
A eetée-náx̱ haa ya-tee. We need it. AH 16
haa x̱oo-dáx̱ from among us JM 4
haa daa on us JD 1
yá i yát-x'i-x̱ haa sa-teey-í we who are your children ML1 20

HAA Here; locative base
haa-t kawdiyáa it came here JD 155

HAA
ka-ya-di-haa (st) move
ḵaa jeenáx̱ + ka-ya-haa be in charge of; take charge of; have authority over
ka-di-haa ( ) disappear; appear; move invisibly

• aax̱ áwé du jeet kawdiháa yú.á yá Xixch'i S'áaxw
From there, it's said, he acquired the Frog Hat JD 151
<ka-wu-di-háa
np ap cl st perfective

ji-la-haa (tr) send for, order
a káa + ji-li-haa come upon, find doing, catch in the act, discover doing

- aadéi yaa ajiklaháa áwé as he was sending it there JM 11
<a - ji- ga-la-háa
op np cp cl st
This is a sequential progressive, indicated by the conjugation prefix, "a" classifier, and long, high stem.

sa-di-haa (in) be ready, decide, intend to, want, strongly desire

- chush t'aḵkaadéi asawdihaa du kéek' he wanted his younger brother beside him JM 10
<a sa- wu-di-haa
op np ap cl st perfective

HAAN (Singular; See **NAAḴ**)
ya-haan (in) stand

- Yáa-t aan hán. Here he stands with it. AH 13
- Ḵa yáa-náx̱ á a shóo-dei han aa. And on this side one stands next to it. AH 17
- Haa káx̱ háni yax̱ yatee. It's as if she's standing for us. ML2 13-14
<han-i
st participial
- Yá a shóodei han aa. Someone is standing next to it. JD 26
Note "stolen stress" on hán.
- A shóodei ahán. Someone is standing next to it. JD 30
"A" is a 3rd person subject pronoun without focus.
- Yáat a tóot ahan aa. Here someone stands wearing one; That's the one he's wearing. JD 18, 186
<Yáa-t a tóo-t a-han aa.
lo po op lo po sp st n attributive
This is a confusing line. One might expect "yáat a tóot ahán" (non attributive) someone stands here wearing it, or "yáat a tóot han aa" (attributive) the one who stands here wearing it.

di-haan (in) stand up

- Yanax̲ wudihaan hú tsú. He too stands (stood up) (to face you). JD 190, 194
  <wu-di-haan
  ap cl st perfective

HAASH
li-haash (tr) float, drift
- yei klaháshch it would drift down DK 33
  <yei ga-la-hásh-ch
  dp np cl st occasional progressive
- Yá éil' tlein káx' áyá ulhaashch It would float on this great ocean. DK 36
  <u- la-haash-ch
  ir cl st occasional
- yan ulhaashch it would drift ashore DK 41
  (See above for analysis.)
- yan g̲alaháshín when it drifted to the shore JD 202
  <g̲a-la-hásh-ín
  ap cl st contingent

HAAT Here. (See **HAA**)

HÁHÉ = ÁHÉ It, this

HÁS Plural marker; sometimes the equivalent of an English pronoun. Commonly "steals" the high tone of the word preceding.

Ax̲ sani hás	my paternal uncles AH 2
I sani hás	your paternal uncles AH 10a
ax̲ aat hás	my paternal aunts ML1 3
ldakát hás	all of them ML1 20
has du tuwáx' áyú sigóo	they want ML1 23
hás yá yáa-t	This is them here. WJ 5

HEEK
sha-ya-heek (st) be filled, full
yan sha-ya-heek ( ) be finished, completed, fulfilled
sha-li-heek (tr) fill, finish

- yándei ashagux̲lahéek she will finish this WJ 12
  <a- sha- u- ga-g̲a-la-héek
  op np ir cp ap cl st future
  Note the similarity to the finalitive, but the future here is indicated by the "a" classifier. The position of the irrealis is theoretical here; in reality it affects the positions around it.

- yan ashawlihík yá haa tláach This mother of ours has completed it. ML2 9
  <yan a- sha-wu-li-hík yá haa tláa-ch
  dp op np ap cl st dem pp n- st subject marker
  perfective

HÉEN Water; river

héen-t wudik'ít	it capsized into the water JM 13
héen	water DK 24, 25, 27
yá héen yík	in the water DK 26
tóo hinyawoodaayí áwé	when the river had swollen DK 28

HÉI = HÉ That JM 2

HEIY! Response in oratory, used to acknowledge the speaker DK 9a, 10a, 15a

HÍT House
Yeilkudei Hít X'óow Raven Nest House Robe JD 100

HÚ He; she. 3rd person independent pronoun.
AH 19, 32; JM 15, 18; JD 92, 98

I

I ~ EE You; your. 2nd person singular subject, object, and possessive pronoun

i kéek'	your brother JM 29
i x̲'éi-t	lit. to your mouth AH 10a
i sani hás	your paternal uncles AH 10a
yá i yátx'ix̲ haa sateeyí	we who are your children ML1 17

IT Behind; after (this)
a ít-dáx̲ from this DK 50

J

JEE Hand (see also **JIN** and **JI-**);
(usually with suffixes or verbs of location;
k̲aa + jeewóo to have; to be in the hands of)
ax̲ jee in my hand AH 38
haa jee yéi ya-tee Naatúxjayi this Naatúxjayi whom we have AH 31
ax̲ jee yéi woo-tee it came into my hands AH 22
chance haa jeet yeeyteeyí (that you) give us a chance ML1 4
haa jee-x' for us WJ 7
du jee-x' in his hands JD 92
du jee-t kawdiháa he acquired; it came into his hands JD 151
Weihá jee-dáx̲ aa k'oodás' this shirt from Weihá JD 153

JI- Hand (<JIN); see also **JEE**
ax̲ ji-yís for me WJ 13, 14

JÍN Hand
woosh jín toolshát We're still holding each other's hands DK 59

JIG̲WÉINAA Hand towel AH 38
< ji - g̲wéin - aa
hand - wipe - instrument;
-g̲wéin is the progressive stem of -g̲oo (wipe).

JILK̲ÁAT Chilkat (Place name; see annotations)
Jilk̲áat-dáx̲ from Chilkat JD 33

K

KA Horizontal surface of
ká-x̲ along the surface of WJ 1
a kaa-déi on it DK 27, 46
éil' tlein ká-x' on/in this great ocean DK 36
ká-a ayax̲dateech would blow over it DK 37
a ká-t on it DK 48
k̲áa ká-x' over the person JD 130

KAA (See KA)

KAADÉIK Personal name (of George Dalton); see annotations

KÁAK maternal uncle; mother's brother
ax̲ káak — my mother's brother AH 20
ax̲ káak hás — my mother's brothers DK 23
du káak — her mother's brother JD 144

KÁALK'W Niece or nephew; a woman's brother's child
i káalk'w hás — your brother's children; your nieces and nephews WJ 21
ax̲ káalk'w hás — my brother's children JD 2
ax̲ káalk'w yéet — my brother's daughter's child JD 63

KÁANI in-law; sibling-in-law (of the same sex)
yee káani — your (plural) brother-in-law AH 30
ax̲ kaani hás — my brothers-in-law ML1 6 (note stolen stress)
ax̲ kaani yán — my brothers-in-law WJ 3
Yán is more common a plural marker than hás with káani.

KAATYÉ Personal name (David Kadashan); see annotations.

KAG̲EET Loon
kag̲eet k̲uyéik — loon spirit JD 196

KÁX̲ For
yee tula.eesháan-i ká-x̲ — for your grief AH 32
haa ká-x̲ háni yáx̲ yatee — it is as if she's standing for us ML2 13-14
nich ká-x̲ — for nothing; without honor JD 9
a ká-x̲ áwé — for them JD 11
yee sh tundanóogu káx̲ — for your pain JD 21

KAYAA Like
a kayaa + ya-yaa — be like
a kayaa + A + si-nee — act like, do like
ch'a a kayaa áyá yéi gax̲tusanéi — we will only imitate them DK 82
a kayaa áyá s ootee — they are only imitating them JD 178

KÉEK' Younger sibling of the same sex; his younger brother; her younger sister

du kéek' his younger brother JM 10
i kéek' your younger brother JM 29

KÉET Killer whale
Keet Yaanaayí Personal name (Willie Marks); see annotations. (Note stolen stress.)

KEEWAAX̱.AWTSEIX̱ G̱UWAKAAN Personal name of William Johnson; see annotations and biography

KÉILK' niece or nephew; man's sister's child
ax̱ éesh kéilk' my father's sister's son; my father's nephew JD 66

KEITL Dog
Shaatuḵwáan Keidlí S'áaxw The Mountain Tribe's Dog Hat DK 87b
<keitl-i possessive

KOO
si-koo (tr) know, learn
- ch'a á yeeysikóo yéi yang̱aḵeinin ḵáa yáx̱ you all know when a person might say WJ 9

<wu-yi-si-koo
ap sp cl st perfective
This verb is interesting in form and concept. Note the contraction; this is common in the 2nd person plural perfective. Note also how to "know" is present tense in English, but perfective in Tlingit. Tlingit focuses on the acquisition of the knowledge, which must be prior in time to a person's ability to make a statement about knowing something. The verb "to see" is similar in concept.

KOOWUNAGÁAS' Personal name (of Joe White); see annotations JD 62, 193

KUJÉEN For, because of, at sight or sound of
yee kujéen áwé because of you JD 39

KÚT Nest
Yeilkudei Hít Raven Nest House JD 100

has du kúdi kaadéi   to their nests JD 139

KWEIX' ÉESH   Personal name (of Matthew Lawrence); see annotations and biography

KWSHÉ   How about, maybe. An enclitic, marking rhetorical questions; for example:
daa sá = "what"
daa sákwshé = "I wonder what"
See also gu.aal and gushé.
gu.aal kwshé   my hope is DK 49, 63

K'

K'E   A particle roughly like "hmmm" or "well" in English, "How about if..." or "What if..."
k'e ng̲al'éex'   it would think of breaking / it would decide to break DK 32

K'EEDZÁA   Personal name (Alfred Andrews); see annotations AH 12

K'EET'
ya-k'eet' (tr) eat up, finish, consume

- yaakw du een héent wudik'ít'   the boat swamped/capsized into the water with him JM 13
  <héen-t   wu-di-k'ít'
  n   po ap cl   st   perfective

ka-di-k'eet' (st) all leave, go or come (of a whole group of people); die off leaving only a few

- yanax̲ yeik̲ [has] kawdik'ít'   they have come out JD 12, 14
  <yeik̲   has   ka-wu-di-k'ít'
  dp   pl   np ap cl   st   perfective

K'EI
ya-k'ei (st) be good, fine, pretty

- yak'éi x̲áa   fine indeed JM 30
  <ya-k'éi
  cl st   imperfective
- yak'éiyi l'éiwdei   to a fine sand DK 39
  <ya-k'éi-yi l'éiw-dei
  cl st s n po   attributive;
  Y is inserted between the stem and suffix because the stem ends in a vowel.

K'OODÁS' Shirt
yéil k'oodás'   raven shirt JD 87
du k'oodás'-i   his shirt JD 112
yá Weihá k'oodás'i   Weihá's shirt; this shirt of Weihá JD 93
Geesh daax̲ woogoodi yéil k'oodás'   Raven Who Walked Down Along the Bull Kelp Shirt JD 109

K̲

K̲A And ML1 17, DK 19, AH 17, 23

K̲ÁA Man, person, one
k̲aa eetí sheex'í   last songs from a person; memorial songs JM 22
yá yee yáx̲ sh daa tuwditaani k̲áa áwé   the person who is feeling like you JD 50

K̲AA
ya-ya-k̲aa (in)
A + ya-ya-k̲aa   say, speak, confess, acknowledge, declare, suggest, say thus

- aag̲áa áwé yéi yawdudzik̲aa   that's when they said to him JM 27
  <yéi ya-wu-du-dzi-k̲aa
  ba np ap sp cl st   perfective
- tleigíl ch'a waa sá yakgeek̲aa   aren't you going to say JM 28
  <ya-ga-g̲a-ee-k̲aa
  np cp ap sp st   (future; 2nd person singular)

- yéi yanga̱ḵéinín like when a person speaks thus / might say WJ 9

  <yéi ya-na-ga̱-ḵaa-ín
  ba np cp ap st contingent

  The progressive stem ḵein- is used in this form.

x̱'a-ya-ya-ḵaa (in)
A + x̱'a-ya-ya-ḵaa say (usually in "present tense")

- wé aadéi x̱'ayaduḵa yé where/when people were saying JM 20

  <x̱'a-ya-du-ḵa
  np np sp st imperfective; note stolen stress
- gunalchéesh yóo x̱'ayax̱aḵá I keep saying thank you JD 158

  <yóo x̱'a-ya-x̱a-ḵá
  ba np np sp st imperfective
- yá yee léelk'w hás aadéi x̱'ayaḵaayi yé what your grandparents said JD 180

  <x̱'a-ya-ḵaa-yi
  np np st s attributive

ḴAAKWSAK'AA Personal name (David Williams); see annotations. JD 73

ḴÁAK'W ÉESH Personal name; see annotations.

ḴAATOOSHTÓOW Personal name (John F. Wilson); see annotations. JD 72

ḴÓO People
ḵóo-dax̱ away from people JM 20

ḴOOX̱
ya-ḵoox̱ (in) travel by boat or car, come by boat or car

- a yát yakw.uḵoox̱ch they would go by boat to its face JD 51

  <yakw-u-ḵoox̱-ch
  np ir st occasional

  Note use of irrealis with Ø conjugation verb, and the relatively uncommon use of the noun yaakw (boat) as a nominal prefix in the verb.

- T'aaḵú wátdei...wooḵoox̱ he went by boat to the mouth of Taku JD 147
  <wu-ya-ḵoox̱
  ap cl st perfective

ḴU.AA However, but
hu ḵu.aa but he... JM 15, 18

ḴUT'AAYG̱ÁA Warm season
- yá ḵut'aayg̱áa during the warm season JD 160
  <ḵu-t'aa-g̱aa **<ḵu-ya-t'aa** (im) to be warm (of weather)
  np st po

ḴÚTL'KW Earth, mud, river bank
yá ḵútl'kw the earth DK 30

ḴUYÉIK Shaman spirit; see Introduction
kag̱eet ḵuyéik loon spirit JD 196

ḴWAAN Tribe; group of people from a place
- Shaatuḵwáan Mountain Tribe; tribe inside the mountain
  <shaa-tu-ḵwáan

Ḵ'

Ḵ'AADÓO Personal name; see annotations JM 5

Ḵ'EIḴ'W tern; see also note following
yá ḵ'eiḵ'w the tern(s) JD 127, 129
Ḵ'eiḵ'w X'óow the Tern Robe JD 48

Note on ḵ'eiḵ'w. There is twofold confusion regarding the identification and translation of this bird in everyday English. Technically, ḵ'eiḵ'w is kittywake, popularly called "sea pigeon," and mainly an offshore bird with a biologically and culturally important rookery at G̱aanax̱aa, on the outer coast of Glacier Bay National Monument. It is probably the black legged kittywake (*Rissa tridactyla*) and not the red legged kittywake (*Rissa brevirostris*, which breeds in the Pribilof Islands), although some Tlingit designs show red legs on the bird. The kittywake or sea pigeon is popularly confused with gulls and terns, both of which are grouped in Tlingit under the single term kéidladi or kéitlyadi. The arctic tern (*Sterna paradisaea*) is common in SE Alaska, and is characterized by red legs, black cap, and forked tail, as well as by its flight behavior. There are several gulls in SE Alaska, of which Bonaparte's is similar in flight and appearance to the tern and kittywake. We have used the word "tern" in the English of Jessie Dalton's speech, in deference to common usage, although kittywake is technically more correct. The confusion increases with the reference to k̲'eik̲'w as crest or at.óow, where it is commonly referred to as "sea gull" in English. Thus the group of T'ak̲deintaan women known in Tlingit as K̲'eik̲'w Sháa is most often called "Sea Gull Ladies" or "Tern Women" in English. See the Introduction for more on this group.

L

L ~ TLEIL Not

L ch'u yee wak̲shiyee k̲waasháadi át. I can't even find anything to show you. AH 7

This may also be said wak̲shiyeet, but -t is not required. The verb indicates hasty actions, and conveys the image of a person grabbing among possessions, trying desperately to find something of value.

LAX̲ÉITL Luck, gift

- ha tlax̲ wáa lax̲éitlx̲ sá haa wootee what a great gift we have ML2 10

< verb **li-x̲eitl** (tr) be blessed, lucky

-x̲ is predicate nominative or object compliment marker

LDAKÁT All

ldakát yéidei in all ways, in many ways AH 11
ldakát hás all of them ML1 20
ldakát yeewáan all of you JD 120

LÉELK'W Grandparent

ax̲ léelk'w my grandfather (grandparent) JM 26
ax̲ léelk'w yátx'i my grandfather's children WJ 2
i léelk'w hás your grandfathers WJ 16

LEI

ya-lei (st) be far, distant (in space or time)
A -x̱ + ya lei   high, far to the top
- ch'a ḵóodáx̱ sh nadliléiyi yáx̱ áwé   it is just as if he is distancing himself from people; holding himself distant JM 20
<sh na-dli-léi-yi
op cp cl st participial

LINGIT'AANÍ World
- yá lingit'aaní kaadéi áwé tundatánch   it would think of going into the world DK 35
<tu-na-da-tán-ch
np cp cl st occasional
Contrast: lingit'aaní   world
lingít aaní   Tlingit land

LTU.ÁA Lituya (Place Name) JM 12

LUTÁḴL Personal name; see annotations JD 35

LYEEDAYÉIK Personal name; see annotations JD 29

L'

L'AX̱KEIT Mask
ax̱ léelk'w hás l'ax̱keid-í   my grandparents' mask JD 208

L'EEX'

ya-l'eex' (tr) break (general, solid object)
- yéi tundatánch k'e ngal'éex'   it would think of breaking; it would decide to break DK 32
<na-ga-l'éex'
cp ap st desiderative
- wool'éex'idáx̱ áwé   having broken; when it had broken; after it had broken DK 33
<wu-ya-l'éex'-i- dax̱
ap cl st par po participial

L'ÉIW Sand
l'éiw-dei   to the sand DK 39
l'éiw   sand DK 40

N

NAA TLÁA   Personal name (Jessie Dalton);
<Naa = moiety + tláa = mother

NAAK̲   (plural; see also **HAAN**)
di-naak̲ (in) stand
ya-naak̲ (in) stand up
- wéix̲ has yaawanák̲   they're standing there   WJ 18
  <ya-wu-ya-nák̲
    np ap cl st   perfective
- yándei gax̲yeenáak̲   you will stand   DK 70
  <ga-ga-yee-náak̲
    cp ap sp st   future; 2nd person plural
- a tóot has nák̲   they're standing in these   DK 84
  <a tóo-t has nák̲
    op lo po pl   st
- yee dayéen aan has nági yáa yeedát   that they are standing in front of you at this moment   JD 158
  <has nák̲- i
    pl   st participial

NAATÚXJAYI   Personal name (of Chilkat Tunic);
see annotations   AH 31

NAAWÉIYAA   Personal name (of Harry Marvin);
see annotations

NAAXEIN   Chilkat robe; Chilkat blanket
naaxein   Chilkat robe   JD 34
du naaxein-í   his Chilkat robe   JD 38

NANÉIYI   Dead; departed (<na-néi)
haa nanéiyi   our dead   DK 60
This is a verbal noun from yéi woonee or yéi woonei "died."
The noun could also be listed under the stem **NEE** or **NEI**.

-NAX̲   Through; along
eetéenax̲ + yatee = to need

a tóo-náx̱ through it; from it JD 214
G̱éelák'w tóo-náx̱ through (from) G̱éelák'w JD 216
yi yadaa-náx̱ along your faces ML2 22

- A eetée-náx̱ haa ya-tee. We need them. AH 16
<a eetée-náx̱ haa ya-tee
pp lo po op cl st

NEE (See also NEI)
ya-nee (st); A + ya-nee happen, occur
yan ya-nee be permanent; happen for good; be finished, complete, ready; be prepared
a kayaa + ya-yaa = be similar, like

- yan née áwé when it was finished JM 21
<yan née
dp st sequential

si-nee (tr); A + si-nee do
a kayaa + A si-nee = to act like; do like

- ch'a a kayaa áyá yéi gax̱tusanéi we will only imitate them; we will just do an imitation DK 82
<yéi ga-g̱a-tu-sa-néi
av cp ap sp cl st future

NEI (See also NEE)
ji-ya-nei (in);
yéi + ji-ya-nei work; do

- yan yéi jiwtuwanéi we completed JD 85
<yan yéí ji- wu-tu-ya-néi
dp ba np ap sp cl st perfective
Note that ya classifier appears as wa after u.

daa-ya-nei (tr);
yéi + daa-ya-nei do; perform an action

- yee yáx' yéi hás a daanéi noojéen they used to show you (do to your face) DK 75
<yee yá-x' yéi hás a daa-néi nooch-éen
pp lo po ba pl op np st hv decessive

- hél aadéi has yee daangwaanéiyi yé   there is no way they can do anything for you DK 83
  <hél aa-déi has yee daa-u -na-ga-ya-néi-yi yé
  neg lo po pl   op   np ir cp ap cl   st   s   n
  attributive potential

NEIX
si-neix (tr) save; heal; cure
- hú ku.aa áwé sh wudzineix   but he saved himself JM 15
  <sh wu-dzi-neix
  op ap cl   st   perfective

NICH   In vain; for nothing; (contraction of **NEECH**)
nichká-x   or nothing; without honor JD 9

NOOCH   (See **NOOK**)

NOOK   Helping verb. The helping verb nook is inflected. It appears with the suffixes: -ch -j -een -nee -in -un. Here are some of its forms:

nóok	
nooch = nuch = nukch	would (occasional)
noojéen	used to (decessive)
núknee	if (conditional)
ganúgun	whenever (contingent)

- áa yan yoo latitgi nuch   it would be pounded here DK 41, 42
  <á- a yan yoo la-tit-k-i nuch
  lo po dp dp cl st s s hv   durative with occ. hv
  "K" is a durative suffix, indicating duration of action; "i" is a "peg vowel" for ease in pronunciation.

NOOK (1)
ya-nook (in) sit, sit down, act of sitting

- ganúkch   he would sit JM 18, 20
  <ga-núk-ch
  cp st occasional
- yanax daak guganóok   he will burrow (sit back) down JD 169
  <gu-ga-nóok
  cp ap st   future

NOOK (2)

ya-nook (tr) to feel (physical and emotional)
too + ya-nook

- tóox' áyá tuwanook   we are feeling DK 3
  <tóo-x' áyá tu- ya-nook
  lo po – np cl st   imperfective
- ách áyá x̲át tsú yi jiyís yéi sh x̲adinook   this is why I too feel for you DK 55
  <yéi sh x̲a-di-nook
  ba op sp cl st   imperfective
- yee ée sh danóogu   your feelings; your pain DK 4
  <yee ée sh da-nóok-ú
  pp lo op cl st s   verbal noun
  Note use of base ée with possessive pronoun yee:
  ax̲ sh danóogu   my pain
  haa sh danóogu   our pain
  but, yee ée sh danóogu   your pain
  The phrase may also be spoken without "ée": yee sh danóogu.
- yee sh tudanóogu káx̲   for your pain JD 21
  <yee sh tu-da-nóok-u ká-x̲
  pp op np cl st s lo po   verbal noun
- tléil tóo kwdunook nuch   it (down) would not be felt JD 135
  <tléil tú- u ka-u- du-nook nuch
  neg lo po np ir sp st   hv   imperfective with occ hv
  The nominal prefix ka is used to denote a small object (down); du is 4th person subject pronoun, used also to express passive voice; nuch is the occasional form of the helping verb nook.

si-nook (tr) to feel (directionally), to locate by feeling, to feel at a point; homophonous with one of the themes in nook (1):
si-nook (tr) to carry or take a live creature

a yát + sh + dzi-nook = to feel better, be healed

- a yát sh gayisnoogóot ágé   not that it can heal you / not that it will make you feel better JD 172
  <a yá-t sh ga-yi- s-nook-óot
  op lo po op ap sp cl st purposive
  This is a difficult phrase to analyze. It is not attested in the Naish-Story dictionary with the meaning of "heal" or "feel."

It patterns as a verb of motion, with -t in the progressive, -déi in the future and -x̱ in the customary. It may also be interpreted as a causative of ya-nook. The d-component is required by the reflexive. If the phrase derives from "to carry a live creature," it is highly metaphorical, and would refer to the orator's metaphorically transporting the audience to the face of the rookery or Mt. Fairweather for spiritual healing. In that case, the phrase translates literally as "in order for you folks to carry yourselves to the face of it."

ka-si-nook (st?) to feel (?)
tu + ka-si-nook (?)

- yáa yeedát tlax̱ haa tukayeeysinúk   at this moment how much we feel your stirring (trembling, as from a wind) ML1 15

<haa tu- ka-wu-yee-si-núk
op np np ap sp cl st   perfective
Note wu + yee = yeey

ḵu-ya-nook (in) behave like; do, act
A + ḵu-ya-nook

- aadéi s ḵunoogu yé yéeyi   what they used to do DK 71

<ḵu-nook-u yé yéeyi
np st s n decessive attributive
Note the use of -u and yéeyi when the decessive is not the main verb.

NUCH (See NOOK)

O

.OO

ḵu-di-.oo (in?) turn into; remain; be left

- Ch'a oowayáa jig̱wéinaa yáx̱ ax̱ jee ḵuwda.oowú.   It is as if it has just become a towel in my hand; let it be as if it has become a towel in my hand. AH 38

<ḵu-wu-da-oo-wú
np ap cl st participial   perfective
Oowayáa (oo-ya-yaa) is the main verb; ḵuwda.oowú is a

perfective form in the subordinate clause, therefore has the -wú suffix and the da classifier.

S

S (See **HAS**)

SAA
dli-saa (in) rest
• wudlisáa he rested DK 88c
<wu-dli-sáa
ap cl st perfective

SAAY
ya-saay (tr) call roll; list names
• dusáaych áwé they would call; the name would be called JD 56
<du-sáay-ch
sp st occasional
• ch'a oowayáa ldakát yeewáan yee x̲wasaayí It will be just as if I will have named all of you. JD 120
<yee wu-x̲a-ya-saa -yi
op ap sp cl st participial

SAAYINA.AAT Personal name; see annotations JD 46

SAGÓO Joy; see also **-GOO**
• sagóox̲ nax̲satee let it turn to joy DK 65
<sa-góo-x̲ na-g̲a-sa-tee
cl st s cp ap cl st desiderative
The -x̲ suffix is a predicate nominative marker. Sagóo is a noun, but formed of stem and classifier.

SÁNI Paternal uncle; father's brother
ax̲ sani hás my father's brothers AH 2
Note stolen stress; note also this can be translated as "my fathers' brothers."

SÉEW Rain DK 27

SÉI AKDULX̲ÉITL' Personal name (of David McKinley);
see annotations JD 40a

SÍGÉ Rhetorical marker
sígé wasn't it JD 15

S'

S'ÁAXW Hat
yá xíxch'-i s'áaxw the frog hat DK 87a, JD 151
yá s'áaxw this hat ML2 17
du s'áaxu his hat JD 144, 167
yú s'áaxw that hat JD 147

S'IGEIDI Beaver
s'igeidi x'óow áwé it is the beaver robe/blanket JD 32

S'EILSHÉIX̲' Personal name (of Eva Davis);
see annotations JD 31b

S'OOTAAT Morning
s'ootaat-x' in the morning DK 46, 47

SH

SH Object pronoun; reflexive pronoun; self
sh tóo-tx̲ from us; from ourselves DK 60

SHAA Mountain
• yee éesh hás shaayí tóodei into your fathers' mountain ML2 25
<shaa-yí tóo-dei
n s lo po
Shaa-tu-k̲wáan keidl-í Mountain Tribe's Dog JD 19

SHAA
ya-shaa (tr) bark at
ya-li-shaa (tr) bark at; begin barking
• yee sh tundanóogu káx̲ ashaayi yáx̲ áwé it is as if it is

barking for your pain JD 21
<a- shaa- yi
op st participial

SHAAT

ka-ya-shaat (tr) catch, grab

- k̲waasháadi át (lit) a caught thing, a grasped thing AH 7
<u- g̲a- x̲a- ya- shaat- i
ir ap sp cl st attributive potential

li-shaat (tr) hold, retain in grasp

- woosh jín toolshát yeisú we're still holding each other's hands DK 59
<woosh jín too-l -shát
rp n sp cl st positional imperfective

SHAKEE.ÁT Dance headdress; frontlet; literally "head-top-thing."

G̲éelák'w Shakee.át G̲éelák'w Headdress JD 212
yá shakee.át this headdress JD 219
du shakee.ád-i his headdress JD 220

SHÁT Wife

ax̲ éek' shát my brother's wife JD 75

SH DANÓOGU Pain; deep feelings; (see **NOOK**)

SHEE ~ SHÍ Song

k̲aa eetí sheex'i memorial songs JM 16, 17
wé shí the song JM 34
x'íxch'i s'áaxw daa sheeyí song about the frog hat DK 87a, b
Note how short high vowel becomes long low.

SHEE

ka-li-shee (tr) compose songs (esp. about opp. clan)

- kadulsheex̲ people are/were composing songs JM 16
<ka-du-l- shee-x̲
np sp cl st durative

ka-ya-shee (tr)

kei ka-ya-shee start singing, break into song, especially ceremonial songs

- aadéi áwé kéi a kaawashée wé shí   he began to sing the song JM 34
  <kei a ka-wu-ya-shée
  dp op np ap cl st   perfective
- kei kawduwashée   they sang them; were sung DK 87a
  <kei ka-wu-du-ya-shée
  dp np ap sp cl st   perfective

SHÍ Song; See also **SHEE**

SHOO End; (also **SHU**)

a shóo-dei han aa	one is standing toward the end AH 17
yá a shóodei han aa	someone is standing next to this JD 26
a shóodei ahán	someone is standing next to it JD 30

SHÓOGU Same; very same

ch'u shóogu á   just the same one JD 116

SH TUDANÓOGU Pain; See **NOOK**

SHUNAAYÁ End

a shunaayá-t   the end of it JD 150

T

-T To, arriving at (with verbs of motion); positioned in, on, or within extent of (with verbs of location)

haa-t	here AH 6
i x̲'éi-t	to you (your mouth) AH 10a
x̲oo-t	among AH 15
yáa-t	here AH 13
yáa-d-u	here AH 13 (<yáa-t-u)
héen-t wudik'ít	capsized into the water JM 13
chance haa jee-t yeeyteeyí	gave us a chance ML1 24
yáa-t	here WJ 5
a ká-t	on it DK 48
a tóo-t hás nák̲	they're standing in these DK 84
yáa-t a tóo-t ahan aa	here one stands in one JD 18
a yá-t	to its face JD 51
wéi-t	there JD 86
a t'ak̲ká-t áwé	along side it JD 152

TAAN

si-taan (st)

daak si-taan fall (of natural precipitation); rain, snow

- séew áyá a kaadéi daak ustaanch the rain would fall on it DK 27

<u- s- taan- ch
ir cl st occasional
Note use of irrealis (u) with Ø conjugation verb in the occasional.

ya-taan (tr) carry, take (usually a container or hollow object); lie

- áa yan utaanch it would lie there DK 45

<u-taan-ch
ir st occasional
Reference here is to a log lying on beach. Note use of the irrealis (u) with the Ø conjugation verb in the occasional.

tu-di-taan (?) think, feel, decide

A + tu-di-taan (in) decide, make up one's mind

There are two parallel themes each for "think" and "speak".

tu-di-taan	think	x̲'a-di-taan	speak
tu-ya-taan	think	x̲'a-ya-taan	speak

- yá yee yáx̲ sh daa tuwditaani k̲áa áwé the person who is feeling about him/her self like you JD 50
- yá eeshan déin sh daa tuwditaani k̲áa the person who is feeling grief JD 57

<tu-wu-di-taan-i
np ap cl st attributive perfective

- aag̲áa áwé yéi tundatánch that's when it would think (decide) DK 31

<yéi tu- na-da-tán-ch
ba np cp cl st occasional

- yá lingit'aaní kaadéi áwé tundatánch it would think of going to the world DK 35

<tu-na-da-tán-ch
np cp cl st occasional

- yéi áyá ... tux̲datán I think/wish DK 65

<yéi tu- x̲a-da-tán
ba np sp cl st imperfective

tu-ya-taan (in)
a daa + tu-ya-taan think over; consider, make up one's mind about

- yee sh tundanóogu káx̲ ashaayi yáx̲ áwé daa yóo tux̲aatánk
  it is as if it's barking for your pain is how I'm thinking about it JD 21
- gági yawdixuni yáx̲ has du daa yóo tux̲aatánk as if they're revealing their faces is how I am thinking about them JD 78
  < ... daa yóo tu- x̲a-ya-tán-k
  po ba np sp cl st durative
  Note contraction of x̲a-ya to -x̲aa, and the use of the durative suffix -k.
- á áwé tléil yéi adaa yoo toox̲atánk kaawagaan áyá yóo
  that's the one there; but I don't feel that it burned JD 114
  <yóo tu- u -x̲a-tán-k
  ba np ir sp st durative
  Note the contraction of the irrealis.

x̲'a-di-taan (in) speak, talk, make a speech

- Ax̲ tuwáa sigóo x̲'ax̲wdataaní. I want to speak. ML1 1, AH 2, ML2 7-8
  <x̲'a-wu-x̲a-da-taan-í
  np ap sp cl st participial
  Note contraction of wu and x̲a; also use of the "a" classifier because the verb is a participial form in the subordinate clause. This is a clear and easy example of a main and subordinate clause in Tlingit, ax̲ tuwáa sigóo being the main verb.
- wáa yadali át yáx̲ sáyú nateech...hé aa x̲'awdataan how it is like a heavy burden...(for them) to speak. WJ 6-8
  <x̲'a-wu-da-taan
  np ap cl st perfective verbal noun
  This is difficult to analyze. It looks like a verbal noun, but "aa" seems anomalous. One might expect "áa", but the low tone is correct.

x̲'a-ya-taan (?) speak, talk

- yoo x̲'atángi noojéen he always used to speak AH 11
  <yoo x̲'a-tán-k-i nooch-éen
  ba np st s s hv dec im with dec occ hv
- tlax̲ wáa sá yoo x̲'atángeen a daax' how much he used to speak of it AH 14
  <yoo x̲'a-tán-k-een
  ba np st s decessive imperfective

TAYEE Under
yá aas tayeex̲ áwé under the tree DK 28

TEE 1

Note: the numbers after the stem refer to categories in the Naish-Story *Tlingit Verb Dictionary.* TEE is one of the most important verb stems in Tlingit, and appears in many forms with different affixes and in different syntactic patterns.

ya-tee (st)
A + ya-tee be (a certain way)
A-x' + yéi ya-tee be at, stay, live at, dwell, remain

1) Xwaayeenák̲ áwé yéi yatee this is the way Xwaayeenák̲ is DK 57
<ya-tee
cl st imperfective
2) a yáx̲ yatee ax̲ dláak' my sister is like that WJ 11
3) haa káx̲ háni yáx̲ yatee it is as if she is standing for us ML2 13-14
4) yéi kwg̲atée thus it will be ML1 25a, JD 211a, b
<yéi u -ga-g̲a-tée
ba ir cp ap st future
5) nateech it is WJ 6
<na-tee-ch
cp st occasional
6) yá haa x̲oox' yéi teeyí yá haa tláa that this mother of ours is among us ML2 11-12
<haa x̲oo-x' yéi tee-yí
op lo po ba st participial
7) Eeshandéin ax̲ toowú yatee. I feel grief. AH 5
(Lit. grief is in my mind/feelings)

8) Yéi áyá x̲át tsú ax̲ toowú yatee. This is how I feel too. AH 39
<ax̲ too-wu ya-tee
pp lo po cl st imperfective

9) ch'a ldakát áwé gági yawdixuni yáx̲ áwé ax̲ tuwáa yatee
all of them seem to me as if they are revealing their faces
JD 43

10) Yéi yee ng̲atéenín áyú. Whenever this would happen to you. AH 11
(lit. you would be thus whenever this would happen to you)
<na-g̲a-téen-ín
cp ap st contingent
Note use of the progressive stem TEEN in contingent.

11) yéi at nag̲atéenín when things were thus AH 15
<na-g̲a-téen-ín
cp ap st contingent

12) gu.aal kwshé yee tóodei wuxoogu yáx̲ wooteek̲ my hope is (your grief) be like it's drying to your core JD 210
<woo-tee-k̲
ap st optative

13) Yá tléix' yateeyi aa. There is one thing. AH 23
(lit. this being one thing)
<ya-tee-yi
cl st attributive

14) yéi yateeyi át such a thing ("a such thing") DK 20
<yéi ya-tee-yi
ba cl st attributive

15) Tléil yáa yéi wootee. It wasn't here. AH 27
<yáa -ø yéi u-wu-tee
lo po ba ir ap st perfective negative
Yáa = yáax'; -x' has the Ø allomorph here.

16) yá haa jee yéi yatee[yi] Naatúxjayi This Naatúxjayi whom we have AH 31
<yéi ya - tee -[yi]
ba cl st s attributive
The attributive suffix -yi was not audible on the tape. One would expect it here, but it is also possible, although less common, to omit it here.

17) gu.aal kwshé yéi yee wooteeyík̲ my hope is that you become like it (thus) DK 49
<yéi yee u- wu-tee-yik̲
ba sp ir ap st optative

k̲aa wak̲sheeyeex' + yéi + ya-tee to appear

áwé ch'a oowayáa yee wak̲sheeyeex' gági gútx̲i yáx̲ áwé yatee yeedát this moment it is as if he will be coming out for you to see JD 94

a eetéenáx̲ + ya-tee need; lack; require

a eetée-náx̲ haa yatee we need them AH 16
- a eetéenáx̲ áyá haa wootee ax̲ káak hás we are in need of my mother's brothers DK 22-23
  <woo-tee
  ap st perfective

ka-dzi-tee (?)
sh tuwaa-g̲áa + ka-dzi-tee to feel proud; to be one's own liking

- tlax̲ waa sá aan sh tuwaag̲áa kastéeyin how proud he used to feel wearing it (lit. how very much with it for his own liking he was) JD 96-98
  <sh tu-ya-g̲áa ka- s-tée-yin
  op lo lo po np cl st decessive

k̲u-dzi-tee (in) be, be in existence, live, be born

- áx' áwé du yee tl'átgi k̲uwdzitee it was there he got his land (his land came from) JM 6-7
  <k̲u-wu-dzi-tee
  np ap cl st perfective
- has k̲ustéeyin they were once alive ML1 11, 12
  <k̲u- s-tée-yin
  np cl st decessive
- tléil ... k̲oostí there is nothing ML1 16
  <k̲u-u- s- tí
  np ir cl st negative imperfective
- yá a eetée k̲ux̲dziteeyi aa yeedát the people I am living in place of now DK 77
  <k̲u-x̲a-dzi-tee-yi
  np sp cl st attributive

si-tee (st) A-x̱ + sitee be (member of a set); become

- yá i yátx'ix̱ haa sateeyí we who are your children ML1 17
  <i yát-x'-ix̱ haa sa-tee-yi
  pp n pl s op cl st participial
- sagóox̱ nax̱satee let it turn to joy DK 65
  <sagóo-x̱ na-g̱a-sa-tee
  n s cp ap cl st desiderative
- ax̱ sani hásx̱ siteeyi aa those who are my father's brothers DK 80
  <sáni hás-x̱ si-tee-yi
  n pl s cl st attributive
- ax̱ kaani yánx̱ siteeyi aa those who are my sisters-in-law JD 121
  <káani yán-x̱ si-tee-yi
  n pl s cl st attributive

tu-si-tee (st?) A + tu-si-tee to seem
(Note: this seems to be a new theme not attested in the N-S verb dictionary.)

- gági uwagudi yáx̱ ax̱ tusitee it seems to me as if he came out JD 164
  <ax̱ tu- si-tee
  pp np cl st imperfective

tu-ya-tee (st) want to do, feel like doing
a daa + tu-ya-tee think about

- i daa ax̱ tuwatee I am thinking about you WJ 10
  <ax̱ tu- ya-tee
  op np cl st imperfective
  Note how ya classifier appears as wa after vowel u.
- eeshandéin ágé haa daa tuwatee uhaan tsú? does it take pity on us too? JD 1
  <haa tu- ya-tee
  op np cl st imperfective
- tléil eeshandéin haa daa tootí uháan tsú it does not take pity on us either JD 5
  <tu- u- tí
  np ir st negative imperfective

- eeshandéin tuwateeyi k̲aa káx' over the person who is feeling grief JD 130, 134
  <tu-ya-tee-yi
  np cl st attributive

TEE 2

ya-tee (tr) carry, take, lie, bring, give

- Du eetéetx̲ ax̲ jee yéi wootee. I own it in place of him. AH 22
  (Lit. From in place of him, it came to lie in my hand)
  <yéi woo-tee
  ba ap st perfective
- chance haa jeet yeeyteeyí that you will give us a chance ML1 24
  <haa jee-t wu-yee-tee-yi
  pp lo po ap sp st participial
- kéi ag̲atee to remove it / take it away AH 36
  <kéi a- g̲a-tee
  dp op ap st desiderative
- yá at wuduwateeyí this thing which has been held ML2 16
  <wu-du-ya-tee-yi
  ap sp cl st participial
- tléil sh tóotx̲ yóo tudateek ooháan tsú haa nanéiyi
  we too don't overlook (take out; reject, put off from us) our dead DK 60
  <yoo tu- da-tee-k
  dp sp cl st durative imperfective
  Note "d" classifier required by the reflexive "sh".

a-ya-di-tee (im?) storm, be stormy, rough (of weather)

- a káa ayax̲dateech it (the wind) would blow over it DK 37
  <ká-a a- ya- g̲a-da-tee-ch
  lo po op np cp cl st occasional
- a káa ayax̲dateex' when it (wind) would blow over it DK 38
  <ká-a a- ya- g̲a-da-tee-x'
  lo po op np ap cl st sequential
  In both phrases, we have restored the "a" in a káa. It is not audible on the tape but is probably there. In the first case, the word preceding is áyá, and flows into the káa. In the second, the beginning of the sentence overlaps with a response

in 37a. We do not completely understand the use of the locative -x' in this consequential construction.

TEE 3

ya-tee (tr) imitate actions

- has ootee they are imitating them JD 178
  <has a- u -tee
  pl op ir st

x̲'a-ya-tee (tr) imitate speech, quote

- ax̲ káak áyá x̲'akk̲watee I will imitate my mother's brother DK 6, 11, 16
  <x̲'a- u- ga- g̲a-x̲a-tee
  np ir cp ap sp st future (first person singular)
  Here, as in the preceding verb, Leer considers -u- to be part of the theme. Thus, u-ya-tee and x̲'a-u-ya-tee would be the theoretical forms.

TEEN

ya-teen (tr) see

- ha yeeytéen áyá a tóot hás nák̲ you can see them now standing in these DK 84
  <wu-yee-ya-téen
  ap sp cl st perfective (second person plural)

TÉEN ~ TÍN With (see also **TÍN**)

TEET

li-teet (st) be afloat, be carried by waves, drift

- gunayéi ultéetch it would begin to roll/drift DK 38
  <u- l- teet-ch
  ir cl st occasional
  (Note irrealis with Ø conjugation verb).
- át g̲alatídín áwé l'éiw when it rolled/drifted to the sand DK 40
  <g̲a-la-teet-in
  ap cl st contingent

- áa yan yoo latitgi nuch   there it would be pounded by the waves DK 41, 42
  <á- a yan yoo la-teet-k- i nuch
  lo po dp dp cl st s s hv   dur imperfective with occ hv

  This is a very expressive verb form. Yan means "ashore", yoo means "back and forth", -k is a durative suffix expressing action of long duration. I is a "peg vowel" for ease in pronunciation; the main verb is imperfective and the helping verb nook appears in the occasional.

- yaa gax̲latídin yóo aas   how that tree rolled on the waves JD 201 (lit. "whenever")
  <ga-g̲a-la-teet-in
  cp ap cl st con(tingent)   contingent progressive

TÍN ~ TÉEN   With
yee tula.eesháani tín áwé   with your grief JD 138

TOO ~ TU   Inside

yee tóo-dáx̲	from inside you AH 35
ax̲ tu-wáa si-goo	I want (on my mind desires) AH 1
ax̲ too-wú ya-tee	I feel (in my mind is) AH 5, 39
Tsalx̲aan tóo-dei	to inside Mt. Fairweather ML2 20
tóo-x' áyá	inside (in our minds) DK 3
sh too-tx̲	from inside ourselves DK 60
a tóo-dei	to inside it DK 63
yee too-wú	your feelings, insides DK 74
a tóo-t hás nák̲	they're standing in these DK 84
Shaa-tu-k̲wáan	Tribe Inside the Mountain DK 87b, JD 19
a tóo-náx̲	from it, through it JD 214
G̲éelák'w tóo-náx̲	from (through) G̲éelák'w JD 216

TU   Mind
ax̲ tu-wáa sigóo   I want; "my mind desires" ML1 1
has du tu-wáx' áyú sigóo   they want ML1 23

TULA.EESHÁANI   Grief (obligatorily possessed)
<tu-la-eesháan-i
np cl st poss
yee tula.eesháani   your grief ML2 21

yee tula.eesháani káx̲ — for your grief AH 32, JD 69
yee tula.eesháani tín — with your grief JD 138

-TX̲ = DAX̲ From
aa-tx̲ — from there DK 37
a yee-tx̲ — from under it DK 43, 44
sh too-tx̲ — from inside ourselves DK 60

T'

T'AA
ya-t'aa (st) be warm, hot
si-t'aa (tr) warm (water)
li-t'aa (tr) warm (a person)
k̲aa toowóo + li-t'aa comfort

Note how the transitive (tr) stems cause someone or something to be or become warm; the stative stem (st) implies that something is warm. Note also the different classifiers for animate and inanimate things. This stem is a good example of the systematic alternation of classifiers in Tlingit.

• yee toowú daa oox̲lit'aayi átx' — these are the things that might warm your feelings (comfort you) DK 74
<a - u - g̲a-li-t'aa-yi
op ir ap cl st — attributive potential

T'AAK̲Ú Taku; Taku River (place name)
T'aak̲óo-náx̲ — from (through) Taku JD 155
T'aak̲ú wát-dei — to the mouth of Taku JD 146

T'AK̲(KÁ) Beside, along side
chush t'ak̲kaa-déi — to (go) beside him JM 10
a t'ak̲ká-t áwé — along side it JD 152

T'EEX'
ya-t'eex' (st) be hard (abstract), difficult
• yat'éex'i át áyá — it is a hard thing DK 18
<ya-t'eex'-i
cl st — attributive

TL

TLÁA Mother
ax̲ tláa — my mother JD 45
yá haa tláa — this our mother / mother of ours ML2 12
• yá haa tláach — this our mother ML2 9
<haa tláa-ch
pp n subject marker

TLÁKW Always

TLAX̲ Very; how much
tlax̲ wáa sáyú — how very much JD 68
tlax̲ wáa sá — how very much AH 4

TLEI Then, at that time

TLEIGÍL Isn't there, wasn't there, haven't you
<tléik' - gí - l
"no" * neg
(* = interrogative)

TLÉIL not
<tléik' - l
"no" neg
tléil yáa yéi wootee — it wasn't here AH 27
tléil eeshandéin haa daa tootí uháan tsú — it does not take pity on us either JD 5

TLÉIX' One, united, all together
yá tléix' yateeyi aa — one thing AH 23
tsu tleíx' — all (together) DK 2
ch'a tléix' — all (one) JD 4

TLIYÁA(NAX̲) On the far side
tliyaanax̲ á aa k̲u.aa áwé — but on the far side there is JD 102

TL'

TL'ÁTK   Land
- du yee tl'átgi   the land under him   JM 7
  <du yee tl'átk-i
     pp lo   n   possessive

TL'OOḴ
  ka-doo-ya-tl'ooḵ ( ) drip slowly
- kawduwatl'oogu aa   those things which fell/dripped   ML2 23
  <ka-wu-du-ya-tl'ooḵ-u
     np ap sp cl   st   attributive

TS

TSAGWÁLT   Personal name (Jack David); see annotations   AH 20

TSALX̱AAN   Mount Fairweather (place name; see annotations)

TSALX̱AAN G̱UWAKAAN   Personal name (George Dalton); see annotations   AH 23a, ML2 19b
Tsalx̱áan = Mt. Fairweather
G̱uwakaan = Peace Maker, hostage, deer

TSOOW   (Plural stem. Singular is **TSAAḴ**)
  ya-tsoow (tr) place upright (especially a stick-like object)
- gagaanch áwé a kát x̱'us.utsóowch   the sun would put its rays (feet) on it   JD 203
  <x̱'us u- tsóow-ch
     np ir st   occasional

TSÚ   Also, too
  yee yátx'i tsú   your children too   ML1 10
  uháan tsú   us too   JD 1, 5
  x̱at tsú   me too, I also   AH 2, 5
  hú tsú   he, too   AH 32
  Normally tsú (with tone) means "also" or "too," and tsu (without tone) means "again." However, the tone may be "stolen" by hú:
  tsu hú   he, too   AH 19, JD 88

TS'

TS'ÍGWAA
ka-li-ts'ígwaa (tr) need to treat delicately
(st) be delicate; need diplomacy; be a touchy subject; require tact
• k̲a kwlits'ígwaa and sensitive DK 21
<ku-li-ts'ígwaa
np cl st
The form "ka-li-ts'ígwaa" is more common, but "ku-li-ts'ígwaa" is also used, as shown here.

U

-U Post position; location in; also possessive suffix
yáa-t-u here (locative) AH 13
ax̲ too-wú yatee I feel; on my mind is (poss. suffix) AH 5, 39

UHÁAN Us; we. (independent pronoun) DK 60, JD 1

W

WÁA (SÁ) how
tlax̲ wáa sá how very much AH 4
wáa yadali át yáx̲ sáyú nateech how it is like a heavy burden WJ 6
tlax̲ wáa lax̲éitlx̲ sá what a great gift ML2 10
tlax̲ wáa sáyú how very much JD 68

WAAL'
li-waal' (tr) break (rare)
sha-li-waal' ( ) to cave in, break away, crumble away
(Not attributed in N-S dictionary with this prefix)
• yá k̲útl'kw áwé aax̲ shalawal' nuch the earth would crumble away DK 30
<sha-la-waal' nuch
np cl st hv durative

WAATL' (See YAATL')

WAK̲HÉENI Tear
yee wak̲héeni your tears JD 10
<waak̲ (eye) + héen (water)

WAK̲SHIYEE In a person's sight or presence
<waák̲-shu-yee below the eye(s)
yee wak̲shiyee to show you AH 7
yee wak̲shiyee-x' for you to see JD 94

WANÁAK Away from; separate from
k̲aa wanáak away from people JM 18

WÁT Mouth (of river or bay)
yá Ltu.áa wat-yee-x' at the mouth of Lituya Bay JM 12
T'aak̲ú wát-dei áwé to the mouth of Taku JD 146

WÉ That; the; there. Demonstrative and locative.
wé x'óow that blanket; the blanket AH 37
wei-x̲ along there WJ 18
wéi-t there JD 86
wéi-x' there JD 116

WEIHÁ Personal name; see annotations JD 89

WOOK̲
ya-wook̲ (st) move, fall (esp. of textiles; often a gradual, rippling movement)
- a t'ak̲kát áwé uwawúk̲ along side of it came JD 152
<wu-ya-wúk̲
ap cl st perfective

WOOS'
x̲'a-ya-woos' (tr) ask, question (usually a specific person)
- aag̲áa áwé x̲'awduwawóos' that's when he was asked JM 23
<x̲'a-wu-du-ya-wóos'
np ap sp cl st perfective
Du (4th person subject pronoun) is often translated with English passive voice.

WOOSH Each other
woosh jin toolshát yeisú we're still holding each other's hands DK 59

WOOTEEYEIT Event, happening JD 8

WOOX̲
di-woox̲ (st) become smaller (of tide)
- a yeetx̲ yaa kdawúx̲ch the tide would leave it dry / from under it the tide would go down DK 43, 44
<yaa-ga-da-wúx̲-ch
dp cp cl st occasional

X

XAACH
a-li-xaach (in) despair, give up hope; put off, defer, delay doing, give up
- dei ch'a ch'áakw áwé has du ée antulaxáchch we have long since given up hope for their return JD 105
<a-na-tu-la-xách-ch
op cp sp cl st occasional

XEEX
ya-xeex (st) fall, drop (small, compact object)
- tle tlax̲ ch'a nichkáx̲ aa wooxéexg̲aa so that it not (did not) fall in vain (for nothing) JD 9
<aa-w-ya-xéex-g̲aa
op ap cl st po negative perfective
Aa is an object pronoun here. Literally, "lest any/some (part of it) fall in vain."

XÍXCH' Frog
Xíxch'i S'áaxw Frog Hat DK 87a, JD 151

XOOK
ya-xook (st) be dry, dried (general)
- yaa gaxúkch it would begin to dry out DK 48
<yaa ga-xúk-ch
dp cp st occasional

- a tóodei wuxoogóok   that it will dry out DK 63
  <wu-xook-óok
  ap st   optative perfective
- du tóodei áwé yaa gaxúkch   it would dry (its grief) to the core JD 205
  <yaa ga-xúk-ch
  dp cp st   occasional progressive
- gu.aal kwshé yee tóodei wuxoogu yáx wooteek   my hope is (your grief) be like it is drying to your core JD 210
  <wu-xook-u
  ap st   attributive

XOON
ya-di-xoon (in) show faces (as entering in ceremonial dance); peer, peep

- ch'a ldakát áwé gági yawdixuni yáx áwé   all of them seem (to me) as if they are revealing their faces JD 43
- gági yawdixuni yáx has du daa yoo tuxaatánk   as if they are revealing their faces is how I am thinking about them JD 78
  <ya-wu-di-xun-i
  np ap cl st   participial
- gági yawdixún i aat hás   your father's sisters are revealing their faces JD 70
- gági has yawdixún   they are revealing their faces JD 81
  <ya-wu-di-xún
  np ap cl st   perfective
- a tóonáx áwé daak woodaxoonch yee aat hás   from it your father's sisters would reveal their faces JD 214-215
  <ya-u- da-xoon-ch
  np ir cl st   occasional

XWAAYEENÁK   Personal name; see annotations DK 57

X'

-X'   Plural marker
átx'   things DK 74

-X'   Location in, at, on; of, about;
it also has a Ø allomorph, as in AH 27

yáa-x' here AH 9
yáa here AH 27
a daa-x' about it, of it AH 14
á-x' áwé it was there JM 6
yá Ltu.aa wat-yee-x' at the mouth of Lituya Bay JM 12
haa x̲oo-x' among us ML2 11
yá éil' tlein kax' on the great ocean DK 36
yá lingit'aaní g̲ei-x' in this world DK 58
yee yáx' yéi has a daanéi noojéen they used to show you DK 75
k̲áa ká-x' over the person JD 130
has du tuwá-x' ...sigóo they want ML1 23
wéi-x' there JD 116
du jee-x' in his hands JD 92

X'AA Peninsula, point of land
yee éesh hás x'aayí your fathers' point of land JD 53

X'ÓOW Robe, blanket
wé x'óow the blanket AH 37
• du x'óow-u his robe AH 13, 20
<du x'óow -u
pp n ps
K̲'eik̲'w X'óow The Tern Robe JD 48
Lyeedayéik x'óowu robe of Lyeedayéik JD 29

X'WÁN Won't you? will you? for sure; certainly (rhetorical)
yáa x'wán won't you? WJ 16, 17
i gu.aa yáx̲ x'wán dlák' have courage, sister WJ 15

X̲

-X̲ Predicate nominative marker
yá i yátx'i-x̲ haa sateeyí we who are your children ML1 17
k̲a yá i dachx̲anx'i yán-x̲ haa sateeyi and we who are your grandchildren ML1 17
ha tlax̲ wáa lax̲éitlx̲ sá haa wootee what a great gift we have ML2 10
ch'a aadéi-x̲ siteeyi aa whoever is one DK 52
sagóo-x̲ nax̲satee let it turn to joy DK 65

ax sani hás-x siteeyi aa DK 80 — those who are my paternal uncles

ax kaani yán-x siteeyi aa JD 121 — those who are my sisters-in-law

-X Along (locational)

yee yadaa-x — along your faces DK 64, WJ 1, JD 10
wéi-x has yaawanák — they're standing there WJ 18
aax shalawal' nuch — would crumble away (along the edge of it) DK 30
héen yí-x — along (in) the water DK 33-34
geesh daa-x — along the kelp JD 27

XÁ You know, indeed, surely

yak'éi xá — sure, fine JM 30
tleigíl ch'a wáa sá…xá — indeed JM 28-29
yéi kgwatée xá — thus it will be DK 64a

XAT I, me (object pronoun; subject pronoun with stative verbs)

xát tsú — me too; I also AH 2
xat yeeyliyéx — you created me DK 53, 54

XÉITL See **LAXÉITL**

XOO Among

du aat hás xoo-t — among his aunts AH 15
haa xoo-dáx — from among us JM 4
haa xoo-x' — among us ML2 11
du léelk'w hás xoo-déi — to among his grandparents JD 148, 149

XOOX

ya-xoox (tr) call, summon
A-x + ya-xoox ask for

- chush daadéi áwé kuwdixoox — he summoned people around him JM 32

<ku-wu-di-xoox
np ap cl st perfective
(Not attested in N-S Dictionary with ku prefix. Leer considers this stem to have a u-theme: u-ya-xoox.)

X̲OOX̲KEI.ANA.ÁT Personal name (of Pete Johnson); see annotations JD 67

X̲'

X̲'É Mouth
I x̲'éi-t wu-si-.áx̲ i sani hás. Your paternal uncles are listening to you. AH 10a

X̲'US Foot; contracted from x̲'oos
gagaanch áwé a kát x̲'us.utsóowch the sun would place its rays (feet) on it JD 203
X̲'oos is used here as a nominal prefix, a noun incorporated into the verb complex. See analysis under -tsoow.

X̲'WÁAL' Down (feathers)
has du x̲'wáal'-i their down JD 132, 136

Y

YÁ This; the. Demonstrative. See also **YÁA**
Yá K'eedzáa This K'eedzáa AH 12
Yá yee káani This your brother-in-law AH 30
Yáa yeedát Now; this moment AH 8

YÁ face; vertical face of
a yá-t to the face of JD 51
yee yá-x' yéi hás a daanéi noojéen they used to show you DK 75

YÁA This, here (Locative base; = **YÁ**)
yaa yeedát now; this moment ML1 5
yáa-t here WJ 5, JD 18
yáa-d-u here AH 13, JD 15
yáa-náx̲ á here, this (end) closer through here, on this side AH 17, JD 30
tléil yá-a yéi woo-tee it wasn't here AH 27
tsú yáa-x' here too AH 33
yáa-t'-aa this one ML2 15
yáa-x' áwé (it is) here DK 43

YAA (directional prefix) along
yaa a jiklaháa áwé while he was going there JM 11

YAA
ya-yaa (tr) resemble; look like
• ch'a oowayáa jigwéinaa (may it) resemble a towel AH 38
<a- u- ya-yaa
op ir cl st imperfective
The irrealis is part of the verb theme. If the verb itself were negative, the form would be tlél oowaa, with the zero form of the ya classifier. See also **TEE 3**.
• ch'a oowayáa it is just as if JD 94
• ch'u oowayáa áwé it is just as if JD 20
(See above analysis.)

ka-di-yaa (st) move, travel, happen
a yá<u>x</u> + ka-di-yaa be fulfilled; come true; be like
(Leer considers -u- to be part of the theme: ka-u-di-yaa.)

• Yaakwdáatdei áwé kawdiyaa he went to Yakutat JM 2-3
<ka-wu-di-yaa
np ap cl st perfective
• tlákw áyú yéi kwdayéin it has always been this way ML1 4
<yéi ka- u-da-yein
ba np ir cl st perfective
• yáax' haat <u>x</u>at kawdayaayí that I am here (have arrived here) AH 6
<ka-wu-da-yaa-yi
np ap cl st participial
• yéi koona<u>x</u>dayeinín whenever such things happened DK 72
<yéi ka- u- na-<u>g</u>a-da-yein-ín
ba np ir cp ap cl st contingent
Koo is a contraction of ka + u.
• haat kawdiyáa it came (here) JD 155
<ka-wu-di-yáa
np ap cl st perfective

YÁADU Here; (see **YAA**)

YAAKAAYINDUL.ÁT Personal name; see annotations JD 103

YAAKW Boat, canoe JM 13

YAAKWDÁAT Place name; (Yakutat)
Yaakwdáat-dei to Yakutat JM 2

YAAK̲W
li-yaak̲w (tr) represent as, portray, liken to, explain

- has du yáa x'wán nalyaak̲w you will explain these for them WJ 16
  <na-l- yaak̲w
  cp cl st imperative
- ax̲ tuwáa sigóo yáat'aa x̲walayaag̲ú I would like to explain this ML2 15
  <wu-x̲a-la-yaak̲w-ú
  ap sp cl st participial perfective
- ch'a kk̲walayaak̲w I will just explain it AH 26
  <u- ga-g̲a-x̲a-la-yaak̲w
  ir cp ap sp cl st future
- tléil yan ux̲layaak̲wch I haven't completely explained JD 127
  <yan u- wu-x̲a-la-yaak̲w-ch
  dp ir ap sp cl st durative perfective
- yá dziyáak yá ax̲ éek'ch wuliyaag̲u aa the one this brother of mine explained a while ago JD 200
  <wu-li-yaak̲w-u
  ap cl st attributive

YAANAAYÍ Enemy
Keet Yaanaayí Personal name (Willie Marks); see annotations AH 22a

YÁANÁX̲ Beyond, closer (see also YÁA)
a áwé yáanáx̲ á that is the closer one JD 30

YÁAT'AA This one (see also **YÁA**)

YAATL'
ya-yaatl' (st) to be short
yee-ya-yaatl' (st) to be short (of time)

- ch'a yéi yiguwáatl' just a short time ML2 6
  <yee- ga-u- yáatl'
  no cp ir st verbal noun

YADAA Face (see also **YÁ** and **DAA**)
yee yadaa-x̱ along your faces WJ 1
yee yadaa-náx̱ along your faces ML2 22

YADÁL See **DAAL**

YÁDI Child
i yádi your child (singular) DK 8
yee yadí your child (plural) DK 16

YAKW Nominal prefix; by boat <yaakw
yakw.uk̲oox̱ch would go by boat JD 51

YAKWDEIYÍ G̱UWAKAAN Personal name;
see annotations DK 10

YÁN Plural marker
ax̱ kaani yán my brothers-in-law WJ 3
i dachx̱anx'i yánx̱ haa sateeyí we who are your grandchildren ML1 17

YAN Directional prefix indicating finished action; shore; end
yándei a shagux̱lahéek she will complete this WJ 12
yan ulhaashch it would drift ashore DK 41
áa yan yóo latitgi nuch it would be pounded there DK 41
yándei gax̱yeenáak̲ you will stand DK 70

YANAX̱ Along the ground, underground
yanax̱ yeik̲ kawdik'ít' they have come out JD 12, 14
yanax̱ daak̲ guganóok he will burrow back down out of sight JD 171
yanax̱ wudihaan hú tsú he too stood up to face you JD 190

YÁTX'I Children (plural of **YÉET** or **YÁDI**)
yee yátx'i your children (plural) ML1 10
i yátx'i your children (singular) WJ 20

YAX̲ Like, as if; often modifies an entire verb phrase.
waa a yá-x̲ like it, like this JD 7
yee yá-x̲ like you JD 50
Jig̲wéinaa ya-x̲ like a towel AH 38
yadali át yá-x̲ ... nateech like a heavy burden WJ 6
has ayakawdliyiji yá-x̲ áwé as if they are flying (to face) JD 140

YÉ Place, thing, what. This word often patterns with attributive verbs. Stress is usually "stolen" from the verb.
wé aadéi x̲'ayaduk̲a yé what people were saying JM 19

YEE Under; below; inside a building
du yee tl'átgi the land under him JM 7
yá Ltu.aa wat-yee-x' at the mouth of Lituya Bay (outside, below the mouth of the Bay) JM 12
a yee-tx̲ yaa kdawúx̲ch the tide would go down from under it DK 43, 44

YEE ~ YI You, your (plural); 2nd person plural subject and possessive pronoun; you-all's

yee éesh hás	your (y'all's) fathers ML1 9
yee yátx'i	your children ML1 10
yee tula.eesháani	your grief ML2 18
yee yáx̲	like you JD 50
yee aat	your aunt JD 103
yá yee káani	this your brother-in-law AH 30

YEECH (basically plural; see **K̲EEN** for singular)
ka-dli-yeech (st?) fly

- daak koolyeechch they would fly out JD 130
  <ka- u - l- yeech-ch
  np ir cl st occasional
  Note use of irrealis instead of conjugation prefix for Ø conjugation verbs.

- has ayakawdliyiji yáx̲ áwé as if they are turning back in flight JD 140
  <a- ya-ka- wu-dli-yich-i
  op np np ap cl st participial

This is hard to translate. The idea is of turning back so that one is moving in the direction whence one came. There are parallels with other verbs of motion:
ayawdigút   turned back (walking)
ayawdik̲úx̲   turned back in a boat

YEEDÁT Now; moment
yáa yeedát   now; this moment ML1 5, AH 8, 16

YÉET Son
du yéet   his son DK 7
ax̲ léelk'w yéet   my grandfather's son JD 61

YEEWÁAN You (plural; independent pronoun)
ldakát yeewáan   all of you JD 120

YÉEYEE ~ YÉEYI Former; formerly; once (in past);
Yéeyi also patterns with the decessive when the verb is not in the main clause.
du x'óow-u yéeyi   once his blanket JD 37
du naaxein-í yéeyi   once his Chilkat robe JD 38

YEI Down
(directional prefix; note contrast to bound adverb **YÉI**)

YÉI Thus; (also, bound adverb)
yéi áyá   Thus it is AH 39
ldakát yéidei   in all ways AH 11
yéi wootee   it lay AH 27
aag̲áa áwé yéi yawdudzik̲áa   that's when they said to him JM 27
yéi áyá   thus it is ML1 25
yéi kwag̲atée   thus it will be ML1 25a

YEIK̲ Down to shore; from the interior (directional prefix)

YÉIL Raven
geesh daax̲ woogoodi yéil   Raven who walked down along the bull kelp JD 27

YEILKUDEI Raven Nest; Proper name of Clan House; see annotations; <yéil + kut

YEIN (See **YAA**)

YEISÚ Recently; just now
ch'a yeisú áwé it was just recently JD 83
woosh jin toolshát yeisú we're still holding each other's hands DK 59

YEIX̲
li-yeix̲ (tr) build, make, construct

- awliyex̲i shí the song he had made JM 35
  <a- wu-li-yéx̲-i
  op ap cl st attributive
- x̲at yeeyliyéx̲, Chookaneidí you created me, Chookaneidí
  <x̲at wu-yee-li-yéx̲
  op ap sp cl st perfective

YÍK In (open container)
yá héen yí-k in the water DK 26

YÍS For (post-position)
- ax̲ ji-yís for me WJ 13
  <ax̲ ji- yís
  pp lo po
- yee ji-yís for you DK 55

YÍX̲ In (See also **YÍK**)
héen yí-x̲ along in the water, down the river DK 33, 34

YÓO Thus (bound adverb)

YOOK̲IS'KOOK̲ÉIK Personal name; see annotations JD 187

YÚ = YÓO That one (demonstrative pronoun)

YÚ.Á Particle: "they say"; "it's said" JD 151

Biographies

Jessie Dalton / Naa Tláa
Born: April 12, 1903
Raven; T'aḵdeintaan; Wooshkeetaan yádi

Lithograph of Jessie Dalton, "Naa Tlaa," by R. T. Wallen, Juneau. Reproduced courtesy of R. T. Wallen.

Jessie Starr Dalton was born in Tenakee on April 12, 1903, the only child of Mary and Thomas Starr, their son having died as a child in an accident. Of the Yéil Kudei Hít Taan (Raven Nest House), Jessie was born into the T'aḵdeintaan clan of the Raven moiety, and is a child of the Wooshkeetaan. Her mother's Tlingit name is Shaawát G̱eig̱éi. Her father's Tlingit name is Yeexaas; he was of the Hinka Hít of Angoon.

Jessie's memories of childhood are of lavish attention and boundless love from both parents. The family cash income derived from fishing, cannery work and occasional boat building, but traditional subsistence activities were an important part of her upbringing, and she learned how to gather and prepare the regional specialties of Tlingit cuisine. Missing that, she complains, is one of the hardest parts of growing old.

Jessie married George Dalton on May 18, 1919, an arranged marriage that took her out of Sheldon Jackson School and into adult life earlier than she would have wished. But she complied with her parents' wishes, and she and George lived in Tenakee, near her parents, for the first years of their life together. The first five of her fourteen children were born there. And in Tenakee her father and her husband built the *Tlingit*, the Dalton couple's first boat. The young couple moved to Hoonah, George's home, in 1926 and have made that their home base ever since.

Jessie's life has been an active one, raising her children, taking care of her household, gathering foods in season and putting them up for winter, and earning a cash income from cannery work. The full schedule of Jessie's life has left little time to follow personal pursuits, but she still managed to become a successful beadworker, selling moccasins and other beaded items for cash from time to time.

Jessie wanted to be educated in the Sheldon Jackson School and cajoled her indulgent father into letting her go. But even then, eager as she was to learn the new ways, she had the independence of judgement to realize that the prohibition against the speaking of Tlingit was a bad policy. And she rebelled against it, carefully, by deliberately speaking her language whenever she was out of earshot of the school authorities. She learned to read and write in English, but she maintained her fluency in Tlingit, and cultivated her knowledge of Tlingit traditions. Her mastery is reflected in her public speaking. She is a primary spokesperson for her generation, and, as a member of the paternal grandparent clan of the deceased, was a major speaker at the memorial for Jim Marks.

Jessie has a flexibility rarely found, and always admired, that gives her the conviction to hold on to the principles and values of her traditional culture while still embracing the conveniences and pleasures of the new. She has survived on her selectivity.

The editors thank Lynn and Skip Wallen for the contribution of this biography.

George Davis / Kichnáalx̲; Lk'aanaaw
(May 7, 1899 - January 20, 1985)
Deisheetaan; Kaagwaantaan yádi; Shdeen Hít

George Alexander Davis was born May 7, 1899, in Angoon, where he lived most of his life. He was of the Raven moiety, Deisheetaan clan, and of the Shdeen Hít (Steel House) of which he later became a caretaker. His father was Alexander Davis, a man of the Kake Kaagwaantaan, and child of Deisheetaan. His maternal uncle was "Chief Jake" of Killisnoo, also called "Saginaw Jake," whose Tlingit name was Kichnáalx̲. He was a significant figure and appears in several historical photographs (Kan 1985:XIV and Wyatt 1989:32,46). See also the notes to lines 22-29 of Charlie Jim's speech.

George was married twice. He had twelve children, of whom three daughters survive. He had thirty-eight grandchildren and great-grandchildren. Upon the death of his first wife, he married Eva Davis in 1960, and moved to Hoonah, where he lived until his death.

George was active in community affairs, and was the first president of the Angoon Public Utility District Town Council. He was a charter member of Alaska Native Brotherhood Camp 7 in Angoon, and a lifetime member of the ANB camps in Angoon and Hoonah. George served as an officer from time to time. He was involved with the Hoonah Chapter of the American Legion. George worked in Washington, D.C. for ten years after his first wife died, advocating Alaska Native causes.

He was a commercial fisherman, a crewmember on William Johnson's seiner *Gypsy Queen,* and had two boats of his own. He fished all of his life, handtrolling and seining. He was also active in subsistence activities such as hunting, berry picking, gathering cockles and clams, fishing and drying fish.

George was a leader in Tlingit ceremonial life. He was a "Lingít tlein" or "big man" and was a steward of the Deisheetaan at.óow. George served many times as "naa káani," the traditional master of ceremonies and ceremonial brother-in-law of the host, and this is part of his role in the speeches from the elders conference featured in this book.

George was well-versed as a tradition bearer. He was one of the original organizers of the Sealaska Heritage Foundation, working endlessly for its creation and lending support to its activities. He was also involved in many elders conferences, such as the one documented in this book. He spent many hours with Nora Dauenhauer and others documenting Tlingit culture and heritage. He often commented, "When I'm dead, you can't come to me at my grave and ask me." As with many others of his generation, we lost a world of knowledge with the passing of George Davis. George Davis is featured in the movie *Haa Shagóon* (Kawagey 1981) where he makes a speech and poses a traditional riddle.

George Davis, Sitka 1982, participating in Native Awareness Week. Photo courtesy of Tlingit and Haida Central Council Archives.

George died at Mt. Edgecumbe Hospital on January 20, 1985. His passing was noted by the Alaska State Legislature in February 1985. He was Orthodox, baptized Alexander, and was buried from the Russian Othodox Church in Angoon. The editors thank Eva Davis for her help in researching this biography.

Jimmie George / Wóochx̱ Kaduhaa
Born: November 30, 1889
Eagle; Dak̲l'aweidí; Deisheetaan yádi
Kéet Hít / Killer Whale House

The life of Jimmy George originates in Juneau. He is a grandson of Wooshkeetaan, the "Shark" clan of the Eagle moiety. His grandfather was John Paul, Aandax̱léich, Wooshkeetaan of Noow Hít, Fort House of Angoon. His father was L'ax̱kéikw. His mother was Shaawat Goox̱, a woman of the Dak̲l'aweidí. Her English name was Mrs. Albert George.

Of his education, Jimmie recalls, "I sneaked off to school. My mother didn't want me to go to school in Sitka. A number of events combined to cut his education short. The most tragic of these was when his father died, and there was no one to take care of his four younger brothers. He began to work for a living as the sole support of his family.

Jimmie George (L) with Lydia George and Charlie Joseph (of Angoon) during ceremonies for the dedication of the Wolf Crest Plaque in memory of Ivan Gamble, Angoon, October 1987. Photo by Peter Metcalfe, courtesy of Kootznoowoo, Inc.

Jimmie's early years were spent in the village of Killisnoo, where he lived until the village burned in June 1928. After the fire, he made the most important move of his life when he relocated to Angoon to become caretaker of Kéet Ooxú Hít—Killer Whale Tooth House. He has been active in Tlingit ceremonial life ever since. He was a song leader for the Angoon Dak̲l'aweidí during the Sealaska Heritage Foundation Celebration '88, and on September 3, 1988, he was the main speaker for the Dak̲l'aweidí at one of their gatherings in Klukwan. In October 1989 he and his wife were active song leaders for parts of the Kaagwaantaan memorial in Juneau. The speech in this book is an example of his cultural involvement.

Jimmie and Lydia have been married for fifty years, and are a fine example of a traditionally arranged marriage. Lydia was very young when she married Jimmie. They have eight children, (four boys and four girls) and about fourteen grandchildren. To support his family, Jimmie worked at a variety of jobs in his lifetime, including logging. At one time he was an engineer on the cannery tender *Chilkoot* for Chatham Cannery. Jimmie became a church reader in 1916 and has been actively involved with the Orthodox Church ever since, singing tenor in the choir.

The ANB was founded in Sitka in 1912, and other communities, including Angoon, began organizing camps. Jimmie served as the ANB recording secretary. The work of many people like Jimmie and Lydia George with the ANB eventually led to involvement in the land claims issue and formation of the Tlingit and Haida Central Council. The activities of the ANB and Tlingit and Haida led to the Alaska Native Claims Settlement Act of 1971.

At the age of 100, Jimmie is now retired from political life but remains very active on the cultural front. He recently served as a consultant to Sealaska Heritage Foundation's Naa Kahidi Theater, travelling to a meeting at the Portland Art Museum. Jimmie was a principal elder at the Killer Whale memorial in Juneau in September 1989, where part of the food distributed by the hosts was a large birthday cake in honor of Jimmie's upcoming 100th birthday.

The editors thank Jimmie and Lydia George for their help with this biography.

Austin Hammond / Daanawáak
Born: October 18, 1910
Raven; Lukaax̱.ádi; Kaagwaantaan yádi

Austin Hammond, spring 1989. Photo by David Gelotte, courtesy of Sealaska Heritage Foundation.

Austin Hammond was born October 18, 1910, in Daayasáank'i, a settlement across Lynn Canal from Haines. His parents were Jennie Marks, a woman of the Lukaax̱.ádi named K̲ultuyax̱ Sée, and Tom Phillips, a Kaagwaantaan man, Lukaax̱.ádi yádi, of the Killer Whale House (Kéet Hít) of Klukwan, whose Tlingit name was Neechḵu.oowú. Tom Phillips died when Austin was three years old and Jennie later married Willis Hammond (Shaadahéix̱), a Chookaneidí man from Hoonah, who adopted Austin. Willis and Jennie had two children, Austin's sister Wooshḵu.oowú, Eva in English, and his brother Horace Marks. After his father's death, Austin was raised by his maternal grandparents Jim and Martha David.

In 1930, Austin married Ḵaakwdagaan, Katherine James, a woman of the Kaagwaantaan, daughter of John James and Jennie Thlunaut. Five daughters were born: Elizabeth Hammond, Louise Light, Dorothy Breaks, Josephine Winders, and Phoebe Warren. "I lost count of the grandchildren," Austin confesses. Katherine died in 1940. In 1941 he met Lillian, Yankawgé, of the L'uknax̱.ádi, who later became his second wife. Austin and Lillian raised three sons: Tommy Jimmy, Charlie Jimmy, and Austin (Ozzie) Hammond, Jr.

As a fisherman, Austin owned several boats, including the *North Star*, which he rebuilt in 1932, the *Morning Star (1950)*, and the *Seabird*, which he and his brother Horace rebuilt.

Austin is the steward of Raven House in Haines, and leader of the Lukaax̱.ádi. As a leader, Austin is active in Tlingit ceremonials as well as contemporary issues. He fights tirelessly to prevent continued erosion of Tlingit land and rights. Austin has dedicated much time and effort to education in the last decade, visiting classrooms as part of the Juneau Indian Studies program, where he is "grandfather" to hundreds of elementary students.

His efforts have been recognized by the Native and non-Native communities alike. He is a founder of the Sealaska Heritage Foundation and serves on its Traditional Advisory Council. He has received many awards, including the Alaska State Council on the Arts Governor's Award for Contribution to the Arts (1986). In recognition of his contribution to education, Austin was awarded the honorary degree of Doctor of Humanities from the University of Alaska-Southeast, May 5, 1989.

The editors thank Horace and John Marks, and Richard and Julie Folta for their assistance, and especially Austin Hammond himself for his patience and help in researching this biography.

Johnny C. Jackson / G̲ooch Éesh
(April 20, 1893 - January 13, 1985)
Raven; K̲aach.ádi; Sit'k̲weidí yádi

Johnny C. Jackson was born April 20, 1893, in Sumdum Bay to Charlie and Jenny Sumdum, S'aawdáan in Tlingit. He was born into the K̲aach.ádi clan of the Raven moiety. His father was of the Eagle moiety and Sit'k̲weidí clan, originating in Snettisham. He came from a very large family from Kake.

Lithograph of Johnny C. Jackson, "G̲ooch Éesh," by R. T. Wallen, Juneau. Reproduced courtesy of R. T. Wallen.

Johnny C. Jackson was a fisherman and had a thirty-two foot troller named *Hazel* most of his adult life. He is remembered as a very good fisherman, a troller who made his living at it. He also hunted and trapped, using his power boat as a base. He was active in the Salvation Army, which he joined while he was working in Skagway. He was also a lifetime member of the Alaska Native Brotherhood.

Johnny C. Jackson was well-known as a Tlingit tradition bearer. His relatives remember him as a gifted storyteller, who would tell stories for hours on end. He also composed Tlingit songs, and was a well-known singer and an excellent ceremonial dancer. He was well-known for his Tlingit speech making.

He was also an historian, and calculated that he was the seventh in his line of transmission. He used to emphasize to his family, "This is not my knowledge, but my ancestors'." He explained that their group, the K̲aach.ádi, were once part of the Lukaax̲.ádi, and separated on their migration from the southern part of Alaska. The two clan houses mentioned in his speech derive their names from the K̲aach.ádi settlement at Phybus Bay, across from Kake.

Johnny C. Jackson was married twice. His first wife was Emma Jackson, a woman of the Tsaagweidí and mother, by previous marriage, of his stepdaughter Bessie. His second wife's name was Mary. After fifteen years of marriage, she passed away. Johnny C. Jackson had no children of his own, but, as is common in Tlingit tradition, he and his wife helped his brother Scotty raise some of his children and grandchildren, and he was very close to them. Johnny died in 1985 at the age of ninety-one.

The editors thank the relatives and friends of Johnny C. Jackson, especially Thomas Jackson, Gordon Jackson, Clarence Jackson, Elsie Austin Green, and Vern Metcalfe for their help in researching this biography. We have also translated excerpts from a tape recorded interview of Johnny C. Jackson by Judson Brown, archived at the Sealaska Heritage Foundation. We appreciate his foresight in conducting the interview, and his generosity in archiving the tapes for scholarly use.

Charlie Jim, Sr. / Tóok'
(January 16, 1912 - October 29, 1988)
Raven; Deisheetaan; Dak̲l'aweidí yádi

Charlie Jim was from Angoon. He was of the Raven moiety and Deisheetaan clan. His mother, whose Tlingit name was Saani, was part of the Tsaxweil Sháa—the "Crow Women." His father, Náalk, was a well-known man of the Dak̲l'aweidí clan from Chilkat.

Charlie was primarily self-educated. He spent only a small part of his younger life in school, and was a fifth grader when his maternal uncle's wife died. His maternal uncle became ill after his wife's death, and to help his uncle, Charlie quit school. Following the deaths of Charlie Jim's maternal uncles from Deishú Hít, Charlie became the steward of the house.

Charlie worked in the Alaska Juneau gold mine for a while, and he worked in the cannery each season, before fishing began. He worked on fish traps, when they were still in use. He learned how to do a little mechanical and carpentry work when his eyesight was still good. Charlie was a fisherman, and fished all his life, especially purse seining in Chatham Straits. Like many of his contemporaries, Charlie Jim was also an athlete in his day and played basketball for the Angoon ANB for ten years.

Charlie pointed out with a smile that he was as old as the Alaska Native Brotherhood. Both came into being in 1912. When he was sixteen, his brothers joined him up and paid his dues for him. He went to conventions as a delegate for thirty years. Charlie's life was one of service to his people—service reflected in action on the political and cultural fronts. He participated in the major social and political campaigns of his generation, and in the ceremonial events of Tlingit life. He was one of the delegates who went to Washington D.C. in the mid 1960's to ask for payment for the naval bombardment of Angoon.

Like many of his generation, Charlie was concerned with the well-being of his grandchildren. He was concerned that something be left for them—especially the land and traditions of his people. Charlie and his wife Jenny raised fifteen children, and had many grandchildren and great-grandchildren. He was a generous and gracious man, and an elegant speaker. He passed away on October 29, 1988, at Mt. Edgecumbe Hospital.

Charlie Jim, Sr., Angoon, November 1985, at the rededication of the totem poles during the commemorative ceremonies marking the anniversary of the U.S. Naval bombardment of Angoon (October 26, 1882). Photo by Peter Metcalfe, courtesy of Kootznoowoo, Inc.

George Jim / Keik̲óok'w
Born: May 15, 1902
Eagle; Wooshkeetaan; L'uknax̲.ádi yádi

George Jim was born in Juneau, into the Thunderbird House of the Wooshkeetaan clan of the Eagle moiety, on May 15, 1902. His mother's name was Neikee Tláa. Her father's name was Tuyiknahaa, a Kaagwaantaan yádi from Xeitl Hít, Thunderbird House of Juneau. George's father's names were G̲eek'ee and Nadzaan. He was a man of the L'uknax̲.ádi from Swanson Harbor. He was Wooshkeetaan yádi, which makes George chushgadachx̲án, "grandchild of himself."

George Jim speaks at length about the various Wooshkeetaan community houses, most of which grew out of the earlier Xeitl Hít, Thunderbird House, also called Hít Tlein, "The Large House." George considers his home village to be Juneau, even though there are no more community houses left. He mentions that there are many grandchildren from these houses.

At.óow are important in his life, and he expressed himself eloquently on the subject. "We don't like to see words go to waste. We lay our at.óow for the words to fall on. This is when the opposite clan knows its words have been received." He explains this in the context of exchange of speeches. The guests name people in their speeches; the individuals who are named are those who make speeches in return. George has served as steward of many at.óow. He explains, "When my wife Adeline's father died, I received all of his at.óow.

He trolled for about sixty years, and he was about seventeen years old when he started seining. Like most others of his generation, he was active in hunting, fishing, and a range of community activities. About sixty years ago he was involved with basketball and was manager of the Angoon ANB team. George often hunted with John Fawcett, getting bear, deer, and other animals for subsistence food. George was a member of the Salvation Army while he lived in Kake. He has been active in the Orthodox Church for fifty years, and sings tenor.

George has traveled widely. During World War II he worked for the Army Corps of Engineers in the Alaska War Department and was stationed at Adak in the Aleutians.

George Jim has lived an interesting life, fully involved in Tlingit tradition and the modern age. He was curious about how we use computers to word process Tlingit for the books we produce, and remains in contact with people from around the world.

George moved to Angoon after World War II, and married Adeline Walter, of the T'ak̲deintaan. Her parents were Charlie and Annie Walter of Tenakee. With a few exceptions, all of his old friends have died off. His relatives are also all gone. Only his wife Adeline and their children remain.

George Jim, 1940's. Photo courtesy of George Jim.

Andrew P. Johnson / Íx̱t'ik' Éesh
(May 31, 1898 - January 8, 1986)
Kiks.ádi; Kaagwaantaan yádi

A. P. Johnson, Sitka, June 1971, during the first Tlingit Language Workshop at Sheldon Jackson College, at which he delivered the speech included in this book. Photo by R. Dauenhauer.

Andrew P. Johnson was born in Sitka, Alaska on May 31, 1898, into the Kiks.ádi clan of the Raven moiety, the son of Peter and Bessie Johnson. His ancestors trace back to before the Russian occupation of Sitka. Raised as a traditional Tlingit, he was educated in the old ways by his ancestors.

Orphaned at thirteen, he was placed in the Russian orphanage and later went to Sheldon Jackson School, where he was the valedictorian of the first Sheldon Jackson High School graduating class in the spring of 1921. He went on to Park College in Missouri. Under the auspices of the Presbyterian Church, he studied for the ministry and was ordained as a field evangelist by the Presbytery of Northern Arizona, and worked on the Navajo Reservation as an evangelist from 1925 to 1936.

On June 1, 1925, Andrew married Rose Peshlakai. They reared three sons: Elliott Peter, Steve Peshlakai, and Sterling Philip. After twenty-six years outside, the Johnsons returned to Alaska, and Andrew worked in the crafts department at Mt. Edgecumbe High School from 1947 to 1968. Andrew Johnson served his people as minister, teacher, and officer in Native organizations. He served as president of the Sitka Alaska Native Brotherhood, grand vice-president of the Grand Camp ANB, President of the Tlingit-Haida Association, and member of the Tlingit-Haida Central Council.

From 1968 to 1971, he was director of the Alaska Native Brotherhood Center at the National Park Visitor's Center in Sitka. He was on the staff of Sheldon Jackson College from 1968, where he developed materials and taught courses in Tlingit language and culture. He was involved from the very beginning with the Tlingit Language Workshops held annually on the Sheldon Jackson Campus in the early 1970's. At the first of these workshops, in June 1971, he delivered the short speech with which we open this book.

The Johnson's marriage of fifty-five years ended with the death of Rose Edith Johnson on December 25, 1980. On February 20, 1982, A. P. Johnson married Etta P. Dalton. As his own end drew near, he prepared for death with the dignity of a traditional elder. In his last days he sang for his assembled family one of the spiritual songs he called the "National Anthem" of his clan and house group. He then retired to his bed where he passed away on Wednesday, January 8, 1986, at the age of eighty-seven.

The editors thank Evelyn Bonner and Steve Johnson for their help with this biography.

William Johnson / Keewax̲.awtseix̲ Guwakaan; Kíts' Éesh
(June 5, 1900 - April 6, 1982)
Raven; T'ak̲deintaan; Wooshkeetaan yádi; Yeil kudei hít taan

William Johnson was born June 5, 1900, at Glacier Bay into the Raven moiety, the T'ak̲deintaan clan, and the Yeil kudei hít taan (Raven Nest House Group). His parents were Irene St. Clair and William McKinley. He married Mary Johnson, his wife of fifty-five years, on December 4, 1926.

During World War Two, he was a lieutenant in the Territorial Guard, serving from January 6, 1944, to March 31, 1947. During the war he was also a piledriver foreman, but they released him to go fishing, because food was important for the war effort, too.

William was a well-known fisherman, for many years a seineboat captain and a "highliner." A picture of his seiner *Gypsy Queen* appeared in the *National Geographic Magazine* (June 1965, p. 788). He also fished the seiners *Norma, Clarice, Marie H.* and *Mary Joanne*, and the troller *Leader*.

William and Mary led a rich subsistence lifestyle that included berry picking, gathering seaweed, hunting, trapping, and seal hunting in Glacier Bay. They were fond of sea gull eggs, and William always managed to be in Glacier Bay on his birthday to pick sea gull eggs. The watchman at Bartlett Cove gave him a lifetime pass to go up to the bay.

A community tragedy having cultural impact on Hoonah was the fire of 1944, that destroyed the entire village. The town burned rapidly because it was summer, everything was bone dry, and most of the people were out of town fishing or working at canneries. Most of the T'ak̲deintaan at.óow were lost in the fire. William commissioned David Williams to carve a replica to replace the Frog Hat lost in the Hoonah fire. William was also a steward of the Raven Shirt of Weihá, passed to him after the death of Jim Fox, who also gave the Frog Hat song to William.

William Johnson led a full Tlingit ceremonial life. He served as a Naa Káani for all the Eagle clans of Hoonah. In 1958 he became a peacemaker, G̲uwakaan. His speeches in this book reflect his involvement in traditional ceremonial life as well as the more innovative format of the elders conference. He features prominently in the ceremonial speeches and photographs in this book because he was brother-in-law to Jim and Willie Marks, and a member of their paternal grandparent clan. He worked for the passing on of Tlingit culture through traditional as well as newer institutions, and was a prime mover in organizing Sealaska Heritage Foundation.

The editors thank Mary Johnson for her help in researching this biography.

William and Mary Johnson, Juneau, May 1976, at the fiftieth wedding anniversary of Willie and Emma Marks. Photo by R. Dauenhauer.

Charlie Joseph / K̲aal.átk'
(December 18, 1895 - July 5, 1986)
Eagle; Kaagwaantaan; L'uknax̲.ádi yádi; K̲ook Hít taan

Charlie Joseph was born in Sitka. His mother was Tas.oo, of the Kaagwaantaan, and his father was Jak̲keinduwish, of the L'uknax̲.ádi. At the age of two, his family moved to his father's home village, Ltu.áa, called Lituya Bay in English. At that time not one person spoke English there. Raised in a traditional lifestyle, Charlie recalls, "In the evening, stories were told. I don't remember when we missed an evening of telling stories. It was like going to school today, when my grandfather told all the stories, the ancient stories [tláagu] we remember throughout our lives."

In 1916, Charlie's marriage to K̲ool.át was arranged. He and his wife had six girls and three boys. Early on, his sons were taught to fish.

Charlie lived the traditional lifestyle that was the basis of the Tlingit values he taught to his children, grandchildren, and students. The songs and dances that Charlie taught to the G̲ajaa Héen Dancers were learned from his mother and father from the time Charlie was old enough to understand. The personality and inspiration of Charlie Joseph are at the heart of the third set of speeches in this book, the theme of which is the passing on of culture, and taking personal action and responsibility to ensure that traditions live.

Charlie lived a full and exciting life. In 1954, he and his wife survived a plane crash that took the life of the pilot. From 1975 until his death in 1986, Charlie spent many hours taping songs which have been transcribed and are used as song books by the young people today. Charlie enriched not only his immediate family, but also a new generation of Tlingit youth. His leadership also inspired many of his fellow elders, as we see in the speeches they addressed to him.

Charlie died July 5, 1986. His widow, Annie Joseph, followed him in death, passing away in Sitka on December 28, 1989.

The editors thank Charlie's daughter Ethel Makinen and the staff of the Sitka Native Education Program for their help in this biography.

Charlie Joseph wearing his Bear Shirt, late 1970's. Each shirt passed from generation to generation is an at.óow and is held in common ownership under the stewardship of a group leader. Charlie was the fourth steward of the Bear Shirt, estimated to be 150 years old. Caption information courtesy of Sitka Native Education Program. Photo courtesy of Tlingit and Haida Central Council Archives.

David Kadashan / Kaatyé
(June 5, 1893 - October 14, 1976)
Raven; T'a<u>k</u>deintaan; Shangukeidí yádi

David Paul Kadashan was born in Juneau on June 5, 1893. He was of the Raven moiety and the T'a<u>k</u>deintaan clan, and a child of the Shangukeidí. His father was Paul Kadashan from Haines. His mother was Deiwjee, a T'a<u>k</u>deintaan woman from Ta<u>x</u>' Hít (Snail House); she was Kaagwaantaan yádi. David is also a grandchild of Chookaneidí.

David Kadashan, 1950's, wearing his Alaska Native Brotherhood hat and koogéinaa (ceremonial sash). Photo courtesy of Ida Kadashan.

David was married briefly, for a year, before he married Ida, his wife of thirty-four years in 1942. David and Ida were married in the traditional way. Ida recalls that she first knew David as her paternal uncle. The couple had no children together, but David helped Ida raise her children. He referred to his wife's children as his grandfather's children. He adopted the youngest of the children, and Ida's children all refer to him as their father. David was proud of the children, and said in a metaphor, "I will take the full bucket from her and carry it."

During the First World War, David was trained to be a medic at Chemawa. He had just finished his training when the war ended. For many years, David was involved in community work and service. He served in the Territorial Guard as a sergeant.

David was also an avid musician, and was a master of contemporary Western music as well as Tlingit. Not only did he drum both Tlingit and Western dance band music, but one elder recalls how David had a snare drum in the marching band; he cut the bottom off and converted it to a Tlingit drum!

David was fully active in Tlingit tradition. He and Ida were involved in subsistence as well as wage economies. They had a small boat and both fished from it. They hunted deer, gathered berries, and dried fish for their family. As a child and young man he was an assistant to his grandmother who was a shaman. As an adult he became a song leader and orator of note and standing, and was active in traditional Tlingit ceremonial life. As a leader of the paternal grandparent clan of the departed, he delivered the major speech at the memorial for Jim Marks, included here.

David was involved with ANB literally until the end of his life. At the age of eighty-two, he offered the opening prayer at the Hoonah convention of October 1976, included in this book, and a few days later he contracted pneumonia and died.

The editors thank Ida Kadashan for her help in researching this biography.

Matthew Lawrence / Kweix' Éesh
(July 8, 1902 - January 5, 1981)
Raven; T'akdeintaan; Chookaneidí yádi; Tax' Hít (Snail House)

Matthew Lawrence, whose Tlingit name was Kweix' Éesh, was born into the Raven moiety, the T'akdeintaan clan, and the Snail House of Hoonah, Alaska, and lived all his life in Hoonah. He was the son of David Lawrence (Koonwuhaan) and Eliza Hopkins (Lyayidayéik).

His wife, Annie, (in Tlingit, Kaach.oo) was a woman of the Kaagwaantaan clan and Wolf House (Gooch Hít) of Hoonah. Annie D. Lawrence, born August 21, 1902, was the daughter of John Donwalk and Annie Hanson. Annie is best remembered as a recognized master of spruce root basket weaving. The young couple eloped in their mid-teens, and their marriage lasted sixty-three years, ending with the death of Annie on November 25, 1979. The couple had four children; surviving daughters are Martha Horten and Annabell Revels.

In his younger days, Matthew played basketball and baseball, and was a referee for basketball games in Hoonah. He was also a vocalist during the heyday of the Hoonah Brass Band that played for holidays and funerals in the decades before World War II. Matthew was active in the Alaska Native Brotherhood and served as president.

Like many of his contemporaries, Matthew was involved in commercial fishing as well as subsistence activities. For subsistence, Matthew hunted seal and deer, and the family picked seaweed and all kinds of berries. The family also gathered sea gull eggs. This was a very important seasonal part of the traditional subsistence diet, and Tlingit cultural values and physical needs came into conflict with federal law when the taking of sea gull eggs was declared illegal.

Matthew became one of the leaders of the T'akdeintaan and the Snail House, and was one of the respected tradition bearers in Hoonah. He was active in memorials as a speaker and singer. As a leader of the paternal grandparent clan of the deceased, Matthew ceremonially opened and closed the important Widow's

Cry section of the memorial for Jim Marks. Frank O. Williams, Jr., now of Sitka, Matthew's oldest nephew, was selected by him to carry on the family tradition, and Frank O. Williams is now the custodian of the Snail House at.óow.

Matthew Lawrence, 1977, holding the Tsalx̲aantu Sháawu S'áaxw (Woman in Mt. Fairweather Hat), an important at.óow of the T'ak̲deintaan, carved by Willie Marks. Photo by Anthony Pope, courtesy of Annabell Revels.

Emma Marks / Seigeigéi
Born: August 10, 1913
Raven: Lukaax̱.ádi; Shangukeidí yádi

Emma Marks at her fiftieth wedding anniversary, Juneau, May 1976. Photo by R. Dauenhauer.

Emma Frances Marks was born August 10, 1913, in Yakutat to Katy Frances (Leetkwéi), a woman of the Alsek Lukaax̱.ádi, and George Frances (Naagéi) of the Shangukeidí of the Italio River Kawdliyaayi Hít, House Lowered from the Sun. Emma is Raven,

Lukaax̱.ádi of the Alsek River Shaka Hít (Canoe Prow House). Her Tlingit name is Seigeigéi, after her maternal grandmother. Emma's people were called G̱unaax̱u ḵwáan. Because her group has largely died off, the main point of her speech in this book is to clarify the relationship of the remnants.

Emma's early years were spent in the Alsek River (Aalseix̱) and Dry Bay (Kunaaga.áa) areas in a place called Italio River in English and Ḵeilxwáa in Tlingit. Emma talks about how beautiful Italio River was and how as a child she picked many different kinds of flowers. The image of flowers made a lasting impression, and is reflected today in the floral designs in her beadwork. Her memories of an idyllic childhood come to an end with the death of her father, to whom she was very close, who died of food poison from canned food.

In June of 1926, Emma married Willie Marks, the youngest of her stepfather's cousins. Willie was twenty-five years old, and Emma claimed to be sixteen. Throughout her long marriage, Emma shared in the subsistence lifestyle of her husband and his family, and had many adventures. Emma and Willie had sixteen children together, some of whom died in infancy, but many of whom married and had children of their own.

Emma is acclaimed as one of the finest beadworkers in Alaska, and has received many awards for her work, including an individual artist's fellowship grant from the Alaska State Council on the Arts in the early 1980's, and the prestigious Alaska Governor's Award in the Arts in 1989. In March 1988 she was honored with a one person show at the Alaska State Museum in Juneau, during which her most valuable pieces were assembled from private collections and displayed.

As Emma notes in her speech in this book, she is a very shy person by nature. Her personality is characterized by inner strength. About fifty years ago, realizing that her life was being destroyed by alcohol, she made a decision for Christ and for sobriety. She is a member of the Pentecostal Church, tithes ten per-cent of the income from her art, and does not bead on Sunday. Acceptance of Christ was a turning point, and faith has been the core of her life since that decision.

We thank Emma Marks for her endless patience and good humor in helping research this biography.

Jim Marks / K̲uháanx'; Goox̲ G̲uwakaan
(1881 - October 24, 1967)
Chookaneidí; Lukaax̲.ádi yádi; Brown Bear House

Jim Marks was born in 1881, in Hoonah, Alaska, to Jak̲wteen (Jim Marks, also known as Jim Nag̲ataak'w) and Tl'óon Tláa (Eliza Marks). He was of the Eagle moiety, a Chookaneidí from Hoonah. His mother was of Xoots S'aagí Hít, Brown Bear Nest House. His father, Jak̲wteen, was a Lukaax̲.ádi of G̲eesán Hít

Jim Marks at Marks Trail, Juneau, early 1960's. Photo courtesy of Emma Marks.

(Mt. Ḵeesán House) of Yandeist'aḵyé, a village about four miles north of Haines. Jim considered Hoonah his home village, but he lived much of his life in Juneau at the Marks Trail homesite.

He was married three times. After the death of his first wife and a brief marriage to his second wife, Jim's third marriage was to Ḵultuyax̱ Sée, Jennie, the mother of Austin Hammond and Horace Marks. Following tradition, Jim married the widow of the deceased leader and assumed his position as the hít s'aatí or steward of the Brown Bear House of Hoonah. Being a child of Lukaax̱.ádi, Jim had personal and historical connections to the Chilkat and Chilkoot areas, and these family ties were strengthened by his marriage to Jennie. The marriage lasted over fifty years, and the couple accomplished many things together. Though Jim had no children of his own, he reared Jennie's three children and was actively involved in the lives of his many nieces and nephews.

Jim's life was closely connected to boats, of which the *North Pass* was the most memorable. Jim was a "highliner," and recalled many memorable seasons. In addition to using their boats for commercial seining and trolling, the Marks family lived on their boats and used them for hunting, trapping, and for subsistence fishing. The family was known for living a traditional life when it was no longer the trend.

Jim Marks was a fine carver who strived for perfection. He and his brothers and nephews came from a long line of artists. He was a ceremonial leader, a tradition bearer, and a song composer. Before his death, he recorded the speech included here and the cry song to be played at his own memorial, a song composed by his ancestor Ḵ'aadóo as a lament for the death of Xwaayeenáḵ, his younger brother.

Jim's brother Willie, who inherited Jim's position as tradition bearer, hosted the memorial for his departed brother in Hoonah in October 1968, at which time the speeches comprising the central section of this book were delivered.

The editors thank the family of Jim Marks, especially his sons Horace and John, his sister-in-law Emma Marks, his nieces Betty Govina and Florence Sheakley, his nephew's wife Mamie Williams, and his nephews Ron Williams, Jim Marks and Peter Marks for their help in researching this biography.

Willie Marks / Kéet Yaanaayí
(July 4, 1902 - August 7, 1981)
Chookaneidí; Lukaax̱.ádi yádi

The youngest of six children, Willie Marks came into the world at Marks Trail on Douglas Island across from Juneau on July 4, 1902. He was of the Eagle moiety and the Chookaneidí clan. He was the survivor of two houses; the Brown Bear Nest House and Brown Bear House of Hoonah. His father, Jak̲wteen, was Lukaax̱.ádi from Yandeist'ak̲yé in Chilkat. His mother was Tl'óon Tláa, Chookan sháa from Hoonah.

Willie and his parents lived a subsistence lifestyle, following the seasons of the resources. The family maintained

Willie Marks, Juneau, May 1976, on his fiftieth wedding anniversary. Photo by R. Dauenhauer.

conservative traditions at a time when traditional ways of living were discouraged by missionaries and government institutions.

He married Emma Frances of Yakutat in 1926. They reared sixteen children in the same traditions, living seasonally at Marks Trail and on their boats along the southeast coast of Alaska for many years, months on end, until the government restricted their travel at the outbreak of World War II.

Willie was a fisherman all of his life. He purse seined on the *Anny*, his mother and father's first seine boat. He was also a boat builder. The hull of the second boat named *New Anny* was built in Juneau in 1939 and he helped rebuild the *North Pass* and *Tennessee*, both his brother Jim's boats. As a young man he built the *Nora*.

Willie was a well-known carver, following the tradition of his namesakes in the Brown Bear Nest House. He was commissioned to replicate many of the at.óow lost in the Hoonah fire of 1944. Willie was a ceremonial leader of the Brown Bear House and the Brown Bear Nest House of the Hoonah Chookaneidí. His oldest brother, Jim, inherited the position of "Lingít tlein" or "hít s'aatí" of Brown Bear House, and Willie assisted him in the ceremonies he gave. In 1968, when Jim Marks died, Willie inherited his brother's position as house leader. Willie gave the memorial for Jim Marks in Hoonah in October 1968, at which time he became steward of the clan at.óow.

Willie was a member of the Alaska Native Brotherhood, and with his brother Jim Marks was involved in fund raising for the old ANB Hall in Juneau. During the early years of the Juneau Indian Studies program, Willie taught carving to the elementary grades, and was a storyteller.

In December of 1980, Willie became very ill and was rushed to the hospital. Tests confirmed cancer. The doctor predicted that Willie would not survive the night. He passed away eight months later on August 7, 1981, one month after the untimely death of his youngest child, Eva. During the lasts months of his life, Willie never lost his gift of humor, often saying or doing something to lift the burden of others. He is survived by his wife Emma, and eight of their sixteen children.

Tom Peters / Yeilnaawú
(July 1, 1892 - April 20, 1984)
Tuk.weidí; Yanyeidí yádi

Tom Peters, an inland Tlingit, was born to Sam and Mollie Peters on July 1, 1892, at the head of the Taku River, and lived

Tom Peters, Teslin, 1966, wearing his at.óow, the Deisheetaan Beaver Shirt and beaver fur hat, ceremonial dress inherited from Jake Jackson. Photo by Catharine McClellan.

most of his life in Teslin. He was Raven moiety, of the Tuḵ.weidí clan, an offshoot of the Deisheetaan. His mother's name was X̱waansán, of the Tuḵ.weidí. Tom had only one maternal uncle, who was responsible for his upbringing. His mother's family consisted of just the three of them—Tom's mother, his maternal aunt, and his maternal uncle. Tom was too young to remember when his father died, but he recalled, "There used to be many of my uncles on my father's side."

Tom worked as a trapper and fishing guide at Teslin. He had contact with the White world beginning with the building of the Alaska Highway during World War II. In 1951 he worked with Catharine McClellan, and, among other things, told a version of the "Woman Who Married the Bear" that is analyzed in detail in McClellan's monograph of 1970. (See *Haa Shuká* for more on this, as well as a 1972 telling of the story.) In 1952, he also guided McClellan on an archeological survey, and taped more songs and stories.

As he grew older, Tom Peters became increasingly interested in his group's ties to the coastal Tlingit. He eventually became head of the Tuḵ.weidí, inheriting Jake Jackson's ceremonial dress in which he is photographed here. As a tradition bearer he was very humble and quiet, and very knowledgeable. He took pleasure in hearing the published versions of his work. Others in Teslin (such as Virginia Smarch) enjoy telling the story of Tom's experiencing his story read back to him.

Tom was married twice. The name of his first wife is not available at present; his second wife's name was Alice Sidney Peters, Ḵaashdáx̱ Tláa, a woman of the Yanyeidí clan. There are eight children. Alice died on August 20, 1970. Tom Peters lived a long and active life. His relative, Elizabeth Nyman of Atlin, whose maternal uncle was Tom Peters' father, commented, "He walked straight and packed his water two buckets at a time." Then, suddenly, he had a stroke, lingered a while in the hospital, and died on April 20, 1984, about two months short of his ninety-second birthday.

The editors thank the Yukon Native Languages Center in Whitehorse for help in researching this biographical sketch.

Jennie Thlunaut / Shax'saani Kéek'
(May 18, 1890 - July 16, 1986)
Eagle; Kaagwaantaan; G̲aanax̲teidí yádi

Jennie was born May 18, 1890 in Lax̲acht'aak in the Chilkat area to Yaandak̲in Yéil (Matthew Johnson) and K̲aakwdagáan (Esther Johnson) both of Klukwan, Alaska.

In 1923 she married Lunaat', who died in 1952. He was Yandeist'ak̲yé K̲wáan, a Lukaax̲.ádi of Yeil Hít (Raven House). His English name was John Mark. At one point, Jennie Mark took the name Thlunaut, the English spelling of Lunaat', as her surname. Jennie had nine children with her first husband and two girls with her second husband, and many descendants.

All her life Jennie was surrounded by Tlingit art and at.óow, some of it now world famous through historical photographs and various publications, among the most recent of which are Kaplan and Barsness (1986), Jonaitis (1986), and Wyatt (1989). As a Chilkat weaver, Jennie dedicated three quarters of a century to continuing this art. The art formed her life, and she in turn gave form to traditional art, weaving over fifty robes, shirts, and tunics.

Jennie was active in the Alaska Native Sisterhood and the Presbyterian Church. She received many honors and awards during her long lifetime. In 1974 she was invited by Harvard University to participate in ceremonies for the opening of a new Northwest Coast exhibit at Peabody Museum organized by Rosita Worl and Peter Corey. In 1983 Governor Sheffield declared a Jennie Thlunaut Day, which she requested be changed to Yanwaa Sháa Day, so that she could share the honor with her clanswomen. In 1984 Jennie demonstrated at the Festival of American Folklife on the National Mall in Washington, D.C., co-sponsored by the Smithsonian Institution and the National Park Service. In 1984 she also received a Governor's Award for the Arts, and in 1986 she was one of twelve American artists selected to receive a National Heritage Fellowship Award from the National Endowment for the Arts.

In February and March 1985, just prior to her ninety-fifth birthday, Jennie taught at a Chilkat Weaving Workshop at Raven House in Haines, which she opened with the welcoming speech and prayer included in this book. Her life and work are described by Worl and Smythe (1986) and on the video tape *In Memory of Jennie Thlunaut* (Dauenhauer and Scollon 1988).

In late spring of 1986, Jennie was taken seriously ill, and was flown to Anchorage for diagnosis, which was cancer. Respecting her wish to die at home, Jennie was flown back to Southeast Alaska, and on July 16, 1986, passed away on the airplane returning to her home village of Klukwan. At her funeral on July 19, which was attended by many local and state officials including Governor Bill Sheffield, Jennie was described as being a strong woman of peace, respected by all who knew her.

Jennie Thlunaut, 1985. Photo by Barry J. McWayne, courtesy of the University of Alaska Musuem.

Thomas Young / K̲aajeetg̲uxeex
Born: April 15, 1906
Raven; G̲aanax̲teidí; Shangukeidí yádi

Thomas Young was born April 15, 1906, in Klukwan, the heart of the Chilkat weaving tradition. His Tlingit name is K̲aajeetg̲uxeex, the namesake of the man who built the Frog House. His mother's name was Sa.áax̲w, Frances Young in English. She was G̲aanax̲teidí, and was a Chilkat weaver. Thomas Young's father was K̲indagein, a Shangukeidí man from Klukwan, who was the maternal uncle of Joe White, host of the memorial at which Thomas delivered the speech included here.

In 1918 Thomas entered Sheldon Jackson School in Sitka. Of his school days, he comments, "I went as high as the third grade. I flunked it three times!" He joined the boy scouts at the age of nine, and learned how to read charts and use a compass, but he had difficulty with English. Despite his limited formal education, he passed the Navy navigation tests with flying colors. He was a navigator and a fisherman all his life.

In 1935 Thomas married Charlotte Littlefield, the daughter of John and Annie Littlefield. Their marriage of nearly fifty years ended with the passing of Charlotte in 1982.

Religion has played a very important role in Thomas Young's life. He was introduced to the various books of the Bible in school, but his real conversion came in the mid 1960's with a physical and spiritual healing from tuberculosis. Since then, Thomas dedicated himself to church work. He has served for many years as Starosta of St. Michael's Cathedral in Sitka. When the Cathedral burned in 1966, he was active in its reconstruction. He did much of the interior carpentry in the new Cathedral, including the finished framing of the icons. He also built the altar table according to ancient specifications, all pegged, without nails.

Like many other traditional elders of his generation, firmly grounded in both Tlingit and Christian spirituality, Thomas Young sees no conflict between the two. The point he often makes in his teaching, as well as in the speech included here, is that traditional Tlingit and traditional Christian spirituality are not in conflict with each other, but are in conflict with a secular world view that undermines both, denies spiritual reality, and results in loss of identity, the sale of one's heritage.

The editors thank Thomas Young for his time and patience in helping us research this biography.

Thomas Young, wearing his stikharion and ecclesiastical awards, including the St. Herman Cross, at the consecration of the chapel to St. Innocent in the Cathedral of St. Michael the Archangel, Sitka, October 1978. Photo by R. Dauenhauer.

References

This bibliography lists the references mentioned in this book. No attempt is made at a complete listing of works in anthropology, folklore, ethnopoetics, or linguistics. The bibliographies of the most recent works cited here provide a good starting place for further study.

Astrov, Margot
1962 *American Indian Prose and Poetry: An Anthology.* (Originally published in 1945 as *The Winged Serpent.*) New York: Capricorn Books.

Bahr, Donald
1975 *Pima and Papago Ritual Oratory, a Study of Three Texts.* San Francisco: Indian Historian Press.
n.d. "Oratory, or Public Speaking." Forthcoming in Andrew Wiget, *Dictionary of Native American Literature.*

Bauman, Richard, and Joel Sherzer
1989 *Explorations in the Ethnography of Speaking.* Cambridge: Cambridge University Press. Originally published in 1974.

Berry, Wendell
1983 *Standing by Words.* San Francisco: North Point Press.

Bierhorst, John
1971 *In the Trail of the Wind: American Indian Poems and Ritual Orations.* New York: Farrar, Straus and Giroux.
1974 *Four Masterworks of American Indian Literature.* New York: Farrar, Straus and Giroux.

Boelscher, Marianne
1989 *The Curtain Within: Haida Social and Mythical Discourse.* Vancouver: University of British Columbia Press.

Bowers, C. A.
1987 *Elements of a Post-Liberal Theory of Education.* New York and London: Teachers College Press, Columbia University.

Brunvand, Jan Harold
1978 *The Study of American Folklore: An Introduction.* 2d ed. New York: W. W. Norton.

Campbell, J., with Bill Moyers
1988*a* *The Power of Myth.* New York: Mystic Fire Video. (Videotape).
1988*b* *The Power of Myth.* New York: Doubleday.

Chafe, Wallace L.
1961 *Seneca Thanksgiving Rituals.* Smithsonian Institution. Bureau of American Ethnology Bulletin 183. Washington, D.C.: U.S. Government Printing Office.

Codere, Helen
1950 *Fighting with Property: A Study of Kwakiutl Potlatching and Warfare 1792–1930.* Seattle: University of Washington Press.

Dauenhauer, Nora Marks
1975 "Levels of Mediation in Tlingit Oratory." Paper read at the Alaska Anthropology Association meetings, University of Alaska-Fairbanks, 1975, and in revised form at the Simon Fraser University Northwest Coast Conference, Burnaby, B.C., 1976.
1986 "Context and Display in Northwest Coast Art." *Voices of the First America: Text and Context in the New World.* Special issue of *New Scholar* 10 (1,2):419–32.

Dauenhauer, Nora M. and Richard Dauenhauer
1976 *Beginning Tlingit.* 2d ed. Tlingit Readers, Inc. Distributed by Sealaska Heritage Foundation, Juneau, Alaska. (A third edition, revised, accompanied by audiocassette tapes is forthcoming from the University of Washington Press.)
1981 "Because We Cherish You . . .": Sealaska Elders Speak to the Future. Juneau: Sealaska Heritage Foundation.

1984*a* *Tlingit Spelling Book.* 3d ed. Juneau: Sealaska Heritage Foundation.

1984*b* Audiocassette tape for *Tlingit Spelling Book.* Juneau: Sealaska Heritage Foundation.

1987 *Haa Shuká, Our Ancestors: Tlingit Oral Narratives.* Seattle: University of Washington Press.

1989 "Treatment of Shaman Spirits in Contemporary Tlingit Oratory." In Hoppál and von Sadovszky (1989:317-329).

Dauenhauer, Nora M., Richard Dauenhauer, and Gary Holthaus

1986 *Alaska Native Writers, Storytellers and Orators.* (Special Issue of *Alaska Quarterly Review*). University of Alaska, Anchorage.

Dauenhauer, Nora M., and Suzanne Scollon, prod.

1988 *In Memory of Jennie Thlunaut (1890-1986).* A video tape on Chilkat weaving. Juneau: Sealaska Heritage Foundation.

Dauenhauer, Richard

1975 Text and Context of Tlingit Oral Tradition. Ph.D. diss., University of Wisconsin, Madison.

1982 *Conflicting Visions in Alaskan Education.* Center for Cross-Cultural Studies Occasional Paper no. 3. University of Alaska, Fairbanks.

de Laguna, Frederica

1972 *Under Mount Saint Elias.* Smithsonian Contributions to Anthropology. Vol. 7 (in 3 parts) Washington, D.C.: Smithsonian Institution Press.

1987 "Atna and Tlingit Shamanism: Witchcraft on the Northwest Coast." *Arctic Anthropology* 20 (2):47–59.

1988*a* "Tlingit: People of the Wolf and Raven." In Fitzhugh and Crowell, *Crossroads of Continents* (1988):58-63.

1988*b* "Potlatch Ceremonialism on the Northwest Coast." In Fitzhugh and Crowell, *Crossroads of Continents* (1988):271-80.

Dorson, Richard M.

1972 *Folklore and Folklife: An Introduction.* Chicago: University of Chicago Press.

Drucker, Philip
1958 *The Native Brotherhoods: Modern Intertribal Organizations on the Northwest Coast.* Bureau of American Ethnology Bulletin 168. Smithsonian Institution, Washington, D.C.

Dürr, Michael, Wolfgang Oleschinski, and Egon Renner, eds.
1990 *Festschrift Jürgen Pinnow.* Berlin. Forthcoming.

Eliade, Mircea
1964 *Shamanism: Archaic Techniques of Ecstasy.* Princeton: Princeton University Press.

Emmons, George T.
1907 "The Chilkat Blanket." *Memoirs of the American Museum of Natural History* 3(4):329-401.
1916 "The Whale House of the Chilkat." *Anthropological Papers of the American Museum of Natural History* 19(1)1-33.

Fitzhugh, William and Aron Crowell.
1988 *Crossroads of Continents.* Washington, D.C.: Smithsonian Institution Press.

Foster, Michael K.
1974*a* *From the Earth to Beyond the Sky: An Ethnographic Approach to Four Longhouse Iroquois Speech Events.* Canadian Ethnology Service Paper no. 20. National Museum of Man Mercury Series. Ottawa: National Museums of Canada.
1974*b* "When Words Become Deeds: An Analysis of Three Iroquois Longhouse Speech Events." In Bauman and Sherzer 1974; 1989:354–67.
1978 *The Recovery and Translation of Native Speeches Accompanying Ancient Iroquois-White Treaties.* Canadian National Museum of Man, Ethnology Division, Canadian Studies Report 5 e-f. Ottawa.

Goldman, Irving
1975 *The Mouth of Heaven: An Introduction to Kwakiutl Religious Thought.* New York: Wiley-Interscience.

Golovin, P. N.
1863 "Iz putevykh pisem P. N. Golovina." In *Morskoi Sbornik.*

1983 *Civil and Savage Encounters. The Worldly Travel Letters of an Imperial Russian Navy Officer 1860–1861.* Translated and annotated by Basil Dmytryshyn and E. A. P. Crownhart-Vaughan. Portland: Oregon Historical Society.

Grim, J. A.

1987 *The Shaman: Patterns of Religious Healing among the Ojibway Indians.* Norman: University of Oklahoma Press. Originally published in 1983.

Hinckley, Ted C.

1970 "'The Canoe Rocks—We Do Not Know What Will Become of Us': The complete transcript of a meeting between Governor John Green Brady of Alaska and a group of Tlingit Chiefs, Juneau, December 14, 1898." *Western Historical Quarterly* (July 1970):265–90.

Holmberg, Heinrich Johan

1985 *Holmberg's Ethnographic Sketches.* Edited by Marvin W. Falk. Translated by Fritz Jaensch. Fairbanks: University of Alaska Press. Originally published in Russian, 1855–63.

Hope, Andrew, III

1975 *Founders of the Alaska Native Brotherhood.* Sitka: David Howard Memorial Fund.

Hoppál, Mihály, ed.

1984 *Shamanism in Eurasia.* 2 vols. Göttingen: Edition Herodot.

Hoppál, Mihály, and Otto von Sadovszky, ed.

1989 *Shamanism: Past and Present.* Budapest and Los Angeles/Fullerton: ISTOR Books 1-2.

Hyde, Lewis

1983 *The Gift: Imagination and the Erotic Life of Property.* New York: Vintage Books.

Hymes, Dell

1981 *In Vain I Tried to Tell You: Essays in Native American Ethnopoetics.* Philadelphia: University of Pennsylvania Press.

Jackman, S. W., ed.

1978 *The Journal of William Sturgis.* Victoria: Sono Nis Press.

Jonaitis, Aldona

1986 *Art of the Northern Tlingit.* Seattle: University of Washington Press.

Jones, Suzi, ed.

1986 *The Artists Behind the Work: Life Histories of Nick Charles, Sr., Frances Demientieff, Lena Sours, Jennie Thlunaut.* Fairbanks: University of Alaska Museum.

Kan, Sergei

1982 *Wrap Your Father's Brothers in Kind Words: An Analysis of the Nineteenth-Century Tlingit Mortuary and Memorial Rituals.* Ph.D. diss., University of Chicago.

1983 "Words that Heal the Soul: Analysis of the Tlingit Potlatch Oratory." *Arctic Anthropology* 20 (2):47-59.

1985 "Russian Orthodox Brotherhoods among the Tlingit: Missionary Gods and Native Response." *Ethnohistory* 32 (3):196–223.

1986*a* "The Nineteenth-Century Tlingit Potlatch: A New Perspective." *American Ethnologist* 13 (2):191-212.

1986*b* "Review of *Alaskan John G. Brady* by Ted C. Hinckley." *Alaska Native Magazine.* (May/June 1986):14-15.

1987*a* "Memory Eternal: Orthodox Christianity and the Tlingit Mortuary Complex." *Arctic Anthropology 24 (1):32-55.*

1987*b* "Potlatch Songs outside the Potlatch." Paper presented at the 86th annual meeting of the American Anthropological Association. Chicago, Ill., November 22, 1987. Forthcoming in *American Indian Quarterly.*

1989 *Symbolic Immortality: Tlingit Potlatch of the Nineteenth Century.* Washington D.C.: Smithsonian Institution Press.

Kaplan, Susan, and Kristin J. Barsness

1986 *Raven's Journey.* Philadelphia: University of Pennsylvania Press.

Kawagey, Joseph, prod.

1981 *Haa Shagóon.* Film. 16 mm. 29 min. Distributed by Chilkat Indian Association, Haines, Alaska. Also available in VHS cassette from the Alaska State Film Library, Juneau.

Kirk, Ruth

1986 *Tradition & Change on the Northwest Coast.* Seattle: University of Washington Press.

Kittlitz, Friedrich H. von
1987 "Extract from *Denkwürdigkeiten einer Reise nach dem russischen Amerika.*" In Frederic Litke, *A Voyage Around the World. 1826–1829.* Edited by R. Pierce. Kingston, Ontario: Limestone Press. Originally published in 1858.

Krause, Aurel
1956 *The Tlingit Indians.* Translated by Erna Gunther. Seattle: University of Washington Press.

Léon-Portilla, Miguel
1985 "Nahua Literature." In *Supplement to the Handbook of Middle American Indians.* Vol. 3. *Literatures.* Munro S. Edmonson, ed. 7-43. Austin: University of Texas Press.

Lewis, I. M.
1984 "What is a Shaman?" In Hoppál (1984):3-12.

Lisianski, Yuri
1947 *Puteshestvie vokrug sveta na korable Neva v 1803-1806 godakh.* Moskva. Originally published in 1812.

Lord, Albert B.
1954 *Serbocroatian Heroic Songs.* Vol. 1. *Novi Pazar: English Translations.* Cambridge and Belgrade: The Harvard University Press and the Serbian Academy of Sciences.

Marvin, Amy
1987 "Glacier Bay History." In Dauenhauer and Dauenhauer, *Haa Shuká* (1987):260-91.

Mauss, Marcel
1967 *The Gift: Forms and Functions of Exchange in Archaic Societies.* Translated by Ian Cunnison. New York: Norton.

McClellan, Catharine
1954 "The Interrelations of Social Structure with Northern Tlingit Ceremonialism." *Southwestern Journal of Anthropology* 10 (1):75-96.

1956 "Shamanistic Syncretism in Southern Yukon Territory." *Transactions of the New York Academy of Science,* 2d series, Vol. 19 (2):130–37.

1975 *My Old People Say: An Ethnographic Survey of Southern Yukon Territory.* National Museums of Canada. National Museum of Man. Publications in Ethnology, no. 6. Ottawa.

1987 *Part of the Land, Part of the Water: A History of the Yukon Indians.* Vancouver and Toronto: Douglas & McIntyre.

Michael, Henry N.

1963 *Studies in Siberian Shamanism.* Arctic Institute of North America. *Anthropology of the North: Translations from Russian Sources no. 4.* Toronto: University of Toronto Press.

Mousalimas, Soterios

1987 "Russian Orthodox Missionaries and Southern Alaskan Shamans: Interaction and Analysis." Paper presented at the Second International Conference on Russian America, at Sitka, Alaska, August 19-22, 1987.

1988*a* "Shamans of Old in Southern Alaska." Paper presented at the 12th International Congress of Anthropological and Ethnological Sciences, Symposium on Shamanism, at Zagreb, Yugoslavia, July 24-31, 1988.

1988*b* "Patristics in Missionary Work: An Example from the Russian Orthodox Mission in Alaska." *Greek Orthodox Theological Review.* Vol. 33, no. 3 (Fall 1988):327-34. First presented as a paper entitled "Patristics and Russian Orthodox Missionary Work in Alaska," at the Tenth International Conference in Patristic Studies, at Oxford, England, August 24-29, 1987.

Naish, Constance M.

1979 *A Syntactic Study of Tlingit.* Dallas, Texas: Summer Institute of Linguistics. Microfiche. (Revision of 1963 M.A. thesis.)

Nichols, John

1988 *"Statement Made by the Indians": A bilingual petition of the Chippewas of Lake Superior, 1864.* Text + Series no. 1. Studies in the Interpretation of Canadian Languages and Cultures. London, Ontario: University of Western Ontario.

Oleksa, Michael

1987 *Alaskan Missionary Spirituality.* New York and Mahwah, N. J.: Paulist Press.

Olson, R. L.

1967 *Social Structure and Social Life of the Tlingit in Alaska.* Anthropological Records Vol. 26. Berkeley and London: University of California Press.

Ostyn, C., prod.
1981 *Kaal.átk'*. Video tape about Charlie Joseph. Sitka: Sitka Native Education Program.
Rosman, Abraham, and Paula Rubel
1971 *Feasting with Mine Enemy: Rank and Exchange Among Northwest Coast Societies.* New York and London: Columbia University Press.
Rothenberg, Jerome
1968 *Technicians of the Sacred.* Garden City, N.Y.: Anchor Books.
1972 *Shaking the Pumpkin: Traditional Poetry of the Indian North Americas.* Garden City, N.Y.: Anchor Books.
Rothenberg, Jerome and Diane Rothenberg
1983 *Symposium of the Whole: A Range of Discourse Toward an Ethnopoetics.* Berkeley and London: University of California Press.
Samuel, Cheryl
1982 *The Chilkat Dancing Blanket.* Seattle: Pacific Search Press.
Schuhmacher, Wilfried
1979 "Aftermath of the Sitka Massacre of 1802." *The Alaska Journal.* Vol. 9, no. 1 (Winter 1979):58-61. Extracts from the Sydney, [Australia] *Gazette,* 29 May 1803, 18 November 1804, and 9 December 1804.
Scollon, Ron and Suzanne Scollon
1987 *How to Teach Thematic Comparative Literature: A Curriculum Note for Secondary Teachers.* Haines, Alaska: Black Current Press.
Seguin, Margaret
1985 *Interpretive Contexts for Traditional and Current Coast Tsimshian Feasts.* Canadian Ethnology Service Paper no. 98. National Museum of Man Mercury Series. Ottawa: National Museums of Canada.
Sherzer, Joel
1983 *Kuna Ways of Speaking: An Ethnographic Perspective.* Austin: University of Texas Press.
1987 "Poetic Structuring of Kuna Discourse: The Line." In Sherzer and Woodbury 1987:103-39.

Sherzer, Joel, and Anthony C. Woodbury
1987 *Native American Discourse: Poetics and Rhetoric.* Cambridge Studies in Oral and Literate Culture, no. 13. Cambridge: Cambridge University Press.
Shils, Edward
1981 *Tradition.* Chicago: University of Chicago Press.
Shotridge, Louis
1913 "Chilkat Houses." *The Museum Journal.* University of Pennsylvania Museum. Vol. 4, no. 3 (September 1913): 81-94.
Siikala, Anna-Leena
1978 *The Rite Technique of the Siberian Shaman.* Folklore Fellows Communications, no. 220. Helsinki: Suomalainen Tiedeakatemia.
Spencer, Katherine
1957 *Mythology and Values: An Analysis of Navaho Chantway Myths.* Philadelphia: American Folklore Society.
Steltzer, Ulli
1984 *A Haida Potlatch.* Seattle: University of Washington Press.
Story, Gillian,
1979 *A Morphological Study of Tlingit.* Dallas, Texas: Summer Institute of Linguistics. Microfiche. (Revision of 1963 M.A. thesis.)
1990 "An Analysed Tlingit Procedural Text." Forthcoming in Dürr et al. *Festchrift Jürgen Pinnow.* Berlin.
Story, Gillian, and Constance Naish
1973 *Tlingit Verb Dictionary.* Fairbanks: Alaska Native Language Center, University of Alaska.
1976 *Tlingit Noun Dictionary.* 2d ed. Revised and expanded by Henry Davis and Jeff Leer. Sitka: Sheldon Jackson College.
Swann, Brian
1983 *Smoothing the Ground: Essays on Native American Oral Literature.* Berkeley and London: University of California Press.
Swanton, John
1970*a* *Social Conditions, Beliefs, and Linguistic Relationship of the Tlingit Indians.* New York and London: Johnson Reprint Corporation. Originally published in 1908.

1970*b* *Tlingit Myths and Texts.* Smithsonian Institution. Bureau of American Ethnology Bulletin 39. New York and London: Johnson Reprint Corporation. Originally published in 1909.

Tedlock, Dennis

1972 *Finding the Center: Narrative Poetry of the Zuni Indians.* New York: Dial Press.

1983 *The Spoken Word and the Work of Interpretation.* Philadelphia: University of Pennsylvania Press.

Toelken, Barre

1979 *The Dynamics of Folklore.* Boston: Houghton Mifflin.

Underhill, Ruth M., with Donald Bahr, Baptisto Lopez, Jose Pancho, and David Lopez

1979 *Rainhouse and Ocean: Speeches for the Papago Year.* Flagstaff: Museum of Northern Arizona Press.

Vanderwerth, W. C.

1971 *Indian Oratory: Famous Speeches by Noted Indian Chieftains.* New York: Ballantine Books.

Veniaminov, Ivan

1984 *Notes on the Islands of the Unalashka District.* Translated by Lydia T. Black and R. H. Geoghegan. Edited with an Introduction by Richard A. Pierce. Kingston: Limestone Press. Originally published in Russia in 1840.

Walens, Stanley

1981 *Feasting with Cannibals: An Essay on Kwakiutl Cosmology.* Princeton: Princeton University Press.

Worl, Rosita and Charles Smythe

1986 "Jennie Thlunaut: Master Chilkat Blanket Artist." In Jones 1986:123-46.

Wyatt, Victoria

1989 *Images from the Inside Passage: An Alaskan Portrait by Winter & Pond.* Seattle and London: University of Washington Press.

This book was produced on the Apple family of computers. The earliest drafts were word processed in Tlingit and English on Apple //+ and Apple //e computers using The Writer's Assistant, UCSD Pascal–based software created by Inter Learn (Cardiff-by-the-Sea, California), and modified at various stages by James Levin (Inter Learn) to interface with firmware developed by Ron Scollon (Gutenberg Dump Ltd., Haines, Alaska) and Allan Rogers (Hands on Training Co., Bonita, California) to permit fluent word processing, screen display, and printing in two languages with different character sets. When Apple Macintosh hardware and software became more available, the Apple // files were downloaded to a Macintosh using the Red Ryder telecommunication program.

The book is printed in ten point Palatino and in a Tlingit font created by Tim Wilson and Michael D. Travis using Altsys Corporation's Fontographer and based on Adobe's version of Palatino. All of the final editing and layout was done by Michael Travis using Microsoft Word, with the exception of the charts, which were created with Aldus Freehand, a Postscript drawing program.

The hardware used for the final editing and layout was an Apple Macintosh SE with a Radius Two Page Display monitor. The camera–ready manuscript was printed on an Apple LaserWriter II NTX.

www.ingramcontent.com/pod-product-compliance
Lightning Source LLC
Chambersburg PA
CBHW021713300426
44114CB00009B/122